AF673488

NCERT SOLUTIONS

with Chapterwise **Study Notes**

CHEMISTRY 12th

Fully Updated as per
Latest NCERT Textbook

NCERT SOLUTIONS

with Chapterwise **Study Notes**

CHEMISTRY 12th

Author

Tarnija Midha
Shikha Soni

arihant
SUCCESS AND NOTHING LESS

Including Selected Questions of **DIKSHA**

ARIHANT PRAKASHAN (Series), MEERUT

卐 **Administrative & Production Offices**

Regd. Office

'Ramchhaya' 4577/15, Agarwal Road, Darya Ganj, New Delhi -110002
Tele: 011- 47630600, 43518550

卐 **Head Office**

Kalindi, TP Nagar, Meerut (UP) - 250002
Tel: 0121-7156203, 7156204

卐 **Sales & Support Offices**

Agra, Ahmedabad, Bengaluru, Bareilly, Chennai, Delhi, Guwahati, Hyderabad, Jaipur, Jhansi, Kolkata, Lucknow, Nagpur & Pune.

卐 **PRICE** ₹375.00

卐 **PO No :** TXT-59-T071458-6-26

Published by Arihant Publications (India) Ltd.

For further information about the books published by Arihant, log on to www.arihantbooks.com or e-mail at info@arihantbooks.com

Follow us on

Preface

Feeling the immense importance and value of NCERT books, we are presenting this book, having the **NCERT Exercises Solutions**. For the overall benefit of the students we have made this book unique in such a way that it presents not only solutions but also detailed explanations. Through these detailed and through explanations, students can learn the concepts which will enhance their thinking and learning abilities.

We have introduced some Additional Features with the solutions which are given below:

- **Explanatory Solutions** Along with the solutions to questions we have given all the points that tell how to approach to solve a problem. Here we have tried to cover all those loopholes which may lead to confusion. All formulae and hints are discussed in full detail.
- Also included **Thinking Process** and **Mistake Alert** to understanding 'How to solve question' and points of mistakes.
- **Note** We have provided notes also to solutions in which special points are mentioned which are of great value for the students.

Apart from all those who helped in the compilation of this book a special note of thanks to all. With the hope that this book will be of great help to the students, we wish great success to our readers.

Tarnija Midha
Shikha Soni

Contents

Solutions

CHAPTER 01

Important Points

01 A **solution** is a homogeneous mixture of two of more substances. The component lesser in amount is called **solute** and the component present in larger amount known as **solvent.** There can be gaseous, liquid or solid solutions.

02 **Henry's law** states that at constant temperature, the solubility of a gas in a liquid is directly proportional to the pressure of the gas.

or

The partial pressure (p) of a gas in vapour phase is proportional to the mole fraction (x) of the gas.

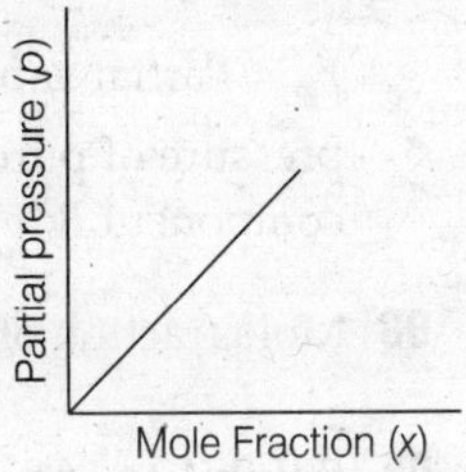

$$p = K_H x$$

K_H = Henry's law constant

03 (a) Mass % of solute $= \dfrac{W_B}{W_A + W_B} \times 100$ $\left[\begin{array}{l} W_A = \text{Mass of solvent} \\ W_B = \text{Mass of solute} \end{array}\right]$

(b) Volume % of solute $= \dfrac{V_B}{V} \times 100$ $\left[\begin{array}{l} V_B = \text{Volume of solute} \\ V = \text{Volume of solution} \end{array}\right]$

(c) Mass by volume % of solute $= \dfrac{W_B}{V} \times 100$

(d) Parts per million (ppm) $= \dfrac{W_B}{W_A + W_B} \times 10^6$

(e) Mole fraction of $A(x_A) = \dfrac{n_A}{n_A + n_B}$ $\left[\begin{array}{l} n_A = \text{no. of moles of } A \\ n_B = \text{no. of moles of } B \end{array}\right]$

$\Rightarrow \qquad x_A + x_B = 1$

Note $x_1 + x_2 + \ldots + x_i = 1$

04 Molarity $(M) = \dfrac{\text{Moles of solute}}{\text{Volume of solution (in L)}} = \dfrac{W_B}{M_B \times V}$ mol L^{-1}

[M_B = Molar mass of solute]

05 Molality $(m) = \dfrac{\text{Moles of solute}}{\text{Mass of solvent (kg)}} = \dfrac{W_B}{M_B \times W_A}$ mol kg^{-1}

06 Dilution formulae : $M_1V_1 = M_2V_2$; $N_1V_1 = N_2V_2$

07 **Raoult's law for volatile solute**

Raoult's law states that for a solution of volatile liquids, the partial vapour pressure of each component of the solution is directly proportional to its mole fraction in solution.

$$p_A = p_A^\circ x_A \text{ and } p_B = p_B^\circ x_B$$

According to **Dalton's law of partial pressure,**

$$p = p_A + p_B = p_A^\circ x_A + p_B^\circ x_B$$

p_A = Partial vapour pressure of component A; p_A° = Vapour pressure of pure component A; p_B = Partial vapour pressure of component B; p_B° = Vapour pressure of pure component B

08 Mole fraction of A in vapour phase, $X_A = \dfrac{p_A}{p_A + p_B} = \dfrac{p_A}{p_{\text{Total}}}$

09 **Solubility** of a substance can be defined as the maximum amount of solute that can be dissolved in a specific amount of solvent at a specified temperature.

10 **Saturated solution** is a solution in which no more solute can be dissolved at the same temperature and pressure.

11 Factors affecting solubility are :

(a) Nature of solute and solvent (like dissolves like)

(b) Temperature (Temperature $\propto$ Solubility)

(c) Pressure (no significant effect)

12 (i) **Ideal Solution** They obey Raoult's law. Force of attraction between $A-A$ and $B-B$ is nearly equal to $A-B$. They have $\Delta_{\text{mix}}H = 0$ and $\Delta_{\text{mix}}V = 0$. **Example** *n*-hexane and *n*-heptane, benzene and toluene, chlorobenzene and bromobenzene, etc.

(ii) **Non-ideal solution** They does not obey Raoult's law and have $\Delta_{mix}H \neq 0$ and $\Delta_{mix}V \neq 0$. The force of attraction between $A-A$ and $B-B$ is not equal to $A-B$

(a) **Positive Deviation** $A-B$ interactions are weaker than the $A-A$ and $B-B$ interactions, this leads to increase in vapour pressure. For example, water and ethanol, chloroform and water, ethanol and CCl_4, etc.

(b) **Negative Deviation** $A-B$ interactions are stronger than the $A-A$ and $B-B$ interactions, this leads to decrease in vapour pressure. For example, chloroform and acetone, water and nitric acid, etc.

13 **Azeotropes**
Liquid mixtures which have the same composition in liquid and vapour phase and boil at a constant temperature.

Minimum boiling azeotropes
The solution which show a large positive deviation from Raoult's law form minimum boiling azeotrops at a specific composition. For example ethanol and water, water and benzene, etc.

Maximum boiling azeotropes
The solutions which show a large negative deviation from Raoult's law form maximum boiling azeotropes at a specific composition for example, nitric acid and water, etc.

14 Colligative properties depend on the number of solute particles, irrespective of their nature. These are : relative lowering of vapour pressure, elevatinon in boiling point, depression in freezing point and osmotic pressure.

$$\frac{p_A - p}{p_A^\circ} = x_B = \frac{n_B}{n_A + n_B} = \frac{n_B}{n_A} = \frac{W_B}{M_B} \times \frac{M_A}{W_A}$$

[For very dilute solution $n_B << n_A$]

15 **Elevation in boiling point.** $\Delta T_b = K_b \times m$

$$\Delta T_b = \frac{K_b \times W_B \times 1000}{M_B \times W_A}; \quad \Delta T_b = T_b - T_b^\circ$$

Where, T_b^0 = Boiling point of pure solvent, T_b = Boiling point of solution, K_b = Boiling point elevation constant or molal elevation constant (Ebullioscopic constant).

Depression in freezing point. $\Delta T_f = K_f \times m$

$$\Delta T_f = \frac{K_f \times W_B \times 1000}{M_B \times W_A}; \Delta T_f = T_f^\circ - T_f$$

K_f = Freezing point depression constant or Molal depression constant (cryoscopic constant), T_f^0 = Freezing point of pure solvent, T_f = Freezing point when non-volatile solute is dissolved solvent.

16 $K_b = \dfrac{R \times M_A \times T_b^2}{1000 \times \Delta_{vap} H}$ [R = Gas constant, $\Delta_{vap}H$ = enthalpy of vapourisation of the solvent]

17 $K_f = \dfrac{R \times M_A \times T_f^2}{1000 \times \Delta_{fus} H}$ [$\Delta_{fus}H$ = enthalpy of fusion of the solvent]

18 Osmotic pressure $(\pi) = CRT = \dfrac{n_B RT}{V} = \dfrac{W_B \times R \times T}{M_B \times V}$

[C = Concentration (Molarity)]

19 The direction of osmosis can be reversed if a pressure larger than the osmotic pressure is applied to the solution side. Now, the pure solvent flows out of the solution through the semipermeable membrane. This phenomenon is called **reverse osmosis.**

20 **van't Hoff factor** (i)

$$i = \frac{\text{Normal molecular mass}}{\text{Observed molecular mass}}$$

or $$i = \frac{\text{Observed colligative property}}{\text{Calculated colligative property}}$$

or $$i = \frac{\text{Total number of moles of particles after dissociation}}{\text{Number of moles of particles before dissociation}}$$

(i) $\dfrac{p_A^\circ - p_A}{p_A^\circ} = i\, x_B$; (ii) $\Delta T_b = i\, K_b m$

(iii) $\Delta T_f = i\, K_f m$; (iv) $\pi V = i n_B RT$

21 $\alpha = \dfrac{i-1}{n-1}$; α = Degree of dissociation;

n = Number of ions produced per formula of the compound

Intext Questions

Question 1 Calculate the mass percentage of benzene (C_6H_6) and carbon tetrachloride (CCl_4) if 22 g of benzene is dissolved in 122 g carbon tetrachloride.

◎ *Thinking Process*

(i) We have mass of C_6H_6 and CCl_4, so calculate the mass of solution by adding these two.

(ii) Then, calculate the mass percentage from the formula,

$$\text{Mass \%} = \frac{\text{Mass of one component}}{\text{Mass of solution}} \times 100$$

Sol. Mass of benzene = 22 g; Mass of CCl_4 = 122 g

$$\text{Mass of solution} = 22 + 122 = 144 \text{ g}$$

$$\text{Mass \% of benzene} = \frac{22}{144} \times 100 = 15.28\%$$

$$\text{Mass \% of } CCl_4 = 100 - 15.28 = 84.72\%$$

Quick Solution

Mass percent of CCl_4 can also be calculated by using the formula as:

$$\text{Mass \% of } CCl_4 = \frac{122}{144} \times 100 = 84.72\%$$

Question 2 Calculate the mole fraction of benzene in solution containing 30% by mass in carbon tetrachloride.

◎ *Thinking Process*

(i) Concentration 30% by mass shows that 30 g C_6H_6 is dissolved in 100 g solution or 70 g CCl_4. So, calculate the moles of each by dividing their mass with their molecular mass.

(ii) Then calculate the mole fraction by using the formula,

$$\text{Mole fraction of a component} = \frac{\text{Number of moles of the component}}{\text{Total number of moles of all components}}$$

$$x_A = \frac{n_A}{n_A + n_B}$$

Sol. Let the mass of solution = 100 g

Mass of benzene = 30 g

Mass of carbon tetrachloride = 100 − 30 = 70 g

Molar mass of benzene (C_6H_6) = $(12 \times 6) + (6 \times 1) = 72 + 6 = 78 \text{ g mol}^{-1}$

Moles of benzene, $n_{C_6H_6} = \dfrac{\text{Mass}}{\text{Molar mass}} = \dfrac{30\text{ g}}{78\text{ g mol}^{-1}} = 0.385\text{ mol}$

Molar mass of carbon tetrachloride $(CCl_4) = 12 + (35.5 \times 4)$

$= 12 + 142.0 = 154\text{ g mol}^{-1}$

Moles of CCl_4, $n_{CCl_4} = \dfrac{70\text{ g}}{(154\text{ g mol}^{-1})} = 0.454\text{ mol}$

Mole fraction of benzene, $x_{C_6H_6} = \dfrac{n_{C_6H_6}}{n_{C_6H_6} + n_{CCl_4}}$

$= \dfrac{0.385\text{ mol}}{(0.385 + 0.454)\text{ mol}} = 0.459$

Question 3 Calculate the molarity of each of the following solutions :

(a) 30 g of $Co(NO_3)_2 \cdot 6H_2O$ in 4.3 L of solution.

(b) 30 mL of 0.5 M H_2SO_4 diluted to 500 mL.

◎ ***Thinking Process***

(a) Molarity $= \dfrac{\text{Moles of solute}}{\text{Volume of solution in litre}}$

and moles of solute $= \dfrac{\text{Mass of solute}}{\text{Molar mass of solute}}$

So, first find molar mass by adding atomic masses of different elements, then find moles of solute and then molarity.

(b) Use molarity equation for dilution,

$$\underset{\text{(Before dilution)}}{M_1V_1} = \underset{\text{(After dilution)}}{M_2V_2}$$

Sol. (a) Molar mass of $Co(NO_3)_2 \cdot 6H_2O$

$= (58.7) + 2(14 + 48) + (6 \times 18)\text{ g mol}^{-1}$

$= 58.7 + 124 + 108 = 290.7 \approx 291\text{ g mol}^{-1}$

Mole of $Co(NO_3)_2 \cdot 6H_2O = \dfrac{30\text{ g}}{291\text{ g mol}^{-1}} = 0.103$ mole

Volume of solution = 4.3 L

Molarity $(M) = \dfrac{0.103\text{ mol}}{4.3\text{ L}} = 0.024\text{ mol L}^{-1} = 0.024\text{ M}$

(b) Volume of undiluted H_2SO_4 solution $(V_1) = 30$ mL

Molarity of undiluted H_2SO_4 solution $(M_1) = 0.5$ M

Volume of diluted H_2SO_4 solution $(V_2) = 500$ mL

We know that $M_1V_1 = M_2V_2$

$\therefore \quad M_2 = \dfrac{M_1V_1}{V_2} = \dfrac{(0.5\text{ M}) \times (30\text{ mL})}{500\text{ mL}} = 0.03\text{ M}$

Quick Solution

No. of moles of H_2SO_4 in 1000 mL of 0.5 M H_2SO_4 = 0.5 mol

No. of moles of H_2SO_4 in 30 mL of 0.5 M $H_2SO_4 = \frac{0.5 \times 30}{1000}$ mol

$= 0.015$ mol

Volume of solution = 500 mL = 0.5 L

$$\text{Molarity} = \frac{0.015\,\text{mol}}{0.5\,\text{L}} = 0.03\ \text{mol L}^{-1} = 0.03\ \text{M}$$

Question 4 Calculate the mass of urea (NH_2CONH_2) required in making 2.5 kg of 0.25 molal aqueous solution.

◎ *Thinking Process*

We know that $\text{molality}\ (m) = \frac{\text{Moles of solute}}{\text{Mass of solvent in kg}}$

and $\text{moles of solute} = \frac{\text{Mass of solute}}{\text{Molar mass of solute}}$

So, find the molar mass of solute by adding atomic masses of different element present in it and then find mass by using the formula,

$$\text{Molality} = \frac{\text{Mass of solute / molar mass of solute}}{\text{Mass of solvent in kg}}$$

Sol. Molality of the solution = 0.25 m = 0.25 mol kg^{-1}

Molar mass of urea (NH_2CONH_2) = $(14 \times 2) + (1 \times 4) + 12 + 16$

$= 60\ \text{g mol}^{-1}$

0.25 molal aqueous solution of urea means 1000 g (or 1 kg) water contains 0.25 mol = 0.25×60 = 15 g urea

So, 1000 + 15 = 1015 g = 1.015 kg solution contains 15 g urea

$\therefore$ 2.5 kg solution contains $\frac{2.5 \times 15}{1.015}$ g = 36.95 g ≈ 37 g urea

Question 5 Calculate (a) molality (b) molarity and (c) mole fraction of KI if the density of 20% (mass/mass) aqueous KI is 1.202 g mL^{-1}.

◎ *Thinking Process*

(i) As density and % by mass is given, so find the mass of solute and solvent (as x % solution contains x g solute in $(100 - x)$ g solvent).

(ii) Find volume of the solution by using, $\text{Volume} = \frac{\text{Mass}}{\text{Density}}$

(iii) Recall the formulae of molality, molarity and mole fraction, to calculate them.

Sol. (a) **Molality** Let mass of solution of KI in water = 100 g

Weight of KI in solution = 20 g

Weight of water in the solution = 100 − 20 = 80 g = 0.08 kg

Molar mass of KI = 39 + 127 = 166 g mol^{-1}

$$\text{Molality of the solution } (m) = \frac{\text{Number of moles of KI}}{\text{Mass of water in kg}}$$

$$= \frac{(20\text{ g})/(166\text{ g mol}^{-1})}{(0.08\text{ kg})}$$

$$= 1.506 \text{ mol kg}^{-1}$$

$$= 1.506 \text{ m} \approx 1.51 \text{ m}$$

(b) **Molarity**

Weight of the solution = 100 g

Density of the solution = 1.202 g mL^{-1}

$$\text{Volume of the solution} = \frac{\text{Weight of solution}}{\text{Density}}$$

$$= \frac{(100\text{ g})}{(1.202\text{ g mL}^{-1})}$$

$$= 83.19 \text{ mL} = 0.083 \text{ L}$$

$$\text{Molarity of the solution } (M) = \frac{\text{Number of gram moles of KI}}{\text{Volume of solution in litres}}$$

$$= \frac{(20\text{ g})/(166\text{ g mol}^{-1})}{(0.083\text{ L})}$$

$$= 1.45 \text{ mol L}^{-1}$$

$$= 1.45 \text{ M}$$

(c) **Mole fraction of KI**

$$\text{Number of moles of KI, } n_{KI} = \frac{\text{Mass of KI}}{\text{Molar mass of KI}}$$

$$= \frac{(20\text{ g})}{(166\text{ g mol}^{-1})} = 0.12 \text{ mol}$$

$$\text{Number of moles of water, } n_{H_2O} = \frac{\text{Mass of water}}{\text{Molar mass of water}}$$

$$= \frac{(80\text{ g})}{(18\text{ g mol}^{-1})} = 4.44 \text{ mol}$$

$$\text{Mole fraction of KI, } x_{KI} = \frac{n_{KI}}{n_{KI} + n_{H_2O}} = \frac{(0.12\text{ mol})}{(0.12 + 4.44)\text{ mol}}$$

$$= \frac{0.12}{4.56} = 0.0263$$

Question 6 H_2S, a toxic gas with rotten egg like smell, is used for the qualitative analysis. If the solubility of H_2S in water at STP is 0.195 m, calculate Henry's law constant.

Thinking Process

(i) Molality is the moles present in 1000 g of water so find the moles of H_2S, if molality is 0.195 m.

(ii) Calculate the moles of water n_{H_2O} as we know from molality its mass is 1000 g.

(iii) Calculate the mole fraction of H_2S using the formula,

$$x_{H_2S} = \frac{n_{H_2S}}{n_{H_2S} + n_{H_2O}}$$

(iv) Calculate Henry's law constant K_H by using Henry's law $p = K_H \times x_{H_2S}$.

Sol. (a) **Calculation of mole fraction of H_2S** 0.195 m means that 0.195 mole of H_2S are dissolved in 1000 g of water.

Number of moles of water in 1000 g, $(n_{H_2O}) = \frac{(1000 \text{ g})}{(18 \text{ g mol}^{-1})}$

$$= 55.55 \text{ mol}$$

$$\text{Mole fraction } H_2S\ (x_{H_2S}) = \frac{n_{H_2S}}{n_{H_2S} + n_{H_2O}}$$

$$= \frac{(0.195 \text{ mol})}{(0.195 + 55.55) \text{ mol}}$$

$$= \frac{(0.195 \text{ mol})}{(55.745 \text{ mol})}$$

$$= 0.0035$$

(b) **Calculation of Henry's law constant**

According to Henry's law, $p_{H_2S} = K_H \times x_{H_2S}$

$$K_H \text{ for } H_2S = \frac{\text{Partial pressure of } H_2S \text{ at STP}}{x_{H_2S}}$$

$$= \frac{(0.987 \text{ bar})}{(0.0035)}$$

$$= 282 \text{ bar}$$

Note At STP, Pressure $(P) = 0.987$ bar

Mistake Alert Unit of K_H (Henry's law constant) is bar.

Question 7 Henry's law constant for CO_2 in water is 1.67×10^8 Pa at 298 K. Calculate the quantity of CO_2 in 500 mL of soda water when packed under 2.5 atm CO_2 pressure at 298 K.

◎ ***Thinking Process*** To calculate the mass of CO_2 dissolved, calculate the mole fraction of CO_2 by using Henry's law,

$$p = K_H \times x \quad \text{or} \quad x = \frac{p}{K_H}$$

Then calculate the number of moles and finally the mass.

Sol. **Step I Calculation of number of moles of CO_2**

According to Henry's law, $p_{CO_2} = K_H \times x_{CO_2}$

$$\text{Mole fraction of } CO_2\ (x_{CO_2}) = \frac{\text{Partial pressure of } CO_2}{K_H \text{ for } CO_2}$$

$$K_H = 1.67 \times 10^8 \text{ Pa} = \frac{(1 \text{ atm})}{(101325 \text{ Pa})} \times (1.67 \times 10^8 \text{ Pa})$$

$$= 1.648 \times 10^3 \text{ atm}$$

$$x_{CO_2} = \frac{2.5 \text{ atm}}{(1.648 \times 10^3 \text{ atm})} = 1.52 \times 10^{-3}$$

For 500 mL soda water,

⇒ Volume of water = 500 mL

⇒ Mass of water = 500 g

Consider density of water = 1 gmL^{-1}

$$n_{H_2O} = \frac{(500 \text{ g})}{(18 \text{ g mol}^{-1})} = 27.78 \text{ mol}$$

$$x_{CO_2} = \frac{n_{CO_2}}{n_{CO_2} + n_{H_2O}} = \frac{n_{CO_2}}{n_{H_2O}}$$

$$= \frac{n_{CO_2}}{(27.78 \text{ mol})} \qquad [n_{CO_2} << n_{H_2O}]$$

$$n_{CO_2} = x_{CO_2} \times (27.78 \text{ mol})$$

$$= (1.52 \times 10^{-3}) \times (27.78 \text{ mol})$$

$$= 0.0422 \text{ mol}$$

Note • 1 atm = 101325 Pa

• n_{CO_2} is considered negligible due to its little solubility in water.

Step II Calculation of mass of dissolved CO_2 in water

Mass of CO_2 = No · of moles CO_2 × Molar mass of CO_2

$= (0.0422 \text{ mol}) \times (44 \text{ g mol}^{-1})$

$= 1.857$ g

Question 8 The vapour pressure of pure liquids A and B are 450 and 700 mm Hg respectively, at 350 K. Find out the composition of the liquid mixture if total vapour pressure is 600 mm Hg. Also find the composition of the vapour phase.

◎ *Thinking Process* Apply Raoult's law

$p_T = p_A^\circ x_A + p_B^\circ x_B = p_A^\circ x_A + p_B^\circ (1 - x_A)$

to calculate mole fraction of $A(x_A)$ and $B(x_B)$.

In vapour phase, partial pressures are used instead of number of moles.

Sol. **Step I Composition in liquid phase**

Vapour pressure of pure liquid $A\,(p_A^\circ) = 450$ mm

Vapour pressure of pure liquid $B\,(p_B^\circ) = 700$ mm

Total vapour pressure of the solution $(p) = 600$ mm

According to Raoult'a law,

$$p = p_A^\circ x_A + p_B^\circ x_B = p_A^\circ x_A + p_B^\circ (1 - x_A)$$

$$(600 \text{ mm}) = 450 \text{ mm} \times x_A + 700 \text{ mm}\,(1 - x_A)$$

$$= 700 \text{ mm} + x_A \times (450 - 700) \text{ mm}$$

$$= 700 - x_A\,(250 \text{ mm})$$

$$x_A = \frac{(600 - 700)}{-(250 \text{ mm})} = 0.40$$

Mole fraction of $A\,(x_A) = 0.40$

Mole fraction of $B\,(x_B) = 1 - 0.40 = 0.60$

Step II Composition in vapour phase

$$p_A = p_A^\circ x_A = (450 \text{ mm}) \times 0.40 = 180 \text{ mm}$$

$$p_B = p_B^\circ x_B = (700 \text{ mm}) \times 0.60 = 420 \text{ mm}$$

Mole fraction of A in vapour phase $= \dfrac{p_A}{p_A + p_B}$

$$= \frac{(180) \text{ mm}}{(180 + 420) \text{ mm}} = 0.30$$

Mole fraction of B in vapour phase

$$= \frac{p_B}{p_A + p_B} = \frac{(420) \text{ mm}}{(180 + 420) \text{ mm}} = 0.70$$

Note $x_A + x_B = 1$

$\Rightarrow \quad x_B = 1 - x_A$

Question 9 Vapour pressure of pure water at 298 K is 23.8 mm Hg. 50 g urea (NH_2CONH_2) is dissolved in 850 g of water. Calculate the vapour pressure of water for this solution and its relative lowering.

◎ *Thinking Process* Consider Raoult's law and formula for relative lowering in vapour pressure,

$$\frac{p_A^\circ - p_S}{p_A^\circ} = \frac{n_B}{n_A} = \frac{W_B}{M_B} \times \frac{M_A}{W_A} \quad (\text{if } n_A >> n_B)$$

where, $\frac{p_A^\circ - p_S}{p_A^\circ}$ is called relative lowering in vapour pressure.

Sol. **Step I : Calculation of vapour pressure of water for this solution (p_s)**

According to Raoult's law,

$$\frac{p_A^\circ - p_S}{p_A^\circ} = \frac{n_B}{n_A + n_B} = \frac{W_B / M_B}{W_A / M_A + W_B / M_B} \quad \ldots(i)$$

(Pure water) $p_A^\circ = 23.8$ mm;

$$W_B \text{ (urea)} = 50 \text{ g}; W_A \text{ (water)} = 850 \text{ g}$$

$$M_B\text{(urea)} = 60 \text{ g mol}^{-1}; M_A \text{ (water)} = 18 \text{ g mol}^{-1}$$

Placing the values in eq. (i)

$$\frac{p_A^\circ - p_S}{p_A^\circ} = \frac{(50/60)}{(50/60) \times (850/18)} = \frac{0.83}{0.83 + 47.22}$$

$$\frac{23.8 - p_S}{23.8} = 0.0173; 23.8 - p_S = 0.4117$$

$$p_s = 23.388 \approx 23.39 \text{ mm Hg} \approx 23.4 \text{ mm Hg}$$

Step II : Calculation of relative lowering of vapour pressure

Relative lowering in vapour pressure $= \frac{p_A^\circ - p_S}{p_A^\circ}$

$$= \frac{(23.8 - 23.388) \text{ mm}}{(23.8 \text{ mm})}$$

$$= 0.0173$$

Question 10 Boiling point of water 750 mm Hg is 99.63°C. How much sucrose is to be added to 500 g of water such that it boils at 100 °C. [K_b for water is 0.52 K kg mol^{-1}]

◎ *Thinking Process*

(i) Since boiling point is changing, apply the formula for elevation in boiling point, $\Delta T_b = K_b \cdot m$.

(ii) $m = \dfrac{W_B}{M_B \cdot W_A}$

So, $\Delta T_b = \dfrac{K_b \cdot W_B}{M_B \times W_A}$ or $W_B = \dfrac{\Delta T_b \times M_B \times W_A}{K_b}$

(iii) Find ΔT_b as $\Delta T_b = T_b - T_b^\circ$

T_b = Boiling point of solution.

T_b° = Boiling point of pure solvent

Sol. Mass of water (W_A) = 500 g = 0.5 kg

Elevation in boiling point (ΔT_b) = 100°C − 99.63°C = 0.37°C = 0.37 K

Molal elevation constant (K_b) = 0.52 K kg mol^{-1}

Molar mass sucrose $C_{12}H_{22}O_{11}$ (M_B) = (12 × 12) + (22 × 1) + (16 × 11)

$$= 342 \text{ g mol}^{-1}$$

$$\Delta T_b = K_b m = \frac{K_b \cdot W_B}{M_B \times W_A}$$

$$W_B = \frac{M_B \times \Delta T_B \times W_A}{K_b}$$

$$= \frac{(342 \text{ g mol}^{-1}) \times (0.37 \text{ K}) \times (0.5 \text{ kg})}{(0.52 \text{ K kg mol}^{-1})}$$

$$= 121.7 \text{ g}$$

Question 11 Calculate the mass of ascorbic acid (Vitamin C, $C_6H_8O_6$) to be dissolved in 75 g of acetic acid to lower its melting point by 1.5°C. K_f = 3.9 K kg mol^{-1}.

◎ *Thinking Process* Since, lowering of melting point is given apply the formula for lowering of melting point, *i.e.*,

$$\Delta T_f = K_f \cdot m$$

$$\Delta T_f = \frac{K_f \cdot W_B}{M_B \times W_A}$$

or

$$W_B = \frac{\Delta T_f \cdot M_B \cdot W_A}{K_f}$$

Sol. Mass of ascorbic acid $(W_A) = 75 \text{ g} = 0.075 \text{ kg}$

Depression in melting point $(\Delta T_f) = 1.5°\text{ C} = 1.5 \text{ K}$

Molar mass of ascorbic acid $(M_B) = (12 \times 6) + (8 \times 1) + (16 \times 6)$

$= 176 \text{ g mol}^{-1}$

Molal depression constant $(K_f) = 3.9 \text{ K kg mol}^{-1}$

$$\Delta T_f = \frac{K_f \cdot W_B}{M_B W_A}$$

$$W_B = \frac{\Delta T_f \times W_A \times M_B}{K_f}$$

$$W_B = \frac{(176 \text{ g mol}^{-1}) \times (1.5 \text{ K}) \times (0.075 \text{ kg})}{(3.9 \text{ K kg mol}^{-1})}$$

$$= 5.08 \text{ g}$$

Question 12 Calculate the osmotic pressure in pascals exerted by a solution prepared by dissolving 1.0 g of polymer of molar mass 185000 in 450 mL of water at 37°C.

◎ ***Thinking Process*** Use the formula for osmotic pressure $(\pi) = CRT$, and $C = \frac{n}{V}$ and $n = \frac{W_B}{M_B}$

Sol. Mass of polymer $(W_B) = 1.0 \text{ g}$

Molar mass of polymer $(M_B) = 185000 \text{ g mol}^{-1}$

Volume of solution $(V) = 450 \text{ mL} = 0.450 \text{ L}$

Temperature $(T) = 37 + 273 = 310 \text{ K}$

Gas constant $(R) = 8.314 \times 10^3 \text{ Pa L K}^{-1} \text{ mol}^{-1}$

Osmotic pressure $(\pi) = CRT = nRT / V$

$$= \frac{W_B \times R \times T}{M_B \times V}$$

$$\therefore \quad \pi = \frac{(1.0 \text{ g}) \times (8.314 \times 10^3 \text{ Pa L K}^{-1} \text{ mol}^{-1}) \times (310 \text{ K})}{(185000 \text{ g mol}^{-1}) \times (0.450 \text{ L})}$$

$$= 30.96 \text{ Pa}$$

Exercises

Question 1 Define the term solution. How many types of solutions are formed? Write briefly about each type with an example.

◎ *Thinking Process* Solution is the homogeneous mixture of 2 or more components. Define and classify them on the basis of difference in their components.

Sol. A solution is a homogeneous mixture of two or more pure substances. It means their composition and properties are uniform throughout the solution. Solute and solvent are two components of a solution.

Types of solutions On the basis of different states of solute and solvent, solutions are of three types mainly, which are further categorized into three.

These are listed in the following table with examples.

Types of solutions	Solute	Solvent	Examples
1. Gaseous solutions	(a) Gas	Gas	Mixture of oxygen and nitrogen gases.
	(b) Liquid	Gas	Moisture in air.
	(c) Solid	Gas	Camphor in nitrogen gas.
2. Liquid solutions	(a) Gas	Liquid	Oxygen dissolved in water.
	(b) Liquid	Liquid	Ethanol dissolved in water.
	(c) Solid	Liquid	Glucose dissolved in water.
3. Solid solutions	(a) Gas	Solid	Solution of hydrogen in palladium.
	(b) Liquid	Solid	Amalgam of mercury with sodium.
	(c) Solid	Solid	Alloys

Question 2 Given an example of a solid solution in which the solute is a gas.

Sol. Solution of hydrogen (solute) in palladium (solvent).

Question 3 Define the following terms.

(i) Mole fraction (ii) Molality
(iii) Molarity (iv) Mass percentage

Sol. (i) **Mole fraction** Mole fraction may be defined as the ratio of the number of moles of one component (solute or solvent) to the total number of all the components present in the solution.

Mole fraction of a component

$$= \frac{\text{Number of moles of component}}{\text{Total number of moles of all the components}}$$

For example, in a binary mixture, if the number of moles of A and B are n_A and n_B respectively, the mole fraction of A and B will be x_A and x_B. [Mole fraction is a ratio, so it has no unit.]

$$x_A = \frac{n_A}{n_A + n_B}; \quad x_B = \frac{n_B}{n_A + n_B}$$

(ii) **Molality** The number of moles of the solute (n) per kilogram (kg) of the solvent is known as molality (m).

$$\text{Molality}(m) = \frac{\text{Moles of solute}}{\text{Mass of solvent in kg}}$$

Unit of molality is **mol kg^{-1}** or **m (molal)**

(iii) **Molarity** Molarity (M) is defined as 'the number of moles of solute dissolved in one litre (or one cubic decimetre) of solution.

$$\text{Molarity}(M) = \frac{\text{Moles of solute}}{\text{Volume of solution in litre}}$$

Unit of molarity is **mol L^{-1}** or M **(Molar)**

(iv) **Mass percentage** It may be defined as mass of solute per 100 g of solution.

$$\text{Mass \% of solute} = \frac{\text{Mass of solute}}{\text{Mass of solution}} \times 100$$

Question 4 Concentrated nitric acid used in laboratory work is 68% nitric acid by mass in aqueous solution. What should be the molarity of such a sample of the acid if the density of the solution is 1.504 g mL^{-1}?

◎ Thinking Process

(i) Since mass percentage *i.e.*, mass of solute (HNO_3) in 100 g solution is given, find mass of HNO_3; then calculate its molar mass and number of moles.

(ii) From density, find the volume of solution.

(iii) Calculate the molarity by applying the formula,

$$\text{Molarity} = \frac{\text{Moles of solute}}{\text{Volume of solution (in L)}}$$

Sol. 68% HNO_3 by mass means

$$\text{Mass of nitric acid} = 68\text{ g}$$
$$\text{Mass of solution} = 100\text{ g}$$
$$\text{Molar mass of } HNO_3 = (1) + (14) + (16 \times 3) = 63\text{ g mol}^{-1}$$
$$\text{Number of moles of } HNO_3(n_{HNO_3}) = \frac{W}{M} = \frac{(68\text{ g})}{(63\text{ g/mol})} = 1.079\text{ mol}$$
$$\text{Density of solution} = 1.504\text{ g mL}^{-1}$$
$$\text{Volume of solution} = \frac{\text{Mass}}{\text{Density}} = \frac{(100\text{ g})}{(1.504\text{ g mL}^{-1})}$$
$$= 66.5\text{ mL or } 0.0665\text{ L}$$
$$\text{Molarity} = \frac{\text{Moles of solute}}{\text{Volume of solution in litres}}$$
$$= \frac{(1.079\text{ mol})}{(0.0665\text{ L})}$$
$$= 16.23\text{ mol L}^{-1}\text{ or } 16.23\text{ M}$$

Question 5 A solution of glucose in water is labelled as 10% *w*/ *w*. What should be the molality and mole fraction of each component in the solution? If the density of solution is 1.2 g mL^{-1}, then what shall be the molarity of the solution?

◎ Thinking Process

(i) As percentage by weight is given find weight of solute (W_B) and solvent (W_A) from it and calculate molar mass of solute (glucose), M_B by adding atomic masses of different elements.

(ii) Calculate molality by using, $m = \dfrac{W_B / M_B}{W_A}$.

(iii) In order to calculate mole fraction, calculate the number of moles of solute and solvent.

(iv) Calculate the volume by the formula of density and then molarity by using moles of solute and volume of solution.

Sol. **Calculation of molality of the solution**

10% w/w glucose solution means

$$W_B = \text{Mass of glucose} = 10\text{ g}$$
$$\text{Mass of solution} = 100\text{ g}$$
$$W_A = \text{Mass of water (solvent)}$$
$$= 100 - 10 = 90\text{ g} = 0.09\text{ kg}$$
$$M_B = \text{Molar mass of glucose } (C_6H_{12}O_6)$$
$$= (12 \times 6) + (1 \times 12) + (16 \times 6)$$
$$= 72 + 12 + 96 = 180\text{ g mol}^{-1}$$

$$\text{Molality of solution } (m) = \frac{W_B / M_B}{W_A} = \frac{(10\text{ g})/(180\text{ g mol}^{-1})}{(0.09\text{ kg})}$$

$$= \frac{(10\text{ g})}{(180\text{ g mol}^{-1}) \times (0.09\text{ kg})}$$

$$= 0.617\text{ mol kg}^{-1} \text{ or } 0.617\text{ m}$$

Calculation of mole fraction (solute and solvent both)

$$\text{Number of moles of glucose } (n_B) = \frac{W_B}{M_B} = \frac{(10\text{ g})}{(180\text{ g mol}^{-1})} = 0.055\text{ mol}$$

$$\text{Number of moles of water } (n_A) = \frac{W_A}{M_A} = \frac{(90\text{ g})}{(18\text{ g mol}^{-1})} = 5.0\text{ mol}$$

$$\text{Mole fraction of glucose } (x_B) = \frac{n_B}{n_B + n_A} = \frac{0.055\text{ mol}}{(0.055 + 5.0)\text{ mol}} = 0.01$$

$$\text{Mole fraction of water } (x_A) = \frac{n_A}{n_B + n_A} = \frac{(5.0\text{ mol})}{(0.055 + 5.0)\text{ mol}} = 0.99$$

Calculation of molarity of the solution

Mass of solution = 100 g

Density of solution = 1.2 g mL^{-1}

$$\text{Volume of solution} = \frac{\text{Mass}}{\text{Density}} = \frac{(100\text{ g})}{(1.2\text{ g mL}^{-1})}$$

$$= 83.33\text{ mL} = 0.0833\text{ L}$$

Molarity of solution

$$(M) = \frac{\text{Mass of glucose / Molar mass of glucose}}{\text{Volume of solution in litres}}$$

$$= \frac{(10\text{ g})/(180\text{ g mol}^{-1})}{(0.08333\text{ L})}$$

$$= 0.67\text{ mol L}^{-1} = 0.67\text{ M}$$

Question 6 How many mL of 0.1 M HCl are required to react completely with 1 g mixture of Na_2CO_3 and $NaHCO_3$ containing equimolar amounts of both?

◎ Thinking Process

(i) Find the moles of Na_2CO_3 and $NaHCO_3$ by assuming mass of Na_2CO_3 is x, calculate the mass of Na_2CO_3 and $NaHCO_3$ as Na_2CO_3 and $NaHCO_3$ are equimolar.

(ii) Calculate the total mass of HCl required by unitary method.]

(iii) Finally calculate the volume of HCl required, from the formula of molarity, as we know the molarity of solution.

Sol. **Step I** Calculating the mass of Na_2CO_3 and $NaHCO_3$

Mass of the mixture = 1.0 g

Let the mass of Na_2CO_3 = x g

Then the mass of $NaHCO_3$ = $(1 - x)$ g

$$\text{Moles of } Na_2CO_3 = \frac{\text{Mass}}{\text{Molar mass}}$$

$$= \frac{x \text{ g}}{[(23 \times 2) + (12) + (16 \times 3)] \text{ g mol}^{-1}}$$

$$= \frac{x}{106} \text{ mol}$$

$$\text{Moles of } NaHCO_3 = \frac{\text{Mass}}{\text{Molar mass}}$$

$$= \frac{(1 - x) \text{ g}}{[(23) + (1) + (12) + (16 \times 3)] \text{ g mol}^{-1}}$$

$$= \frac{(1 - x)}{84} \text{ mol}$$

According to the question, the mixture contains equimolar amounts of Na_2CO_3 and $NaHCO_3$.

$$\text{Moles of } Na_2CO_3 = \text{Moles of } NaHCO_3$$

$$\frac{x}{106} \text{ mol} = \frac{(1 - x)}{84} \text{ mol}$$

$$84x = 106 - 106\,x;\ 106x + 84x = 106$$

$$190x = 106;\ x = \frac{106}{190} = 0.558 \text{ g}$$

$\therefore$ Mass of Na_2CO_3 = 0.558 g

Mass of $NaHCO_3$ = (1 − 0.558) = 0.442 g

Step II Calculating total mass of HCl required

$$Na_2CO_3(s) + 2\,HCl(aq) \rightarrow 2\,NaCl(aq) + H_2O\,(l) + CO_2x\,(g)$$

106 g   73 g

According to the above equation

$\because$ 106 g Na_2CO_3 require HCl to react completely = 73 g

$\because$ 0.558 g $NaCO_3$ require HCl to react completely = $\frac{73 \times 0.558}{106}$ g

= 0.384 g

$$NaHCO_3(s) + HCl\,(aq) \longrightarrow NaCl\,(aq) + H_2O\,(l) + CO_2(g)$$

84 g   36.5 g

$\because$ 84 g $NaHCO_3$ require HCl = 36.5 g

$\therefore$ 0.442 g $NaHCO_3$ require HCl = $\frac{36.5 \times 0.442}{84}$ g = 0.192 g

Total mass of HCl required = (0.384 + 0.192) g = 0.576 g

Step III Calculating volume of HCl required

Mass of HCl required = 0.576 g

Molarity of HCl solution = 0.1 M

$$\text{Molarity }(M) = \frac{\text{Mass/Molar mass}}{\text{Volume of HCl in litres}}$$

$$(0.1 \text{ mol L}^{-1}) = \frac{(0.576 \text{ g})/(36.5 \text{ g mol}^{-1})}{\text{Volume in litres}}$$

$$\text{Volume }(V) = \frac{0.576}{36.5 \times 0.1} = 0.1578 \text{ L} = 157.8 \text{ mL}$$

Question 7 A solution is obtained by mixing 300 g of 25% solution and 400 g of 40% solution by mass. Calculate the mass percentage of the resulting solution.

◎ ***Thinking Process***

(i) Calculate the masses of solute in both the solutions separately.
(ii) Find the mass of solute and solution after mixing.
(iii) And then mass % of solute and solvent in the resulting solution.

Sol. Mass of solute in I solution $= \frac{25}{100} \times 300 \text{ g} = 75 \text{ g}$

Mass of solute in II solution $= \frac{40}{100} \times 400 \text{ g} = 160 \text{ g}$

After mixing both solutions,

Total mass of solute = (75 + 160) g = 235 g

Total mass of solution = (300 + 400) g = 700 g

Mass % of solute in final solution $= \frac{(235 \text{ g})}{(700 \text{ g})} \times 100 = 33.57\%$

Mass % solvent in final solution = 100 − 33.57 = 66.43%

Question 8 An antifreeze solution is prepared from 222.6 g of ethylene glycol ($C_2H_6O_2$) and 200 g of water. Calculate the molality of the solution. If the density of the solution is 1.072 g m L^{-1}, then what shall be the molarity of the solution?

◎ ***Thinking Process***

(i) In order to find molality, moles of ethylene glycol is required. So, first calculate the molar mass of ethylene glycol and then convert the mass (222.6 g) into moles by dividing it by molar mass.

(ii) Then, calculate molality (m) using the formula, $m = \frac{n \times 1000}{W(\text{g})}$

(iii) In order to calculate molarity, volume (V) is required which is calculated from density, then calculate molarity (M) by using the formula;

$$M = \frac{n \times 1000}{V(\text{ml})}$$

Sol. **Step I : Calculation of molality of the solution**

Mass of ethylene glycol = 222.6 g

Molar mass of ethylene glycol ($C_2H_6O_2$)

$$= (12 \times 2) + (1 \times 6) + (16 \times 2)$$

$$= 24 + 6 + 32 = 62 \text{ g mol}^{-1}$$

Mass of water = 200 g = 0.2 kg

$$\text{Molality } (m) = \frac{\text{Mass of ethylene glycol / Molar mass}}{\text{Mass of solvent in kg}}$$

$$= \frac{(222.6 \text{ g})/(62 \text{ g mol}^{-1})}{0.2 \text{ kg}} = 17.95 \text{ mol kg}^{-1}$$

$$= 17.95 \text{ m}$$

Step II : Calculation of molarity of the solution

Density of the solution = 1.072 g mL^{-1}

Mass of solution = Mass of solute + Mass of solution

$$= 222.6 \text{ g} + 200 \text{ g} = 422.6 \text{ g}$$

$$\text{Volume} = \frac{\text{Mass}}{\text{Density}} = \frac{422.6 \text{ g}}{1.072 \text{ g mL}^{-1}} = 394.22 \text{ mL}$$

$$= 0.39422 \text{ L}$$

$$\text{Molarity } (M) = \frac{\text{Mass of ethylene glycol / Molar mass}}{\text{Volume in litres}}$$

$$= \frac{(222.6 \text{ g})/(62 \text{ g mol}^{-1})}{0.39422}$$

$$= 9.107 \text{ mol L}^{-1} = 9.11 \text{ M}$$

Question 9 A sample of drinking water was found to be severely contaminated with chloroform ($CHCl_3$) supposed to a carcinogen. The level of contamination was 15 ppm (by mass) :

(i) Express this in per cent by mass.

(ii) Determine the molality of chloroform in the water sample.

Thinking Process ppm = parts per million – 10^6 units

Determine mass % and molality as in previous problems.

Sol. (i) Percentage (%) by mass of $CHCl_3$

$$= \frac{\text{Mass of CHCl}_3}{\text{Mass of solution}} \times 100$$

$$= \frac{(15.0 \text{ g})}{(10^6 \text{ g})} \times 100 = 1.5 \times 10^{-3}\%$$

(ii) Molality of solution $(m) = \dfrac{\text{Mass of CHCl}_3/\text{Molar mass}}{\text{Mass of water in kg}}$

$$= \frac{15/(12 + 1 + 106.5)}{10^6/1000 \text{ kg}}$$

$$= \frac{(15 \text{ g})}{(119.5 \text{ g mol}^{-1})} \times \frac{1000}{10^6 \text{ kg}}$$

$$= 1.255 \times 10^{-4} \text{ mol kg}^{-1}$$

$$= 1.255 \times 10^{-4} \text{ m}$$

Question 10 What role does the molecular interaction play in a solution of alcohol and water?

◎ ***Thinking Process*** Alcohols and water have O—H bond, because of which they are capable to form H-bonds.

Sol. Between the molecules of alcohol as well as water, hydrogen bonding is one of the interactive forces between the molecules. When alcohol and water are mixed together, new H-bonds also develop between alcohol and water molecules but these are weaker than the previous ones. So, the magnitude of attractive forces tends to decrease and the solution shows positive deviation from Raoult's law. This will lead to increase in vapour pressure of the solution and also decrease in its boiling point.

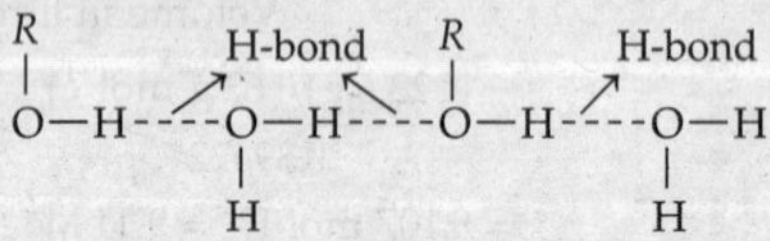

Question 11 Why do gases always tend to be less soluble in liquids as the temperature is raised?

◎ ***Thinking Process*** Consider the heat exchange during dissolution of gases in liquids and give answer on the basis of Le-Chatelier's principle.

Sol. Gas + Liquid $\rightleftharpoons$ Dissolving gas; $\Delta H = -$ ve.

Dissolution of gas is an exothermic process. As the temperature is raised, the equilibrium shifts in reverse direction (Le-Chatelier's principle). It results in decrease of solubility of gases in liquid.

Question 12 State Henry's law and mention some important applications?

◎ ***Thinking Process*** Henry's law is, $p \propto x$. State this in the form of statement and give its applications, like dissolution of CO_2 in soda water, less oxygen intake at high altitudes, etc.

Sol. **Henry's law** This law states that 'the solubility of a gas in a liquid at a particular temperature is directly proportional to the pressure of the gas in equilibrium with the liquid at that temperature.'

or

'The partial pressure of the gas in vapour phase (p) is proportional to the mole fraction of the gas (x) in the solution'. It is expressed as

$$p = K_H x$$

where, K_H = Henry's law constant

p = Partial pressure of the gas in vapour phase

x = Mole fraction of the gas

Applications of Henry's law

(i) To increase the solubility of CO_2 in soda water and soft drinks, the bottle is sealed under high pressure.

(ii) Scuba divers have high concentrations of dissolved gases of air in blood as the pressure is high underwater. But, when divers come towards the surface, the pressure decreases gradually, which causes the release of dissolved gases and leads to the formation of bubbles of nitrogen in the blood. This blocks the capillaries and creates bends (medical condition), which are painful and dangerous to life. To avoid the toxic effects of high concentration of nitrogen in the blood, the tanks used by scuba divers are filled with air diluted with helium (11.7% helium, 56.2% nitrogen and 32.1% oxygen).

(iii) At high altitudes, the partial pressure of oxygen is less than that at the ground level, so it leads to low blood oxygen which causes climbers to become weak and make them unable to think clearly, these are symptoms of a condition known as anoxia.

Question 13 The partial pressure of ethane over a solution containing 6.56×10^{-3} g of ethane is 1 bar. If the solution contains 5.00×10^{-2} g of ethane, then what shall be the partial pressure of gas?

Thinking Process According to Henry's law $m \propto p$ (at constant T), so compare the pressures for two different mole fractions (or masses) as solute is same.

Sol. According to Henry's law, The mass of the gas (m) dissolved in solution $\propto$ Partial pressure (p) (At constant temperature)

$$\therefore \quad (6.56 \times 10^{-3} \text{ g}) \propto 1 \text{ bar}$$

$$6.56 \times 10^{-3} \text{ g} = K_H \times 1 \text{ bar}$$

$$K_H = 6.56 \times 10^{-3} \text{ g bar}^{-1}$$

$$\Rightarrow \quad (5.00 \times 10^{-2} \text{ g}) \propto p$$

$$5 \times 10^{-2} g = K_H p \text{ or } p = \frac{(5.0 \times 10^{-2} \text{ g})}{(6.56 \times 10^{-3} \text{ g})} \times (1 \text{ bar}) = 7.62 \text{ bar}$$

Question 14 What is meant by positive and negative deviations from Raoult's law and how the sign of $\Delta_{mix} H$ related to positive and negative deviations from Raoult's law?

◎ *Thinking Process* Positive deviation means A—B interaction are weaker than A—A and B—B interaction while opposite is true in case of negative deviation. Also give the related expressions and graphs.

Sol. **Positive deviation** 'When the vapour pressure of a solution is higher than the predicted value by Raoult's law, it is called positive deviation'. In such cases intermolecular interactions between solute and solvent particles (A and B) are weaker than those between solute-solute ($A-A$) and solvent-solvent ($B-B$). Hence, the molecules (of A or B) will escape more easily from the surface of solution than in their pure state. Therefore, the vapour pressure of the solution will be higher.

Characteristics of a solution showing positive deviation

(i) $p_A > p_A^\circ x_A$; $p_B > p_B^\circ x_B$
(ii) $\Delta H_{mix} > 0$; *i.e.*, +ve
(iii) $\Delta V_{mix} > 0$, *i.e.*, +ve

Examples of solutions showing positive deviation

(i) Ethyl alcohol and water
(ii) Acetone and carbon disulphide
(iii) Carbon tetrachloride and benzene
(iv) Acetone and benzene

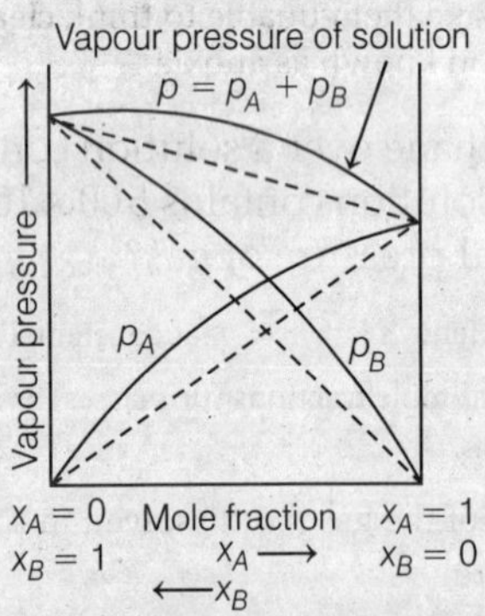

Vapour pressure diagram showing positive deviation

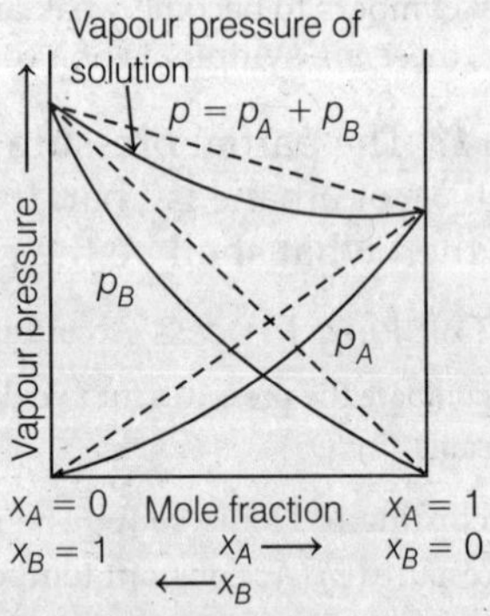

Vapour pressure diagram showing negative deviation

Negative deviation 'When the vapour pressure of a solution is lower than the predicted value by Raoult's law, it is called negative deviation.' In case of negative deviation the intermolecular attractive forces between $A-A$ and $B-B$ are weaker than those between $A-B$. It leads to decrease in vapour pressure resulting in negative deviation.

Characteristics of a solution showing negative deviation

1. $p_A < \overset{\circ}{p}_A x_A$: $p_B < \overset{\circ}{p}_B x_B$
2. $\Delta H_{mix} < 0$; *i.e.*, – ve; because weak $A - A$ and $B - B$ bonds are broken and strong $A - B$ bonds is formed. Heat is consequently released.
3. $\Delta V_{mix} < 0$; *i.e.*,–ve

Examples of solutions showing negative deviation

(i) HNO_3 and water
(ii) Chloroform and acetone
(iii) Acetic acid and pyridine
(iv) Hydrochloric acid and water.

Question 15 An aqueous solution of 2% non-volatile solute exerts a pressure of 1.004 bar at the normal boiling point of the solvent. What is the molar mass of the solute?

◎ *Thinking Process* Normal vapour pressure of pure water = 1.013 bar and vapour pressure of solution = 1.004 bar

As vapour pressure is changing, use the formula of relative lowering in vapour pressure, and calculate the molar mass by substituting the other values.

Sol. Relative lowering in vapour pressure.

$$\frac{\overset{\circ}{p}_A - p_S}{\overset{\circ}{p}_A} = \frac{n_B}{n_A} = \frac{W_B}{M_B} \times \frac{M_A}{W_A} \quad \ldots(i)$$

$\overset{\circ}{p}_A$ (water) = 1.013 bar; $W_B = 2$ g; $M_A = 18$ g mol^{-1}

p_S (water) = 1.004 bar ; $W_A = (100 - 2) = 98$ g; $M_B = ?$

Placing the values in equation (i)

$$\frac{(1.013 - 1.004) \text{ bar}}{(1.013 \text{ bar})} = \frac{(2\text{ g}) \times (18 \text{ g mol}^{-1})}{M_B \times (98\text{g})}$$

$$M_B = \frac{(2\text{ g}) \times (18\text{ g mol}^{-1}) \times (1.013 \text{ bar})}{(0.009 \text{ bar}) \times (98\text{g})}$$

$$= 41.35 \text{ g mol}^{-1}$$

Question 16 Heptane and octane form an ideal solution. At 373 K, the vapour pressure, of the two liquid components are 105.2 kPa and 46.8 kPa respectively. What will be the vapour pressure of a mixture of 26.0 g of heptane and 35 g of octane?

◎ *Thinking Process*

(i) In order to calculate the mole fractions of heptane and octane first calculate their molar masses and moles and then use the formula of mole fraction, $x_A = \frac{n_A}{n_A + n_B}$.

(ii) Then calculate the vapour pressures, by using Raoult's law $p = p^0 x$.

Sol. Number of moles of octane $(n_A) = \dfrac{\text{Mass}}{\text{Molar mass}} = \dfrac{35\text{ g}}{114\text{ g mol}^{-1}}$

$= 0.307\text{ mol}$

[Molar mass of octane $C_8H_{18} = (12 \times 8) + (1 \times 18) = 114\text{ g mol}^{-1}$]

Number of moles of heptane $(n_B) = \dfrac{26\text{ g}}{100\text{ g mol}^{-1}} = 0.26\text{ mol}$

[Molar mass of heptane $C_7H_{16} = (12 \times 7) + 16 = 100\text{ g mol}^{-1}$]

Mole fraction of octane $(x_A) = \dfrac{n_A}{n_A + n_B} = \dfrac{(0.307\text{ mol})}{(0.307 + 0.26)\text{ mol}} = 0.541$

Mole fraction of heptane $(x_B) = \dfrac{n_B}{n_A + n_B} = \dfrac{(0.26\text{ mol})}{(0.307 + 0.26)\text{ mol}} = 0.459$

Vapour pressure of pure heptane $(p_B^\circ) = 105.2\text{ kPa}$

Vapour pressure of pure octane $(p_A^\circ) = 46.8\text{ kPa}$

In the mixture of 26.0 g heptane and 35.0 g octane

(i) Vapour pressure of heptane $(p_B) = p_B^\circ\, x_B$

$= (105.2\text{ kPa} \times 0.459)$

$= 48.29\text{ kPa}$

(ii) Vapour pressure of octane $(p_A) = p_A^\circ\, x_A = (46.8\text{ kPa} \times 0.541)$

$= 25.32\text{ kPa}$

(iii) Total vapour pressure of the mixture $(p) = p_A + p_B$

$= 25.32 + 48.29 = 73.61\text{ kPa}$

Question 17 The vapour pressure of water is 12.3 kPa at 300 K. Calculate vapour pressure of 1 molal solution of a non-volatile solute in it.

◎ ***Thinking Process***

(i) In order to calculate vapour pressure, mole fraction is required but we have molality. So, convert molality into mole fraction by using following steps.

(a) Find the moles of solute and mass of solvent from molality.

(b) Find of moles of solvent, *i.e.*, water by dividing its mass by molar mass.

(c) Find mole fraction of solute, $x_B = \dfrac{n_B}{n_A + n_B}$

(ii) Find mole fraction of solvent x_A as $x_A + x_B = 1$

(iii) Finally calculate the vapour pressure by using Raolut's law, $p = p^\circ x$.

Sol. Molality of solution is 1 m. It means that one mole of solute is dissolved in 1000 g of water.

Number of moles of solute (n_B) = 1 mol

Number of moles of water

$$(n_A) = \frac{\text{Mass of water}}{\text{Molar mass}} = \frac{(1000\text{ g})}{(18\text{ g mol}^{-1})}$$

$$= 55.55 \text{ mol}$$

Mole fraction of solute

$$(x_B) = \frac{n_B}{n_A + n_B} = \frac{(1\text{ mol})}{(55.55 + 1.0)\text{ mol}} = \frac{1}{56.55} = 0.0177$$

Mole fraction water $(x_A) = 1 - 0.0177 = 0.9823$

Vapour pressure of solution

$$(p_A) = p_A^\circ\, x_A = (12.3\text{ kPa}) \times 0.9823 = 12.08\text{ kPa}$$

Question 18 Calculate the mass of a non-volatile solute (molar mass 40 g mol^{-1}) which should be dissolved in 114 g octane to reduce its vapour pressure to 80%.

◎ ***Thinking Process*** As vapour pressure in changing, calculate the mass by using the formula of relative lowering of vapour pressure,

$$\frac{p^\circ - p_S}{p_S} = \frac{W_B}{M_B} \times \frac{M_A}{W_A}.$$

Sol. According to Raoult's law, relative lowering of vapour pressure,

$$\frac{p_A^\circ - p_S}{p_A^\circ} = x_B \qquad \text{...(i)}$$

$$x_B = \frac{n_B}{n_B + n_A} = \frac{W_B/M_B}{\frac{W_B}{M_B} + \frac{W_A}{M_A}} \qquad \text{...(ii)}$$

Given Vapour pressure is reduced to 80% when non-volatile solute is dissolved in octane. It means

If $p_A^\circ = 1$ atm then $p_S = 0.8$ atm; $p_A^\circ - p_S = 0.2$ atm;

$M_A\,(C_8H_{18}) = 114\text{ g mol}^{-1}$; $W_A = 114$ g; $M_B = 40\text{ g mol}^{-1}$; $W_B = ?$

Applying equation (ii)

$$0.2 = \frac{W_B/40}{\frac{W_B}{40} + \frac{114}{114}} = \frac{W_B/40}{\frac{W_B}{40} + 1}$$

$$0.2 = \frac{W_B}{W_B + 40}$$

$$0.2W_B + 8 = W_B$$

$$W_B = 10\text{ g}$$

Question 19 A solution containing 30 g of non-volatile solute exactly in 90 g of water has a vapour pressure of 2.8 kPa at 298 K. Further, 18 g of water is then added to the solution and the new vapour pressure becomes 2.9 kPa at 298 K. Calculate (i) molar mass of the solute (ii) vapour pressure of water at 298 K.

Thinking Process

(i) In the equation of Raoult's law ($p_A = p_A^\circ x_A$), mole fraction is required, so first find the moles of solute and solvent and then mole fraction in case first.

(ii) Now put the value of mole fraction in the equation of Raoult's law.

(iii) Make another equation in the similar way as mentioned above, when 18 g water is added (so the mass of water will become $= 90 + 18 = 108$ g).

(iv) Solve two equation to find molar mass.

(v) Put the value of molar mass in any of the two equations to find vapour pressure.

Sol. **Step I : Calculation of molar mass of the solute**

Case I Number of mole of solute

$$(n_B) = \frac{\text{Mass}}{\text{Molar mass}} = \frac{(30\text{ g})}{(M\text{ g mol}^{-1})} = \frac{30}{M}\text{ mol}$$

Number of moles of water

$$(n_A) = \frac{\text{Mass}}{\text{Molar mass}} = \frac{(90\text{ g})}{(18\text{ g mol}^{-1})} = 5\text{ mol}$$

Mole fraction of water

$$(x_A) = \frac{n_A}{n_A + n_B} = \frac{(5\text{ mol})}{\left(5\text{ mol} + \frac{30}{M}\text{ mol}\right)} = \frac{M}{(6 + M)}$$

Vapour pressure of Ist solution (p_A) = 2.8 kPa

According to Raoult's law, $p_A = p_A^\circ x_A$

$$(2.8\text{ kPa}) = p_A^\circ \times \frac{M}{(6 + M)} \quad \ldots\text{(i)}$$

Case II Number of moles of solute $(n_B) = \frac{30}{M}$ mol

Mass of water = (90 + 18)g = 108 g

Number of moles of water

$$(n_A) = \frac{\text{Mass}}{\text{Molar mass}} = \frac{(108\text{ g})}{(18\text{ g mol}^{-1})} = 6\text{ mol}$$

$$\text{Mole fraction of water } (x_A) = \frac{n_A}{n_A + n_B} = \frac{(6\text{ mol})}{\left(6\text{ mol} + \frac{30}{M}\text{ mol}\right)}$$

$$= \frac{M}{(5 + M)}$$

Vapour pressure of solution $(p_A) = 2.9$ kPa
According to Raoult's law, $p_A = p_A^\circ x_A$

$$(2.9 \text{ kPa}) = p_A^\circ \times \frac{M}{(5+M)} \quad \text{... (ii)}$$

Dividing Eq. (i) by Eq. (ii)

$$\frac{(2.8 \text{ kPa})}{(2.9 \text{ kPa})} = \frac{(5+M)}{(6+M)}$$

$$0.9655 = \frac{(5+M)}{(6+M)}$$

$$(0.9655 \times 6) + 0.9655 \text{ M} = 5 + M$$

$$0.0345 \text{ M} = 0.793$$

$$M = \frac{0.793}{0.0345} = 23 \text{ g mol}^{-1}$$

Step II : Calculation of vapour pressure of water
According to Rauolt's law, $p_A = p_A^\circ x_A$

or $$(2.8 \text{ kPa}) = p_A^\circ = \frac{M}{(6+M)} \quad \text{...(iii)}$$

Placing the value of M in Eq. (i)

$$2.8 \text{ kPa} = p_A^\circ \times \frac{(23 \text{ g mol}^{-1})}{(6+23) \text{ g mol}^{-1}}$$

$$p_A^\circ = \frac{2.8 \times 29}{23}$$

$$= \frac{81.2}{23} = 3.53 \text{ kPa}$$

Question 20 A 5% solution (by mass) of cane sugar in water has freezing point 271 K. Calculate freezing point of 5% glucose in water if freezing point of pure water is 273.15 K.

◎ ***Thinking Process*** Freezing point of pure water is 273.15 K (0°C) and that of given solution is 271 K, *i.e.*, we have depression in freezing point.
So,

(i) Apply the formula of depression in freezing point for cane sugar and make it eq (i)

(ii) Similarly, find the depression in freezing point for glucose and make it eq (ii)

(iii) Compare the two equations to find the freezing point of glucose.

Sol. **For cane sugar solution**

W_B (sugar) = 5 g; W_A (water) = 100 − 5 = 95 g

M_B (sugar) = 342 g mol^{-1}; ΔT_f = (273.15 − 271.00) K = 2.15 K

$$\Delta T_f = \frac{K_f \times W_B}{M_B \times W_A}$$

$$(2.15\ \text{K}) = \frac{K_f \times (5\ \text{g}) \times 1000}{(342\ \text{g mol}^{-1}) \times (95\ \text{g})} \qquad \text{....(i)}$$

$$K_f = \frac{(2.15\ \text{K})\ (342\ \text{g mol}^{-1})\ (95\ \text{g})\ (1\ \text{kg})}{(5\ \text{g}) \times (1000\ \text{g})} = 13.971\ \text{K kg mol}^{-1}$$

For glucose solution

W_B (glucose) = 5 g; W_A (water) = 100 − 5 = 95 g

M_B (glucose) = 180 g mol^{-1}; ΔT_f = ?

$$\Delta T_f = \frac{K_f \times (5\ \text{g}) \times 1000}{(180\ \text{g mol}^{-1}) \times (95\ \text{g})} \qquad \text{...(ii)}$$

Put the value of K_f,

$$\Delta T_f = \frac{(13.971\ \text{K kg mol}^{-1}) \times (5\ \text{g}) \times (1000\ \text{g})}{(180\ \text{g mol}^{-1})\ (95\ \text{g})\ (1\ \text{kg})}$$

$$\Delta T_f = 4.085\ \text{K}$$

Freezing point temperature for 5% glucose solution

$$= (273.15 - 4.085)\ \text{K} = 269.07\ \text{K}$$

Question 21 Two elements *A* and *B* form compounds having formula AB_2 and AB_4. When dissolved in 20 g of benzene (C_6H_6), 1 g AB_2 lowers the freezing point by 2.3 K whereas 1.0 g of AB_4 lowers it by 1.3 K. The molar depression constant for benzene is 5.1 K kg mol^{-1}. Calculate atomic masses of *A* and *B*.

◎ ***Thinking Process*** Since, depression in freezing point is given, calculate

(i) molecular masses of AB_2 and AB_4.

(ii) atomic masses of elements *A* and *B*, from their molecular masses.

Sol. **Step I : Calculation of molecular masses of compounds AB_2 and AB_4**

For compound AB_2

$W_B\ (AB_2) = 1\ \text{g}$; $W_A\ (C_6H_6) = 20\ \text{g}$; $\Delta T_f = 2.3\ \text{K}$

$K_f = 5.1\ \text{K kg mol}^{-1} = 5.1 \times 1000\ \text{K g mol}^{-1}$

$$M_B = \frac{K_f \times W_B}{\Delta T_f \times W_A} = \frac{(5.1 \times 1000\ \text{K g mol}^{-1}) \times (1\ \text{g})}{(2.3\ \text{K}) \times (20\ \text{g})}$$

$$= 110.87\ \text{g mol}^{-1}$$

For compound AB_4

$W_B\ (AB_4) = 1\ \text{g}$; $W_A\ (C_6H_6) = 20\ \text{g}$; $\Delta T_f = 1.3\ \text{K}$

$K_f = 5.1\ \text{K kg mol}^{-1}$

$$M_B = \frac{(5.1\ \text{K} \times 1000\ \text{kg mol}^{-1}) \times (1\ \text{g})}{(1.3\ \text{K}) \times (20\ \text{g})} = 196.15\ \text{g mol}^{-1}$$

Step II : Calculation of the atomic masses of elements *A* and *B*

Let the atomic mass of element $A = a$

Let the atomic mass of element $B = b$

$$\text{Molecular mass of } AB_2 = a + 2b$$
$$\text{Molecular mass of } AB_4 = a + 4b$$

According to the available data

$$a + 2b = 110.87 \quad \text{... (i)}$$
$$a + 4b = 196.15 \quad \text{... (ii)}$$

Substract Eq. (i) from Eq. (ii)

$$a + 4b - a - 2b = 196.15 - 110.87$$
$$2b = 85.28;\ b = \frac{85.28}{2} = 42.64$$

Substituting the value of *b* in Eq. (i)

$$a + 2 \times 42.64 = 110.87$$
$$a + 85.28 = 110.87;\ a = 110.87 - 85.28 = 25.59$$

Thus, atomic mass of element $A = 25.59$ g/mol

Atomic mass of element $B = 42.64$ g/mol

Question 22 At 300 K, 36 g of glucose present in a litre of its solution has an osmotic pressure of 4.98 bar. If the osmotic pressure of the solution is 1.52 bar at the same temperature, what would be its concentration?

◎ ***Thinking Process*** Apply $\pi = CRT$ and $C = \frac{n}{V} = \frac{W_B}{M_B \times V}$ $\left(\because n = \frac{W_B}{M_B}\right)$

Sol. $\pi = CRT = \frac{W_B \times R \times T}{M_B \times V}$

For both solutions, *R*, *T* and *V* are constants.

For I solution

$$(4.98 \text{ bar}) = \frac{(36 \text{ g}) \times R \times T}{(180 \text{ g mol}^{-1}) \times V} \quad \text{...(i)}$$

For II solution

$$(1.52 \text{ bar}) = \frac{W_B \times R \times T}{M_B \times V} \quad \text{... (ii)}$$

On dividing Eq. (ii) by Eq. (i), we get

$$\frac{(1.52 \text{ bar})}{(4.98 \text{ bar})} = \frac{W_B \times R \times T}{M_B \times V} \times \frac{180 \times V}{36 \times R \times T}$$
$$\frac{W_B}{M_B} = \frac{1.52}{4.98 \times 5} = 0.0610 \text{ mol}$$

[Since, volume of the solution is 1 L.]

Concentration of solution = 0.061 M

Question 23 Suggest the most important type of intermolecular attractive interaction in the following pairs.

(i) *n*-hexane and *n*-octane

(ii) I_2 and CCl_4

(iii) $NaClO_4$ and water

(iv) Methanol and acetone

(v) Acetonitrile (CH_3CN) and acetone (C_3H_6O)

◎ **Thinking Process** Recall different types of intermolecular forces. London's forces exist between the non-polar molecules, ionic interactions are found in ionic compound and dipole interactions are found in polar compounds. —OH, —NH or HF bond if present, the molecule can form H-bond.

Sol. (i) London's forces/van der Waal's forces

(ii) London's forces/van der Waal's forces

(iii) Ion-dipole interactions

(iv) Intermolecular hydrogen bonding

(v) Dipole-dipole interactions

Question 24 Based on solute-solvent interactions, arrange the following in order of increasing solubility in *n*-octane and explain. Cyclohexane, KCl, CH_3OH, CH_3CN.

◎ **Thinking Process** 'Like dissolves like, *i.e.*, polar substance dissolves in polar solvent and non-polar solute dissolves in non-polar solvent.

Sol. (i) Cyclohexane and *n*-octane both are non-polar. So, they mix completely in all proportions.

(ii) KCl is an ionic compound, but *n*-octane is non-polar. So, KCl does not dissolve in *n*-octane.

(iii) CH_3OH and CH_3CN both are polar but CH_3CN is less polar than CH_3OH. As the solvent is non-polar, CH_3CN will dissolve more than CH_3OH in *n*-octane.

Order of solubility is $KCl < CH_3OH < CH_3CN <$ cyclohexane.

Question 25 Among the following compounds, identify which are insoluble, partially soluble and highly soluble in water?

(i) Phenol (ii) Toluene

(iii) Formic acid (iv) Ethylene glycol

(v) Chloroform (vi) Pentanol

◎ **Thinking Process** Consider different types of molecular forces.

Sol. (i) **Phenol : Partially soluble** (Reason : Phenol has polar –OH group and non-polar C_6H_5 – group).
(ii) **Toluene : Insoluble** (Reason : Toluene is non-polar, water is polar).
(iii) **Formic acid : Highly soluble** (Reason : Hydrogen bonding).
(iv) **Ethylene glycol : Highly soluble** (Reason : Hydrogen bonding).
(v) **Chloroform : Insoluble** (Reason : Chloroform is an organic liquid).
(vi) **Pentanol : Partially soluble** (Reason : –OH group is polar but long hydrocarbon part is non-polar).

Question 26 If the density of some lake water is 1.25 g mL^{-1} and contains 92 g of Na^+ ions per kg of water, calculate the molarity of Na^+ ions in the lake.

◎ *Thinking Process* Apply the formula for molarity, *i.e.*, find concentration in mol/L.

Sol. Mass of solution = mass of solute + mass of water

$$= (92 + 1000) \text{ g} = 1092 \text{ g}$$

$$\text{Volume of solution} = \frac{\text{mass of solution}}{\text{density of solution}}$$

$$= \frac{1092 \text{ g}}{1.25 \text{ g mL}^{-1}} = 873.6 \text{ mL}$$

$$\text{Molarity of Na}^+ \text{ ions } (M) = \frac{\text{Moles of Na}^+ \text{ ions}}{\text{Volume of solution (L)}}$$

$$= \frac{(92 \text{ g} / 23 \text{ g mol}^{-1})}{(873.6) \text{ mL}} \times 1000 = 4.579 \text{ M} \approx 4.58 \text{ M}$$

Question 27 If the solubility product of CuS is 6×10^{-6}, calculate the maximum molarity of CuS in aqueous solution.

◎ *Thinking Process* Write the reaction for dissociation of CuS. Find the concentration (molarity) according to it.
(See Chap. equilibrium of XI part I)

Sol. Chemical equation for the dissociation of CuS in aqueous solution is a follows :

$$\text{CuS}(s) \overset{H_2O}{\rightleftharpoons} \text{Cu}^{2+}(aq) + \text{S}^{2-}(aq)$$

Molar concentration, $[S]$ $[S]$ $[S]$

Solubility product, $K_{sp} = [\text{Cu}^{2+}][\text{S}^{2-}] = S \times S = S^2$

$$6 \times 10^{-16} = S^2$$

$$S = \sqrt{6 \times 10^{-16}} \text{ or } (6 \times 10^{-16})^{1/2}$$

$$= 2.45 \times 10^{-8} \text{ mol L}^{-1} \text{ or } 2.45 \times 10^{-8} \text{ M}$$

Question 28 Calculate the mass percentage of aspirin ($C_9H_8O_4$) in acetonitrile (CH_3CN) when 6.5 g of $C_9H_8O_4$ is dissolved in 450 g of CH_3CN.

◎ ***Thinking Process*** We know that mass % $= \dfrac{\text{Mass of solute}}{\text{Mass of solution}} \times 100$

and mass of solution = mass of solute + mass of solvent.
So, calculate mass of solution and then mass percentage.

Sol. Mass of aspirin = 6.5 g

Mass of acetonitrile = 450 g

Mass of solution = (6.5 + 450) g = 456.5 g

$$\text{Mass }\% = \frac{(6.5\text{ g})}{(456.5\text{ g})} \times 100 = 1.424\%$$

Question 29 Nalorphene ($C_{19}H_{21}NO_3$), similar to morphine, is used to combat withdrawal symptoms in narcotic users. Dose of nalorphene generally given is 1.5 mg. Calculate the mass of 1.5×10^{-3} m aqueous solution required for the above dose.

◎ ***Thinking Process***

(i) As molality is given, apply the formula for molality to calculate the mass of solvent.

(ii) Calculate molecular mass of $C_{19}H_{21}NO_3$ by adding atomic masses of all the atoms present in it.

Sol. $m = 1.5 \times 10^{-3}$ m or 1.5×10^{-3} mol kg^{-1}

Mass of solute = 1.5×10^{-3} g or 1.5 mg

Mass of solvent = ?

Molar mass of solute

$$(C_{19}H_{21}NO_3) = (12 \times 19) + (1 \times 21) + (14) + (16 \times 3)$$
$$= 311\text{ g mol}^{-1}$$

$$\text{Number of moles of solute} = \frac{\text{Mass}}{\text{Molar mass}} = \frac{(1.5 \times 10^{-3}\text{ g})}{(311\text{ g mol}^{-1})}$$

$$\text{Molality }(m) = \frac{\text{Number of moles}}{\text{Mass of solvent in kg}}$$

$$\text{Mass of solvent} = \frac{\text{Number of moles}}{\text{Molality}}$$

$$= \frac{(1.5 \times 10^{-3}\text{ g})}{(311\text{ g mol}^{-1})} \times \frac{1}{(1.5 \times 10^{-3}\text{ mol kg}^{-1})}$$

$$= \frac{1}{311} = 0.0032\text{ kg or } 3.2\text{ g}$$

Question 30 Calculate the amount of benzoic acid (C_6H_5COOH) required for preparing 250 mL of 0.15 M solution in methanol.

◎ ***Thinking Process*** As molarity is given, apply the formula for molarity, to find the mass of benzoic acid.

Sol. Molarity = 0.15 M or 0.15 mol L^{-1}, Volume solution = 250 mL = 0.25 L

Molar mass of solute = $(12 \times 6) + (1 \times 5) + (12) + (16 \times 2) + (1) = 122 \text{ g mol}^{-1}$

$$\text{Molarity} = \frac{\text{Mass}}{\text{Molar mass}} \times \frac{1}{\text{Volume (L)}};$$

$$(0.15 \text{ mol L}^{-1}) = \frac{W}{(122 \text{ g mol}^{-1})} \times \frac{1}{(0.25 \text{ L})}$$

Mass of solute (Benzoic acid) = $(0.15 \times 122 \times 0.25)$ g = 4.575 g

Question 31 The depression in freezing point of water observed for the same amount of acetic acid, trichloroacetic acid and trifluoroacetic acid increases in the order given above. Explain briefly.

◎ ***Thinking Process*** Depression in freezing point of a solvent due to the dissolution of a solute is dependent on the degree of dissociation (α). ΔT_f is directly proportional to α.

Sol. The depression in freezing point of a solute in water depends upon the number of particles or ions in its aqueous solution or its degree of dissociation (α). Three acids are arranged in the order of their increasing acidic strengths as follows :

$$CH_3COOH < CCl_3COOH < CF_3COOH$$

This is the order in which acids easily lose H^+ ions and gets ionized to produce more ions.

Fluorine is more electronegative than chlorine. So, trifluoroacetic acid is stronger acid than trichloroacetic acid which in turn is stronger than acetic acid. The order of depression in freezing point is also the same.

Question 32 Calculate the depression in the freezing point of water when 10 g of $CH_3CH_2CHCl\ COOH$ is added to 250 g of water. $K_a = 1.4 \times 10^{-3}$; $K_f = 1.86 \text{ K kg mol}^{-1}$.

◎ ***Thinking Process*** Depression in freezing point (ΔT_f) can be given as

$\Delta T_f = i \cdot K_f \cdot m$, so the required quantities are α, i and m.

(a) First calculate molality (m) and the degree of dissociation (α) by using $\alpha = \frac{K_a}{C}$ (Here C = molality).

(b) Then calculate van't Hoff factor (i) by using ($i = 1 + \alpha$).

(c) Finally put all the above value in the expression of ΔT_f to calculate depression in freezing point (ΔT_f).

Sol. **Step I : Calculation of degree of dissociation**

Mass of solute = 10 g

Molar mass of solute

$$(CH_3CH_2CHClCOOH) = (12 \times 4) + (1 \times 7) + (35.5) + (16 \times 2)$$
$$= 48 + 7 + 35.5 + 32 = 122.5 \text{ g mol}^{-1}$$

$$\text{Molal concentration of solution} = \frac{\text{Mass / Molar mass}}{\text{Mass of solvent (kg)}}$$
$$= \frac{(10 \text{ g})}{(122.5 \text{ g mol}^{-1}) \times (0.25 \text{ kg})}$$
$$= 0.326 \text{ m}$$

If α is the degree of dissociation of $CH_3CH_2CHClCOOH$, then

$$CH_3CH_2CHClCOOH \rightleftharpoons CH_3CHClCOO^- + H^+$$

Initial conc.	$C \text{ mol}^{-1}$ kg	0	0
At equilibrium	$C(1-\alpha)$	$C\alpha$	$C\alpha$

$$\therefore \quad K_a = \frac{C\alpha \times C\alpha}{C(1-\alpha)} = C\alpha^2$$

[Considering $(1-\alpha) = 1$ for dilute solutions]

$$\alpha^2 = \frac{K_a}{C} \quad \text{or} \quad \alpha = \sqrt{\frac{K_a}{C}}$$

$$\text{So,} \quad \alpha = \sqrt{\frac{1.4 \times 10^{-3}}{0.326}} = \sqrt{42.9 \times 10^{-4}}$$
$$= 6.55 \times 10^{-2} = 0.065$$

Step II : Calculation of van't Hoff factor (*i*)

$$CH_3CH_2CHClCOOH \rightleftharpoons CH_3CH_2CHCl\,COO^- + H^+$$

Initial no. of moles	1	0	0
Moles at equilibrium	$1-\alpha$	α	α

Total number of moles after dissociation

$$= (1-\alpha) + (\alpha) + (\alpha) = (1+\alpha)$$

van't Hoff factor

$$(i) = \frac{\text{Total number of moles after dissocation}}{\text{Number of moles before dissocation}}$$

$$i = \frac{(1+\alpha)}{1} = (1+\alpha)$$
$$= 1 + 0.065 = 1.065$$

Step III : Calculation of depression in freezing point (ΔT_f)

$$\Delta T_f = i\,K_f\,m = (1.065) \times (1.86 \text{ K kg mol}^{-1}) \times (0.326 \text{ mol kg}^{-1})$$
$$\Delta T_f = 0.65 \text{ K}$$

Question 33 19.5 g of CH_2FCOOH is dissolved in 500 g of water. The depression in the freezing point of water observed is $1.0^\circ C$. Calculate the van't Hoff factor and dissociation constant of fluoroacetic acid.

$$K_f = 1.86 \text{ K kg mol}^{-1}$$

◎ *Thinking Process* As in previous question.

Sol. **Step I : Calculation of van't Hoff factor of acid**

$$\Delta T_f = 1^\circ C = 1 \text{ K}; K_f = 1.86 \text{ K kg mol}^{-1}$$

$$\Delta T_f = i K_f m$$

or $$i = \frac{\Delta T_f}{K_f m} \quad \text{...(i)}$$

$$m = \frac{W_B}{M_B \times W_A}$$

[Molecular mass of $CH_2FCOOH = 78 \text{gmol}^{-1}$]

$$= \frac{(19.5 \text{ g})}{(78 \text{ g mol}^{-1}) \times (0.5 \text{ kg})}$$

$$= 0.5 \text{ mol kg}^{-1} \quad \text{... (ii)}$$

Placing the values in Eq. (i), we find the value of van't Hoff factor (i)

$$i = \frac{1}{(1.86 \text{ K kg mol}^{-1}) \times (0.5 \text{ mol kg}^{-1})}$$

$$= 1.0753$$

Step II : Calculation of degree of dissociation of the acid

Suppose degree of dissociation at the given concentration is α.

$$CH_2FCOOH \xrightleftharpoons{aq} CH_2FCOO^- + H^+$$

	CH_2FCOOH	CH_2FCOO^-	H^+
Initial conc.	$C \text{ mol kg}^{-1}$	0	0
At equilibrium	$C(1-\alpha)$	$C\alpha$	$C\alpha$

$$\text{Total} = C(1+\alpha)$$

$$\therefore \quad i = \frac{C(1+\alpha)}{C} = 1 + \alpha$$

$$\alpha = i - 1 = 1.0753 - 1 = 0.0753$$

Step III : Calculation of dissociation constant for the acid

$$\text{(Molal) } C = 0.5 \text{ m} \quad \text{(From Eq. (ii))}$$

$$K_a = \frac{[CH_2FCOO^-][H^+]}{[CH_2FCOOH]} = \frac{C\alpha \cdot C\alpha}{C(1-\alpha)} = \frac{C\alpha^2}{(1-\alpha)}$$

$$K_a = \frac{(0.5)(0.0753)^2}{(1-0.0753)} = \frac{(0.5) \times (0.0753)^2}{(0.9247)} = 3.07 \times 10^{-3}$$

Question 34 Vapour pressure of water at 293 K is 17.535 mm Hg. Calculate the vapour pressure of water at 293 K when 25 g of glucose is dissolved in 450 g of water.

◎ *Thinking Process* As vapour pressure is changing, apply Raoult's law for the relative lowering of vapour pressure to calculate vapour pressure of water.

Sol. W_B (solute) = 25 g ; $M_B = 180$ g mol^{-1}; $p_A^\circ = 17.535$ mm

W_A (water) = 450 g; M_A = 18 g mol ;

$$p_S = ?$$

$$\frac{p_A^\circ - p_S}{p_A^\circ} = x_B = \frac{n_B}{n_B + n_A}$$

$$n_B = \frac{W_B}{M_B} = \frac{25}{180} = 0.1389$$

$$n_A = \frac{W_A}{M_A} = \frac{450}{18} = 25$$

$$\frac{17.535 - p_S}{17.535} = \frac{0.1389}{0.1389 + 25}$$

$$\frac{17.535 - p_S}{17.535} = 0.00552$$

$$p_S = 17.535 - 0.097$$

$$p_S = 17.438 \text{ mm Hg}$$

Question 35 Henry's law constant for the molality of methane in benzene at 298 K is 4.27×10^5 mm Hg. Calculate the solubility of methane in benzene at 298 K under 760 mm Hg.

◎ *Thinking Process* Apply Henry's law, $p = K_H \cdot x$

Sol. $K_H = 4.27 \times 10^5$ mm Hg (at 298 K),

$p = 760$ mm

Applying Henry's law

$$p = K_H\, x \qquad [x = \text{Mole fraction /solubility of methane}]$$

$$x = \frac{p}{K_H}$$

$$= \frac{(760 \text{ mm})}{(4.27 \times 10^5 \text{ mm})}$$

$$= 178 \times 10^{-5}$$

$$= 1.78 \times 10^{-3}$$

Question 36 100 g of liquid A (molar mass 140 g mol^{-1}) was dissolved in 1000 g of liquid B (molar mass 180 g mol^{-1}). The vapour pressure of pure liquid B was found to be 500 torr. Calculate the vapour pressure of pure liquid A and its vapour pressure in the solution if the total vapour pressure of the solution is 475 torr.

◎ Thinking Process

(i) For the solution of two liquids (A and B) Raoult's law is

$$p = p_A^\circ x_A + p_B^\circ x_B$$

We have total pressure (p) and vapour pressure of B (p_B°). So, the required quantities are mole fractions of A and B.

(ii) First find moles of A and B from their masses and then find their mole fraction.

(iii) Put the values of mole fraction in the equation of Raoult's law to find vapour pressure of A.

(iv) Apply $p_A = p_A^\circ x_A$ to find p_A (vapour pressure in the solution).

Sol. Step I : Calculation of vapour pressure of pure liquid A (p_A°)

Number of moles of liquid A

$$(n_A) = \frac{W_A}{M_A} = \frac{(100\text{ g})}{(140\text{ g mol}^{-1})} = 0.7143\text{ mol}$$

Number of moles of liquid B

$$(n_B) = \frac{W_B}{M_B} = \frac{(1000\text{ g})}{(180\text{ g mol}^{-1})} = 5.5556\text{ mol}$$

Mole fraction of A

$$(x_A) = \frac{n_A}{n_A + n_B} = \frac{(0.7143\text{ mol})}{(0.7143 + 5.5556)\text{ mol}} = \frac{0.7143}{6.2699} = 0.1139$$

Mole fraction of B $(x_B) = 1 - 0.1139 = 0.8861$

Vapour pressure of pure liquid B $(p_B^\circ) = 500$ torr

Total vapour pressure of solution $(p) = 475$ torr

According to the Raoult's law,

$$p = p_A^\circ x_A + p_B^\circ x_B$$

$$475\text{ torr} = p_A^\circ \times (0.1139) + 500\text{ torr} \times (0.8861)$$

$$475\text{ torr} = p_A^\circ \times (0.1139) + 443.05\text{ torr}$$

$$p_A^\circ = \frac{(475 - 443.05)\text{ torr}}{(0.1139)} = \frac{31.95}{0.1139}\text{ torr} = 280.5\text{ torr}$$

Step II : Calculation of vapour pressure of A in the solution (p_A)

According to Raoult's law,

$$p_A = p_A^\circ x_A = (280.5\text{ torr}) \times (0.1139)$$

$$p_A = 32.0\text{ torr}$$

Question 37 Vapour pressures of pure acetone and chloroform at 328 K are 741.8 mm Hg and 632.8 mm Hg respectively. Assuming that they form ideal solution over the entire range of composition, plot p_{total}, $p_{chloroform}$ and $p_{acetone}$ as function of $x_{acetone}$. The experimental data observed for different compositions of mixture is :

$100\ x_{acetone}$	0	11.8	23.4	36.0	50.8	58.2	64.5	72.1
$p_{acetone}$ / mm Hg	0	54.9	110.1	202.4	322.7	405.9	454.1	521.1
$p_{chloroform}$ / mm Hg	632.8	548.1	469.4	359.7	257.7	193.6	161.2	120.7

Plot this data also on the same graph paper. Indicate whether it has positive deviation or negative deviation from the ideal solution.

Thinking Process Find p_{total} and $x_{acetone}$ and then plot the graph.

Sol.

$x_{acetone}$	0	0.118	0.234	0.360	0.508	0.582	0.645	0.721
$p_{acetone}$ / mm Hg	0	54.9	110.1	202.4	322.7	405.9	454.1	521.1
$p_{choroform}$ / mm Hg	632.8	548.1	469.4	359.7	257.7	193.6	161.2	120.7
p_{total}	632.8	603.0	579.5	562.1	580.4	599.5	615.3	641.8

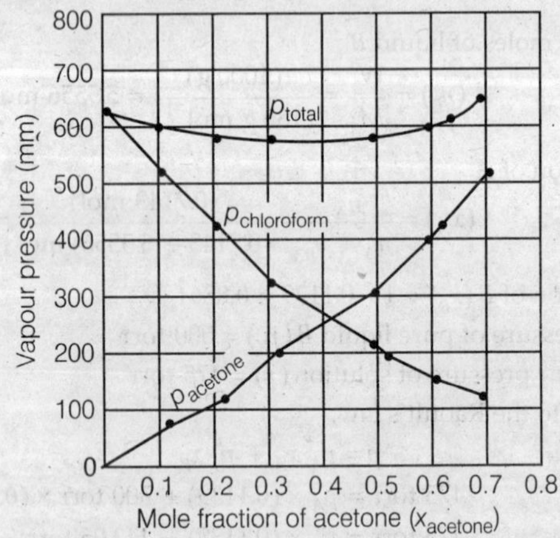

Since, the plot p_{total} dips downwards, the solution shows **negative deviation** from Raoult's law.

Question 38 Benzene and toluene form ideal solution over the entire range of composition. The vapour pressure of pure benzene and toluene at 300 K are 50.71 mm Hg and 32.06 mm Hg respectively. Calculate the mole fraction of benzene in vapour phase if 80 g of benzene is mixed with 100 g of toluene.

Thinking Process For ideal solution, Raoult's law is $p_T = p_A^\circ x_A + p_B^\circ x_B$

and vapour pressure in vapour phase $= \dfrac{p_A^\circ x_A}{p_T}$

Thus, the required quantities are x_A, x_B and p_T as we know p_A° and p_B°.

(i) Find x_A ($x_{C_6H_6}$) and x_B ($x_{C_7H_8}$) by first finding their moles.

(ii) Find p_T by subtitling the values of other quantities.

(iii) Find vapour pressure in vapour phase from the values of p_T, p_A° and x_A.

Sol. Molar mass of benzene (C_6H_6) = 78 g mol^{-1}

Molar mass of toluene (C_7H_8) = 92 g mol^{-1}

$n_{C_6H_6}$ (Number of moles of benzene) $= \dfrac{80\text{ g}}{(78\text{ g mol}^{-1})} = 1.026$ mol

$n_{C_7H_8}$ (Number of moles of toluene) $= \dfrac{(100\text{ g})}{(92\text{ g mol}^{-1})} = 1.087$ mol

Mole fraction of benzene $(x_{C_6H_6}) = \dfrac{(1.026\text{ mol})}{(1.026 + 1.087)\text{ mol}} = 0.486$

Mole fraction of toluene $(x_{C_7H_8}) = 1 - 0.486 = 0.514$

Applying Raoult's law,

Partial vapour pressure of benzene in solution $(p_{C_6H_6})$

$$= p^\circ_{C_6H_6} \times x_{C_6H_6} = (50.71\text{ mm}) \times (0.486) = 24.64\text{ mm}$$

Partial vapour pressure of toluene in solution

$$(p_{C_7H_8}) = p^\circ_{(C_7H_8)} \times x_{C_7H_8} = (32.06\text{ mm}) \times (0.514) = 16.48\text{ mm}$$

Total vapour pressure of solution $(p) = (24.64 + 16.48)$ mm = 41.12 mm

Mole fraction of benzene in vapour phase

$$= \frac{x_{C_6H_6} \times p^\circ_{C_6H_6}}{p_{\text{total}}}$$

$$= \frac{0.486 \times (50.71\text{ mm})}{(41.12\text{ mm})} = 0.599 \approx 0.60$$

Mole fraction of toluene in vapour phase $= \dfrac{x_{C_7H_8} \times p^\circ_{{}_7H_8}}{p_{\text{total}}}$

$$= \frac{0.514 \times (32.06\text{ mm})}{(41.12\text{ mm})}$$

$$= 0.401 \approx 0.40$$

Question 39 The air is a mixture of a number of gases. The major components are oxygen and nitrogen with approximate proportion of 20% is to 79% by volume at 298 K. The water is in equilibrium with air at a pressure of 10 atm. At 298 K if the Henry's law constants for oxygen and nitrogen at 298 K are 3.30×10^7 mm and 6.51×10^7 mm respectively, calculate the composition of these gases in water.

◎ ***Thinking Process*** First find the partial pressure of oxygen and nitrogen from Henry's law, $p = K_H \cdot x$ and the find their mole fraction (again applying the Henry's law).

Sol. **Step I : Calculation of partial pressure of oxygen and nitrogen**

Partial pressure of O_2 (p_{O_2}) $= (10 \text{ atm}) \times \frac{20}{100} = 2 \text{ atm} = 2 \times 760 \text{ mm}$

Partial pressure of N_2 (p_{N_2}) $= (10 \text{ atm}) \times \frac{79}{100} = 7.9 \text{ atm} = 7.9 \times 760 \text{ mm}$

Step II : Composition of O_2 and N_2 dissolved in water

The amount of gases dissolved in water is calculated in terms of their mole fractions.

$$x_{O_2} = \frac{p_{O_2}}{K_H}$$

$$= \frac{(2 \times 760 \text{ mm})}{(3.30 \times 10^7 \text{ mm})}$$

$$= 4.6 \times 10^{-5}$$

$$x_{N_2} = \frac{p_{N_2}}{K_H} = \frac{(7.9 \times 760 \text{ mm})}{(6.51 \times 10^7 \text{ mm})}$$

$$= 9.22 \times 10^{-5}$$

Question 40 Determine the amount of $CaCl_2$ ($i = 2.47$) dissolved in 2.5 L of water such that its osmotic pressure is 0.75 atm at 27°C.

◎ ***Thinking Process*** First calculate the moles of $CaCl_2$ by applying van't Hoff equation, $\pi = iCRT$ and $C = \frac{n_B}{V}$

Then calculate amount of $CaCl_2$ by multiplying the moles with molar mass.

Sol. According to van't Hoff equation,

$$\text{Osmotic pressure } (\pi) = i\,CRT = \frac{i n_B RT}{V}$$

$$i = 2.47; \quad V = 2.5 \text{ L}; \quad R = 0.0821 \text{ L atm K}^{-1}\text{mol}^{-1}$$

$$T = 27 + 273 = 300 \text{ K}; \quad \pi = 0.75 \text{ atm}$$

$$n_B = \frac{\pi V}{iRT}$$

$$= \frac{(0.75 \text{ atm}) \times (2.5 \text{ L})}{(2.47) \times (0.0821 \text{ L atm K}^{-1}\text{mol}^{-1}) \times (300 \text{ K})} = 0.0308 \text{ mol}$$

Amount of $CaCl_2$ dissolved $= n_B \times M_B$

$$= (0.0308 \text{ mol}) \times (111 \text{ g mol}^{-1})$$

$$= 3.42 \text{ g}$$

Question 41 Determine the osmotic pressure of a solution prepared by dissolving 25 mg of K_2SO_4 in 2 L of water at 25°C, assuming that it is completely dissociated.

◎ ***Thinking Process*** Apply van't Hoff equation, $\pi = iCRT$, where, i = Number of ions produced by K_2SO_4).

Sol. Amount of K_2SO_4 dissolved = 25 mg = 0.025 g

Volume of solution = 2 L

$T = 25°C = 25 + 273 \text{ K} = 298 \text{ K}$

Molar mass of $K_2SO_4 = (2 \times 39) + (32) + (4 \times 16) = 174 \text{ g mol}^{-1}$

Since, K_2SO_4 dissociates completely as

$$K_2SO_4 \xrightarrow{aq} 2K^+ + SO_4^{2-}$$

Total ions produced after dissociation (per mole) = 3

So, $i = 3$, $\pi = iCRT = i \times \frac{n}{V} RT = \frac{i \times W \times R \times T}{M \times V}$

$$= \frac{3 \times (0.025 \text{ g}) \times (0.0821 \text{ L atm K}^{-1}\text{mol}^{-1}) \times (298 \text{ K})}{(174 \text{ g mol}^{-1}) \times (2 \text{ L})}$$

$$= 5.27 \times 10^{-3} \text{ atm}$$

DIKSHA APP Questions

Multiple Choice Questions

Q.1 Effect of adding a non-volatile solute to a solvent is

(a) to lower the vapour pressure. (b) to increase the freezing point.
(c) to decrease the boiling point. (d) to decrease the osmotic pressure.

Sol. (a) Adding a non-volatile solute to a solvent lowers the solvent's vapour pressure because the solute particles occupy space at the surface, reducing the number of solvent molecules that can escape into the gas phase. This phenomenon is explained by Raoult's law.

Q.2 At equilibrium, the rate of dissolution of a solid solute in a volatile liquid solvent is

(a) less than the rate of crystallisation.
(b) greater than the rate of crystallisation.
(c) equal to the rate of crystallisation.
(d) zero.

Sol. (c) At equilibrium, the rate of dissolution of a solid solute is equal to the rate of crystallisation. This dynamic equilibrium occurs when the amount of solute dissolving into the solution is exactly balanced by the amount crystallising back from the solution, resulting in no net change in the concentration of the solute.

Q.3 The value of Henry's constant K_H is

(a) larger for gases with high solubility.
(b) large for gases with lower solubility.
(c) constant for all gases.
(d) not related to the solubility of gases.

Sol. (b) The solubility of a gas in a liquid is directly proportional to the partial pressure of the gas above the liquid at constant temperature. This relationship is described by Henry's law, which can be expressed as:

$$P = K_H x$$

Where, P is the pressure, x is the solubility of the gas in liquid and K_H is Henry's law constant. This equation can be rewritten as, $x = \frac{P}{K_H}$

From this equation, we can see that the Henry's constant (K_H) is inversely proportional to the solubility (x) of the gas. Therefore, gases with lower solubility in a liquid will have a higher value of Henry's constant.

Q.4 In which mode of expression the concentration of solution remains independent of temperature?

(a) Molarity (b) Normality (c) Formality (d) Molality

Sol. (d) The concentration of a solution in molality remains independent of temperature because molality is defined as the number of moles of solute per kilogram of solvent. Unlikc molarity, which depends on the volume of the solution (and can change with temperature due to expansion or contraction), molality depends only on the mass of the solvent, which does not change with temperature.

Q.5 Amalgams are the example of

(a) liquid in solid solutions. (b) solid in solid solutions.
(c) gas in solid solutions. (d) liquid in liquid solutions.

Sol. (a) An amalgam is a type of solution where a liquid (usually mercury) is dissolved in a solid (typically a metal). In this case, mercury is the solute, and the metal it dissolves into (such as gold or silver) is the solvent.

Q.6 Which one of the following solutions represent the solution of solid in a solid?

(a) Boron (b) Brass (c) Beryllium (d) Bread

Sol. (b) Brass is an alloy, which is a solution of a solid solute (usually zinc) dissolved in a solid solvent (typically copper). In this case, copper is the solvent, and zinc is the solute, forming a homogeneous mixture of metals.

Q.7 Colligative properties depend on

(a) the nature of solute particles dissolved in solutions.
(b) the number of solute particles in solution.
(c) the physical properties of solute particles dissolved in solutions.
(d) the nature of solvent particles.

Sol. (b) Colligative properties are the properties of a solution that depend on the number of solute particles in a solution, but not on the nature of the solute particles. These include vapour pressure lowering, boiling point elevation, freezing point depression and osmotic pressure.

Q.8 At a given temperature, osmotic pressure of a concentrated solution of a substance

(a) is higher than at a dilute solution.
(b) is lower than at a dilute solution.
(c) is same as that of a dilute solution.
(d) cannot be compared with osmotic pressure of dilute solution.

Sol. (a) At a given temperature, the osmotic pressure of a solution is directly proportional to the concentration of solute particles. Therefore, a concentrated solution will have a higher osmotic pressure than a dilute solution. This relationship is described by the formula

$$\pi = iCRT$$

where π is the osmotic pressure, C is the molarity of the solution, i is the van't Hoff factor (number of particles into which the solute dissociates), R is the gas constant and T is the temperature.

☐ Short Answer Type

Q.1 (a) Why is an increase in temperature observed on mixing chloroform and acetone?

(b) Why does common salt solution freeze at a lower temperature than water?

Sol. (a) The increase in temperature observed when mixing chloroform and acetone is due to an exothermic solution process. When these two liquids are mixed, intermolecular interactions between chloroform and acetone molecules are formed, which release energy in the form of heat. This occurs because the molecular interactions between the two substances are stronger than the interactions in the pure liquids. The process of mixing leads to a net release of energy, which manifests as an increase in temperature. This is an example of negative enthalpy change ($\Delta H < 0$), where the heat of mixing is released, making the solution warmer.

(b) A common salt solution freezes at a lower temperature than water due to depression in freezing point, a colligative property. The presence of salt (solute) in water reduces the number of water molecules at the surface available to form ice, thus lowering the temperature at which the solution can freeze.

☐ Long Answer Type

Q.1 (i) The molecular masses of polymer are determined by osmotic pressure method and not by measuring other colligative properties given reasons.

(ii) At 300 K, 20g of glucose, $C_6H_{12}O_6$ present per litre in its solution has a osmotic pressure of 2.86 bar. If the osmotic pressure of another glucose solution is 1.43 bar at the same temperature, calculate the concentration of other solution.

Sol. (i) The molecular masses of polymers are determined by osmotic pressure method and not by measuring other colligative properties because: Osmotic pressure is measured at room temperature and it has appreciable value which can be measured easily while, the changes observed in elevation in boiling point, depression in freezing point and relative lowering in vapor pressure are very small and difficult to measure.

(ii) **First solution**

- Osmotic pressure $\pi_1 = 2.86$ bar
- Molar mass of glucose = 180 g/mol
- Mass of glucose = 20 g
- Volume = 1 L
- Moles of glucose = $\dfrac{20\text{g}}{180\text{g / mol}} = 0.1111\,\text{mol}$

- Molarity $C_1 = \frac{0.1111 \text{ mol}}{1\text{L}} = 0.1111\text{M}$

Second solution

- Osmotic pressure $\pi_2 = 1.43$ bar

Osmotic pressure is directly proportional to molarity, so.

$$\frac{\pi_2}{\pi_1} = \frac{C_2}{C_1}$$

$$\frac{1.43}{2.86} = \frac{C_2}{0.1111}, C_2 = 0.0556 \text{ M}$$

∴ The concentration of the second solution is 0.0556 M

Q.2 (a) State Rasoult's law for a solution containing volatile components. How does Raoult's law become a special case of Henry's law?

(b) 2.00 g of a non-electrolyte solution dissolved in 100 g of benzene lowered the freezing point of benzene by 0.80 K. Find the molar mass of the solute. (K_f for benzene = 5.12 K kg mol^{-1})

Sol. (a) Raoult's law states that the partial vapour pressure of each component is directly proportional to its mole fraction when both solute and solvent are volatile.

$$p_A \propto x_A$$

$$p_A = p_A^{\circ} x_A \text{ and}$$

$$p_B \propto x_B$$

$$p_B = p_B^{\circ} x_B$$

In both the cases, partial pressure of volatile component is directly proportional to its mole fraction in solution. Only the proportionality constant K_H differs from p_A°. Thus, Raoult's law is a special case of Henry's law

(b)
- Mass of a non-electrolyte substance $(W_1) = 2.00$ g
- Mass of the solvent $(W_2) = 100$ g
- Freezing point depression constant $(K_f) = 5.12 \text{K kg mol}^{-1}$
- Depression in freezing point of benzene $\Delta T_f = 0.40$ K
- Depression in freezing point, $\Delta T_f = K_f \times m$
  where, m = molality = moles of solute per kg of solvent
- $\Delta T_f = K_f \times \frac{W_1 \times 1000}{M \times W_2}$ (where, $m = \frac{W_1 \times 1000}{M \times W_2}$ and M = molar mass of solute)
- $0.40 = 5.12 \times \frac{2 \times 1000}{M \times 100}$
- $M = 256 \text{ g mol}^{-1}$

Thus, the molar mass of non-electrolyte solute is 256 g mol^{-1}.

Electrochemistry

CHAPTER 02

Important Points

01 **Electrochemistry** is the study of the chemical reactions which produce electrical energy or those chemical reactions which take place on passing electricity.

02 The potential difference between the electrode and the electrolyte is known as **electrode potential.** When the concentration of all the species involved in a half cell is unity at 25°C and 1 bar pressure, then the electrode potential is called **standard electrode potential (E°).**

03 EMF of the cell, $E^\circ_{cell} = E^\circ_{cathode} - E^\circ_{anode} = E^\circ_{Right} - E^\circ_{Left}$

04 Nernst equation : $E_{cell} = E^\circ_{cell} - \frac{0.0591}{n} \log \frac{[\text{Anode}]}{[\text{Cathode}]}$

For concentration cell; $E = \frac{0.0591}{n} \log \frac{C_1}{C_2}$

05 Standard Gibb's energy of the reaction :

$$\Delta_r G^\circ = -nFE^\circ_{cell} = -2.303\, RT \log K$$

06 The series in which the standard electrode potential are arranged in increasing order is known as **electrochemical series.**

07 **Conductance (G)** is the reciprocal of resistance and may be defined as the ease with the electric current flows through the conductor, $G = \frac{1}{R}$ [SI unit = Siemen (S) or ohm^{-1}]

08 **Molar conductivity (Λ_m)** is defined as the conducting power of all the ions produced by dissolving one gram mole of an electrolytes placed between two large electrodes placed at a distance of one centimetre.

09 **Conductivity** of an electrolytic solution may be defined as the conductance of a solution of 1 cm length with area of cross section equal to 1 cm^2.

10 Conductivity decreases with decrease in concentration because the number of ions per unit volume decreases.

11 Molar conductivity increases with decrease in concentration because the total volume having one mole electrolyte increases.

12 $R = \rho\left[\frac{l}{A}\right] = \rho \times$ cell constant

where, R = Resistance ; ρ = Resistivity ; l = Length and A = Area of cross section of electrolyte.

13 Conductivity or specific conductance (κ) = $\frac{1}{R} \times$ cell constant.

14 $\Lambda_m = \frac{\kappa \times 1000}{C}$ where, Λ_m = Molar conductivity; C = Molarity of solution.

15 A substance that dissociates in a solution to produce ions and conducts electricity in dissolved or molten state is called an **electrolyte.** There are two types of electrolytes:

(i) **Weak electrolytes** (do not dissociate completely) — CH_3COOH, HCN, etc.

(ii) **Strong electrolytes** (dissociate completely)—NaCl, $MgCl_2$, etc.

16 Mathematical form of **Kohlrausch's law**

$$\Lambda^{\infty}_m(A_x B_y) = x\lambda^{\infty}_m(A^{y-}) + y\lambda^{\infty}_m(B^{x-})$$

where, Λ^{∞}_m is the molar conductivity at infinite dilution; x and y = No. of cations and anions produced by one unit formula of electrolyte on complete dissociation.

Kohlrausch's law states that limiting molar conductivity of an electrolyte at infinite dilution is the sum of contributions from its individual ions. This is only valid for weak electrolytes. For strong electrolytes, Debye-Huckel-Onsager equation is followed

$$\Lambda = \Lambda° - A\sqrt{C} \qquad (A = \text{constant})$$

17 Degree of dissociation, $\alpha = \frac{\Lambda^c_m}{\Lambda^\circ_m}$

[Λ^c_m = molar conductivity at a given concentration, Λ°_m = limiting molar conductivity].

18 Dissociation constant, $K_a = \frac{C\alpha^2}{(1-\alpha)}$ (for weak electrolyte)

[C = Concentration, α = Degree of dissociation]

19 Quantity of charge in Coulombs

$$Q = \text{Current}\,(I) \times \text{Time}\,(t)$$

Unit = Ampere-sec or Coulomb.

20 1 Faraday = 96500 Coulomb.

21 **Faraday's first law of electrolysis** During electrolysis, amount of substance (w) liberated at electrode = $Z \times i \times t$.

22 **Faraday's second law of electrolysis :**

$$\frac{w_1}{w_2} = \frac{E_1}{E_2}$$

[w_1 and w_2 are the amount of substances produced at different electrodes. E_1 and E_2 = Equivalent masses]

23 **Salt bridge** is an inverted U-tube, containing a salt paste. It completes the inner cell circuit and maintains the electrical neutrality of the electrolytes in the two half-cells, without mixing them.

24 **Battery** is used as a source of electrical energy, in which a combination of galvanic cells are connected in series. There are two types of batteries :

(i) **Primary battery**— In primary batteries, the reaction occurs only once and after use over a period of time, battery becomes dead and cannot be reused. For example, dry cell (Leclanche cell).

(ii) **Secondary battery**— It can be reused and recharged by passing current through it in the opposite direction. For example, lead storage battery.

25 **Fuel cells** are galvanic cells that are designed to convert the combustion energy of fuels like, hydrogen, methane, methanol, etc., directly into electrical energy.

26 **Corrosion** is the process of slow conversion of metals into their oxides by reaction with moisture and oxygen present in the atmosphere. Corrosion can be prevented by —

(i) covering the surface with paint or by some chemicals (bisphenol).

(ii) covering the surface by other metals (Sn, Zn, etc.) which are inert or react to save the object. This is called **sacrificial protection,** in which the metal corrodes itself to save the object.

(iii) alloying.

Intext Questions

Question 1 How would you determine the standard electrode potential of the system Mg^{2+}/Mg?

◎ *Thinking Process* It is not possible to find the $E°$ for a single electrode so construct an electrochemical cell, with a reference electrode to find $E°_{Mg^{2+}/Mg}$.

Sol. $E°$ value of Mg^{2+}/Mg electrode is determined by setting up an electrochemical cell. For this purpose, a Mg electrode is dipped in 1M $MgSO_4$ solution, which acts as one half cell *i.e,* oxidation half-cell. In the same way, the standard hydrogen electrode acts as the other half-cell i.e., reduction half cell.

The deflection of voltmeter placed in the cell circuit is towards the Mg electrode which indicates the direction of flow of current.

The cell may be represented as :

$$Mg|Mg^{2+}(M)||H^+(1\,M)|H_2(1\,atm), Pt$$

The reading as given by voltmeter gives $E°_{cell}$

$$E°_{cell} = E°_{(H^+/1/2H_2)} - E°_{(Mg^{2+}/Mg)}$$

$$= 0 - E°_{(Mg^{2+}/Mg)}$$

$$= -E°_{(Mg^{2+}/Mg)}$$

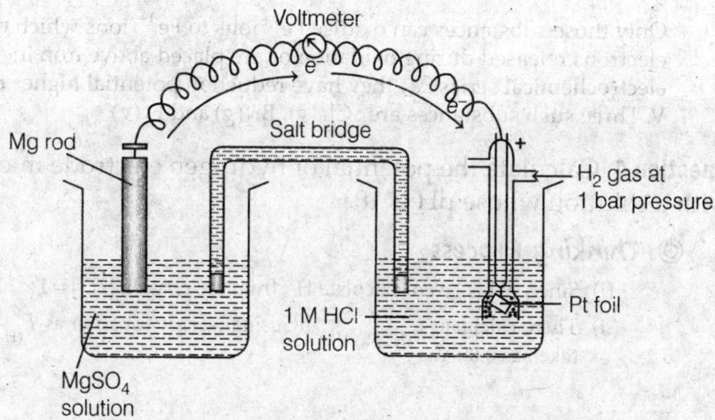

Question 2 Can you store copper sulphate solutions in a zinc pot?

◎ *Thinking Process* Consider the E° values of copper and zinc. More negative the value of E°, higher is the reactivity and a more reactive metal can displace a less reactive metal from its salt solution.

Sol. No, zinc pot cannot store copper sulphate solutions because the standard electrode potential (E°) value of zinc is less than that of copper. So, zinc is a stronger reducing agent than copper and is more reactive than copper.

$$Zn^{2+}(aq) + 2e^- \longrightarrow Zn(s); \quad E^\circ = -0.76\text{V}$$

$$Cu^{2+}(aq) + 2e^- \longrightarrow Cu(s); \quad E^\circ = +0.34\text{V}$$

So, zinc will lose electrons to Cu^{2+} ions and redox reaction will occur as follows:

$$Zn(s) + Cu^{2+}(aq) \longrightarrow Zn^{2+}(aq) + Cu(s)$$

Mistake Alert More negative $E^0_{M+/M}$ suggests that metal undergoes oxidation faster to form an ion.

Question 3 Consult the table on standard electrode potentials and suggest three substances that can oxidise ferrous ions under suitable condition.

◎ *Thinking Process* Select good oxidising agent having positive values of E° greater than 0.77 V, as E° for ferrous ion is 0.77 V.

Sol. Fe^{2+} (ferrous) ion gets oxidised to Fe^{3+} (ferric) ion as follows

$$Fe^{2+} \longrightarrow Fe^{3+} + e^-; \qquad E^\circ_{ox} = -0.77\text{V}$$

Only those substances can oxidise Fe^{2+} ions to Fe^{3+} ions which can accept electrons released during oxidation or are placed above iron in electrochemical series *i.e.,* they have reduction potential higher than +0.77 V. Three such substances are : $Cl_2(g)$, $Br_2(g)$ and $F_2(g)$.

Question 4 Calculate the potential of hydrogen electrode in contact with a solution whose pH is 10.

◎ *Thinking Process*

(i) Since, pH is given, calculate H^+ from the relation $[H^+] = 1 \times 10^{-pH}$.

(ii) Then, calculate $E_{(H^+/1/2H_2)}$ by using Nernst equation as $E^\circ_{(H^+/1/2H_2)}$ is taken as 0.00 V.

Sol. For hydrogen electrode, $H^+ + e^- \longrightarrow \frac{1}{2}H_2$

Applying Nernst equation,

$$E_{(H^+/1/2H_2)} = E^\circ_{(H^+/1/2H_2)} - \frac{0.0591}{n}\log\frac{1}{[H^+]}$$

$$= 0 - \frac{0.0591}{1}\log\frac{1}{(10^{-10})} \qquad [pH = 10\ ; [H^+] = 10^{-10} M]$$

$$= 0 - \frac{0.0591}{1}\times(10\log 10) = -0.591V$$

$$E_{(H^+/1/2H_2)} = -0.591V$$

Question 5 Calculate the emf of the cell in which the following reaction takes place :

$$Ni(s) + 2\,Ag^+\,(0.002\text{ M}) \longrightarrow Ni^{2+}\,(0.160\text{ M}) + 2Ag(s)$$

Given that $E^\circ_{cell} = 1.05V$

Sol. From the given cell reaction and Nernst equation.

$$E_{cell} = E^\circ_{cell} - \frac{0.0591}{n}\log\frac{[Ni^{2+}]}{[Ag^+]^2} = 1.05V - \frac{0.0591}{2}\log\frac{[0.160]}{[0.002]^2}$$

$$= 1.05 - \frac{0.0591}{2}\log(4\times10^4) = 1.05 - \frac{0.0591}{2}(4.6021)$$

$$= 1.05 - 0.14 = 0.91V,\ E_{cell} = 0.91V$$

Question 6 The cell in which the following reaction occurs,

$$2\,Fe^{3+}(aq) + 2I^-(aq) \longrightarrow 2\,Fe^{2+}(aq) + I_2(s)$$

has $E^\circ_{cell} = 0.236V$ at 298 K, calculate the standard Gibbs energy and the equilibrium constant of the cell reaction.

◎ *Thinking Process*

(i) Gibbs energy, $\Delta_r G^\circ = -nFE^\circ_{cell}$ where, n is the number of electons taking part in the reaction, so write two half reactions to find the value of n and then calculate the standard Gibbs energy by using the formula.

(ii) Equilibrium constant is related to Gibbs energy as $\log K_c = \frac{\Delta G^\circ}{2.030\,RT}$.

So, calculate K_c by using this formula.

Sol. Two half reactions for the given redox reaction may be written as :

$$2Fe^{3+}(aq) + 2e^- \longrightarrow 2Fe^{2+}(aq); \quad 2I^- \longrightarrow I_2 + 2e^-$$

2 moles of electrons are involved in the reaction, so $n = 2$.

$$\Delta_r G^\circ = -nFE^\circ_{cell} = (-2\text{ mol})\times(96500\text{ C mol}^{-1})\times(0.236\text{ V})$$

$$= -45548\text{ CV} = -45548\text{ J}$$

$$\Delta_r G^\circ = -45.55 \text{ kJ}$$

$$\log K_c = -\frac{\Delta G^\circ}{2.303\,RT} = -\frac{(-45.55 \text{ kJ})}{2.303 \times (8.314 \times 10^{-3} \text{ kJK}^{-1}) \times (298 \text{ K})} = 7.983$$

$$K_c = \text{Antilog}\,(7.983) = 9.616 \times 10^7$$

$$K_c = 9.616 \times 10^7$$

Question 7 Why does the conductivity of a solution decrease with dilution?

◎ *Thinking Process* Conductivity ∝ Number of ions per unit volume.

Sol. The conductivity of a solution is related with the number of ions present per unit volume of the solution. When the solution is diluted, the number of ions per unit volume decreases. Hence, conductivity or specific conductance of the solution also decreases.

Question 8 Suggest a way to determine the Λ°_m for water.

◎ *Thinking Process* Recall Kohlrausch's law, to find the conductance of weak electrolyte.

Sol. The molar conductance of water at infinite dilution can be obtained from the knowledge of molar conductances at infinite dilution of sodium hydroxide, hydrochloric acid and sodium chloride (all strong electrolytes). This is in accordance with Kohlrausch's law.

$$\Lambda^\circ_{m(H_2O)} = \Lambda^\circ_{m\,(NaOH)} + \Lambda^\circ_{m\,(HCl)} - \Lambda^\circ_{m\,(NaCl)}$$

$$\Lambda^\circ_{m\,(HCl)} = \lambda^\circ_{m\,(H^+)} + \lambda^\circ_{m\,(Cl^-)}$$

$$\Lambda^\circ_{m\,(NaOH)} = \lambda^\circ_{m\,(Na^+)} + \lambda^\circ_{m\,(OH^-)} \Rightarrow \Lambda^\circ_{m\,(NaCl)} = \lambda^\circ_{m\,(Na^+)} + \lambda^\circ_{m\,(Cl^-)}$$

$$\Rightarrow \quad \Lambda^\circ_{m\,(H_2O)} = \lambda^\circ_{m\,(H^+)} + \lambda^\circ_{m\,(Cl^-)} + \lambda^\circ_{m\,(Na^+)} + \lambda^\circ_{m\,(OH^-)} - \lambda^\circ_{m\,(Na^+)} - \lambda^\circ_{m\,(Cl^-)}$$

$$\Lambda^\circ_{m\,(H_2O)} = \lambda^\circ_{m\,(H^+)} + \lambda^\circ_{m\,(OH^-)}$$

Question 9 The molar conductivity of 0.025 mol L^{-1} methanoic acid is 46.1 $Scm^2 mol^{-1}$. Calculate its degree of dissociation and dissociation constant.

Given, $\lambda^\circ(H^+) = 349.6 \text{ S cm}^2 \text{mol}^{-1}$

and $\lambda^\circ(HCOO^-) = 54.6 \text{ S cm}^2 \text{mol}^{-1}$.

◎ *Thinking Process*

(i) Degree of dissociation, α is related to conductivity as $\alpha = \dfrac{\Lambda^c_m}{\Lambda^\circ_m}$

Λ^c_m is given. Calculate Λ°_m by using Kohlrausch's law.

(ii) Calculate K_a as $K_a = \dfrac{C\alpha^2}{(1-\alpha)}$ and we know C and α both.

Sol. **Step I : Calculation of degree of dissociation (α) of HCOOH**

$$\Lambda^c_m = 46.1 \text{ S cm}^2 \text{ mol}^{-1}$$

$$\Lambda^\circ_{m\,(HCOOH)} = \lambda^\circ_{m\,(HCOO^-)} + \lambda^\circ_{m\,(H^+)}$$

$$= (54.6 + 349.6) \text{ S cm}^2 \text{ mol}^{-1}$$

$$= 404.2 \text{ S cm}^2 \text{ mol}^{-1}$$

$$\alpha = \frac{\Lambda^c_m}{\Lambda^\circ_m} = \frac{(46.1) \text{ S cm}^2 \text{ mol}^{-1}}{(404.2) \text{ S cm}^2 \text{ mol}^{-1}} = 0.1140 = 11.4\%$$

Step II : Calculation of dissociation constant

$$HCOOH(aq) \underset{}{\overset{\text{Water}}{\rightleftharpoons}} HCOO^-(aq) + H^+(aq)$$

Initial conc.	C	0	0
Equilibrium conc.	C(1 − α)	Cα	Cα

$$\text{Dissociation constant, } K_a = \frac{[HCOO^-][H^+]}{[HCOOH]} = \frac{C\alpha \times C\alpha}{C(1-\alpha)} = \frac{C\alpha^2}{(1-\alpha)}$$

Placing values
$$K_a = \frac{(0.025 \text{ mol L}^{-1}) \times (0.114)^2}{(1 - 0.114)}$$

$$= \frac{(3.249 \times 10^{-4} \text{ mol L}^{-1})}{(0.886)}$$

$$= 3.67 \times 10^{-4} \text{ mol L}^{-1}$$

$$\alpha = 0.114$$

$$K_a = 3.67 \times 10^{-4} \text{ mol L}^{-1}$$

Question 10 If a current of 0.5 ampere flows through a metallic wire for 2 h, then how many electrons would flow through the wire?

◎ Thinking Process

(i) Find charge by using, $Q = It$.

(ii) When charge 1 Faraday (96500 C) flows; number of electrons is equal to 6.022×10^{23}. So, calculate the number of electrons when charge is Q by unitary method.

Sol. Quantity of charge (Q) passed = Current (I) × Time (t)

$$= (0.5\text{A}) \times (2 \times 60 \times 60\text{s})$$

$$= (3600) \text{ Ampere sec} = 3600 \text{ C}$$

Number of electrons flowing through the wire on passing charge of one Faraday (96500 C) = 6.022×10^{23}

Number of electrons flowing through the wire on passing a charge of 3600 C

$$= \frac{6.022 \times 10^{23} \times (3600\text{C})}{(96500\text{C})} = 2.246 \times 10^{22}$$

Number of electrons = 2.246×10^{22}

Question 11 Suggest a list to metals that are extracted electrolytically.

◎ *Thinking Process* Metals which are very reactive (large –ve E°) are extracted electrolytically, as no reducing agent is available for their reduction.

Sol. Those metals which are highly reactive and have large negative E° values can be extracted electrolytically.This type of metals are powerful reducing agents. *e.g.*, sodium, potassium, calcium, magnesium, etc.

Question 12 Consider the reaction,

$$Cr_2O_7^{2-} + 14H^+ + 6e^- \longrightarrow 2Cr^{3+} + 7H_2O$$

What is the quantity of electricity in coulombs needed to reduce 1 mole of $Cr_2O_7^{2-}$?

◎ *Thinking Process* Consider the given equation; $6e^-$ means 6 Faraday.

Sol. 1 mole $Cr_2O_7^{2-}$ require 6 Faraday electricity (6 F)

$$= 6 \times 96500 \text{ C}$$

$$= 5.79 \times 10^5 \text{ C}$$

Quantity of electricity = 5.79×10^5 coulomb

Question 13 Write the chemistry of recharging the lead storage battery, highlighting all the materials that are involved during recharging.

◎ *Thinking Process* Recall the reactions during use of battery and reverse them.

Sol. When lead storage battery is recharged, electrical energy is supplied to the cell from the external source ; *i.e.*, the cell operates as an electrolytic cell during recharging. All the chemical reactions, which take place during the use of battery, are reversed at this time.

At anode $PbSO_4(s) + 2e^- \longrightarrow Pb(s) + SO_4^{2-}(aq)$

At cathode $PbSO_4(s) + 2H_2O(l) \longrightarrow PbO_2(s) + SO_4^{2-}(aq) + 4H^+(aq) + 2e^-$

Overall reaction $2PbSO_4(s) + 2H_2O(l) \longrightarrow Pb(s) + PbO_2(s) + 2H_2SO_4(aq)$

Question 14 Suggest two materials other than hydrogen that can be used as fuels in fuel cells.

Sol. Methane (CH_4) and methanol (CH_3OH).

Question 15 Explain how rusting of iron is envisaged as setting up of an electrochemical cell.

◎ *Thinking Process* Rusting of iron is a redox reaction, it involves the oxidation of Fe to Fe^{2+} and reduction of O_2.

Sol. In corrosion, a metal is oxidised by loss of electrons to oxygen with the formation of oxides. So, an electrochemical cell is set up. *e.g.*, **Rusting of iron** involves following steps :

(i) The water layer present on the surface of iron dissolves acidic oxides from air like CO_2 and forms acid to produce H^+ ions.

$$H_2O + CO_2 \longrightarrow H_2CO_3 \rightleftharpoons 2H^+ + CO_3^{2-}$$

(ii) In the presence of H^+ ions, iron starts losing electrons at some spot to form ferrous ions. This spot behaves as anode.

$$Fe(s) \xrightarrow{\text{Oxidation}} Fe^{2+}(aq) + 2e^-; \quad [E^\circ_{(Fe^{2+}/Fe)} = -0.44V]$$

(iii) The electrons released at anode move to another spot, where H^+ ions and the dissolved oxygen gain these electrons. This spot becomes a cathode.

$$O_2(g) + 4H^+(aq) + 4e^- \xrightarrow{\text{Reduction}} 2H_2O(l); \quad [E^\circ_{(H^+/O_2/H_2O)} = 1.23V]$$

(iv) Overall reaction, *i.e.*, redox reaction is :

$$2Fe(s) + O_2(g) + 4H^+(aq) \longrightarrow 2Fe^{2+}(aq) + 2H_2O(l);$$
$$[E^\circ_{cell} = 1.67V]$$

(v) Ferrous ions are further oxidised by the atmospheric oxygen to ferric ions which combine with water molecules to form hydrated ferric oxide, $\cdot x$ (Rust)

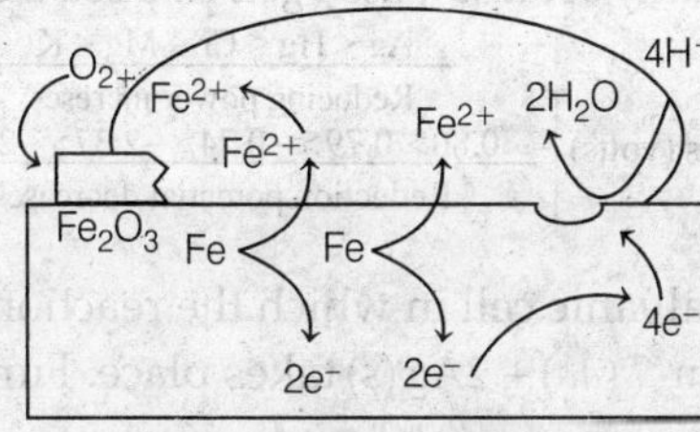

Corrosion of iron in atmosphere

Oxidation : $Fe(s) \longrightarrow Fe^{2+}(aq) + 2e^-$

Reduction : $O_2(g) + 4H^+(aq) + 4e^- \longrightarrow 2H_2O(l)$

Atmospheric

Oxidation : $2Fe^{2+}(aq) + 2H_2O(l) + \frac{1}{2}O_2(g) \longrightarrow Fe_2O_3(s) + 4H^+(aq)$

Exercises

Question 1 Arrange the following metals in the order in which they displace each other from the solution of their salts. Al, Cu, Fe, Mg and Zn.

◎ ***Thinking Process*** Consider the order of reactivity of metals, as a more reactive metal can displace the less reactive metal from its salt solution.

Sol. Mg > Al > Zn > Fe > Cu

It means that every metal on the left side can displace the next one (*s*) from its salt solution.

Question 2 Given the standard electrode potentials,

$K^+/K = -2.93$ V, $Ag^+/Ag = 0.80$ V

$Hg^{2+}/Hg = 0.79$V,

$Mg^{2+}/Mg = -2.37$ V,

$Cr^{3+}/Cr = -0.74$ V

Arrange these metals in their increasing order of reducing power.

◎ ***Thinking Process*** Reducing power $\propto \dfrac{1}{\text{Reduction potential}}$ *i.e.*, as the reduction potential decreases, reducting power increases. So, arrange the given metals on this basis.

Sol. Metal which has lower reduction potential (more negative E° value) has greater reducing capacity because it itself gets oxidised more easily.

Metals	Ag < Hg < Cr < Mg < K $\longrightarrow$ Reducing power increses
Reduction, potentials (volts)	0.80> 0.79> −0.74> −2.37> −2.93 $\longrightarrow$ Reduction potential decreases

Question 3 Depict the galvanic cell in which the reaction, $Zn(s) + 2Ag^+(aq) \longrightarrow Zn^{2+}(aq) + 2Ag(s)$ takes place. Further show :

(i) Which of the electrode is negatively charged?

(ii) The carriers of the current in the cell.

(iii) Individual reaction at each electrode.

◎ ***Thinking Process*** Anode is negative electrode and cathode is positive electrode. Anode is always the site of oxidation and cathode is the site of reduction. In a galvanic cell, anode half-cell is written on the left and cathode half-cell on right. Salt bridge is represented as || (parallel lines).

Sol. (i) Cell equation : $Mg(s) + Cu^{2+}(aq) \longrightarrow Mg^{2+}(aq) + Cu(s)$ $(n = 2)$

Nernst equation : $E_{cell} = E^{\circ}_{cell} - \frac{0.0591}{2}\log\frac{[Mg^{2+}]}{[Cu^{2+}]}$

EMF of the cell, $E_{cell} = [0.34 - (-2.37)] - \frac{0.0591}{2}\log\frac{[10^{-3}]}{[10^{-4}]}$

$= 2.71 - 0.02955$

$= 2.68V$

EMF = 2.68 V

(ii) Cell equation : $Fe(s) + 2H^{+}(aq) \longrightarrow Fe^{2+}(aq) + H_2(g)$ $(n = 2)$

Nernst equation : $E_{cell} = E^{\circ}_{cell} - \frac{0.0591}{2}\log\frac{[Fe^{2+}]}{[H^{+}]^2}$

EMF of the cell, $E_{cell} = [0-(-0.44)] - \frac{0.0591}{2}\log\frac{[10^{-3}]}{[1]^2}$

$= 0.44 - \frac{0.591}{2}\times(-3)$

$= 0.44 + 0.0887$

$= 0.5287\text{ V} \approx 0.53\text{ V}$

EMF = 0.53 V

(iii) Cell Equation : $Sn(s) + 2H^{+}(aq) \longrightarrow Sn^{2+}(aq) + H_2(g)$ $(n = 2)$

Nernst equation : $E_{cell} = E^{\circ}_{cell} - \frac{0.0591}{2}\log\frac{[Sn^{2+}]}{[H^{+}]^2}$

EMF of the cell, $E_{cell} = [0-(-0.14)] - \frac{0.0591}{2}\log\frac{[0.05]}{[0.02]^2}$

$= 0.14 - \frac{0.0591}{2}\times(2.097)$

$= 0.14 - 0.0620$

$= 0.08\text{ V}$

EMF = 0.08 V

(iv) Cell equation : $2Br^{-}(l) + 2H^{+}(aq) \longrightarrow Br_2(l) + H_2(g)$ $(n = 2)$

Nernst equation : $E_{cell} = E^{\circ}_{cell} - \frac{0.0591}{2}\log\frac{1}{[Br^{-}]^2[H^{+}]^2}$

EMF of the cell,

$$E_{cell} = [0 - 1.08] - \frac{0.0591}{2} \log \frac{1}{(0.01)^2 \times (0.03)^2}$$
$$= -1.08 - \frac{0.0591}{2} \log(1.111 \times 10^7)$$
$$= -1.08 - \frac{0.0591}{2} (7.0457)$$
$$= -1.08 - 0.208 = -1.288 \text{ V}$$
$$\text{EMF} = -1.288 \text{ V}$$

($\because$ Oxidation will occur at hydrogen electrode and reduction at Br_2 electrode.)

Question 6 In the button cell widely used in watches and other devices the following reaction takes place :

$$Zn(s) + Ag_2O(s) + H_2O(l) \longrightarrow Zn^{2+}(aq) + 2Ag(s) + 2OH^-(aq)$$

Determine $\Delta_r G^\circ$ and E° for the reaction.

[Given, $E^\circ_{Zn/Zn^{2+}} = -0.76$ V and $E^\circ_{Ag^+/Ag}$ $+0.34$ V]

◎ *Thinking Process*

(i) Write half-cell equations and calculate E°_{cell} by using $E^\circ_{cell} = E^\circ_{cathode} - E^\circ_{anode}$

(ii) Find number of electrons (n) taking part in the reaction to calculate ΔG° from the formula $\Delta G^\circ = -nFE^\circ$.

Sol. [Given, $Zn \longrightarrow Zn^{2+} + 2e^-, E^\circ = -0.76$ V

$Ag_2O + H_2O + 2e^- \longrightarrow 2Ag + 2OH^-; E^\circ = 0.344$ V]

In the given electrochemical cell, zinc is oxidised and silver ions are reduced.

$$E^\circ_{cell} = E^\circ_{cathode} - E^\circ_{anode}$$
$$E^\circ_{cell} = [0.344 - (-0.76)] = 1.104 \text{ V} \approx 1.1 \text{ V}$$

Reactions :

At anode $\quad Zn(s) \longrightarrow Zn^{2+}(aq) + 2e^-$

At cathode $\quad Ag_2O(s) + H_2O(l) + 2e^- \longrightarrow 2Ag(s) + 2OH^-(aq)$

$$\Delta_r G^\circ = -nFE^\circ$$
$$= -2 \times (96500 \text{ C}) \times (1.104 \text{ V})$$
$$= -213072 \text{ CV (or J)}$$
$$= -2.13 \times 10^5 \text{ J}$$

$\therefore$
$$E^\circ = 1.11\text{V};$$
$$\Delta_r G^\circ = -2.131 \times 10^5 \text{ J}$$

Sol. The galvanic cell for the reaction is represented as

$$Zn(s)|\,Zn^{2+}(aq)\,||\,Ag^{+}(aq)|\,Ag(s)$$

(i) Zinc electrode (anode) is negatively charged.

(ii) Electrons and ions are the carriers of the current in the cell.

(iii) **Anode :** $Zn(s) \xrightarrow{\text{Oxidation}} Zn^{2+}(aq) + 2e^-$

Cathode : $2Ag(aq) + 2e^- \xrightarrow{\text{Reduction}} 2Ag(s)$

Question 4 Calculate the standard cell potentials of galvanic cell in which the following reactions take place:

(i) $2Cr(s) + 3Cd^{2+}(aq) \longrightarrow 2Cr^{3+}(aq) + 3Cd$

(ii) $Fe^{2+}(aq) + Ag^{+}(aq) \longrightarrow Fe^{3+}(aq) + Ag(s)$

Calculate the $\Delta_r G°$ and equilibrium constant for the reactions.

◎ ***Thinking Process*** Calculate

(i) E°_{cell} from $E^{\circ}_{cathode}$ and E°_{anode} as $E^{\circ}_{cell} = E^{\circ}_{cathode} - E^{\circ}_{anode}$

(ii) $\Delta_r G°$ by using the formula $\Delta G° = -nFE^{\circ}_{cell}$.

(iii) K_c for both reactions by using the formula $\Delta_r G^0 = -2.303\, RT \log K_c$.

Sol. (i) Given $E^{\circ}_{Cr^{3+}/Cr} = -0.74V$; $E^{\circ}_{(Cd^{2+}/Cd)} = -0.40V$

Galvanic cell : $Cr(s) \mid Cr^{3+} \mid\mid cd^{2+}(aq) \mid cd\,(s)$

(a) Calculation of standard cell potential (E°)

$$E^{\circ}_{cell} = E^{\circ}_{cathode} - E^{\circ}_{anode}$$

$$= (-0.40) - (-0.74) = +\,0.34V$$

$$E^{\circ}_{cell} = +\,0.34V$$

(b) Calculation of $\Delta_r G°$

$$\Delta_r G° = -nFE^{\circ}_{cell} \text{ [here, } n = 6]$$

$$= -(6 \text{ mol}) \times (96500\,Cmol^{-1}) \times (0.34\text{ V})$$

$$= -196860\,C\,V = -196860\text{ J} = -196.86\text{ kJ}$$

$$\Delta_r G° = -196.86\,kJ$$

(c) Calculation of equilibrium constant (K_c)

$$\Delta_r G° = -2.303\,RT \log K_c$$

$$\log K_c = \frac{-\Delta_r G°}{2.303\,RT}$$

$$= (-)\frac{(-196860\,J)}{2.303 \times (8.314\text{ JK}^{-1}) \times (298\text{ K})}$$

$$= 34.501$$

$$K_c = \text{Antilog }(34.501) = 3.17 \times 10^{34}$$

$$K_c = 3.17 \times 10^{34}$$

(ii) Given $E^\circ_{(Ag^+/Ag)} = 0.80\ V$; $E^\circ_{(Fe^{3+}/Fe^{2+})} = 0.77V$

Galvanic cell : $Fe^{2+}(aq)\ |Fe^{3+}(aq)\ ||Ag^+(aq)\ |\ Ag_{(s)}$

(a) Calculation of standard cell potential (E°)

$$E^\circ_{celll} = E^\circ_{cathode} - E^\circ_{anode} = (0.80) - (0.77)V = 0.03V$$

$$E^\circ_{cell} = +\ 0.03V$$

(b) Calculation of $\Delta_r G^\circ$

$$\Delta_r G^\circ = nFE^\circ_{cell} \qquad \text{[here, } n = 1]$$

$$= -(1\ mol) \times (96500\ C\ mol^{-1}) \times (0.03V)$$

$$= -2895\ CV = -2895\ J = -2.895\ kJ$$

$$\Delta_r G^\circ = -2.895$$

(c) Calculation of equilibrium constant (K_c)

$$\Delta_r G^\circ = 2.303\, RT \log K_c$$

$$\log K_c = \frac{\Delta_r G^\circ}{2.303RT}$$

$$= (-)\frac{(-2895\ J)}{2.303 \times (8.314\ JK^{-1}) \times (298\ K)} = 0.5074$$

$$K_c = \text{Antilog}\,(0.5074) = 3.22$$

$$K_c = 3.22$$

Question 5 Write the Nernst equation and emf of the following cells at 298 K :

(i) $Mg(s)|Mg^{2+}\,(0.001M)||\,Cu^{2+}\,(0.0001M)|Cu(s)$

(ii) $Fe\,(s)|Fe^{2+}\,(0.001M)||H^+\,(1M)|H_2\,(g)\,(1\ bar)|Pt(s)$

(iii) $Sn(s)\,|Sn^{2+}\,(0.050\ M)\,||H^+\,(0.020\ M)\,|H_2\,(g)(1\ bar)|\,Pt(s)$

(iv) $Pt(s)\,|Br^-\,0.010\ M\,|Br_2\,(l)\,||\,H^+\,(0.030\ M)\,||H_2\,(g)(1bar)Pt(s)$

Given :

$$E^\circ_{(Mg^{2+}/Mg)} = -2.37V;$$

$$E^\circ_{(Cu^{2+}/Cu)} = +0.34V;$$

$$E^\circ_{(Fe^{2+}/Fe)} = -0.44V;$$

$$E^\circ_{(Sn^{2+}/Sn)} = -0.14V;$$

$$E^\circ_{(1/2Br_2/Br^-)} = +1.08V.$$

◎ Thinking Process

(i) Write the balanced equation for each cell to find number of electrons taking part in the reaction and oxidised and reduced ions.

(ii) Write Nernst equation to find emf.

Sol. $\frac{1\ \text{S cm}^{-1}}{100\ \text{S m}^{-1}} = 1$ (Unit conversion factor)

Conc. (M)	$C^{1/2}(M^{1/2})$	κ (S m^{-1})	κ (S cm^{-1})	$\Lambda_m^c = \frac{1000 \times \kappa}{\text{Molarity}}$ (S cm^2 mol^{-1})
10^{-3}	0.03162	1.237×10^{-2}	1.237×10^{-4}	$\frac{1000 \times 1.237 \times 10^{-4}}{10^{-3}} = 123.7$
10^{-2}	0.100	11.85×10^{-2}	11.85×10^{-4}	$\frac{1000 \times 11.85 \times 10^{-4}}{10^{-2}} = 118.5$
2×10^{-2}	0.141	23.15×10^{-2}	23.15×10^{-4}	$\frac{1000 \times 23.15 \times 10^{-4}}{2 \times 10^{-2}} = 115.8$
5×10^{-2}	0.224	55.53×10^{-2}	55.53×10^{-4}	$\frac{1000 \times 55.53 \times 10^{-4}}{5 \times 10^{-2}} = 111.1$
10^{-1}	0.316	106.74×10^{-2}	106.74×10^{-4}	$\frac{1000 \times 106.74 \times 10^{-4}}{10^{-1}} = 106.7$

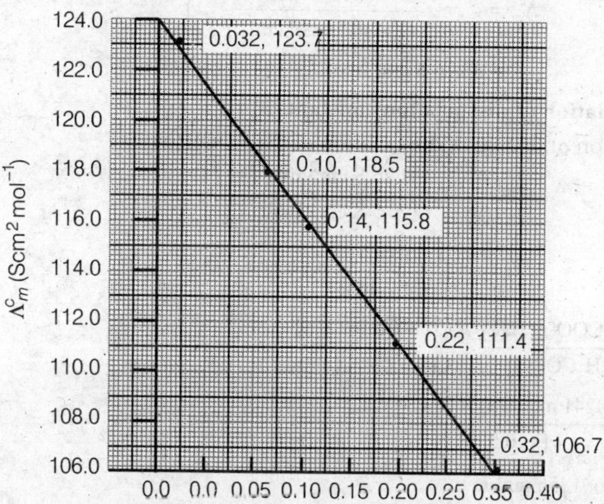

Λ_m° = Intercept on the Λ_m^c axis $= 124.05\ \text{S cm}^2\ \text{mol}^{-1}$

Mistake Alert This type of graph is only observed for strong electrolytes and not for weak electrolytes.

Question 11 Conductivity of 0.00241M acetic acid is 7.896×10^{-5} S cm^{-1}

Calculate its molar conductivity. If Λ°_m for acetic acid is 390.5 S cm^2 mol^{-1}, what is its dissociation constant?

◎ *Thinking Process*

Use the formula $\Lambda^c_m = \dfrac{\kappa}{C}$ to find molar conductivity;

$K_a = \dfrac{C\alpha^2}{(1-\alpha)}$ so calculate K_a (dissociation constant) as you know C and α.

Sol. Step I : Calculation of molar conductivity (Λ^c_m)

$$\kappa = 7.896\times10^{-5}\text{ S cm}^{-1};$$

$$C = 0.00241\text{mol L}^{-1} = \frac{0.00241}{10^3}\text{ mol cm}^{-3}$$

$$= 241\times10^{-8}\text{mol cm}^{-3}$$

$$\Lambda^c_m = \frac{\kappa}{C} = \frac{(7.896\times 10^{-5}\text{ S cm}^{-1})}{(241\times 10^{-8}\text{ mol cm}^{-3})}$$

$$= 32.76\text{ S cm}^2\text{ mol}^{-1}$$

Step II : Calculation of dissociation constant (K_a)

(a) Calculation of degree of dissociation of $CH_3COOH(\alpha)$

$$\alpha = \frac{\Lambda^c_m}{\Lambda^\circ_m} = \frac{(32.76\text{ S cm}^2\text{ mol}^{-1})}{(390.5\text{ S cm}^2\text{ mol}^{-1})}$$

$$= 0.084$$

$$= 8.4\times 10^{-2}$$

(b) $$K_a = \frac{[CH_3COO^-]\,[H^+]}{[CH_3COOH]} = \frac{C\alpha\times C\alpha}{C(1-\alpha)} = \frac{C\alpha^2}{(1-\alpha)}$$

$$= \frac{(0.00241\text{ mol L}^{-1})\times(0.084)^2}{(1-0.084)}$$

$$= 0.00001856\text{ mol L}^{-1}$$

$$= 1.86\times 10^{-5}\text{ mol L}^{-1}$$

Molar conductivity (Λ^c_m) = 32.76 S cm^2 mol^{-1}

Dissociation constant (K_a) = 1.86×10^{-5}mol L^{-1}

Mistake Alert Always convert concentration (C) from mol L^{-1} to mol cm^{-3}, to calculate Λ^c_m.

Question 7 Define conductivity and molar conductivity for the solution of an electrolyte. Discuss their variation with concentration.

Sol. **Conductivity (κ)** The inverse of resistivity (ρ), is called conductivity.

$$\kappa = \frac{1}{\rho} = \frac{1}{R} \times \frac{l}{A}$$

$$= G \times \frac{l}{A}$$

[G = conductance, l = length, A = cross-section area, R = resistance]

If $l = 1$ cm and $A = 1\text{cm}^2$, then $\kappa = G$,

So, conductivity of an electrolytic solution may be defined as the conductance of a solution of 1 cm length with area of cross-section equal to 1cm^2. Its unit is $\text{ohm}^{-1}\text{cm}^{-1}$ or S cm^{-1}.

Molar conductivity (Λ_m) Molar conductivity of a solution at a given concentration is the conductance of the volume (V) of solution containing one mole of electrolyte kept between two electrodes with area of cross section A and at a distance of unit length.

$$\Lambda_m = \frac{\kappa A}{l} = \kappa$$

Since, $l = 1$ and $A = V$; $\Lambda_m = \kappa V$

Its unit is $\text{ohm}^{-1}\ \text{cm}^2\ \text{mol}^{-1}$ or $\text{S cm}^2\ \text{mol}^{-1}$.

Variation of conductivity and molar conductivity with concentration

Conductivity always decreases with decrease in concentration both, for weak and strong electrolytes. This is so because the number of ions per unit volume that carry the current in a solution decreases on dilution.

Molar conductivity increases with decrease in concentration. This is because the total volume, V of solution containing one mole of electrolyte also increases.

It has been found that decrease in κ on dilution of a solution is more than compensated by increase in its volume.

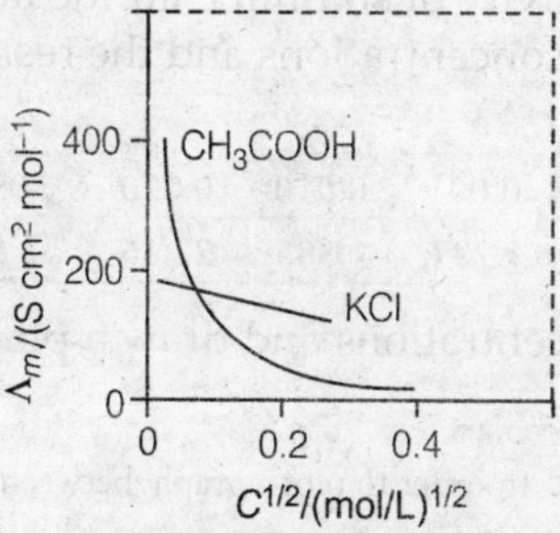

Molar conductivity versus $C^{1/2}$ for acetic acid (weak electrolyte) and potassium chloride (strong electrolyte) in aqueous solutions.

Question 8 The conductivity of 020M solution of KCl at 298K is 0.0248 S cm^{-1}. Calculate its molar conductivity.

Thinking Process Molar conductivity is calculated as $\Lambda_m = \frac{\kappa}{C} \Omega^{-1}\ mol^{-1} cm^2$. So, first convert concentration (mol/L) into mol cm^{-3} and then calculate molar conductivity.

Sol. Conductivity $(\kappa) = 0.0248\ S\ cm^{-1} = 0.0248\ ohm^{-1}\ cm^{-1}$

$$\text{Molar concentration (C)} = 0.20\ mol\ L^{-1} = \frac{(0.2\ mol)}{(1000\ cm^3)} = 2.0 \times 10^{-4}\ mol\ cm^{-3}$$

$$\text{Molar conductivity } (\Lambda_m) = \frac{\kappa}{C} = \frac{(0.0248\ ohm^{-1}\ cm^{-1})}{(2.0 \times 10^{-4}\ mol\ cm^{-3})}$$

$$= 124\ ohm^{-1} mol^{-1} cm^2$$

$$\text{or } 124\ S\ mol^{-1}\ cm^2$$

$$\text{Molar conductivity} = 124\ S\ mol^{-1}\ cm^2$$

Question 9 The resistance of a conductivity cell containing 0.001 M KCl solution at 298 K is 1500 Ω. What is the cell constant if conductivity of 0.001 M KCl solution at 298 K is $0.146 \times 10^{-3}\ S\ cm^{-1}$.

Thinking Process Cell constant = Conductivity × Resistance

Sol. $R = 1500\Omega$; $\kappa = 0.146 \times 10^{-3} S\ cm^{-1}$

$$\text{Cell constant} = R \times \kappa = (1500\ \Omega) \times (0.146 \times 10^{-3}\ S\ cm^{-1}) = 0.219\ cm^{-1}$$

$$\text{Cell constant} = 0.219\ cm^{-1}$$

Question 10 The conductivity of sodium chloride at 298 K has been determined at different concentrations and the results are given below :

Concentration/ M	0.001	0.010	0.020	0.050	0.100
$10^{-2} \times \kappa / Sm^{-1}$	1.237	11.85	23.15	55.53	106.74

Calculate Λ_m for all concentrations and draw a plot between Λ_m and $C^{1/2}$. Find the value of Λ°_m.

Thinking Process In order to plot a graph between Λ_m and $\sqrt{C}$ first find the values of $C^{1/2}$ and Λ^c_m and plot the graph. After that find Λ°_m from the graph, as it is equal to the intercept on the Λ^c_m axis.

Question 16 Three electrolytic cells *A, B, C* containing solutions of $ZnSO_4, AgNO_3$ and $CuSO_4$ respectively are connected in series. A steady current of 1.5 amperes was passed through them until 1.45 g of silver deposited at the cathode of cell *B*. How long did the current flow? What mass of copper and zinc were deposited? [Atomic masses; Cu= 63.5, Zn= 65.3 ; Ag= 108]

◎ *Thinking Process*

(i) We know that $Q = nF$ and $Q = I \times t$, so find t by using, $t = \frac{Q}{I}$.

(ii) Apply mole concept to find the amount of Zn and Cu.

Sol. (a) $\underset{}{Ag^+(aq)} + \underset{1\,\text{mol}}{e^-} \longrightarrow \underset{\substack{1\,\text{mol} \\ (108\,\text{g})}}{Ag(s)}$

108 g silver are deposited by electricity = 96500 C

1.45 g silver are deposited by electricity

$$= \frac{(96500\text{C}) \times (1.45\,\text{g})}{(108\,\text{g})}$$

$$= 1295.6\ \text{C}$$

Current (I) = 1.5 amperes

$$\text{Time}\ (t) = \frac{Q}{I} = \frac{(1295.6\ \text{C})}{(1.5\ \text{A})} = 863.7\text{s}$$

$$= 14\ \text{min}\ 39\,\text{s}$$

(b) $Cu^{2+}(aq) + \underset{\substack{2\text{F} \\ (2 \times 96500\text{C})}}{2e^-} \longrightarrow \underset{63.5\,\text{g}}{Cu(s)}$

On passing electricity of $(2 \times 96500\text{C})$; Cu deposited = 63.5 g

On passing electricity of 1295.6 C; Cu deposited

$$= \frac{(63.5) \times (1295.6\ \text{C})}{(2 \times 96500\ \text{C})} = 0.426\,\text{g}$$

$Zn^{2+}(aq) + \underset{\substack{2\text{F} \\ (2 \times 96500\text{C})}}{2e^-} \longrightarrow \underset{65.3\,\text{g}}{Zn(s)}$

On passing electricity of (2×96500) C;

Zn deposited = 65.3 g

On passing electricity of 1295.6 C; Zn deposited

$$= \frac{(65.3\ \text{g}) \times (12956\text{C})}{(2 \times 96500\ \text{C})} = 0.438\ \text{g}$$

$\therefore$ Deposited Cu= 0.426g

Deposited Zn= 0.438g

Question 17 Using the standard electrode potential values; predict if the reaction between the following is feasible:

(i) $Fe^{3+}(aq)$ and $I^-(aq)$
(ii) $Ag^+(aq)$ and $Cu(s)$
(iii) $Fe^{3+}(aq)$ and $Br^-(aq)$
(iv) $Ag(s)$ and $Fe^{3+}(aq)$
(v) $Br_2(aq)$ and $Fe^{2+}(aq)$

Given standard electrode potentials

$$E^\circ_{(1/2I_2/I^-)} = +0.541\text{ V}$$
$$E^\circ_{(Cu^{2+}/Cu)} = +0.34\text{ V}$$
$$E^\circ_{(1/2Br_2/Br^-)} = +1.09\text{ V}$$
$$E^\circ_{(Ag^+/Ag)} = +0.80\text{ V}$$
$$E^\circ_{(Fe^{3+}/Fe^{2+})} = +0.77\text{ V}$$

◎ ***Thinking Process*** For feasibility of the reaction, E°_{cell} should be positive. So, find E°_{cell} for all the reactions to find feasibility of the reaction.

Sol. A reaction is feasible, if its E°_{cell} value is positive.

(i) $Fe^{3+}(aq) + I^-(aq) \longrightarrow Fe^{2+}(aq) + \frac{1}{2}I_2(g)$

$$E^\circ_{cell} = E^\circ_{(Fe^{3+}/Fe^{2+})} - E^\circ_{1/2I_2/I^-} = 0.77 - 0.54 = 0.23\text{ V}$$

The reaction is feasible.

(ii) $Cu(s) + 2Ag^+(aq) \longrightarrow 2Ag(s) + Cu^{2+}(aq)$

$$E^\circ_{cell} = E^\circ_{(Ag^+/Ag)} - E^\circ_{Cu^{2+}/Cu} = 0.80 - 0.34 = 0.46\text{ V}$$

The reaction is feasible.

(iii) $Fe^{3+}(aq) + Br^-(aq) \longrightarrow Fe^{2+}(aq) + 1/2\,Br_2(g)$

$$E^\circ_{cell} = E^\circ_{(Fe^{3+}/Fe^{2+})} = E^\circ_{(1/2Br_2/Br^-)} = 0.77 - 1.09 = -0.32\text{V}$$

The reaction is not feasible.

(iv) $Ag(s) + Fe^{3+}(aq) \longrightarrow Ag^+(aq) + Fe^{2+}(aq)$

$$E^\circ_{cell} = E^\circ_{(Fe^{3+}/Fe^{2+})} - E^\circ_{(Ag^+/Ag)} = 0.77 - 0.80 = -0.03\text{ V}$$

The reaction is not feasible.

(v) $\frac{1}{2}Br_2(aq) + Fe^{2+}(aq) \longrightarrow Br^-(aq) + Fe^{3+}(aq)$

$$E^\circ_{cell} = E^\circ_{(1/2Br_2/Br^-)} - E^\circ_{(Fe^{3+}/Fe^{2+})} = 1.09 - 0.77 = 0.32\text{V}$$

The reaction is feasible.

Question 12 How much charge is required for the following reductions :

(i) 1 mole of Al^{3+} to Al? (ii) 1 mole of Cu^{2+} to Cu?

(iii) 1 mole of MnO_4^- to Mn^{2+}?

◎ *Thinking Process* Write electrode reaction (balanced), to find the number of electron taking part in the reaction and then calculate Q by using, $Q = n \times 96500\,C$.

Sol. (i) **1 mole of Al^{3+} to Al**

Electrode reaction : $\underset{1\,mol}{Al^{3+}(aq)} + \underset{3\,mol}{3e^-} \longrightarrow Al(s)$

Quantity of charge required for reduction of 1 mole of Al^{3+} = 3 Faraday = $3 \times 96500\,C = 289500\,C$ or $2.895 \times 10^5\,C$

(ii) **1 mole Cu^{2+} to Cu**

Electrode reaction : $\underset{1\,mol}{Cu^{2+}(aq)} + \underset{2\,mol.}{2e^-} \longrightarrow Cu(s)$

Quantity of charge required for reducing 1 mole Cu^{2+} to Cu $= 2\,F = 2 \times 96500\,C = 193000\,C = 1.93 \times 10^5\,C$

(iii) **1 mole MnO_4^- to Mn^{2+}**

Electrode reaction : $\underset{\substack{\text{(ox.no. of Mn= 7)} \\ \text{1 mol}}}{MnO_4^-} + \underset{5\,mol}{5e^-} \longrightarrow \underset{\text{(ox.no.of Mn= 2)}}{Mn^{2+}}$

Quantity of charge required for reducing 1 mole MnO_4^- to $Mn^{2+} = 5\,F = 5 \times 96500 = 482500\,C = 4.825 \times 10^5\,C$

Question 13 How much electricity in terms of Faraday is required to produce.

(i) 20.0 g of Ca from molten $CaCl_2$?

(ii) 40.0 g of Al from molten Al_2O_3?

◎ *Thinking Process* Same as in question 12.

Sol. (i) Electrode reaction : $Ca^{2+}(aq) + \underset{2F}{2e^-} \longrightarrow \underset{40\,g}{Ca(s)}$

To produce 40g of Ca from molten $CaCl_2$, electricity required = 2F

To produce 20 g Ca from $CaCl_2$, electricity required = 1F

(ii) Electrode reaction : $Al_2O_3(l) + \underset{6F}{6e^-} \longrightarrow \underset{[(2\times 27) = 54g]}{2Al} + 3O^{2-}$

To produce 54 g Al from molten Al_2O_3, electricity required = 6F

To produce 40 g Al from molten Al_2O_3, electricity required

$$= \frac{(6F) \times (40g)}{(54g)} = 4.44F$$

Question 14 How much electricity is required in coulomb for the oxidation of

(i) 1 mole of H_2O to O_2?
(ii) 1 mole of FeO to Fe_2O_3?

Thinking Process Same as is question 12.

Sol. (i) $\underset{1\,\text{mol}}{H_2O} \longrightarrow 2H^+ + \frac{1}{2}O_2 + \underset{2F}{2e^-}$

Electricity required to oxidize 1 mol H_2O to O_2 = 2 F

$= 2 \times (96500\,C) = 193000\,C$

$= 1.93 \times 10^5\,C$

(ii) $FeO + \frac{1}{2}O_2 \longrightarrow \frac{1}{2}Fe_2O_3$

$\underset{1\,\text{mol}}{Fe^{2+}} \longrightarrow Fe^{3+} + \underset{1F}{2e^-}$

Electricity required to oxidize 1 mole FeO to Fe_2O_3 = 1F = 96500 C = 9.65×10^4 C

Question 15 A solution of $Ni(NO_3)_2$ is electrolysed between platinum electrodes using a current of 5 amperes for 20 min. What mass of Ni is deposited at the cathode? (Atomic mass of Ni = 58.7)

Thinking Process

(i) Find the quantity of electricity used by the formula, $Q = I \times t$.
(ii) Write the balanced equation for the electrolysis of $Ni(NO_3)_2$ to find the quantity of electricity used to deposit 1 mole (58.7 g mol^{-1}) Ni.
(iii) Apply the mole concept for calculating the mass of Ni.

Sol. Quantity of electricity used = Current in amperes × Time in second

$= 5A \times (20 \times 60)\,s$

$= 6000\,C$

Chemical equation for the reaction during electrolysis :

$$Ni(NO_3)_2(aq) + 2H^+ + \underset{2F}{2e^-} \longrightarrow \underset{58.7g}{Ni} + 2HNO_3$$

Charge Q on n moles of electrons is given by : $Q = nF$

Charge required to deposit 1 mole nickel = 2F = 2 × 96500 C

$= 1.93 \times 10^5\,C$

Molar mass of nickel = 58.7g mol^{-1}

1.93×10^5 C of charge produces nickel = 58.7g

6000 C of charge produces nickel $= \dfrac{(58.7g) \times (6000\,C)}{(1.93 \times 10^5\,C)}$

$= 1.825\,g$

DIKSHA APP Questions

Q.1 Galvanization is a method to

(a) Protect iron metal from corrosion

(b) Extract iron from its ore

(c) Protect food from rancidity

(d) Improve the ductility of the metal

Sol. (a) Galvanization is a method to protect iron metal from corrosion. It is a process in which iron or steel is coated with a thin layer of zinc to protect it from rusting. The zinc acts as a sacrificial anode, preventing corrosion by forming a protective barrier and by corroding in place of the iron.

Q.2 The representation of the galvanic cell made up by Cu and Ag electrode in which the following reaction takes place is

$Cu(s) + 2Ag^+(aq) \rightarrow Cu^{2+}(aq) + 2Ag(s)$

(a) $Cu(s)|Cu^{2+}(aq)||Ag(s)|Ag^+(aq)$

(b) $Cu(s)|Cu^{2+}(aq)||Ag^+(aq)|Ag(s)$

(c) $Cu^{2+}(aq)|Cu(s)||Ag^+(aq)|Ag(s)$

(d) $Ag^+(aq)|Ag(s)||Cu^{2+}(aq)|Cu(s)$

Sol. (b) In a galvanic cell for the reaction.

$$Cu + 2Ag^+ \rightarrow 2Ag + Cu^{2+}$$

- Anode (Copper Electrode) : Copper (Cu) is oxidized to copper ions (Cu^{2+}), releasing electrons.

$$Cu \rightarrow Cu^{2+} + 2e^-$$

- Cathode (Silver Electrode) : Silver ions (Ag^+) are reduced to silver metal (Ag), gaining electrons.

$$Ag^+ + e^- \rightarrow Ag$$

- Salt Bridge : Maintains charge balance by allowing ion flow between the half-cells.

The overall reaction generates electrical energy as electrons flow from the anode to the cathode.

The cell representation is

$$Cu(s)|Cu^{2+}(aq)||Ag^+(aq)|Ag(s)$$

Q.3 Corrosion can be prevented by

(a) Alloying (b) Galvanizing

(c) Tinning (d) All of these

Sol. (d) Corrosion can be prevented by:

- **Alloying** Mixing metals with other elements (*e.g.*, stainless steel) to improve resistance to corrosion.
- **Tinning** Coating metal (usually iron) with a layer of tin to protect it from rusting.
- **Galvanizing** Coating iron or steel with zinc to prevent rust, as zinc acts as a sacrificial anode.

Q.4 The role of platinum or palladium metal used in fuel cells are

(a) To increase the rate of electrode reaction
(b) Used as cathode anode
(c) Used as an electrolyte
(d) Used as anode

Sol. (a) Catalysts like finely divided platinum or palladium metal are incorporated into the electrodes of fuel cells for increasing the rate of electrode reactions.

Q.5 A fuel cell is used to convert chemical energy into

(a) Mechanical energy (b) Solar energy
(c) Electrical energy (d) potential energy

Sol. (c) Galvanic cells that are designed to convert the energy of combustion of fuels like hydrogen, methane, methanol, etc., (chemical energy) directly into electrical energy are called fuel cells.

Q.6 The cell suitable for hearing aids, watches etc. is

(a) Mercury cell (b) Fuel cell
(c) Dry cell (d) Nickel cadmium cell

Sol. (a) Mercury cells are used in hearing aids and watches because they provide a stable, long-lasting voltage and have a high energy density in a small size. Their compact design allows them to fit into small devices, and they maintain constant cell potential during its life as the overall reaction does not involve any ion in solution whose concentration can change during its life time, making them ideal for precision instruments like hearing aids and watches where reliable, long-term power is essential.

Q.7 Lead storage battery consists of

(a) Lead anode and lead sulphate cathode
(b) Lead anode and lead dioxide cathode
(c) Lead oxide anode and lead cathode
(d) Lead sulphate anode and Lead cathode

Sol. (b) Lead storage battery consists of a lead anode and a grid of lead packed with lead dioxide (PbO_2) as cathode. A 38% solution of sulphuric acid is used as an electrolyte.

Note For a reaction to be feasible

$$E^{\circ}_{cell} > 0$$

as, $\Delta G^{\circ} = -nFE^{\circ}_{cell}$

So, $\Delta G^{\circ} < 0$ if $E^{\circ}_{cell} > 0$

$\Delta G^{\circ} < 0$ means reaction is spontaneous (feasible).

Question 18 Predict the products of electrolysis in each of the following :

(i) An aqueous solution of $AgNO_3$ with silver electrodes.
(ii) An aqueous solution of $AgNO_3$ with platinum electrodes.
(iii) A dilute solution of H_2SO_4 with platinum electrodes.
(iv) An aqueous solution of $CuCl_2$ with platinum electrodes.

◎ *Thinking Process* Consider the electron transfer on both electrodes (cathode and anode), write the equations and find the products.

Sol. (i) An aqueous solution of $AgNO_3$ with silver electrodes.

In aqueous solution, ionisation of $AgNO_3$ and H_2O takes place.

$$AgNO_3(s) \xrightleftharpoons{(aq)} Ag^+(aq) + NO_3^-(aq)$$

$$H_2O(l) \rightleftharpoons H^+(aq) + OH^-(aq)$$

At cathode Ag^+ ions have higher E^0 value than H^+ ions so silver will be deposited at cathode.

$$Ag^+(aq) + e^- \longrightarrow Ag(s) \qquad E^0 = 0.080\text{ V}$$

$$H^+ + e^- \longrightarrow \frac{1}{2}H_2(g) \qquad E^0 = 0.00\text{ V}$$

At anode An equivalent amount of silver will be oxidised to Ag^+ ions by releasing electrons.

$$Ag(s) \longrightarrow Ag^+(aq) + e^-$$

Ag anode is attacked by NO_3^- ions, so it will also produce Ag^+ in the solution.

(ii) An aqueous solution of $AgNO_3$ with platinum electrodes.

In aqueous solution, ionisation of $AgNO_3$ and H_2O occurs

$$AgNO_3(s) \xrightleftharpoons{(aq)} Ag^+(aq) + NO_3^-(aq)$$

$$H_2O(l) \rightleftharpoons H^+(aq) + OH^-(aq)$$

As platinum electrodes are non-attackable electrodes, they will not be reacted upon by NO_3^- ions.

At cathode Ag will be deposited at cathode, due to higher E^0 value than H^+

$$Ag^+(aq) + e^- \longrightarrow Ag(s) \qquad E^0 = 0.080\text{ V}$$

$$H^+ + e^- \longrightarrow \frac{1}{2}H_2(g) \qquad E^0 = 0.00\text{ V}$$

At anode Out of NO_3^- and OH^- ions, only OH^- ions will be oxidised (due to less discharge potential) preferentially and NO_3^- ions will remain in the solution.

$$OH^-(aq) \longrightarrow OH + e^-$$
$$4OH \longrightarrow 2H_2O(l) + O_2(g)$$

So, oxygen gas is produced at anode. The solution remains acidic due to the presence of HNO_3.

$$H^+(aq) + NO_3^-(aq) \rightleftharpoons HNO_3(aq)$$

(iii) A dilute solution of H_2SO_4 with platinum electrodes.

Both H_2SO_4 and water ionise in the solution.

$$H_2SO_4(aq) \rightleftharpoons 2H^+(aq) + SO_4^{2-}(aq)$$
$$H_2O(l) \rightleftharpoons 2H^+(aq) + OH^-(aq)$$

At cathode H^+ ions will be reduced and hydrogen gas is produced at cathode.

$$H^+(aq) + e^- \longrightarrow \frac{1}{2}H(g)$$

At anode The following reactions are possible :

(a) $2H_2O \longrightarrow O_2 + 4H^+ + 4e^-$ $E° = +1.23\text{ V}$

(b) $SO_4^{2-} \longrightarrow S_2O_6^{2-} + 2e^-$ $E° = +1.96\text{ V}$

For dil. H_2SO_4, reaction (a) is preferred and O_2 is produced at anode. But for conc. H_2SO_4, reaction (b) is preferred.

(iv) An aqueous solution of $CuCl_2$ with platinum electrodes.

Both $CuCl_2$ and water ionise as usual.

$$CuCl_2 \xrightleftharpoons{(aq)} Cu^{2+}(aq) + 2Cl^-(aq)$$
$$H_2O(l) \rightleftharpoons 2H^+(aq) + OH^-(aq)$$

At cathode Cu^{2+} ions will be reduced preferentially due to high E^0 values than H^+ ions.

$$Cu^{2+}(aq) + 2e^- \longrightarrow Cu(s) \qquad E° = 0.34\text{ V}$$
$$H^+ + e^- \longrightarrow \frac{1}{2}H_2; \qquad E° = 0.00\text{ V}$$

Copper metal is deposited at cathode.

At anode The following oxidation reactions are possible :

$$Cl^- \longrightarrow \frac{1}{2}Cl_2 + e^-;\ E° = +1.36\text{ V}$$
$$2H_2O(l) \longrightarrow O_2 + 4H^+ + 4e^-;\ E° = 1.23\text{ V}$$

At anode, reaction with lower $E°$ is preferred, but due to over-potential of oxygen, Cl^- gets oxidised and we get $Cl_2(g)$ at anode.

Chemical Kinetics

CHAPTER 03

Important Points

01 **Chemical kinetics** is the branch of chemistry which deals with the study of the rates of chemical reactions and their mechanism.

02 **Rate of chemical reaction** is the change in molar concentration of the species taking part in the chemical reaction per unit time.

03 **Instantaneous rate of reaction** is the rate of change of concentration of any one of the species involved in the reaction at a particular instant of time. Whereas, **average rate of reaction** is the rate of reaction measured over a long time interval.

04 Rate of reaction $= \dfrac{\text{Decrease in concentration of reactant}}{\text{Time taken}} = \dfrac{-\Delta[A]}{\Delta t}$

$[A \rightarrow B]$

or $= \dfrac{\text{Increase in concentration of product}}{\text{Time taken}} = \dfrac{\Delta[B]}{\Delta t}$

Units of rate = mol $L^{-1}s^{-1}$ or atm s^{-1} (in gaseous state)

05 For a general reaction : $aA + bB \rightarrow cC + dD$

$$\text{Instantaneous rate} = -\frac{1}{a}\frac{d[A]}{dt} = -\frac{1}{b}\frac{d[B]}{dt} = \frac{1}{c}\frac{d[C]}{dt} = \frac{1}{d}\frac{d[D]}{dt}$$

06 **Rate law** relates the rate of reaction with the concentration of reactants.

$$\text{Rate} = k[A]^m[B]^n$$

Rate law for any reaction cannot be predicted by merely looking at the balanced chemical equation; *i.e.*, theoretically but must be determined experimentally.

07 **Order** of a chemical reaction is the sum of coefficients of reacting species that are involved in the rate equation for the reaction. Order of a reaction $= x + y$; if rate $= k[A]^x[B]^y$.

08 The overall rate of the reaction is controlled by the slowest step in the reaction, known as the **rate determining step.**

A chemical reaction in which one or more of the reactants react to form products directly in a single step and with a single transition state, is called as an **elementary reaction.**

09 Rate of reaction is affected by some factors like temperature, concentration of reactants/products, catalyst, surface area of the reactants, etc.

10 **Molecularity** of a reaction is the number of the reacting species that collide simultaneously to bring about a chemical reaction.

11 **Units of rate constant** $(k) = (\text{mol L}^{-1})^{1-n}\ \text{s}^{-1}$

For Ist order reaction $k = \text{s}^{-1}$

IInd order reaction $k = \text{mol}^{-1}\ \text{L s}^{-1}$

IIIrd order reaction $k = \text{mol}^{-2}\ \text{L}^2\ \text{s}^{-1}$

Zero order reaction $k = \text{mol L}^{-1}\ \text{s}^{-1}$

12 Integrated rate equation for zero order reaction $k = \dfrac{[A]_0 - [A]}{t}$.

13 Half-life period for zero order reaction $(t_{1/2}) = \dfrac{[A]_0}{2k}$.

14 Integrated rate equation for Ist order reaction $k = \dfrac{2.303}{t} \log \dfrac{a}{a-x}$.

15 Half-life period for Ist order reaction $t_{1/2} = \dfrac{0.693}{t}$.

16 For gaseous reaction : $k = \dfrac{2.303}{t} \log \dfrac{p_i}{2p_i - p_t}$.

17 If a reaction is not truly of first order, but under certain conditions it becomes a first order reaction, then it is called a **pseudo first order reaction.** Examples include, hydrolysis of ester, inversion of cane sugar, etc.

Q.8 Molten NaCl conducts electricity due the presence of

(a) Free electrons (b) Free Molecules
(c) Atoms of Na and Cl (d) Free ions

Sol. (d) Molten sodium chloride (NaCl) conducts electricity because, in its molten state, NaCl dissociates into free ions. When solid NaCl is heated to its melting point, the ionic bonds between sodium (Na^+) and chloride (Cl^-) ions are broken, allowing the ions to move freely within the liquid. These free-moving ions (Na^+ and Cl^-) are able to carry charge, making molten NaCl an effective conductor of electricity.

Q.9 The unit of cell constant is represented as

(a) $ohm^{-2}cm^{-1}$ (b) cm^2
(c) cm^{-1} (d) $ohm\,cm^{-1}$

Sol. (c) The quantity l/A is called cell constant denoted by the symbol, G*. It depends on the distance between the electrodes and their area of cross-section and has the dimension of $length^{-1}$ and can be calculated if we know l and A. Its unit is represented as cm^{-1}.

Q.10 Arrange the following species in the increasing order of their reducing power on the basis of standard electrode potential values given below

(I) $K^+/K = -2.93V$
(II) $Ni^{2+}/Ni = -0.25V$
(III) $Ag^+/Ag = 0.80\,V$

(a) I < II < III (b) II < III < I
(c) III < II < I (d) III < I < II

Sol. (c) The lower or more negative the electrode potential, the stronger is the reducing agent. Therefore, the increasing order of the reducing power of the given metals is Ag < Ni < K.
Therefore, the correct order of reducing power is III < II < I.

Q.11 Which of the given statements is correct for a Daniel cell made up by Zn and Cu electrode, which $E_{ext} > 1.1\,V$?

(a) Electrons flow from Cu to Zn and current flows from Zn to Cu.
(b) Electrons flow from Zn to Cu and current flows from Cu to Zn
(c) No flow of electrons or current
(d) Zn dissolves at anode and Cu deposits at cathode.

Sol. (b) In a Daniel Cell, the reactions at the electrodes are as follows

1. **At the Anode (Zinc Electrode, Zn)**
   - Zinc undergoes oxidation, losing electrons
     $$Zn(s) \rightarrow Zn^{2+}(aq) + 2e^-$$
   - Electrons flow from the Zn electrode to the external circuit.
2. **At the cathode (Copper Electrode, Cu)**
   - Copper ions (Cu^{2+}) in solution are reduced by gaining electrons to form copper metal.
   - $Cu^{2+}(aq) + 2e^- \rightarrow Cu(s)$
   - Electrons flow from Zn (anode) to Cu (cathode) through the external circuit.
   - Current flow from Cu (cathode) to Zn (anode) in the external circuit (opposite to the flow of electrons)

□ Short Answer Type

Q.1 The standard electrode potential (E^0) for Daniell cell is +1.1 V. Calculate the standerd Gibbs energy for the reaction.

$Zn(s) + Cu^{2+}(aq) \longrightarrow Zn^{2+}(aq) + Cu(s)$ Given ;$1F = 96500 Cmol^{-1}$

Sol. For the reaction, $n = 2$

Given, $F = 96500$ C/mol and $E^0 = +1.1$ V

By applying the formula, $\Delta G° = -nFE°$

Substitute the values $\Delta G° = -(2) \times (96485 C/mol) \times (1.1 V)$

$$\Delta G° = -2 \times 96485 \times 1.1$$

$$\Delta G° = -212,267 J/mol, \Delta G° = -212.3 kJ/mol$$

□ Long Answer Type

Q.1 State Kohlrausch law and mention any two application of this law.

Sol. Kohlrausch law of independent migration of ions states that limiting molar conductivity of an electrolyte can be represented as the sum of the individual contributions of the anion and cation of the electrolyte. Two applications; (1) Using Kohlrausch law limiting molar conductivity of weak electrolytes can be calculated. If an electrolyte on dissociation gives $+ve$ cations and $-ve$ anions then its limiting molar conductivity is given by

$$\Lambda°_m = v_+ \overset{\circ}{\lambda}_+ + v_-{}^-\lambda°_-$$

Here, $\overset{\circ}{\lambda}_+$ and $\overset{\circ}{\lambda}_-$ are the limiting molar conductivities of the cation and anion respectively. Using kohlrausch law dissociation constant of weak electrolytes can be calculated.

At any concentration c, if α is the degree of dissociationthen it can be approximated to the ratio of molar conductivity Λ_m at the concentration c to limiting molar conductivity, $\Lambda°_m$. Thus we have:

$$\alpha = \frac{\Lambda_m}{\overset{\circ}{\Lambda}_m}$$

Intext Questions

Question 1 For the reaction, $R \longrightarrow P$, the concentration of a reactant changes from 0.03 M to 0.02 M in 25 minutes. Calculate the average rate of reaction using units of time both in minutes and seconds.

◎ ***Thinking Process*** Average rate of reaction

$$= \text{Rate of change of } [R] \text{ or } [P] = \frac{\text{Change in concentration of } [R] \text{ or } [P]}{\text{Time taken}}$$

Sol. For the reaction $R \longrightarrow P$

$$\text{Average rate of reaction} = \frac{\text{Change in concentration of reactant/ product}}{\text{Time taken}}$$

$$= \frac{-\Delta[R]}{\Delta t}$$

$$= -\frac{[R_2]-[R_1]}{t_2 - t_1}$$

$$= -\frac{(0.02 - 0.03)\text{ M}}{(25 \times 60)\text{ s}} = -\frac{(-0.01)\text{ M}}{(1500)\text{ s}}$$

$$= 6.67 \times 10^{-6}\ \text{Ms}^{-1}$$

$$= 6.67 \times 10^{-6}\ \text{mol L}^{-1}\ \text{s}^{-1}$$

Question 2 In a reaction, $2A \longrightarrow$ products, the concentration of A decreases from 0.5 mol L^{-1} to 0.4 mol L^{-1} in 10 minutes. Calculate the rate during this interval.

Sol. Rate of reaction = rate of disappearance of A

$$= -\frac{1}{2}\frac{\Delta[A]}{\Delta t} = -\frac{1}{2}\frac{(0.4 - 0.5)\text{ mol L}^{-1}}{10\text{ min}}$$

$$= 0.005\ \text{mol L}^{-1}\ \text{min}^{-1}$$

$$= 5 \times 10^{-3}\ \text{M min}^{-1}$$

Question 3 For a reaction, $A + B \longrightarrow$ product; the rate law is given by, $r = k\,[A]^{1/2}\,[B]^2$. What is the order of the reaction?

◎ ***Thinking Process*** Order = Sum of powers of the concentration of reactants.

Sol. Order of reaction $= \frac{1}{2} + 2 = \frac{5}{2} = 2.5$

$$\text{Order} = \frac{5}{2} = 2.5$$

Question 4 The conversion of molecules x to y follows second order kinetics. If concentration of x is increased to three times how will it affect the rate of formation of y?

◎ *Thinking Process* For II order kinetics, rate $= k\,[\text{reactant}]^2$, so make two equation first by taking initial rate and concentration, second by taking tripled concentration and unknown rate (r'). Compare them to find a relation between r and r'.

Sol. For the reaction $x \longrightarrow y$

$$\text{Reaction rate}\,(r) = k\,[x]^2 \quad \ldots\text{(i)}$$

If the concentration of x is increased three times, then

$$\text{Reaction rate}\,(r') = k\,[3x]^2 = k \times [9x^2] \quad \ldots\text{(ii)}$$

Dividing Eq. (ii) by Eq. (i);

$$\frac{r'}{r} = \frac{k \times [9x^2]}{k \times [x^2]} = 9$$

It means that the rate of formation of y will increase by **nine times.**

Question 5 A first order reaction has a rate constant $1.15 \times 10^{-3}\ \text{s}^{-1}$. How long will 5 g of this reactant take to reduce to 3 g?

◎ *Thinking Process* For Ist order reaction ;

$k = \frac{2.303}{t} \log \frac{[R]_0}{[R]}$, so calculate t by using, $t = \frac{2.303}{k} \log \frac{[R]_0}{[R]}$

Sol. Rate constant $(k) = 1.15 \times 10^{-3}\ \text{s}^{-1}$

Initial amount $[R]_0 = 5\ \text{g}$

Final amount $[R] = 3\ \text{g}$

$$t = \frac{2.303}{k} \log \frac{[R]_0}{[R]}$$

$$= \frac{2.303}{(1.15 \times 10^{-3}\ \text{s}^{-1})} \times \log \frac{(5\ \text{g})}{(3\ \text{g})}$$

$$= \frac{2.303}{(1.15 \times 10^{-3}\ \text{s}^{-1})} (\log 5 - \log 3)$$

$$= \frac{2.303}{(1.15 \times 10^{-3}\ \text{s}^{-1})} (0.6990 - 0.4771)$$

$$= 2.0 \times 10^3 \times 0.2219\ \text{s}$$

$$= 443.8\ \text{s}$$

$$\text{Time} = 444\ \text{s}$$

18 Some important graphs of the chapter are :

(a)

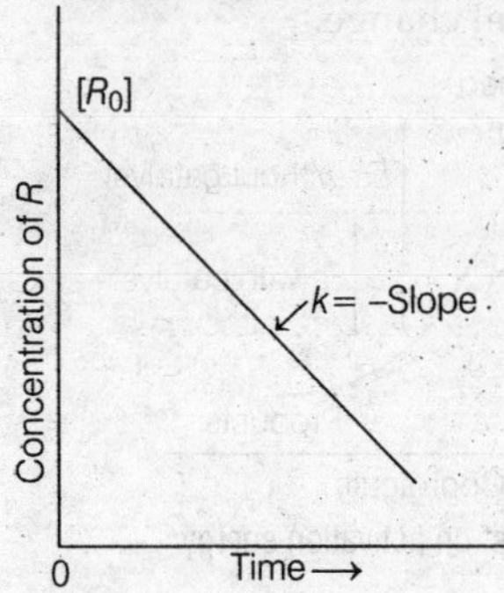

▲ Variation in the concentration *vs* time plot for a zero order reaction

(b)

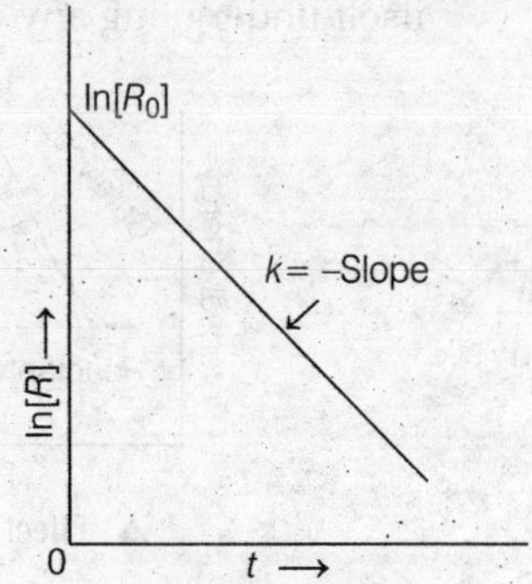

▲ A plot between $\ln [R]$ and t for a first order reaction

(c)

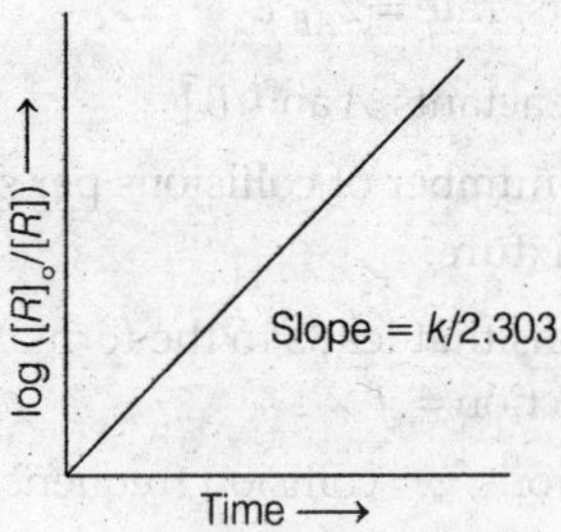

▲ Plot of $\log([R]/[R_0])$ *vs* time for a first order reaction

(d)

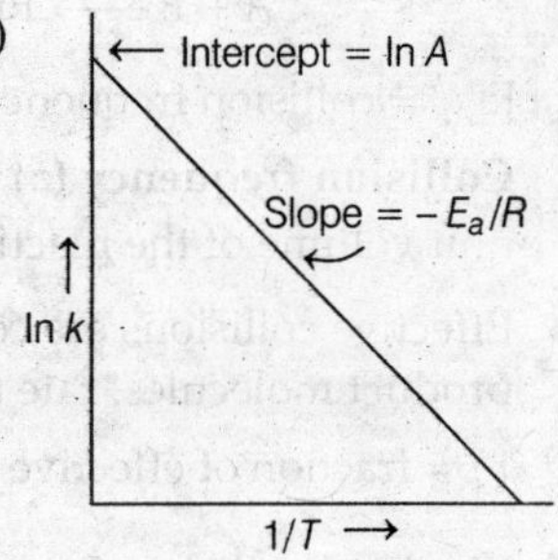

▲ A plot between $\ln k$ and $1/T$

19 Arrhenius equation for activation energy is :

$$k = Ae^{-E_a/RT}$$

$$\log k = \log A - \frac{E_a}{2.303\,RT}$$

where, A = Arrhenius factor or frequency factor

E_a = Activation energy

$$\log \frac{k_2}{k_1} = \frac{E_a}{2.303\,R}\left[\frac{1}{T_1} - \frac{1}{T_2}\right]$$

20 **Activation energy** is the extra amount of energy which has to be supplied to the reacting species in their normal energy state to make their energy equal to threshold energy.

21 For a chemical reaction with rise in temperature by 10°, the rate constant is nearly doubled.

22 **Catalyst** is a substance that increases the rate of reaction without itself undergoing any chemical change.

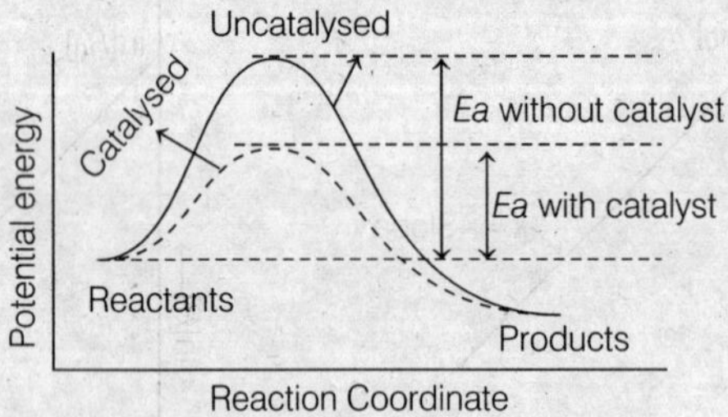

▲ Effect of catalyst on activation energy

23 For a bimolecular elementary reaction,

$$A + B \longrightarrow \text{Products, rate} = z_{AB}\, e^{-\frac{Ea}{RT}}$$

[z_{AB} = collision frequency of reactants A and B]

Collision frequency (z) is the number of collisions per second per unit volume of the reaction mixture.

24 Effective collisions are collisions that leads to the formation of product molecules. rate of reaction = $f \times z$

[f = fraction of effective collisions, z = collision frequency]

25 Modified collision theory, Rate = $PZ_{AB}\, e^{-\frac{Ea}{RT}}$

[P = probability or steric factor; It accounts for proper orientation of colliding molecules $e^{-\frac{Ea}{RT}}$ = fraction of molecules having energies equal to or greater than E_a].

26

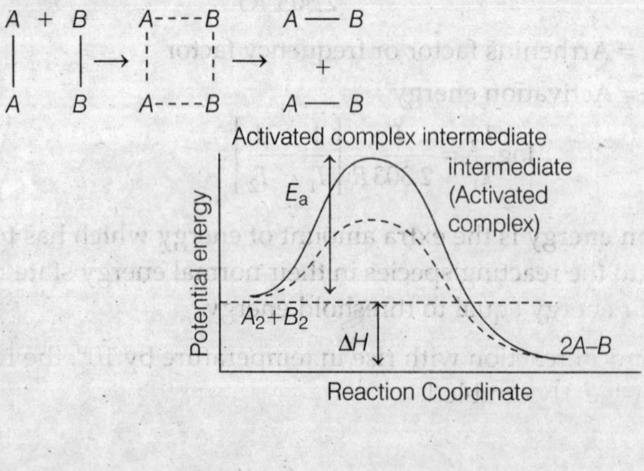

Sol. (i) Rate $= k[NO]^2$, Order of reaction = 2

Units (Dimensions) of rate constant

$$(k) = \frac{\text{Rate}}{[NO]^2} = \frac{\text{mol L}^{-1}\text{ s}^{-1}}{(\text{mol L}^{-1})^2} = \text{mol}^{-1}\text{ L s}^{-1}$$

(ii) Rate $= k[H_2O_2][I^-]$

Order of reaction = 1 + 1 = 2

$$\text{Dimensions of } k = \frac{\text{Rate}}{[H_2O_2][I^-]} = \frac{\text{mol L}^{-1}\text{ s}^{-1}}{(\text{mol L}^{-1})(\text{mol L}^{-1})} = \text{mol}^{-1}\text{ L s}^{-1}$$

(iii) Rate $= k[CH_3CHO]^{3/2}$

Order of reaction $= \frac{3}{2}$

$$\text{Dimensions of } k = \frac{\text{Rate}}{[CH_3CHO]^{3/2}} = \frac{\text{mol L}^{-1}\text{ s}^{-1}}{(\text{mol L}^{-1})^{3/2}} = \text{mol}^{-1/2}\text{ L}^{1/2}\text{ s}^{-1}$$

(iv) Rate $= k[C_2H_5Cl]$

Order of reaction = 1

$$\text{Dimensions of } k = \frac{\text{Rate}}{[C_2H_5Cl]} = \frac{\text{mol L}^{-1}\text{s}^{-1}}{\text{mol L}^{-1}} = \text{s}^{-1}$$

Mistake Alert The coefficient of reactant in the chemical equation is not equal to its order.

Question 2 For the reaction, $2A + B \longrightarrow A_2B$ the rate $= k[A][B]^2$ with $k = 2.0 \times 10^{-6}$ mol^{-2} L^2 s^{-1}. Calculate the initial rate of reaction when $[A] = 0.1$ mol L^{-1}, $[B] = 0.2$ mol L^{-1}. Calculate the rate of reaction after $[A]$ is reduced to 0.06 mol L^{-1}.

Thinking Process

- Calculate rate by using rate $= k[A][B]^2$ as you know k, $[A]$ and $[B]$.
- In second case, calculate the amount of B left with the help of the equation $2A + B \rightarrow A_2B$ and then further calculate rate by using the changed $[A]$ and $[B]$.

Sol. (i) **Case I** Rate $= k[A][B]^2$

$$= (2.0 \times 10^{-6}\text{ mol}^{-2}\text{ L}^{-2}\text{ s}^{-1}) \times (0.1\text{ mol L}^{-1}) \times (0.2\text{ mol L}^{-1})^2$$

$$= 8.0 \times 10^{-9}\text{ mol L}^{-1}\text{ s}^{-1}$$

(ii) **Case II** Concentration of A at a particular time = 0.06 mol L^{-1} $[A]$

Amount of A reacted = (0.1 − 0.06) = 0.04 mol L^{-1}

Amount of B reacted $= \frac{1}{2} \times 0.04$ mol L^{-1} = 0.02 mol L^{-1}

Concentration of B at a particular time = $[B]$

$$= (0.2 - 0.02)\text{ mol L}^{-1} = 0.18\text{ mol L}^{-1}$$

Rate $= k[A][B]^2$

$$= (2.0 \times 10^{-6}\text{ mol}^{-2}\text{ L}^2\text{ s}^{-1}) \times (0.06\text{ mol L}^{-1}) \times (0.18\text{ mol L}^{-1})^2$$

$$= 3.89 \times 10^{-9}\text{ mol L}^{-1}\text{ s}^{-1}$$

Question 3 The decomposition of NH_3 on platinum surface is zero order reaction. What are the rates of production of N_2 and H_2 if $k = 2.5 \times 10^{-4}\ mol^{-1}Ls^{-1}$?

Thinking Process

(i) To find the relation between the rate of decomposition of NH_3 and rate of production of N_2 and H_2. Write the chemical equation for the decomposition of NH_3 and write the expressions for rate of production of N_2 and H_2.

(ii) Do calculation by placing the values, in these expression.

Sol.

$$2NH_3 \longrightarrow N_2 + 3H_2$$

By dividing the equation by 2,

$$NH_3 \longrightarrow \frac{1}{2}N_2 + \frac{3}{2}H_2$$

$$\text{Rate} = -\frac{d[NH_3]}{dt} = +\frac{2d[N_2]}{dt} = \frac{2}{3}\frac{d[H_2]}{dt}$$

For zero order reaction, rate = $k = 2.5 \times 10^{-4}$ mol $L^{-1}s^{-1}$

So,

$$\frac{-d[NH_3]}{dt} = \frac{2d[N_2]}{dt} = \frac{2}{3}\frac{d[H_2]}{dt}$$

$$= 2.5 \times 10^{-4} \text{ mol } L^{-1}s^{-1}$$

$\therefore$ Rate of production of $N_2 = \frac{d[N_2]}{dt}$

$$= \frac{(2.5 \times 10^{-4} \text{ mol } L^{-1}s^{-1})}{2}$$

$$= 1.25 \times 10^{-4} \text{ mol } L^{-1}s^{-1}$$

$\therefore$ Rate of production of $H_2 = \frac{d[H_2]}{dt} = \frac{3}{2} \times (2.5 \times 10^{-4} \text{ mol } L^{-1}s^{-1})$

$$= 3.75 \times 10^{-4} \text{ mol } L^{-1}s^{-1}$$

Question 4 The decomposition of dimethyl ether leads to the formation of CH_4, H_2 and CO and the reaction rate is given by : Rate $= k[CH_3OCH_3]^{3/2}$. The rate of reaction is followed by increase in pressure in a closed vessel, so the rate can also be expressed in terms of the partial pressure of dimethyl ether *i.e*, Rate $= k\,(p_{CH_3OCH_3})^{3/2}$. If the pressure is measured in bar and time in minutes, then what are the units of rate and rate constants?

Thinking Process

(i) In terms of pressure, units of rate = bar min^{-1}.

(ii) $k = \frac{\text{Rate}}{(p_{CH_3OCH_3})^{3/2}}$. Put the units of rate and $p_{CH_3OCH_3}$ to find the units of k.

Question 6 Time required to decompose SO_2Cl_2 to half of its initial amount is 60 minutes. If the decomposition is a first order reaction, calculate the rate constant of the reaction.

◎ *Thinking Process* The time in which a substance is reduced to half of its original quantity is called its half-life, $t_{1/2}$. We have $t_{1/2}$ so calculate k from the formula, $k = 0.693 / t_{1/2}$ (for Ist order reaction)

Sol. For the first order reaction,

$$\text{Rate constant } (k) = \frac{0.693}{t_{1/2}} = \frac{0.693}{60\,\text{min}} = \frac{0.693}{(60 \times 60)\,\text{s}} = 1.925 \times 10^{-4}\ \text{s}^{-1}$$

$$k = 1.925 \times 10^{-4}\ \text{s}^{-1}$$

Question 7 What will be the effect of temperature on rate constant?

◎ *Thinking Process* Recall Arrhenius equation, $k = Ae^{-E_a/RT}$ to show the effect of temperature on rate constant.

Sol. The rate constant for a reaction is nearly doubled with about 10° rise in temperature. The reason is that the number of effective collision becomes almost double. The exact dependence of the rate of reaction can be given by Arrhenius equation; $k = Ae^{-E_a/RT}$. Where, A is called the frequency factor or Arrhenius factor and E_a is the activation energy of the reaction.

Question 8 The rate of the chemical reaction doubles for an increase of 10 K in absolute temperature from 298 K. Calculate E_a.

◎ *Thinking Process* To calculate E_a, apply Arrhenius equation,

$$\log\frac{k_2}{k_1} = \frac{E_a}{2.303}\left[\frac{1}{T_1} - \frac{1}{T_2}\right]$$

Sol. According to Arrhenius equation,

$$\log\frac{k_2}{k_1} = \frac{E_a}{2.303R}\left[\frac{1}{T_1} - \frac{1}{T_2}\right]$$

$$\frac{k_2}{k_1} = 2;\ T_1 = 298\ \text{K};\ T_2 = 308\ \text{K};\ R = 8.314\ \text{JK}^{-1}\ \text{mol}^{-1}$$

$$\therefore \quad \log 2 = \frac{E_a}{2.303 \times (8.314\ \text{JK}^{-1}\ \text{mol}^{-1})}\left[\frac{1}{298\,\text{K}} - \frac{1}{308\ \text{K}}\right]$$

$$\text{or} \quad 0.3010 = \frac{E_a}{2.303 \times (8.314\ \text{J mol}^{-1})} \times \frac{(10)}{298 \times 308}$$

$$E_a = \frac{0.3010 \times 2.303 \times 8.314 \times 298 \times 308}{10}\ (\text{J mol}^{-1})$$

$$= 52897.78\ \text{J mol}^{-1} \text{ or } 52.9\ \text{kJ mol}^{-1}$$

Activation energy for the reaction = $52.9\ \text{kJ mol}^{-1}$

Question 9 The activation energy for the reaction

$$2\,HI(g) \longrightarrow H_2(g) + I_2(g) \text{ is } 209.5 \text{ kJ mol}^{-1} \text{ at } 581 \text{ K.}$$

Calculate the fraction of molecules of reactants having energy equal to or greater than activation energy.

◎ ***Thinking Process*** The fraction of molecules having energy equal to E_a is related to E_a as $x = n / N = e^{-E_a/RT}$.

Sol. Fraction of molecules (x) having energy equal to or more than activation energy may be calculated as follows :

$$x = n/N = e^{-E_a/RT}$$

$$\ln x = \frac{-E_a}{RT} \text{ or } \log x = -\frac{E_a}{2.303\,RT}$$

[Given, $Ea = 209.5$ kJ/mol, $T = 581$ K, $R = 8.314$ J K^{-1} mol^{-1}]

$$\text{or} \quad \log x = -\frac{209.5 \times 10^3 \text{ J mol}^{-1}}{2.303 \times (8.314 \text{ JK}^{-1} \text{ mol}^{-1}) \times 581 \text{ K}}$$

$$= -18.8323$$

$$x = \text{Antilog}(-18.8324) = \text{Antilog } \overline{19}.1677$$

$$= 1.471 \times 10^{-19}$$

$$\text{Fraction of molecules} = 1.471 \times 10^{-19}$$

Mistake Alert Always convert activation energy from kJ mol^{-1} to J mol^{-1} to put in the Arrhenius equation.

Exercises

Question 1 From the rate expression for the following reactions, determine their order of reaction and the dimensions of the rate constants.

(i) $3NO(g) \longrightarrow N_2O(g)$; Rate $= k\,[NO]^2$

(ii) $H_2O_2\,(aq) + 3I^-\,(aq) + 2H^+ \longrightarrow 2H_2O(l) + I_3^-$;
Rate $= k\,[H_2O_2][I^-]$

(iii) $CH_3CHO(g) \longrightarrow CH_4\,(g) + CO(g)$; Rate $= k\,[CH_3CHO]^{3/2}$

(iv) $C_2H_5Cl\,(g) \longrightarrow C_2H_4\,(g) + HCl\,(g)$; Rate $= k\,[C_2H_5Cl]$

◎ ***Thinking Process***

(a) If rate $= k\,[A]^x\,[B]^y$, then order of reaction $= x + y$; so find order from rate law.

(b) $k = \text{Rate}/\,[A]^x\,[B]^y$, calculate units of k in the similar manner.

Sol. (i) Rate $= k[A][B]^2$

The different rate equation will be $\frac{-d[R]}{dt} = k[A][B]^2$

(ii) Rate $= k[A][3B]^2 = 9k[A][B]^2$ Rate of reaction becomes 9 times if the concentration of B is increased 3 times

(iii) Rate $= k[2A][2B]^2 = 8k[A][B]^2$ Rate of reaction becomes 8 times if the concentrations of both A and B are doubled.

Question 10 In a reaction between A and B the initial rate of reaction (r_0) was measured for different initial concentrations of A and B as given below:

A / mol L^{-1}	0.20	0.20	0.40
B / mol L^{-1}	0.30	0.10	0.05
r_0 / mol L^{-1}s^{-1}	5.07×10^{-5}	5.07×10^{-5}	1.43×10^{-5}

What is the order to the reaction with respect to A and B?

◎ Thinking Process

(i) Rate of reaction $= k[A]^x[B]^y$; Order $= x$ (with respect to A) and y (with respect to B)

(ii) Make three equations for the three experiments by putting the value of and r_o and solve them to find the value of x and y.

Sol. Rate law states that

$$\text{Rate} = k[A]^x[B]^y$$

$$(\text{Rate})_1 = k[0.20]^x[0.30]^y = 5.07 \times 10^{-5} \quad \ldots(\text{i})$$

$$(\text{Rate})_2 = k[0.20]^x[0.10]^y = 5.07 \times 10^{-5} \quad \ldots(\text{ii})$$

$$(\text{Rate})_3 = k[0.40]^x[0.05]^y = 1.43 \times 10^{-4} \quad \ldots(\text{iii})$$

Dividing equation (i) by equation (ii)

$$\frac{(\text{Rate})_1}{(\text{Rate})_2} = \frac{k[0.20]^x[0.30]^y}{k[0.40]^x[0.10]^y} = \frac{5.07 \times 10^{-5}}{5.07 \times 10^{-5}} = 1$$

$$[3]^y = [3]^0 = 1;\ y = 0$$

Now dividing equation (ii) by equation (iii)

$$\frac{(\text{Rate})_2}{(\text{Rate})_3} = \frac{k[0.20]^x[0.10]^0}{k[0.40]^x[0.05]^0} = \frac{5.07 \times 10^{-5}}{1.43 \times 10^{-4}}$$

$$\left[\frac{1}{2}\right]^x = \frac{1}{2.82}$$

$$2^x = 2.82$$

$$x \log 2 = \log 2.82$$

$$\therefore \quad x = 1.4957 \simeq 1.5$$

Order with respect to $A = 1.5$

Order with respect to $B = 0$

Question 11 The following results have been obtained during the kinetic studies of the reaction, $2A + B \longrightarrow C + D$

Experiment	$[A]$ mol L^{-1}	$[B]$ mol L^{-1}	Initial rate of formation of D / mol L^{-1} min^{-1}
I	0.1	0.1	6.0×10^{-3}
II	0.3	0.2	7.2×10^{-2}
III	0.3	0.4	2.88×10^{-1}
IV	0.4	0.1	2.40×10^{-2}

Determine the rate law and the rate constant for the reaction.

◎ ***Thinking Process***

(i) Same as Q. 10.

(ii) Calculate rate constant by putting the other quantities in any of the four equations.

Sol. Rate law may be expressed as

$$\text{Rate} = k[A]^x [B]^y$$

$$(\text{Rate})_1 = 6.0 \times 10^{-3} = k(0.1)^x (0.1)^y \quad \ldots(i)$$

$$(\text{Rate})_2 = 7.2 \times 10^{-2} = k(0.3)^x (0.2)^y \quad \ldots(ii)$$

$$(\text{Rate})_3 = 2.88 \times 10^{-1} = k(0.3)^x (0.4)^y \quad \ldots(iii)$$

$$(\text{Rate})_4 = 2.40 \times 10^{-2} = k(0.4)^x (0.1)^y \quad \ldots(iv)$$

$$\frac{(\text{Rate})_1}{(\text{Rate})_4} = \frac{6.0 \times 10^{-3}}{2.40 \times 10^{-2}} = \frac{k(0.1)^x (0.1)^y}{k(0.4)^x (0.1)^y}$$

or $$\frac{1}{4} = \frac{(0.1)^x}{(0.4)^x} = \left(\frac{1}{4}\right)^x$$

$\therefore$ $$x = 1$$

$$\frac{(\text{Rate})_2}{(\text{Rate})_3} = \frac{7.2 \times 10^{-2}}{2.88 \times 10^{-1}} = \frac{k(0.3)^x (0.2)^y}{k(0.3)^x (0.4)^y}$$

or $$\frac{1}{4} = \frac{(0.2)^y}{(0.4)^y} = \left(\frac{1}{2}\right)^y$$

$\therefore$ $$y = 2$$

Rate law expression is given by

$$\text{Rate} = k[A][B]^2$$

Rate constant k can be determined by placing the values of A, B and rate of formation of D. By taking the values from experiment II.

$$\text{Rate} = k[A][B]^2$$

$$k = \frac{\text{Rate}}{[A][B]^2} = \frac{7.2 \times 10^{-2} \text{ mol L}^{-1}\text{min}^{-1}}{(0.3 \text{ mol L}^{-1})(0.2 \text{ mol L}^{-1})^2}$$

$$= 6.0 \text{ mol}^{-2} \text{L}^2 \text{ min}^{-1}$$

$$k = 6.0 \text{ mol}^{-2} \text{ L}^2 \text{ min}^{-1}$$

Sol. Unit of rate = bar min^{-1}

$$\text{Rate} = k(p_{CH_3OCH_3})^{3/2}$$

$$\text{Unit of } k = \frac{\text{Rate}}{(p_{CH_3OCH_3})^{3/2}} = \frac{\text{bar min}^{-1}}{(\text{bar})^{3/2}} = \text{bar}^{-1/2}\ \text{min}^{-1}$$

Question 5 Mention the factors that affect the rate of a chemical reaction.

Sol. Following factors affect the rate of a chemical reaction.

(a) **Nature of reactants** Ionic substances react more rapidly than covalent compounds because ions produced after dissociation are immediately available for reaction.

(b) **Concentration of reactants** Rate of reaction increases when concentration of reactants is increased.

(c) **Temperature** Generally rate of reaction increases on increasing the temperature.

(d) **Surface area of the reactants** Rate of reaction increases with increase in surface area of the reactants. That is why powdered form of reactants is preferred than their granular form.

(e) **Catalyst** Presence of catalyst also effects the rate of reaction. It decreases the activation energy by forming a reaction intermediate and hence lowers the potential energy barrier. So, rate of reaction increases.

Question 6 A reaction is second order with respect to a reactant. How is the rate of reaction affected if the concentration of the reaction is

(i) doubled (ii) reduced to half?

◎ ***Thinking Process*** For II order reaction, rate $= k[A]^2$. Find the rate expression when concentration is doubled or reduced to half and compare it with the normal rate.

Sol. For a reaction, $A \longrightarrow$ Products

$$\text{Rate} = k[A]^2 = ka^2$$

(i) When concentration of A is doubled

i.e.,
$$[A] = 2a$$
$$\text{Rate} = k(2a)^2 = 4ka^2$$

Rate of reaction becomes 4 times

(ii) When concentration of A is reduced to $\frac{1}{2}$

i.e.,
$$[A] = \frac{1}{2}a$$
$$\text{Rate} = k\left(\frac{a}{2}\right)^2 = \frac{1}{4}ka^2$$

Rate of reaction becomes $\frac{1}{4}$ times *i.e.,* reduced to one fourth.

Question 7 What is the effect of temperature on the rate constant of a reaction? How can this effect of temperature on rate constant be represented quantitatively?

◎ *Thinking Process* Arrhenius equation gives a relation between rate constant and temperature, $k = Ae^{-E_a/RT}$.

Sol. The rate constant of a reaction increases with increase in temperature and becomes nearly double for every 10° rise in temperature. The effect can be represented quantitatively by Arrhenius equation,

$$k = Ae^{-E_a/RT}$$

Where, E_a is the activation energy of the reaction and A represents the frequency factor.

Question 8 In a pseudo first order reaction in water, the following results were obtained.

t/s	0	30	60	90
[Ester]/mol L^{-1}	0.55	0.31	0.17	0.085

Calculate the average rate of reaction between the time interval 30 to 60 seconds.

◎ *Thinking Process* Calculate average rate from the relation, Average rate = Change in concentration / Time taken.

Sol. Average rate during the interval 30 – 60 s $= -\dfrac{C_2 - C_1}{t_2 - t_1}$

$$= \frac{(0.17 - 0.31)\text{ mol L}^{-1}}{(60 - 30)\text{ s}}$$

$$= \frac{0.14}{30}\text{ mol L}^{-1}\text{s}^{-1}$$

$$\text{Average rate} = 4.67 \times 10^{-3}\text{ mol L}^{-1}\text{s}^{-1}$$

Question 9 A reaction is first order in A and second order in B.

(i) Write the differential rate equation.

(ii) How is the rate affected on increasing the concentration of B three times?

(iii) How is the rate affected when the concentrations of both A and B are doubled?

◎ *Thinking Process*

(i) Order is written as a superscript of the concentration terms. So, rate $= k[A][B]^2$

(ii) Find rate when concentration of only B is tripled and compare it with the rate equation, to find the effect on rate.

(iii) Find rate when concentration of A and B both are doubled and compare.

Question 12 The reaction between A and B is first order with respect to A and zero order with respect to B. Fill in the blanks in the following table :

Experiment	$[A]$ mol L^{-1}	$[B]$ mol L^{-1}	Initial rate mol L^{-1} min^{-1}
I	0.1	0.1	2.0×10^{-2}
II	—	0.2	4.0×10^{-2}
III	0.4	0.4	—
IV	—	0.2	2.0×10^{-2}

Thinking Process

(i) Write the rate law, when order w.r.t. A is 1 and w.r.t. B is 0.

(ii) By the reading of Ist experiment, determine the value of k and use this value for other experiments.

Sol. The rate expression

$$\text{Rate} = k[A]^1[B]^0 = k[A]$$

For Ist experiment, $[A] = 0.1 \text{ mol L}^{-1}$

So, $$\text{Rate} = 2.0\times 10^{-2} = k[0.1 \text{mol L}^{-1}]$$

$$k = \frac{2.0\times 10^{-2} \text{ mol L}^{-1}\text{min}^{-1}}{0.1 \text{ mol L}^{-1}} = 0.2 \text{ min}^{-1}$$

For IInd experiment, $4.0\times 10^{-2} \text{ mol L}^{-1} \text{ min}^{-1} = 0.2 \text{ min}^{-1}[A]$

$$[A] = \frac{4.0\times 10^{-2} \text{ mol L}^{-1}\text{min}^{-1}}{0.2 \text{ min}^{-1}} = 0.2 \text{ mol L}^{-1}$$

$$[A] = 0.2 \text{ mol L}^{-1}$$

For IIIrd experiment, $\text{Rate} = k[A]$

$$\text{Rate} = 0.2 \text{ min}^{-1} \times 0.4 \text{ mol L}^{-1}$$

$$\text{Rate} = 8\times 10^{-2} \text{ mol L}^{-1}\text{min}^{-1}$$

For IVth experiment, $\text{Rate} = k[A]; [A] = \frac{\text{Rate}}{k}$

$$[A] = \frac{2.0\times 10^{-2} \text{mol L}^{-1}\text{min}^{-1}}{0.2 \text{ min}^{-1}}$$

$$= 0.1 \text{mol L}^{-1}$$

$$[A] = 0.1 \text{ mol L}^{-1}$$

Question 13 Calculate the half-life of a first order reaction from their rate constants given below :

(i) 200 s^{-1} (ii) 2 min^{-1} (iii) 4 $years^{-1}$

◎ ***Thinking Process*** We know that half-life, $t_{1/2} = 0.693 / k$ (where, k = rate constant)

Sol. Half-life period for first order reaction

$$t_{1/2} = \frac{0.693}{k}$$

(i) $t_{1/2} = \frac{0.693}{200\ s^{-1}} = 0.346 \times 10^{-2}\ s = 3.46 \times 10^{-3}\ s$

(ii) $t_{1/2} = \frac{0.693}{2\ min^{-1}} = 0.346\ min = 3.46 \times 10^{-1}\ min$

(iii) $t_{1/2} = \frac{0.693}{4\ yr^{-1}} = 0.173\ year = 1.73 \times 10^{-1}\ year$

Question 14 The half-life for radioactive decay of ^{14}C is 5730 yr. An archaeological artifact containing wood had only 80% of the ^{14}C found in a living tree. Estimate the age of the sample.

◎ ***Thinking Process***

(i) Since, all the radioactive processes follow first order kinetics, calculate rate constant from $t_{1/2}$ as $k = 0.693 / t_{1/2}$.

(ii) Then, put the value of k in the expression of first order rate constant to find t.

Sol. Decay constant $(k) = \frac{0.693}{t_{1/2}} = \frac{0.693}{5730}\ yr^{-1}$

Radioactive decays follow first order kinetics

$$t = \frac{2.303}{k} \log \frac{[A]_0}{[A]}$$

Given, $[A] = 80\%$

It means that $[A]_0 = 100\%$

$$t = \frac{2.303 \times 5730}{0.693} \times \log \frac{100}{80}$$

$$= \frac{2.303 \times 5730 \times 0.0969}{0.693}$$

$$= 1845 \text{ years}$$

Estimated age = 1845 years

Note All radioactive processes follow first order kinetics.

Question 15 The experimental data for decomposition of N_2O_5 $[2N_2O_5 \longrightarrow 4NO_2 + O_2]$ in gas phase at 318 K are given below :

t / s	0	400	800	1200	1600	2000	2400	2800	3200
$10^{+2} \times [N_2O_5]$ / mol L^{-1}	1.63	1.36	1.14	0.93	0.78	0.64	0.53	0.43	0.35

(i) Plot $[N_2O_5]$ against t.
(ii) Find the half-life period for the reaction.
(iii) Draw a graph between $\log[N_2O_5]$ and t.
(iv) What is the rate law?
(v) Calculate the rate constant.
(vi) Calculate the half-life period from k and compare it with (ii).

Sol. (i) The plot of $[N_2O_5]$ against time is given below.

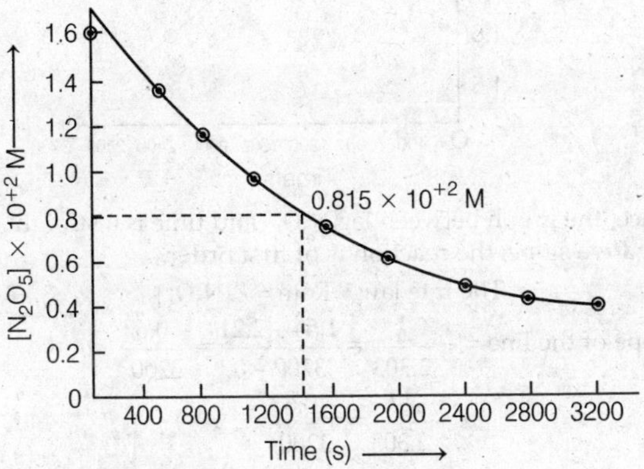

(ii) Initial concentration of $N_2O_5 = 1.63 \times 10^2$ M

Half of initial concentration $= \dfrac{1.63 \times 10^2}{2} = 0.815 \times 10^2$ M

Half-life period = Time corresponding to the above amount in the graph

= 1440 s (approximately)

(iii) For graph between log $[N_2O_5]$ and time, we first find the values of $\log[N_2O_5]$.

Time (s)	0	400	800	1200	1600	2000	2400	2800	3200
$[N_2O_5] \times 10^{+2}$ mol L^{-1}	1.63	1.36	1.14	0.93	0.78	0.64	0.53	0.43	0.35
$\log [N_2O_5]$	2.21	2.13	2.06	1.97	1.89	1.81	1.72	1.63	1.54

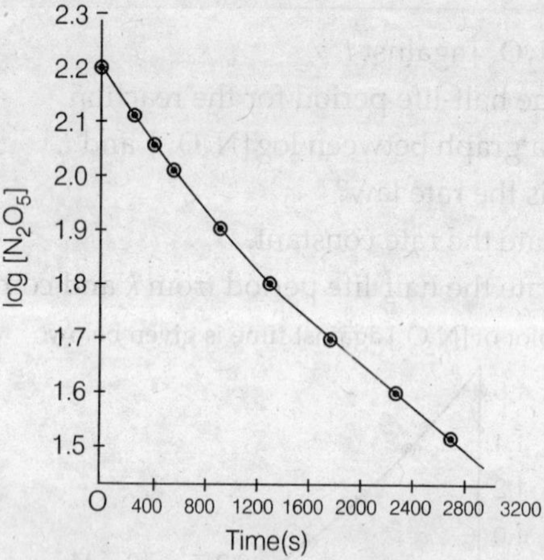

(iv) Since, the graph between $\log[N_2O_5]$ and time is a straight line with negative slope, the reaction is of first order.

The rate law : Rate $= k[N_2O_5]$

(v) Slope of the line $= -\dfrac{k}{2.303} = \dfrac{1.54 - 2.21}{3200 - 0} = \dfrac{-0.67}{3200}$

$$\frac{-k}{2.303} = \frac{-0.67}{3200}$$

$$k = \frac{0.67 \times 2.303}{3200}$$

or $$k = 4.82 \times 10^{-4}\ s^{-1}$$

(vi) Half-life period $(t_{1/2}) = \dfrac{0.693}{k} = \dfrac{0.693}{4.82 \times 10^{-4}\ s^{-1}} = 1438$ s

Half-life period $(t_{1/2})$ as calculated from the formula and slope are approximately the same.

Note For a first order reaction, $\log[A] = -\dfrac{kt}{2.303} + \log[A]_0$

So, the slope of graph between $\log[A]$ and time will be $\dfrac{-k}{2.303}$

Question 16 The rate constant for a first order reaction is 60 s^{-1}. How much time will it take to reduce the initial concentration of the reactant to its $1/16^{th}$ value?

◎ *Thinking Process* For Ist order reaction, time, $t = \frac{2.303}{k} \log \frac{a}{(a-x)}$

Sol. For Ist order reaction

$$t = \frac{2.303}{k} \log \frac{a}{(a-x)} \quad \ldots(i)$$

Given, $(a - x) = \frac{a}{16}$; $k = 60\ s^{-1}$

Put the values in equation (i)

$$t = \frac{2.303}{60\ s^{-1}} \log \frac{a \times 16}{a} = \frac{2.303}{60\ s^{-1}} \log 16 = \frac{2.303}{60\ s^{-1}} \log 2^4$$

$$= \frac{2.303}{60\ s^{-1}} \times 4 \log 2 = \frac{2.303}{60\ s^{-1}} \times 4 \times 0.3010 = 4.62 \times 10^{-2}\ s$$

Time $= 4.62 \times 10^{-2}$ s

Question 17 During nuclear explosion one of the products is ^{90}Sr with half-life of 28.1 years. If 1 μg of ^{90}Sr was absorbed in the bones of a newly born baby instead of calcium, how much of it will remain after 10 years and 60 years if it is not lost metabolically?

◎ *Thinking Process* Radioactive phenomenon follows first order kinetics, so use the integrated rate equation for the first order reaction, *i.e.*, $t = \frac{2.303}{k} \log \frac{a}{(a-x)}$ to find $(a-x)$ after 10 years and 60 years respectively.

Sol. $t_{1/2} = 28.1$ years ; $k = \frac{0.693}{t_{1/2}} = \frac{0.693}{28.1}\ yr^{-1}$

For Ist order reactions, $t = \frac{2.303}{k} \log \frac{a}{(a-x)}$

Case I $a = 1\mu g$; $t = 10$ years; $k = \frac{0.693}{28.1}\ yr^{-1}$

$$10 = \frac{2.303}{0.693} \times 28.1 \log \frac{a}{(a-x)}$$

$$\log \frac{a}{(a-x)} = \frac{10 \times 0.693}{2.303 \times 28.1} = 0.107$$

$$\frac{a}{(a-x)} = \text{Antilog}(0.107) = 1.279$$

$$(a-x) = \frac{a}{1.279} = \frac{(1\ \mu g)}{1.279} = 0.7819\mu g$$

Amount left after 10 years = 0.7819 μg

Case II $a = 1\mu g$, $t = 60$ yr ; $k = \frac{0.693}{28.1}$ yr^{-1}

$$60 = \frac{2.303}{0.693/28.1} \times \log \frac{a}{(a-x)}$$

$$\log \frac{a}{(a-x)} = \frac{(60) \times 0.693/28.1)}{2.303} = 0.642$$

$$\frac{a}{(a-x)} = \text{Antilog } 0.642 = 4.385$$

$$(a-x) = \frac{a}{4.385} = \frac{(1\,\mu g)}{4.385} = 0.2280\,\mu g$$

Amount left after 60 years = 0.2280 μg

Question 18 For a first order reaction, show that time required for 99% completion is twice the time required for the completion of 90% of reaction.

◎ *Thinking Process*

(i) Find t for the 99% completion of reaction by using, $t = \frac{2.303}{k} \log \frac{a}{a-x}$.

(ii) Similarly find t for 90% completion.

(iii) Compare the above two values to find a relation between $t_{99\%}$ and $t_{90\%}$.

Sol. **Case I** If $a = 100$; $(a-x) = (100-99) = 1$

For 99% completion of the reaction

$$t_{99\%} = \frac{2.303}{k} \log \frac{100}{1} = \frac{2.303}{k} \log 10^2$$

$$= \frac{2.303 \times 2}{k}$$

$$t_{99\%} = \frac{4.606}{k} \quad \text{...(i)}$$

Case II If $a = 100$; $(a-x) = (100-90) = 10$

For 90% completion of the reaction

$$t_{90\%} = \frac{2.303}{k} \log \frac{100}{10} = \frac{2.303}{k} \log 10 = \frac{2.303}{k} \quad \text{...(ii)}$$

On dividing Eq. (i) by Eq. (ii), we get

$$\frac{t_{99\%}}{t_{90\%}} = \frac{4.606}{k} \times \frac{k}{2.303} = 2$$

It means that time required for 99% completion of the reaction is twice the time required to complete 90% of the reaction.

Question 19 A first order reaction takes 40 min for 30% decomposition. Calculate $t_{1/2}$.

Thinking Process To calculate $t_{1/2}$ for a first order reaction, k is required, so first calculate, k by using $t = \frac{2.303}{k} \log \frac{a}{a-x}$ and calculate $t_{1/2}$ as $t_{1/2} = \frac{0.693}{k}$.

Sol. $a = 100$; $a - x = 100 - 30 = 70$; $t = 40$ min

$$k = \frac{2.303}{t} \log \frac{a}{(a-x)} = \frac{2.303}{40} \log \frac{100}{70}$$

$$= \frac{2.303}{40} \log \frac{10}{7}$$

$$= \frac{2.303}{40} \log 1.4286 = \frac{2.303}{40} \times 0.1549$$

$$k = 8.918 \times 10^{-3} \text{ min}^{-1}$$

$$t_{1/2} = \frac{0.693}{k} = \frac{0.693}{8.918 \times 10^{-3} \text{ min}^{-1}} = 77.708 \text{ min} \approx 77.7 \text{ min}$$

$$t_{1/2} = 77.7 \text{ minutes}$$

Question 20 For the decomposition of azoisopropane to hexane and nitrogen at 543 K, the following data are obtained. Calculate the rate constant.

t (s)	p (mm of Hg)
0	35.0
360	54.0
720	63.0

Thinking Process Use the relation $k = \frac{2.303}{t} \log \left(\frac{p_i}{2p_i - p_t} \right)$ to calculate rate constants and then find average rate constant.

Sol. $(CH_3)_2CHN{=}NCH(CH_3)_2\,(g) \longrightarrow N_2(g) + C_6H_{14}\,(g)$

Initial pressure	p_i	0	0
After time t	$p_i - p$	p	p

Total pressure after time t, *i.e.*, $(p_t) = (p_i - p) + p + p = p_i + p$

or $$p = p_t - p_i$$

$a = p_i$; $(a - x) = p_i - p$, on substituting the values of p;

$$(a - x) = p_i - (p_t - p_i), \text{ i.e., } (a - x) = 2p_i - p_t$$

The decomposition reaction is a first order reaction and the rate constant k can be calculated as :

$$k = \frac{2.303}{t} \log \frac{a}{a - x}$$

substitution of value of a and $(a - x)$ gives $k = \frac{2.303}{t} \log \left(\frac{p_i}{2p_i - p_t} \right)$

(i) Rate constant after 360 s = k_1

$$k_1 = \frac{2.303}{(360 \text{ s})} \log \frac{(35 \text{ atm})}{(70 - 54) \text{ atm}}$$

$$= \frac{2.303}{(360 \text{ s})} \log \frac{35}{16} = \frac{2.303}{(360 \text{ s})} \log 2.1875$$

$$= \frac{2.303 \times 0.33995}{(360 \text{ s})} = 2.175 \times 10^{-3} \text{ s}^{-1}$$

(ii) Rate constant after 720 s = k_2

$$k_2 = \frac{2.303}{(720 \text{ s})} \log \frac{(35 \text{ atm})}{(70 - 63) \text{ atm}}$$

$$= \frac{2.303}{(720 \text{ s})} \log 5 = \frac{2.303 \times 0.6990}{(720 \text{ s})} = 2.236 \times 10^{-3} \text{ s}^{-1}$$

Average rate constant $k = \frac{(2.175 + 2.236) \times 10^{-3} \text{ s}^{-1}}{2}$

$$k = 2.2055 \times 10^{-3} \text{ s}^{-1} \approx 2.21 \times 10^{-3} \text{ s}^{-1}$$

Question 21 The following data were obtained during the first order thermal decomposition of SO_2Cl_2 at a constant volume.

$$SO_2Cl_2(g) \longrightarrow SO_2(g) + Cl_2(g)$$

Experiment	Time/s^{-1}	Total pressure/atm
1	0	0.5
2	100	0.6

Calculate the rate of the reaction when total pressure is 0.65 atm.

Sol. $SO_2Cl_2(g) \longrightarrow SO_2(g) + Cl_2(g)$

	$SO_2Cl_2(g)$	$SO_2(g)$	$Cl_2(g)$
Initially	p_i	0	0
After time t	$p_i - p$	p	p

Total pressure after time t, *i.e.*,

$$p_t = p_i - p + p + p = p_i + p$$

$$p = p_t - p_i$$

So, $a = p_i$

$$a - x = p_i - (p_t - p_i) \qquad [\text{as } (a - x) = p_i - p]$$

$$= p_i - p_t + p_i$$

$$= 2p_i - p_t$$

Substitutions of the value of a and $(a - x)$ gives $k = \frac{2.303}{t} \log \frac{p_i}{(2p_i - p_t)}$

(a) Calculation of rate constant k

Given, $p_i = 0.5$ atm ; $p_t = 0.6$ atm,

$$k = \frac{2.303}{t} \log \frac{p_i}{(2p_i - p_t)} = \frac{2.303}{(100\text{ s})} \log \frac{0.5\text{ atm}}{0.4\text{ atm}}$$

$$= \frac{2.303}{(100\text{ s})} \log 1.25 = \frac{2.303}{(100\text{ s})} \times 0.0969 = 2.23 \times 10^{-3}\text{ s}^{-1}$$

(b) Calculation of reaction rate when total pressure is 0.65 atm ($p_t = 0.65$ atm) $p_{SO_2Cl_2}$ at time is :

$$p_{SO_2Cl_2} = p_i - p - [p = p_t - p_i] \Rightarrow p_{SO_2Cl_2} = p_i - (p_t - p_i) = 2p_i - p_t$$

$$\Rightarrow \quad p_{SO_2Cl_2} = 2 \times 0.50 - 0.65$$

$$\Rightarrow \quad p_{SO_2Cl_2} = 0.35\text{ atm} \Rightarrow k = 2.23 \times 10^{-3}\text{ s}^{-1}$$

$$\text{Rate} = k \times p_{SO_2Cl_2} = (2.23 \times 10^{-3}\text{ s}^{-1}) \times (0.35\text{ atm})$$

$$\text{Rate} = 7.8 \times 10^{-4}\text{ atm s}^{-1}$$

Question 22 The rate constant for the decomposition of N_2O_5 at various temperatures is given below :

$T/°C$	0	20	40	60	80
$10^5 \times k/s^{-1}$	0.0787	1.70	25.7	178	2140

Draw a graph between ln k and $1/T$ and calculate the values of A and E_a. Predict the rate constant at 50° and 30°C.

Thinking Process To draw a graph between k and $1/T$, find the values of $1/T$ and log$k$ and proceed.

Sol. (a) To draw the graph between log k *versus* $1/T$ we rewrite the data as follows.

T (K)	273	293	313	333	353
$1/T$	0.003663	0.003413	0.003213	0.003003	0.002833
log$k$	3.896	5.230	6.410	7.250	8.330

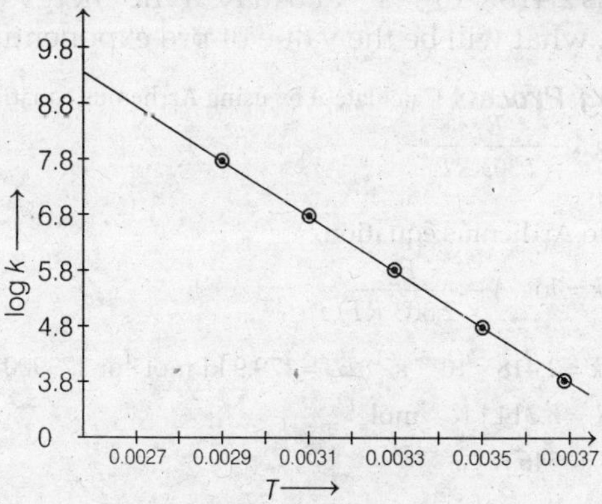

(b) As we know that according to arrhenius equation,

$$k = Ae^{\frac{-E_a}{RT}} \Rightarrow \log k = \log A - \frac{E_a}{2.303\,RT}$$

From the graph, b/w log k and $1/T$ we find the slope.

$$\text{Slope} = \frac{-E_a}{2.303R} = \frac{8.330 - 3.896}{0.002833 - 0.003663} = -\frac{4.434}{0.00083}$$

$$\therefore \text{ Activation energy } (E_a) = \frac{4.434 \times 2.303 \times 8.314 \text{ J mol}^{-1}}{0.00083}$$

$$= 102287.262 \text{ J mol}^{-1} = 102.287 \text{ kJ mol}^{-1}$$

$$E_a = 102.287 \text{ kJ mol}^{-1}$$

(c) We know that

$$\log k = \log A - \frac{E_a}{2.303\,RT}$$

On comparing it with $y = mx + c$, the equation of line in intercept form;

$$\log k = \left(-\frac{E_a}{2.303R}\right)\frac{1}{T} + \log A$$

$\log A$ = Value of intercept on y-axis, *i.e*, on the log k-axis

$$\text{Frequency factor } A = \text{Antilog } 9.3 = 1.9953 \times 10^9$$

$$= 1.995 \times 10^9 \text{ collisions s}^{-1}$$

$$A = 1.995 \times 10^9 \text{ collisions s}^{-1}$$

(d) Value of rate constant k can be find by the study of graph.

T (K)	$1/T$	Values of log$k$ from graph	Values of k
303	0.003300	5.8	6.31×10^5 s^{-1}
323	0.003096	6.6	3.98×10^6 s^{-1}

Question 23 The rate constant for the decomposition of hydrocarbons is 2.418×10^{-5} s^{-1} at 546 K. If the energy of activation is 179.9 kJ/mol, what will be the value of pre-exponential factor?

◎ *Thinking Process* Calculate A by using Arrhenius equation, $\log k = \log A - \frac{E_a}{2.303\,RT}$.

Sol. According to Arrhenius equation,

$$\log k = \log A - \frac{E_a}{2.303\,RT}$$

$$k = 2.418 \times 10^{-5} \text{ s}^{-1};\ E_a = 179.9 \text{ kJ mol}^{-1} \text{or } 179900 \text{ J mol}^{-1}$$

$$R = 8.314 \text{ J K}^{-1} \text{ mol}^{-1}$$

$$T = 546 \text{ K}$$

$$\log A = \log k + \frac{E_a}{2.303\,RT}$$

$$= \log(2.418 \times 10^{-5}\ \text{s}^{-1}) + \frac{179900\ \text{J mol}^{-1}}{2.303 \times (8.314\ \text{JK}^{-1}\text{mol}^{-1}) \times 546\ \text{K}}$$

$$= -4.6184 + 17.21 = 12.5916$$

$$A = \text{Antilog } 12.5916 = 3.9 \times 10^{12}\ \text{s}^{-1}$$

$$A = 3.9 \times 10^{12}\ \text{s}^{-1}$$

Question 24 Consider a certain reaction; $A \longrightarrow$ products with $k = 2.0 \times 10^{-2}\ \text{s}^{-1}$. Calculate the concentration of A remaining after 100 s, if the initial concentration of A is $1.0\ \text{mol L}^{-1}$.

◎ ***Thinking Process*** It is a first order reaction so, calculate $[A]$ or $(a - x)$ by using first order integrated equation $t = \frac{2.303}{k} \log \frac{[A]_0}{[A]}$.

Sol. For the first order reaction

$$t = \frac{2.303}{k} \log \frac{[A]_0}{[A]} \text{ or } \log \frac{[A]_0}{[A]} = \frac{k \times t}{2.303}$$

$$k = 2.0 \times 10^{-2}\ \text{s}^{-1};\ t = 100\ \text{s};\ [A]_0 = 1.0\ \text{mol L}^{-1} = 1.0\ \text{M}$$

$$\log \frac{[A]_0}{[A]} = \frac{(2.0 \times 10^{-2}\ \text{s}^{-1}) \times (100\ \text{s})}{2.303} = 0.8684$$

$$\frac{[A]_0}{[A]} = \text{Antilog } 0.8684 = 7.3858$$

$$[A] = \frac{[A]_0}{7.3858} = \frac{[1\text{M}]}{7.3858} = 0.135\ \text{M}$$

$$[A] = 0.135\text{M}$$

Question 25 Sucrose decomposes in acid solution into glucose and fructose according to the first order rate law, with $t_{1/2} = 3.00$ hours. What fraction of sample of sucrose remains after 8 hours?

◎ ***Thinking Process*** $t_{1/2} = \frac{0.693}{k}$; $t = \frac{2.303}{k} \log \frac{[A]_0}{[A]}$ (for Ist order reactions) So, calculate $[A]$ from the above relations.

Sol. For Ist order reactions

$$k = \frac{0.693}{t_{1/2}} = \frac{0.693}{(3.0)}$$

$$t = \frac{2.303}{k} \log \frac{[A]_0}{[A]}$$

or $$\log \frac{[A]_0}{[A]} = \frac{k \times t}{2.303}$$

$$\log \frac{[A]_0}{[A]} = \frac{0.693}{3} \times \frac{(8)}{2.303} = 0.8024$$

$$\frac{[A]_0}{[A]} = \text{Antilog } 0.8024 = 6.345$$

$$[A]_0 = 1\text{M}; [A] = \frac{[A]_0}{6.345} = \frac{1\text{M}}{6.345} = 0.1576 \text{ M}$$

After 8 hours, sucrose left = 0.1576 M

Question 26 The decomposition of hydrocarbon follows the equation $k = (4.5 \times 10^{11} \text{ s}^{-1}) e^{-28000} K/T$. Calculate the activation energy E_a.

◎ ***Thinking Process*** Compare the given equation with the Arrhenius equation, $k = Ae^{-Ea/RT}$ to find the value of E_a.

Sol. According to Arrhenius equation

$$k = Ae^{-E_a/RT} \quad \text{...(i)}$$

According to the available data

$$k = (4.5 \times 10^{11} \text{s}^{-1}) e^{-28000 K/T} \quad \text{...(ii)}$$

On comparing both equations;

$$-\frac{E_a}{RT} = \frac{-28000 \text{ K}}{T}$$

$$E_a = (28000 \text{ K}) \times R = (28000 \text{ K}) \times (8.314 \text{ K}^{-1}\text{J mol}^{-1})$$

$$= 232792 \text{ J mol}^{-1}$$

$$E_a = 232.792 \text{ kJ mol}^{-1}$$

Question 27 The rate constant for the first order decomposition of H_2O_2 is given by the following equation, $\log k = 14.34 - 1.25 \times 10^4$ K/T. Calculate E_a for this reaction and at what temperature will its half-life period be 256 minutes?

◎ ***Thinking Process***

(i) Compare the given equation with the Arrhenius equation $\log k = \log A - \frac{E_a}{2.303 RT}$ to find the value of E_a.

(ii) Find k from $t_{1/2}$ as $k = \frac{0.693}{t_{1/2}}$ and use Arrhenius equation $k = Ae^{-E_a/RT}$ to find the value of T.

Sol. (a) **Calcuation of activation energy E_a**

According to Arrhenius equation; $k = Ae^{-E_a/RT}$

$$\log k = \log A - \frac{E_a}{2.303\ RT} \quad \ldots(i)$$

$$\log k = 14.34 - \frac{1.25 \times 10^4 \text{ K}}{T} \quad \text{[Given]} \quad \ldots(ii)$$

On comparing both equations.

$$\frac{E_a}{2.303RT} = \frac{1.25 \times 10^4 \text{ K}}{T}$$

$$E_a = 1.25 \times 10^4 \text{ K} \times 2.303 \times 8.314 \text{ (J K}^{-1} \text{ mol}^{-1})$$

$$= 23.93 \times 10^4 \text{ J mol}^{-1} = 239.3 \text{ kJ mol}^{-1}$$

(b) **Calculation of required temperature** If $t_{1/2} = 256$ min.

For Ist order reaction ;

$$k = \frac{0.693}{t_{1/2}} = \frac{0.693}{(256 \text{ min})} = \frac{0.693}{256 \times 60 \text{ s}} = 4.51 \times 10^{-5} \text{ s}^{-1}$$

According to Arrhenius theory,

$$\log k = 14.34 - \frac{1.25 \times 10^4 \text{ K}}{T}$$

$$\log (4.51 \times 10^{-5}) = 14.34 - \frac{1.25 \times 10^4 \text{ K}}{T}$$

$$-4.35 = 14.34 - \frac{1.25 \times 10^4 \text{ K}}{T}$$

$$\frac{1.25 \times 10^4}{T} = 14.34 + 4.35 = 18.69$$

$$T = \frac{1.25 \times 10^4}{18.69} = 669 \text{ K}$$

$$E_a = 239.3 \text{ kJ mol}^{-1}$$

$$T = 669 \text{ K}$$

Question 28 The decomposition of A into product has values of k as $4.5 \times 10^3 \text{ s}^{-1}$ at 10°C and energy of activation 60 kJ mol^{-1}. At what temperature would k bc $1.5 \times 10^4 \text{ s}^{-1}$.

◎ ***Thinking Process*** Find T_2 by putting values of other quantities in the Arrhenius equation $\log \frac{k_2}{k_1} = \frac{E_a}{2.303\ R} \times \frac{T_2 - T_1}{T_1\ T_2}$.

Sol. According to Arrhenius equation

$$\log \frac{k_2}{k_1} = \frac{E_a}{2.303\ R} \times \frac{T_2 - T_1}{T_1\ T_2}$$

$k_1 = 4.5 \times 10^3 \text{s}^{-1}$; $k_2 = 1.5 \times 10^4 \text{s}^{-1}$; $T_1 = 10°\text{C} = 283 \text{K}$,

$E_a = 60 \text{ kJ mol}^{-1} = 60.000 \text{ J mol}^{-1}$

$$\log \frac{1.5\times 10^4}{4.5\times 10^3} = \frac{(60{,}000\ \text{J mol}^{-1})}{2.303\times(8.314\ \text{J mol}^{-1})}\left(\frac{T_2-283}{283\ T_2}\right)$$

$$\log 3.333 = 3133.62\left(\frac{T_2-283}{283\ T_2}\right)$$

$$\frac{0.5288}{3133.62} = \frac{T_2-283}{283\,T_2}$$

$$\frac{0.5288\times 283}{3133.62} = \frac{T_2-283}{T_2}$$

$$1-\frac{283}{T_2} = 0.04776$$

or $$T_2 = \frac{283}{1-0.04776} = \frac{283}{0.95224}$$

$$T_2 = 297.19\ \text{K} = (297.19-273.0) = 24.19°\text{C}$$

Temperature = 24.19°C

Question 29 The time required for 10% completion of a first order reaction at 298 K is equal to that required for its 25% completion at 308 K. If the value of A is $4\times 10^{10}\ \text{s}^{-1}$. Calculate k at 318 K and E_a.

◎ *Thinking Process*

(i) First find the relation between k_1 (for 90% completion) and k_2 (for 25% completion) by using the integrated rate equation $k = \frac{2.303}{t}\log\frac{[A]_0}{[A]}$.

(ii) Use the ratio of $\frac{k_2}{k_1}$ in the Arrhenius equation to find E_a.

(iii) Calculate k by using Arrhenius equation (taking temperature 318 K).

Sol. (a) **Calculation of activation energy (E_a)**

For Ist order reaction : $k = \frac{2.303}{t}\log\frac{[A]_0}{[A]}$

At 298 K; $k_1 = \frac{2.303}{t}\log\frac{100}{90} \Rightarrow t = \frac{2.303}{k_1}\log\frac{100}{90}$ ...(i)

At 308 K; $k_2 = \frac{2.303}{t^1}\log\frac{100}{75} \Rightarrow t' = \frac{2.303}{k_2}\log\frac{100}{75}$ ...(ii)

As per question $t = t'$

$$\Rightarrow \frac{2.303}{k_1}\log\frac{100}{90} = \frac{2.303}{k_2}\log\frac{100}{75}$$

$$\Rightarrow \frac{k_2}{k_1} = \frac{\log\frac{100}{75}}{\log\frac{100}{90}} = \frac{0.1249}{0.0458} = 2.727 \approx 2.73$$

According to Arrhenius theory;

$$\log \frac{k_2}{k_1} = \frac{E_a}{2.303\,R} \times \frac{T_2 - T_1}{T_1\,T_2}$$

$$\log 2.73 = \frac{E_a}{2.303\,R}\left[\frac{308 - 298}{298 \times 308}\right]$$

$$E_a = \frac{0.4361 \times 2.303 \times (8.314\ \text{J mol}^{-1}) \times 298 \times 308}{10}$$

$$E_a = 76651.28\ \text{Jmol}^{-1} = 76.651\ \text{kJ mol}^{-1}$$

(b) **Calculation of rate constant (k)**

According to Arrhenius equation

$$\log k = \log A - \frac{E_a}{2.303\,RT}$$

$$\log k = \log(4 \times 10^{10}) - \frac{76651.28\ \text{J mol}^{-1}}{2.303 \times (8.314\ \text{J mol}^{-1}\text{K}^{-1}) \times (318\ \text{K})}$$

$$\log k = 10.6021 - 12.5890 = -1.9869$$

$$k = \text{Antilog}\,(-1.9849) = \text{Antilog}\,(\bar{2}.0151) = 0.010306\ \text{s}^{-1} \approx 1.031 \times 10^{-2}\ \text{s}^{-1}$$

$$E_a = 76.651\ \text{kJ mol}^{-1},\ k = 1.03 \times 10^{-2}\ \text{s}^{-1}$$

Question 30 The rate of a reaction quadruples when the temperature changes from 293 K to 313 K. Calculate the energy of activation of the reaction assuming that it does not change with temperature.

Sol. According to Arrhenius equation,

$$\log \frac{k_2}{k_1} = \frac{E_a}{2.303\,R}\left[\frac{1}{T_1} - \frac{1}{T_2}\right]$$

[Given $T_1 = 293\text{K}$; $T_2 = 313\text{K}$; $T_2 - T_1 = 20\text{K}$] [$k_2 = 4k_1$]

$$\log \frac{4}{1} = \frac{\text{E}_\text{a}}{2.303 \times (8.314\ \text{J mol}^{-1}\ \text{K}^{-1})} \times \frac{20}{293 \times 313}$$

$$0.6021 = \frac{\text{E}_\text{a}}{2.303 \times (8.314\ \text{J mol}^{-1})} \times \frac{20}{293 \times 313}$$

$$E_a = \frac{0.6021 \times 2.303 \times 8.314 \times 293 \times 313}{20}\ \text{J mol}^{-1} = 52863.33\ \text{J mol}^{-1}$$

$$E_a = 52.863\ \text{kJ mol}^{-1}$$

DIKSHA APP Questions

□ Multiple Choice Questions

Q.1 Which of the following is not the characteristic of a catalyst?

(a) It changes the equilibrium constant.
(b) It alters the reaction path.
(c) It increases the rate of reaction.
(d) It does not effect the Gibbs energy.

Sol. (a) A catalyst is a substance which increases the rate of a reaction without itself undergoing any permanent chemical change. It is believed that the catalyst provides an alternate pathway or reaction mechanism by reducing the activation energy between reactants and products and hence lowering the potential energy barrier.

A catalyst does not alter Gibbs energy, ΔG of a reaction. It catalyses the spontaneous reactions but does not catalyse non-spontaneous reactions. It is also found that a catalyst does not change the equilibrium constant of a reaction rather, it helps in attaining the equilibrium faster, that is, it catalyses the forward as well as the backward reactions to the same extent so that the equilibrium state remains same but is reached earlier.

Q.2 Which of the following influences the rate of a chemical reaction performed in solution?

(a) Temperature
(b) Activation energy
(c) Presence of a catalyst
(d) All of the above

Sol. (d) The rate of a chemical reaction depends on temperature, activation energy and presence of a catalyst.

(a) As temperature increases, the rate of reaction generally increases. This is because higher temperatures provide more energy to the molecules, causing them to collide more frequently and with greater energy, increasing the chances of overcoming the activation energy barrier.

(b) A lower activation energy leads to a faster reaction rate, as it's easier for molecules to reach the energy needed to react.

(c) A catalyst speeds up the reaction by lowering the activation energy without being consumed in the process. It provides an alternative reaction pathway with a lower energy barrier, increasing the reaction rate.

Q.3 On increasing the temperature, the rate of the reaction increases because of

(a) decrease in the number of collisions.
(b) decrease in the energy of activation.
(c) decrease in the number of activated molecules.
(d) increase in the number of effective collision.

Sol. (d) On increasing the temperature, the rate of reaction generally increases. This is because higher temperatures provide more energy to the molecules, causing them to collide more frequently and with greater energy, increasing the chances of overcoming the activation energy barrier. Thus, this leads to increase in number of effective collisions.

Q.4 For a chemical reaction the rate constant at 25°C is represented as K, than what will be the rate constant of the reaction at 35°C.

(a) Remain same (b) Become double

(c) Become half (d) None of these

Sol. (b) For a chemical reaction, the rate constant is nearly doubled with rise in temperature by 10° (25°C to 35°C).

Q.5 The time required for 100% competion of a zero order reaction is

(a) $[R_0]/2k$ (b) $R_0 k$ (c) $2k/[R_0]$ (d) $[R_0]/k$

Sol. (d) For a zero-order reaction, the time required for 100% completion can be calculated using the integrated rate law for zero-order reactions.

$[R] = [R_0] - kt$

Where

- $[R]$ is the concentration of the reactant at time t,
- $[R_0]$ is the initial concentration of the reactant,
- k is the rate constant,
- t is the time

For 100% completion, the concentration of the reactant $[R]$ will become zero, so the equation becomes :

$$0 = [R_0] - kt$$

Solving for time t.

$$t = \frac{[R_0]}{k}$$

Q.6 The rate constant for first order reaction whose half-life is 480 sec is

(a) $2.88 \times 10^{-3} s^{-1}$ (b) $2.72 \times 10^{-2} s^{-1}$ (c) $1.44 \times 10^{-3} s^{-1}$ (d) $1.44 s^{-1}$

Sol. (c) For a **first-order reaction,** the relationship between the half-life ($t_{1/2}$) and the rate constant (k) is given by the formula.

$$t_{1/2} \frac{0.693}{k}$$

Where, $t_{1/2}$ is the half-life of the reaction and k is the rate constant

Given, $t_{1/2} = 480\ s$

Solving for k:

$$k = \frac{0.693}{t_{1/2}} = \frac{0.693}{480s} = 0.00144 s^{-1} = 144 \times 10^{-3} s^{-1}$$

Q.7 If the rate of a gaseous reaction is independent of pressure, the order to the reaction is

(a) zero (b) one (c) two (d) 1/2

Sol. (a) If the rate of a gaseous reaction is independent of pressure, the order of the reaction is zero. For a zero-order reaction, the rate law is of the form:
Rate= k

where k is the rate constant. So, the rate does not depend on the concentration or pressure of the reactants.

☐ Short Answer Type

Q.1 Define the following

(a) Elementary step in a reaction
(b) Rate of a reaction

Sol. (a) Elementary step in a reaction : Those reactions that take place in one step are called elementary reactions.
(b) Rate of a reaction : The change in the concentration of any one of the reactants or products per unit time is called rate of reaction.

☐ Long Answer Type

Q.1 A first order reaction takes 10 minutes for 25% decomposition. Calculate $t_{1/2}$ for reaction.

Sol. Given : Time for 25% decomposition = 10 minutes

The reaction is first-order, so the integrated rate law is.

$$\log\left(\frac{[A_0]}{[A]}\right) = \frac{k}{2.303}\cdot t$$

Where, $[A_0]$ is the initial concentration, $[A]$ is the concentration after time, k is the rate constant and t is the time.

For 25% decomposition, 75% of the original concentration remains, so,

$$[A_0] = 100 \text{ and } [A] = 75$$

$$[A]/[A_0] = 0.75$$

Therefore, the rate law becomes :

$$\log\left(\frac{1}{0.75}\right) = \frac{k}{2.303}\cdot 10$$

$$\log(1.3333) = \frac{k}{2.303}\cdot 10$$

Using the logarithmic value

$$\log(1.3333) \approx 0.1249$$

$$0.1249 = \frac{k}{2.303}\cdot 10$$

Solving for k

$$k = \frac{0.1249 \times 2.303}{10} = 0.02877 \text{min}^{-1}$$

For a first-order reaction, the half-life is given by the formula.

$$t_{1/2} = \frac{0.693}{k}$$

Substitute the value of k,

$$t_{1/2} = \frac{0.693}{0.02877} = 24.09 \text{ minutes}$$

Q.2 (a) For a reaction $2NH_3 \rightarrow N_2 + 3H_2$ (in the presence of Pt catalyst at 1130 K), Rate = k write the order of the reaction and unit of the rate constant of the reaction

(b) Write three differences between order of reaction and molecularity of the reaction.

Sol. (a) Rate is independent of the concentration of the reactants as, rate= k, so the order of reaction is zero and the unit of rate constant (k) is mol $L^{-1}s^{-1}$.

(b)

Order of reaction	Molecularity
1. The sum of power of the concentration of the reactants in the rate law expression is called the order of reaction.	The number of reacting species taking part in an elementary reaction is called molecularity of the reaction.
2. It can be fractional or zero.	It is always a whole number and cannot be zero.
3. It is determined experimentally.	It can be calculated by simply adding the molecules of the slowest step.

The *d*-and *f*-Block Elements

CHAPTER 04

Important Points

01 *d*-block elements or transition elements are those elements which have incompletely filled *d*-orbitals in their ground state or in any of its excited states.

02 There are three transition series in the periodic table and each series contains ten transition metals.

03 General electronic configuration of transition metals is $(n-1)\, d^{1-10}\, ns^{1-2}$.

04 Transition metals show variable oxidation states, form complex compounds and also give coloured ions in aqueous solution, due to *d-d* transition.

05 Magnetic moment $(\mu) = \sqrt{n(n+2)}$ BM. (BM = Bohr magneton)

06 Diamagnetic substances have paired electrons. Paramagnetic substances have atleast one unpaired electron.

07 Transition metals can form interstitial compounds as small atoms of H, B, C, N, etc. can easily occupy positions in the voids present in the crystal lattice of transition metals.

08 *f*-block elements or inner-transition elements have incompletely filled *f*-orbitals. General configuration is $(n-2)\, f^{1-14}\, (n-1)\, d^{0-1}\, ns^2$.

09 The decrease in the atomic and ionic radii of the members of lanthanoid family is called lanthanoid contraction. It is called actinoid contraction in case of actinoids.

10 Oxidation state is +3 generally in lanthanoids although +4 and +2 states are also shown by them occasionally.

11 *d*- and *f*-block elements have wide applications in various fields including steel industry, organic synthesis, etc. They behave as good catalysts and form complexes and alloys too.

Intext Questions

Question 1 Silver atom has completely filled *d*-orbitals ($4d^{10}$) in its ground state. How can you say that it is a transition element?

Thinking Process Transition elements have incomplete *d*-orbital in its any oxidation state +2 state of Ag atom has incomplete 4*d*-orbital.

Sol. Silver ($Z = 47$) has completely filled *d*-orbitals in its ground state ($4d^{10} 5s^1$). Silver in its +1 oxidation state exhibits $4d^{10} 5s^0$ configuration. But in some compounds it also shows +2 oxidation state, *i.e.*, $4d^9 5s^0$ configuration. Here *d*-orbital is not completely filled. Therefore, silver is a transition element.

Question 2 In the series Sc ($Z = 21$) to Zn ($Z = 30$), the enthalpy of atomisation of zinc is the lowest, *i.e.*, 126 kJ mol^{-1}, why?

Thinking Process Enthalpy of atomisation is related to the stability of crystal lattice and strength of metallic bond.

Sol. The extent of metallic bonding decides the enthalpy of atomisation. In zinc ($3d^{10} 4s^2$) *d*-orbital is completely filled so the electrons of *d*-orbital are not involved in bonding. So, metallic bond in zinc is weaker than the other elements of the series, where the electrons of *d*-orbitals are involved in metallic bonds. So, enthalpy of atomisation of zinc is lowest in its transition series.

Question 3 Which of the 3*d* series of the transition metals exhibits the largest number of oxidation states and why?

Sol. Manganese (atomic no. = 25) has electronic configuration [Ar] $3d^5 4s^2$. It shows maximum number of oxidation states, *i.e.*, from +2 to +7 (+2, +3, +4, +5, +6, +7) in its compounds, due to maximum number of unpaired electrons in *d*-orbital.

Question 4 The $E°(M^{2+}/M)$ value for copper is positive (+0.34 V). What is possibly the reason for this?
(**Hint** Consider its high $\Delta_a H°$ and low $\Delta_{hyd} H°$)

Thinking Process Consider the factors on which $E°$ value depends, like ionisation enthalpy, hydration enthalpy and enthalpy of atomisation.

Sol. $E°(M^{2+}/M)$ value for any metal depends on three factors :

(i) $\Delta_a H$ (Enthalpy of atomisation);

$$M(s) + \Delta_a H \longrightarrow M(g)$$

(ii) $\Delta_i H$ (Enthalpy of ionisation);

$$M(g) + \Delta_i H \longrightarrow M^{2+}(g)$$

(iii) $\Delta_{hyd} H$ (Hydration enthalpy);

$$M^{2+}(g) + (aq) \longrightarrow M^{2+}(aq)$$

Copper has high value of enthalpy of atomisation and low value of enthalpy of hydration. It means that $\Delta_i H$ required is not compensated by the energy released.

Therefore, $E^\circ_{(Cu^{2+}/Cu)}$ is positive.

Question 5 How would you account for the irregular variation of ionisation enthalpies (first and second) in the first series of the transition elements?

Sol. In the first transition series, there is irregular variation of ionisation enthalpies because the stability of 3*d* configuration differs to some extent. Generally, the ionisation enthalpy increases with increase in effective nuclear charge. The configurations like d^0, d^5 and d^{10} are exceptionally stable. So, they have high ionisation enthalpies.

Question 6 Why is the highest oxidation state of a metal exhibited in its oxide or fluoride only?

◎ ***Thinking Process*** Consider high electronegativity of F and O.

Sol. Oxygen as well as fluorine both have high values of electronegativity. So, in their compounds (oxides and fluorides) they can oxidise the metal to their highest oxidation states.

Question 7 Which is a stronger reducing agent Cr^{2+} or Fe^{2+} and why?

◎ ***Thinking Process*** Consider E° values and reducing agent is stronger if it gets oxidised easily.

Sol. Cr^{2+} is a stronger reducing agent than Fe^{2+}. The E° values are

$$E^\circ_{(Cr^{3+}/Cr^{2+})} = -0.41 \text{ V and } E^\circ_{(Fe^{3+}/Fe^{2+})} = 0.77 \text{ V}$$

Transition $\underset{(3d^4)}{Cr^{2+}} \longrightarrow \underset{(3d^3)}{Cr^{3+}}$ is easier than $\underset{(3d^6)}{Fe^{2+}} \longrightarrow \underset{(3d^5)}{Fe^{3+}}$ because according to the E° values Cr^{2+} can be easily oxidised to Cr^{3+}, but Fe^{2+} does not get oxidized easily to Fe^{3+}. Therefore, Cr^{2+} is stronger reducing agent (itself gets oxidised easily) than Fe^{2+}.

Question 8 Calculate the 'spin only' magnetic moment of $M^{2+}(aq)$ ion ($Z=27$).

Thinking Process Spin only magnetic moment depends upon the number of unpaired electrons as $\mu = \sqrt{n(n+2)}$.
So first find the number of unpaired electrons from its electronic configuration to calculate μ.

Sol. Electronic configuration of M ($Z = 27$) is [Ar] $3d^7 4s^2$.

Electronic configuration of M^{2+} = [Ar] $3d^7$

or

↑↓	↑↓	↑	↑	↑

Three unpaired electrons are present in $M^{2+}(aq)$ ion, *i.e.*, $n = 3$. Applying 'spin only' formula for magnetic moment,

$$\mu = \sqrt{n(n+2)} = \sqrt{3(3+2)} = \sqrt{15}\text{ BM} = 3.87\text{ BM}$$

Note Unit of magnetic moment is Bohr Magneton (BM).

Question 9 Explain why Cu^+ ion is not stable in aqueous solutions?

Sol. In aqueous solution, $Cu^+(aq)$ undergoes disproportionation reaction as follows :

$$2Cu^+(aq) \longrightarrow Cu^{2+}(aq) + Cu(s)$$

The higher stability of $Cu^{2+}(aq)$ in aqueous solution is due to higher negative enthalpy of hydration, $\Delta_{hyd}H°$ than that of $Cu^+(aq)$. It compensates the second IE of Cu involved in the formation of Cu^{2+} ion. Hence, Cu^+ ion changes to more stable Cu^{2+} ion in aqueous medium.

Question 10 Actinoid contraction is greater from element to element than lanthanoid contraction. Why?

Thinking Process

(i) General electronic configuration of lanthanoids and actinoids are $4f^{1-14}5d^{0-1}6s^2$ and $5f^{1-14}6d^{0-1}7s^2$ respectively.

(ii) Shielding effect of $4f$-electrons is more than that of $5f$-electrons.

Sol. The decrease in atomic (or ionic) radii in actinoid elements (actinoid contraction) is greater than lanthanoid elements (clanthanoid constraction) because $5f$-electrons have poor shielding effect as compared to $4f$-electrons. Therefore, the effect of increased nuclear charge leading to contraction in size is more in case of actinoid elements.

Mistake Alert Shelding effect order is $4f > 5f$.

Exercise

Question 1 Write down the electronic configuration of

(i) Cr^{3+} (ii) Pm^{3+} (iii) Cu^{+} (iv) Ce^{4+}

(v) Co^{2+} (vi) Lu^{2+} (vii) Mn^{2+} (viii) Th^{4+}

◎ ***Thinking Process*** **Recall the atomic number of each element and write their electronic configuration then, remove the electrons from the outer most shell according to positive charge present on the ion.**

Sol. (i) $_{24}Cr = 1s^2\,2s^2\,2p^6\,3s^2\,3p^6\,3d^5\,4s^1$ or $[Ar]3d^5\,4s^1$

$Cr^{3+} = 1s^2\,2s^2\,2p^6\,3s^2\,3p^6\,3d^3$ or $[Ar]\,3d^3$

(ii) $_{61}P_m = 1s^2\,2s^2\,2p^6\,3s^2\,3p^6\,3d^{10}\,4s^2\,4p^6\,4d^{10}\,4f^5\,5s^2\,5p^6\,6s^2$ or $[Xe]4f^5\,6s^2$

$P_m = 1s^2\,2s^2\,2p^6\,3s^2\,3p^6\,3d^{10}\,4s^2\,4p^6\,4d^{10}\,4f^4\,5s^2\,5p^6$ or $[Xe]\,4f^4$

(iii) $_{29}Cu = 1s^2\,2s^2\,2p^6\,3s^2\,3p^6\,3d^{10}\,4s^1$ or $[Ar]\,3d^{10}\,4s^1$

$Cu^{+} = 1s^2\,2s^2\,2p^6\,3s^2\,3p^6\,3d^{10}$ or $[Ar]\,3d^{10}$

(iv) $_{58}Ce = 1s^2\,2s^2\,2p^6\,3s^2\,3p^6\,4d^{10}\,4s^2\,4p^6\,4d^{10}\,4f^1\,5s^2\,5p^6\,5d^1\,6s^2$
or $[Xe]4f^1\,5d^1\,6s^2$

$Ce^{4+} = 1s^2\,2s^2\,p^6\,3s^2\,3p^6\,3d^{10}\,4s^2\,4p^6\,d^{10}\,5s^2\,5p^6$ or $[Xe]$

(v) $_{27}Co = 1s^2\,2s^2\,2p^6\,3s^2\,3p^6\,3d^7\,4s^2$ or $[Ar]\,3d^7\,4s^2$

$Co^{2+} = 1s^2\,2s^2\,2p^6\,3s^2\,3p^6\,3d^7$ or $[Ar]\,3d^7$

(vi) $_{71}Lu = 1s^2\,2s^2\,2p^6\,3s^2\,3p^6\,3d^{10}\,4s^2\,4p^6\,4d^{10}\,4f^{14}\,5s^2\,5p^6\,5d^1\,6s^2$
or $[Xe]\,4f^{14}\,5d^1\,6s^2$

$Lu^{2+} = 1s^2\,2s^2\,2p^6\,3s^2\,3p^6\,3d^{10}\,4s^2\,4p^6\,4d^{10}\,4f^{14}, 5s^2\,5p^6\,5d^1$ or $[Xe]\,4f^{14}\,5d^1$

(vii) $_{25}Mn = 1s^2\,2s^2\,2p^6\,3s^2\,3p^6\,3d^5\,4s^2$ or $[Ar]\;3d^5\,4s^2$

$Mn^{2+} = 1s^2\,2s^2\,2p^6\,3s^2\,3p^6\,3d^5$ or $[Ar]\,3d^5$

(viii) $_{90}Th = 1s^2, 2s^2\,2p^6, 3s^2\,3p^6\,3d^{10}, 4s^2\,4p^6\,4d^{10}\,4f^{14}, 5s^2\,5p^6\,5d^{10}\,6s^2\,6p^6\,6d^2\,7s^2$
or $[Rn]\,6d^2, 7s^2$

$Th^{4+} = 1s^2\,2s^2\,2p^6\,3s^2\,3p^6\,3d^{10}\,4s^2\,4p^6\,4d^{10}\,4f^{14}\,5s^2\,5p^6\,5d^{10}\,6s^2\,6p^6$ or $[Rn]$

Question 2 Why are Mn^{2+} compounds more stable than Fe^{2+} towards oxidation to their +3 state?

◎ ***Thinking Process*** **Half-filled orbitals are more stable.**

Sol. $Mn^{2+} = 1s^2\,2s^2\,2p^6\,3s^2\,3p^6\,3d^5$ (half-filled *d*-orbital)

$Fe^{2+} = 1s^2\,2s^2\,2p^6\,3s^2\,3p^6\,3d^6$

Mn^{2+} compounds are more stable due to half-filled *d*-orbitals. Fe^{2+} compounds are comparatively less stable as they have six electrons in their 3*d*-orbital. So, they tend to lose one electrons (form Fe^{3+}) and get stable $3d^5$ configuration.

Question 3 Explain briefly how +2 state becomes more and more stable in the first half of the first row transition elements with increasing atomic number?

◎ *Thinking Process* Stability ∝ number of unpaired electron in *d*-orbitals.

Sol. $Sc^{2+} = 3d^1$, $Ti^{2+} = 3d^2$, $V^{2+} = 3d^3$, $Cr^{2+} = 3d^4$, $Mn^{2+} = 3d^5$

In all the elements listed, the two 4*s* electrons are removed. Since, the number of empty *d*-orbitals decreases or the number of unpaired electrons in 3*d*-orbitals increases with increase in atomic number of cations, so the stability of the cations (M^{2+}) increases from Sc^{2+} to Mn^{2+}.

Question 4 To what extent do the electronic configurations decide the stability of oxidation states in the first series of the transition elements? Illustrate your answer with examples.

Sol. If an orbital is half-filled or completely filled, it imparts stability to an atom or ion.

e.g., (1) $_{25}Mn = [Ar]\ 3d^5 4s^2$

$Mn^{2+} = [Ar]\ 3d^5$ (Most stable)

$Mn^{3+} = [Ar]\ 3d^4$, $Mn^{4+} = [Ar]\ 3d^3$

e.g., (2) $_{29}Cu = [Ar] = 3d^{10} 4s^1$

$Cu^+ = [Ar]\ 3d^{10}$ (Most stable), $Cu^{2+} = [Ar]\ 3d^9$

In manganese, Mn^{2+} ion is more stable due to symmetry and half-filled *d*-orbitals. In the same way in copper, Cu^+ ion is more stable due to symmetry and completely filled *d*-orbitals.

Question 5 What may be the stable oxidation state of the transition element with the following *d*-electron configuration in the ground state of their atoms : $3d^3, 3d^5, 3d^8$ and $3d^4$?

◎ *Thinking Process*

(i) In case of d block elements upto 7 group, the maximum oxidation state $= ns + (n-1)d$ unpaired electrons.

(ii) Minimum oxidation state is generally +2, but in chromium it is +3.

(iii) Write the outer shell configuration of the atoms having the given configuration to find the stable oxidation states.

Sol. Stable oxidation states :

$3d^3$: Vanadium ($3d^3 4s^2$) : Common oxidation states +2, +3, +4 and +5. Stable oxidation state +2

$3d^5$: Chromium ($3d^5 4s^1$) : Common oxidation states +3, +4 and +6. Stable oxidation state +3

$3d^5$: Manganese ($3d^5 4s^2$): Common oxidation states (+2, +4, +6, +7). Stable oxidation state +2

$3d^8$: Nickel ($3d^8 4s^2$) : Common oxidation states +2, +3 (in complexes) Stable oxidation state +2

$3d^4$: Such configuration does not exist in ground state [exists as $3d^5 4s^1$].

Question 6 Name the oxometal anions of the first series of the transition metals in which the metal exhibits the oxidation state equal to its group number.

Sol. $[ScO_2]^-$; Group number = Oxidation state of Sc = 3

$[TiO_3]^{2-}$; Group number = Oxidation state of Ti = 4

$[VO_3]^-$; Group number = Oxidation state of V = 5

$[Cr_2O_7]^{2-}$; Group number = Oxidation state of Cr = 6

$[CrO_4]^{2-}$; Group number = Oxidation state of Cr = 6

$[MnO_4]^-$; Group number = Oxidation state of Mn = 7

Mistake Alert Oxidation number of 3*d*-transition metal element is sum of number of electrons in (*ns*) and $(n-1)\,d$ shell.

Question 7 What is lanthanoid contraction? What are the consequences of lanthanoid contraction?

Sol. **Lanthanoid contraction** The overall decrease in atomic and ionic radii from lanthanum to leutetium is observed in the lanthanoids. This phenomenon is called lanthanoid contraction. It is due to the fact that with every additional proton in the nucleus, the corresponding electron goes into a 4*f*-subshell.

The 4*f* electrons have poor shielding effect. Hence, the attraction of the nucleus for the outermost electrons increases steadily with the atomic number. This results in decrease in size of lanthanoids with increase in the atomic number.

Consequences of Lanthanoid Contraction The important consequences of lanthanoid contraction are as follows :

(i) **Basic character of oxides and hydroxides** Due to the lanthanoid contraction, the covalent nature of La – OH bond increases and thus, the basic character of oxides and hydroxides decreases from $La(OH)_3$ to $Lu(OH)_3$.

(ii) **Similarity in the size of elements of second and third transition series** Because of lanthanoid contraction, elements which follow the third transition series are considerably smaller than would otherwise be expected. The normal size increases from $Sc \rightarrow Y \rightarrow La$ and disappears after lanthanides.

Thus, pairs of elements such as Zr / Hf, Nb / Ta and Mo / W are almost identical in size.

Due to almost similar size, such pairs have very similar properties which makes their separation difficult.

(iii) **Separation of lanthanoids** Due to lanthanoid contraction, there is a difference in some properties of lanthanoid like solubility, degree of hydration and complex formation. These difference enable the separation of lanthanoids by ion exchange method.

Question 8 What are the characteristics of the transition elements and why are they called transition elements? Which of the *d*-block elements may not be regarded as the transition elements?

◎ *Thinking Process* Transition elements are placed between *s* and *p* block elements in the Period Table and have incompletely filled *d*-orbital in neutral state or in any of the oxidation states.

Sol. Characteristics of the transition elements (*d*-Block)

(i) **Electronic configuration** General configuration of these elements $(n-1)\,d^{1-10}ns^{1-2}$.

(ii) **Physical properties** These elements have metallic properties such as metallic lustre, high tensile strength, ductility, malleability, high thermal and electrical conductivity, low volatility (except Zn, Cd, Hg), hardness, etc. Their melting points are high.

(iii) **Atomic and ionic size** In a given series, there is a progressive decrease in radius with increasing atomic number.

(iv) **Ionisation enthalpies** Due to an increase in nuclear charge which accompanies the filling of inner *d*-orbitals, there is an increase in ionisation enthalpy along each series of the transition elements from left to right.

(v) **Oxidation states** These elements exhibit variable oxidation states. *e.g.*, **I Transition series :**

Sc	Ti	V	Cr	Mn	Fe	Co	Ni	Cu	Zn
	+2	+2	+2	+2	+2	+2	+2	+1	+2
+3	+3	+3	+3	+3	+3	+3	+3	+2	
	+4	+4	+4	+4	+4	+4	+4		
		+5	+5	+5					
			+6	+6	+6				
				+7					

(vi) **Trends in $M^{2+}/ME°$ values** The general trend towards less negative $E°$ values across the series is related to the general increase in the sum of the first and second ionisation enthalpies.

(vii) **Trends in $M^{3+}/M^{2+}E°$ values** Low value of $E°$ shows the stability of ion (either d^5 or d^{10} configuration).

(viii) **Magnetic properties** These elements show diamagnetism and paramagnetism.

(ix) **Formation of coloured salts** The compounds of transition elements form coloured ions, *e.g.*, Mn^{3+} violet; Fe^{2+} green, etc.

(x) **Complex formation** These elements form complex compounds due to their small size and high charge density. *e.g.*, $[PtCl_4]^{2-}$

(xi) **Catalyst** Many of these elements are used as catalyst *e.g.*, V_2O_5 is used as a catalyst in contact process for the manufacture of H_2SO_4.

(xii) **Interstitial compound formation** Transition elements form interstitial compounds. It means the compounds in which H, C or N etc. are trapped inside the crystal lattices of metals.

(xiii) **Alloy formation** Because of similar radii and other characteristics alloys are readily formed by these metals.

(xiv) (a) **The *d*-block elements are called transition elements** Because these elements represent change or transition in properties from *s*-block to *p*-block elements.

(b) The electronic configuration of **Zn, Cd and Hg** is represented by the general formula $(n-1)\, d^{10} ns^2$. These elements have completely filled *d*-orbitals in ground state as well as in their common oxidation states. Therefore, they may not be regarded as the transition elements.

Question 9 In what way is the electronic configuration of the transition elements different from that of non-transition elements?

Sol. Transition elements have incomplete *d*-orbital, *i.e.*, their electronic configuration is $(n-1)\, n^{1-10} ns^{1-2}$. In non-transition elements, *d*-orbital is absent or completely filled and they have ns^{1-2} or $ns^2 np^{1-6}$ type electronic configuration.

Question 10 What are the different oxidation states exhibited by lanthanoids?

Sol. +2, +3 and +4 (Most common is +3).

Question 11 Explain giving reasons.

(i) Transition metals and many of their compounds show paramagnetic behaviour.

(ii) The enthalpies of atomisation of the transition metals are high.

(iii) The transition metals generally form coloured compounds.

(iv) Transition metals and their many compounds act as good catalyst.

Sol. (i) Transition elements have unpaired electrons. Each unpaired electron has a magnetic moment associated with its spin angular momentum and orbital angular momentum. This is the reason of paramagnetism in transition metals.

(ii) The reason for the high enthalpy of atomisation is the presence of large number of unpaired electrons in their atoms. These atoms have strong interatomic interaction and hence, stronger metallic bonding between them.

(iii) Formation of coloured compounds by transition metals is due to the presence of unpaired electrons, these electrons undergo *d-d* transitions by absorbing light (visible light) and giving complementary colour.

(iv) Transition metal ions show **variable oxidation states,** so they are effective catalysts. Also, transition metals have large surface and can form an intermediate by bonding to the reactants, which leads to formation of products.

Question 12 What are the interstitial compounds? Why are such compounds well known for transition metals?

Sol. The compounds in which small atoms like H, C, N, etc., occupy the interstitial sites in the crystal lattice are called interstitial compounds. These compounds are well known for transition metals because small atoms can easily occupy the positions in the voids present in the crystal lattices of transition metals.

Question 13 How is the variability in oxidation states of transition metals different from that of non-transition metals? Illustrate with examples.

Sol. In transition elements the oxidation states vary by unity (due to incomplete filling of *d*-orbitals) *e.g.,* Mn exhibits +2, +3, +4, +5, +6 and +7 all differing by 1. In non-transition element, this variation is selective, always differing by 2. *e.g.,* S exhibits 2, 4, 6 oxidation states. N exhibits 3, 5, etc.

Question 14 Describe the preparation of potassium dichromate from iron chromite ore. What is the effect of increasing pH on a solution of potassium dichromate?

Sol. (i) **Preparation of $K_2Cr_2O_7$ from chromite ore**

(a) Potassium dichromate is obtained by the fusion of chromite ore ($FeCr_2O_4$) with sodium (or potassium) carbonate in the presence of excess of air.

$$4FeCr_2O_4 + 8Na_2CO_3 + 7O_2 \longrightarrow \underset{\text{(Yellow solution)}}{8Na_2CrO_4} + 2Fe_2O_3 + 8CO_2$$

(b) The solution is filtered and treated with sulphuric acid.

$$2Na_2CrO_4 + \underset{\text{(From } H_2SO_4)}{2H^+} \longrightarrow \underset{\substack{\text{Sodium}\\\text{dichromate}\\\text{(orange)}}}{Na_2Cr_2O_7(s)} + 2Na^+ + H_2O$$

(c) Now sodium dichromate is treated with potassium chloride. As a result, potassium dichromate is produced.

$$Na_2Cr_2O_7 + 2KCl \longrightarrow \underset{\substack{\text{Potassium}\\\text{dichromate}\\\text{crystals}}}{K_2Cr_2O_7} + 2NaCl$$

(ii) **Effect of increasing pH on $K_2Cr_2O_7$ solution**

$$\underset{\text{Orange}}{Cr_2O_7^{2-}} + 2OH^- \longrightarrow \underset{\text{Yellow}}{2CrO_4^{2-}} + H_2O$$

On increasing pH; $K_2Cr_2O_7$ changes into K_2CrO_4 (orange to yellow).

Question 15 Describe the oxidising action of potassium dichromate and write the ionic equations for its reaction with

(i) iodide (ii) iron (II) solution (iii) H_2S

Thinking Process Potassium dichromate being a strong oxidising agent, oxidises (i) I^- into I_2. (ii) Fe^{2+} into Fe^{3+} and (iii) H_2S into S and itself gets reduced to Cr^{3+}.

Sol. Potassium dichromate is a strong oxidising agent. In acidic solution, its oxidising action may be represented as :

$$Cr_2O_7^{2-} + 14H^+ + 6e^- \longrightarrow 2Cr^{3+} + 7H_2O (E° = 1.33\ V)$$

Ionic Equations

(i) Reaction of $K_2Cr_2O_7$ with I^-

$$Cr_2O_7^{2-} + 14H^+ + 6I^- \longrightarrow 2Cr^{3+} + 3I_2 + 7H_2O$$

(ii) Reaction of $K_2Cr_2O_7$ with $Fe^{2+}(aq)$

$$Cr_2O_7^{2-} + 14H^+ + 6Fe^{2+} \longrightarrow 2Cr^{3+} + 6Fe^{3+} + 7H_2O$$

(iii) Reaction of $K_2Cr_2O_7$ with H_2S

$$Cr_2O_7^{2-} + 8H^+ + 3H_2S \longrightarrow 2Cr^{3+} + 3S + 7H_2O$$

Question 16 Describe the preparation of potassium permanganate. How does the acidified permanagate solution react with (i) iron (II) ions (ii) SO_2 and (iii) oxalic acid?
Write the ionic equations for the reactions.

Thinking Process In acidic medium $KMnO_4$ is a good oxidising agent. It oxidises

(i) Fe^{2+} into Fe^{3+} (ii) SO_2 into SO_4^{2-}

(ii) $(COOH)_2$ into CO_2 and itself gets reduced to Mn^{2+} ion.

Sol. (a) **Preparation of** $KMnO_4$ Potassium permanganate is prepared by the fusion of Pyrolusite (MnO_2) with an alkali metal hydroxide and an oxidising agent like KNO_3. It forms dark green, K_2MnO_4 which dispro portionates in a neutral or acidic solution to give permanganate.

(i) $2MnO_2 + 4KOH + O_2 \xrightarrow{KNO_3} 2K_2MnO_4 + 2H_2O$

(ii) $3MnO_4^{2-} + 4H^+ \longrightarrow 2MnO_4^- + MnO_2 + 2H_2O$

or $3K_2MnO_4 + 2H_2SO_4 \longrightarrow \underset{\text{Potassium permanganate}}{2KMnO_4} + 2K_2SO_4 + MnO_2 + 2H_2O$

(b) **Reactions of $KMnO_4$ in acidic medium**

$$MnO_4^- + 8H^+ + 5e^- \longrightarrow Mn^{2+} + 4H_2O \quad ...(i)$$

(i) **Iron (II) ions** Ferrous is oxidised to ferric.

$$[Fe^{2+} \longrightarrow Fe^{3+} + e^-]\times 5 \quad ...(ii)$$

From Eq. (i) and (ii)

$$5Fe^{2+} + MnO_4^- + 8H^+ \longrightarrow Mn^{2+} + 4H_2O + 5Fe^{3+}$$

(ii) **SO_2** It is oxidised to SO_4^{2-} by acidified $KMnO_4$.

$$SO_2 + 2H_2O \longrightarrow SO_4^{2-} + 4H^+ + 2e^- \quad ...(iii)$$

From Eq. (i) and (iii)

$$5SO_2 + 2MnO_4^- + 2H_2O \longrightarrow 2Mn^{2+} + 4H^+ + 5SO_4^{2-}$$

(iii) **Oxalic acid**

$$C_2O_4^{2-} \longrightarrow 2CO_2 + 2e^- \quad ...(iv)$$

From Eq. (i) and (iv)

$$5C_2O_4^{2-} + 2MnO_4^- + 16H^+ \longrightarrow 2Mn^{2+} + 8H_2O + 10\,CO_2$$

Question 17 For M^{2+}/M and M^{3+}/M^{2+} systems the $E°$ values for some metals are as follows :

$Cr^{2+}/Cr -0.9$ V; Cr^{3+}/Cr^{2+} -0.4 V

$Mn^{2+}/Mn -1.2$ V; Mn^{3+}/Mn^{2+} $+1.5$ V

$Fe^{2+}/Fe -0.4$ V; Fe^{3+}/Fe^{2+} $+0.8$ V

Use this data to comment upon

(i) the stability of Fe^{3+} in acid solution as compared to that of Cr^{3+} or Mn^{3+} and

(ii) the ease with which iron can be oxidised as compared to a similar process for either chromium or manganese metal.

Thinking Process

(i) Negative value of $E°$ means more stability and less reactivity.

(ii) More negative $E°$ value, more the ease of oxidation of metal.

Sol. (i) $E°_{(Cr^{3+}/Cr^{2+})}$ is negative (-0.4 V). It shows the stability of Cr^{3+} ions, *i.e.*, Cr^{3+} in solution cannot be reduced to Cr^{2+} ions. Further Mn^{3+} has high positive E° value so it is easily converted to Mn^{2+} as compared to the conversion of Fe^{3+} into Fe^{2+}. Thus, the order of relative stabilities of different ions is $Mn^{3+} < Fe^{3+} < Cr^{3+}$

(ii) From the E° values, the order of oxidation of the metal to the divalent cation is : Mn > Cr > Fe

Mn^{2+}/Mn has most negative reduction potential (E°), so it is oxidised most easily.

Question 18 Predict which of the following will be coloured in aqueous solution? Ti^{3+}, V^{3+}, Cu^{+}, Sc^{3+}, Mn^{2+}, Fe^{3+} and Co^{2+}. Give reasons for each.

◎ *Thinking Process* Incomplete *d*-orbitals are responsible for producing colour in aqueous solution. So write electronic configuration of all the ions to find the number of unpaired electrons.

Sol. Only those ions will be coloured which have incomplete *d*-orbitals i.e., they have unpaired electron in *d*-orbital, which can undergo *d*-*d* transition. Ions which have complete or vacant *d*-orbitals are colourless.

Ion	Colour
$Ti^{3+}=[Ar]\,3d^1$	Purple
$V^{3+}=[Ar]\,3d^2$	Green
$Cu^{+}=[Ar]\,3d^{10}$	Colourless
$Sc^{3+}=[Ar]$	Colourless
$Mn^{2+}=[Ar]\,3d^5$	Pink
$Fe^{3+}=[Ar]\,3d^5$	Brown
$Co^{2+}=[Ar]\,3d^7$	Pink

As Sc^{3+} and Cu^{+} have $3d^0$ and $3d^{10}$ configuration in their valence shell, so their aqueous solutions are colourless. All others, *i.e.*, Ti^{3+}, V^{3+}, Mn^{2+}, Fe^{3+} and Co^{2+} are coloured in aqueous medium.

Question 19 Compare the stability of +2 oxidation state for the elements of the first transition series.

◎ *Thinking Process* Write the valence shell electronic configuration of first transition series for M^{2+}. Compare the stability on the basis of half-filled and completely filled *d*-orbitals.

Sol. Remaining answer same as in question 3 of exercise.

Question 20 Compare the chemistry of actinoids with that of the lanthanoids with special reference to

(i) electronic configuration
(ii) atomic and ionic sizes
(iii) oxidation state
(iv) chemical reactivity

Sol.

S. No.	Lanthanoids	Actinoids
(i)	Electronic configuration $[Xe]_{54} 4f^{1-14} 5d^{0-1} 6s^2$ e.g., $_{57}La = [Xe] 5d^1 6s^2$ $_{58}Ce = [Xe] 4f^1 5d^1 6s^2$	Electronic configuration $[Rn]_{86} 5f^{1-14} 6d^{0-1} 7s^2$ e.g., $_{89}Ac = [Rn] 6d^1 7s^2$ $_{90}Th = [Rn] 6d^2 7s^2$
(ii)	**Oxidation state(s)** Most common oxidation state = + 3 Other oxidation states = + 2, + 4.	**Oxidation state(s)** Most common oxidation state = + 3 Other oxidation states = +4, +5, +6.
(iii)	**Atomic and ionic size** Size of atom/ion decreases across the period. In the group, size of a lanthanoid element is smaller than the actinoid of its own group.	**Atomic and ionic size** Size of atom/ion decreases along the period. Actinoid has largest size in its own group.
(iv)	**Chemical reactivity** (a) Less tendency towards complex formation. (b) Except promethium, they are non-radioactive. (c) They do not form oxocations. (d) Oxides and hydroxides are less basic.	**Chemical reactivity** (a) Stronger tendency towards complex formation. (b) All the actinoids are radioactive. (c) They form oxocations like UO_2^{2+}, PuO_2^{2+}, UO^+, etc. (d) Oxides and hydroxides are more basic.

Question 21 How would you account for the following.

(i) Of the d^4 species, Cr^{2+} is strongly reducing while manganese (III) is strongly oxidising.

(ii) Cobalt (II) is stable in aqueous solution but in the presence of complexing reagents it is easily oxidised.

(iii) The d^1 configuration is very unstable in ions.

Sol. (i) $E°$ value of Cr^{3+} / Cr^{2+} is negative (–0.41 V) while that of Mn^{3+} / Mn^{2+} is positive (+1.57 V). This means that Cr^{2+} ions can lose electrons to form Cr^{3+} ions and act as a reducing agent while Mn^{3+} ions can accept electrons and can act as an oxidising agent.

(ii) Cobalt (III) ion has greater tendency to form complexes than cobalt (II) ion. Therefore, Co (II) ion, being stable in aqueous solution, changes to Co (III) ion, in the presence of complexing reagents and gets oxidised.

(iii) Ions of transition metals with d^1 configuration tend to lose one electron to acquire d^0 configuration that is quite stable. Therefore, such ions (with d^1) undergo either oxidation or disproportionation, hence unstable.

Question 22 What is meant by 'disproportionation'? Give two examples of disproportionation reaction in aqueous solution.

Sol. In a disproportionation reaction, same substance undergoes oxidation (increase in oxidation number) as well as reduction (decrease in oxidation number) resulting in the formation of two different products.

In other words, same substance is behaving as oxidising agent for one molecule and at the same time as reducing agent for another molecule.

e.g., (i) $\underset{(+6)}{3MnO_4^{2-}} + 4H^+ \longrightarrow \underset{(+7)}{2MnO_4^-} + \underset{(+4)}{MnO_2} + 2H_2O$

(ii) $\underset{(+5)}{3CrO_4^{3-}} + 8H^+ \longrightarrow \underset{(+6)}{2CrO_4^{2-}} + \underset{(+3)}{Cr^{3+}} + 4H_2O$

Question 23 Which metal in the first series of transition metals exhibits +1 oxidation state most frequently and why?

Sol. $Cu = [Ar]\,3d^{10}4s^1$. When copper atom loses 1 electron, it exhibits +1 oxidation state and forms Cu^+ ion with stable $3d^{10}$ configuration. So, copper metal in the first transition series tends to have +1 oxidation state to achieve a stable configuration.

Question 24 Calculate the number of unpaired electrons in the following gaseous ions; Mn^{3+}, Cr^{3+}, V^{3+} and Ti^{3+}. Which one of these is the most stable in aqueous solution?

◎ ***Thinking Process*** Write the electronic configuration of given ions to find the number of unpaired electrons.

Sol.

	3*d* orbitals	No. of unpaired e^-
Mn^{3+} (Z = 25) = $[Ar]\,3d^4$	↿ ↿ ↿ ↿ □	4
Cr^{3+} (Z = 24) = $[Ar]\,3d^3$	↿ ↿ ↿ □ □	3
V^{3+} (Z = 23) = $[Ar]\,3d^2$	↿ ↿ □ □ □	2
Ti^{3+} (Z = 22) = $[Ar]\,3d^1$	↿ □ □ □ □	1

Out of these species, Cr^{3+} is most stable in aqueous solution due to its tendency of complex formation. [or have half filled t_{2g} level (t_{2g}^3)]

Question 25 Give examples and suggest reasons for the following features of the transition metal chemistry.

(i) The lowest oxide of transition metal is basic, the highest is amphoteric/acidic.

(ii) A transition metal exhibits highest oxidation state in oxides and fluorides.

(iii) The highest oxidation state is exhibited in oxoanions of a metal.

Sol. (i) Acidic strength of oxides increases with the increase in oxidation state of the element *e.g.*, MnO(Mn^{2+}) is basic whereas is acidic in nature.

(ii) Both oxygen and fluorine being highly electronegative can increase the oxidation state of a particular transition metal. For example, +5 oxidation state of vanadium in V_2O_5 and +6 oxidation state of osmium in OsF_6.

(iii) This is also due to high electronegativity of oxygen *e.g.*, chromium exhibits oxidation states of +6 in oxoanion $[CrO_4]^{2-}$ and manganese shows oxidation state of +7 in oxoanion $[MnO_4]^-$.

Question 26 Indicate the steps in the preparation of :

(i) $K_2Cr_2O_7$ from chromite ore

(ii) $KMnO_4$ from pyrolusite ore (MnO_2)

Sol. (i) Same as question 14 Part (i) of Exercise

(ii) Same as question 16 Part (i) of Exercise

Question 27 What are alloys? Name an important alloy which contains some of the lanthanoid metals. Mention its uses.

Sol. (i) **Alloys** An alloy is a homogeneous mixture of two or more metals or non-metals. It is prepared by blending the metals (and/or non-metal) in molten state.

(ii) **An important alloy containing lanthanoid metal (~ 95%)**, iron (~5%), traces of S, C, Ca and Al is **mischmetal.**

(iii) **Mischmetal is used** in Mg-based alloy to produce bullets, shell and lighter flint.

Question 28 What are inner-transition elements? Decide which of the following atomic numbers are the atomic numbers of the inner-transition elements : 29, 59, 74, 95, 102, 104?

◎ *Thinking Process*

(i) Inner-transition means their $(n-2)f$ sub-shell is filled by electrons.

(ii) Write electronic configuration for all the given atomic numbers. If the last electron enters in $(n-2)f$ sub-shell, it is an inner-transition element, otherwise not.

Sol. (i) **Inner-transition elements** Inner transition elements (or *f*-block elements) include lanthanoids ($Z = 58$ to 71) and actinoids ($Z = 90$ to 103). These elements have incomplete *f*-orbital in penultimate shell of their atoms. Their last electron enters in the *f*-orbital.

(ii) The electronic configuration of given atomic number are as

$29 = [Ar]\, 4s^1 3d^{10}$ (*d*-block element or transition element)

$59 = [Xe]\, 6s^2 4f^3$ (*f*-block element or inner transition element)

$74 = [Xe]\, 6s^1 4f^{14} 5d^5$ (*d*-block element or inner transition element)

$95 = [Rn]\, 7s^2 5f^7 6d^0$ (*f*-block element or inner transition element)

$102 = [Rn]\, 7s^2 5f^{14}$ (*f*-block element or inner transition element)

$104 = [Rn]\, 7s^2 5f^{14} 6d^2$ (*d*-block element)

Thus, **atomic numbers** 59 (lanthanoid), 95 and 102 (actinoids) are included among inner transition elements.

Question 29 The chemistry of the actinoid elements is not so smooth as that of the lanthanoids. Justify this statement by giving some examples from the oxidation state of these elements.

Sol. Actinoids shows +3 oxidation state in general. There is a greater range of oxidation states varying from +3 to +7. This variation is due to the fact that $5f$, $6d$ and $7s$ levels are of comparable energies. Due to uneven distribution of oxidation states among actinoid elements, their study becomes somewhat difficult. Also, actinoids are radioactive. Early members of actinoids have relatively long half-lives but the latter ones have half-life ranging from a day to 3 minutes for lawrencium ($Z = 103$). The high radioactivity makes their study more difficult.

Question 30 Which is the last element in the series of the actinoids? Write the electronic configuration of this element. Comment on the possible oxidation state of this element.

◎ *Thinking Process* Actinoids = $_{89}$Ac to $_{103}$Lr.

Sol. Lawrencium (Lr; $Z = 103$) is the last element of actinoids series.

Configuration : $_{103}Lr = [Rn]\, 5f^{14} 6d^1 7s^2$

Its possible oxidation state = + 3 [as Lr attains stable electronic configuration after losing 3 electrons].

Question 31 Use Hund's rule to derive the electronic configuration of Ce^{3+} ion, and calculate its magnetic moment on the basis of 'spin only' formula.

◎ *Thinking Process*

(i) Write the configuration of Ce and Ce^{3+}.

(ii) Find the number of unpaired electrons and calculate μ.

Sol. Ce (Z = 58) = [Xe] $4f^1 5d^1 6s^2$, Ce^{3+} = [Xe] $4f^1$ (only one unpaired electron)

By 'spin-only' formula;

Magnetic moment of Ce^{3+} $(\mu) = \sqrt{n(n+2)}$ [$\because n=1$(1 unpaired electron)]

$= \sqrt{1(1+2)} = \sqrt{3} = 1.732$ BM

Question 32 Name the members of the lanthanoid series which exhibit +4 oxidation states and those which exhibit +2 oxidation states. Try to correlate this type of behaviour with the electronic configurations of these elements.

◎ *Thinking Process* Empty, half-filled or completely filled shells are more stable than partially filled shells.

Sol. +4 oxidation states exists in $_{58}Ce$, $_{59}Pr$ and $_{65}Tb$

+2 oxidation states exists in $_{60}Nd$, $_{62}Sm$, $_{63}Eu$, $_{69}Tm$ and $_{70}Yb$.

Generally +2 oxidation state is exhibited by the elements with configuration $5d^0 6s^2$ so that two electrons may be easily lost. Similarly +4 oxidation state is shown by the elements which after losing four electrons acquire configuration either close to $4f^0$ or $4f^7$.

Question 33 Compare the chemistry of the actinoids with that of lanthanoids with reference to: (i) electronic configuration (ii) oxidation states and (iii) chemical reactivity.

Sol. Difference between lanthanoids and actinoids

	Property	Lanthanoids	Actinoids
(i)	**General electronic configuration**	$6s^2 5d^{0-1} 4f^{1-14}$	$5f^{1-14} 6d^{0-1} 7s^2$
(ii)	**Oxidation state**	They show mainly +3 oxidation state, +2 and +4 oxidation states also exist.	In addition to +3 oxidation state, they also show higher oxidation states like +4, +5 and +6 and +7.
(iii)	**Chemical reactivity**		
	(a) Tendency to form complex	less	more
	(b) Radioactivity	Except promethium these are non-radioactive substances.	These are radioactive substances.
	(c) Basic character	There are less basic.	These are more basic.

Question 34 Write the electronic configuration of the elements with the atomic numbers 61, 91, 101 and 109.

Sol. Promethium or Pm (Z = 61) = [Xe] $4f^5 5d^0 6s^2$

Protactinium or Pa (Z = 91) = [Rn] $5f^2 6d^1 7s^2$

Mendelevium or Md (Z = 101) = [Rn] $5f^{13} 6d^0 7s^2$

Meitnerium or Mt (Z = 109) = [Rn] $5f^{14} 6d^7 7s^2$

Question 35 Compare the general characteristics of the first series of the transition metals with those of the second and third series metals in the respective vertical columns. Give special emphasis on the following points

(i) Electronic configuration
(ii) Oxidation states
(iii) Ionisation enthalpies
(iv) Atomic sizes

Sol. (i) **Electronic configuration** The elements in the same vertical column generally have similar electronic configurations. In first transition series, electrons enter 3*d*-orbital. In second and third transition series, electrons enter 4*d*- and 5*d*-orbitals, respectively. Although **the first series** has only two **exceptions.**

(a) $Cr = 3d^5 4s^1$ and (b) $Cu = 3d^{10} 4s^1$

Second transition series has five exceptions :

(a) $Mo = 4d^5 5s^1$; (b) $Nb = 4d^4 5s^1$; (c) $Rh = 4d^8 5s^1$
(d) $Pd = 4d^{10} 5s^0$ (e) $Ag = 4d^{10} 5s^1$

Third transition series have three exceptions :

(a) $W = 4f^{14} 5d^4 6s^2$;
(b) $Pt = 4f^{14} 5d^9 6s^1$;
(c) $Au = 4f^{14} 5d^{10} 6s^1$

(ii) **Oxidation states** Elements show variable oxidation state in all the transition series. In 3*d* series, +2 and +3 oxidation states are common but 4*d* and 5*d* series elements are stable in higher oxidation state.

(iii) **Ionisation enthalpies** The first ionisation enthalpies in each series generally increase gradually as we move from left to right though some exceptions are observed in each series. The first ionisation enthalpies of some elements in the second (4*d*) series are higher while some of them have lower value than the elements of 3*d* series in the same vertical column.

However, the first ionisation enthalpies of third transition series (5*d* series) are higher than those of 3*d* and 4*d* series. This is because of weak shielding of nucleus of 4*f* electrons in the 5*d* series.

(iv) **Atomic size** Generally, ions of the same charge or atoms in a given series show progressive decrease are in radius with increasing atomic number though the decrease is quite small. But the size of the atoms of the 4*d* series is larger than the corresponding elements of the 3*d* series whereas those of corresponding elements of the 5*d* series are nearly the same as those of 4*d* series due to lanthanoid contraction.

Question 36 Write down the number of 3*d* electrons in each of the following ions : Ti^{2+}, V^{2+}, Cr^{3+}, Mn^{2+}, Fe^{2+}, Fe^{3+}, Co^{2+}, Ni^{2+} and Cu^{2+}. Indicate how would you expect the five 3*d* orbitals to be occupied for these hydrated ions? (octahedral).

◎ ***Thinking Process*** All the ions form complex of the type $[M(H_2O)_6]^{n+}$ water is a weak field ligand so in case of octahedral complex pairing takes place when each t_{2g} and e_g *orbital is singly occupied.* t_{2g} (d_{xy}, d_{yz}, d_{zx}) *set is of lower energy and* e_g $(d_{z^2}, d_{x^2-y^2})$ is of higher energy.

Sol.

	Ions	Configurations	Number of 3*d* electrons		Occupancy of 3*d*-orbitals
(i)	Ti^{2+}	$3d^2$	2	t_{2g}^2	e_g: [ ][ ] t_{2g}: [↑][↑][ ]
(ii)	V^{2+}	$3d^3$	3	t_{2g}^3	e_g: [ ][ ] t_{2g}: [↑][↑][↑]
(iii)	Cr^{3+}	$3d^3$	3	t_{2g}^3	e_g: [ ][ ] t_{2g}: [↑][↑][↑]
(iv)	Mn^{2+}	$3d^5$	5	$t_{2g}^3 e_g^2$	e_g: [↑][↑] t_{2g}: [↑][↑][↑]
(v)	Fe^{2+}	$3d^6$	6	$t_{2g}^4 e_g^2$	e_g: [↑][↑] t_{2g}: [↑↓][↑][↑]
(vi)	Fe^{3+}	$3d^5$	5	$t_{2g}^3 e_g^2$	e_g: [↑][↑] t_{2g}: [↑][↑][↑]
(vii)	Co^{2+}	$3d^7$	7	$t_{2g}^5 e_g^2$	e_g: [↑][↑] t_{2g}: [↑↓][↑↓][↑]
(viii)	Ni^{2+}	$3d^8$	8	$t_{2g}^6 e_g^2$	e_g: [↑][↑] t_{2g}: [↑↓][↑↓][↑↓]
(ix)	Cu^{2+}	$3d^9$	9	$t_{2g}^6 e_g^3$	e_g: [↑↓][↑] t_{2g}: [↑↓][↑↓][↑↓]

Question 37 Comment on the statement that elements of the first transition series possess many properties different from those of heavier transition elements.

Sol. The heavier transition elements belong to second (4*d*), third (5*d*) and fourth (6*d*) transition series. Their properties are expected to be different from the elements belonging to the first (3*d*) series due to the following reasons :

(i) Atomic radii of heavier transition elements (4*d* and 5*d* series) are larger than those of the corresponding elements of the first transition series though those of 4*d* and 5*d* series are very close to each other (due to lanthanoid contraction)

(ii) Ionisation enthalpies of 5*d* series are higher than the corresponding elements of 3*d* and 4*d* series.

(iii) Enthalpies of atomisation of 4*d* and 5*d* series are higher than the corresponding elements of the first series.

(iv) Melting and boiling points of heavier transition elements are greater than those of the first transition series due to stronger intermetallic bonding.

(v) First transition series elements show +2 and +3 oxidation states. Heavier transition state elements show higher oxidation states.

Question 38 What can be inferred from the magnetic moment values of the following complex species?

Example	Magnetic moment (BM)
$K_4[Mn(CN)_6]$	2.2
$[Fe(H_2O)_6]^{2+}$	5.3
$K_2[MnCl_4]$	5.9

◎ ***Thinking Process*** Magnetic moment is related to the number of unpaired electrons as

$\mu = \sqrt{n(n+2)}$ BM (When, n = number of unpaired electrons)

So find the number of unpaired electrons and thus, the oxidation state (having that number of unpaired electrons) of the metal atom present in the complex.

Now give the hybridisation and structure of complex.

Sol. Magnetic moment $(\mu) = \sqrt{n(n+2)}$ BM

For $n = 1$, $\mu = \sqrt{1(1+2)} = \sqrt{3} = 1.73$ BM

For $n = 2$, $\mu = \sqrt{2(2+2)} = \sqrt{8} = 2.83$ BM

For $n = 3$, $\mu = \sqrt{3(3+2)} = \sqrt{15} = 3.87$ BM

For $n = 4$, $\mu = \sqrt{4(4+2)} = \sqrt{24} = 4.90$ BM

For $n = 5$, $\mu = \sqrt{5(5+2)} = \sqrt{35} = 5.92$ BM

$K_4[Mn(CN)_6]$

In this compound, Mn is in +2 oxidation state, *i.e.,* given value of μ (2.2 BM) indicates the presence of one unpaired electron. Hence, when CN^- ligands approach Mn^{2+} ion, the electrons in 3*d* pair up. Thus, CN^- is a strong field ligand. Hybridization involved is d^2sp^3 forming inner orbital octahedral complex.

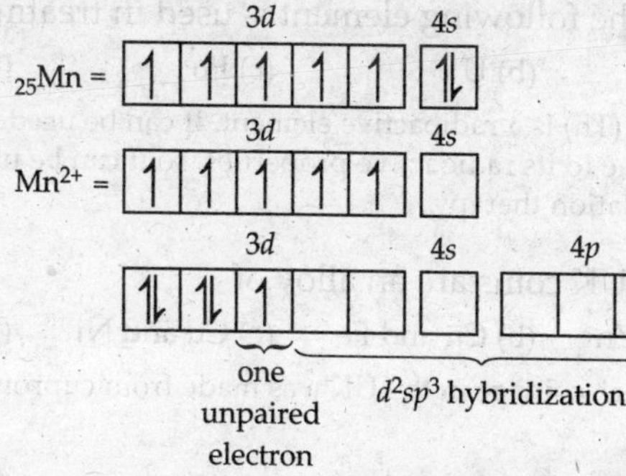

$[Fe(H_2O)_6]^{2+}$ In this compound Fe is in +2 state. Given, $\mu = 5.3$ BM shows that there are four unpaired electrons. This means that the electrons in 3*d* do not pair up when the ligands, H_2O molecules, approach. Hence, H_2O is a weak ligand. To accommodate the electrons donated by H_2O molecules, the hybridization is sp^3d^2. Hence, it will be an outer orbital octahedral complex.

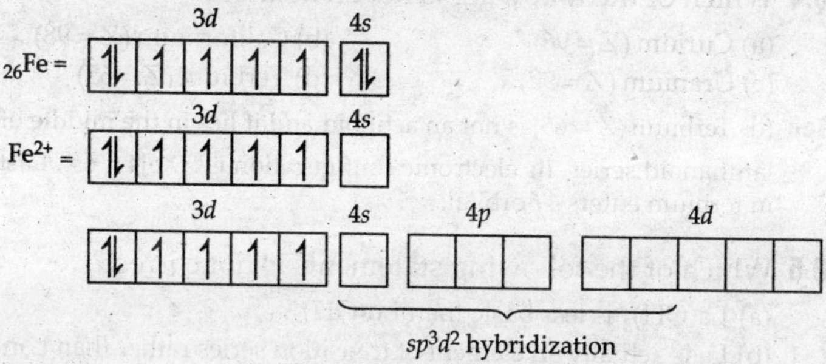

$K_2[MnCl_4]$ In this compound, Mn is in +2 state (Mn^{+2}). $\mu = 5.9$ BM shows the presence of five unpaired electrons. Hence, the hybridization involved will be sp^3 and the complex will be tetrahedral.

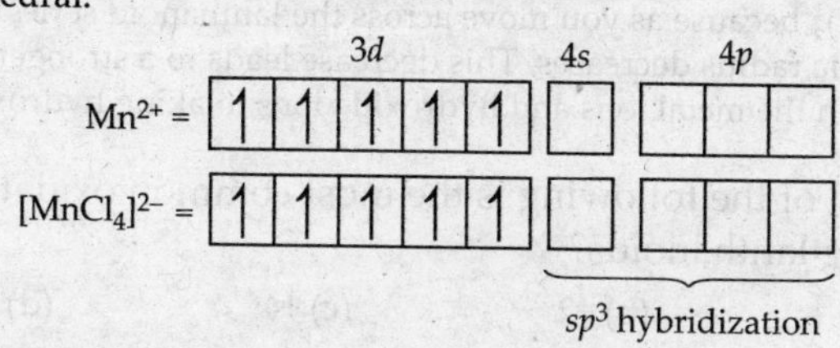

DIKSHA APP *Questions*

Multiple Choice Questions

Q.1 Which of the following element is used in treatment of cancer?

(a) Th (b) U (c) Pu (d) Np

Sol. (a) Thorium (Th) is a radioactive element. It can be used in cancer treatment due to its radioactive properties, so it can be used in certain types of radiation therapy.

Q.2 The silver UK coins are an alloy of

(a) Cu and Zn (b) Cu and Fe (c) Cu and Ni (d) Cu and Al

Sol. (c) All "silver" coinage in the UK was made from cupronickel or Copper and nickel.

Q.3 Among the following actinide pairs, the maximum oxidation states is shown by

(a) U and Np (b) Np and Pu (c) Pu and Th (d) U and Pa

Sol. (b) Np and Pu shows the oxidation state of +7 which is maximum.

Q.4 Which of the following is not an actinoid?

(a) Curium (Z = 96) (b) Californium (Z = 98)
(c) Uranium (Z = 92) (d) Terbium (Z = 65)

Sol. (d) Terbium (Z = 65) is not an actinoid and it lies in the middle of the lanthanoid series. Its electronic configuration is : $[Xe]4f^9 6s^2$. Last electron in terbium enters $4f$ orbital.

Q.5 Which of the following statements is not correct?

(a) $La(OH)_3$ is less basic than $Lu(OH)_3$.

(b) La is actually an element of transition series rather than Lanthanoids.

(c) Atomic radius of Zr and Hf is same.

(d) In Lanthanoid series, the ionic radius of Lu^{3+} is smallest.

Sol. (a) Lanthanum hydroxide $La(OH)_3$ is more basic than Lutetium hydroxide $Lu(OH)_3$ because as you move across the lanthanoid series from La to Lu, the ionic radius decreases. This decrease leads to a stronger attraction between the metal ions and hydroxide ions, making hydroxides less basic.

Q.6 Which of the following is the most common oxidation state among lanthanoids?

(a) +3 (b) +2 (c) +4 (d) +5

Sol. (a) Lanthanoids commonly exhibit a stable +3 oxidation state because achieving this state involves removing two outer 6*s* electrons and one 4*f* electron, which is energetically favorable. The +3 state is preferred from others due to the significant energy required to remove additional electrons from the 4*f* subshell, as these electrons are more tightly bound compared to the 6*s* electrons. This energy difference makes the +3 oxidation state more stable and common among the lanthanoids.

Q.7 Name the gas that can readily decolourise acidified $KMnO_4$ solution?

(a) CO_2 (b) SO_2 (c) NO_2 (d) P_2O_5

Sol. (b) SO_2 can decolourises acidified $KMnO_4$. This occurs because SO_2 acts as a reducing agent and reduces the purple permanganate ions (MnO_4^-) in $KMnO_4$ to colourless Mn^{2+} ions, causing the solution to lose its purple colour.

$$\underset{\text{Potassium permanganate}}{2K\overset{+7}{Mn}O_4(s)} + \underset{\text{Sulphur dioxide}}{5SO_2(g)} + \underset{\text{Water}}{2H_2O(l)} \longrightarrow \underset{\text{Potassium sulphate}}{K_2SO_4(s)} + \underset{\text{Manganese sulphate}}{2\overset{+2}{Mn}SO_4(s)} + \underset{\text{Sulphuric acid}}{2H_2SO_4(l)}$$

Q.8 In chromite ore, the oxidation number of iron and chromium are respectively

(a) +3, +2 (b) +3, +6 (c) +2, +6 (d) +2, +3

Sol. (d) In chromite ore ($FeCr_2O_4$) the oxidation number of iron is +2 and the oxidation number of chromium is +3. This is determined by the fact that the overall charge of the chromite ion is neutral, with the iron and chromium balancing the charge of the oxygen atoms.

Q.9 Among the following pairs of ions, the lower oxidation state in aqueous solution is more stable than other, in

(a) Tl^+, Tl^{3+} (b) Cu^+, Cu^{2+} (c) Cr^{2+}, Cr^{3+} (d) V^{2+}, VO^{2+}

Sol. (a) In aqueous solution, Tl^+ is more stable than Tl^{3+} due to inert pair effect. In this effect the valence *s* electron (in the 6 s orbital) are less available for bonding because they are held more tightly due to poor shielding by the inner *d* and *f* electrons. This makes the +1 oxidation state more stable as compared to the +3 oxidation state, where the *s* electron are involved, leading to increased energy and in stability. Electronic configuration of the species involved are

$Tl = [Xe]4f^{14}5d^{10}6s^2 6p^1$

$Tl^+ = [Xe]4f^{14}5d^{10}6s^2$

$Tl^{3+} = [Xe]4f^{14}5d^{10}$

Q.10 Magnetic moment of 2.84 BM is given by:

(a) Cr^{2+} (b) Co^{2+} (c) Ni^{2+} (d) Ti^{3+}

Sol. (c) The electronic configuration of the given ions is :

Ni^{2+} = [Ar] $3d^8 4s^0$ (two unpaired electron)

Ti^{3+} = [Ar] $3d^1 4s^0$ (one unpaired electron)

Cr^{3+} = [Ar] $3d^3$ (three unpaired electrons)

Co^{2+} = [Ar] $3d^7 4s^0$ (three unpaired electrons)

Magnetic moment (μ) = $\sqrt{n(n+2)}$ BM where,

n = number of unpaired electrons

μ = 2.84 (given)

$$2.84 = \sqrt{n(n+2)} \text{ B.M,}$$

$$(2.84)^2 = n(n+2)$$

$$8 = n^2 + 2n$$

$$n^2 + 2n - 8 = 0$$

Solving the equation

$$n^2 + 4n - 2n - 8 = 0$$

$$n(n+4) - 2(n+4) = 0$$

$$n = 2$$

Since, Ni^{2+} has two unpaired electrons, so its magnetic moment is equal to 2.83 BM.

Q.11 Which of the following is not regarded as *d*-block element?

(a) Y (b) Rf (c) Db (d) Cn

Sol. (d) $Cn = [Rn]5f^{14}6d^{10}7s^2$

Cn (Copernicium) is not considered a *d*-block element because it has completely filled *d*-orbital, so it is not considered as a transition element.

Q.12 Which of the following ion has the electronic configuration $3d^6$?

(a) Ni^{3+} (b) Mn^{3+} (c) Fe^{2+} (d) Co^{2+}

Sol. (c) Ni^{3+} has electronic configuration of [Ar] $3d^7$.

Mn^{3+} has electronic configuration of [Ar] $3d^4$.

Fe^{2+} has electronic configuration of [Ar] $3d^6$.

Co^{2+} has electronic configuration of [Ar] $3d^7$.

Fe^{2+} has electronic configuration of $3d^6$.

Q.13 What is the atomic no of Osmium?

(a) 73 (b) 74 (c) 75 (d) 76

Sol. (d) Osmium is a chemical element with symbol Os and atomic number 76.

Q.14 What is the atomic no of Zirconium?

(a) 39 (b) 40 (c) 41 (d) 42

Sol. (b) Zirconium is a chemical element with symbol Zr and atomic number 40.

☐ Short Answer Type

Q.1 What happens when acidified $KMnO_4$ reacts with (in acidic medium).

(i) H_2S

(ii) Oxalic acid

(iii) KNO_2

Sol. (i) When acidified $KMnO_4$ reacts with H_2S in acidic medium:

$KMnO_4$ acts as oxidising agent and oxidises H_2S to sulphur.

The redox reactions are as follows:

$$MnO_4^- + 8H^+ + 5e^- \longrightarrow Mn^{2+} + 4H_2O] \times 2$$

$$H_2S \longrightarrow 2H^+ + S + 2e^-] \times 5$$

The overall reaction is as follows:

$$2MnO_4^- + 5H_2S + 6H^+ \longrightarrow 2Mn^{2+} + 5S + 8H_2O$$

(ii) When acidified $KMnO_4$ reacts with oxalic acid in acidic medium:

Acidified $KMnO_4$ oxidises oxalate to carbon dioxide. The redox reactions are:

$$\overset{+3}{C}_2O_4^{2-} \longrightarrow 2\overset{+4}{C}O_2 + 2e^-] \times 5$$

$$5e^- + \overset{+7}{Mn}O_4^- + 8H^+ \longrightarrow Mn^{2+} + 4H_2O] \times 2$$

Reaction of acidified permanganate solution with oxalic acid:

$$2MnO_4^- + 16H^+ + 5C_2O_4^{2-} \longrightarrow 2Mn^{2+} + 8H_2O + 10CO_2$$

(iii) When acidified $KMnO_4$ reacts with KNO_2 in acidic medium:

Acidified potassium permanganate oxidises nitrite ion to nitrate ion and reduces itself into manganese (II) by the following reactions.

The redox reactions are :

$$MnO_4^- + 8H^+ + 5e \longrightarrow Mn^{2+} + 4H_2O] \times 2$$

$$NO_2^- + H_2O \longrightarrow NO_3^- + 2H^+ + 2e^-] \times 5$$

$$5NO_2^- + 2MnO_4^- + 6H^+ \longrightarrow 2Mn^{2+} + 5NO_3^- + 3H_2O$$

Q.2 The melting and boiling points of Zn, Cd and Hg are low. Why?

Sol. In Zn, Cd and Hg, all the electrons in *d*-subshell are paired. Hence, the metallic bonds present in them are weak. That is why they have low melting and boiling points.

☐ Long Answer Type

Q.1 Answer the following questions.

(a) Describe how potassium permangnate is made from pyrolusite. Write the chemical equations for the reactions involved.

(b) What is Misch Metal? Give it's one use.

(c) Why many transition elements and their compound can act as a good catalysts.

Sol. (a) Preparation of $KMnO_4$ Potassium permanganate is prepared by the fusion of pyrolusite (MnO_2) with an alkali metal hydroxide and an oxidising agent like KNO_3. It forms dark green, K_2MnO_4 which disproportionates in a neutral or acidic solution to give permanganate.

(i) $2MnO_2 + 4KOH + O_2 \xrightarrow{KNO_3} 2K_2MnO_4 + 2H_2O$

(ii) $3MnO_4^{2-} + 4H^+ \longrightarrow 2MnO_4^- + MnO_2 + 2H_2O$

or $3K_2MnO_4 + 2H_2SO_4 \longrightarrow \underset{\text{Potassium permanganate}}{2KMnO_4} + 2K_2SO_4 + MnO_2 + 2H_2O$

(b) Misch metal is an alloy of Ln, Fe, S, C, Ca, Al which is used in making bullets, shells, lighter flints, etc.

(c) Transition metal ions show variable oxidation states, so they can act as effective catalysts. Also, transition metals have large surface and can form an intermediate by bonding to the reactants, which leads to formation of products.

Q.2 Answer the following questions.

(a) Out of Ag_2SO_4, CuF_2, MgF_2 and CuCl which compound will be coloured and why?

(b) Explain

(i) CrO_4^{2-} is a strong oxidising agent while MnO_4^{2-} is not.

(ii) Zr and Hf have identical sizes.

(iii) The lowest oxidation state of manganese in basic while the highest in acidic.

(iv) Mn (II) shows maximum paramagnetic character amongst the divalent ions of the first transition series.

Sol. (a) In Ag_2SO_4, silver is in the +1 oxidation state (Ag^+), which has a filled *d*-orbital (d^{10}) and does not exhibit colour.

Ag : [Kr] $4d^{10} 5s^1$ $\quad$ Ag^+ : [Kr] $4d^{10} 5s^0$

In CuF_2 copper is in the +2 oxidation state (Cu^{2+}). This oxidation state results in a partially filled 3*d* subshell ($3d^9$) with an unpaired electron, which can absorb visible light and thus show colour. Cu^{2+} compounds are often coloured due to *d-d* transition.

Cu : [Ar] $3d^{10} 4s^1$ $\quad$ Cu^{+2} : [Ar] $3d^9$

Magnesium in MgF_2 is in the +2 oxidation state (Mg^{2+}), with a filled $2p$ subshell and it has no d-orbital to show transitions to absorb visible light, so it is colourless.

Mg : $1s^2 2s^2 2p^6 3s^2$ $\quad$ Mg^{2+} : $1s^2 2s^2 2p^6$

In CuCl, copper is in the +1 oxidation state (Cu^+). This oxidation state also has a filled $3d$ orbital ($3d^{10}$) and does not exhibit colour.

Cu : [Ar] $3d^{10} 4s^1$ $\quad$ Cu^{1+} : [Ar] $3d^{10}$

(b) (i) CrO_4^{2-} (chromate ion) is a strong oxidising agent because chromium is in its highest oxidation state, *i.e.* +6. It can be easily reduced to +3, showing high oxidising power. In contrast, MnO_4^{2-} is not a strong oxidising agent because manganese is in +4 oxidation state and it is not in its highest +7 oxidation state. So, it is less effective at accepting electrons and does not show high oxidising power.

(ii) Zr and Hf have identical size due to lanthanoid contraction. In Hf, the attraction of nucleus on outer shell electrons (effective nuclear charge) increase, due to poor shielding of elctrons in the f-subshell. This leads to the decrease in size of Hf and size of Zr and Hf becomes identical.

(iii) The lowest oxidation state of manganese is +2. In this state, manganese (Mn^{2+}) is basic. It tends to lose electrons to increase its oxidation state, which aligns with its basic nature. For example, $Mn(OH)_2$ is basic in nature. The highest oxidation state of manganese is +7. In this state, manganese (MnO_4^-, permanganate) is acidic because it has a strong tendency to accept electrons (be reduced) rather than lose any more. This reflects its acidic behaviour in acidic solutions.

(iv) Mn^{2+} shows maximum paramagnetic character among the divalent cations of first row transition series because Mn^{2+} has maximum number of unpaired electrons in the half-filled $3d$ orbital (5 unpaired electrons).

Element	Symbol	Divalent Cation	Electronic Configuration of Cation	Number of Unpaired Electrons
Scandium	Sc	Sc^{2+}	[Ar] $3d^1$	1
Titanium	Ti	Ti^{2+}	[Ar] $3d^2$	2
Vanadium	V	V^{2+}	[Ar] $3d^3$	3
Chromium	Cr	Cr^{2+}	[Ar] $3d^4$	4
Manganese	Mn	Mn^{2+}	[Ar] $3d^5$	5
Iron	Fe	Fe^{2+}	[Ar] $3d^6$	4
Cobalt	Co	Co^{2+}	[Ar] $3d^7$	3
Nickel	Ni	Ni^{2+}	[Ar] $3d^8$	2
Copper	Cu	Cu^{2+}	[Ar] $3d^9$	1
Zinc	Zn	Zn^{2+}	[Ar] $3d^{10}$	0

Coordination Compounds

CHAPTER 05

Important Points

01 **Coordination compounds** are those in which a central metal atom or ion is attached with a fixed number of groups or molecules (ligands) through **coordinate bonds.** In other words, these compounds contain complex ions.

02 **Double salts** are formed when two or more salts are added to form a stable compound. They dissociate into simple ions completely when dissolved in water.

03 A molecule or ion which donates electron pairs is called **ligand.**

04 The spatial arrangement of ligand atoms directly attached to the central atom is called **coordination polyhedron.**

05 The number of ligating groups or coordinating atoms in a ligand is called **denticity.**

06 Ligands are of various types :

(a) **Unidentate ligand** Contain single donor atom. Examples, Cl^-, H_2O, NH_3 etc.

(b) **Didentate ligand** Contain two donor atoms. Examples, $C_2O_4^{2-}$, en, etc.

(c) **Polydentate ligand** Contain several donor atoms. Examples, EDTA (ethylene diamine tetraacetic acid).

(d) **Ambidentate ligand** Contain two different donor atoms, but either one of them ligates. Examples, SCN^-, NO_2^-, etc.

(e) **Chelate ligand** When a di- or polydentate ligand uses its two or more donor atoms simultaneously to bind a single metal ion, it is said to be a chelate ligand.

07 Coordination number (CN) of a metal atom/ion represents the number of ligands attached to it.

08 **Homoleptic complex** has only one type of ligands linked to the central metal atom/ion.

09 **Heteroleptic complex** has more than one type of ligands linked to the central metal atom/ion.

10 The nature of bonding in coordination compounds may be explained on the basis of Werner's theory, valence bond theory and crystal field theory.

11 Octahedral complexes show both geometrical as well as optical isomerism.

12 **Isomers** are two or more coordination compounds which have the same molecular formula but different arrangement of atoms. There are two types of isomerism :

(i) **Structural isomerism** (They have different bonds)

(a) **Linkage isomerism** Isomers having the same molecular formula but different linking atoms, due to the presence of ambidentate ligands. For example, $[Co(NH_3)_5(NO_2)]^{2+}$ and $[Co(NH_3)_5(ONO)]^{2+}$.

(b) **Coordination isomerism** This type of isomerism arises from the interchange of ligands between cationic and anionic entities of different metal ions present in a complex. For example, $[Co(NH_3)_6][Cr(C_2O_4)_2]$ and $[Cr(NH_3)_6][Co(C_2O_4)_3]$.

(c) **Ionisation isomerism** In this type of isomerism, the counter ion in a complex salt is itself a potential ligand and can displace a ligand which can becomes a counter ion. For example, $[Co(NH_3)_5(SO_4)]Br$ and $[Co(NH_3)_5Br]SO_4$.

(d) **Solvate isomerism** Solvate isomers (hydrate isomers) differ by whether or not a solvent molecules is directly bonded to the metal ion or merely present as free solvent molecules in the crystal lattice. For example, $[Cr(H_2O)_5Cl]Cl_2 \cdot H_2O$ and $[Cr(H_2O)_6]Cl_3$.

(ii) **Stereoisomerism** (They have same chemical formula and chemical bonds but they have a different spatial arrangement.)

(a) **Geometric isomerism** This occurs due to different possible geometric arrangements of the ligands. For example, *cis-/trans-* and *fac-/mer-* isomers.

(b) **Optical isomerism** Optical isomers are mirror images that cannot be superimposed on one another. These are called **enantiomers** and they are chiral. The two forms are called **dextro** (*d*) and **laevo** (*l*), depending upon the direction in which they rotate the plane polarised light in a polarimeter (*d* rotates to the right, *l* to the left).

13 The complex having d^2sp^3 hybridisation has inner *d*-orbital involved in the hybridisation and this complex is called **inner orbital** or **low spin or spin paired complex.**

The complex having sp^3d^2 hybridisation has outer *d*-orbital involved in the hybridisation and this complex is called **outer orbitals** or **high spin or spin free complex.**

14 The splitting of the degenerate *d*-orbitals of the coordination compounds into three orbitals of lower energy, t_{2g} and two orbitals of higher energy, e_g due to the presence of ligands in a definite geometry (which causes ligand electron-metal electron repulsions) is called as **crystal field splitting.** The energy associated with it is called **crystal field splitting energy (CFSE)** and it is denoted by Δ_0. This can be shown by :

(a)

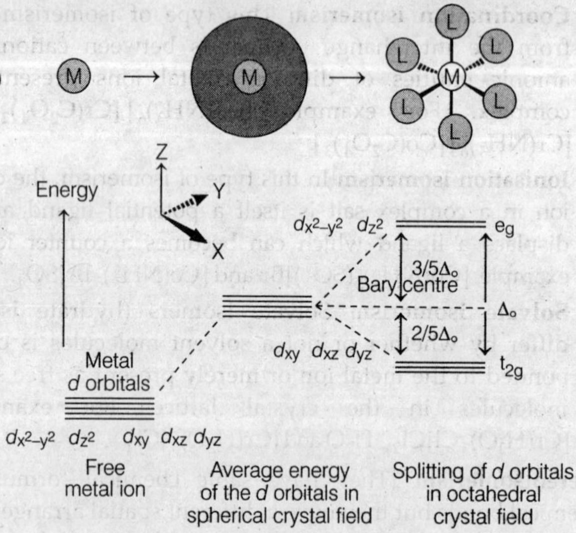

▲ *d* orbital splitting in an octachedral crystal field

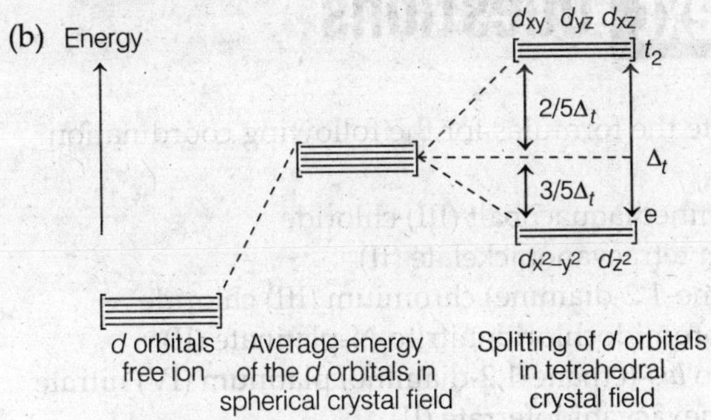

▲ *d* orbital splitting in a tetrahedral crystal field

15 (a) The ligands with a small value of CFSE (Δ_0) are called **weak field ligands.** For these ligands, $\Delta_0 < P$ (P = Pairing energy). The fourth electron enters one of the e_g orbital giving $t_{2g}^3 e_g^1$. They form high spin complexes.

(b) The ligands with large value of CFSE (Δ_0) are called **strong field ligands.** For these ligands, $\Delta_0 > P$, the fourth electron enters t_{2g} orbitals giving $t_{2g}^4 e_g^0$. They form low spin complexes.

16 The arrangement of ligands in order of their increasing field strengths, *i.e.*, increasing crystal field splitting energy (CFSE) values is called **spectrochemical series.**

$$I^- < Br^- < SCN^- < Cl^- < S^{2-} < F^- < OH^- < ox < H_2O < NCS^- < EDTA^{4-} < NH_3 < en < CN^- < CO.$$

17 The relative stabilities of coordination complexes can be compared in terms of stability constant (K), also denoted by β.

For a reaction, $M^{n+} + nL^{x^-} \longrightarrow [ML_n]^{b+}$

$$K = \frac{[ML_n]^{b+}}{[M^{n+}][L^{x^-}]^n}$$

18 In metal carbonyls, the oxidation state of metal is zero.

19 Both sigma as well as pi-bonds are present between the metal and CO in metal carbonyls.

Intext Questions

Question 1 Write the formulas for the following coordination compounds :

(i) Tetraamminediaquacobalt (III) chloride
(ii) Potassium tetracyanonickelate (II)
(iii) *Tris*-(ethane-1,2-diamine) chromium (III) chloride
(iv) Amminebromidochloridonitrito-N-platinate (II)
(v) Dichlorido *bis*-(ethane-1,2-diamine) platinum (IV) nitrate
(vi) Iron (III) hexacyanidoferrate (II)

Thinking Process

(i) If complex name starts with metal, it is an anionic complex and if starts with ligand name or number, the complex is cationic.

(ii) The formula of the cationic complex is written as [metal symbol + ligand (with their number as subscript)] counter ion satisfying the valency of metal or oxidation state of complex.

(iii) The formula of the anionic complex is written as counter ion satisfying valency of metal [metal symbol + ligand (with their number as subscript)]

Sol. (i) $\underbrace{\text{Tetraamminediaqua}}_{\text{Ligand}}\ \underbrace{\text{Cobalt(III)}}_{\text{Metal}}\ \underbrace{\text{Chloride}}_{\text{Counter ion}}$

$$\overset{\text{III}}{[Co(NH_3)_4(H_2O)_2]Cl_x}$$

To find the value of x, we have to find the charge on the complex.

$$\overset{\text{III}}{[Co(NH_3)_4(H_2O)_2]^{x+}}$$

$$+3 + 4 \times 0 + 2 \times 0 = x \Rightarrow x = +3$$

So, the formula of the complex is $[Co(NH_3)_4(H_2O)_2]Cl_3$.

(ii) $\underbrace{\text{Potassium}}_{\text{Counter ion}}\ \underbrace{\text{Tetracyano}}_{\text{Ligand}}\ \underbrace{\text{Nickelate(II)}}_{\text{Metal}}$

$$K_x[\overset{\text{II}}{Ni}(CN)_4]$$

To find the value of x, find the charge on the complex.

$$[Ni(CN)_4]^{x-} \quad (\text{as } K^+ \text{ is positive})$$

$$+2 + (-1) \times 4 = -x \Rightarrow -x = -2 \text{ or } x = +2$$

So, the formula of the complex is $K_2[Ni(CN)_4]$.

Similarly

(iii) $[Cr(en)_3]Cl_3$

(iv) $[Pt(NH_3)BrCl(NO_2)]^-$

(v) $[PtCl_2(en)_2](NO_3)_2$

(vi) $Fe_4[Fe(CN)_6]_3$

Question 2 Write down the IUPAC names of the following coordination compounds :

(i) $[Co(NH_3)_6]Cl_3$ (ii) $[Co(NH_3)_5Cl]Cl_2$
(iii) $K_3[Fe(CN)_6]$ (iv) $K_3[Fe(C_2O_4)_3]$
(v) $K_2[PdCl_4]$ (vi) $[Pt(NH_3)_2Cl(NH_2CH_3)]Cl$

Thinking Process

(i) To write the name of cationic complex, the general formula is
ligand number + ligand names (alphabetically) + metal name + metal oxidation state in parenthesis + counter ion name (counter ion is present outside the coordination sphere.)

(ii) To write the name of anionic complex, the general formula is
counter ion + number of ligands + ligand names (alphabetically) + metal name + 'ate' + (oxidation state of metal).

Sol. (i)

$$[Co(NH_3)_6]Cl_3$$

Metal atom | Ligand | Ligand number | Counter ion

Let the oxidation state of Co be x.

$$x + (0)6 + (-1) \times 3 = 0$$
$$x + 0 - 3 = 0 \Rightarrow x = +3$$

So, the name of this complex is hexaamminecobalt (III) chloride.

(ii) $[Co(NH_3)_5Cl]Cl_2$

$$x + (0) \times 5 + (-1) \times 1 + (-1) \times 2 = 0$$
$$x + 0 - 3 = 0 \Rightarrow x = +3$$

So, the name of the complex is pentaamminechloridocobalt (III) chloride.

(iii)

$$K_3[Fe(CN)_6]$$

Counter ion | Metal | Ligand

Let the oxidation state of Fe is x.

$$(+1)3 + x + (-1)6 = 0$$
$$+3 + x - 6 = 0$$
$$x = +3$$

So, the name of the complex is potassium hexacyanoferrate (III).

(iv)

$$K_3[Fe(C_2O_4)_3]$$

Counter ion | Metal | Ligand

Let the oxidation state of Fe is x.

$$(+1)\,3 + x + (-2)\,3 = 0$$

[$\because$ Oxalate ion ($C_2O_4^{2-}$) bears – 2 charge.]

$$3 + x - 6 = 0$$
$$x = +3$$

So, the name of the complex is potassium trioxalatoferrate (III).

(v) $K_2[PdCl_4]$

Counter ion → K_2; Metal atom → Pd; Ligand → Cl_4

Let the oxidation state of Pd is x.

$$(+1)\,2 + x + (-1)\,4 = 0$$
$$2 + x - 4 = 0$$
$$x = +2$$

So, the name of the complex is potassium tetrachloridopalladate (II).

(vi) $[Pt(NH_3)_2Cl(NH_2CH_3)]Cl$

Metal → Pt; Ligands → $(NH_3)_2Cl(NH_2CH_3)$; Counter ion → Cl

Let the oxidation state of Pt is x.

$$x + (0)\,2 + (-1) \times 1 + (0) + (-1) \times 1 = 0$$
$$x + 0 - 1 + 0 - 1 = 0$$
$$x - 2 = 0$$
$$x = +2$$

So, the name of the complex is diamminechlorido(methylamine) platinum (II) chloride.

Mistake Alert One can make a mistake of not writing the oxidation state of metal in parenthesis.

Question 3 Indicate the types of isomerism exhibited by the following complexes and draw the structures for these isomers :

(i) $K[Cr(H_2O)_2(C_2O_4)_2]$ (ii) $[Co(en)_3]Cl_3$

(iii) $[Co(NH_3)_5(NO_2)](NO_3)_2$ (iv) $[Pt(NH_3)(H_2O)Cl_2]$

Thinking Process

(i) Complexes of the type $[MA_2(AA)_2]$, $(MABC_2)$ (where, M = central metal, A, B and C are unidentate ligands and AA is bidentate ligand) exhibit geometrical isomerism.

(ii) Complexes of the type $[MA_2(AA)_2]$, $[M(AA)_3]$ exhibit optical isomerism.

(iii) Complexes having presence of ambidentate ligands like NO_2, SCN exhibit linkage isomerism, as such ligands have two coordination sites. Ionization isomers give different ions when subjected to ionisation.

Sol. (i) **$K[Cr(H_2O)_2(C_2O_4)_2]$** or **$K[Cr(H_2O)_2(ox)_2]$** (where, ox = oxalate ion)

(a) It exists as geometrical isomers : *cis* and *trans* forms.

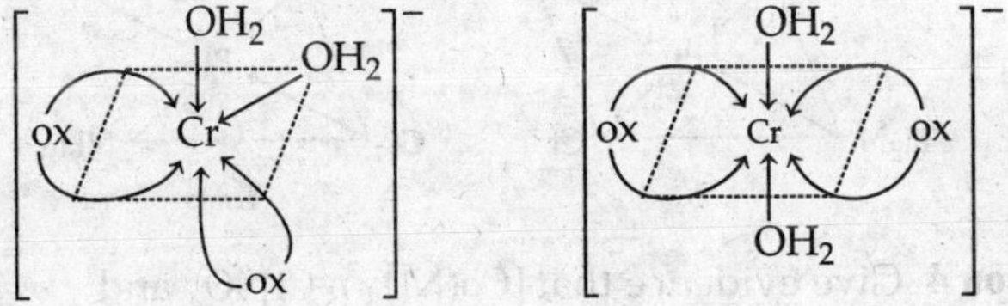

Cis *Trans*

(In *cis* form, the same groups occupy adjacent positions while in *trans* form, they are present at alternate/opposite positions.)

(b) The *cis* isomer can also exist as a pair of optical isomers (*i.e.*, *d*- and *l*- forms) (due to absence of plane of symmetry).

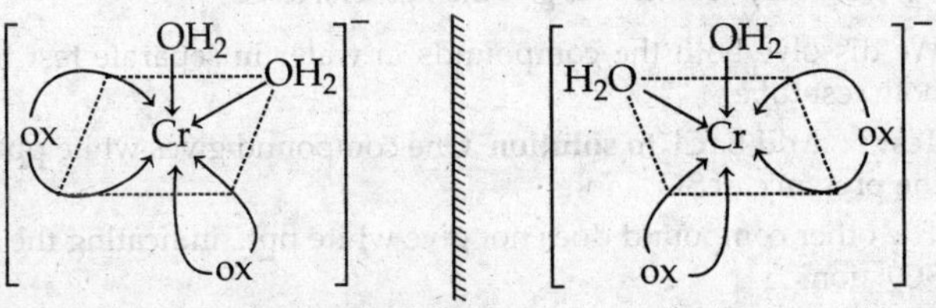

Mirror

(ii) **$[Co(en)_3]Cl_3$** It has two optical isomers (*i.e.* *d*-and *l*-forms)

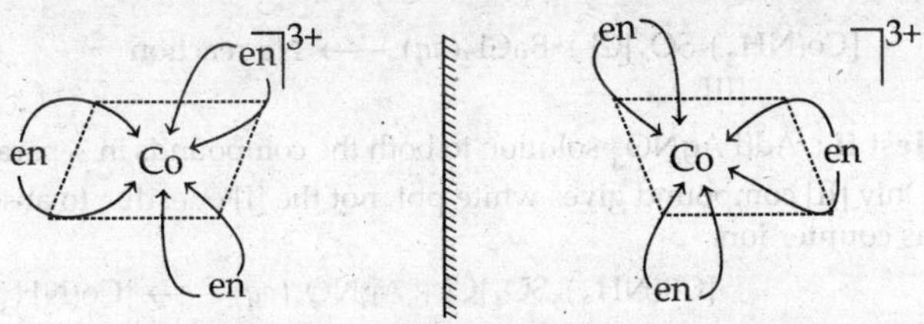

Mirror

(iii) **$[Co(NH_3)_5(NO_2)](NO_3)_2$**

It can exist as a pair of ionisation isomers as well as linkage isomers.

Ionisation isomers

$[Co(NH_3)_5(NO_2)](NO_3)_2$ and $[Co(NH_3)_5(NO_3)](NO_2)(NO_3)$

as they give different ions on ionisation.

$$[Co(NH_3)_5(NO_2)](NO_3)_2 \xrightarrow{\text{Ionisation}} [Co(NH_3)_5(NO_2)]^{2+} + 2NO_3^-$$

$$[Co(NH_3)_5(NO_3)](NO_2)(NO_3) \xrightarrow{\text{Ionisation}} [Co(NH_3)_5NO_3]^{2+} + NO_2^- + NO_3^-$$

Linkage isomers

$[Co(NH_3)_5(NO_2)](NO_3)_2$ and $[Co(NH_3)_5ONO](NO_3)_2$

(iv) **$[Pt(NH_3)(H_2O)Cl_2]$** It can exist as two geometrical isomers.

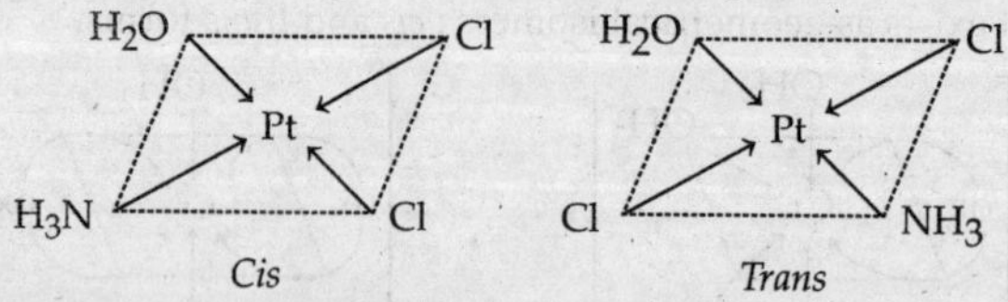

Question 4 Give evidence that $[Co(NH_3)_5Cl]SO_4$ and $[Co(NH_3)_5SO_4]Cl$ are ionisation isomers.

Thinking Process

(i) Ionisation isomers give different ions on ionisation and thus, give different reactions with a reagent.

(ii) Only counter ions give their general tests.

Sol. We dissolve both the compounds in water in separate test tubes. To the both test tube,

Test I : Add $BaCl_2$ to solution One compound gives white ppt., indicating the presence of SO_4^{2-} ions.

The other compound does not give white ppt., indicating the absence of SO_4^{2-} ions.

$$\underset{[I]}{[Co(NH_3)_5Cl]SO_4} + BaCl_2(aq) \longrightarrow [Co(NH_3)_5Cl]Cl_2 + \underset{\text{White ppt.}}{BaSO_4(s)}$$

$$\underset{[II]}{[Co(NH_3)_5SO_4]Cl} + BaCl_2(aq) \longrightarrow \text{No reaction}$$

Test II : Add $AgNO_3$ solution to both the compounds in separate test tubes Only [II] compound gives white ppt, not the [I] one, due to absence of Cl^- as counter ion.

$$\underset{[II]}{[Co(NH_3)_5SO_4]Cl} + AgNO_3(aq) \longrightarrow [Co(NH_3)_5SO_4]NO_3 + \underset{\text{White ppt.}}{AgCl(s)}$$

$$[Co(NH_3)_5Cl]SO_4 + AgNO_3(aq) \longrightarrow \text{No reaction}$$

These two tests prove that the given two compounds are a pair of ionisation isomers.

Question 5 Explain on the basis of valence bond theory that $[Ni(CN)_4]^{2-}$ ion with square planar structure is diamagnetic and the $[NiCl_4]^{2-}$ ion with tetrahedral geometry is paramagnetic.

Thinking Process

(i) Write the outer configuration of Ni and Ni^{2+} ions.

(ii) CN^- being strong field ligand, causes pairing whereas Cl^- does not.

(iii) Diamagnetic compounds have no unpaired electrons whereas in case of paramagnetic compounds unpaired electrons are present.

Sol.

	3d⁸					4s²	4p		
Outer configuration of $_{28}$Ni atom =	1l	1l	1l	1	1	1l			

	3d⁸					4s⁰			
Ni^{2+} ion =	1l	1l	1l	1	1				

(CN^- being strong field ligand paired up the *d*-electrons of metal atom.)

$[Ni(CN)_4]^{2-}$ ion =	1l	1l	1l	1l	××	××	××	××	
					CN^-	CN^-	CN^-	CN^-	

*dsp*² hybridisation

⇒ square planar structure

The complex ion is **diamagnetic** in nature as it has **no unpaired electrons.**

	3d⁸					4s²	4p		
Outer configuration of $_{28}$Ni atom =	1l	1l	1l	1	1	1l			

	3d⁸								
Ni^{2+} ion =	1l	1l	1l	1	1				

(Cl^- being weak field ligand, cannot cause pairing.)

$[NiCl_4]^{2-}$ =	1l	1l	1l	1	1	××	××	××	××
						Cl^-	Cl^-	Cl^-	Cl^-

*sp*³ hybridisation

⇒ tetrahedral geometry

$[NiCl_4]^{2-}$ ion is **paramagnetic** in nature as it has **two unpaired electrons.**

Mistake Alert One can make a mistake in confusing the hybridisation of square planar and tetrahedral complexes.
Tetrahedral geometry = sp^3 hybridisation.
Square planar geometry = dsp^2 hybridisation.
d-orbital is involved in square planar and not in tetrahedral geometry.

Question 6 $[NiCl_4]^{2-}$ is paramagnetic while $[Ni(CO)_4]$ is diamagnetic though both are tetrahedral. Why?

Thinking Process

(i) CO is a strong field ligand and Cl^- is a weak field ligand.

(ii) Same as in previous question.

Sol. In the complex $[NiCl_4]^{2-}$, Ni is in +2 oxidation state and has the configuration $3d^8 4s^0$. The Cl^- ion being a weak field ligand cannot pair the two unpaired electrons present in 3*d*-orbitals. This means that 3*d*-orbitals are not involved in hybridisation. Thus, the complex is sp^3 hybridised (tetrahedral) and is **paramagnetic** in nature.

Outer configuration of Ni atom = $3d^8\ 4s^2$

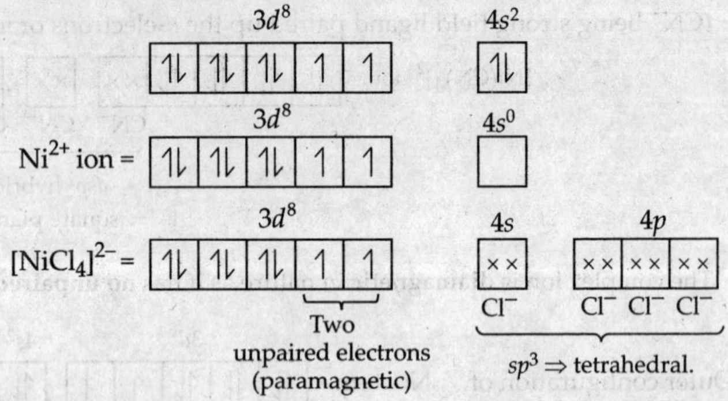

In the complex $[Ni(CO)_4]$, the oxidation state of nickel is zero and electronic configuration is $3d^8 4s^2$. In the presence of the ligand CO, the 4*s*-electrons shift to the two half-filled 3*d*-orbitals and make all the electrons paired. The valence 4*s* and 4*p*-orbitals are involved in hybridisation. Thus, the complex is tetrahedral but diamagnetic in nature.

Outer configuration of Ni atom = $3d^8\ 4s^2$.

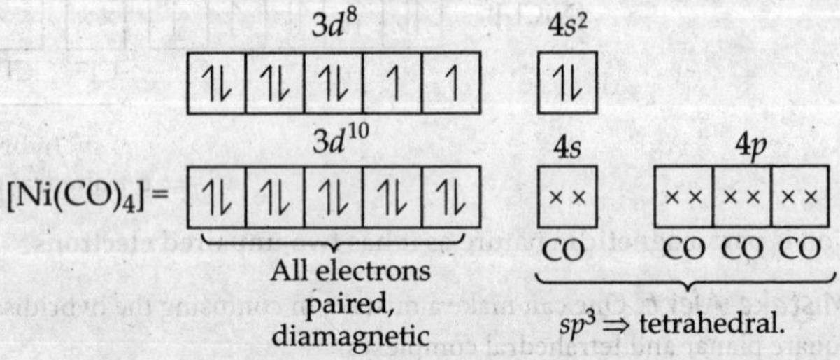

Question 7 $[Fe(H_2O)_6]^{3+}$ is strongly paramagnetic whereas $[Fe(CN)_6]^{3-}$ is weakly paramagnetic. Explain.

Thinking Process

(i) CN^- is a strong field ligand while H_2O is a weak field ligand.

(ii) Paramagnetism depends upon the number of unpaired electrons. Higher the number of unpaired electrons, more is the paramagnetic character.

Sol. Outer configuration of $_{26}Fe = 3d^6\ 4s^2$. In both the complexes Fe is present as Fe^{3+} ion. Fe^{3+} ion $= 3d^5\ 4s^0$

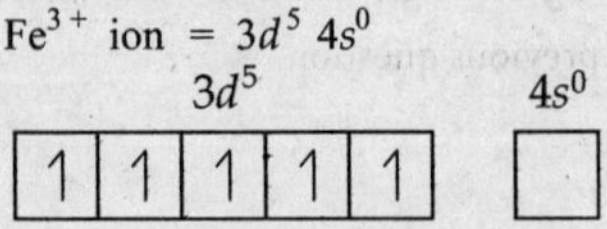

In the presence of CN^- (a strong field ligand) the $3d$-electrons pair up, leaving only one unpaired electron. The hybridisation is d^2sp^3 forming an inner orbital complex.

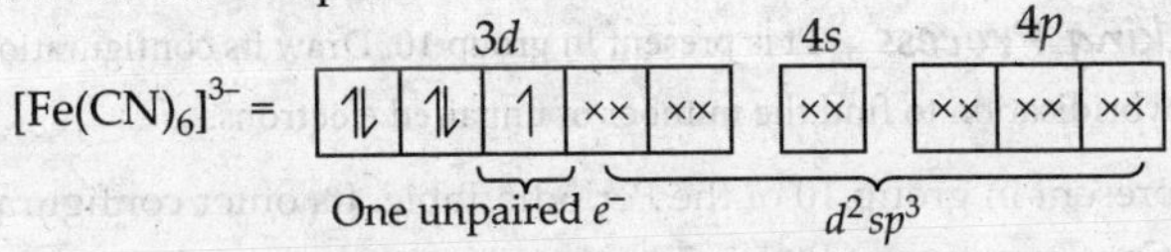

In the presence of H_2O, (a weak field ligand), $3d$-electrons do not pair up. The hybridization is sp^3d^2 forming an outer orbital complex containing five unpaired electrons. Hence, it is strongly paramagnetic.

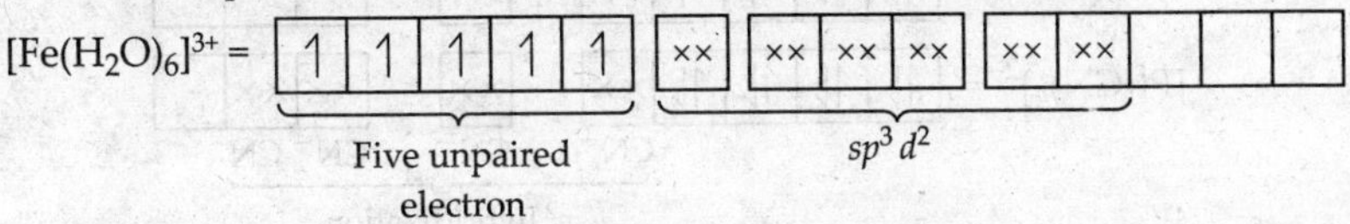

Question 8 Explain $[Co(NH_3)_6]^{3+}$ is an inner orbital complex whereas $[Ni(NH_3)_6]^{2+}$ is an outer orbital complex.

◎ ***Thinking Process*** In inner orbital complexes $(n-1)$ d-orbitals are used and in outer orbital complexes nd-orbitals are used for hybridisation. So, find the hybridisation of both the complexes.

Sol. In $[Co(NH_3)_6]^{3+}$, Co is present as Co^{3+} and has $3d^6$ configuration. In the presence of NH_3, the $3d$-electrons pair up leaving two d-orbitals empty to be involved in d^2sp^3 hybridisation forming inner orbital complex in the case of $[Co(NH_3)_6]^{3+}$.

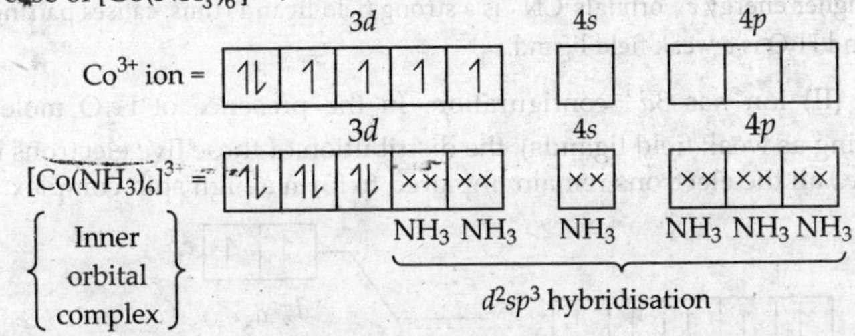

In $[Ni(NH_3)_6]^{2+}$, Ni is in +2 oxidation state and has $3d^8$ configuration.

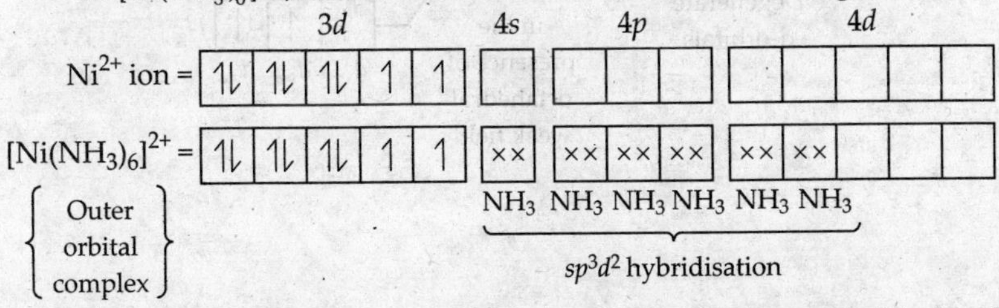

Since, $(n-1)$ d-orbitals are not available but the d-orbitals are used in bond formation *i.e.*, in hybridisation, so the complex is called outer orbital complex.

Question 9 Predict the number of unpaired electrons in the square planar $[Pt(CN)_4]^{2-}$ ion.

◎ ***Thinking Process*** $_{78}Pt$ is present in group 10. Draw its configuration and find hybridisation to find the number of unpaired electrons.

Sol. $_{78}Pt$ is present in group 10 of the Periodic Table. Its outer configuration is $5d^9 6s^1$. Configuration of Pt^{2+} is $5d^8$

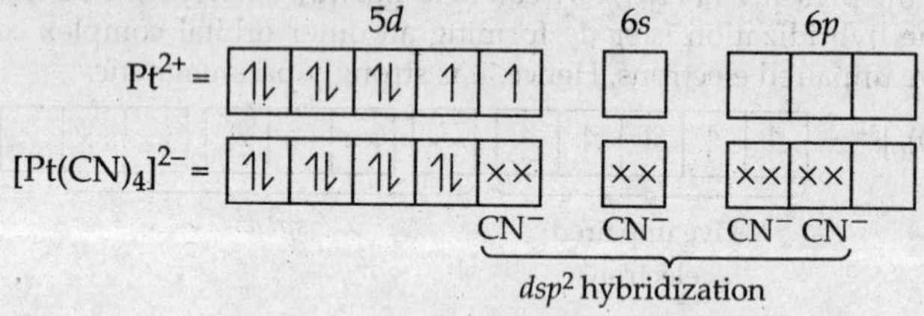

For square planar shape, the hybridisation is dsp^2. Hence, the unpaired electrons in $5d$-orbital pair up to make one d-orbital empty for dsp^2 hybridisation. Thus, there is **no unpaired electron.**

Question 10 The hexaaquamanganese (II) ion contains five unpaired electrons, while the hexacyano ion contains only one unpaired electron. Explain using crystal field theory.

◎ ***Thinking Process*** Because of the presence of six ligands the complex is octahedral and thus, d-orbitals split up into lower energy t_{2g} orbitals and higher energy e_g orbitals. CN^- is a strong field ligand (thus, causes pairing) and H_2O is a weak field ligand.

Sol. Mn (II) ion has $3d^5$ configuration. In the presence of H_2O molecules (acting as weak field ligands), the distribution of these five electrons is t_{2g}^3 e_g^2 i.e., all the electrons remain unpaired to form a high spin complex.

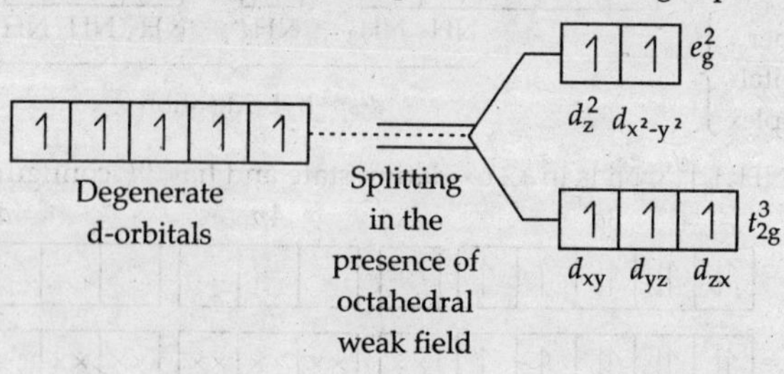

However, in the presence of CN^- (acting as strong field ligands), the distribution of these electrons is $t_{2g}^5 e_g^0$, *i.e.*, two t_{2g} orbitals contain paired electrons while the third t_{2g} orbital contains one unpaired electron. The complex formed is a low spin complex.

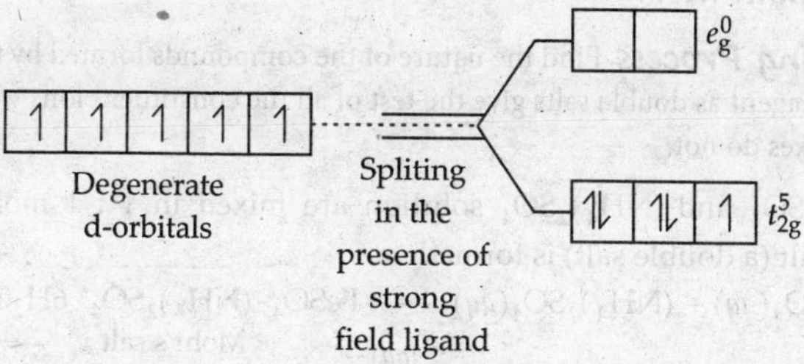

Exercises

Question 1 Explain the bonding in coordination compounds in terms of Werner's postulates.

Sol. Main postulates of Werner's theory are :

(i) In coordination compounds metals show two types of linkages (valencies)—primary and secondary.

(ii) The primary valencies are normally ionisable and are satisfied by negative ions.

(iii) The secondary valencies are non-ionisable. These are satisfied by neutral molecules or negative ions. The secondary valency is equal to the coordination number and is fixed for a metal.

(iv) The ions/groups bound by the secondary linkages to the metal have characteristic spatial arrangements corresponding to different coordination numbers.

e.g., Structure of $[CoCl_2(NH_3)_4]^+Cl^-$ is as follows :

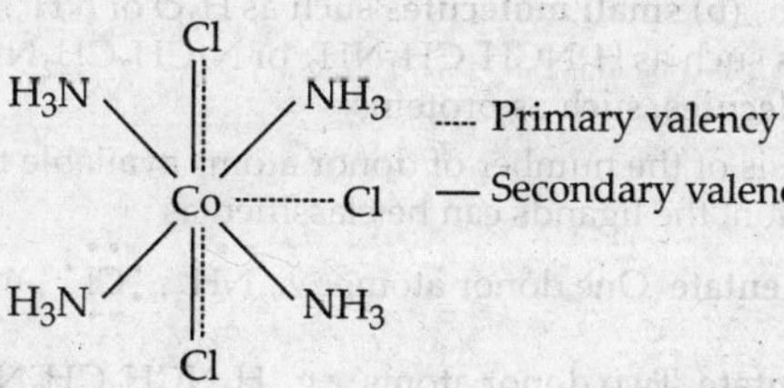

Question 2 $FeSO_4$ solution mixed with $(NH_4)_2SO_4$ solution in 1 : 1 molar ratio gives the test of Fe^{2+} ion but $CuSO_4$ solution mixed with aqueous ammonia in 1 : 4 molar ratio does not give the test of Cu^{2+} ion. Explain why?

◎ *Thinking Process* Find the nature of the compounds formed by the given reagent as double salts give the test of all the constituent ions whereas complexes do not.

Sol. When $FeSO_4$ and $(NH_4)_2SO_4$ solution are mixed in 1 : 1 molar ratio, Mohr's salt (a double salt) is formed.

$$FeSO_4(aq) + (NH_4)_2SO_4(aq) \longrightarrow \underset{\text{Mohr's salt}}{FeSO_4 \cdot (NH_4)_2SO_4 \cdot 6H_2O}$$

$$FeSO_4 \cdot (NH_4)_2SO_4 \cdot 6H_2O \overset{(aq)}{\rightleftharpoons} Fe^{2+}(aq) + 2NH_4^+(aq) + 2SO_4^{2-}(aq) + 6H_2O$$

Because Fe^{2+} ions are formed on dissolution of Mohr's salt, its aqueous solution gives the test of Fe^{2+} ions.

But when $CuSO_4(aq)$ is mixed with $NH_3(aq)$, complex formation takes place.

$$CuSO_4(aq) + NH_3(aq) \longrightarrow [Cu(NH_3)_4]SO_4$$

This complex does not produce Cu^{2+} ions on dissolution as Cu has now become a part of $[Cu(NH_3)_4]^{2+}$ complex ion, so, the solution of $CuSO_4$ and NH_3 does not give the test of Cu^{2+} ion.

Question 3 Explain with two examples each of the following : Coordination entity, ligand, coordination number, coordination polyhedron, homoleptic and heteroleptic.

Sol. (i) **Coordination entity** A central metal atom or ion bonded to a fixed number of molecules or ions (ligands) is known as coordination entity. For example $[CoCl_3(NH_3)_3]$, $[Ni(CO)_4]$, etc.

(ii) **Ligand** The ions or molecules bound to the central atom/ion in the coordination entity are called ligands. These may be (a) **simple ions** such as Cl^-, (b) **small molecules** such as H_2O or NH_3, (c) **large molecules** such as $H_2NCH_2CH_2NH_2$ or $N(CH_2CH_2NH_2)_3$ or even (d) **macromolecules**, such as proteins.

On the basis of the number of donor atoms available for coordination, the ligands can be classified as :

(a) **Unidentate** One donor atom, *e.g.*, $\ddot{N}H_3$, $:\ddot{\underset{..}{Cl}}:^-$, etc.

(b) **Bidentate** Two donor atoms, *e.g.*, $H_2NCH_2CH_2NH_2$ (ethane-1,2-diamine or en), $C_2O_4^{2-}$ (oxalate), etc.

(c) **Polydentate** More than two donor atoms, *e.g.*, $N(CH_2CH_2NH_2)_3$, EDTA, etc.

(iii) **Coordination number** The coordination number (CN) of a metal ion in a complex can be defined as the number of ligands or donor atoms to which the metal is directly bonded. *e.g.*, In $[PtCl_6]^{2-}$, CN of Pt – 6; In$[Ni(NH_3)_4]^{2+}$, CN of Ni = 4.

(iv) **Coordination polyhedron** The spatial arrangement of the ligand atoms which are directly attached to the central atom or ion is called coordination polyhedron about the central atom. Octahedral, square planar, tetrahedral are some common coordination polyhedra. *e.g.*, $[Co(NH_3)_6]^{3+}$ is octahedral; $[Ni(CO)_4]$ is tetrahedral; $[PtCl_4]^{2-}$ is square planar.

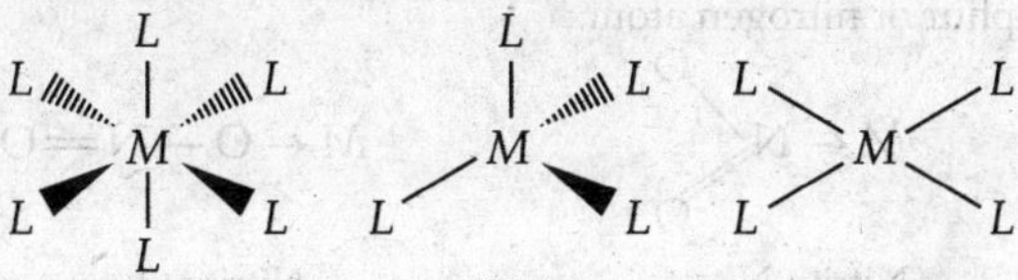

Octahedral Tetrahedral Square planar

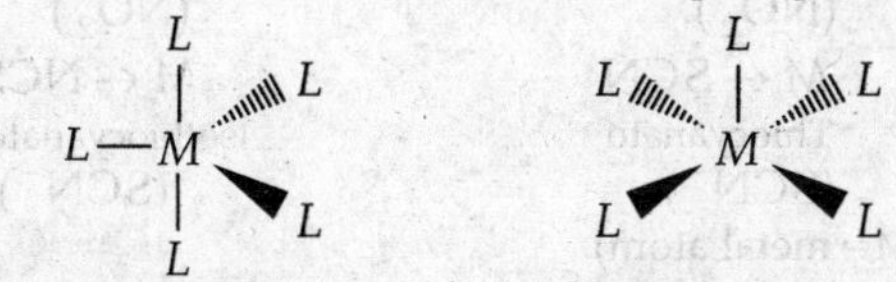

Trigonal-bipyramidal Square-pyramidal

Where, *M* represents the metal atom and *L* represents the ligands.
i.e.,

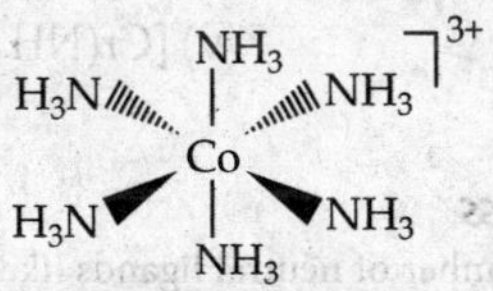

(v) **Homoleptic** Complexes in which a metal is bound to only one kind of donor groups are called homoleptic complexes. *e.g.*, $[Co(NH_3)_6]^{3+}$.

(vi) **Heteroleptic** Complexes in which a metal is bound to more than one kind of donor groups are known as heteroleptic complexes. *e.g.*, $[Co(NH_3)_4Cl_2]$

Question 4 What is meant by unidentate, didentate and ambidentate ligands? Give two examples for each.

◎ *Thinking Process* Uni = 1; Di = 2; Ambi = two different; dentate means donor atoms.

Sol. (i) **Unidentate** The negative ion or neutral molecule having only one donor atom is called unidentate ligand *e.g.*, $\ddot{N}H_3$, $:\ddot{Cl}:^-$, $H_2\ddot{O}:$ etc.

(ii) **Bidentate (or didentate)** The ions or molecules having two donor atoms are called bidentate ligands. *e.g.*, $\begin{matrix} COO^- \\ | \\ COO^- \end{matrix}$ oxalate ion, $\begin{matrix} CH_2\ddot{N}H_2 \\ | \\ CH_2\ddot{N}H_2 \end{matrix}$ ethylene diamine (en).

(iii) **Ambidentate** Ligand which can ligate through two different atoms is called ambidentate ligand. *e.g.*, NO_2^-, SCN^- ions. NO_2^- ion can coordinate either through nitrogen or through oxygen to a central metal atom/ion. Similarly, SCN^- ion can coordinate through the sulphur or nitrogen atom.

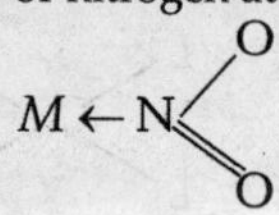

$M \leftarrow O - N = O$

Nitrito-N (NO_2^-)	Nitrito-O (NO_2^-)
$M \leftarrow SCN$	$M \leftarrow NCS$
Thiocyanato (SCN^-)	Isothiocyanato (SCN^-)

(where, M = metal atom)

Question 5 Specify the oxidation numbers of the metals in the following coordination entities :

(i) $[Co(H_2O)(CN)(en)_2]^{2+}$
(ii) $[CoBr_2(en)_2]^+$
(iii) $[PtCl_4]^{2-}$
(iv) $K_3[Fe(CN)_6]$
(v) $[Cr(NH_3)_3Cl_3]$

Thinking Process

(i) Oxidation number of neutral ligands like H_2O, en, NH_3, etc. is 0. It is -1 for CN, Cl and Br.
(ii) In a neutral complex, the sum of oxidation states of all the atoms present in the complex is equal to zero.
(iii) In case of complex ion, the sum is equal to the charge on the ion.

Sol. Let the oxidation number of metal be x.

(i) $[Co(H_2O)(CN)(en)_2]^{2+}$

$\Rightarrow x + 0 + (-1) + (2 \times 0) = +2 \Rightarrow x = 2 + 1 = +3$

(ii) $[CoBr_2(en)_2]^+$

$x + 2 \times (-1) + (2 \times 0) = +1 \Rightarrow x = 1 + 2 = +3$

(iii) $[PtCl_4]^{2-}$

$x + (-1)4 = -2 \Rightarrow x - 4 = -2 \Rightarrow x = -2 + 4 = +2$

(iv) $K_3Fe(CN)_6$

$(+1) \times 3 + x + (-1) \times 6 = 0 \Rightarrow 3 + x - 6 = 0 \Rightarrow x - 3 = 0$

$x = +3$

(v) $[Cr(NH_3)_3Cl_3]$ $x + (3 \times 0) + (3 \times -1) = 0 \Rightarrow x = +3$

Question 6 Using IUPAC norms write the formulas of the following :

(i) Tetrahydroxidozincate (II)
(ii) Potassium tetrachloridopalladate (II)
(iii) Diamminedichlorido platinum (II)
(iv) Potassium tetracyanidonickelate (II)
(v) Pentaamminenitro-O-cobalt (III)
(vi) Hexaamminecobalt (III) sulphate
(vii) Potassiumtri(oxalato) chromate (III)
(viii) Hexaammineplatinum (IV)
(ix) Tetrabromidocuprate (II)
(x) Pentaamminenitrito-N-cobalt (III)

◎ ***Thinking Process*** As in Q. 2 of intext questions.

Sol. (i) $[Zn(OH)_4]^{2-}$ (ii) $K_2[PdCl_4]$

(iii) $[Pt(NH_3)_2Cl_2]$ (iv) $K_2[Ni(CN)_4]$

(v) $[Co(NH_3)_5(ONO)]^{2+}$ (O represents that NO_2 group binds to the metal atom through oxygen.)

(vi) $[Co(NH_3)_6]_2(SO_4)_3$ (vii) $K_3[Cr(C_2O_4)_3]$

(viii) $[Pt(NH_3)_6]^{4+}$ (ix) $[CuBr_4]^{2-}$

(x) $[Co(NH_3)_5(NO_2)]^{2+}$ (N represents that NO_2 group binds to the metal atom through nitrogen.)

Question 7 Using IUPAC norms write the systematic names of the following :

(i) $[Co(NH_3)_6]Cl_3$ (ii) $[Pt(NH_3)_2Cl(NH_2CH_3)]Cl$
(iii) $[Ti(H_2O)_6]^{3+}$ (iv) $[Co(NH_3)_4Cl(NO_2)]Cl$
(v) $[Mn(H_2O)_6]^{2+}$ (vi) $[NiCl_4]^{2-}$
(vii) $[Ni(NH_3)_6]Cl_2$ (viii) $[Co(en)_3]^{3+}$
(ix) $[Ni(CO)_4]$

◎ ***Thinking Process*** As in Q. 1 of intext questions.

Sol. (i) Hexamminecobalt (III) chloride.

(ii) Diamminechlorido (methyl amine) platinum (II) chloride.

(iii) Hexaaquatitanium (III) ion.

(iv) Tetramminechloridonitrito-N-cobalt (III) chloride.

(v) Hexaaquamanganese (II) ion.

(vi) Tetrachloridonickelate (II) ion.

(vii) Hexaammine nickel (II) chloride.

(viii) *Tris*-(ethane-1,2-diamine) cobalt (III) ion.

(ix) Tetracarbonyl nickel (0).

Question 8 List various types of isomerism possible for coordination compounds, giving an example of each.

Sol. Isomerism in coordination compounds is mainly of two types :

1. **Structural isomerism**
   (a) Linkage isomerism
   (b) Coordination isomerism
   (c) Ionisation isomerism
   (d) Solvate isomerism

2. **Stereo isomerism**
   (a) Geometrical isomerism
   (b) Optical isomerism

Examples :

1. (a) **Linkage isomerism :**

(i) $[Co(NH_3)_5NO_2]Cl_2$ and $[Co(NH_3)_5ONO]Cl_2$

(ii) $[Mn(CO)_5SCN]$ and $[Mn(CO)_5NCS]$

(b) **Coordination isomerism :**

(i) $[Co(NH_3)_6][Cr(CN)_6]$ and $[Cr(NH_3)_6][Co(CN)_6]$

(c) **Ionisation isomerism :**

(i) $[Co(NH_3)_5SO_4]Br$ and $[Co(NH_3)_5Br]SO_4$

(d) **Solvate isomerism :**

(i) $[Cr(H_2O)_6]Cl_3$ (violet) and $[Cr(H_2O)_5]Cl]Cl_2 \cdot H_2O$ (grey-green)

2. (a) **Geometrical isomerism :**

(i) *cis*- and *trans*-isomers of $[CoCl_2(en)_2]$

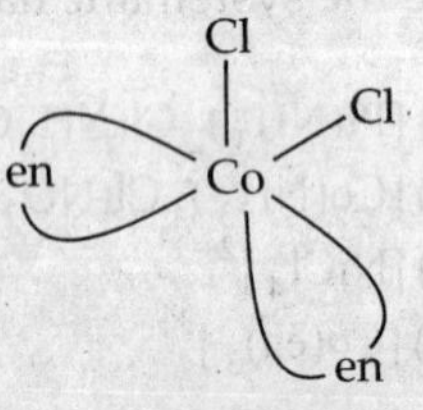

Cis-form

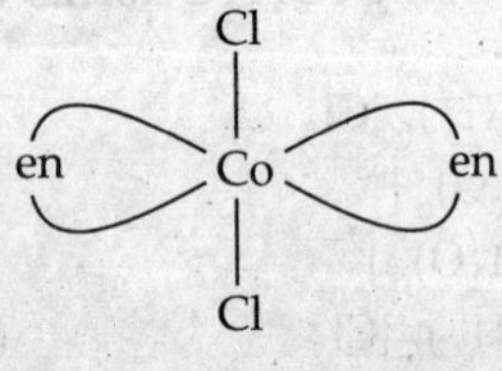

Trans-form

(b) **Optical isomerism**

(i) *dextro*- and *laevo*-rotatory forms of $[Co(en)_3]^{3+}$

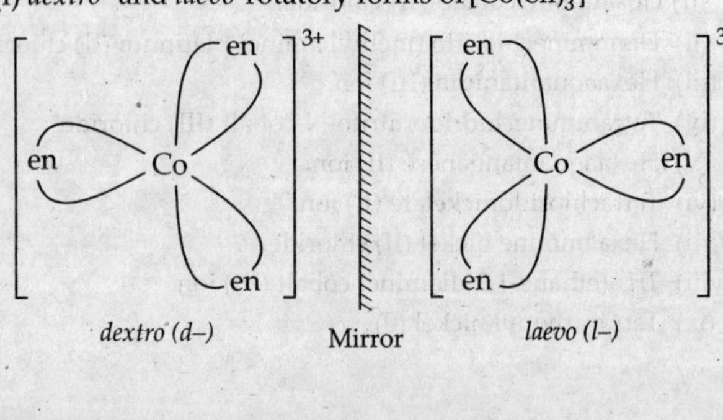

dextro (d–) Mirror *laevo (l–)*

Question 9 How many geometrical isomers are possible in the following coordination entities?

(i) $[Cr(C_2O_4)_3]^{3-}$ (ii) $[Co(NH_3)_3Cl_3]$

◎ *Thinking Process*

(i) Geometrical isomerism is exhibited by octahedral complexes of the type $[MA_3B_3]$, $[MA_2B_4]$ etc, where A and B are monodentate ligands.

(ii) $[M(AA)_3]$ type complex does not exhibit geometrical isomerism, they exhibit optical isomerism.

(iii) When the similar groups occupy adjacent positions, the isomer is called *fac* or *cis*-form, if not, it is called *mer* or *trans*-form.

Sol. (i) No geometrical isomer is possible.

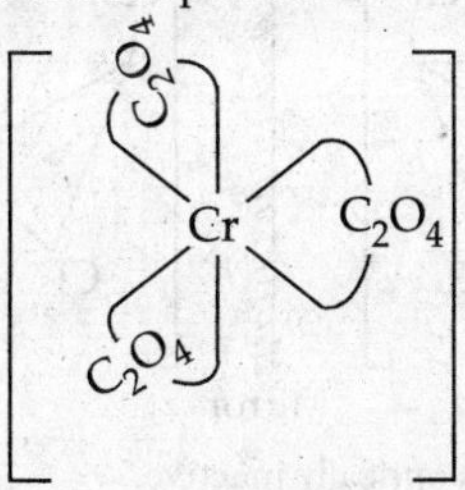

(ii) Two geometrical isomers are possible for $[Co(NH_3)_3Cl_3]$

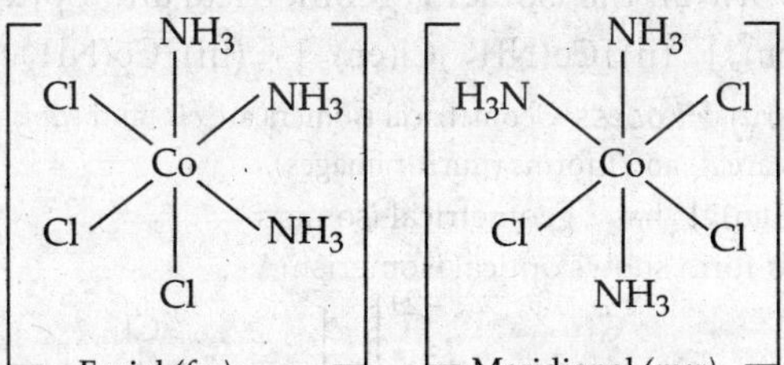

Facial (*fac*) Meridional (*mer*)

Question 10. Draw the structures of optical isomers of :

(i) $[Cr(C_2O_4)_3]^{3-}$ (ii) $[PtCl_2(en)_2]^{2+}$ (iii) $[Cr(NH_3)_2Cl_2(en)]^+$

Sol. (i) $[Cr(C_2O_4)_3]^{3-}$

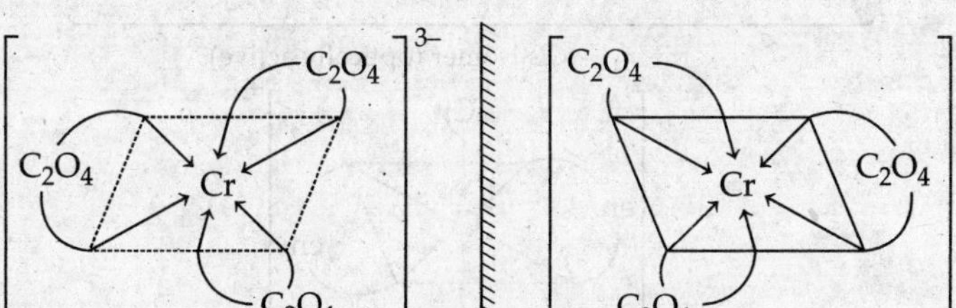

Mirror

(ii) ***Cis*-**

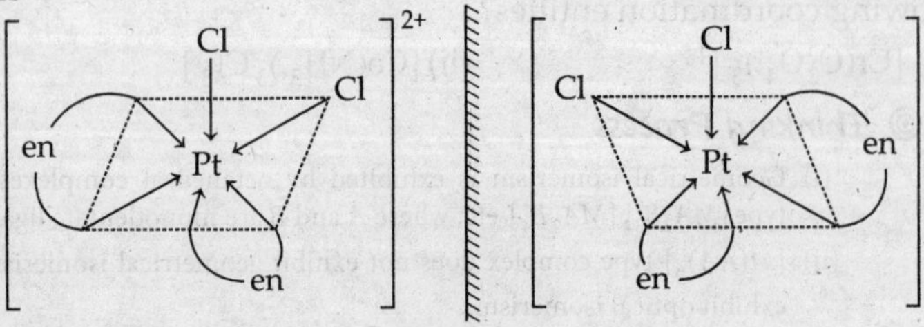

Mirror

(iii) ***Cis*-**

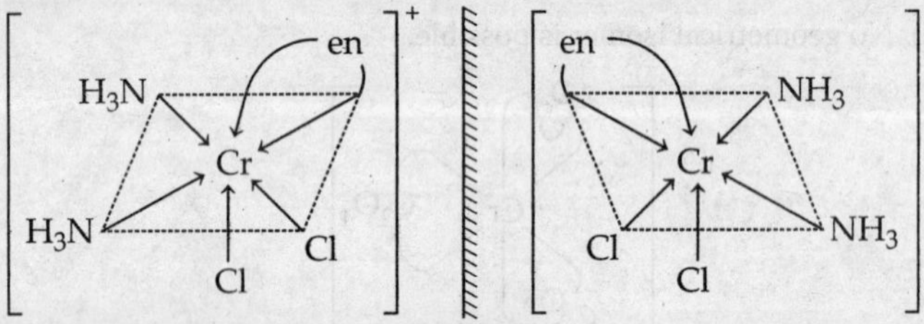

Mirror

Note *Trans*-$[PtCl_2(en)_2]^{2+}$ is optically inactive.

Question 11 Draw all the isomers (geometrical and optical) of :

(i) $[CoCl_2(en)_2]^+$ (ii) $[Co(NH_3)Cl(en)_2]^{2+}$ (iii) $[Co(NH_3)_2Cl_2(en)]^+$

◎ *Thinking Process* Geometrical isomers are *cis*- and *trans*-forms. Optical isomers are *d*- and *l*-forms (mirror images).

Sol. (i) $[CoCl_2(en)_2]^+$ has 2 geometrical isomers.

Further *cis*-form shows optical isomerism.

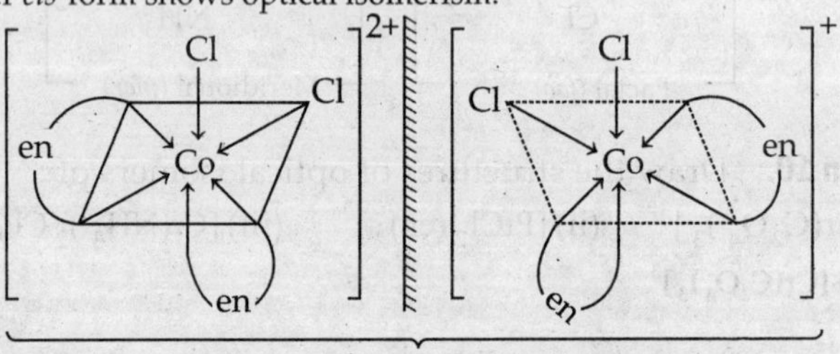

Cis-isomer (optically active)

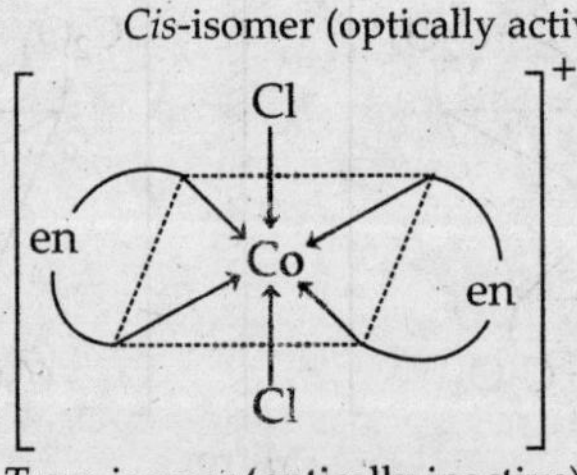

Trans-isomer (optically inactive)

(ii) $[Co(NH_3)Cl(en)_2]^{2+}$

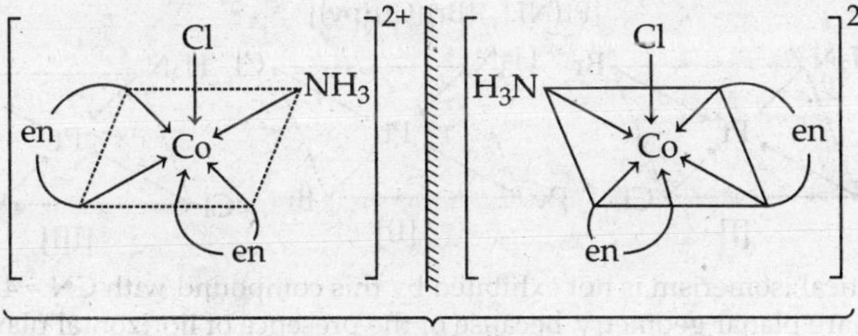

Cis-isomer (optically active)

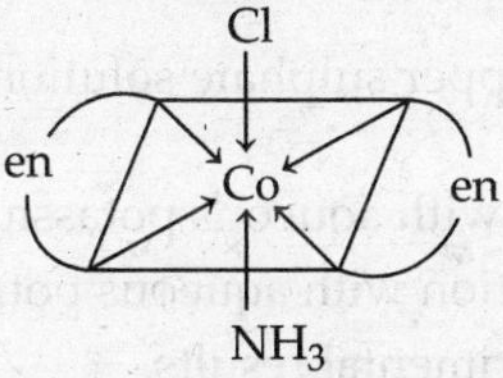

Trans-isomer (optically inactive)

(iii) $[Co(NH_3)_2Cl_2(en)]$

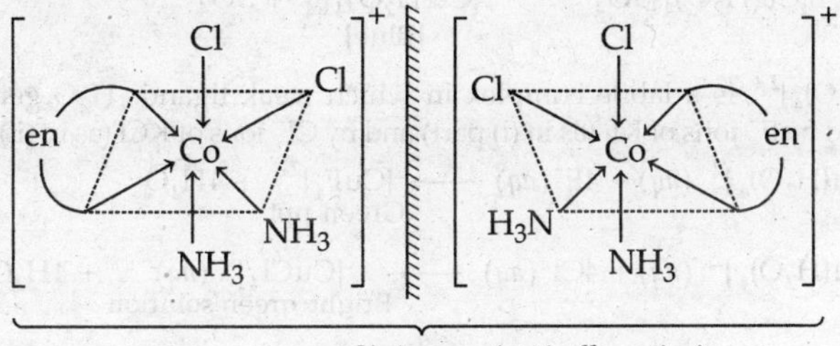

Cis-isomer (optically active)

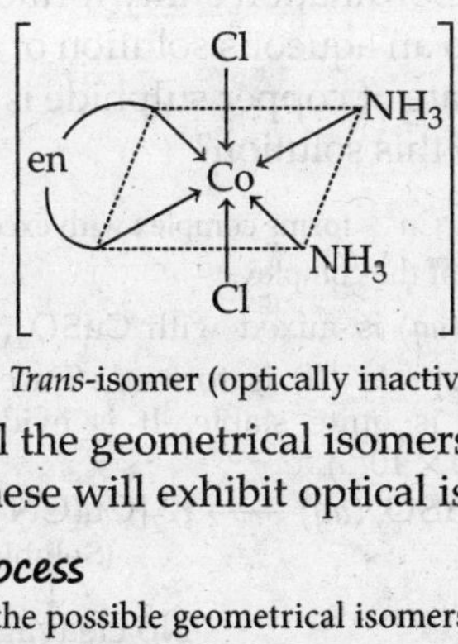

Trans-isomer (optically inactive)

Question 12 Write all the geometrical isomers of $[Pt(NH_3)(Br)(Cl)(py)]$ and how many of these will exhibit optical isomers?

◎ ***Thinking Process***

(i) Draw all the possible geometrical isomers and find which of these have any symmetry element.

(ii) Compounds in which symmetry elements are present, are optically inactive, *i.e.*, does not exhibit optical isomerism.

Sol. Three geometrical isomers are possible for

$[Pt(NH_3)(Br)(Cl)(py)]$

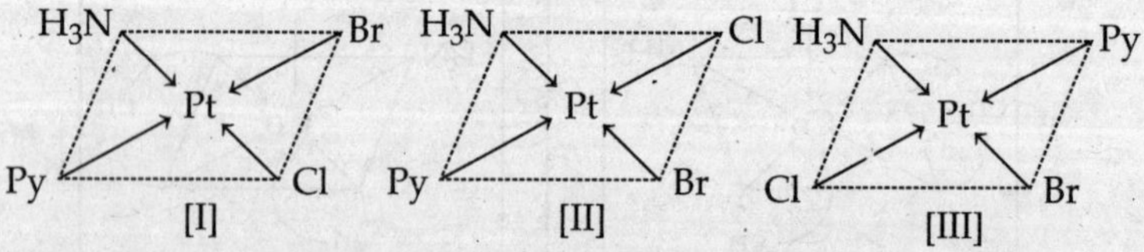

Optical isomerism is not exhibited by this compound with CN = 4 and square planar geometry, because of the presence of horizontal plane of symmetry.

Question 13 Aqueous copper sulphate solution (blue in colour) gives :

(i) a green precipitate with aqueous potassium fluoride and.

(ii) a bright green solution with aqueous potassium chloride.

Explain these experimental results.

Sol. Aqueous copper sulphate (blue) is $[Cu(H_2O)_4]SO_4$

$$[Cu(H_2O)_4]SO_4 \xrightleftharpoons{aq} \underset{[\text{Blue}]}{[Cu(H_2O)_4]^{2+}} + SO_4^{2-}$$

$[Cu(H_2O)_4]^{2+}$ is a labile complex in which weak ligands H_2O get easily replaced by F^- ions of KF (as in (i) part) and by Cl^- ions of KCl (as in (ii) part).

(i) $[Cu(H_2O)_4]^{2+}(aq) + 4F^-(aq) \longrightarrow \underset{\text{Green ppt.}}{[CuF_4]^{2-}} + 4H_2O$

(ii) $[Cu(H_2O)_4]^{2+}(aq) + 4Cl^-(aq) \longrightarrow \underset{\text{Bright green solution}}{[CuCl_4]^{2-}(aq)} + 4H_2O$

Question 14 What is the coordination entity formed when excess of aqueous KCN is added to an aqueous solution of copper sulphate? Why is it that no precipitate of copper sulphide is obtained when $H_2S\,(g)$ is passed through this solution?

◎ ***Thinking Process*** Cu^{2+} forms complex with excess KCN. Cu^{2+} ions are absent in the solution of the complex.

Sol. When excess of KCN(aq) is mixed with $CuSO_4(aq)$, a complex named potassiumtetracyanocuprate (II) is formed. Since, CN^- ions are strong ligands, the complex is quite stable. It is evident from the stability constant value ($K = 2.0 \times 10^{27}$).

$$\underset{(\text{Excess})}{4KCN(aq)} + CuSO_4(aq) \longrightarrow \underset{(\text{Soluble})}{K_2[Cu(CN)_4](aq)} + K_2SO_4\,(aq)$$

↓

No cleavage and no production of Cu^{2+} ions

So, no ppt. of CuS is obtained when H_2S is passed through the solution.

Question 15 Discuss the nature of bonding in the following coordination entities on the basis of valence bond theory :

(i) $[Fe(CN)_6]^{4-}$ (ii) $[FeF_6]^{3-}$

(iii) $[Co(C_2O_4)_3]^{3-}$ (iv) $[CoF_6]^{3-}$

◎ ***Thinking Process*** Finding of hybridisation and bonding involves the following steps

(i) Find the outer shell configuration of central metal atom and ion.

(ii) Find this configuration in the presence of ligand. If ligands are strong, pairing occurs, otherwise not.

(iii) Now fill the ligands in the empty orbitals to find hybridisation.

Sol. (i) $[Fe(CN)_6]^{4-}$ In this complex Fe is present as Fe^{2+}.

$$Fe = [Ar]\ 3d^6\ 4s^2$$

Outer configuration of $Fe^{2+} = 3d^6\ 4s^0$

$3d^6$

⇅	↑	↑	↑	↑

CN^- being strong field ligand, pair up the unpaired d electrons Thus, two $3d$-orbital are now available for CN^- ions.

$[Fe(CN)_6]^{4-}$ =

$3d^6$					$4s$	$4p$		
⇅	⇅	⇅	xx	xx	xx	xx	xx	xx
			CN^-	CN^-	CN^-	CN^-	CN^-	CN^-

No unpaired electron; d^2sp^3 hybridisation ⇒ Octahedral geometry

Since, all the electrons are paired, the complex is diamagnetic. Moreover $(n-1)$ d-orbitals are involved in bonding, so, it is an inner orbital or low spin complex.

(ii) $[FeF_6]^{3-}$ In this complex, the oxidation state of Fe is + 3.

$$Fe^{3+} = 3d^5\ 4s^0$$

Fe^{3+} = $3d^5$

↑	↑	↑	↑	↑

F^- is not a strong field ligand. It is a weak field ligand, so no pairing occurs. Thus, $3d$-orbitals are not available to take part in bonding.

$[FeF_6]^{3-}$ =

$3d$					$4s$	$4p$			$4d$				
↑	↑	↑	↑	↑	xx	xx	xx	xx	xx	xx			
					F^-	F^-	F^-	F^-	F^-	F^-			

Five unpaired electrons; sp^3d^2 hybridisation ⇒ Octahedral geometry

Because of the presence of five unpaired electrons, the complex is paramagnetic.
Moreover, *nd*-orbitals are involved in bonding, so it is an outer orbital or high spin complex.

(iii) $[Co(C_2O_4)_3]^{3-}$ In this complex, the oxidation state of Co is + 3.
Outer configuration of Co = $3d^7\ 4s^2$
$Co^{3+} = 3d^6\ 4s^0$

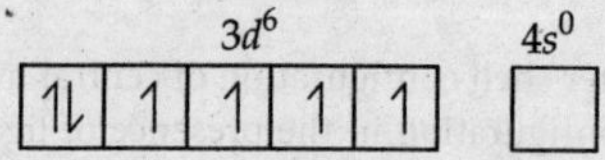

Oxalate ion being a strong field ligand, pairs up the 3*d* electrons, thus two out of the five 3*d*-orbitals are available for oxalate ions.

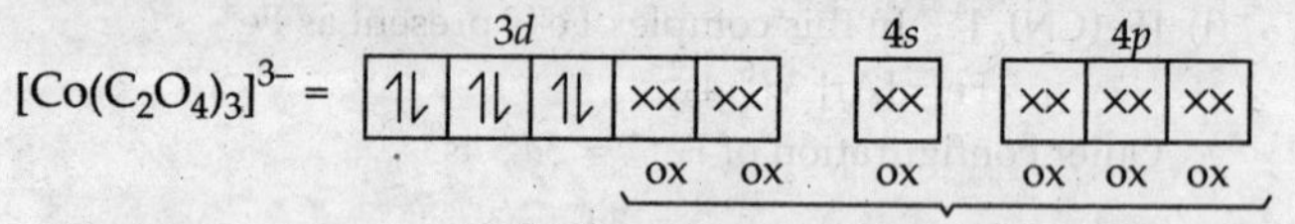

d^2sp^3 hybridisation ⇒ Octahedral geometry

Since, all the electrons are paired, this complex is diamagnetic.
It is an inner orbital complex because of the involvement of $(n-1)$ *d*-orbital for bonding.

(iv) $[CoF_6]^{3-}$ In this complex, Co is present as Co^{3+}.
Outer configuration of $Co^{3+} = 3d^6\ 4s^0$

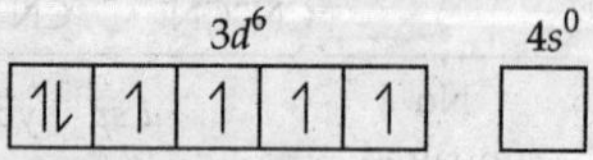

F^- is a weak field ligand, so no pairing occurs and thus, F^- occupy *nd* orbitals as

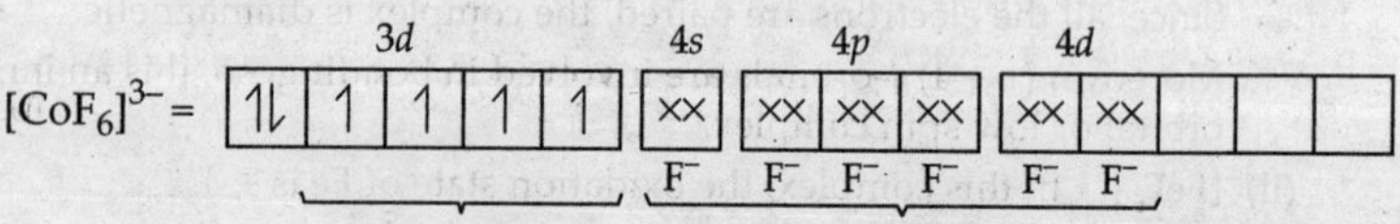

Four unpaired electrons

sp^3d^2 hybridisation ⇒ Octahedral geometry

Because of the presence of four unpaired electrons, the complex is paramagnetic.
Since, *nd* orbitals take part in bonding, it is an outer orbital complex or high spin complex.

Mistake Alert $C_2O_4^{2-}$ (oxalate) ligand behaves as a weak field ligand in all compexes except $[Co(C_2O_4)_3]^{3-}$.

Question 16 Draw figure to show the splitting of *d*-orbitals in an octahedral crystal field.

Sol.

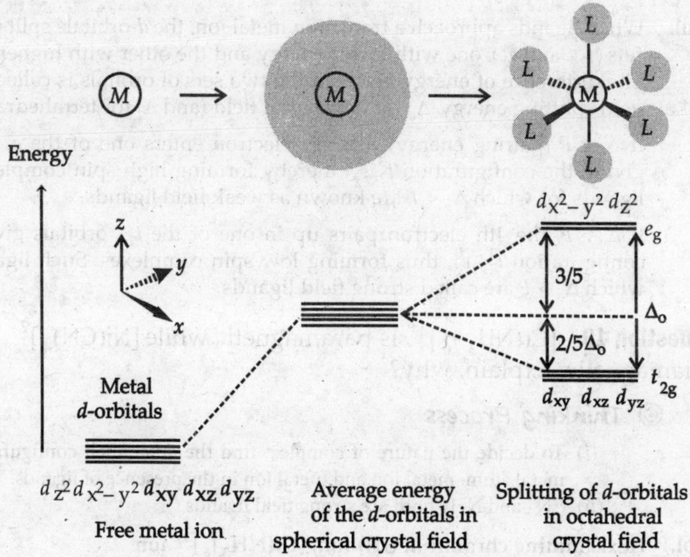

▲ *d*-orbital splitting in an octahedral crystal field

Question 17 What is spectrochemical series? Explain the difference between a weak field ligand and a strong field ligand.

Sol. The arrangement of ligands in order of their increasing field strengths, *i.e.*, increasing crystal field splitting energy (CFSE) values is called spectrochemical series.

$$\underbrace{I^- < Br^- < SCN^- < Cl^- < F^- < OH^- < ox < H_2O < NCS^- < EDTA^{4-} < NH_3 < en < CN^- < CO}_{\text{Spectrochemical series}}$$

The ligands with a small value of CFSE (Δ_o) are called **weak field ligands.** For such ligands $\Delta_o < P$ where P is the pairing energy. They form high spin complexes. Whereas the ligands with a large value of CFSE are called **strong field ligands.** In case of such ligands $\Delta_o > P$. They form low spin complexes.

Question 18 What is crystal field splitting energy? How does the magnitude of Δ_o decide the actual configuration of *d*-orbitals in a coordination entity?

Sol. When ligands approach a transition metal ion, the *d*-orbitals split into two sets (t_{2g} and e_g), one with lower energy and the other with higher energy. The difference of energy between the two sets of orbitals is called crystal field splitting energy, Δ_o for octahedral field (and Δ_t for tetrahedral field)

If $\Delta_o < P$ (pairing energy), the 4th electron enters one of the e_g orbitals giving the configuration $t_{2g}^3 e_g^1$ thereby forming high spin complex. Such ligands for which $\Delta_o < P$ are known as weak field ligands.

If $\Delta_o > P$, the 4th electron pairs up in one of the t_{2g} orbitals giving the configuration $t_{2g}^4 e_g^0$, thus forming low spin complexes. Such ligands for which $\Delta_o > P$ are called strong field ligands.

Question 19 $[Cr(NH_3)_6]^{3+}$ is paramagnetic while $[Ni(CN)_4]^{2-}$ is diamagnetic. Explain, why?

◎ ***Thinking Process***

(i) To decide the nature of complex, find the outer shell configuration of metal atom, metal ion and metal ion in the presence of ligands.
(ii) CN^- and NH_3 both are strong field ligands.

Sol. **Hexaammine chromium (III) ion, $[Cr(NH_3)_6]^{3+}$ ion**

Oxidation state of Cr = +3, $_{24}Cr = [Ar]\ 3d^5 4s^1$, $Cr^{3+} = [Ar]\ 3d^3$

Cr^{3+} provides six empty orbitals to accommodate six electron pairs from six NH_3 molecules. It involves d^2sp^3 hybridisation and hence, forms octahedral complex.

It is paramagnetic due to the presence of three unpaired electrons.

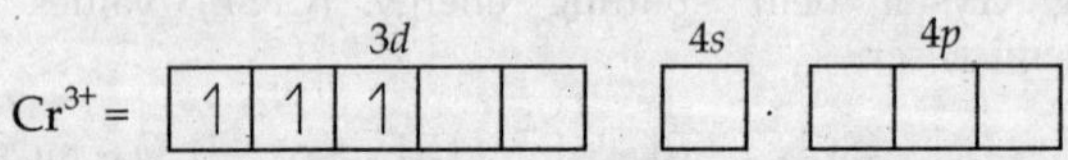

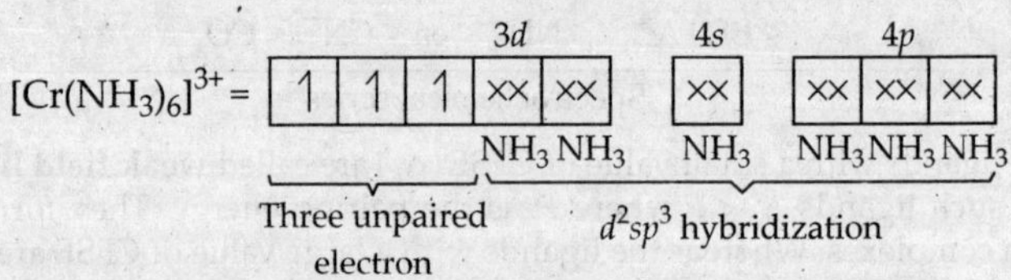

Tetracyanonickelate (II) ion, $[Ni(CN)_4]^{2-}$

$$Ni = [Ar]\ 3d^8 4s^2, \quad Ni^{2+} = [Ar]\ 3d^8$$

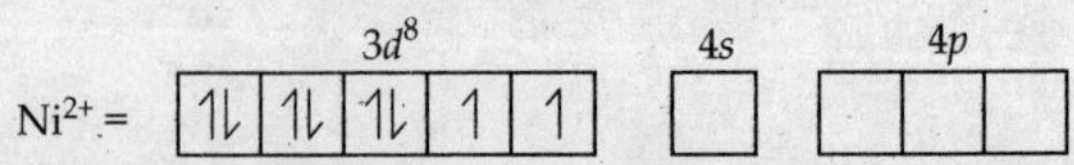

(CN^- being strong field ligand causes pairing of 3*d* electrons thus, one of the 3*d*-orbital becomes empty for CN^- ion.)

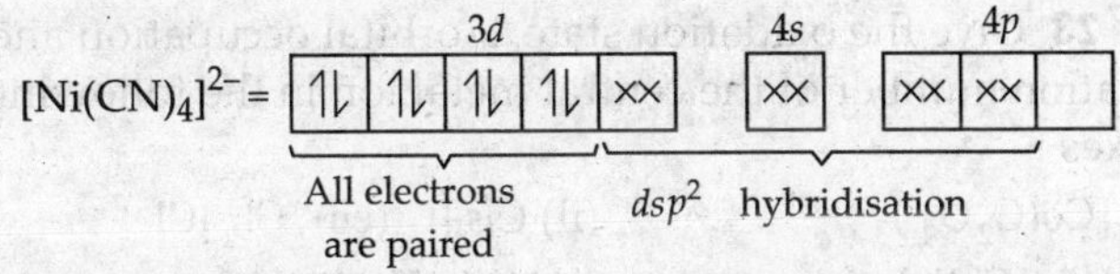

Unpaired electron is not present so it is diamagnetic.

Question 20 A solution of $[Ni(H_2O)_6]^{2+}$ is green but a solution of $[Ni(CN)_4]^{2-}$ is colourless. Explain.

Sol. The configuration of Ni^{2+} ion is

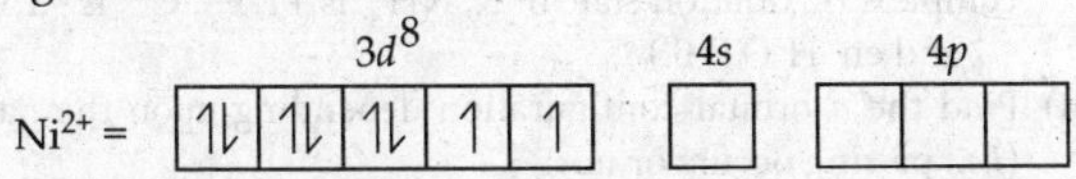

In $[Ni(H_2O)_6]^{2+}$, H_2O molecules are weak field ligands, they do not cause electron pairing. As a result, the complex has two unpaired electrons. Thus, *d–d* transition takes place due to absorption of radiation corresponding to red light and the emission of complementary green colour occurs. Hence, it is green. In $[Ni(CN)_4]^{2-}$, CN^- ions are strong field ligands. So, in the presence of CN^- ions, the two unpaired electrons in the 3*d*-orbitals pair up. Hence, there is no unpaired electron so, no *d-d* transition. Hence, it is colourless.

Question 21 $[Fe(CN)_6]^{4-}$ and $[Fe(H_2O)_6]^{2+}$ are of different colours in dilute solutions. Why?

Sol. In both the complex compounds, Fe is in +2 oxidation state with configuration $3d^6$, *i.e.*, it has four unpaired electrons. In the presence of weak H_2O ligands, the unpaired electrons do not pair up. But in the presence of strong ligand CN^-, they get paired up. Then no unpaired electron is left. Due to this difference in the number of unpaired electrons, both complex ions have different colours.

Question 22 Discuss the nature of bonding in metal carbonyls.

Sol. The metal-carbon bond in metal carbonyls have both sigma (σ) and pi (π) characters. The metal-carbon σ-bond is formed by the donation of lone pair of electrons of the carbonyl carbon to a vacant orbital of the metal. The metal-carbon π-bond is formed by the donation of a pair of electrons from a filled *d*-orbital of metal into the vacant antibonding π-molecular orbital (π*) of carbon monoxide. The metal to ligand bonding creates a synergic effect which strengthens the bond between CO and the metal.

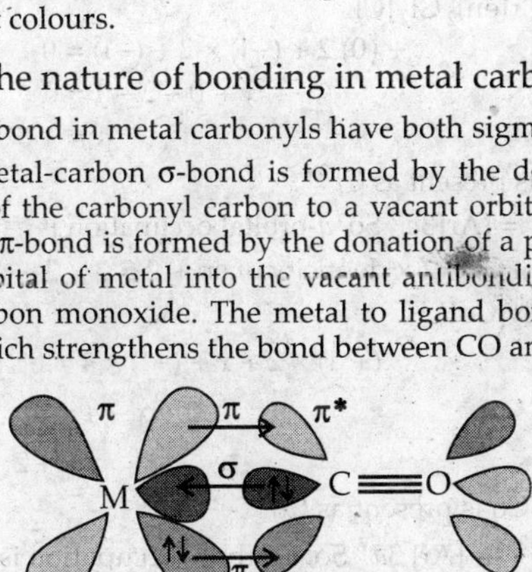

Synergic bonding

▲ Example of synergic bonding interactions in a carbonyl complex

Question 23 Give the oxidation state, *d*-orbital occupation and coordination number of the central metal ion in the following complexes :

(i) $K_3[Co(C_2O_4)_3]$ (ii) *Cis*-$[Cr(en)_2Cl_2]Cl$
(iii) $(NH_4)_2[CoF_4]$ (iv) $[Mn(H_2O)_6]SO_4$

Thinking Process

(i) Calculate the oxidation state of the metal atom by substituting the oxidation states of other species as their sum is equal to zero in case of complex. (Oxidation state of K, NH_4^+ is +1, F^-, Cl^- is −1, $C_2O_4^{2-}$, SO_4^{2-} is −2 and en, H_2O is 0.)
(ii) Find the *d*-orbital configuration depending upon the nature of ligand (*i.e.*, pairing occurs or not).
(iii) Coordination number is equal to number of ligand in case of monodentate ligand while in case of polydentate ligands, it is equal to number of ligands multiplied by its denticity.

Sol. (i) $K_3[Co(C_2O_4)_3]$

$$(+1)\,3 + x + (-2) \times 3 = 0$$
$$+3 + x - 6 = 0$$
$$x = +3$$

Thus, Co is present as Co^{3+}.

$_{27}Co = [Ar]\,3d^7\,4s^2$

$Co^{3+} = [Ar]\,3d^6$ so *d*-orbital occupation is d^6 or $t_{2g}^6\,e_g^0$

(as $C_2O_4^{2-}$ is strong field ligand)

CN of Co = 3 × denticity of C_2O_4

= 3 × 2 (as $C_2O_4^{2-}$ is a bidentate ligand) = 6

(ii) *Cis*-$[Cr(en)_2Cl_2]Cl$

$$x + (0)\,2 + (-1) \times 2 + (-1) = 0$$
$$x + 0 - 2 - 1 = 0$$
$$x = +3$$

Thus, Cr is present as Cr^{3+}.

$Cr^{3+} = [Ar]3d^3$ So, *d*-orbital occupation is d^3 or t_{2g}^3, eg^0

CN of Cr = 2 × denticity of en + 2 = 2 × 2 + 2 = 6

(iii) $(NH_4)_2[CoF_4]$

$$(+1) \times 2 + x + (-1) \times 4 = 0$$
$$2 + x - 4 = 0$$
$$x = +2$$

Thus, Co is present as Co^{2+}

$Co^{2+} = [Ar]\,3d^7$ So, *d*-orbital occupation is d^7 or $t_{2g}^5\,e_g^2$

(as F^- is a weak field ligand)

CN of Co = 4

(iv) $[Mn(H_2O)_6]SO_4$

$$x + (0)\,6 + (-2) = 0$$
$$x = +2$$

Thus, Mn is present as Mn^{2+}.

$Mn^{2+} = [Ar]\,3d^5$ So, d-orbital occupation is d^5 or $t_{2g}^3\ e_g^2$

(H_2O is a weak field ligand)

CN of Mn = 6

Question 24 Write down the IUPAC name for each of the following complexes and indicate the oxidation state, electronic configuration and coordination number. Also give stereochemistry and magnetic moment of the complex :

(i) $K[Cr(H_2O)_2(C_2O_4)_2]\cdot 3H_2O$ (ii) $[Co(NH_3)_5Cl]Cl_2$

(iii) $[CrCl_3(py)_3]$ (iv) $Cs[FeCl_4]$

(v) $K_4[Mn(CN)_6]$

Sol. (i) $K[Cr(H_2O)_2(C_2O_4)_2]\cdot 3H_2O$

IUPAC name : Potassium diaquadioxalatochromate (III) trihydrate;

Coordination number (CN) = 6;

Shape = octahedral

Oxidation state of Cr

$$+1 + x + (0) \times 2 + (-2)\,2 + 3\,(0) = 0$$
$$+1 + x - 4 = 0$$
$$x = +3$$

EC of $Cr^{3+} = 3d^3 = t_{2g}^3 \cdot e_g^0$

Unpaired electrons (n) = 3

Magnetic moment $(\mu) = \sqrt{n(n+2)} = \sqrt{3(3+2)} = 3.87$ BM

This complex exhibits geometrical isomerism and exists in following *cis-trans* forms.

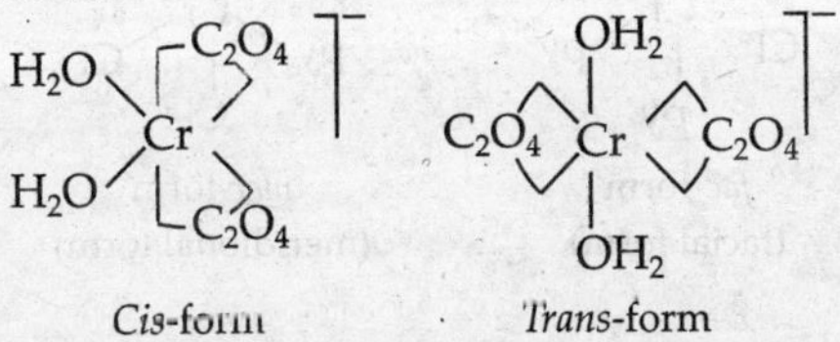

Cis-form *Trans*-form

cis-form can be resolved into d and l-forms (*i.e.*, optical isomers)

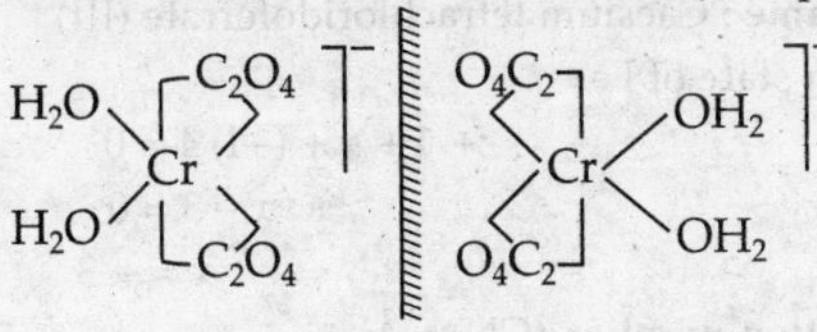

Mirror

(ii) $[Co(NH_3)_5Cl]Cl_2$

IUPAC name: Pentaamminechloridocobalt (III) chloride

Oxidation state of Co can be calculated as

$$x + (0)\,5 + (-1) + (-1)\,2 = 0$$
$$x - 3 = 0$$
$$x = +3$$

Coordination number (CN) = 5 + 1 = 6 (number of monodentate ligands)

Shape = Octahedral

Outer electronic configuration (EN) of $Co^{3+} = 3d^6 = t_{2g}^6\ e_g^0$

Number of unpaired electrons, $n = 0$ (all electrons are paired)

So, **magnetic moment,** $\mu = \sqrt{n\,(n+2)}$ BM = $\sqrt{0\,(0+2)}$ **BM = 0 BM**

This complex does not exhibit geometrical as well as optical isomerism.

(iii) $[CrCl_3(py)_3]$

IUPAC name : Trichloridotripyridinechromium (III)

Oxidation state of Cr

$$x + (-1) \times 3 + (0)\,3 = 0,\ x = +3$$

Coordination number (CN) = 6

shape = Octahedral

Outer electronic configuration of Cr = $3d^3\ (t_{2g}^3\ e_g^0)$

Number of unpaired electrons = 3

So, **magnetic moment,** $\mu = \sqrt{n\,(n+2)}$ BM

$$= \sqrt{3\,(3+2)} = \sqrt{15} = 3.87 \text{ BM}$$

This complex exists in *fac* and *mer* forms, *i.e.*, exhibit geometrical isomerism. (In *fac* form, similar groups occupy adjacent positions while this is not true in case of *mer*-isomer.

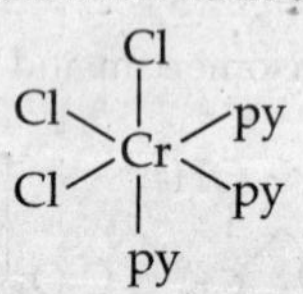

fac-form
(facial form)

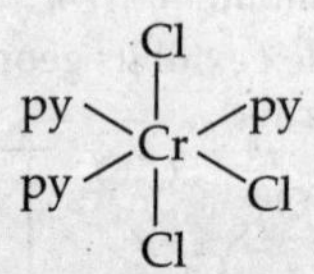

mer-form
(meridional form)

(iv) $Cs[FeCl_4]$

IUPAC name : Caesium tetrachloridoferrate (III)

Oxidation state of Fe

$$+1 + x + (-1)\,4 = 0$$
$$x - 3 = 0$$
$$x = +3$$

Coordination number, (CN) = 4

Shape = Tetrahedral

Outer electronic configuration of Fe = $3d^5$ ($e^2t_2^3$)
Number of unpaired electrons = 5
$\therefore$ **Magnetic moment,** $\mu = \sqrt{n(n+2)}$ BM $= \sqrt{5(5+2)} = \sqrt{35} = 5.92$ BM
It is a tetrahedral complex, so it does not exhibit geometrical or optical isomerism (stereo isomerism).

(v) $K_4[Mn(CN)_6]$
IUPAC name : Potassium hexacyanomanganate (II)
Oxidation state of Mn in K_4 [Mn $(CN)_6$]

$$(+1)4 + x + (-1)6 = 0$$
$$x - 2 = 0, x = +2$$

Coordination number (CN) = 6
shape = Octahedral
Outer electronic configuration of Mn = $3d^5$ [t_{2g}^5 e_g^0]
(as CN^- is a strong field ligand)
Number of unpaired electrons = 1
Magnetic moment, $\mu = \sqrt{n(n+2)}$ BM $= \sqrt{1(1+2)}$ BM
$= \sqrt{3} = 1.73$ BM

This complex does not exhibit geometrical and stereo isomerism.

Note *d-orbitals split up into* t_{2g} *(*d_{xy}, d_{yz}, d_{zx}*) set and* e_g *(*d_{z^2}, $d_{x^2-y^2}$*) set as* : (in octahedral complexes)

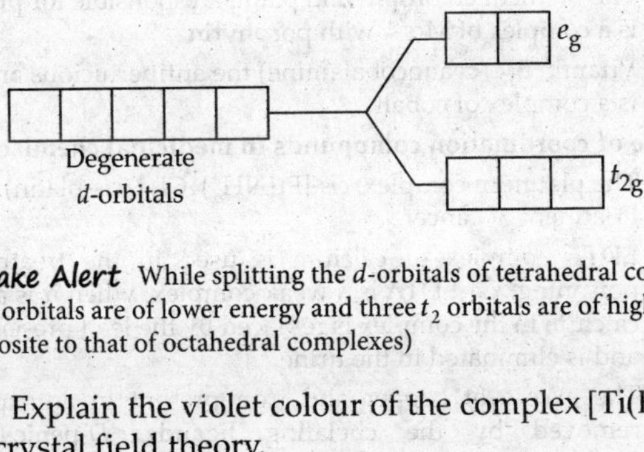

Mistake Alert While splitting the *d*-orbitals of tetrahedral complexes, two *e* orbitals are of lower energy and three t_2 orbitals are of higher energy. (Opposite to that of octahedral complexes)

Question 25 Explain the violet colour of the complex $[Ti(H_2O)_6]^{3+}$ on th basis of crystal field theory.

Sol. In $[Ti(H_2O)_6]^{3+}$ titanium is present in +3 oxidation state.

E.C. of $Ti^{3+} = 3d^1$

E.C. of $[Ti(H_2O)_6]^{3+}$ =

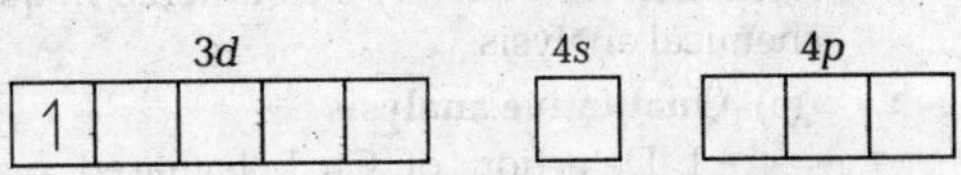

$[Ti(H_2O)_6]^{3+}$ has one unpaired electron. This unpaired electron when excited from t_{2g} level to e_g level absorb yellow light and hence, appears violet coloured.

Question 26 What is meant by the chelate effect? Give an example.

Sol. When a didentate or a polydentate ligand contains donor atoms positioned in such a way that when they coordinate with the central metal ion, a 5- or 6-membered ring is formed, the effect is known as chelate effect. Example

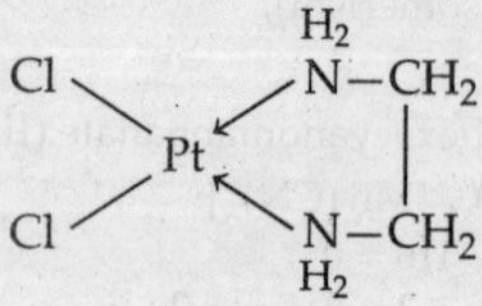

or $[PtCl_2(en)]$

Question 27 Discuss briefly giving an example in each case the role of coordination compounds in

(i) biological systems

(ii) medicinal chemistry

(iii) analytical chemistry

(iv) extraction/metallurgy of metals

Sol. (i) **Role of coordination compounds in biological systems**

(a) Haemoglobin, the oxygen carrier in blood, is a complex of Fe^{2+} with porphyrin.

(b) The pigment chlorophyll in plants, responsible for photosynthesis, is a complex of Mg^{2+} with porphyrin.

(c) Vitamin B_{12} (cyanocobalamine) the antipernicious anaemia factor, is a complex of cobalt.

(ii) **Role of coordination compounds in medicinal chemistry**

(a) The platinum complex, *cis*-$[Pt(NH_3)_2Cl_2]$ (*cis*-platin) is used in the treatment of cancer.

(b) EDTA complex of calcium is used in the treatment of lead poisoning. Ca-EDTA is a weak complex; when it is administered, calcium in the complex is replaced by the lead present in the body and is eliminated in the urine.

(c) The excess of copper and iron present in animal system are removed by the chelating ligands, *D*-penicillamine and desferrioxime *B via* the formation of complexes.

(iii) **Role of coordination compounds in analytical chemistry** Complex formation is frequently encountered in qualitative and quantitative chemical analysis.

(a) **Qualitative analysis**

I. Detection of Cu^{2+} is based on the formation of a blue tetraammine copper (II) ion.

$$Cu^{2+} + 4NH_3 \longrightarrow \underset{\text{Deep blue}}{[Cu(NH_3)_4]^{2+}}$$

II. Ni^{2+} is detected by the formation of a red complex with dimethyl glyoxime (DMG).

$$NiCl_2 + 2DMG + 2NH_4OH \longrightarrow \underset{\substack{\text{Nickel bis}\\ \text{dimethyl glyoximate}\\ \text{(red colour)}}}{[Ni(DMG)_2]} + 2NH_4Cl + 2H_2O$$

III. The separation of Ag^+ and Hg^{2+} in group I is based on the fact that while AgCl dissolves in NH_3, forming a soluble complex, Hg_2Cl_2 forms an insoluble black substance.

$$AgCl(s) + 2NH_3(aq) \longrightarrow \underset{\text{Soluble complex}}{[Ag(NH_3)_2]Cl(aq)}$$

$$Hg_2Cl_2(s) + NH_3 \longrightarrow \underset{\text{Black insoluble substance}}{Hg(NH_2)Cl \cdot Hg} + Cl^-$$

(b) **Quantitative analysis** Gravimetric estimation of Ni^{2+} is carried out by precipitating Ni^{2+} as red nickel dimethyl glyoxime complex in the presence of ammonia.

$$Ni^{2+} + 2DMG \xrightarrow{NH_3} \underset{\text{Red ppt.}}{[Ni(DMG)_2]}$$

EDTA is used in the complexometric determination of several metal ions such as $Ca^{2+}, Zn^{2+}, Fe^{2+}, Co^{2+}, Ni^{2+}$, etc.

(iv) **Role of coordination compounds in extraction/metallurgy of metals** Extraction of various metals from their ore involves complex formation. For example, silver and gold are extracted from their ore by forming cyanide complex.

$$4Au + 8KCN + 2H_2O + O_2 \longrightarrow \underset{\text{Potassium dicyanoaurate (I)}}{4K[Au(CN)_2]} + 4KOH$$

$$2K[Au(CN)_2] + Zn \longrightarrow K_2[Zn(CN)_4] + 2Au\downarrow$$

Purification of some metals can be achieved through complex formation. For example in **Mond process,** impure nickel is converted into $[Ni(CO)_4]$, which is decomposed to yield pure nickel.

Question 28 How many ions are produced from the complex, $Co(NH_3)_6Cl_2$ in solution?

(a) 6 (b) 4

(c) 3 (d) 2

Sol. The complex will dissociate in aqueous solution to produce 3 ions.

$$Co(NH_3)_6Cl_2 \xrightarrow{aq} [Co(NH_3)_6]^{2+} + 2Cl^-$$

Thus, correct answer is (c).

Question 29 Amongst the following ions which one has the highest magnetic moment value?

(a) $[Cr(H_2O)_6]^{3+}$ (b) $[Fe(H_2O)_6]^{2+}$ (c) $[Zn(H_2O)_6]^{2+}$

◎ *Thinking Process* More the number of unpaired electrons, higher is the magnetic moment. So, find the number of unpaired electrons to find magnetic moment.

Sol. The oxidation states of metals in the complexes along with the electronic configuration are given :

(a) Cr^{3+} : $3d^3$ configuration; no. of unpaired electrons (n) = 3

(b) Fe^{2+} : $3d^6$ configuration; $n = 4$

(c) Zn^{2+} : $3d^{10}$ configuration; $n = 0$

The complex $[Fe(H_2O)_6]^{2+}$ with maximum number of unpaired electrons has the highest magnetic moment. Thus, correct answer is (b).

Quick Solution

You can use the formula $\mu = \sqrt{n(n+2)}$ BM, to calculate the magnetic moment of the given three complexes and then compare their values to find out which one has the highest magnetic moment value.

Question 30 Amongst the following, the most stable complex is

(a) $[Fe(H_2O)_6]^{3+}$ (b) $[Fe(NH_3)_6]^{3+}$, (c) $[Fe(C_2O_4)_3]^{3-}$, (d) $[FeCl_6]^{3-}$

Sol. In all these complexes, Fe is in +3 oxidation state. However, the complex (c) is a chelate because three $C_2O_4^{2-}$ ions (bidentate ligand) act as the chelating ligands. Thus, the most stable complex is $[Fe(C_2O_4)_3]^{3-}$.

Thus, correct answer is (c).

Question 31 What will be the correct order for the wavelengths of absorption in the visible region for the following :

$$[Ni(NO_2)_6]^{4-}, [Ni(NH_3)_6]^{2+}, [Ni(H_2O)_6]^{2+}$$

◎ *Thinking Process*

(i) CFSE is higher for the complex having strong field ligand.

(ii) CFSE (crystal field splitting energy) varies inversely with wavelength.

Sol. In all the given complexes, the metal ion is Ni^{2+}. The increasing field strengths of the ligands present as per electrochemical series are in the order :

$$H_2O < NH_3 < NO_2^-$$

The energies absorbed for excitation will be in the order :

$$[Ni(H_2O)_6]^{2+} < [Ni(NH_3)_6]^{2+} < [Ni(NO_2)_6]^{4-}$$

As $E = \frac{hc}{\lambda}$, *i.e.*, $E \propto \frac{1}{\lambda}$; the wavelengths will be in the opposite order, that is as follows

$$[Ni(H_2O)_6]^{2+} > [Ni(NH_3)_6]^{2+} > [Ni(NO_2)_6]^{4-}$$

DIKSHA APP Questions

Multiple Choice Questions

Q.1 EDTA is used for the estimation of

(a) Na^+ and K^+ ions (b) Cu^{2+} and Cs^+ ions
(c) Cl^- and Br^- ions (d) Ca^{2+} and Mg^{2+} ions

Sol. (d) EDTA is used for the estimation of Ca^{2+} and Mg^{2+} ions through complexometric titration, where EDTA binds to these metal ions, forming stable complexes.

Q.2 Which of the following has Magnesium?

(a) Chlorophyll (b) Haemocyanin
(c) Carbonic Anhydrase (d) Vitamin B-12

Sol. (a) Chlorophyll contains a central magnesium ion (Mg^{2+}) coordinated to a porphyrin ring structure. This magnesium ion plays a crucial role in capturing light energy during photosynthesis, enabling the chlorophyll molecule to absorb light and convert it into chemical energy.

Q.3 The correct structure of $Fe(CO)_5$ is

(a) Octahedral (b) Tetrahedral
(c) Square Pyramidal (d) Trigonal Bipyramidal

Sol. (d) The structure of $Fe(CO)_5$ is trigonal bipyramidal due to the coordination of five carbon monoxide (CO) ligands around the iron (Fe) center. The iron atom adopts this geometry to minimize electron repulsion, with three CO ligands in the equatorial positions and two in the axial positions, resulting in a stable configuration.

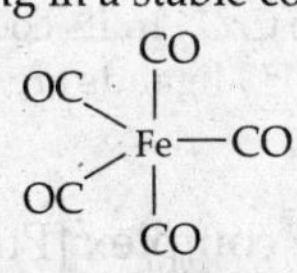

$Fe(CO)_5$
Trigonal bipyramidal

Q.4 Which of the following facts about the complex $[Cr(NH_3)_6]Cl_3$ is incorrect?

(a) The complex involves d^2sp^3 hybridisation and is octahedral in shape.
(b) The complex is paramagnetic.
(c) The complex is an outer orbital complex.
(d) The complex gives white precipitate with $AgNO_3$ solution.

Sol. (c) In $[Cr(NH_3)_6]^{3+}$, Cr exists as Cr^{3+} ion. The outer orbital electronic configuration of Cr is $3d^3\ 4s^0$. The orbital diagram is represented by.

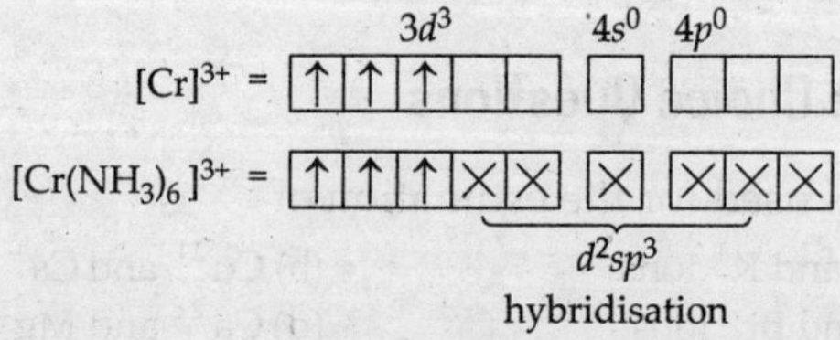

Here ☒ indicates lone pair of NH_3 donated to Cr

For hybridisation, it uses its lower-energy 3*d*, 4*s* and 4*p* orbitals (the inner orbitals), resulting in d^3sp^3 hybridisation, typical of inner orbital complexes. These hybrid orbitals then form bonds with the six ammonia (NH_3) ligands, resulting in an octahedral geometry. Cr^{3+} has three unpaired electrons in its *d*-orbitals, making the complex paramagnetic.

Reaction with $AgNO_3$: When $[Cr(NH_3)_6]Cl_3$ is treated with silver nitrate ($AgNO_3$), the chloride ions react with Ag^+ to form a white precipitate of AgCl. This confirms the presence of chloride ions in the complex.

Reaction:

$$[Cr(NH_3)_6]Cl_3(aq) + 3AgNO_3(aq) \rightarrow 3AgCl(s) + [Cr(NH_3)_6]^{3+}(aq) + 3NO_3^-(aq)$$

Q.5 The complexes $[Co(NH_3)_6][Cr(CN)_6]$ and $[Cr(NH_3)_6][Co(CN)_6]$ are the examples of which types of isomerism?

(a) Linkage Isomerism (b) Ionisation Isomerism

(c) Coordination Isomerism (d) Geometrical Isomerism

Sol. (c) Coordination isomerism arises from the interchange of ligands between cationic and anionic entities of different metal ions present in a complex. For example, in $[Co(NH_3)_6][Cr(CN)_6]$, NH_3 ligands are bound to Co^{3+} and the CN^- ligands to Cr^{3+}. In its coordination isomer $[Cr(NH_3)_6][Co(CN)_6]$,the NH3 ligands are bound to Cr^{3+} and the CN^- ligands to Co^{3+}.

Q.6 The IUPAC name of the complex $[Pt(NH_3)_3Br(NO_2)Cl]Cl$

(a) Triamminechlorobranonitroplatinum (IV) Chloride

(b) Triamminebranonitrochloroplatinum (IV) Chloride

(c) Triamminebromidochloridonitrito -N- Platinum (IV) Chloride

(d) Triamminenitrito -N- ChlorobromoPlatinum (IV) Chloride

Sol. (c) The IUPAC name of $[Pt(NH_3)_3Br(NO_2)Cl]Cl$ complex is:

Triamminebromidochloridonitrito-N-platinum(IV) chloride

Q.7 The correct IUPAC name of $[CO(NH_3)_3(NO_2)_3]$ is

(a) Triamminertrinitrito -N- Cobalt (III)
(b) Triamminetrinitrito -N- Cobalt (II)
(c) TriammineCobalt (III) nitrite
(c) Triaamminetrinitrito -N- Cobaltate (III).

Sol. (a) The IUPAC name of $[Co(NH_3)_3(NO_2)_3]$ complex is: Triaamminetrinitrito-N-cobalt (III).

Q.8 Which of the following is hexadentate ligand?

(a) diene (b) CN^- (c) En (d) EDTA

Sol. (d) EDTA (Ethylenediaminetetraacetic acid) is a hexadentate ligand because it can form six bonds with a central metal ion. It has two amine groups and four carboxylate groups, each donating a lone pair of electrons, resulting in a stable chelate complex.

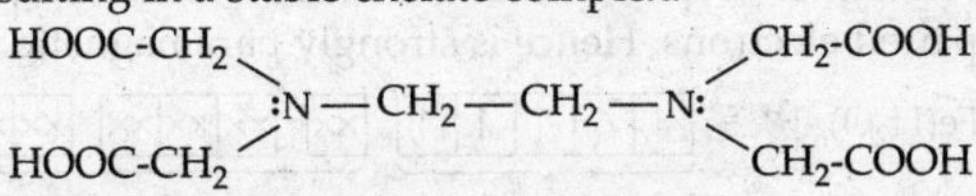

Stucture of EDTA

Q.9 On adding $AgNO_3$ solution to 1 mole of $PdCl_2 \cdot 4NH_3$, two moles of AgCl are formed. The secondary valency of Pd in the complex will be.

(a) 0 (b) 2 (c) 4 (d) 1

Sol. (c) In the complex $PdCl_2 \cdot 4NH_3$, two chloride ions are free and not coordinated to palladium, as evidenced by the formation of 2 moles of AgCl. This indicates that palladium is coordinated to 4 ammonia (NH_3) ligands and it forms $[Pt(NH_3)_4]Cl_2$ complex. Therefore, the secondary valency (coordination number) of palladium is 4.

Q.10 How many ions are produced from $[Co(NH_3)_6]Cl_3$ in solution?

(a) 6 (b) 4 (c) 3 (d) 2

Sol. (b) The complex $[Co(NH_3)_6]Cl_3$ produces four ions in solution.

$$[Co(NH_3)_6]Cl_3 \rightleftharpoons [Co(NH_3)_6]^{3+} + 3Cl^-$$

☐ Short Answer Type

Q.1 Explain why $[Fe(H_2O)_6]^{3+}$ has magnetic value of 5.92 B.M whereas $[Fe(CN)_6]^{3-}$ has a value of only 1.74 B.M?

Sol. Outer configuration of $_{26}Fe = 3d^6\ 4s^2$. In both the complexes Fe is present as Fe^{3+} ion

Fe^{3+} ion $= 3d^5 4s^0$

$3d^5$ $4s^0$

[1 | 1 | 1 | 1 | 1] [ ]

In the the presence of CN^- (a strong field ligand) the $3d$- electrons pair up, leaving only one unpaired electron. The hybridsation is d^2sp^3 forming an inner orbital complex

$3d$ $4s$ $4p$

$[Fe(CN)_6]^{3-}$ = [⥮ | ⥮ | 1 | xx | xx] [xx] [xx | xx | xx]

One unpaired e^- d^2sp^3

For $n = 1$ (1 unpaired electron), the magnetic moment is

$$\mu = \sqrt{1(1+2)} = \sqrt{3} \approx 1.74 \text{ BM.}$$

In the presence of H_2O, (a weak field ligand), 3d- electrons do not pair up. The hybridization is sp^3d^2 forming an outer orbital complex containing five unpaired electrons. Hence is strongly paramagnetic

$[Fe(H_2O)_6]^{3+}$ = [1 | 1 | 1 | 1 | 1] [xx] [xx | xx | xx] [xx | xx | | |]

Five unpaired electron sp^3d^2

for $n = 5$ (5 unpaired electrons), the magnetic moment is

$\mu = \sqrt{5(5+2)} = \sqrt{35} \approx 5.92$ BM

☐ Long Answer Type

Q.1 (a) Explain the following

(i) Low spin octahedral complexes of nickel are unknown.

(ii) $\pi\Delta$ Complexes are known for transition metals only.

(iii) CO is strong ligand than NH_3 for most of the metals.

(b) Calculate the overall complex dissociation equilibrium constant for $[Cu(NH_3)_4]^{2+}$ ion, given that β_4 for the complex is 2.1×10^{13}.

Sol. (a) (i) Ni has an electronic configuration of $3d^8 4s^2$. Ni cannot afford 2 vacant $3d$ orbitals for formation of low spin octahedral complexes, hence d^2sp^3 hybridisation of Ni are unknown.

(ii) Transition metals have vacant d orbitals thus $d\pi - p\pi$ bonding is possible in them and they can form π- complexes

(iii) CO Show back bonding, which is not feasible in case of NH_3, hence NH_3 is a weaker ligand than CO.

(b) Dissociation constant is the reciprocal of the stability constant ($\beta = 1/K$). Overall complex dissociation equilibrium constant,

$$K = \frac{1}{\beta_4} = \frac{1}{2.1 \times 10^{13}} = 4.76 \times 10^{-14}$$

Haloalkanes and Haloarenes

CHAPTER 06

Important Points

01 Alkyl or aryl halides are classified as mono, di or polyhalogen compounds. They are polar in nature.

02 Haloalkanes are prepared by electrophilic addition of halogen acids with alkenes.

$$R—CH{=}CH_2 + HBr \xrightarrow[\text{additions)}]{\text{(Markovnikov's}} R—\underset{}{\overset{\displaystyle Br}{\overset{|}{C}H}}—CH_3$$

$$R—CH{=}CH_2 + HBr \xrightarrow[\text{Peroxide}]{\text{Anti-Markovnikov additions}} R—CH_2—CH_2—Br$$

These are also prepared from alkanes by free radical halogenation.

$$CH_3CH_2CH_3 \xrightarrow[\text{or } \Delta]{Cl_2/h\nu} CH_3CH_2CH_2Cl + \text{isomers}$$

03 Haloalkanes are also prepared by the reaction of alcohols with halogen acids, phosphorus halides and thionyl chloride.

$$R—OH + HCl \xrightarrow{\text{anhyd. } ZnCl_2} R—Cl + H_2O$$

$$3R—OH + PX_3 \longrightarrow 3R—X + H_3PO_3\ (X = Cl, Br)$$

$$R—OH + PCl_5 \longrightarrow RCl + POCl_3 + HCl$$

$$R—OH \xrightarrow[X_2 = Br_2, I_2]{\text{Red P}/X_2} R—X$$

$$R—OH + SOCl_2 \longrightarrow R—Cl + SO_2\uparrow + HCl\uparrow$$

04 Fluorides and iodides are best prepared by halogen exchange method.

(a) $R—X + NaI \xrightarrow[\text{(Finkelstein reaction)}]{\text{Dry acetone}} R—I + NaX\downarrow$

(b) $R—X \xrightarrow[\text{(Swarts reaction)}]{AgF,\ Hg_2F_2,\ CoF_2,\ SbF_3} R—F$

05 Preparation of haloarenes :

(a) From hydrocarbons by electrophilic substitution

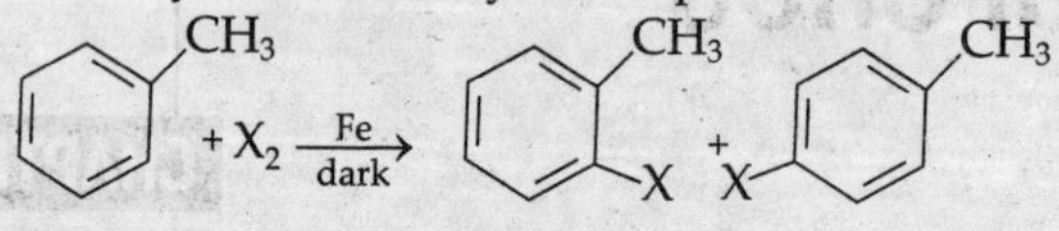

(b) From amines by sandmeyer's reaction

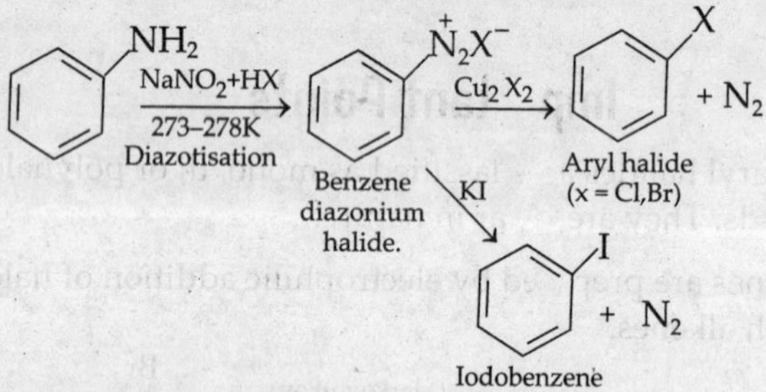

06 Boiling point decreases with increase in branching as surface area decreases, so weak intermolecular forces are present.

Boiling point increases with increasing size and mass of halogens in alkyl halides as magnitude of van der waals forces of attraction increases. So the order of boiling point is:

$$RF < RCl < RBr < RI$$

07 **Melting point** of *p*-isomers of dihalobenzenes is higher as compared to their *o*- and *m*-isomers because *para*-isomers have high symmetry and the fit better into the crystal lattice.

08 **Nucleophiles** are electron rich species. Nucleophile replaces an already present nucleophile in a molecule by nucleophilic substitution reactions. Haloalkanes participate in nucleophilic substitution reactions (S_N) due to the polar C—X bond (X = leaving nucleophile/halide).

09 Nucleophiles like cyanides (CN^-) and nitrites (NO_2^-) have two nucleophilic centres, so they are called **ambident nucleophiles.**

10 Nucleophilic substitution reactions of alkyl halides are

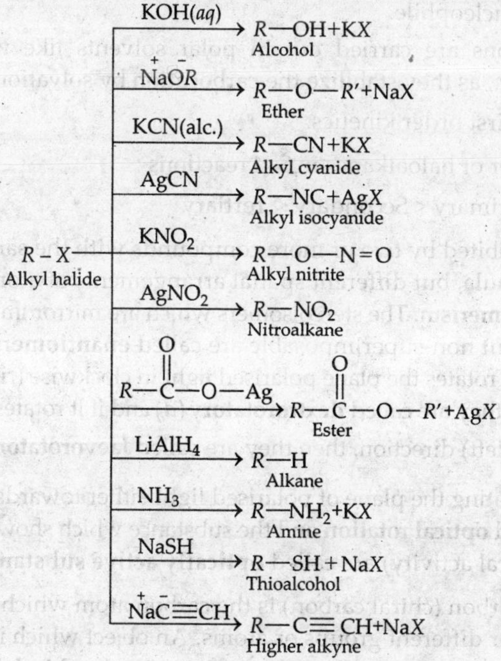

11 S_N2 (Bimolecular nucleophilic substitution reaction)

(a) Rate of the reaction depends on the concentration of two species, alkyl halide and nucleophile.

(b) It occurs in only one step. The backside attack of nucleophile and removal of leaving group takes place simultaneously.

(c) Non-polar solvents favour S_N2 mechanism.

(d) It follows second order kinetics.

12 Reactivity order of haloalkanes in S_N2 reactions :

Primary > Secondary > Tertiary

13 S_N1 (Unimolecular nucleophilic substitution reaction).

(a) Rate of reaction depends upon the concentration of only one of the reactants, *i.e.*, alkyl halides.

(b) The slowest step is the rate determining step, which involves concentration of alkyl halide only.

(c) S_N1 reaction occurs in two steps-carbocation formation and attack of nucleophile.

(d) S_N1 reactions are carried out in polar solvents like water, alcohol, etc., as they stabilize the carbocation by solvation.

(e) It follows first order kinetics.

14 Reactivity order of haloalkanes in S_N1 reactions :

Primary < Secondary < Tertiary

15 Isomerism exhibited by two or more compounds with the same molecular formula, but different spatial arrangements of atoms is called **stereoisomerism.** The stereoisomers which are mirror images of each other but non-superimposable are called **enantiomers.** If the enantiomer rotates the plane polarised light in clockwise (right) direction, then they are called **dextrorotatory** (*d*) and if it rotates it in anti-clockwise (left) direction, then they are called **laevorotatory** (*l*).

16 Property of rotating the plane of polarised light either towards left or right is called **optical rotation** and the substance which show such property (optical activity) are called **optically active substances.**

17 Asymmetric carbon (chiral carbon) is the carbon atom which is attached to four different groups or atoms. An object which is non-superimposable on its mirror image is said to be **chiral.** The non-superimposable on its mirror image is said to be chiral. The property of being chiral is known as **chirality.**

18 **Racemic mixture** is a mixture containing equal amounts of enantiomers (*d*- and *l*-). It does not show optical activity due to external compensation, so racemic mixture is optically inactive. The process of conversion of an enantiomer into racemic mixture is known as **racemisation.**

19 When optically active (*d*)-alkyl halide is treated with OH^- nucleophile, we get optically active (*l*)-alcohol due to backside attack of OH^-. This is **inversion of configuration** (in S_N2 mechanism).

20 Retention of configuration is the preservation of the spatial arrangement of bonds to an assymmetric centre during a chemical reaction.

21 Optical isomerism in these compounds is found due to the presence of chiral carbon atom.

22 S_N2 mechanism leads to inversion of configuration in haloalkanes whereas S_N1 mechanism leads to racemisation.

23 Dehydrohalogentation reaction (β-elimination) or elimination reaction of a haloalkane.

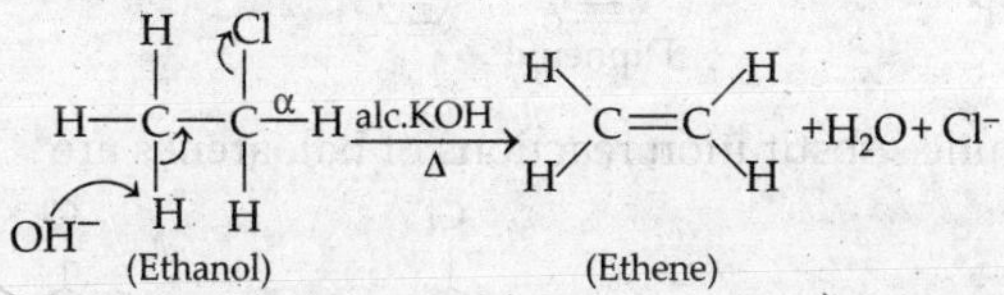

24 (a) Reaction with metals $R—X + Mg \xrightarrow{\text{Dry ether}} RMgX$
Alkyl magnesium halide (Grignard reagent)

(b) $R—X + 2Na + X—R \xrightarrow[\text{(Wurtz reaction)}]{\text{Dry ether}} R—R + 2NaX$

25 Aryl halides are less reactive towards nucleophilic substitution reactions due to resonance effect, instability of phenyl cation and repulsion between electron rich arene and nucleophile. Also, C$-X$ bond is difficult to break as carbon is sp^2 hybridised so the C$-X$ bond is shorter and less reactive towards S_N reactions.

26 Reactions of haloarenes are :

(a)
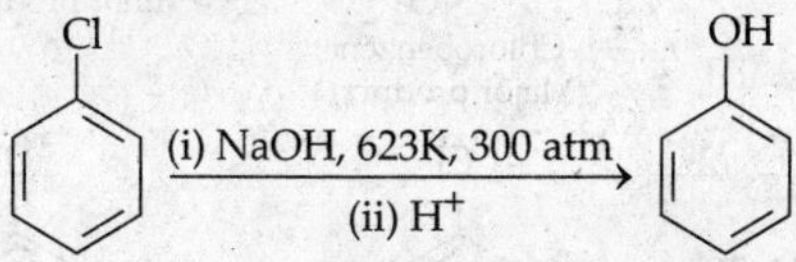

(b)
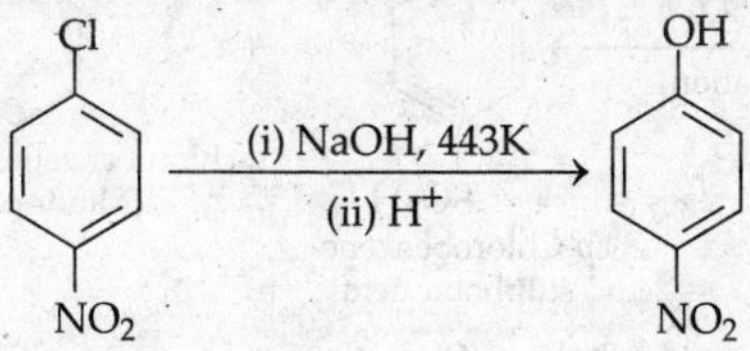

(c)
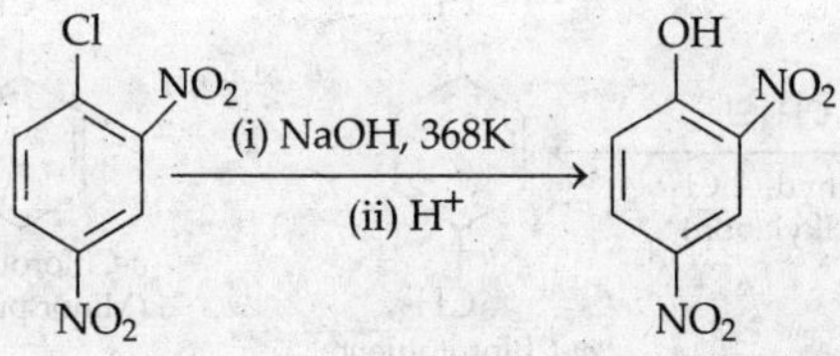

(d)
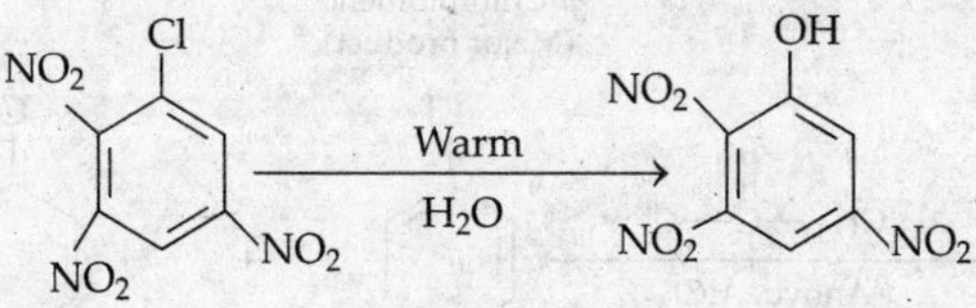

(e)
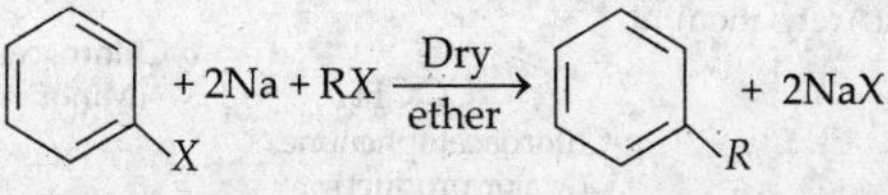

(f) 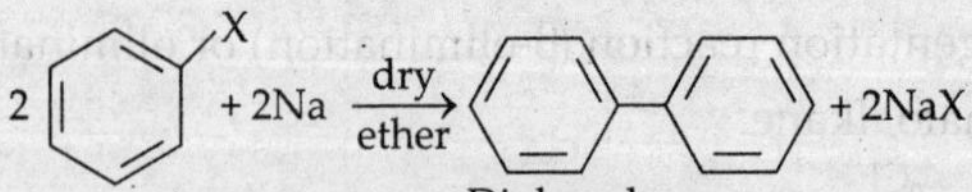

Diphenyl

27 Electrophilic substitution reactions of haloarenes are

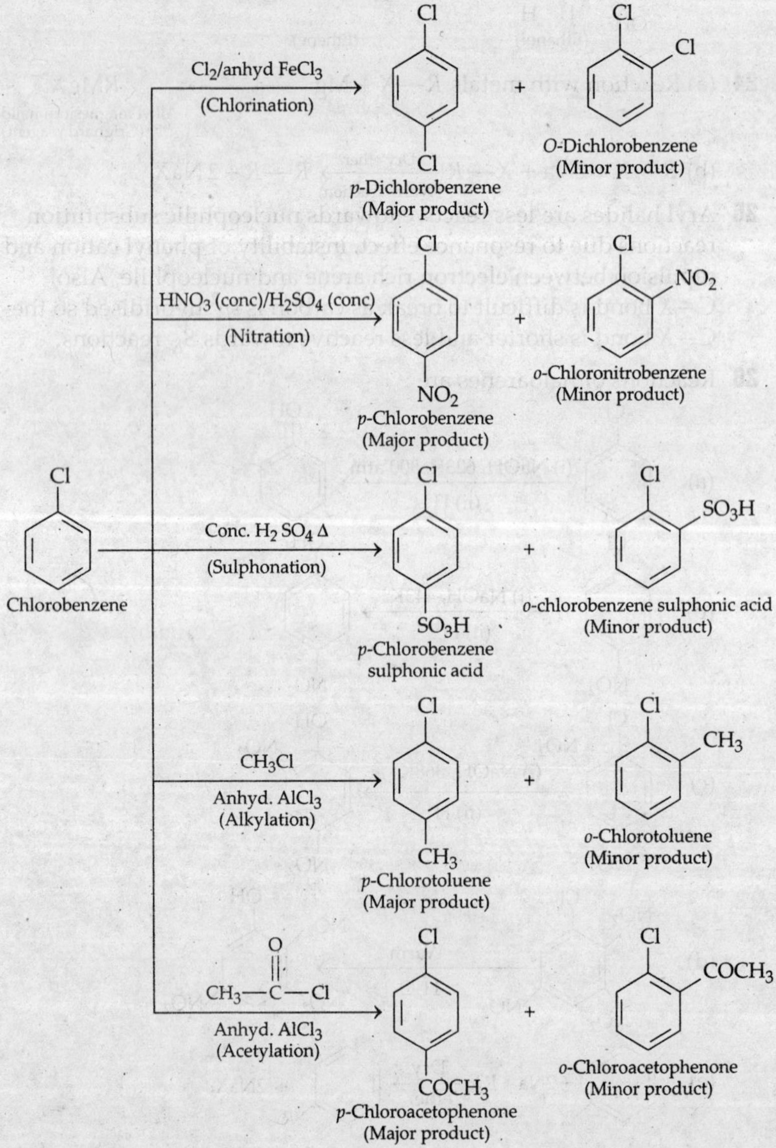

28 Carbon compounds containing more than one halogen atom are usually referred to as **polyhalogen compounds.** These compounds have various industrial applications.

29 Dichloromethane (Methylene chloride) is used as a solvent in pharmaceuticals, paint remover, propellant in aerosols.

30 Chloroform (Trichloromethane) is not used as anaesthetic due to its toxic nature (formation of phosgene gas).

$$\underset{\text{(Chloroform)}}{2CHCl_3} + O_2 \xrightarrow{\text{Light}} \underset{\text{(Phosgene)}}{2COCl_2} + 2HCl$$

Chloroform is used to produce freon refrigerant (R-22). It is used as a solvent for fats, alkaloids, iodine, etc.

31 Iodoform (triiodomethane) is used as an antiseptic for dressing wounds as it produces free iodine. But it has an objectionable smell, so it is being replaced by other antiseptics containing iodine.

32 Carbon tetrachloride (tetrachloromethane, CCl_4) is used in fire extinguishers, preparation of refrigerants and propellants for aerosols cans. It can deplete the ozone layer and cause cancer in humans.

33 The chlorofluorocarbon compounds of methane and ethane are collectively known as freons. They are extremely stable, non-toxic, unreactive, non-corrosive and easily liquefiable gases. Freon is (CCl_2F_2) is commonly used freon in industries. Freons are used as refrigerants but damage the ozone layer. Ozone layer is a protective cover for ultraviolet radiations of sun.

34 *p, p*′-Dichlorodiphenyl trichloroethane (DDT) was used as an insecticide. DDT is not preferred now-a-days due to its non-biodegradable nature and high toxicity.

Intext Questions

Question 1 Write the structures of the following compounds.

(i) 2-Chloro-3-methylpentane
(ii) 1-Chloro-4-ethyl cyclohexane
(iii) 4-Butyl-3-iodoheptane
(iv) 1,4 Dibromobut-2-ene
(v) 1-Bromo-4-sec-butyl-2-methylbenzene

◎ ***Thinking Process*** To write the structure of the compounds, first draw the continuous C–chain according to the name of parent hydrocarbon. Then place the substituents at the positions as mentioned in the name.

(i) C-chain of 5–atoms; —Cl at C-2 and —CH_3 at C-3.
(ii) Cyclic arrangement of 6 C-atoms; —Cl at C-1 and —C_2H_5 at C-4.
(iii) C-chain of 7 atoms; *tert.*-butyl [—$C(CH_3)_3$] at C-4 and —I at C-3.
(iv) C-chain of 4 atoms; —Br at C-1 and C-4; Double bond between C-2 and C-3.
(v) Benzene ring with 6 C-atoms and 3 double bonds at alternate positions; —Br at C-1; —CH_3 at C-2 and *sec.* butyl $\left[\begin{array}{c} —\underset{|}{C}H—CH_2—CH_3 \\ CH_3 \end{array} \right]$ at C-4 position.

Sol. (i) $\overset{1}{C}H_3—\overset{2}{\underset{\underset{Cl}{|}}{C}}H—\overset{3}{\underset{\underset{CH_3}{|}}{C}}H—\overset{4}{C}H_2—\overset{5}{C}H_3$

2-Chloro-3-methylpentane

(ii)

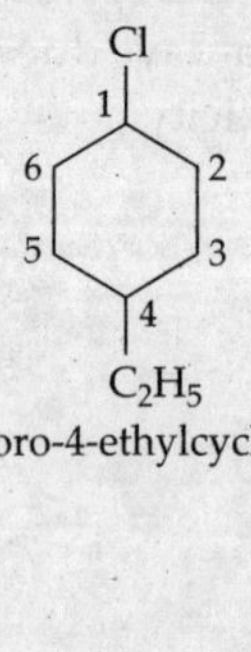

1-Chloro-4-ethylcyclohexane

(iii) 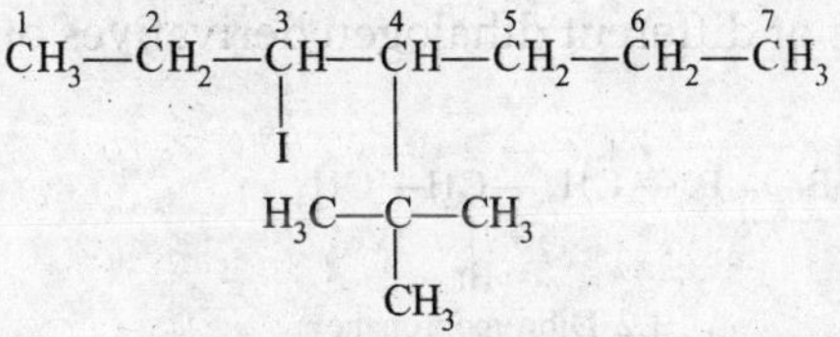

4-*tert*.Butyl-3-iodoheptane

(iv) $\overset{1}{Br—CH_2}—\overset{2}{CH}=\overset{3}{CH}—\overset{4}{CH_2}—Br$

1,4-dibromobut-2-ene

(v) 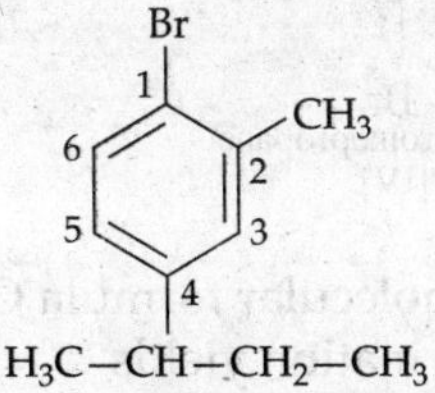

1-Bromo-4-*sec*. butyl-2-methylbenzene

Mistake Alert After drawing the structures, count the valencies of every element and complete them by using H-atoms (if incomplete).

Question 2 Why is sulphuric acid not used during the reaction of alcohols with KI?

Thinking Process Sulphuric acid is a good oxidising agent.

Sol. When KI reacts with H_2SO_4, it produces HI. In order to produce alkyl iodides (R—I), this HI should react with alcohols (R—OH). But the reaction does not take place in this manner as H_2SO_4 oxidises HI to I_2, which in turn does not react with alcohol.

$$KI + H_2SO_4 \xrightarrow{\text{Heat}} KHSO_4 + HI$$

$$H_2SO_4 \longrightarrow H_2O + SO_2 + [O]$$

$$2HI + [O] \longrightarrow H_2O + I_2$$

Note Instead of H_2SO_4, H_3PO_4 can be used to produce alkyl iodides.

Question 3 Write structures of different dihalogen derivatives of propane.

Sol. $Br-\overset{1}{C}H_2-\overset{2}{C}H_2-\overset{3}{C}H_2-Br$

1,3-Dibromopropane
[I]

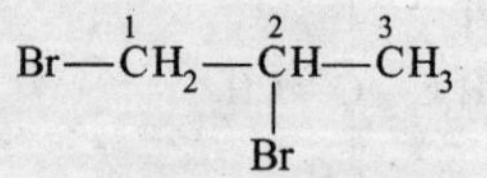

1,2-Dibromopropane
[II]

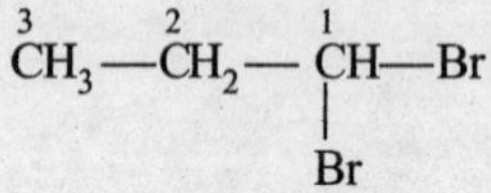

1,1-Dibromopropane
[III]

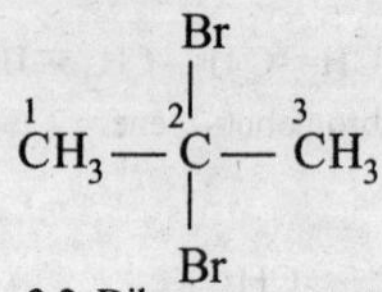

2,2-Dibromopropane
[IV]

Question 4 Among the isomeric alkanes of molecular formula C_5H_{12}, identify the one that on photochemical chlorination yields

(i) a single monochloride
(ii) three isomeric monochlorides
(iii) four isomeric monochlorides.

◎ *Thinking Process*

(i) The molecular formula C_5H_{12} can be represented by three structural isomers. These are

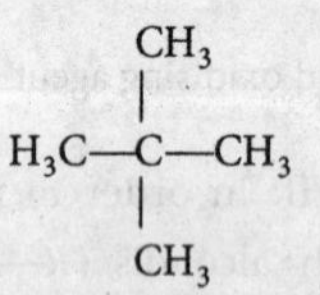

2,2-Dimethylpropane
(neo-pentane)
[I]

$CH_3-CH_2-CH_2-CH_2-CH_3$
Pentane (*n*-pentane)
[II]

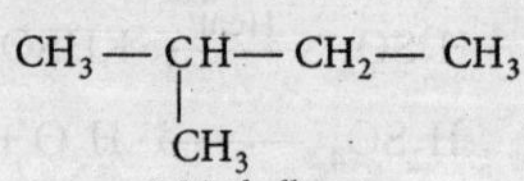

2-Methylbutane
(*iso*-Pentane)
[III]

(ii) Number of monochlorides depends upon the types of hydrogen atoms present in the molecule. So, find the different types of hydrogen atoms and give answer on this basis.

Sol. (i) A single monochloride [IV] can be produced only when all the hydrogen atoms are equivalent. This isomer must be symmetrical. Its structure is given by [I].

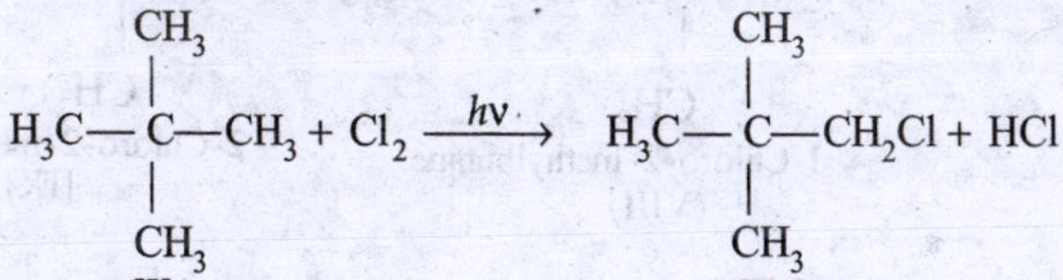

[I] *neo*-Pentane → [IV] 1-Chloro-2, 2-dimethylpropane

(ii) Isomer [II] has three groups of equivalent hydrogen atoms. Therefore, three isomeric monochlorides [V, VI and VII] are produced.

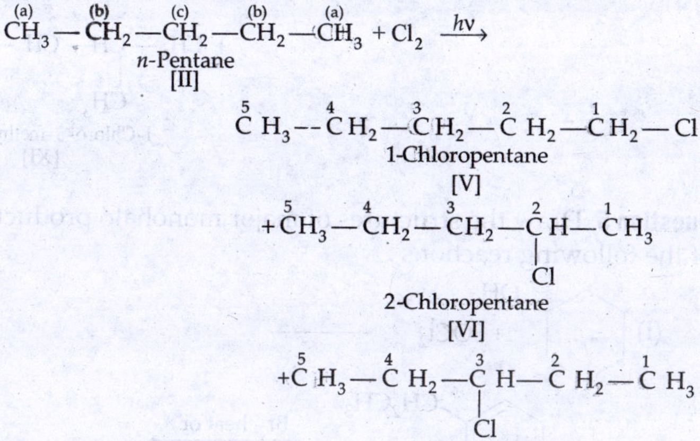

n-Pentane [II]

1-Chloropentane [V]

2-Chloropentane [VI]

3-Chloropentane [VII]

(iii) Isomer [III] has four groups of equivalent hydrogen atoms. Therefore, it can produce four isomeric monochlorides [VIII, IX, X and XI].

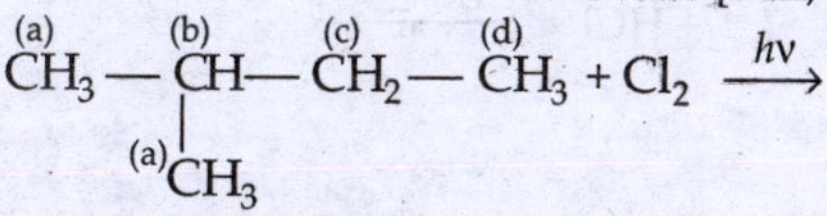

2-Methylbutane [III]

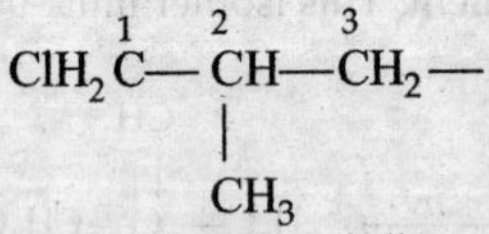

1-Chloro-2-methylbutane
(VIII)

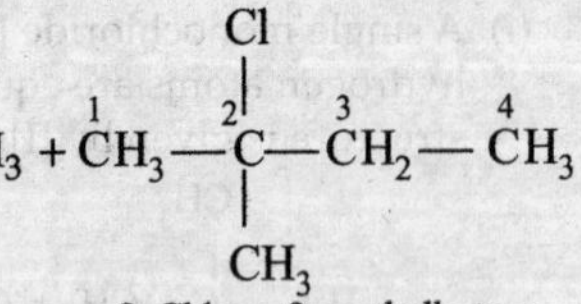

2-Chloro-2-methylbutane
[IX]

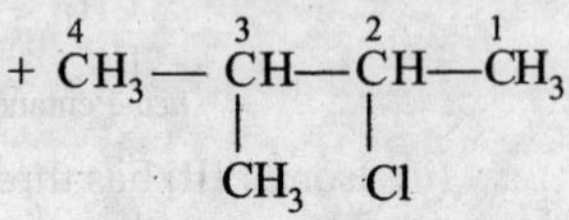

2-Chloro-3-methylbutane
[X]

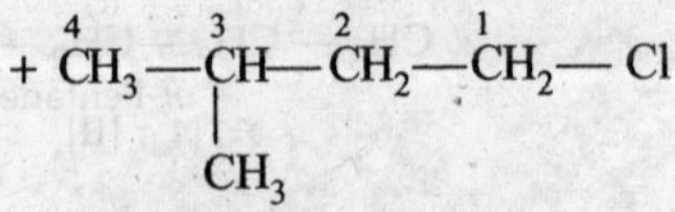

1-Chloro-3-methylbutane
[XI]

Question 5 Draw the structures of major monohalo products in each of the following reactions :

(i) 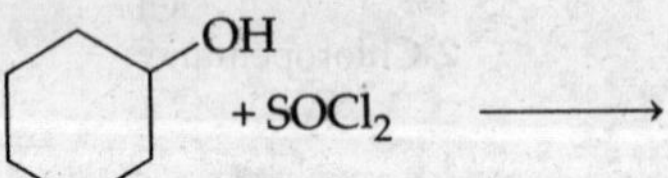

(ii) 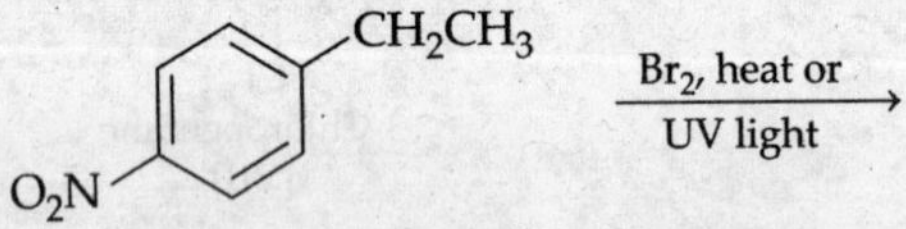

(iii) 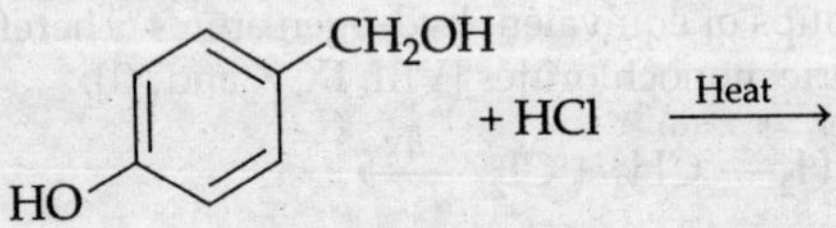

(iv) 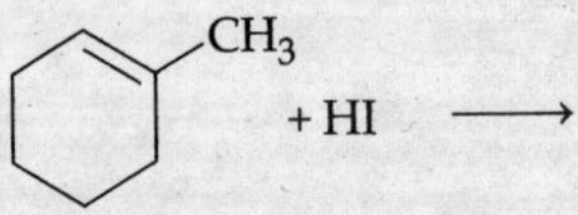

(v) $CH_3CH_2Br + NaI \longrightarrow$

(vi) 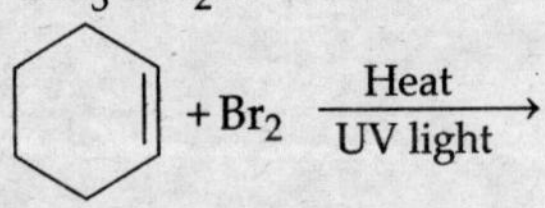

Thinking Process

(i) $SOCl_2$ converts aliphatic —OH group into —Cl.

(ii) In the presence of light allylic substitution takes place *i.e.*, H^- of allylic position is replaced by Br^-.

(iii) HCl at high temperature replaces aliphatic —OH group by —Cl.

(iv) In case of asymmetric unsaturated compounds, addition of HI takes place according to Markovnikov's rule.

(v) It is a halide exchange reaction.

(vi) Same as (ii)

Sol. (i)

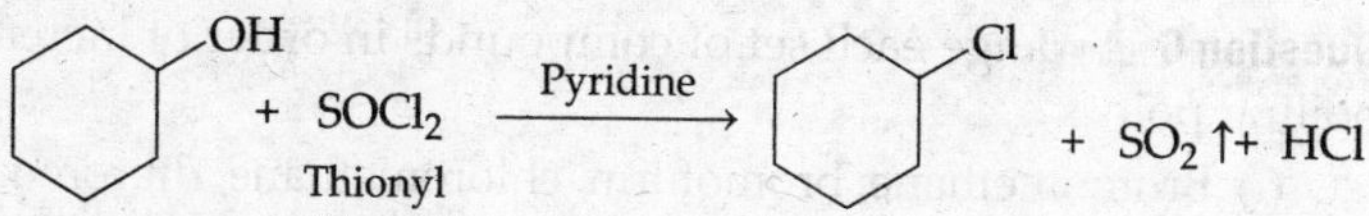

Cyclohexanol Thionyl chloride Chlorocyclohexane

Note The reaction takes place in the presence of pyridine. The method is known as **Darzen's method.**

(ii)

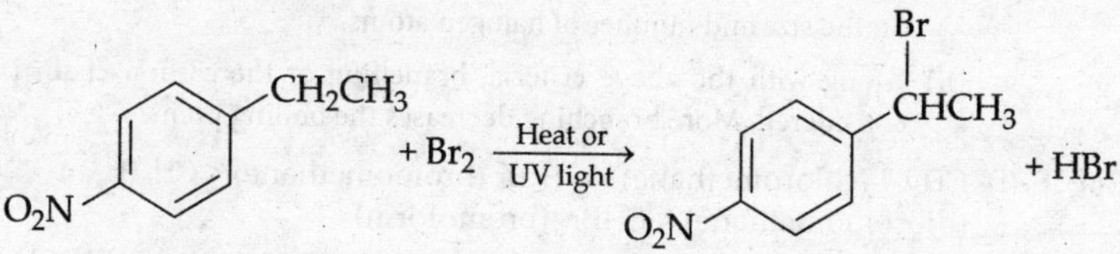

4-nitroethyl benzene 1-bromo-1-(4-nitrophenyl) ethane

Note Bromination does not take place in benzene ring.

(iii)

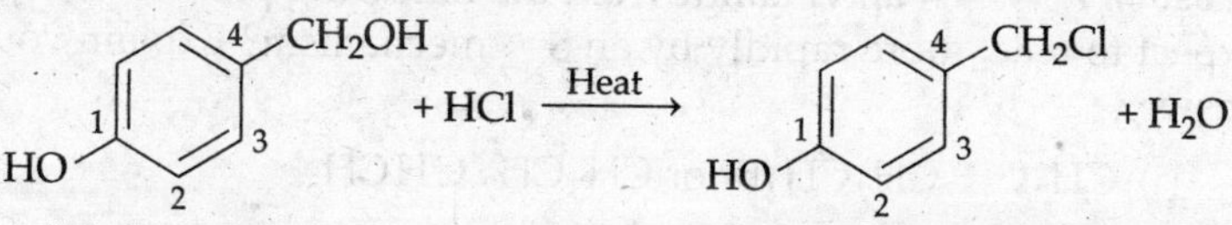

4-Hydroxymethyl phenol 4-Chloromethyl phenol

Note Phenolic —OH group is not replaced by —Cl group.

(iv)

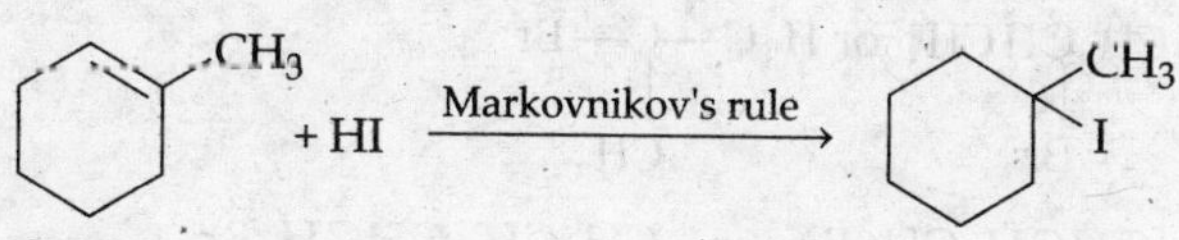

1-Methyl cyclohexene 1-Iodo-1-methyl cyclohexane

Note According to Markovnikov's rule, iodine will add to the carbon atom having less number of hydrogen atoms.

(v) $\underset{\text{Bromoethane}}{CH_3CH_2Br} + NaI \longrightarrow \underset{\text{Iodoethane}}{CH_3CH_2I} + NaBr$

Note Iodide ion is a strong nucleophile so it displaces bromide ion.

(vi) 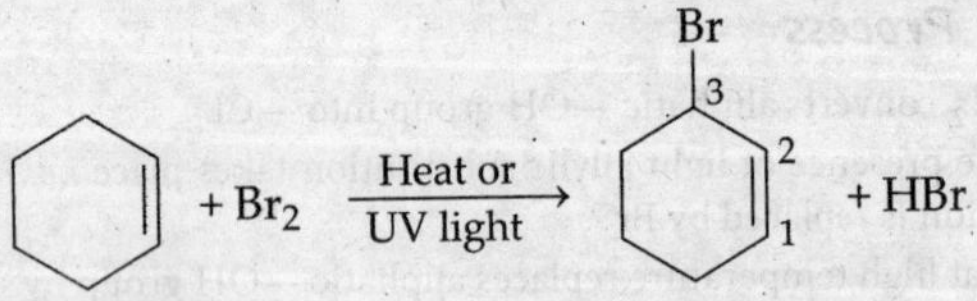

Cyclohexene 3-Bromocyclohexene

Note Under above specified conditions, allylic halogenation takes place. Addition reaction can take place only if reaction is at room temperature.

Question 6 Arrange each set of compounds in order of increasing boiling points

(i) Bromomethane, bromoform, chloromethane, dibromomethane

(ii) 1-Chloropropane, *iso*-propyl chloride, 1-chlorobutane

Thinking Process

(i) Boiling point increases with increase in molecular mass. It also depends on the size and number of halogen atoms.

(ii) Along with the above criteria, branching of the carbon chain is also considered. More branching decreases the boiling point.

Sol. (i) CH_3Cl (chloromethane) < CH_3Br (bromomethane) < CH_2Br_2 (dibromomethane) < $CHBr_3$ (bromoform)

(ii) $(CH_3)_2CHCl$ (*iso*-propylchloride or 2-chloropropane) < $ClCH_2CH_2CH_3$ (1-chloropropane) < $ClCH_2CH_2CH_2CH_3$ (1-chlorobutane).

Question 7 Which alkyl halide from the following pairs would you expect to react more rapidly by an S_N2 mechanism? Explain your answer.

(i) $CH_3CH_2CH_2CH_2Br$ or $CH_3CH_2CH(Br)CH_3$

(ii) $CH_3CH_2CH(Br)CH_3$ or $H_3C—C(CH_3)_2—Br$

(iii) $CH_3CH(CH_3)CH_2CH_2Br$ or $CH_3CH_2CH(CH_3)CH_2Br$

Thinking Process If the leaving group is same in two isomers then the reactivity towards S_N2 reaction decreases with increase in steric hindrance.

Sol. (i) $CH_3CH_2CH_2CH_2Br$

Reason Being a primary halide (less hindered), it is more reactive than the other isomer which is a secondary halide (more hindered).

(ii) $CH_3CH_2\underset{\underset{Br}{|}}{C}HCH_3$

Reason Being a secondary halide, it is more reactive than the tertiary halide. (tertiary halide is more sterically hindered than secondary halide).

(iii) $\overset{4}{C}H_3\underset{\underset{CH_3}{|}}{\overset{3}{C}}H\overset{2}{C}H_2\overset{1}{C}H_2Br$

Reason Here both are primary halides. The presence of methyl group closer to halide group increases the steric hindrance and decreases the rate in $\overset{4}{C}H_3\overset{3}{C}H_2\underset{\underset{CH_3}{|}}{\overset{2}{C}}H\overset{1}{C}H_2Br$.

Question 8 In the following pairs of halogen compounds, which compound undergoes faster $S_{N}1$ reaction?

(i) 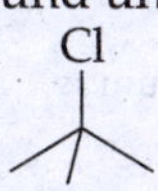 and 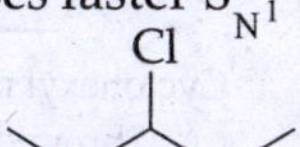

(ii) 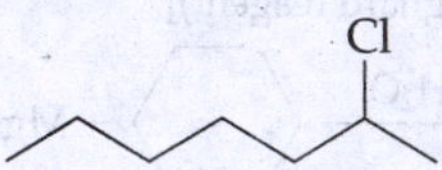 and 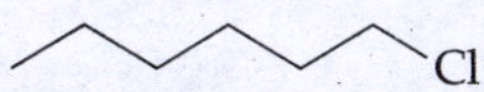

◎ ***Thinking Process*** Reactivity of a halogen derivative towards $S_{N}1$ reaction depends upon the stability of the carbocation formed. So, compare the stability of carbocation formed.

Sol. The order of relative stabilities of carbocations is as follows: Tertiary > Secondary > Primary. (3° > 2° > 1°)

(i) 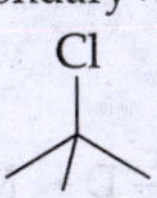 It is a tertiary halide. So, the carbocation formed is comparatively more stable, making the compound more reactive.

(ii) 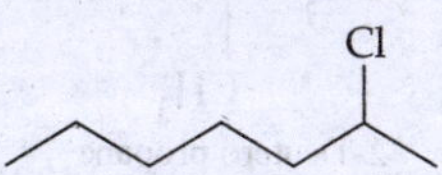

It is a secondary halide. So, its carbocation is more stable than that of the primary halide.

Question 9 Identify *A, B, C, D, E, R* and *R'* in the following :

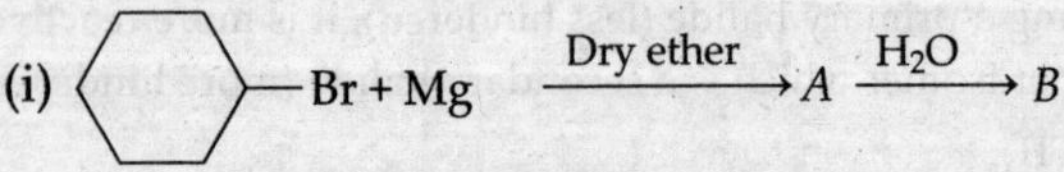

(ii) $R—Br + Mg \xrightarrow{\text{Dry ether}} C \xrightarrow{D_2O} CH_3\underset{\displaystyle D}{\underset{|}{C}}HCH_3$

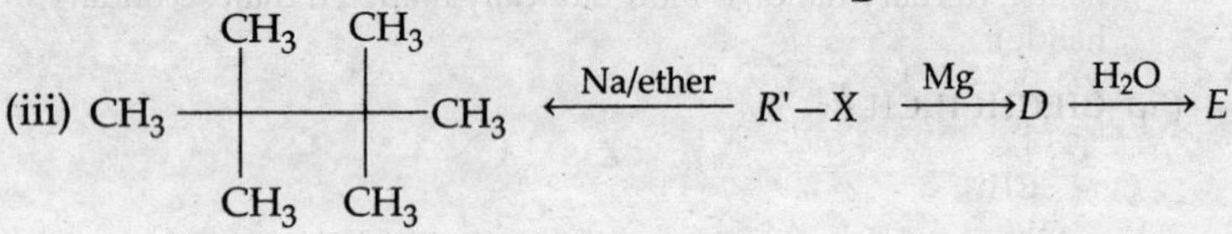

◎ Thinking Process

(i) Haloalkanes react with Mg in dry ether to form Grignard reagents ($RMgX$), which reacts with water to form hydrocarbons.

(ii) Haloalkanes react with Na in dry ether to give hydrocarbons containing double number of C–atoms.

Sol. (i)

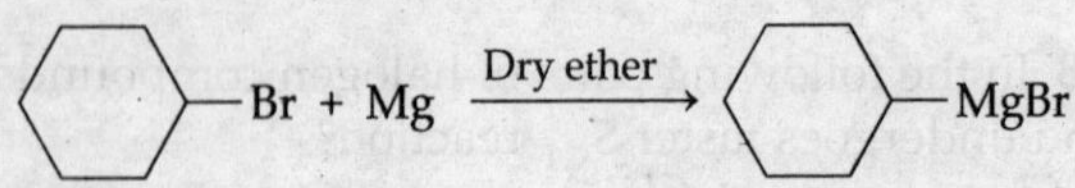

Bromocyclohexane

Cyclohexyl magnesium bromide [*A*] (Grignard reagent)]

Cyclohexane [*B*]

(ii) $CH_3—\underset{\displaystyle CH_3}{\underset{|}{CH}}—Br + Mg \xrightarrow{\text{Dry ether}} CH_3—\underset{\displaystyle CH_3}{\underset{|}{CH}}—MgBr$

Iso-Propyl bromide [*R*-Br]

Iso-Propyl magnesium bromide [*C*] (Grignard reagent)

$\xrightarrow{D_2O} CH_3—\underset{\displaystyle CH_3}{\underset{|}{CH}}—D + Mg(OD)Br$

2-Deutero propane

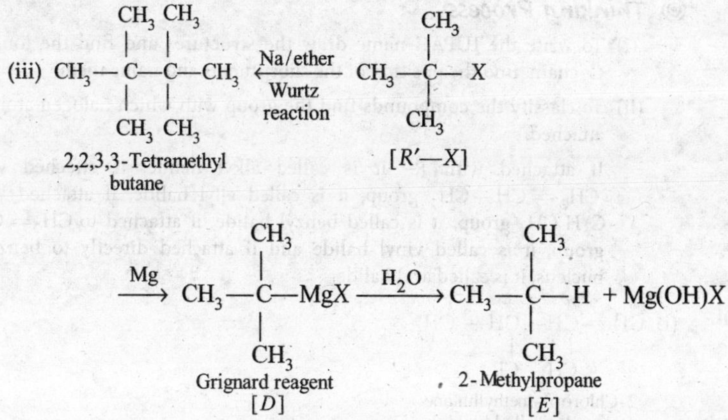

Exercises

Question 1 Name the following halides according to IUPAC system and classify them as alkyl, allyl, benzyl (primary, secondary, tertiary), vinyl or aryl halides :

(i) $(CH_3)_2CHCH(Cl)CH_3$

(ii) $CH_3CH_2CH(CH_3)CH(C_2H_5)Cl$

(iii) $CH_3CH_2C(CH_3)_2CH_2I$

(iv) $(CH_3)_3CCH_2CH(Br)C_6H_5$

(v) $CH_3CH(CH_3)CH(Br)CH_3$

(vi) $CH_3C(C_2H_5)_2CH_2Br$

(vii) $CH_3C(Cl)(C_2H_5)CH_2CH_3$

(viii) $CH_3CH = C(Cl)CH_2CH(CH_3)_2$

(ix) $CH_3CH = CHC(Br)(CH_3)_2$

(x) p-$ClC_6H_4CH_2CH(CH_3)_2$

(xi) m-$ClCH_2C_6H_4CH_2C(CH_3)_3$

(xii) o-$Br—C_6H_4CH(CH_3)CH_2CH_3$

◎ Thinking Process

(i) To write the IUPAC name draw the structures and find the longest C–chain, find the position of the substituents and name them.

(ii) To classify the compounds find the group with which halogen atom is attached.

If attached with *R*– it is called alkyl halide, if attached with $CH_2=CH-CH_2$ group, it is called allyl halide, if attached with $C_6H_5CH_2$-group, it is called benzyl halide, if attached to $CH_2=CH$ group, it is called vinyl halide and if attached directly to benzene nucleus, it is called aryl halide.

Sol. (i) 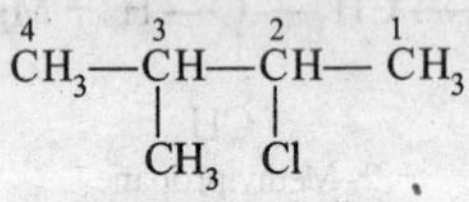

2-Chloro-3-methylbutane
[Secondary alkyl halide]

(ii) 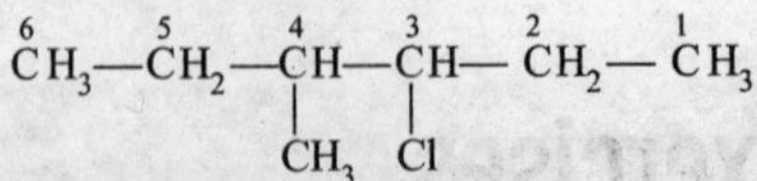

3-Chloro-4-methylhexane
[Secondary alkyl halide]

(iii) 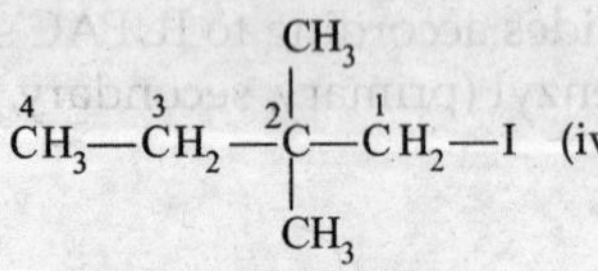

1-Iodo-2,2-dimethylbutane
[Primary alkyl halide]

(iv) 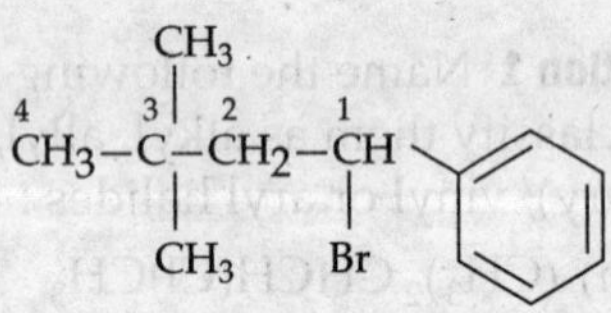

1-Bromo-3,3-dimethyl-1-phenylbutane
[Secondary benzyl halide]

(v) 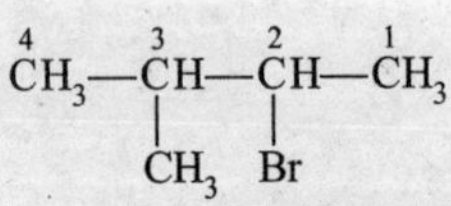

2-Bromo-3-methylbutane
[Secondary alkyl halide]

(vi) 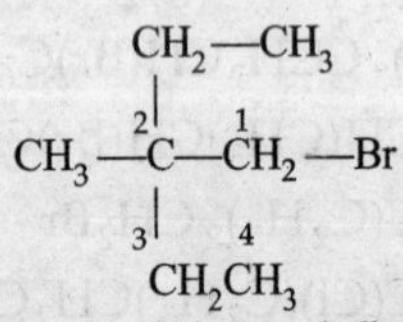

1-Bromo-2-ethyl-2-methylbutane
[Primary alkyl halide]

(vii) 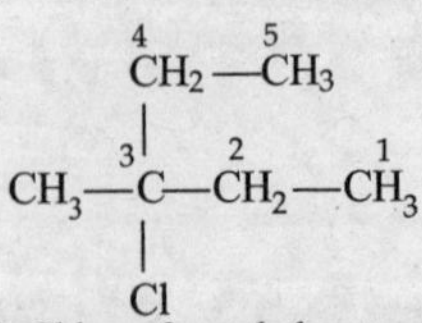

3-Chloro-3-methylpentane
[Tertiary alkyl halide]

(viii) 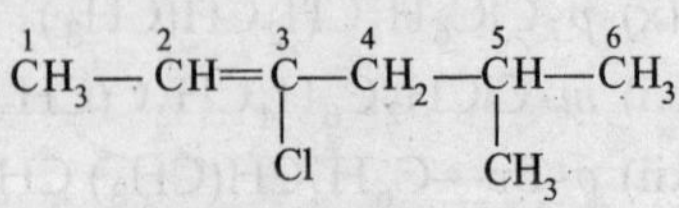

3-Chloro-5-methylhex-2-ene
[Vinyl halide]

(ix) 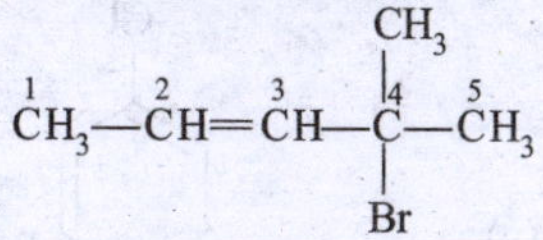

4-Bromo-4-methylpent-2-ene
[Allyl halide]

(x) 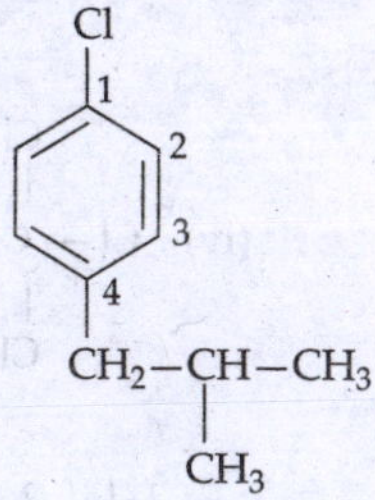

1-Chloro-4-(2-methylpropyl) benzene [Aryl halide]

(xi) 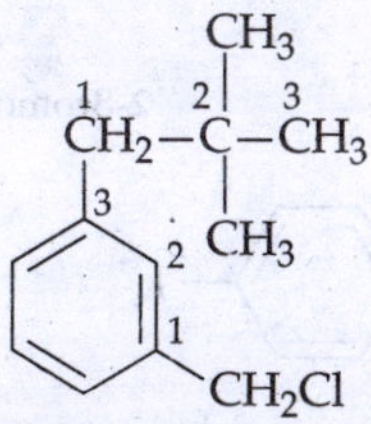

1-Chloromethyl-3-(2, 2-dimethylpropyl) benzene [Benzyl halide]

(xii) 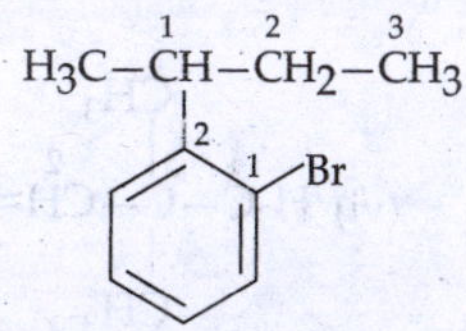

1-Bromo-2-(1-methylpropyl) benzene [Aryl halide]

Question 2 Give the IUPAC names of the following compounds :

(i) $CH_3CH(Cl)CH(Br)CH_3$
(ii) $CHF_2CBrClF$
(iii) $ClCH_2C \equiv CCH_2Br$
(iv) $(CCl_3)_3CCl$
(v) $CH_3C(p\text{-}ClC_6H_4)_2CH(Br)CH_3$
(vi) $(CH_3)_3CCH{=}C{\cdot}ClC_6H_4I\text{-}p$

◎ ***Thinking Process*** To write IUPAC name draw the structures. Find the longest C-chain. Give the numbers and name them.

Sol.

(i) 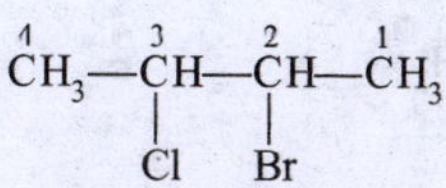

2-Bromo-3-chlorobutane

(ii) 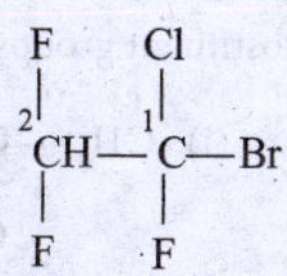

1-Bromo-1-chloro-1,2,2-trifluoroethane

(iii) 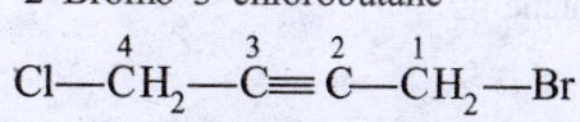

1-Bromo-4-chlorobut-2-yne

(iv) 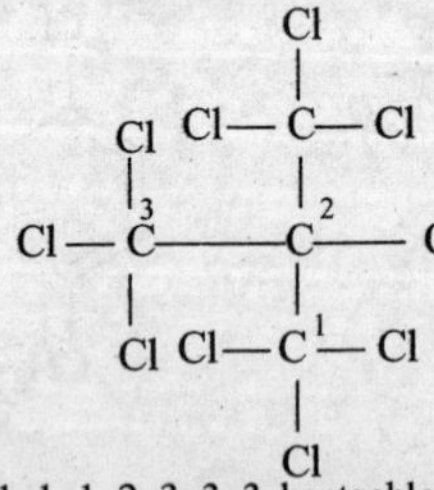

1, 1, 1, 2, 3, 3, 3-heptachloro-2-(trichloromethyl) propane

(v) 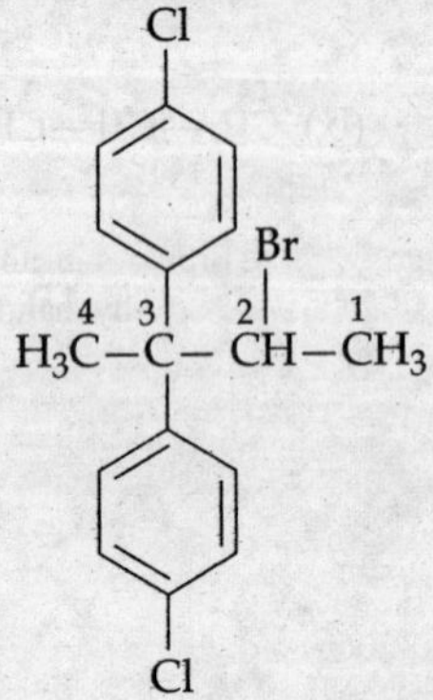

2-Bromo-3, 3-bis (4-chlorophenyl) butane

(vi) 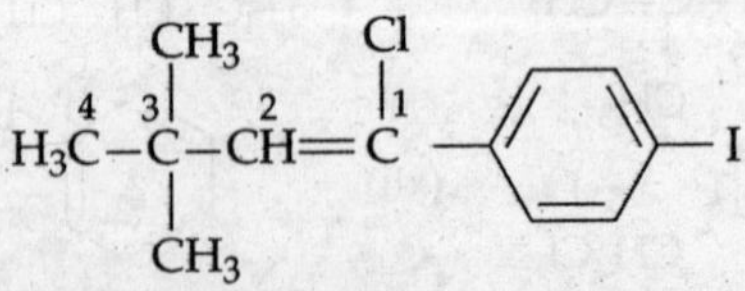

1-Chloro-1-(4-iodophenyl)-3, 3-dimethylbut -1-ene

Question 3 Write the structures of the following organic halogen compounds :

(i) 2-Chloro-3-methylpentane (ii) *p*-Bromochlorobenzene
(iii) 1-Chloro-4-ethylcyclohexane
(iv) 2-(2-chlorophenyl)-1-iodooctane
(v) 2-Bromobutane (vi) 4-tert-butyl-3-iodoheptane
(vii) 1-Bromo-4-sec-butyl-2-methylbenzene
(viii) 1,4-Dibromobut-2-ene

◎ *Thinking Process* To write the structure of organic compound draw the carbon chain according to the parent hydrocarbon. Then, place the substituent groups at their mentioned positions.

Sol. (i) 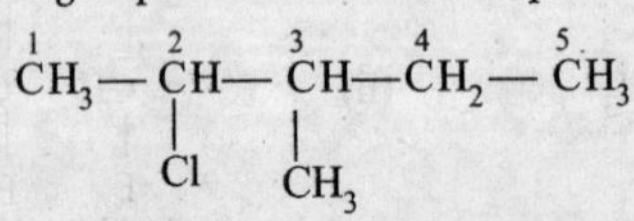

2-Chloro-3-methylpentane

(ii) 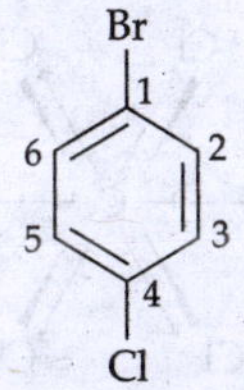

p-bromochlorobenzene

(iii) 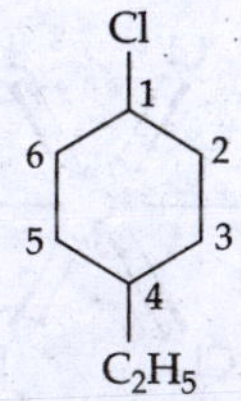

1-Chloro-4-ethylcylohexane

(iv) 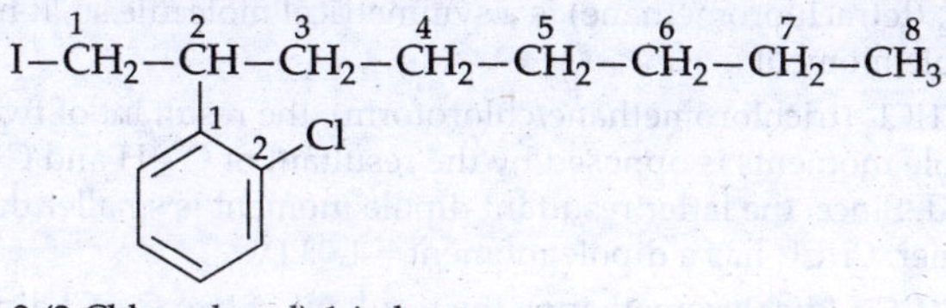

2-(2-Chlorophenyl)-1-iodooctane

(v) $\overset{1}{C}H_3-\overset{2}{C}H(Br)-\overset{3}{C}H_2-\overset{4}{C}H_3$

2-Bromobutane

(vi) $\overset{1}{C}H_3-\overset{2}{C}H_2-\overset{3}{C}H(I)-\overset{4}{C}H(C(CH_3)_3)-\overset{5}{C}H_2-\overset{6}{C}H_2-\overset{7}{C}H_3$

4-*tert*-Butyl-3-iodoheptane

(vii) 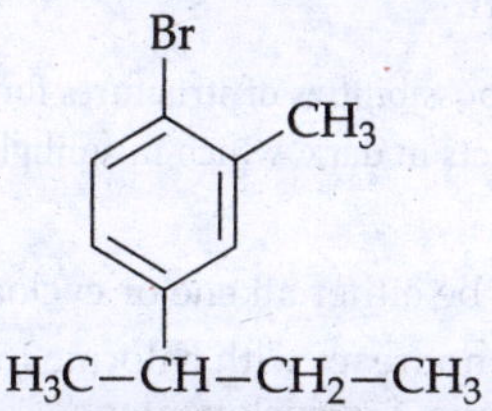

1-bromo-4-sec.butyl-2-methyl benzene

(viii) $\overset{1}{C}H_2(Br)-\overset{2}{C}H=\overset{3}{C}H-\overset{4}{C}H_2(Br)$

1,4-Dibromobut-2-ene

Question 4 Which one of the following has the highest dipole moment?

(i) CH_2Cl_2 (ii) $CHCl_3$ (iii) CCl_4

◎ ***Thinking Process*** **Draw the structures and observe the symmetry of each molecule to find their dipole moment as it is zero for symmetrical molecule.**

Sol.

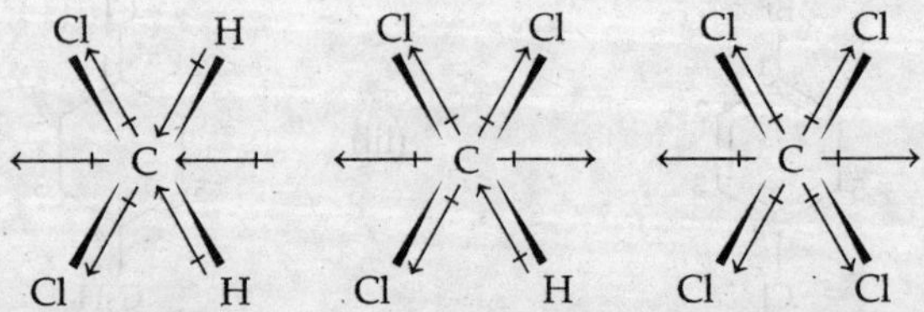

(i) $\mu = 1.62$ D (ii) $\mu = 1.03$ D (iii) $\mu = 0.0$ D

(i) CCl_4 (tetrachloromethane) is a symmetrical molecule so, it has zero dipole moment.

(ii) In $CHCl_3$ (trichloromethane/chloroform), the resultant of two C—Cl dipole moments is opposed by the resultant of C—H and C—Cl bond. Since, the latter resultant dipole moment is smaller than the former, $CHCl_3$ has a dipole moment = 1.03 D.

(iii) In CH_2Cl_2 (dichloromethane), the resultant of two C—Cl dipole moments is reinforced by the resultant of two C—H bonds. Thus, CH_2Cl_2 has a dipole moment = 1.62 D.

Therefore, CH_2Cl_2 has the highest dipole moment amongst the above three molecules.

Note CCl_4 is also called carbon tetrachloride; CH_2Cl_2 is methylene chloride.

Question 5 A hydrocarbon C_5H_{10} does not react with chlorine in dark but gives a single monochloro compound C_5H_9Cl in bright sunlight. Identify the hydrocarbon.

Thinking Process Enlist the possibilities of structures for molecular formula C_5H_{10}. Which isomer reacts in dark, which in sunlight. Then give the reactions.

Sol. (i) Molecular formula C_5H_{10} can be either alkene or cycloalkane.

(ii) Since, the hydrocarbon does not react with chlorine in dark, it is not an alkene. So, it is a cycloalkane, *i.e.*, cyclopentane.

(iii) Since, it forms only single monochloro derivative in bright sunlight, all the H-atoms should be identical. So, it is cyclopentane.

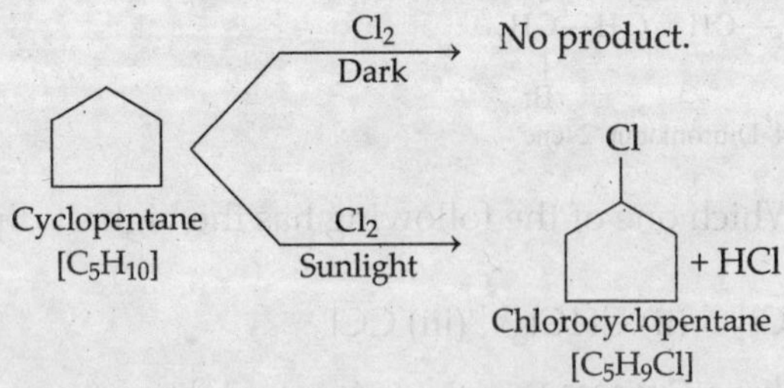

Question 6 Write the isomers of the compound having formula C_4H_9Br.

Sol. There are five isomers of C_4H_9Br. These are :

$$\overset{4}{C}H_3—\overset{3}{C}H_2—\overset{2}{C}H_2—\overset{1}{C}H_2—Br$$

1-Bromobutane
[I]

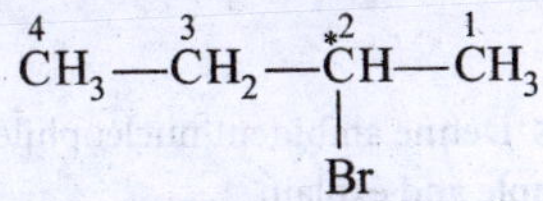

2-Bromobutane
(*d* and *l* form)
[II]

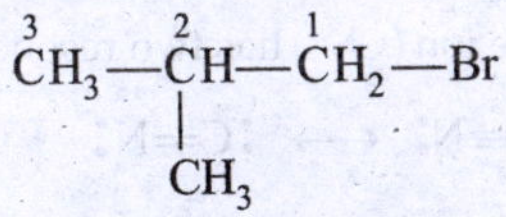

1-Bromo-2-methyl propane
[III]

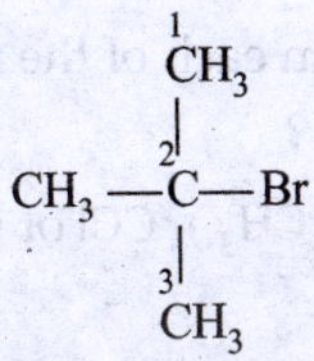

2-Bromo-2-methyl propane
[IV]

Note 2-Bromobutane is expected to exhibit optical isomerism due to the presence of chiral C-atom (C*).

Question 7 Write the equations for the preparation of 1-iodobutane from

(i) 1-butanol (ii) 1-chlorobutane (iii) but-1-ene

◎ *Thinking Process* Reagents

(i) HI will replace —OH by —I.

(ii) NaI will replace —Cl by —I.

(iii) HBr will add to form bromoderivative, then —Br will be replaced by —I by using KI in methanol.

Sol. (i) $\underset{\text{1-Butanol}}{CH_3CH_2CH_2CH_2OH} + HI \xrightarrow{ZnCl_2} \underset{\text{1-Iodobutane}}{CH_3CH_2CH_2CH_2I} + H_2O$

(ii) $CH_3CH_2CH_2CH_2Cl + NaI \xrightarrow[\text{Acetone}]{CH_3OH} CH_3CH_2CH_2CH_2I + NaCl$

(iii) $CH_3CH_2CH{=}CH_2 + HBr \xrightarrow[\text{(Anti-Markovnikov addition)}]{\text{Peroxide}} CH_3CH_2CH_2CH_2Br$

But-1-ene → 1-Bromobutane

$$CH_3CH_2CH_2CH_2Br \xrightarrow{CH_3OH \,|\, KI} CH_3CH_2CH_2CH_2I$$

1-Iodobutane

Question 8 What are ambident nucleophiles? Explain with an example.

Thinking Process Define ambident nucleophile. Draw resonating structures of the example and explain.

Sol. The nucleophiles which have two different electron donor atoms and can attack through two different sites are called **ambident nucleophiles.**

For example : Cyanide ion (CN^-) has two resonating structures :

$$^{-}:C{\equiv}N: \longleftrightarrow :C{=}\ddot{N}:^{-}$$

So, it can attack through carbon to form cyanides and through N to form isocyanides or carbylamines.

Question 9 Which compound in each of the following pairs will react faster in S_N2 reaction with $\bar{O}H$?

(i) CH_3Br or CH_3I (ii) $(CH_3)_3CCl$ or CH_3Cl

Thinking Process

(i) Lesser the bond dissociation energy, faster is the reaction, so find the molecule in which bond dissociation enthalpy is less.

(ii) If both the groups are same, steric hindrance will be considered. More the steric hindrance, lesser the reactivity.

Sol. (i) CH_3—I will react faster because bond dissociation enthalpy of C—I bond is less than that of C—Br bond.

(ii) CH_3Cl will react faster because of less steric hindrance as compared to $(CH_3)_3CCl$.

Question 10 Predict all the alkanes that would be formed by dehydrohalogenation of the following halides with sodium ethoxide in ethanol and identify the major alkene :

(i) 1-Bromo-1-methylcyclohexane

(ii) 2-Chloro-2-methylbutane

(iii) 2,2,3-Trimethyl-3-bromopentane

Thinking Process On reacting with sodium ethoxide in ethanol, the H-atom from β-carbon atom is eliminated. This is called β-elimination. Simultaneously, elimination of halogen atom from α-carbon takes place.

Sol. (i) 1-Bromo-1-methylcyclohexane has two β-hydrogen atoms.

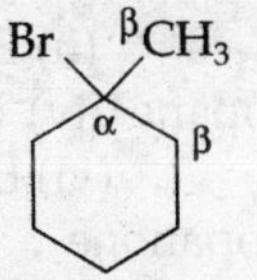

So, two products will be formed.

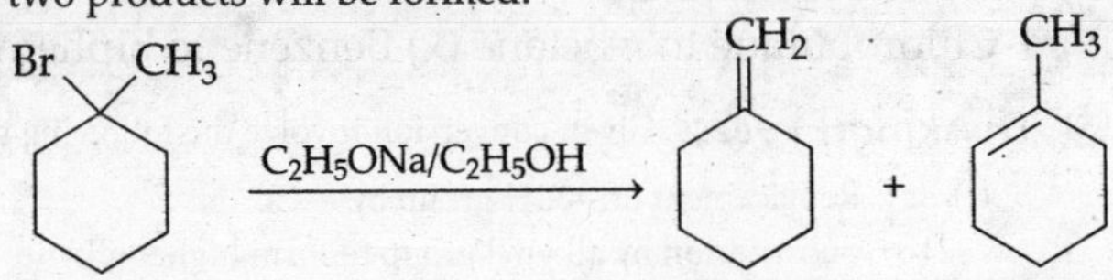

1-Bromo-1-methyl cyclohexane; Methylidene cyclohexene [*A*] (Minor); 1-Methylcyclo hexene [*B*] (Major)

Note **Saytzeff's rule** The product is preferred in which the carbon atoms joined by double bond are more alkyl substituted or alkylated.

(ii)

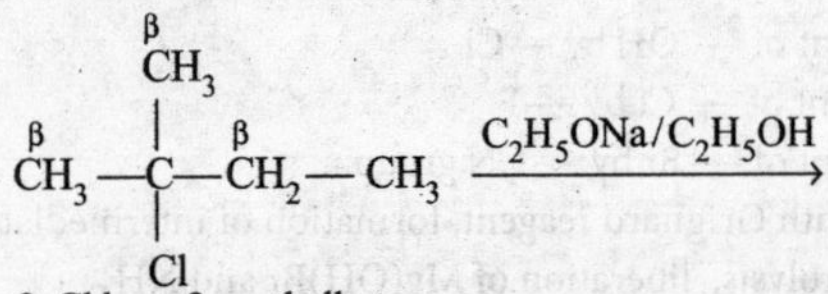

2-Chloro-2-methylbutane

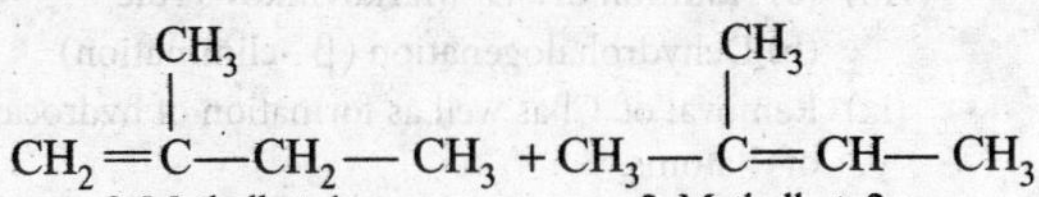

2-Methylbut-1-ene (Minor); 2-Methylbut-2-ene (Major)

(iii)

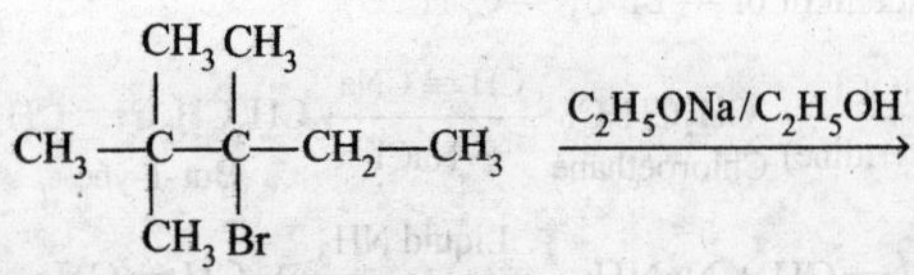

3-Bromo-2,2,3-trimethylpentane

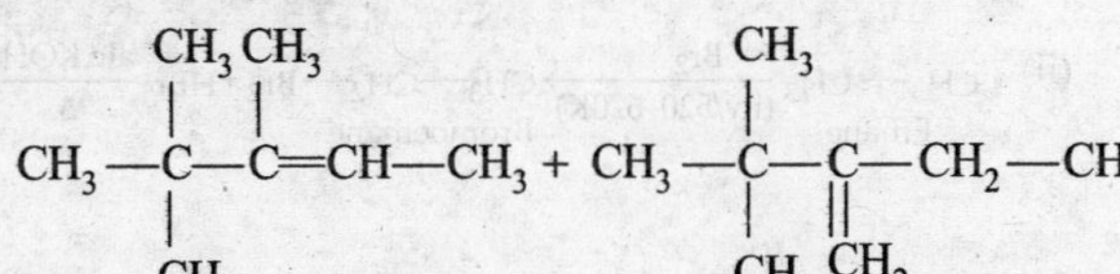

3,4,4-Trimethyl pent-2-ene (Major); 2-Ethyl-3,3-dimethyl but-1-ene (Minor)

Question 11 How will you bring about the following conversions?

(i) Ethanol to but-1-yne (ii) Ethane to bromoethene
(iii) Propene to 1-nitropropane (iv) Toluene to benzyl alcohol
(v) Propene to propyne (vi) Ethanol to ethyl fluoride
(vii) Bromomethane to propanone
(viii) But-1-ene to but-2-ene
(ix) 1-Chlorobutane to *n*-octane (x) Benzene to biphenyl

◎ ***Thinking Process*** Given conversion involve the following steps.

(i) (a) Replacement of —OH group by —Cl.
(b) Substitution by alkynyl group to form higher alkyne.

(ii) Bromination either on heating or in the presence of light.

(iii) (a) Addition of HBr (Anti-Markovnikov's rule or peroxide effect)
(b) Nitration.

(iv) (a) Chlorination of $—CH_3$ group
(b) Hydroxylation (Replacement of —Cl by —OH)

(v) (a) Addition of Br_2 molecule
(b) Reaction with alc. KOH (Dehydrohalogenation)

(vi) (a) Replacement of — OH by —Cl
(b) Replacement of — Cl by —F.

(vii) (a) Replacement of — Br by —CN group.
(b) Reaction with Grignard reagent, formation of intermediate product.
(c) Acidic hydrolysis, liberation of Mg(OH)Br and NH_3.

(viii) (a) Addition of HBr Markovnikov's rule
(b) Dehydrohalogenation (β –elimination)

(ix) Removal of Cl as well as formation of hydrocarbon with double number of C-atoms.

(x) (a) Bromination of benzene
(b) Replacement of —Br by $—C_6H_5$.

Sol. (i)

$$\underset{\text{Ethanol}}{CH_3CH_2OH} \xrightarrow[\text{(Pyridine)}]{SOCl_2} \underset{\text{Chloroethane}}{CH_3CH_2Cl} \xrightarrow[-NaCl]{CH\equiv CNa} \underset{\text{But-1-yne}}{CH_3CH_2C\equiv CH}$$

$$[CH\equiv CH + NaNH_2 \xrightarrow[196\,K]{\text{Liquid } NH_3} CH\equiv CNa + NH_3]$$

(ii)

$$\underset{\text{Ethane}}{CH_3—CH_3} \xrightarrow[(hv/520–670K)]{Br_2} \underset{\text{Bromoethane}}{CH_3—CH_2—Br_2} + HBr \xrightarrow[\Delta]{\text{alc.KOH}} \underset{\text{(Ethene)}}{CH_2=CH_2} + HBr$$

$$\xrightarrow{Br_2/CCl_4} \underset{\text{1, 2-Dibromoethane}}{BrCH_2-CH_2Br} \xrightarrow[\Delta]{\text{alc.KOH}} \underset{\text{Bromoethene}}{CH_2=CHBr} + HBr$$

(iii) $$\underset{\text{Propene}}{CH_3CH{=}CH_2} \xrightarrow[\text{Peroxide}]{HBr} \underset{\text{1-Bromopropane}}{CH_3—CH_2—CH_2—Br} \xrightarrow[-AgBr]{AgNO_2} \underset{\text{1-Nitropropane}}{CH_3—CH_2—CH_2—NO_2}$$

(iv) 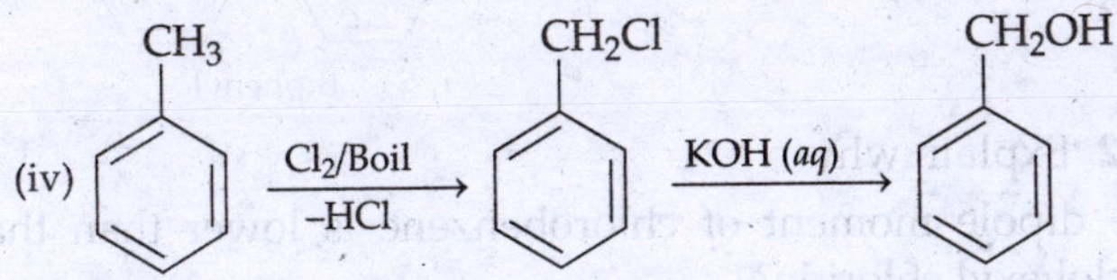

Toluene Benzyl chloride Benzyl alcohol

(v) $$\underset{\text{Propene}}{CH_3—CH{=}CH_2} \xrightarrow{Br_2} \underset{\text{1, 2-Dibromopropane}}{CH_3—\underset{|}{\overset{}{CH}}(Br)—CH_2(Br)} \xrightarrow{KOH(alc)} \underset{\text{Propyne}}{CH_3—C{\equiv}CH}$$

(vi) $$\underset{\text{Ethanol}}{CH_3CH_2OH} \xrightarrow[\text{(pyridine)}]{SOCl_2} \underset{\text{Chloroethane}}{CH_3CH_2Cl} \xrightarrow[-Hg_2Cl_2]{Hg_2F_2} \underset{\text{Fluoroethane (Ethyl fluoride)}}{CH_3CH_2F}$$

(vii) $$\underset{\text{Bromomethane}}{CH_3Br} \xrightarrow[-KBr]{KCN(alc)} \underset{\text{Acetonitrile}}{CH_3C{\equiv}N} \xrightarrow[\text{(ether)}]{CH_3MgBr} \left[CH_3—\underset{\underset{CH_3}{|}}{C}{=}NMgBr \right] \xrightarrow[H_2O/H^+]{-Mg(OH)Br,} \xrightarrow{-NH_3} \underset{\text{Propanone}}{CH_3—\underset{\underset{CH_3}{|}}{C}{=}O}$$

(viii) $$\underset{\text{But-1-ene}}{CH_3—CH_2—CH{=}CH_2} \xrightarrow{HBr} \underset{\text{2-Bromobutane}}{CH_3—CH_2—\underset{\underset{Br}{|}}{CH}—CH_3} \xrightarrow{KOH(alc)} \underset{\text{But-2-ene}}{CH_3—CH{=}CH—CH_3}$$

(ix) $$\underset{\text{1-Chlorobutane}}{2CH_3—CH_2—CH_2—CH_2—Cl} + 2Na \xrightarrow[\text{Wurtz reaction}]{\text{Dry ether}}$$

$$\underset{n\text{-Octane}}{CH_3—CH_2—CH_2—CH_2—CH_2—CH_2—CH_2—CH_3} + 2\,NaCl$$

(x) 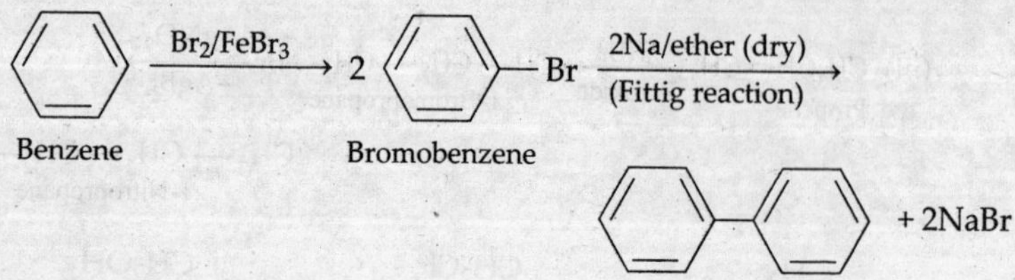

Benzene Bromobenzene Biphenyl

Question 12 Explain why

(i) the dipole moment of chlorobenzene is lower than that of cyclohexyl chloride?

(ii) alkyl halides, though polar, are immiscible with water?

(iii) Grignard reagents should be prepared under anhydrous conditions?

◎ Thinking Process

(i) Find the hybridisation of C-atoms in chlorobenzene and cyclohexyl chloride and electronegativity to find the bond polarity and thus, dipole moment.

(ii) Strong intermolecular H -bonding among water molecules.

(iii) Consider reactive nature of Grignard reagents with water.

Sol. (i) 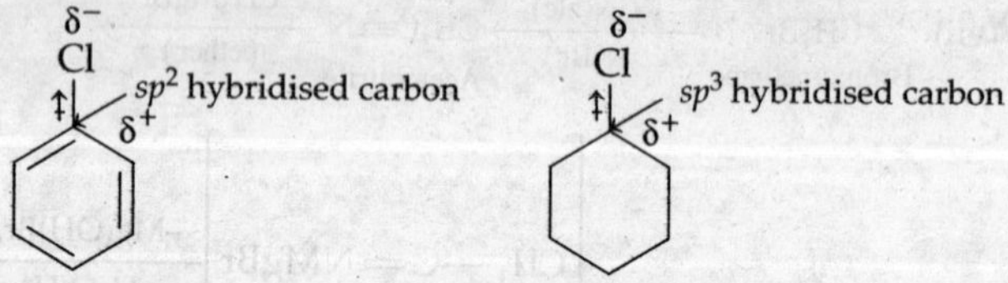

Chlorobenzene Cyclohexyl chloride

Due to sp^2 hybridisation of C-atom in chlorobenzene, C-atom is more electronegative (greater s-character) whereas in cyclohexyl chloride, C-atom is sp^3 hybridised, *i.e.*, less electronegative (lesser s-character). So polarity of C—Cl bond in chlorobenzene is less than the C—Cl bond in cyclohexyl chloride. Therefore, the dipole moment of chlorobenzene is lower than that of cyclohexyl chloride.

(ii) Water molecules have enough strong H-bonding (intermolecular) which is difficult to be broken by alkyl halides, though they are also polar in nature. Therefore, alkyl halides do not dissolve in water and form separate layers.

(iii) Grignard reagents (R—Mg—X) are readily decomposed by water to produce alkanes. That is why they should be prepared under anhydrous conditions. Instead, dry ether is used as a solvent during the preparation of Grignard reagent.

$$R\text{—Mg—}X + H_2O \longrightarrow \underset{\text{Alkane}}{R\text{—H}} + Mg\begin{matrix} X \\ OH \end{matrix}$$

Question 13 Give the uses of freon 12, DDT, carbon tetrachloride and iodoform.

Sol. Uses of freon 12 [CCl_2F_2]

(i) It is used as a refrigerant.
(ii) It is used as propellants in aerosols and foams.
(iii) It is also used for air conditioning purposes.

Uses of DDT [*p, p'*-dichlorodiphenyltrichloroethane]

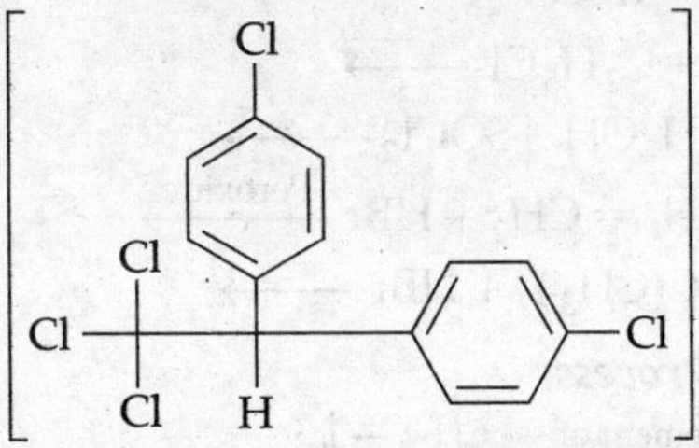

DDT

(i) It is an effective insecticide against the mosquito that spreads malaria and lice that carry typhus.
(ii) It is also used in many countries as insecticide for sugarcane and fodder crops.
[Due to its non-biodegradable nature, its use has been banned in various countries including U.S.A.]

Use of carbon tetrachloride [CCl_4]

(i) It is used in the manufacture of refrigerants.
(ii) It is used in the manufacture of propellants of aerosol cans.
(iii) It is also used as feedstock in synthesis of chlorofluoro carbons and other chemicals.
(iv) It is used as a fire-extinguisher under the name pyrene due to its non-inflammable nature.
(v) It is used as a cleansing agent in home and industries.
(vi) It is also used as an important solvent.

Uses of iodoform [Triodomethane CHI_3]

(i) It is used as an antiseptic, particularly for dressing wounds.

Note Use of freons is not environment friendly, as it damages the ozone layer in the atmosphere.
Due to unpleasant odour of iodoform, its use as an antiseptic is replaced by other iodine containing compounds.

Question 14 Write the structure for the major organic product in each of the following reactions.

(i) $CH_3CH_2CH_2Cl + NaI \xrightarrow[\text{heat}]{\text{Acetone}}$

(ii) $(CH_3)_3CBr + KOH \xrightarrow[\text{heat}]{\text{Ethanol}}$

(iii) $CH_3CH(Br)CH_2CH_3 + NaOH \xrightarrow{\text{Water}}$

(iv) $CH_3CH_2Br + KCN \xrightarrow{aq\cdot\text{ethanol}}$

(v) $C_6H_5ONa + C_2H_5Cl \longrightarrow$

(vi) $CH_3CH_2CH_2OH + SOCl_2 \longrightarrow$

(vii) $CH_3CH_2CH = CH_2 + HBr \xrightarrow{\text{Peroxide}}$

(viii) $CH_3CH{=}C(CH_3)_2 + HBr \longrightarrow$

Thinking Process

(i) Replacement of — Cl by — I.

(ii) Dehydrohalogenation (β-elimination).

(iii) Replacement of — Br by — OH.

(iv) Replacement of — Br by — CN

(v) Elimination of NaCl, formation of ether. (Williamson's synthesis)

(vi) Replacement of —OH by —Cl; formation of alkyl halide.

(vii) Addition of HBr across the double bond (peroxide effect) (Anti-Markovnikov's rule)

(viii) Addition of HBr according to Markovnikov's rule.

Sol. (i) $H_3C—CH_2—CH_2—Cl + NaI \xrightarrow[\text{heat}]{\text{Acetone}} CH_3—CH_2—CH_2—I + NaCl$

1-Chloropropane → 1-Iodopropane

(ii) $H_3C—C(CH_3)_2—Br + KOH \xrightarrow[\text{Heat}]{\text{Ethanol}} CH_3—C(=CH_2)—CH_3 + KBr + H_2O$

2-Bromo-2-methyl propane → 2 - Methylpropene

(iii) $H_3C—CH(Br)—CH_2—CH_3 + NaOH \xrightarrow[\text{hydrolysis}]{\text{Water}} CH_3—CH(OH)—CH_2—CH_3 + NaBr + H_2O$

2-Bromobutane → 2-Butanol or butane –2–ol

(iv) $\underset{\text{Bromoethane}}{CH_3-CH_2-Br} + KCN \xrightarrow{aq.\ \text{ethanol}} \underset{\text{Ethyl cyanide}}{CH_3-CH_2-C\equiv N} + KBr$

(v) $\underset{\text{Sodium phenoxide}}{C_6H_5ONa} + \underset{\text{Chloroethane}}{C_2H_5Cl} \xrightarrow[\text{synthesis}]{\text{Williamson's}} \underset{\text{Phenyl ethyl ether}}{C_6H_5-O-C_2H_5} + NaCl$

(vi) $\underset{\text{Propan-1-ol}}{CH_3-CH_2-CH_2-OH} + SOCl_2 \xrightarrow{\text{Pyridine}}$

$$\underset{\text{1-Chloropropane}}{CH_3-CH_2-CH_2-Cl} + SO_2\uparrow + HCl$$

(vii) $\underset{\text{But-1-ene}}{CH_3-CH_2-CH=CH_2} + HBr \xrightarrow[\text{Anti-Markovnikov's rule}]{\text{Peroxide}}$

$$\underset{\text{1-Bromobutane}}{CH_3-CH_2-CH_2-CH_2Br}$$

(viii) $CH_3-CH=\overset{\overset{\large CH_3}{|}}{C}-CH_3 + HBr \xrightarrow[\text{rule}]{\text{Markovnikov's}}$

$$CH_3-CH_2-\underset{\underset{\large Br}{|}}{\overset{\overset{\large CH_3}{|}}{C}}-CH_3$$

2-Bromo-2-methyl butane

Question 15 Write the mechanism of the following reaction.

$$nBuBr + KCN \xrightarrow{EtOH-H_2O} nBuCN$$

◎ ***Thinking Process***

(i) Write the resonating structures of KCN.

(ii) Due to the presence of polar solvent, find the possibility, which product will be formed preferentially?

Sol. Resonating forms of KCN are the following.

$$\overset{+}{K}[\,:\overset{-}{C}\equiv N:\,] \leftrightarrow [\,:C=\overset{\bullet\bullet\,-}{N}:\,]$$

Cyanide ion is an ambident nucleophile. It can attack through C-atom or through N-atom. Thus, two possible products are cyanides and isocyanides respectively. Here in the presence of the polar solvent, KCN readily ionises to furnish ions. As C—C bond is more stable than C—N bond, so cyanide is predominantly formed.

$$\overset{+\;\;-}{KCN} + \underset{n\text{ butyl bromide}}{CH_3-CH_2-CH_2-\overset{\delta+}{CH_2}-\overset{\delta-}{Br}} \longrightarrow$$

$$\underset{n\text{ butyl cyanide}}{CH_3-CH_2-CH_2-CH_2C\equiv N} + KBr$$

Question 16 Arrange the compounds of each set in order of reactivity towards S_{N^2} displacement :

(i) 2-Bromo-2-methylbutane, 1-bromopentane, 2-bromopentane

(ii) 1-Bromo-3-methylbutane, 2-bromo-2-methylbutane, 2-bromo-3-methylbutane

(iii) 1-Bromobutane, 1-bromo-2, 2-dimethylpropane, 1-bromo-2-methylbutane, 1-bromo-3-methylbutane.

◎ ***Thinking Process*** **S_{N^2} reactions involve the formation of transition state. Higher the steric hindrance, lesser the stability of transition state and so lesser the reactivity towards S_{N^2}.**

Sol. The order of decreasing reactivity of compounds is given as

(i) $CH_3CH_2CH_2CH_2CH_2Br$ (1-Bromopentane(1°)) $> CH_3\underset{\underset{Br}{|}}{C}HCH_2CH_2CH_3$ (2-Bromopentane(2°)) $> CH_3\overset{\overset{Br}{|}}{\underset{\underset{CH_3}{|}}{C}}CH_2CH_3$ (2-Bromo-2-methyl-butane (3°))

(ii) $CH_3\underset{\underset{CH_3}{|}}{C}HCH_2CH_2Br$ (1-Bromo-3-methylbutane (1°)) $>$

$CH_3-\underset{\underset{Br}{|}}{CH}-\underset{\underset{CH_3}{|}}{CH}-CH_3$ (2-Bromo-3-methyl butane (2°)) $> CH_3-\overset{\overset{Br}{|}}{\underset{\underset{CH_3}{|}}{C}}-CH_2-CH_3$ (2-Bromo-2-methylbutane (3°))

(iii) $CH_3CH_2CH_2CH_2Br$ (1-Bromobutane (1°)) $> CH_3\underset{\underset{CH_3}{|}}{C}HCH_2CH_2Br$ (1-Bromo-3-methyl butane (1°))

$> CH_3CH_2\underset{\underset{CH_3}{|}}{C}HCH_2Br$ (1-Bromo-2-methyl butane (1°)) $> CH_3-\overset{\overset{CH_3}{|}}{\underset{\underset{CH_3}{|}}{C}}-CH_2Br$ (1-Bromo-2,2 dimethyl propane (1°))

Question 17 Out of $C_6H_5CHClC_6H_5$ and $C_6H_5CH_2Cl$ which is more easily hydrolysed by aqueous KOH?

Thinking Process In S_N1 reactions, stability of carbocations is responsible for the reactivity. The reaction is more likely to take place by S_N1 reaction.

Sol. The hydrolysis reaction by aqueous KOH proceeds through the formation of carbocation. So, stability of carbocation tells about the ease of hydrolysis by aq. KOH.

$$\underset{\text{1-Chloro-1, 1-diphenyl methane}(2^\circ)}{C_6H_5-\underset{\displaystyle Cl}{\underset{|}{C}H}-C_6H_5} \xrightarrow{\text{Ionisation}} \underset{\substack{\text{Carbocation stabilised}\\ \text{by delocalisation}\\ \text{over } C_6H_5 \text{ rings}\\ \text{(More stable)}}}{C_6H_5-\overset{+}{C}H-C_6H_5} + \overset{-}{Cl}$$

$$\underset{\substack{\text{Benzyl chloride}\\ (1^\circ)}}{C_6H_5CH_2Cl} \xrightarrow{\text{Ionisation}} \underset{\substack{\text{Carbocation}\\ \text{stabilised by}\\ \text{delocalisation over}\\ \text{one } C_6H_5 \text{ ring}\\ \text{(Less stable)}}}{C_6H_5\overset{+}{C}H_2} + \overset{-}{Cl}$$

In S_N1 reaction, reactivity depends upon the stability of carbocations. $C_6H_5-\overset{+}{C}H-C_6H_5$ carbocation is more stable as compared to C_6H_5. Therefore, C_6H_5 $CHClC_6H_5$ gets hydrolysed more easily than C_6H_5CHCl.

Question 18 *p*-dichlorobenzene has higher melting point and than those of *o*-and *m*-isomers. Discuss.

Thinking Process Symmetry of the molecule is related to its crystal lattice structure and hence, to its melting point. A highly symmetrical structure has a higher melting point.

Sol.

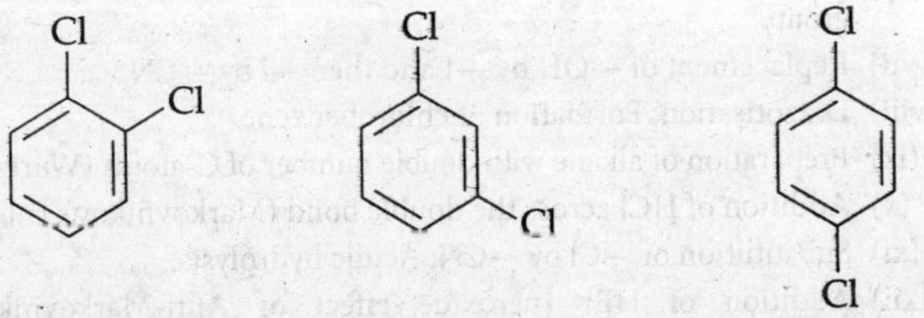

o-dichlorobenzene *m*-dichlorobenzene *p*-dichlorobenzene

Out of the above three isomers of dichlorobenzene, the *p*-isomer is more symmetrical than other two isomers. So, it has more closely packed arrangement of molecules in its crystal lattice. So, *p*-dichlorobenzene has a higher melting point as compared to *ortho* and *meta* isomers.

Question 19 How the following conversions can be carried out?

(i) Propene to propan-1-ol (ii) Ethanol to but-1-yne
(iii) 1-Bromopropane to 2-Bromopropane
(iv) Toluene to benzyl alcohol
(v) Benzene to 4-Bromonitrobenzene
(vi) Benzyl alcohol to 2-Phenyl ethanoic acid
(vii) Ethanol to Propane nitrile (viii) Aniline to chlorobenzene
(ix) 2-Chlorobutane to 3, 4-Dimethylhexane
(x) 2-Methyl-1-propene to 2-Chloro-2-Methylpropane
(xi) Ethyl chloride to Propanoic acid
(xii) But-1-ene to *n*-Butyliodide
(xiii) 2-Chloropropane to 1-Propanol
(xiv) *Iso*-propyl alcohol to Iodoform
(xv) Chlorobenzene to *p*-Nitrophenol
(xvi) 2-Bromopropane to 1-Bromopropane
(xvii) Chloroethane to Butane (xviii) Benzene to diphenyl
(xix) *tert*. Butyl bromide to *iso*-Butyl bromide
(xx) Aniline to Phenylisocyanide

Thinking Process

(i) Addition of HBr (peroxide effect); Replacement of —Br by —OH.
(ii) —OH is substituted by —Cl; then substitution by alkynyl group to form higher alkyne.
(iii) Dehydrohalogenation by alc. KOH (β-elimination), Addition of HBr (Markovnikov's rule)
(iv) Chlorination of $—CH_3$ group; Replacement of —Cl by —OH.
(v) Bromination of benzene; Nitration of bromobenzene at *p*-position.
(vi) Replacement of —OH by —Cl; then —Cl by —CN and at last by —COOH group.
(vii) Replacement of —OH by —I and then —l by —CN.
(viii) Diazotisation; Formation of chlorobenzene.
(ix) Preparation of alkane with double number of C-atoms (Wurtz reaction).
(x) Addition of HCl across the double bond (Markovnikov's rule).
(xi) Substitution of —Cl by —CN; Acidic hydrolysis.
(xii) Addition of HBr (peroxide effect or Anti-Markovnikov's rule); Substitution of —Br by —I.
(xiii) Dehydrohalogenation (β-elimination); Addition of HBr (peroxide effect); Substituting —Br by —OH by aqueous KOH.
(xiv) Oxidation of alcohol to ketone, Iodoform reaction.
(xv) Nitration and then replacement of —Cl by —OH.
(xvi) Dehydrohalogenation (β-elimination); Addition of HBr (peroxide effect).
(xvii) Wurtz reaction-Formation of hydrocarbon with double number of carbon atoms.
(xix) Dehydrohalogenation; Addition of HBr (peroxide effect).
(xx) Carbylamine reaction.

Sol.

(i) $$\underset{\text{Propene}}{CH_3-CH=CH_2} \xrightarrow[R-O-O-R]{HBr}$$

(Anti-Markovnikov's addition)

$$\underset{\text{1-Bromopropane}}{CH_3-CH_2-CH_2-Br} \xrightarrow{KOH(aq)} \underset{\text{Propan-1-ol}}{CH_3-CH_2-CH_2-OH}$$

(ii) $$\underset{\text{Ethanol}}{CH_3CH_2OH} \xrightarrow[\text{Pyridine}]{SO_2Cl_2} \underset{\text{Chloroethane}}{CH_3CH_2Cl} \xrightarrow[-NaCl]{CH\equiv CNa} \underset{\text{But-1-yne}}{CH_3CH_2C\equiv CH}$$

(iii) $$\underset{\text{1-Bromopropane}}{CH_3-CH_2-CH_2-Br} \xrightarrow{KOH(alc.)} \underset{\text{Propene}}{CH_3CH=CH_2} \xrightarrow[\text{(Markovnikov addition)}]{HBr} \underset{\text{2-Bromopropane}}{CH_3-\underset{Br}{\underset{|}{CH}}-CH_3}$$

(iv) 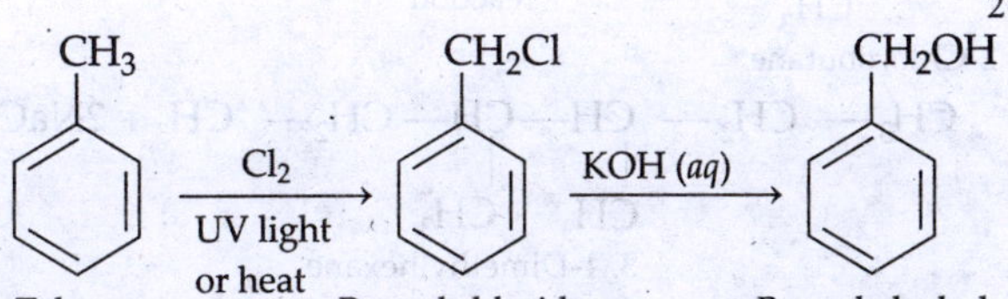

Toluene → Benzyl chloride → Benzyl alcohol

(v) 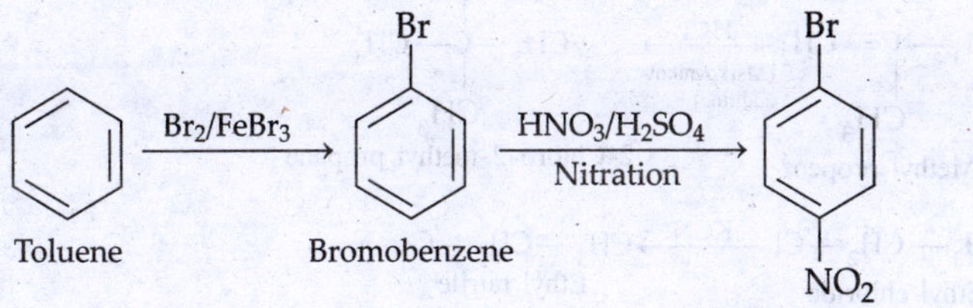

Toluene → Bromobenzene → 4-Bromonitrobenzene

(vi) 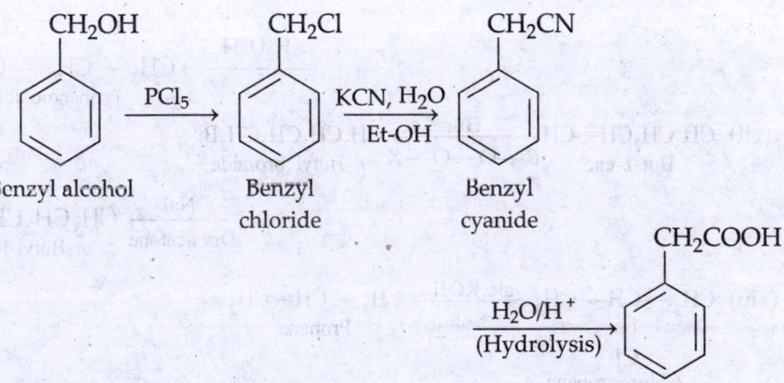

Benzyl alcohol → Benzyl chloride → Benzyl cyanide → 2-Phenyl ethanoic acid

(vii) $CH_3—CH_2—OH \xrightarrow{Red\ P/I_2} CH_3—CH_2—I \xrightarrow{KCN} CH_3—CH_2—CN$

Ethanol   Iodoethane   Propane nitrile

(viii)

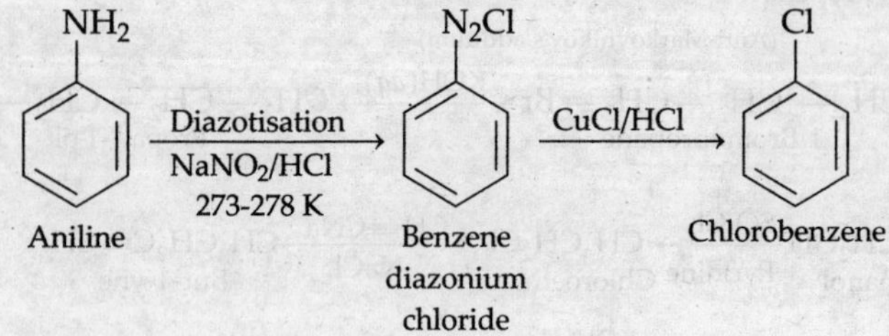

(ix) $2\,CH_3—CH_2—\underset{\underset{CH_3}{|}}{CH}—Cl + 2Na \xrightarrow[\text{Wurtz reaction}]{\text{Dry ether}}$

2-Chlorobutane

$CH_3—CH_2—\underset{\underset{CH_3}{|}}{CH}—\underset{\underset{CH_3}{|}}{CH}—CH_2—CH_3 + 2NaCl$

3, 4-Dimethylhexane

(x) $CH_3—\underset{\underset{CH_3}{|}}{C}=CH_2 \xrightarrow[\text{(Markovnikov addition)}]{HCl} CH_3—\overset{\overset{Cl}{|}}{\underset{\underset{CH_3}{|}}{C}}—CH_3$

2-Methyl propene   2-Chloro-2-methyl propane

(xi) $CH_3—CH_2—Cl \xrightarrow{KCN} CH_3—CH_2—C\equiv N$

Ethyl chloride (chloroethane)   Ethyl nitrile (cyanopropane)

$\xrightarrow{H_2O/H^+} CH_3—CH_2—COOH$

Propanoic acid

(xii) $CH_3CH_2CH=CH \xrightarrow[R—O—O—R]{HBr} CH_3CH_2CH_2CH_2Br$

But-1-ene   *n*-Butyl bromide

$\xrightarrow[\text{Dry acetone}]{NaI} CH_3CH_2CH_2CH_2I$

n-Butyl iodide

(xiii) $CH_3—\underset{\underset{Cl}{|}}{CH}—CH_3 \xrightarrow[\text{heat}]{\text{alc. KOH}} CH_3—CH=CH_2$

2-Chloropropane   Propene

$\xrightarrow[\text{Anti-Markovnikov addition}]{\text{HBr; Peroxide}} CH_3CH_2CH_2Br \xrightarrow[\text{Nucleophilic substitution}]{(aq)\,KOH,\ \Delta} CH_3CH_2CH_2OH$

1-Bromopropane   1-Propanol

(xiv) $\underset{\textit{Iso-propyl alcohol}}{CH_3-\underset{\substack{|\\OH}}{CH}-CH_3} \xrightarrow[\text{[O]}]{K_2Cr_2O_7/H_2SO_4} \underset{\text{Propanone}}{CH_3-\overset{\substack{O\\\|}}{C}-CH_3}$

$\xrightarrow[\text{Iodoform reaction}]{NaOI} \underset{\text{Iodoform}}{CHI_3} + \underset{\text{Sodium ethanoate}}{CH_3COONa}$

(xv) 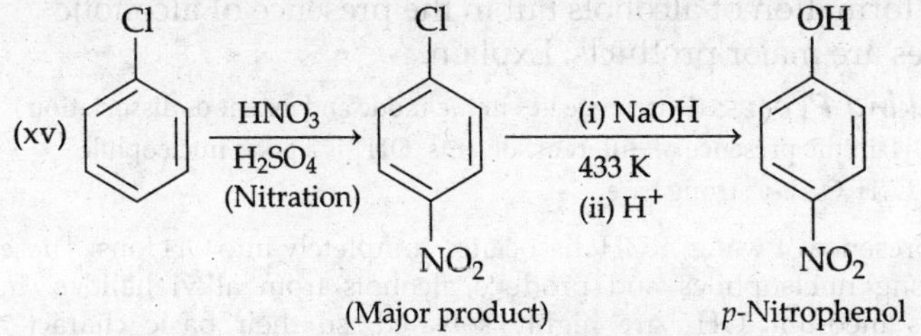

(xvi) $\underset{\text{2-Bromopropane}}{CH_3-\underset{\substack{|\\Br}}{CH}-CH_3} \xrightarrow{alc\ KOH} \underset{\text{Propene}}{CH_3-CH=CH_2}$

$\xrightarrow[R-O-O-R]{\text{HBr (Anti-Markovnikov addition)}} \underset{\text{1-Bromopropane}}{CH_3-CH_2-CH_2-Br}$

(xvii) $CH_3-CH_2-Cl + 2\,Na + Cl-CH_2-CH_3$

$\xrightarrow[\text{Wurtz reaction}]{\text{Dry ether}} \underset{\text{Butane}}{CH_3-CH_2-CH_2-CH_3} + 2NaCl$

(xviii) For answer, consult answer of Q. 11 (part *x*)

(xix) $\underset{\substack{\textit{tert.}\text{ Butyl bromide}\\\text{(or 2-Bromo-2-methylpropane)}}}{CH_3-\overset{\substack{CH_3\\|}}{\underset{\substack{|\\Br}}{C}}-CH_3} \xrightarrow{\text{alc. KOH}} \underset{\substack{\textit{Iso}\text{-Butylene}\\\text{(or 2-methyl 1-propene)}}}{CH_3-\overset{\substack{CH_3\\|}}{C}=CH_2}$

$\xrightarrow[R-O-O-R]{HBr} \underset{\substack{\textit{Iso}\text{-Butyl bromide}\\\text{(or 1-Bromo-2-methyl propane)}}}{CH_3-\overset{\substack{CH_3\\|}}{CH}-CH_2-Br}$

(xx) 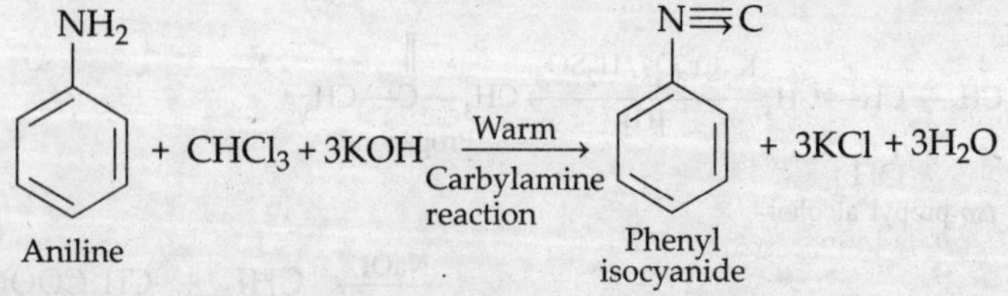

Question 20 The treatment of alkyl chlorides with aqueous KOH leads to the formation of alcohols but in the presence of alcoholic KOH, alkenes are major products. Explain.

◎ *Thinking Process* Difference lies in the mode and extent of dissociation of KOH in the presence of different solvents. OH^- is a good nucleophile while $C_2H_5O^-$ is a strong base.

Sol. In the presence of water, KOH dissociates completely into $\bar{O}H$ ions. These are strong nucleophiles and produce alcohols from alkyl halides. In aqueous medium, OH^- are highly solvated, so their basic character decreases. Therefore, OH^- cannot abstract H^+ from the β-carbon to form alkenes. In alcoholic medium, solution also contains $C_2H_5\bar{O}$, ethoxide ions in addition to $\bar{O}H$ ions. Being a stronger base, they abstract H^+ ion from β-C-atom giving rise to alkene (Dehydrohalogenation).

Question 21 Primary alkyl halide C_4H_9Br (*A*) reacted with alcoholic KOH to give compound (*B*). Compound (*B*) is reacted with HBr to give (*C*) which is an isomer of (*A*). When (*A*) is reacted with sodium metal, it gives compound (*D*), C_8H_{18} which is different from the compound formed when n-butyl bromide is reacted with sodium. Give the structural formula of (*A*) and write the equations for all the reactions.

◎ *Thinking Process*

(i) Write the possible isomers of C_4H_9Br.

(ii) Write the equation for the reaction of *n*-butyl bromide with sodium.

(iii) Write the equation for all possible reactions and identify the compounds (*A*), (*B*), (*C*) and (*D*).

Sol. Two possible isomers of C_4H_9Br (primary halide) are :

$CH_3—CH_2—CH_2—CH_2—Br$
[I]
(1°)

$CH_3—\underset{\underset{CH_3}{|}}{C}H—CH_2—Br$
[II]
(1°)

According to the question, compound (*A*) on reaction with sodium does not give the same product produced by *n*-butyl bromide. So (*A*) cannot be [I].

$$\underset{n\text{-Butylbromide}}{2CH_3—CH_2—CH_2—CH_2—Br} + 2Na \xrightarrow{\text{Ether}}$$

$$\underset{n\text{-Octane (not formed in the reaction) } C_8H_{18}}{CH_3—CH_2—CH_2—CH_2—CH_2—CH_2—CH_2—CH_3}$$

Now, [II] must be the correct isomer.

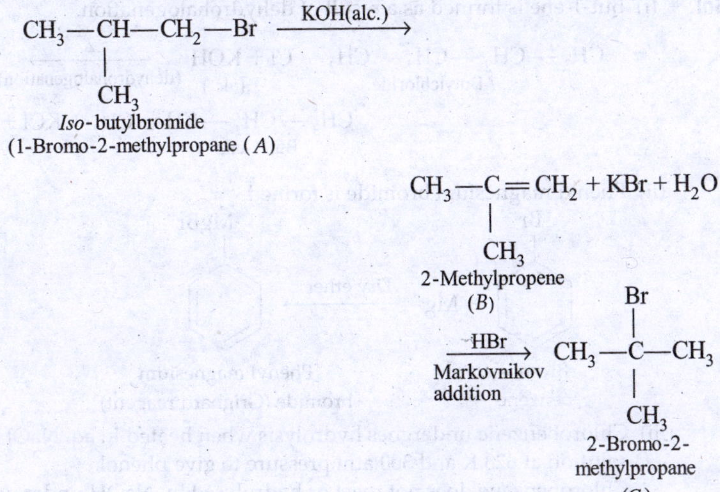

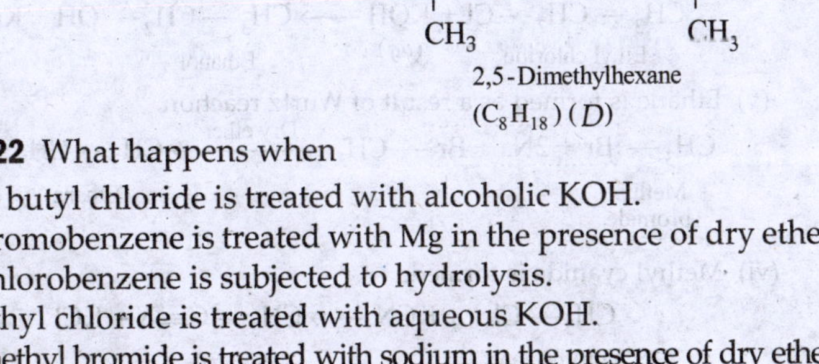

Question 22 What happens when

(i) *n*- butyl chloride is treated with alcoholic KOH.
(ii) bromobenzene is treated with Mg in the presence of dry ether.
(iii) chlorobenzene is subjected to hydrolysis.
(iv) ethyl chloride is treated with aqueous KOH.
(v) methyl bromide is treated with sodium in the presence of dry ether.
(vi) methyl chloride is treated with KCN?

Thinking Process

(i) Dehydrohalogenation (β-elimination) as alc. KOH is a dehydrohalogenating reagent.
(ii) Formation of Grignard reagent.
(iii) No reaction, due to double bond character in C—Cl bond.
(iv) (S_N2)—Cl is replaced by —OH.
(v) Wurtz reaction
(vi) (S_N2)— Cl is replaced by — CN.

Sol. (i) But-1-ene is formed as a result of dehydrohalogenation.

$$\underset{n\text{-Butylchloride}}{CH_3—CH_2—CH_2—CH_2—Cl} + \underset{\text{(alc.)}}{KOH} \xrightarrow[\text{(dehydrohalogenation)}]{\Delta}$$

$$\underset{\text{But-1-ene}}{CH_3—CH_2—CH{=}CH_2} + KCl + H_2O$$

(ii) Phenyl magnesium bromide is formed.

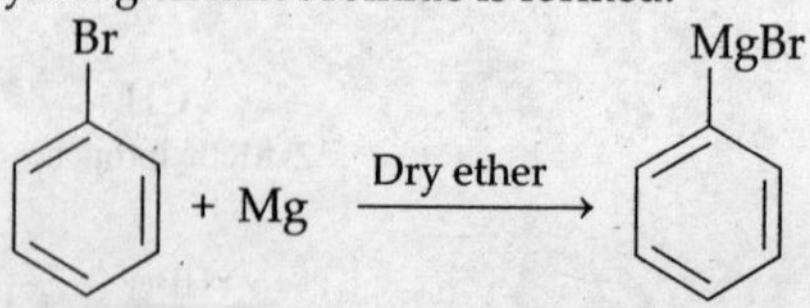

Bromo-benzene — Phenyl magnesium bromide (Grignard reagent)

(iii) Chlorobenzene undergoes hydrolysis when heated in aq. NaOH solution at 623 K and 300 atm pressure to give phenol.
Chlorobenzene does not react or hydrolysed by NaOH under normal conditions.

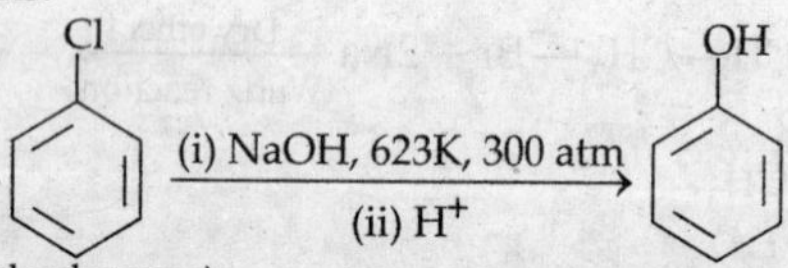

(Chlorobenzene) — (Phenol)

(iv) Ethanol is formed.

$$\underset{\text{Ethyl chloride}}{CH_3—CH_2—Cl} + \underset{(aq)}{KOH} \longrightarrow \underset{\text{Ethanol}}{CH_3—CH_2—OH} + KCl + H_2O$$

(v) Ethane is formed as a result of Wurtz reaction.

$$\underset{\text{Methyl bromide}}{CH_3—Br} + 2Na + Br—CH_3 \xrightarrow{\text{Dry ether}} \underset{\text{Ethane}}{CH_3—CH_3} + 2NaBr$$

(vi) Methyl cyanide is formed.

$$\underset{\text{Chloromethane (Methyl chloride)}}{CH_3—Cl} + KCN \longrightarrow \underset{\text{Acetonitrile (Methylcyanide)}}{CH_3—C{\equiv}N} + KCl$$

DIKSHA APP Questions

☐ Multiple Choice Questions

Q.1 Chronic chloroform exposure may cause damage to liver and kidney due to the formation of

(a) phosgene (b) methylene chloride

(c) methyl chloride (d) carbon tetrachloride

Sol. (a) Chloroform is slowly oxidised in air in the presence of light to form an extremely poisonous gas, phosgene (carbonyl chloride). This causes damage to liver and kidneys.

$$2\,CHCl_3 + O_2 \xrightarrow{\text{Light}} \underset{\text{Phosgene}}{2COCl_2} + 2HCl$$

Q.2 The organic compound used in refrigerators and air conditioners is

(a) DDT (b) Carbon tetrachloride

(c) Freon (d) BHC

Sol. (c) Freons are the organic compounds used in refrigerators and air conditioners. Freons are the chlorofluorocarbon compounds of methane and ethane. They are extremely stable, non-toxic, non-corrosive and easily liquefiable gases. Freon 12 (CCl_2F_2) is one of the most common freons used in industries.

Q.3 Which on of the following undergoes nucleophilic substitution exclusively by S_N1 mechanism?

(a) Ethyl chloride (b) Isopropyl chloride

(c) Chloro benzene (d) Benzyl chloride

Sol. (d) Benzyl chloride undergoes nucleophilic substitution reaction exclusively by S_N1 mechanism because the rate determining step or an important step in S_N1 reaction mechanism is the formation of carbocation. The benzyl chloride forms benzyl carbocation which is very stable as the positive charge is delocalised in the benzene ring by resonance. So, the rate of S_N1 reaction in this case is extremely high.

Q.4 Which of the following reagent produces pure alkyl halides when heated with alcohols?

(a) PCl_5 (b) PCl_3

(c) $SOCl_2$ (d) Dry HCl

Sol. (c) $SOCl_2$ (thionyl chloride) produces pure alkyl halides when treated with alcohols as the side products formed in this reaction are SO_2 and HCl gases. So, these two side products are escapable and hence gives the pure alkyl halides.

$$R\text{—}OH + SOCl_2 \longrightarrow R\text{—}Cl + SO_2 + HCl$$

Q.5 Which of the following has the highest boiling point?

(a) CH_3CH_2Br (b) $CH_3CH_2CH_2CH_2Br$

(c) $(CH_3)_2CHCH_2Br$ (d) $(CH_3)_3CBr$

Sol. (b) Boiling point increases with increase in size and mass of the alkyl halide as the van der waals forces increases. Boiling point decreases with increase in branching as the surface area decreases, so weak inter-molecular forces are present in the branched molecule. Hence, $CH_3CH_2CH_2CH_2Br$ has the highest boiling point from the given options.

Q.6 The decreasing order of boiling points of alkyl halides is

(a) RF > RCl > RBr > RI

(b) RBr > RCl > RI > RF

(c) RI > RBr > RCl > RF

(d) RCl> RF > RI > RBr

Sol. (c) Boiling point increases with increasing size and mass of halogens in alkyl halides as the magnitude of van der waals forces of attraction increases. So the correct order of boiling points of alkyl halides is:

$$RI > RCl > RBr > RF.$$

Q.7 An alkyl iodide is prepared by the reaction of alkyl chloride/alkyl bromide with sodium iodide in dry acetone. This reaction Is known as

(a) Sandmayers reaction (b) Swarts reaction

(c) Finkelstein reaction (d) Wurtz reaction

Sol. (c) Alkyl iodides are often prepared by the reaction of alkyl chlorides/bromides with NaI in dry acetone. This reaction is known as Finkelstein reaction.

$$R\text{—}X + NaI \longrightarrow R\text{—}I + NaX$$

$$(X = Cl, Br)$$

Q.8 The catalyst used in the preparation of an alkyl chloride by the action of dry HCl on an alcohol is

(a) $FeCl_3$
(b) Cu
(c) anhydrous $AlCl_3$
(d) anhydrous $ZnCl_2$

Sol. (d) The catalyst used in the preparation of an alkyl chloride by the action of dry HCl on an alcohol is anhydrous $ZnCl_2$.

$$R—OH + HCl \xrightarrow[\text{anhyd}]{ZnCl_2} R—Cl + H_2O$$

Q.9 C—X bond is strongest in

(a) CH_3I (b) CH_3F
(c) CH_3Br (d) CH_3Cl

Sol. (b) C—X (X = halogen) bonds are polar in nature. As we move from F to I, the size of the halogen increases, thus their C—X bond length increases, so bond strength decreases. Thus, the C—X bond length is strongest in CH_3F.

Q.10 Which one of the following alkyl halide has highest dipole moment?

(a) Methyl fluoride (b) Methyl chloride
(c) Methyl bromide (d) Methyl iodide

Sol. (b) The dipole moment of a molecule is influenced by the electronegativity of the atoms involved and the distance between them. For the given molecules- CH_3F, CH_3Cl, CH_3Br and CH_3I, the dipole moment generally increases with the electronegativity of the halogen atom attached to the carbon. But, the size of F atom is small so the distance or the C—F bond length is small in CH_3F molecule. This decrease in bond length affects the dipole moment more than the increase in electronegativity so, the dipole moment of CH_3F becomes less than CH_3Cl.

Q.11 The IUPAC name of $CH_2{=}CH—CH_2Cl$ is

(a) Vinyl Chloride
(b) Allyl Chloride
(c) 1-Chloroprop-3-ene
(d) 3-Chloroprop-1-ene

Sol. (d) The IUPAC name of the compound is 3-chloroprop-1-ene.

Q.12 The IUPAC name of benzene hexachloride is

(a) 1, 2, 3, 4, 5, 6-hexachlorocyclohexane
(b) 1, 1, 1, 6, 6, 6-hexachlorocyclohexane
(c) 1, 6-phenyl-1, 6-chlorohexane
(d) 1, 1-phenyl-6, 6-chlorohexane

Sol. (a)

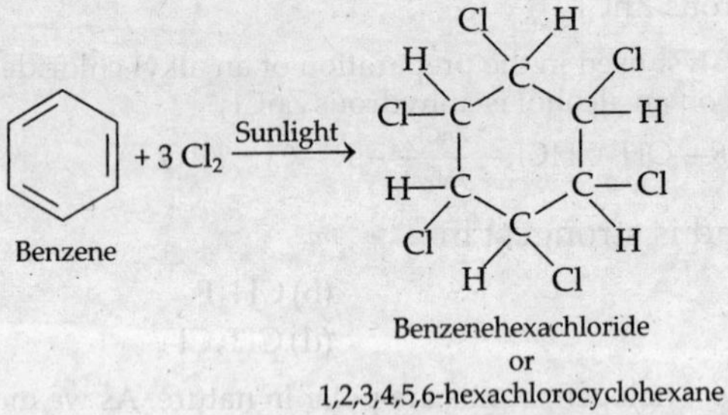

Q.13 Which one of the following is optically active?

(a) Butane (b) 4-Methylheptane
(c) 3-Methylheptane (d) 2-Methylheptane

Sol. (c) 3-.Methylheptane has a chiral carbon or assymettic center present in the molecule. So, it is optically active.

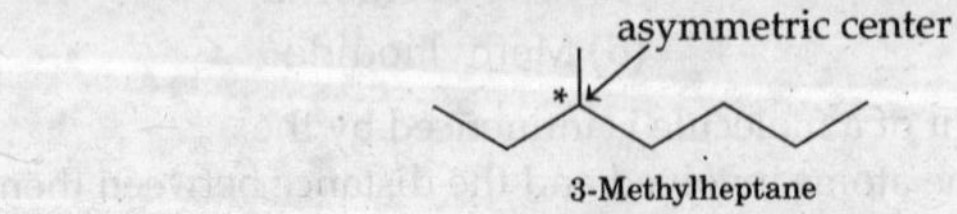

Q.14 Which one of the following is a geminal dihalide?

(a) CH_3CHBr_2 (b) $CH_2Br—CH_2Br$
(c) $CH_3CHBrCH_2Br$ (d) $CH_3CHBrCH_2CH_2Br$

Sol. (a) When both the halogens are present on the same carbon atom of the molecule, then it is called geminal dihalide.

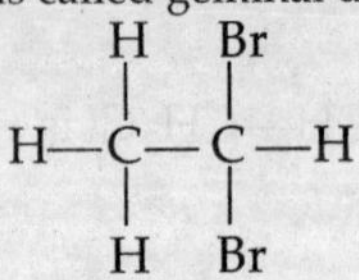

☐ Short Answer Type

Q.1 What do you mean by a chiral compound? Give an example.

Sol. Molecule that is non-superimposable on its mirror imag is said to be chiral and this property is known as chirality. For example, butan-2-ol is a chiral compound.

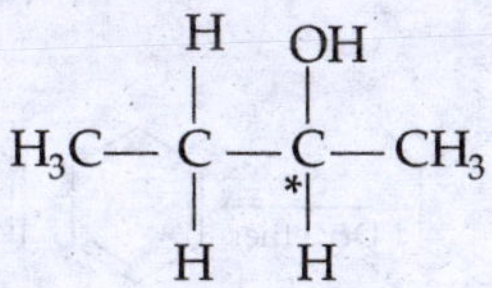

Butan-2-ol

Q.2 Dichlorobenzene has higher melting point, than those of *ortho* and *meta* isomers. Why?

Sol. The *p*-isomer being more symmetrical fits closely in the crystal lattice and thus has stronger intermolecular forces of attraction than those of *ortho* and *meta* isomers. Hence, a large amount of energy is needed to melt *p*-isomer and has higher melting point.

☐ Long Answer Type

Q.1 (a) Write the chemical equations for the conversion of

(i) Propene to Propyne

(ii) But-1-ene to But-2-ene

(iii) Benzene to Biphenyl

(b) How will you distinguish between ethyl chloride and ethyl bromide?

(c) What is the role of lewis acid in the preparation of aryl halide in dark?

Sol. (a) (i) $\underset{\text{Propene}}{CH_3-CH{=}CH_2} \xrightarrow{Br_2/CCl_4} \underset{\text{1, 2-Dibromopropane}}{CH_3-\underset{Br}{\underset{|}{CH}}-\underset{Br}{\underset{|}{CH_2}}} \xrightarrow[\text{Liq. } NH_3]{NaNH_2}$

$\underset{\text{Propyne}}{CH_3C{\equiv}CH}$

(ii) Conversion of but-1-ene to but-2-ene

$$\underset{\text{But-1-ene}}{CH_3CH_2CH{=}CH_2} \xrightarrow{HBr} \underset{\text{2-Bromobutane}}{CH_3CH_2\overset{\displaystyle Br}{\overset{|}{C}H}\,CH_3}$$

$$\xrightarrow[\Delta]{\text{alc. KOH}} \underset{\text{But-2-ene}}{CH_3CH{=}CHCH_3}$$

(iii)

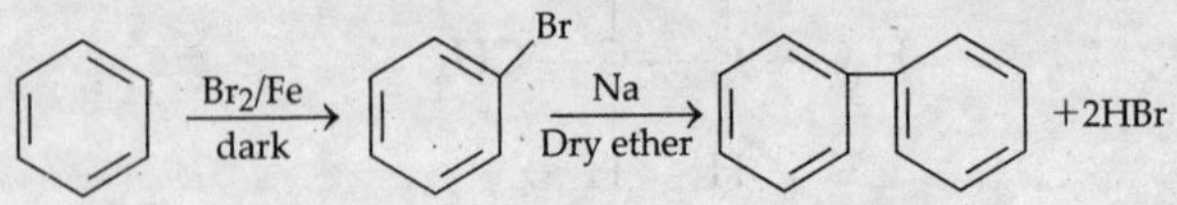

Benzene　　Bromobenzene　　Biphenyl

(b) When ethyl chloride is treated with *aq.* KOH followed by reaction with $AgNO_3$, a white ppt (AgCl) is obtained which is soluble in NH_4OH whereas ethyl bromide reacts to give pale yellow ppt (AgBr) which is insoluble in NH_4OH.

(c) Lewis acid helps in the generation of electrophile from the dihalogens and thus facilitate electrophilic substitution reaction.

Q.2 Give reasons for each of the following:

(a) (i) S_N1 reactions are generally carried out in the presence of polar solvents.

(ii) Allyl chloride is hydrolysed more readily than *n*-propyl chloride.

(b) Compound A with molecular formula C_4H_9Br is treated with *aq.* KOH solution. The rate of this reaction depends upon the concentration of '*A*' only. When another optically active isomer '*B*' of this compound was treated with aq. KOH solution the rate of reaction was found to depend on concentration of both compound and KOH.

(i) Write down the structural formula of both the compounds '*A*' and '*B*'.

(ii) Which one of the two will be converted to the product with inverted configuration?

Sol. (a) (i) Polar solvents stabilise the carbocations formed by solvation and hence favour S_N1 reaction.

(ii) Allyl halide forms allyl carbocation which is stabilised by resonance. Allyl carbocation is more stable than the carbocation formed by n-propylchloride and hence allyl chloride is hydrolysed more easily.

(b) (i) The rate of reaction of compound '*A*' with aq. KOH depends only on the concentration of *A*. This shows that the reaction follows S_N1 pathway and the compound is tertiary alkyl halide. *A* is

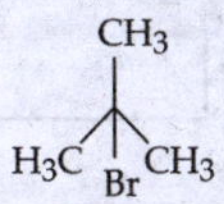

2-Bromo-2-methylpropane

(ii) Since compound *B* is optically active and the rate of its reaction with *aq*. KOH depends on the concentration of both *B* and *aq*. KOH, the reaction occurs by S_N2 mechanism and the compound is 2-Bromobutane.

$$H_3C-\underset{}{\overset{Br}{\overset{|}{C}}}H-CH_2CH_3$$

The reaction of compound *B* with *aq*. KOH follows S_N2 pathway. Hence it will be converted to the product with inverted configuration.

Alcohols, Phenols and Ethers

CHAPTER 07

Important Points

01 Alcohols are prepared by hydration of alkenes in the presence of acid or by hydroboration-oxidation reaction.

(a) $H_2C{=}CH_2 \xrightarrow[H_2O]{H_2SO_4} H_3C{-}CH_2{-}OH$

(b) $3R{-}CH{=}CH_2 + (BH_3)_2 \longrightarrow (R{-}CH_2{-}CH_2)_3B$

$$\xrightarrow[OH^-,\ H_2O]{H_2O_2} R{-}CH_2{-}CH_2{-}OH + H_3BO_3$$

02 Aldehydes form alcohols (primary and secondary) with Grignard reagent whereas ketones give tertiary alcohols. Aldehydes and ketones can also be reduced to alcohols using $NaBH_4$, $LiAlH_4$ or H_2 in Ni/Pd.

(a) $H{-}CHO \xrightarrow{CH_3MgBr} CH_3CH_2OH + Mg(OH)Br$

$$CH_3{-}\overset{\overset{\large O}{\|}}{C}{-}CH_3 \xrightarrow{CH_3MgBr} CH_3{-}\underset{\underset{\large CH_3}{|}}{\overset{\overset{\large OH}{|}}{C}}{-}CH_3 + Mg(OH)Br$$

(b) $CH_3{-}CHO \xrightarrow{H_2/Pd} CH_3CH_2OH$

$$CH_3{-}\overset{\overset{\large O}{\|}}{C}{-}CH_3 \xrightarrow{NaBH_4} H_3C{-}\underset{\underset{\large OH}{|}}{CH}{-}CH_3$$

03 Reduction of carboxylic acids and esters also gives alcohol by using $LiAlH_4$

$$RCOOH \xrightarrow[\text{(ii) } H_2O]{\text{(i) } LiAlH_4} RCH_2OH$$

$$\underset{\text{(acid)}}{RCOOH} \xrightarrow[H^+]{R'OH} \underset{\text{(ester)}}{RCOOR'} \xrightarrow[\text{catalyst}]{H_2} RCH_2OH + R'OH$$

04 Phenols may be prepared from haloarenes, aryl sulphonic acids by substitution reactions and also from diazonium salts.

(a)

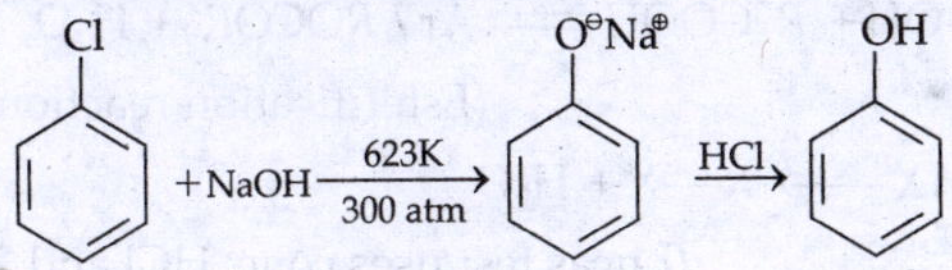

(b)

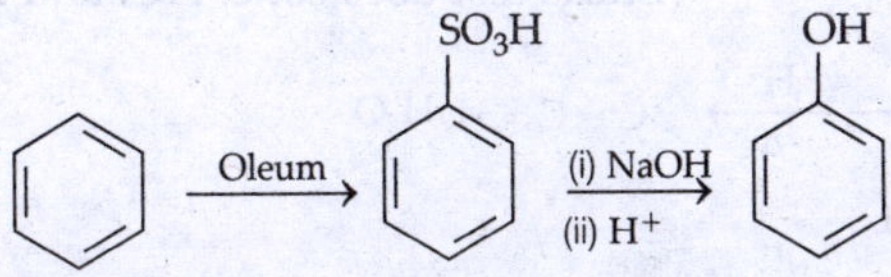

(c)

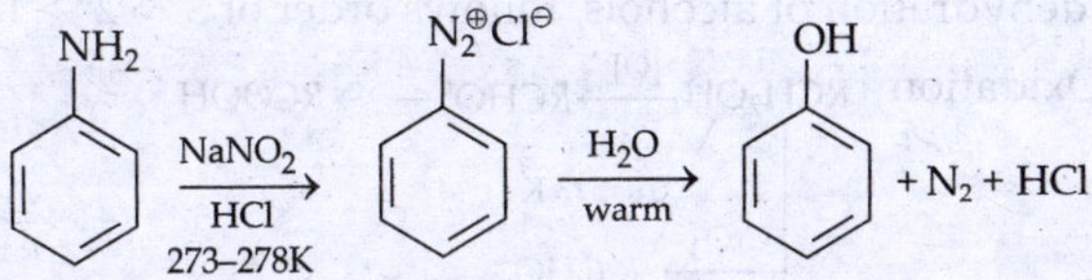

05 Phenols are manufactured from cumene.

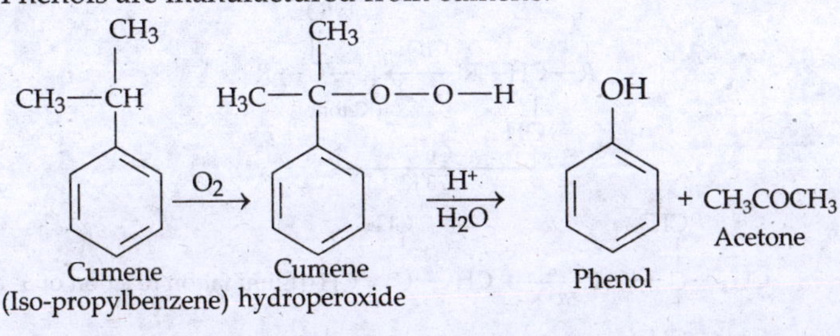

06 The boiling points of alcohols and phenols increases with increase in number of carbon atoms and decreases with increase of branching in carbon chain. Alcohols have higher boiling point than ethers and hydrocarbons because of the presence of intermolecular hydrogen bonding in alcohols, which is absent in hydrocarbons and ethers.

07 Solubility of alcohols and phenols in water also increases due to the presence of H-bonds between alcohols/phenols and water molecules. Solubility of alcohols in water decreases with increase in size of alkyl group.

08 Alcohols and phenols react as both electrophiles and nucleophiles.

09 Alcohols and phenols are acidic in nature.

10 Phenolic —OH group is *ortho* and *para* directing in nature.

11 Some important reactions of alcohols and phenols are :

(a) $2Ar / R—OH + 2Na \longrightarrow 2Ar/R—ONa + H_2 \uparrow$

(b) $Ar / R—OH + R'COOH \overset{H^+}{\rightleftharpoons} Ar / ROCOR' + H_2O$

(Esterification reaction)

(c) $ROH + HX \longrightarrow R—X + H_2O$

(Lucas test uses conc. HCl and $ZnCl_2$)

(d) $—\underset{H}{\overset{|}{\underset{|}{C}}}—\underset{OH}{\overset{|}{\underset{|}{C}}}— \xrightarrow[\Delta]{H^+} \gt C=C \lt + H_2O$

(dehydration of alcohols, follows order of 3° > 2° > 1°)

(e) Oxidation

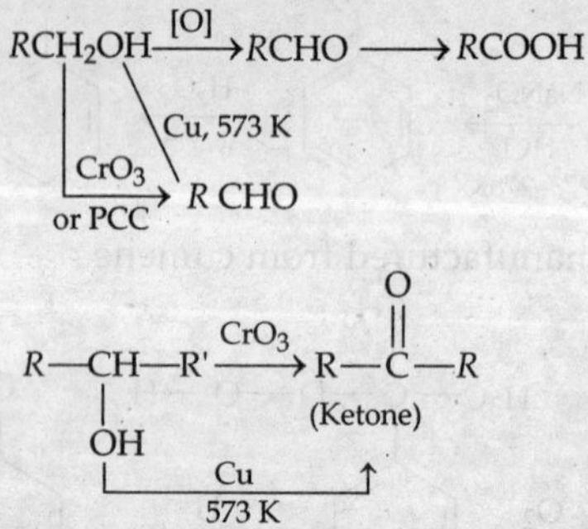

$$CH_3—\underset{CH_3}{\overset{CH_3}{\underset{|}{\overset{|}{C}}}}—OH \xrightarrow[573\ K]{Cu} CH_3—\overset{CH_3}{\overset{|}{C}}=CH_2$$ (Elimination reaction of 3° alcohols)

12 1°, 2° and 3° alcohols are distinguished by Victor Meyer and Lucas tests.

13 Electron withdrawing groups in phenol increase its acidic strength and electron releasing groups decrease it.

14 Phenols undergo electrophilic aromatic substitution reactions as:

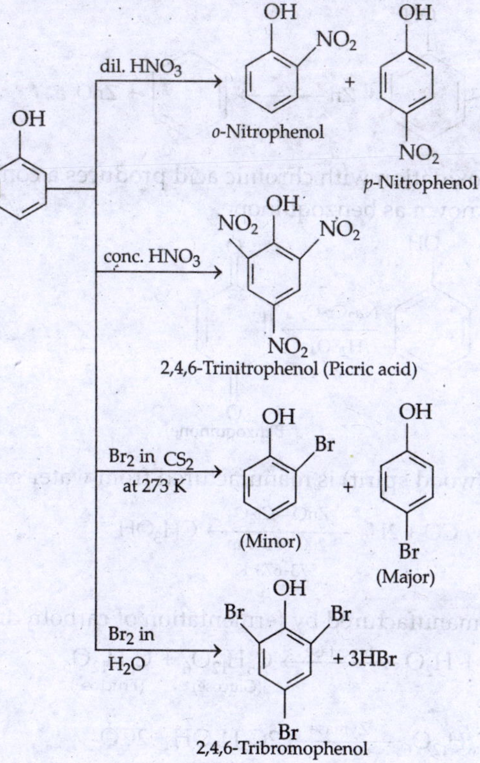

15 Salicylic acid is prepared commercially from phenol by Kolbe's reaction.

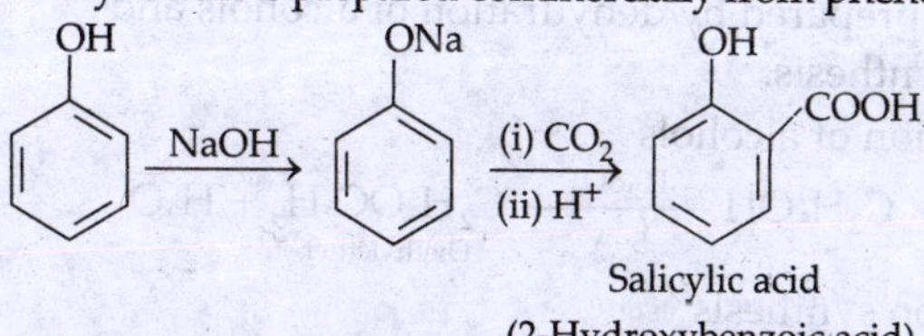

16 Reimer-Tiemann reaction is used to introduce —CHO group at *o*–position in phenol (formation of salicylaldehyde).

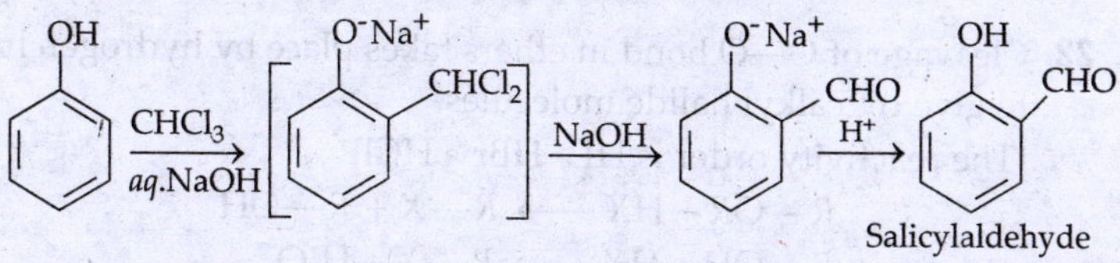

17 Phenol is converted to benzene on heating with zinc dust.

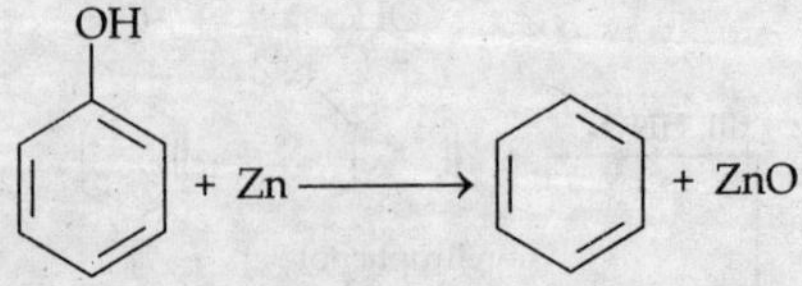

18 Phenol on oxidation with chromic acid produces a conjugated diketone, known as benzoquinone.

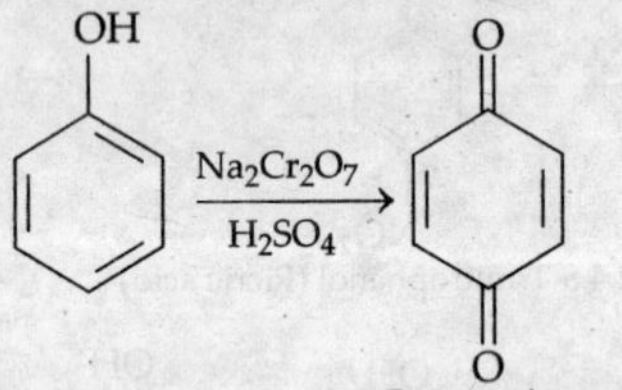

Benzoquinone

19 Methanol (wood spirit) is manufactured from water gas.

$$CO + 2H_2 \xrightarrow[\substack{200\text{-}300\ \text{atm} \\ 573\text{-}673\ \text{K}}]{ZnO-Cr_2O_3} CH_3OH$$

20 Ethanol is manufactured by fermentation of carbohydrates.

$$\underset{\substack{\text{Sugar} \\ \text{(Sucrose)}}}{C_{12}H_{22}O_{11}} + H_2O \xrightarrow{\text{Invertase}} \underset{\text{(Glucose)}}{C_6H_{12}O_6} + \underset{\text{(Fructose)}}{C_6H_{12}O_6}$$

$$C_6H_{12}O_6 \xrightarrow{\text{Zymase}} \underset{\text{(Ethanol)}}{2C_2H_5OH} + 2CO_2$$

21 Ethers can be prepared by dehydration of alcohols and Williamson synthesis.

(a) Dehydration of alcohols

$$\underset{\text{Ethanol}}{C_2H_5OH + C_2H_5OH} \xrightarrow[S_N2]{H_2SO_4} \underset{\text{Diethylether}}{C_2H_5OC_2H_5} + H_2O$$

(b) Williamson synthesis

$$\underset{\substack{\text{Alkyl} \\ \text{halide} \\ \text{(Primary)}}}{R—X} + \underset{\substack{\text{Sodium} \\ \text{alkoxide}}}{R'—O^{\ominus}Na^{\oplus}} \xrightarrow[S_N2]{} \underset{\text{Ether}}{R—O—R'} + NaX$$

22 Cleavage of C—O bond in ethers takes place by hydrogen halides to give two alkyl halide molecules.

[The reactivity order is HI > HBr > HCl]

$$R—OR + HX \longrightarrow R—X + R—OH$$

$$R—OH + HX \longrightarrow R—X + H_2O$$

23 In electrophilic substitution of aromatic ethers, the alkoxy group activates the aromatic ring and directs the incoming group to *ortho* and *para* positions.

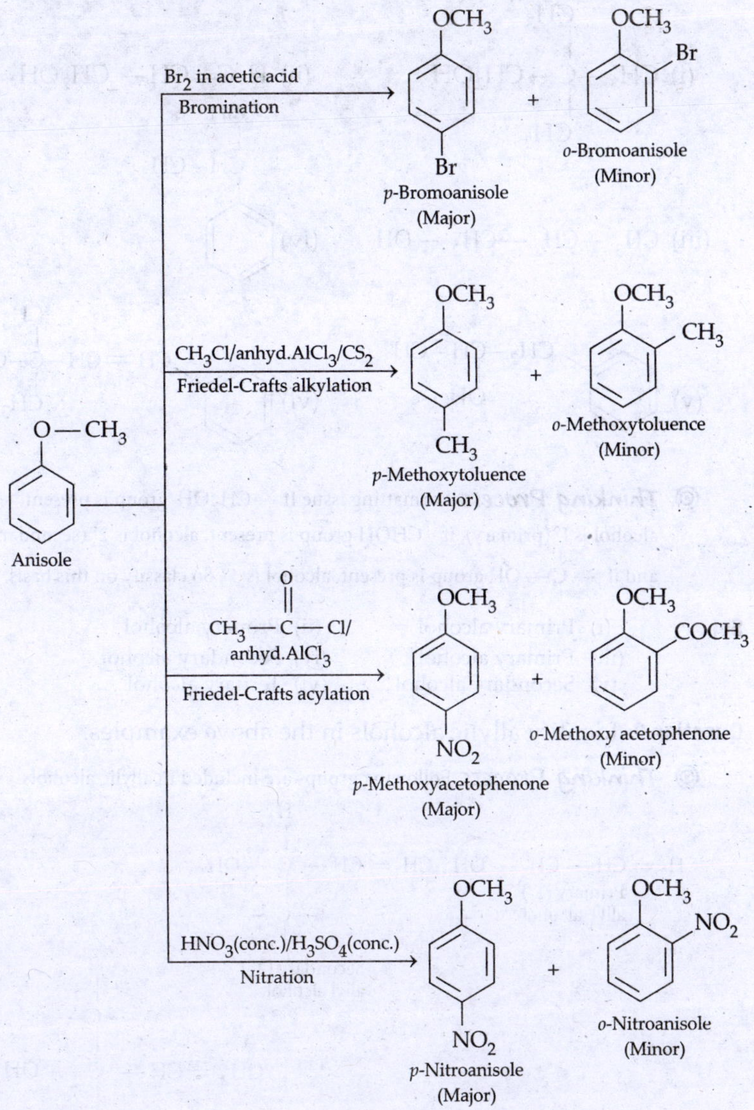

Intext Questions

Question 1 Classify the following as primary, secondary and tertiary alcohols.

(i) $CH_3-\overset{\overset{CH_3}{|}}{\underset{\underset{CH_3}{|}}{C}}-CH_2OH$

(ii) $H_2C=CH-CH_2OH$

(iii) $CH_3-CH_2-CH_2-OH$

(iv) 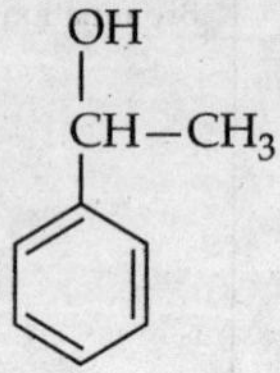

(v) 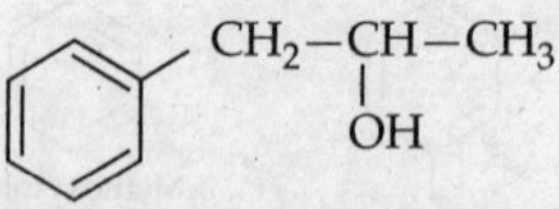

(vi) 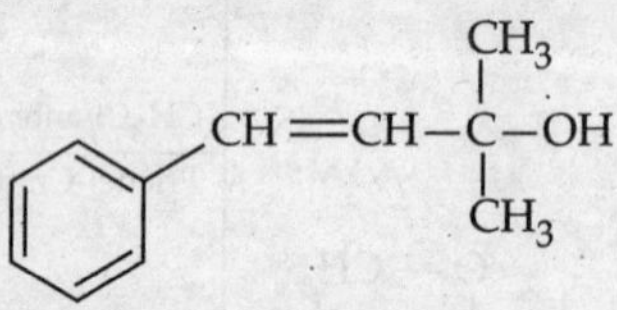

◎ ***Thinking Process*** Formatting issue If $-CH_2OH$ group is present, alcohol is 1° (primary), if CHOH group is present, alcohol is 2° (secondary) and if $-\overset{|}{\underset{|}{C}}-OH$ group is present, alcohol is 3°. So classify on this basis.

Sol. (i) Primary alcohol (ii) Primary alcohol
(iii) Primary alcohol (iv) Secondary alcohol
(v) Secondary alcohol (vi) Tertiary alcohol

Question 2 Identify allylic alcohols in the above examples.

◎ ***Thinking Process*** Following groups are included in allylic alcohols.

$CH_2=CH-CH_2-OH$,
Primary (1°) allyl alcohol

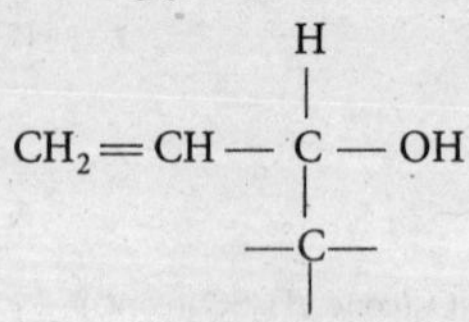

Secondary (2°) allyl alcohol

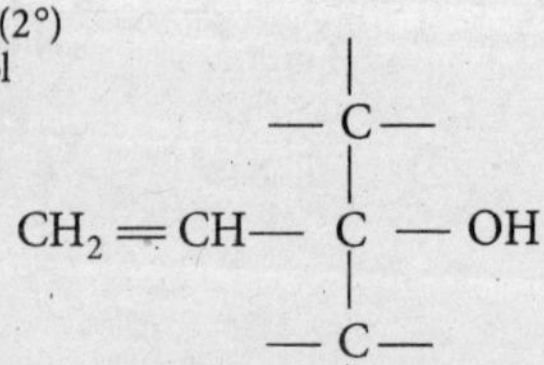

Tertiary (3°) allyl alcohol

Sol. (ii) $H_2C{=}CH{-}CH_2OH$

(vi) 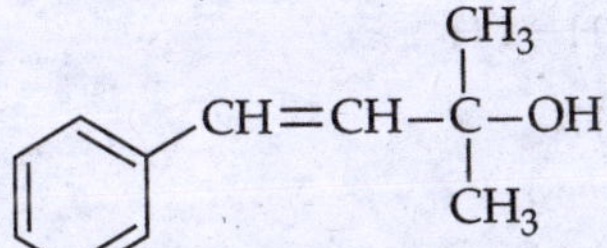

Question 3 Name the following compounds according to the IUPAC system.

(i) $CH_3{-}CH_2{-}CH(CH_2Cl){-}CH(CH_2OH){-}CH(CH_3){-}CH_3$

(ii) $H_3C{-}CH(CH_3){-}CH_2{-}CH(OH){-}CH(CH_2OH){-}CH_3$

(iii) 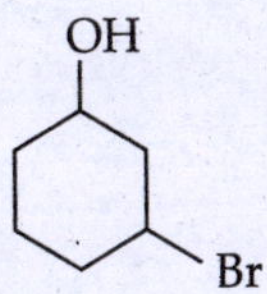

(iv) $H_2C{=}CH{-}CH(OH){-}CH_2{-}CH_2{-}CH_3$

(v) $CH_3{-}C(CH_3){=}C(Br){-}CH_2OH$

◎ ***Thinking Process*** Prefix according to the C-chain; for alcohol add suffix —ol; for double bond —ene; tell the position of substituents, double bond and functional group(s). Then, give the name in the following manner.
Name of substituent with position (in alphabetical order) + parent C-chain name + primary suffix + secondary suffix with position (for main functional group).

Sol.

(i) 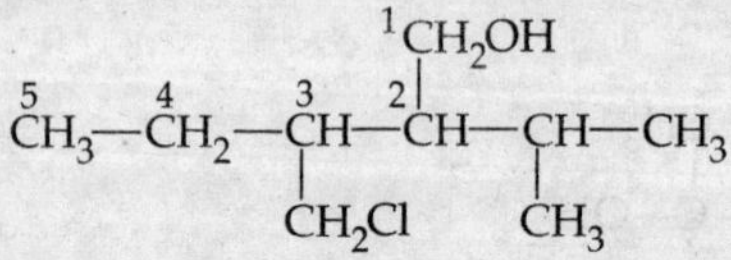

3-Chloromethyl-2-iso-propyl pentan-1-ol

(ii) 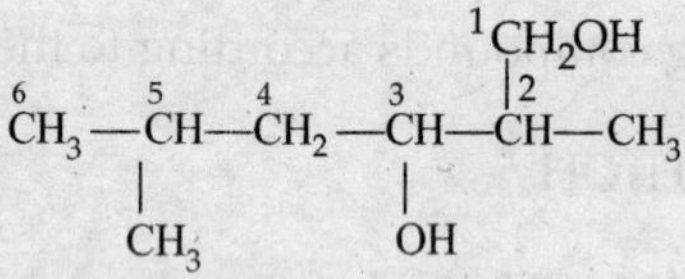

2,5-Dimethylhexan-1,3-diol

(iii) 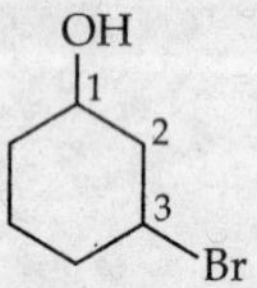

3-Bromocyclohexanol

(iv) 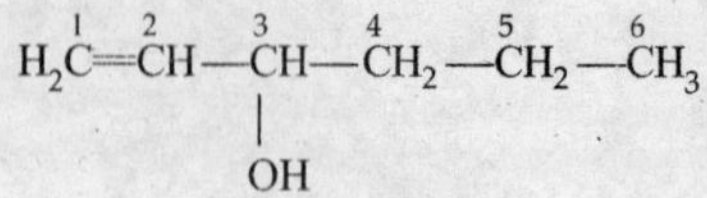

Hex-1-en-3-ol

(v) 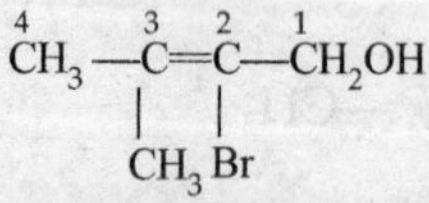

2-Bromo-3-methylbut-2-en-1-ol

Question 4 Show how are the following alcohols prepared by the reaction of a suitable Grignard reagent on methanal?

(i) 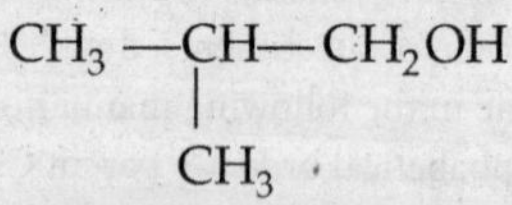 (ii) 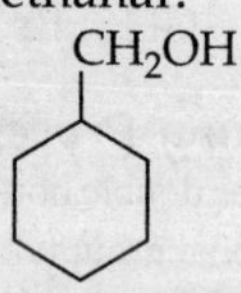

◎ *Thinking Process* $HCHO + RMgX \xrightarrow[H^+]{H_2O} RCH_2OH + Mg(OH)X.$

From here, it is clear that HCHO gives CH_2OH groups, so R of Grignard reagent is the remaining part of given alcohols. Thus, select the suitable Grignard reagent by substituting the value of R.

Sol. (i) $\underset{\text{Methanal}}{HCHO} + \underset{\substack{\text{Isopropyl}\\ \text{magnesium}\\ \text{bromide}}}{(CH_3)_2CH\,MgBr} \xrightarrow{\text{Dry ether}} \underset{\text{Addition compound}}{[(CH_3)_2CH\cdot CH_2OMgBr]}$

$$\xrightarrow[-Mg(Br)OH]{H_2O/H^+} \underset{\substack{\text{Isobutyl alcohol}\\ \text{or 2-Methylpropan-1-ol}}}{(CH_3)_2CH{-}CH_2OH}$$

(ii)

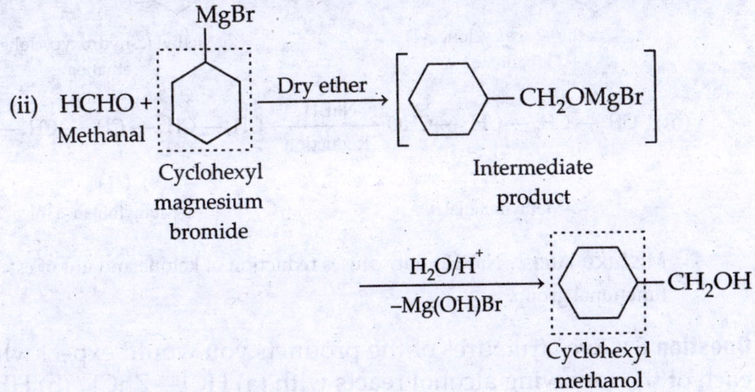

Question 5 Write structures of the products of the following reactions.

(i) $CH_3{-}CH{=}CH_2 \xrightarrow{H_2O/H^+}$

(ii)

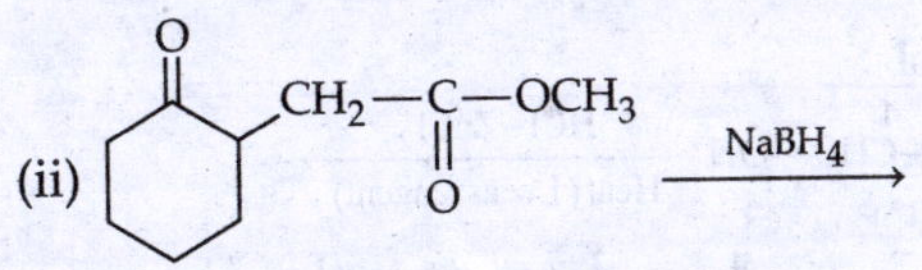

(iii) $CH_3{-}CH_2{-}\underset{\displaystyle CH_3}{\underset{|}{CH}}{-}CHO \xrightarrow{NaBH_4}$

◎ ***Thinking Process***

(i) Acidic hydration of propene *i.e.,* addition of H_2O (according to Markovnikov's rule) result in the formation of alcohol.

(ii) Reduction of $>C{=}O$ group (not in ester group) into —OH.

(iii) Reduction of —CHO group into — CH_2OH.

Sol. (i) $\underset{\text{Propene}}{CH_3-CH=CH_2} \xrightarrow[\text{Markovnikov's rule}]{H_2O/H^+} \underset{\text{Propan-2-ol}}{\overset{1}{C}H_3-\overset{2}{C}H(OH)-\overset{3}{C}H_3}$

(ii) 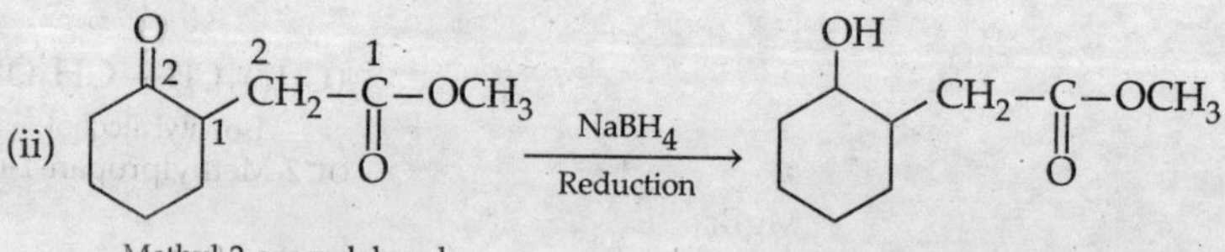

Methyl-2-oxocyclohexyl ethanoate → Methyl (2-hydroxycyclohexyl) ethanoate

(iii) $\underset{\text{2-Methylbutanal}}{\overset{4}{C}H_3-\overset{3}{C}H_2-\overset{2}{C}H(CH_3)-\overset{1}{C}HO} \xrightarrow[\text{Reduction}]{NaBH_4} \underset{\text{2-Methylbutan-1-ol}}{\overset{4}{C}H_3-\overset{3}{C}H_2-\overset{2}{C}H(CH_3)-\overset{1}{C}H_2-OH}$

Mistake Alert $NaBH_4$ only causes reduction of ketone and not of ester functional group.

Question 6 Give structures of the products you would expect when each of the following alcohol reacts with (a) HCl—$ZnCl_2$ (b) HBr and (c) $SOCl_2$

(i) Butan-1-ol (ii) 2-methylbutan-2-ol

Thinking Process Replacement of —OH by (a) —Cl (b) —Br (c) —Cl

Sol. (i) Reactions of butan-1-ol

(a) $\underset{\text{Butan-1-ol}(1^\circ)}{\overset{4}{C}H_3-\overset{3}{C}H_2-\overset{2}{C}H_2-\overset{1}{C}H_2-OH} \xrightarrow[\text{Heat (Lucas reagent)}]{HCl-ZnCl_2}$

$\underset{\text{1-Chlorobutane}}{\overset{4}{C}H_3-\overset{3}{C}H_2-\overset{2}{C}H_2-\overset{1}{C}H_2-Cl} + H_2O$

This reaction does not take place at room temperature.

(b) $\underset{\text{Butan-1-ol}}{CH_3-CH_2-CH_2-CH_2-OH}$

$\xrightarrow[\text{Heat}]{HBr} \underset{\text{1-Bromobutane}}{\overset{4}{C}H_3-\overset{3}{C}H_2-\overset{2}{C}H_2-\overset{1}{C}H_2-Br} + H_2O$

(c) $CH_3-CH_2-CH_2-CH_2-OH \xrightarrow[\text{Heat}]{SOCl_2}$

$\underset{\text{1-Chlorobutane}}{\overset{4}{C}H_3-\overset{3}{C}H_2-\overset{2}{C}H_2-\overset{1}{C}H_2-Cl} + SO_2 + HCl$

(ii) Reactions of 2-methylbutan-2-ol

(a) $\overset{1}{C}H_3-\overset{2}{C}(CH_3)(OH)-\overset{3}{C}H_2-\overset{4}{C}H_3 \xrightarrow[\text{Lucas reagent}]{HCl—ZnCl_2} \overset{1}{C}H_3-\overset{2}{C}(CH_3)(Cl)-\overset{3}{C}H_2-\overset{4}{C}H_3 + H_2O$

2-Methylbutan-2-ol (3°) → 2-Chloro-2-methylbutane

(b) $\overset{1}{C}H_3-\overset{2}{C}(CH_3)(OH)-\overset{3}{C}H_2-\overset{4}{C}H_3 \xrightarrow[\text{Heat}]{HBr} \overset{1}{C}H_3-\overset{2}{C}(CH_3)(Br)-\overset{3}{C}H_2-\overset{4}{C}H_3 + H_2O$

2-Methylbutan-2-ol → 2-Bromo-2-methylbutane

(c) $\overset{1}{C}H_3-\overset{2}{C}(CH_3)(OH)-\overset{3}{C}H_2-\overset{4}{C}H_3 \xrightarrow[\text{Heat}]{SOCl_2} \overset{1}{C}H_3-\overset{2}{C}(CH_3)(Cl)-\overset{3}{C}H_2-\overset{4}{C}H_3 + SO_2 + HCl$

2-Chloro-2-methylbutane

Note • Butan-1-ol, being primary alcohol requires heating with Lucas reagent. 2-Methylbutan-2-ol being tertiary alcohol reacts without heating.

• Lucas test is used to distinguish between primary, secondary and tertiary alcohols.

Question 7 Predict the major product of acid catalysed dehydration of

(i) 1-methylcyclohexanol (ii) butan-1-ol

◎ ***Thinking Process*** In acid catalysed dehydration process a molecule of water is liberated according to Saytzeff's rule *i.e.,* results in the formation of more substituted alkene.

Sol. (i)

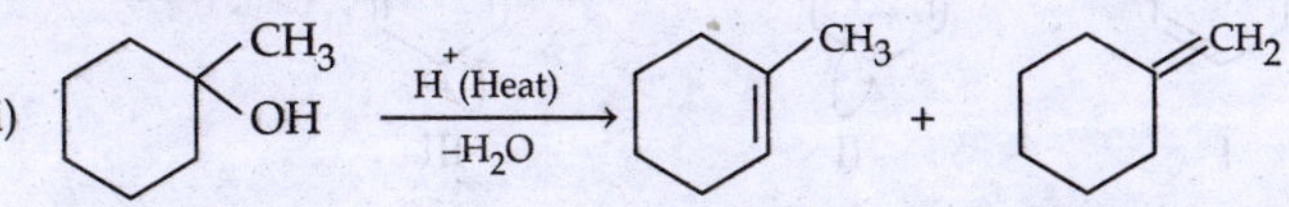

1-Methyl cyclohexanol → 1-Methyl cyclohexene (Major) + 1-Methylene cyclohexane (Minor)

(ii) $CH_3—CH_2—CH_2—CH_2—OH \xrightarrow[-H_2O]{H^+, \text{heat}}$
Butan-1-ol

$CH_3—CH_2—CH=CH_2 + CH_3—CH=CH—CH_3$
But-1-ene (Minor) But-2-ene (Major)

Note —OH from α-C atom and H from β-C atom is eliminated.

- According to Saytzeff's rule, major product is 1-methyl-cyclohexene, since it is more substituted.
- Major product is but-2-ene due to rearrangement to give secondary carbocation, which is more stable.

Mechanism :

$$CH_3—CH_2—CH_2—CH_2—OH \xrightarrow[-H_2O]{H^+} CH_3—CH_2\underset{\underset{H}{|}}{CH}—\overset{+}{C}H_2$$

Butan-1-ol

1º carbocation (Less stable)

$$\xrightarrow[\text{(Rearrangement)}]{H^- \text{ ion shift}} CH_3—CH_2—\overset{\oplus}{C}H—CH_3$$

2° carbocation (More stable)

$$\downarrow -H^+$$

$$CH_3—CH=CH—CH_3$$

But-2-ene

Question 8 *Ortho* and *para* nitrophenols are more acidic than phenol. Draw the resonance structures of the corresponding phenoxide ions.

◎ *Thinking Process* Acidic strength depends on the relative stabilities of corresponding phenoxide ions based on resonance.

Sol. (i) **Phenoxide ion**

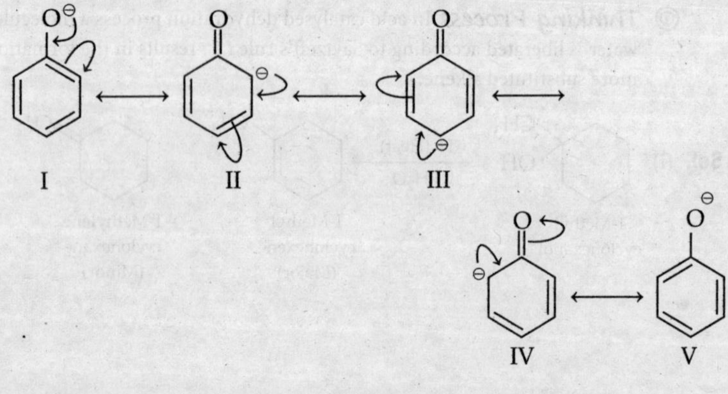

I II III IV V

(ii) *o*-Nitrophenoxide ion

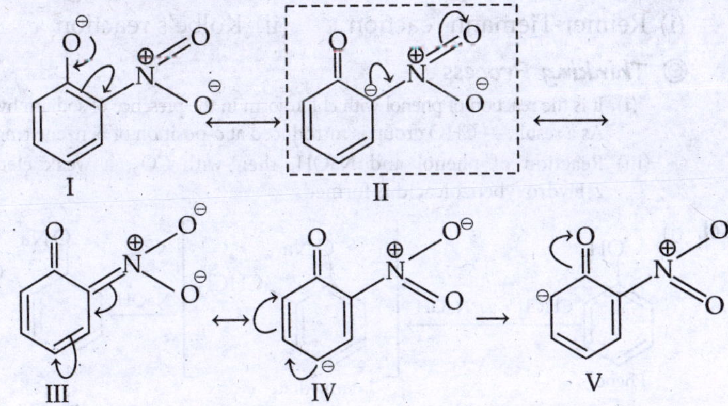

(iii) *p*-Nitrophenoxide ion

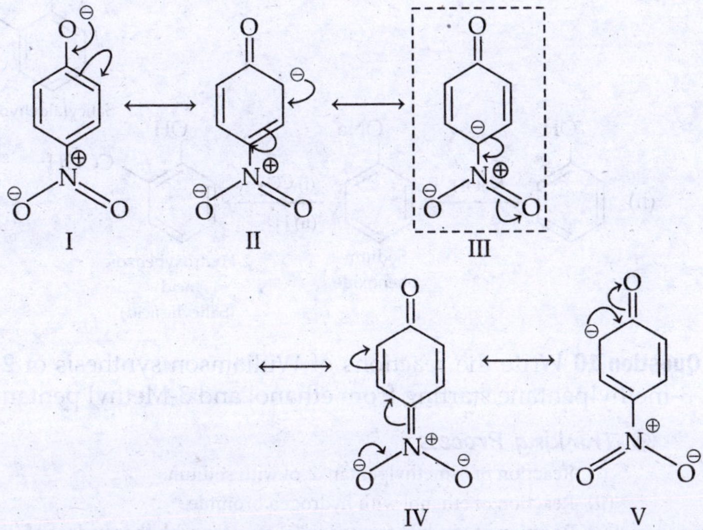

Due to —*R* effect of —NO_2 group, *o*- and *p*-Nitrophenoxide ions are more stable than phenoxide ion. Consequently, both *o*- and *p*-nitrophenols are more acidic than phenol.

Note Structures in boxes have negative charge on that C-atom to which electron withdrawing —NO_2 group is attached. So, these structures contribute more towards the acidic character than the others.

Mistake Alert —NO_2 can be written as 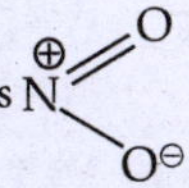

Question 9 Write the equations involved in the following reactions :

(i) Reimer-Tiemann reaction (ii) Kolbe's reaction

◎ *Thinking Process*

(i) It is the reaction of phenol with chloroform in the presence of sodium hydroxide. As a result, —CHO group is introduced at *o*-position of benzene ring.

(iii) Reaction of phenol and NaOH, then with CO_2, a weak electrolyte. 2-Hydroxybenzoicacid is formed.

Sol. (i)

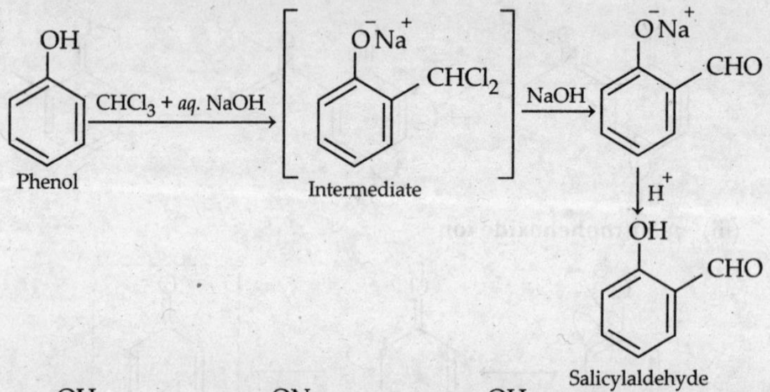

(ii)

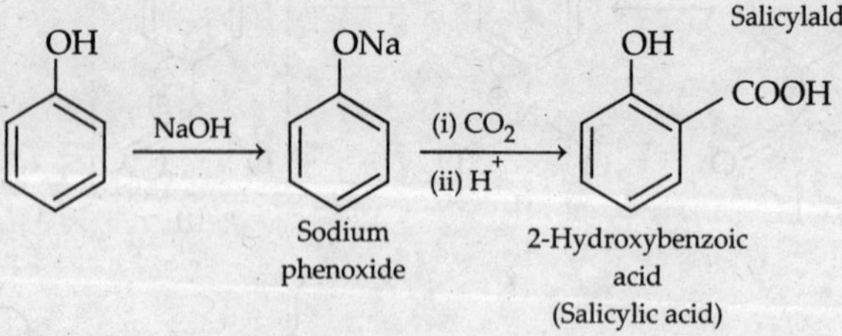

Question 10 Write the reactions of Williamson synthesis of 2-ethoxy -3-methylpentane starting from ethanol and 3-Methyl pentan-2-ol.

◎ *Thinking Process*

(i) Reaction of 3-methylpentan-2-ol with sodium.

(ii) Reaction of ethanol with hydrogen bromide.

(iii) Reaction of product formed in (i) reaction with the product of (ii).

Sol. (i) $\overset{5}{C}H_3—\overset{4}{C}H_2—\overset{3}{C}H(CH_3)—\overset{2}{C}H(OH)—\overset{1}{C}H_3 + Na \longrightarrow$

3-Methylpentan-2-ol

$CH_3—CH_2—CH(CH_3)—CH(ONa)—CH_3$

Sodium-(3-methyl)-pentan-2-oxide

(ii) $C_2H_5OH + HBr \longrightarrow C_2H_5Br + H_2O$
Bromoethane

(iii) $CH_3-CH_2-\underset{CH_3}{\underset{|}{CH}}-\underset{ONa}{\underset{|}{CH}}-CH_3 + C_2H_5Br \longrightarrow CH_3-CH_2-\underset{CH_3}{\underset{|}{CH}}-\underset{OC_2H_5}{\underset{|}{CH}}-CH_3$

2-Ethoxy -3-methylpentane

Question 11 Which of the following is an appropriate set of reactants for the preparation of 1-methoxy-4-nitrobenzene and why?

(i) 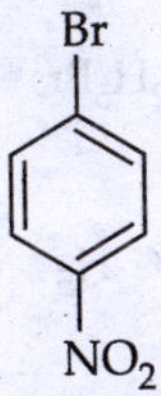 + CH_3ONa

(ii) 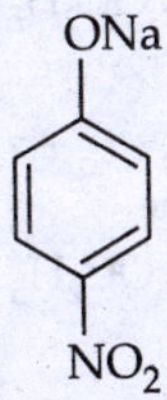 + CH_3Br

◎ *Thinking Process* This reaction involves preparation of ether by Williamson synthesis. It takes place by S_{N^2} attack of an alkoxide ion on primary alkyl halide.

Sol. (ii) 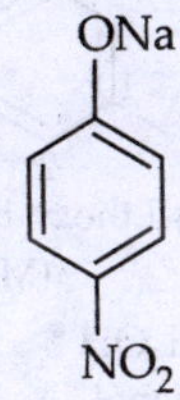 + $CH_3Br \longrightarrow$ 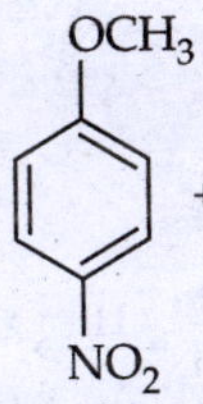 + NaBr

1-Methoxy-4-nitrobenzene

Because here the alkyl halide used is primary. Moreover in method (i) the C – Br bond has some double bond character.

Question 12 Predict the products of the following reactions :

(i) $CH_3-CH_2-CH_2-O-CH_3 + HBr \longrightarrow$

(ii) 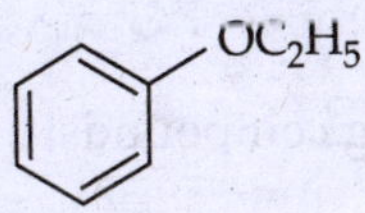 + HBr $\longrightarrow$

(iii) 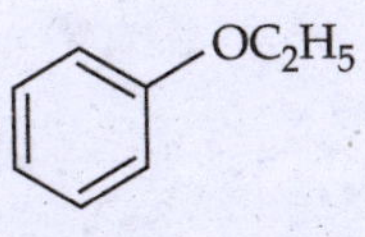 $\xrightarrow[\text{Conc. } HNO_3]{\text{Conc. } H_2SO_4}$

(iv) $(CH_3)_3C-OC_2H_5 \xrightarrow{HI}$

◎ *Thinking Process*

(i) and (ii) $R'—O—R + H \vdots X \longrightarrow R'—OH + R—X$ *i.e.*, primary halide is formed.

(iii) Nitration (introduction of NO_2 group) takes place at *o*- and *p*-positions.

(iv) Tertiary iodide and primary alcohol are formed.

Sol. (i) $CH_3—CH_2—CH_2—O—CH_3 + HBr \longrightarrow$ (Methoxypropane)

$CH_3—CH_2—CH_2—OH + CH_3Br$ (Propanol)

(ii) 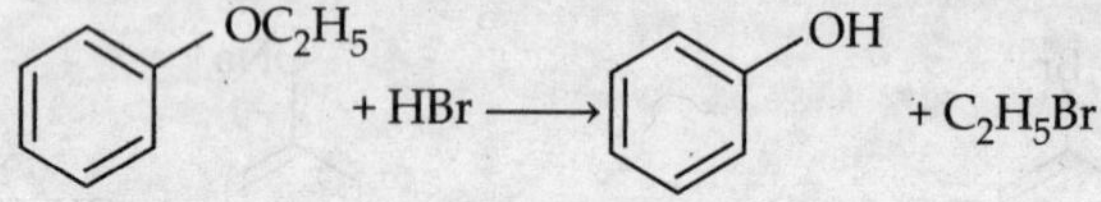

Ethoxy benzene → Phenol

(iii) 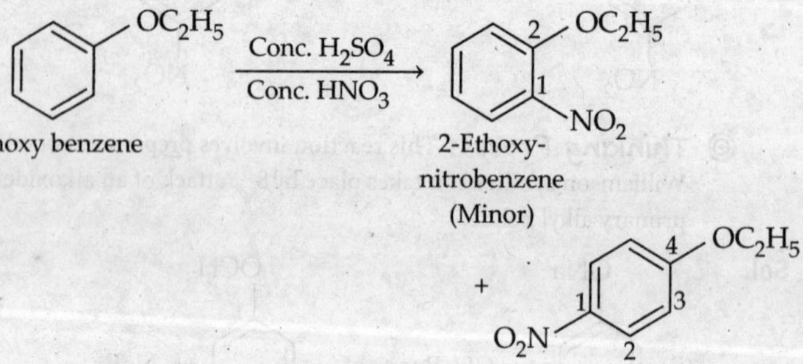

Ethoxy benzene → 2-Ethoxy-nitrobenzene (Minor) + 4-Ethoxy-nitrobenzene (Major)

(iv) $(CH_3)_3C—OC_2H_5 \xrightarrow{HI} (CH_3)_3C—I + C_2H_5OH$

t-butyl ethyl ether → *t*-butyl iodide, Ethanol

Mistake Alert $R'—O \vdots —R$ is cleaved in such a way that R forms a stable carbocation (like 3°).

Exercises

Question 1 Write IUPAC name of the following compounds:

(i) $CH_3—CH(CH_3)—CH(OH)—C(CH_3)_2—CH_3$

(ii) $H_3C-\underset{|\atop OH}{CH}-CH_2-\underset{|\atop OH}{CH}-\underset{|\atop C_2H_5}{CH}-CH_2-CH_3$

(iii) $CH_3-\underset{|\atop OH}{CH}-\underset{|\atop OH}{CH}-CH_3$

(iv) $HO-CH_2-\underset{|\atop OH}{CH}-CH_2-OH$

(v) 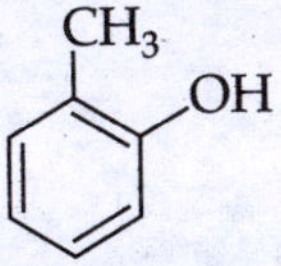

(vi) 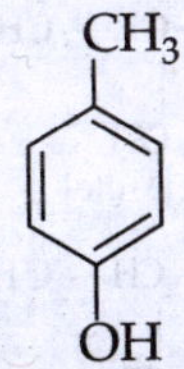

(vii) 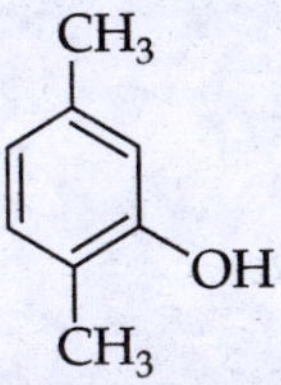

(viii) 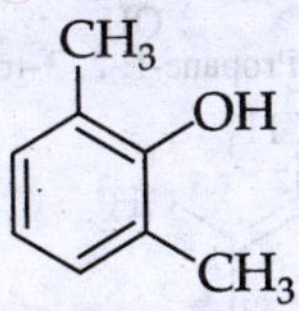

(ix) $CH_3-O-CH_2-\underset{|\atop CH_3}{CH}-CH_3$

(x) $C_6H_5-O-C_2H_5$

(xi) $C_6H_5-O-C_7H_{15}(n-)$

(xii) $CH_3-CH_2-O-\underset{|\atop CH_3}{CH}-CH_2-CH_3$

◎ ***Thinking Process*** Prefix according to the carbon chain; for alcohol (—OH) use suffix -ol; tell the position of substituents and functional group. For ether (—O—), prefix alkoxy is used. For —OH group attached directly to benzene ring, suffix phenol is used.

So, give the name of alcohol as substituent with position (in alphabetical order) + prefix of carbon chain + primary suffix (*ane, ene, yne*) + 'ol' with position and give the name of ether as alkoxy alkane (where alkoxy smaller *R* group and alkane is main chain)

Sol.

(i) 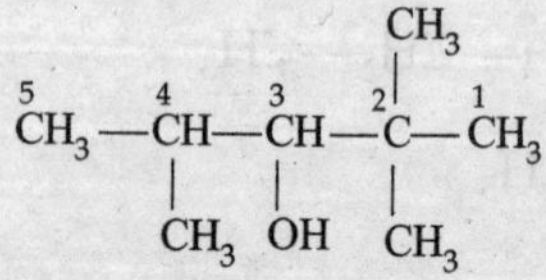

2, 2, 4-Trimethylpentan-3-ol

(ii) 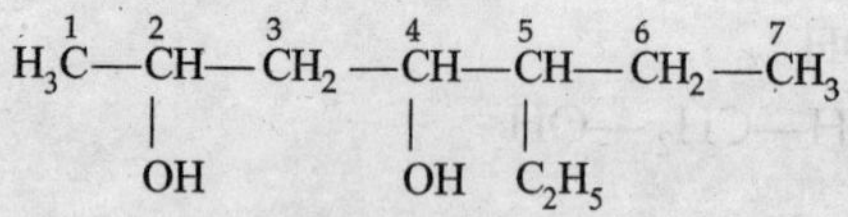

5-Ethylheptane-2, 4-diol

(iii) 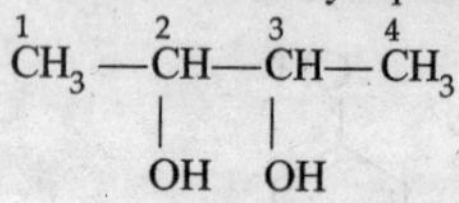

Butane-2, 3-diol

(iv) 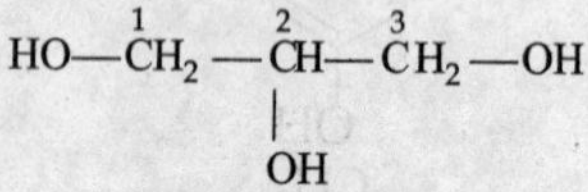

Propane-1, 2, 3-triol

(v) 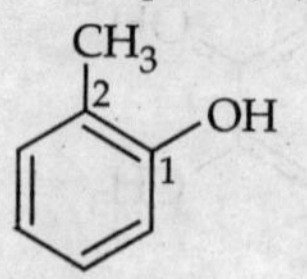

2-Methylphenol

(vi) 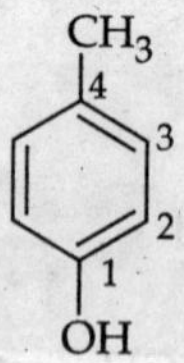

4-Methylphenol

(vii) 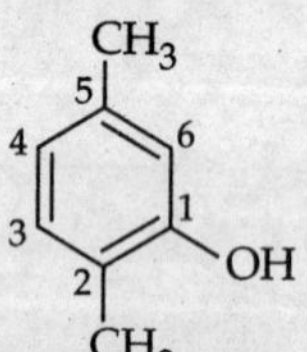

2,5-Dimethylphenol

(viii) 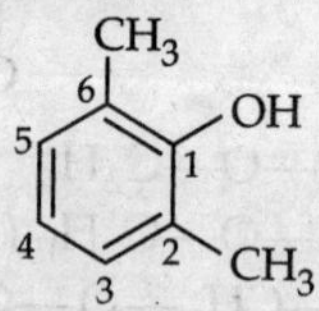

2,6-Dimethylphenol

(ix) 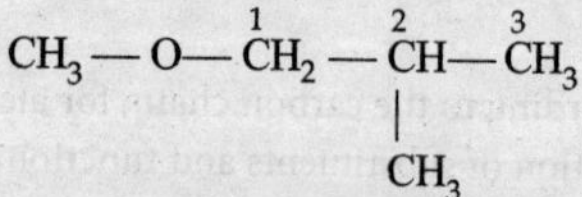

1-Methoxy-2-methylpropane

(x) $C_6H_5-O-C_2H_5$

Ethoxybenzene

(xi) $C_6H_5-O-C_7H_{15}$ $(n-)$

1-Phenoxyheptane

(xii) 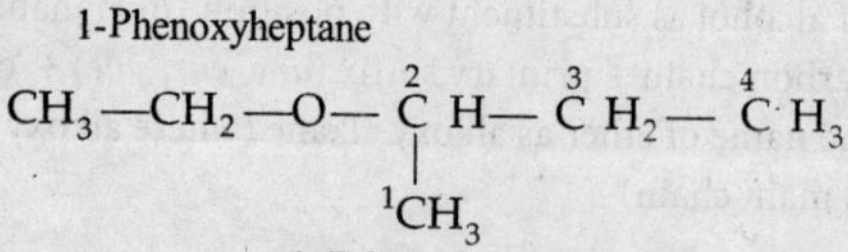

2-Ethoxybutane

Question 2 Write structures of the compounds whose IUPAC names are as follows:

(i) 2-Methylbutan-2-ol
(ii) 1-Phenylpropan-2-ol
(iii) 3, 5-Dimethylhexane-1, 3, 5-triol
(iv) 2,3-Diethylphenol
(v) 1-Ethoxypropane
(vi) 2-Ethoxy-3-methylpentane
(vii) Cyclohexylmethanol
(viii) 3-Cyclohexylpentan-3-ol
(ix) Cyclopent-3-en-1-ol
(x) 4-Chloro-3-ethylbutan-1-ol

◎ Thinking Process

(i) Draw the main carbon chain according to the root word of carbon chain and then attach the other groups according to the positions mentioned.

(ii) Suffix 'al' represents –OH group and prefix 'alkoxy' represents '*RO*' group.

Sol. (i) 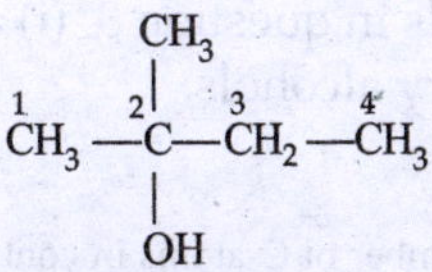

2-Methylbutan-2-ol

(ii) 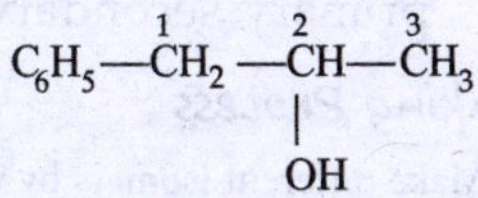

1-Phenylpropan-2-ol

(iii) 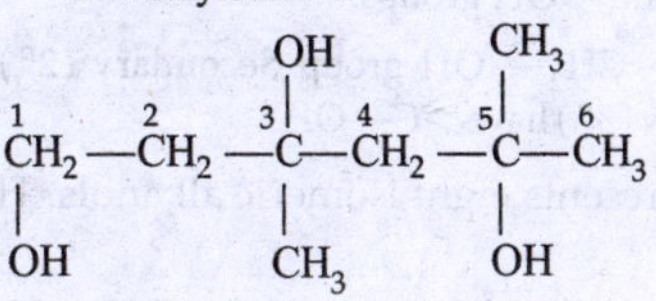

3, 5-Dimethylhexane-1, 3,5-triol

(iv) 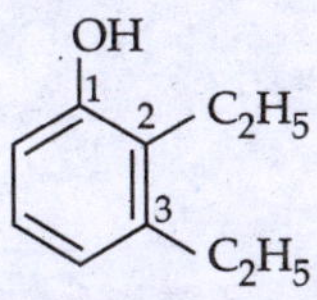

2,3-Diethylphenol

(v) $\overset{}{C_2H_5O}-\overset{1}{CH_2}-\overset{2}{CH_2}-\overset{3}{CH_3}$

1-Ethoxypropane

(vi) 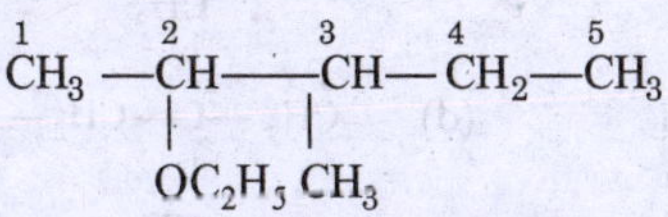

2-Ethoxy-3-methylpentane

(vii) 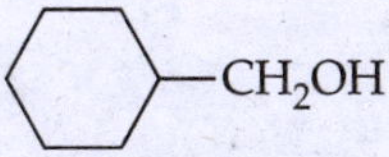

Cyclohexylmethanol

(viii) 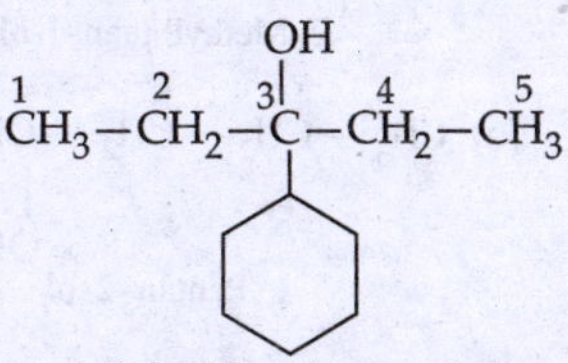

3-Cyclohexylpentan-3-ol

(ix) 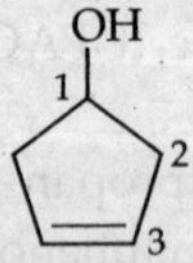

Cyclopent-3-en-1-ol

(x) $\overset{1}{HO—CH_2}—\overset{2}{CH_2}—\overset{3}{CH}(C_2H_5)—\overset{4}{CH_2}—Cl$

4-Chloro-3-ethylbutan-1-ol

Question 3 (i) Draw the structures of all isomeric alcohols of molecular formula $C_5H_{12}O$ and give their IUPAC names.

(ii) Classify the isomers of alcohols in question 3. (i) as primary, secondary and tertiary alcohols.

◎ *Thinking Process*

(i) Make different isomers by varying the number of C-atoms in continuous chain, the position of $—CH_3$ and $—OH$ groups.

(ii) Primary (1°) alcohols have $—CH_2—OH$ group Secondary (2°) have $>CH—OH$ group and Tertiary (3°) have $\geqslant C—OH$.

Sol. (i) Molecular formula $C_5H_{12}O$ represents eight isomeric alkanols. These are :

(a) $\overset{5}{CH_3}—\overset{4}{CH_2}—\overset{3}{CH_2}—\overset{2}{CH_2}—\overset{1}{CH_2}—OH$

Pentan-1-ol

(b) $\overset{4}{CH_3}—\overset{3}{CH}(CH_3)—\overset{2}{CH_2}—\overset{1}{CH_2}—OH$

3-Methyl butan-1-ol

(c) $\overset{4}{CH_3}—\overset{3}{CH_2}—\overset{2}{CH}(CH_3)—\overset{1}{CH_2}—OH$

2-Methylbutan-1-ol

(d) $\overset{3}{CH_3}—\overset{2}{C}(CH_3)_2—\overset{1}{CH_2}—OH$

2, 2-Dimethylpropan-1-ol

(e) $\overset{5}{CH_3}—\overset{4}{CH_2}—\overset{3}{CH_2}—\overset{2}{CH}(OH)—\overset{1}{CH_3}$

Pentan-2-ol

(f) 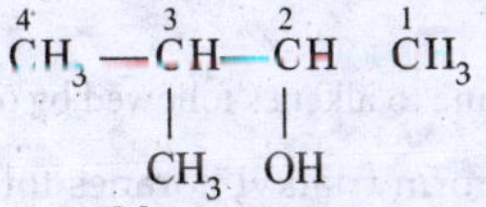

3-Methylbutan-2-ol

(g) 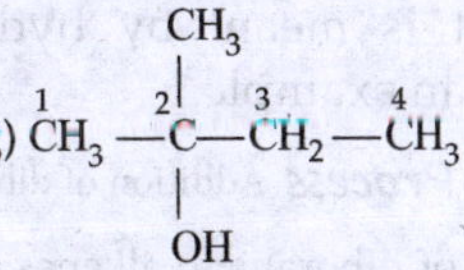

2-Methylbutan-2-ol

(h) 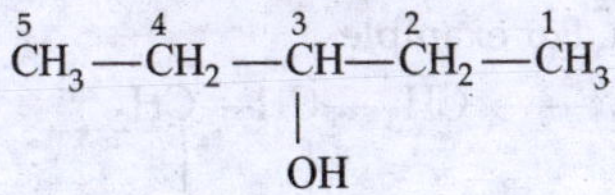

Pentan-3-ol

(ii) Primary : (a), (b), (c) and (d); Secondary (e), (f), (h); Tertiary : (g).

Question 4 Explain why propanol has higher boiling point than that of the hydrocarbon, butane?

◎ ***Thinking Process*** Boiling point is directly proportional to the intermolecular forces existing in a compound.

Sol. Although butane and propanol have comparable molecular masses (58 and 60 respectively) but, in propanol, polar $-OH$ group is present, due to which strong intermolecular hydrogen bonding exists between its molecules. Whereas in butane weak van der Waals' forces of attraction are the only forces between the molecules. Therefore, propanol has higher boiling point (391 K) as compared to that of butane (309 K).

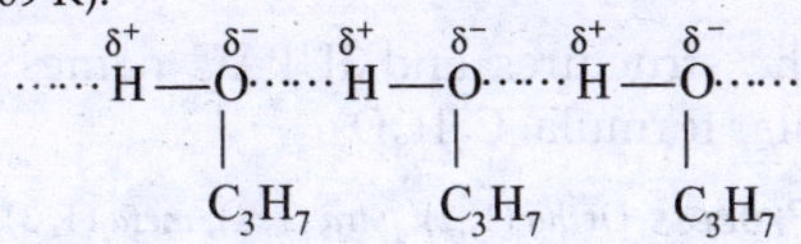

Question 5 Alcohols are comparatively more soluble in water than hydrocarbons of comparable molecular masses. Explain this fact.

◎ ***Thinking Process*** Consider polar nature of water as well as alcohol; presence of hydrogen bonding.

Sol. Water and alcohols both are polar in nature. When an alcohol is dissolved in water, it forms hydrogen bonds with water by breaking the H-bonding already existing between the water molecules. Hydrocarbons are non-polar in nature and do not form H-bonds with water molecules. Therefore, alcohols are readily soluble in water whereas hydrocarbons are not.

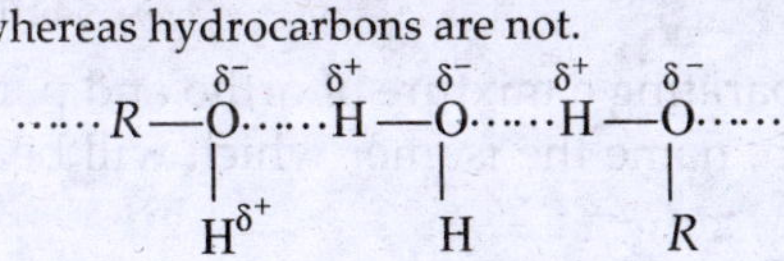

Hydrogen bonding among alcohol and water

Question 6 What is meant by hydroboration-oxidation reaction? Illustrate it with an example.

◉ *Thinking Process* Addition of diborane to alkenes followed by oxidation.

Sol. The addition of diborane to alkenes to form trialkyl boranes followed by their oxidation by alkaline H_2O_2 to form alcohols is known as hydroboration-oxidation reaction. For example

$$\underset{\text{Propene}}{CH_3-CH=CH_2} + \underset{\text{Diborane}}{(H-BH_2)_2} \longrightarrow CH_3-\underset{\displaystyle H}{\underset{|}{CH}}-\underset{\displaystyle BH_2}{\underset{|}{CH_2}}$$

$$\downarrow CH_3-CH=CH_2$$

$$(CH_3-CH_2-CH_2)_3B \xleftarrow{CH_3-CH=CH_2} (CH_3-CH_2-CH_2)_2BH$$

$$\xrightarrow{H_2O,\ 3H_2O_2,\ OH^-} \underset{\text{Propan-1-ol}}{3CH_3-CH_2-CH_2-OH} + \underset{\text{Boric acid}}{B(OH)_3}$$

Alcohol formed by this reaction appears as it has been formed by addition of water in a way contrary to the Markovnikov's rule.

🔔 *Mistake Alert* Three moles of alkene are required for one mole of diborane in hydroboration oxidation reaction.

Question 7 Give the structures and IUPAC names of monohydric phenols of molecular formula, C_7H_8O.

◉ *Thinking Process* *Ortho* (1, 2); *para* (1, 4); *meta* (1, 3). Draw these isomers according to the mentioned positions of —OH and —CH_3 groups.

Sol. Following three isomers are formed from C_7H_8O.

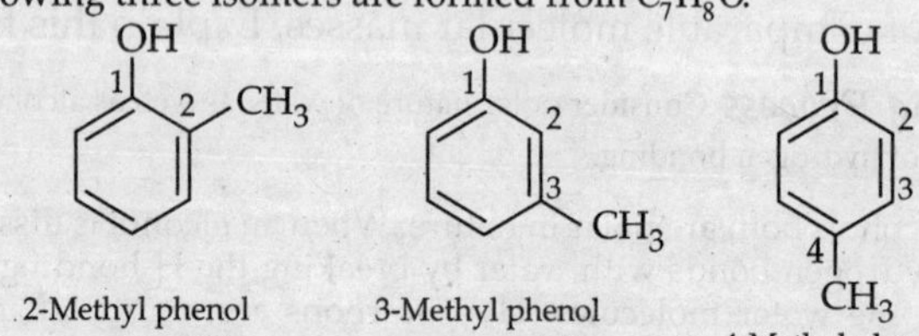

2-Methyl phenol or *o*- cresol (I) | 3-Methyl phenol or *m*- cresol (II) | 4-Methyl phenol or *p*-cresol (III)

Question 8 While separating a mixture of ortho and para nitrophenols by steam distillation, name the isomer which will be steam volatile. Give reason.

◉ *Thinking Process* Isomer, which is steam volatile is less strongly bonded. The other one is strongly bonded by H-bonding.

Sol. *Ortho*-nitrophenol is steam volatile. The reason is intramolecular H-bonding. So, it can be separated by steam distillation from *p*-nitrophenol. *Para*-nitrophenol is not steam volatile due to presence of intermolecular H-bonding, (as intermolecular H-bonding is stronger than intramolecular H-bonding, so, boiling point of compound having intramolecular H-bonding is lower.)

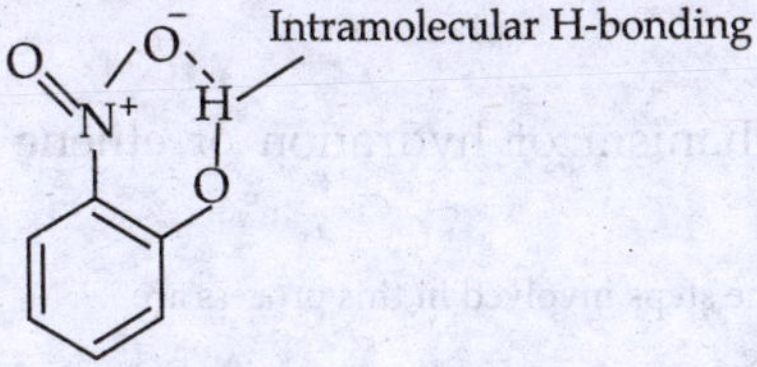

(*o*-nitrophenol)

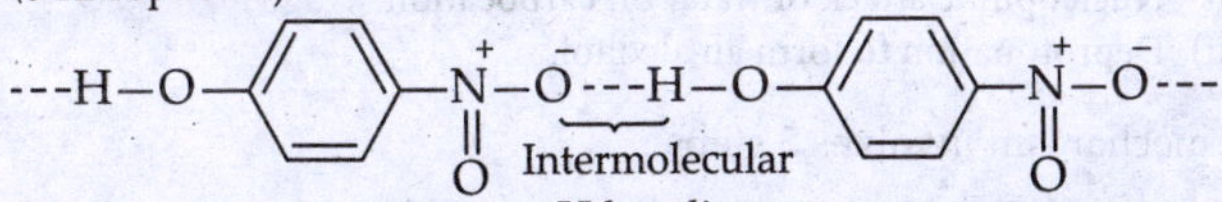

(*p*-nitrophenol)

Question 9 Give the equations of reactions for the preparation of phenol from cumene.

◎ ***Thinking Process*** Oxidation of cumene into cumene hydroperoxide, then acidic hydrolysis.

Sol.

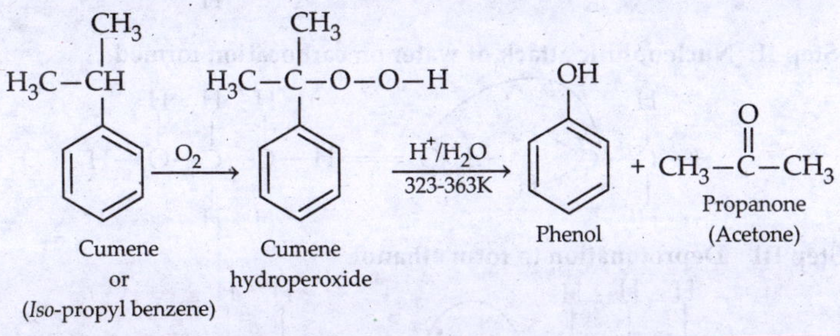

Note This method is employed for the preparation of phenol on commercial scale, as the by product is also an important reagent.

Question 10 Write chemical reaction for the preparation of phenol from chlorobenzene.

◎ ***Thinking Process*** Reaction of chlorobenzene with sodium hydroxide followed by acidification of the product formed.

Sol.

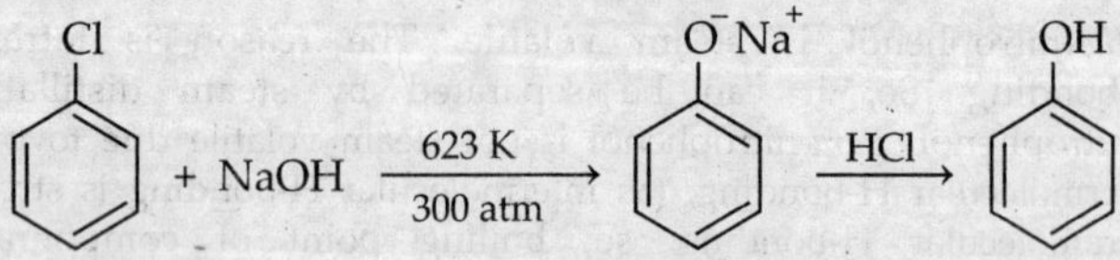

Chloro-benzene Sodium phenoxide Phenol

Question 11 Write the mechanism of hydration of ethene to yield ethanol.

◎ *Thinking Process* The steps involved in this process are

(i) Protonation of alkene.
(ii) Nucleophilic attack of water on carbocation.
(iii) Deprotonation to form an alcohol.

Sol. The mechanism involves 3 steps :

Step I : Protonation of ethene to form carbocation by electrophile attack of H_3O^+.

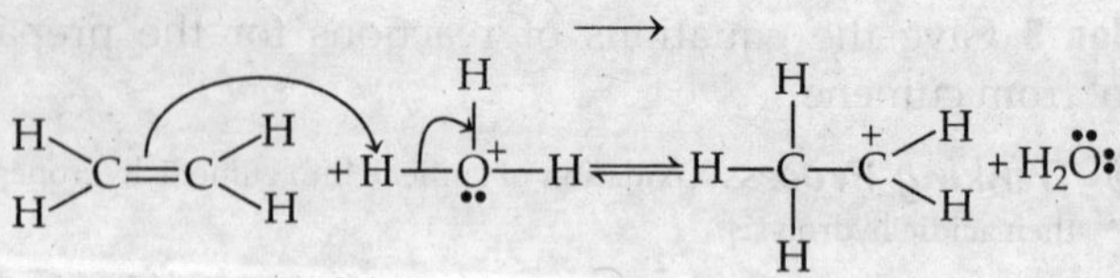

Step II: Nucleophilic attack of water on carbocation formed.

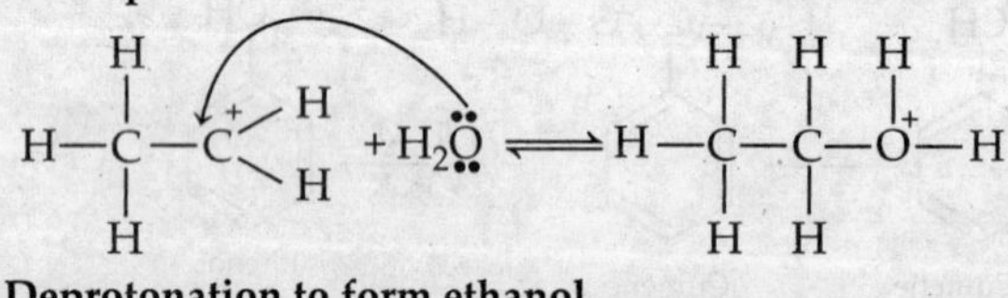

Step III : Deprotonation to form ethanol.

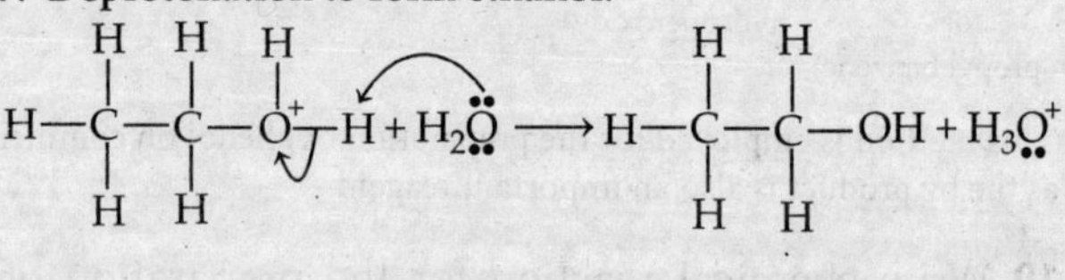

Question 12 You are given benzene, conc. H_2SO_4 and NaOH. Write the equations for the preparation of phenol using these reagents.

◎ *Thinking Process*

(i) Sulphonation of benzene.
(ii) Reaction with NaOH and water.

Sol.

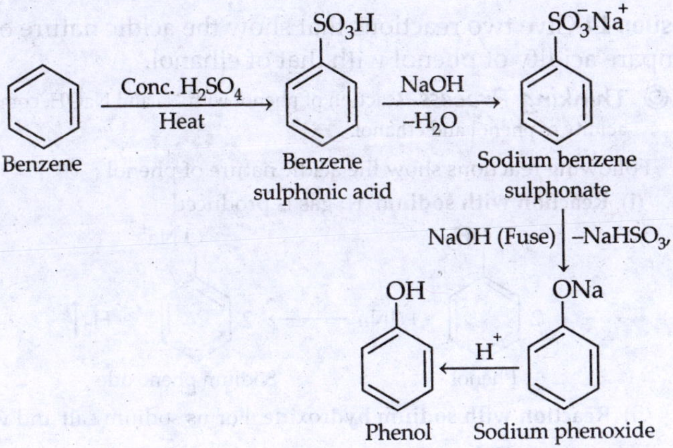

Question 13 Show how will you synthesize :

(i) 1-phenylethanol form a suitable alkene.

(ii) Cyclohexylmethanol using an alkyl halide by an S_N2 reaction.

(iii) pentan-1-ol using a suitable alkyl halide?

◎ ***Thinking Process***

(i) Acidic hydration of ethenyl benzene.

(ii) Alkaline hydrolysis of cyclohexyl methyl bromide.

(iii) Alkaline hydrolysis of 1-bromopentane.

Sol. (i)

$$\underset{\text{Ethenylbenzene (Styrene)}}{C_6H_5—HC=CH_2} + H_2O \xrightarrow[\text{Markovnikov's rule}]{\text{dil.}H_2SO_4} \underset{\text{1-Phenylethanol}}{C_6H_5—\overset{1}{C}H(OH)—\overset{2}{C}H_3}$$

(ii)

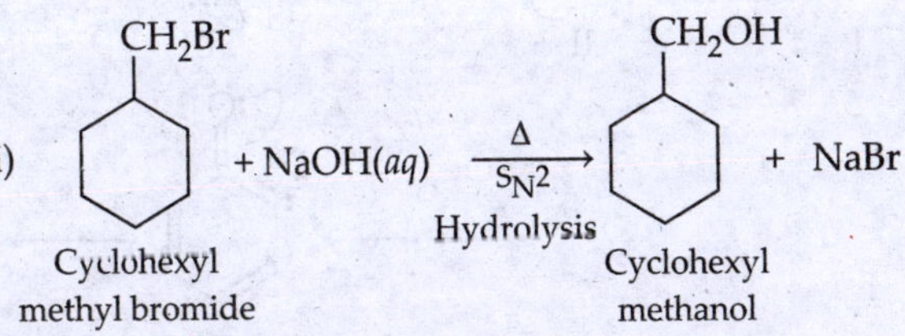

(iii)

$$\underset{\text{1-Bromopentane}}{\overset{5}{C}H_3\overset{4}{C}H_2\overset{3}{C}H_2\overset{2}{C}H_2\overset{1}{C}H_2Br} + \underset{(aq)}{KOH} \xrightarrow[\text{S}_N2\ \text{Hydrolysis}]{\Delta} \underset{\text{Pentan -1-ol}}{\overset{5}{C}H_3\overset{4}{C}H_2\overset{3}{C}H_2\overset{2}{C}H_2\overset{1}{C}H_2OH} + KBr$$

Question 14 Give two reactions that show the acidic nature of phenol. Compare acidity of phenol with that of ethanol.

◎ ***Thinking Process*** Reaction of phenol with Na and NaOH; comparing of acidity of phenol and ethanol.

Sol. Following reactions show the acidic nature of phenol :

(i) **Reaction with sodium** H_2 gas is produced.

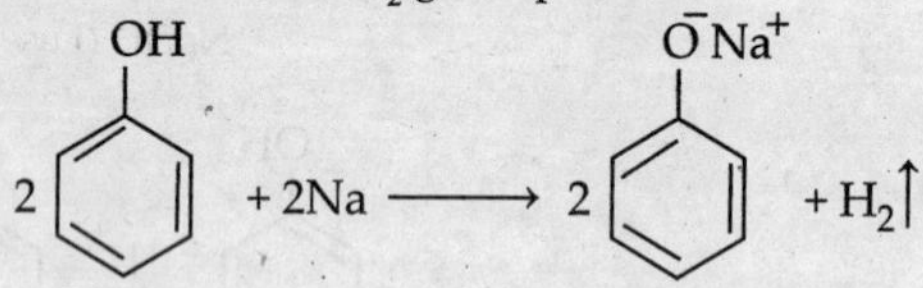

Phenol Sodium phenoxide

(ii) **Reaction with sodium hydroxide** Forms sodium salt and water.

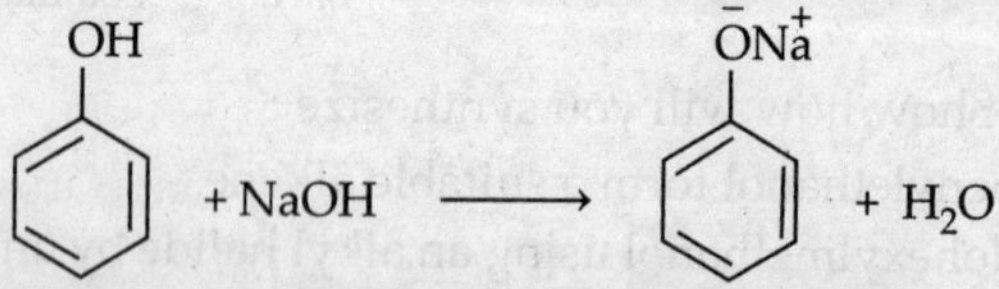

Phenol Sodium phenoxide

Comparison of acidic character of phenol and ethanol

Phenol is more acidic than ethanol because after losing a proton (H^+), phenol forms phenoxide ion which is stabilised by resonance whereas ethoxide ion is not.

(a) $C_2H_5OH \rightleftharpoons C_2H_5O^- + H^+$

(b)

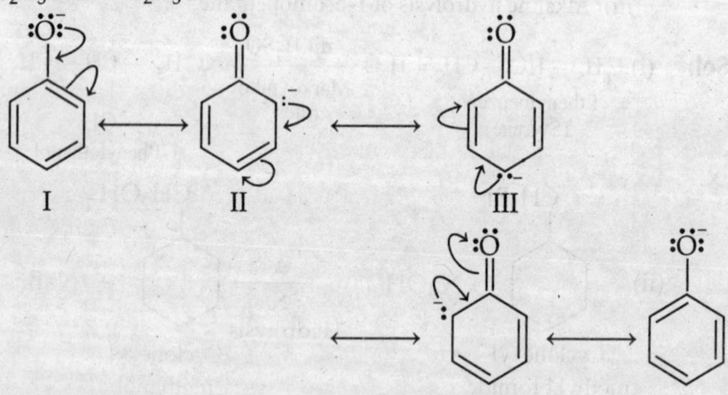

I II III IV V

Question 15 Explain why is *ortho* nitrophenol more acidic than *ortho* methoxyphenol?

◎ ***Thinking Process***

(i) NO_2^-- electron withdrawing group. OCH_3-electron releasing group.

(ii) Presence of electron withdrawing group increases the stability of phenoxide ion while presence of electron releasing group decreases its stability.

(iii) Higher is the stability of phenoxide ion formed, more is the acidic character.

Sol. Nitro (NO_2) group is electron withdrawing whereas methoxy (OCH_3) group is electron releasing in nature. *o*-Nitrophenol produces H^+ ions easily but methoxyphenol does not. This is because *o*-nitrophenoxide ion is stabilised due to resonance. This is not true with *o*-methoxyphenoxide ion. The two negative charges repel each other thereby destabilising it.

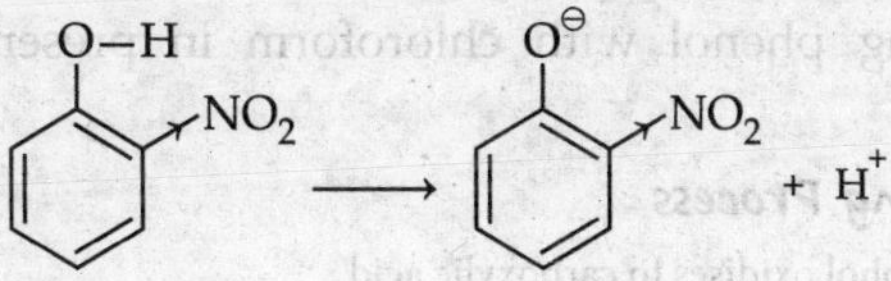

o-Nitrophenol

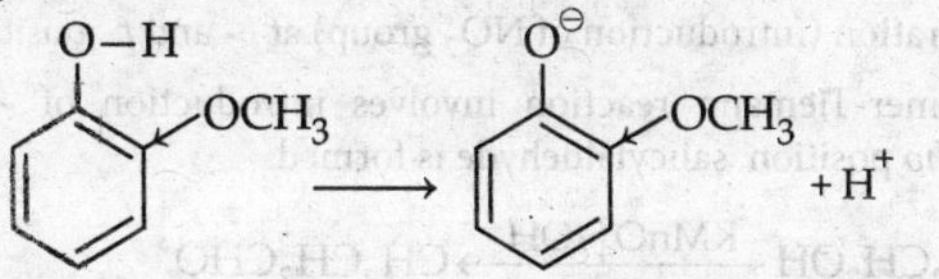

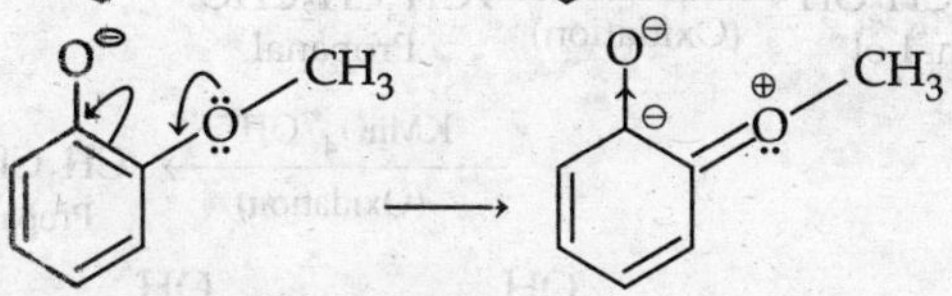

Note Also give resonating structures of o-nitrophenoxide ion for Q. 8 intext questions.

Question 16 Explain how does the —OH group attached to a carbon of benzene ring activate it towards electrophilic substitution?

◎ **Thinking Process** Resonance effect due to, —OH group.

Sol. In the presence of attacking electrophile, —OH group exerts +*R* effect on the benzene ring. So, electron density in the ring increases particularly at the *ortho* and *para* positions and the ring is activated for the substitution of electrophiles at these (*o* and *p*–) positions.

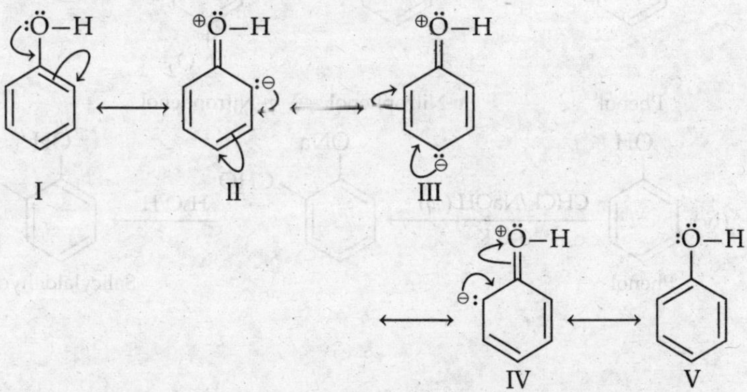

Question 17 Give equation of the following reactions.

(i) Oxidation of propan-1-ol with alkaline $KMnO_4$ solution.

(ii) Bromine in CS_2 with phenol.

(iii) Dilute HNO_3 with phenol.

(iv) Treating phenol with chloroform in presence of aqueous NaOH

◎ Thinking Process

(i) Alcohol oxidises to carboxylic acid.

(ii) *o*-and *p*- bromophenol are formed.

(iii) Nitration (introduction of NO_2 group) at *o*- and *p*- positions.

(iv) Reimer-Tiemann reaction involves introduction of —CHO group at *ortho* position, salicylaldehyde is formed.

Sol. (i) $\underset{\text{Propan-1-ol}}{CH_3CH_2CH_2OH} \xrightarrow[\text{(Oxidation)}]{KMnO_4/OH^-} \underset{\text{Propanal}}{CH_3CH_2CHO}$

$$\xrightarrow[\text{(Oxidation)}]{KMnO_4/OH^-} \underset{\text{Propanoic acid}}{CH_3CH_2COOH}$$

(ii) 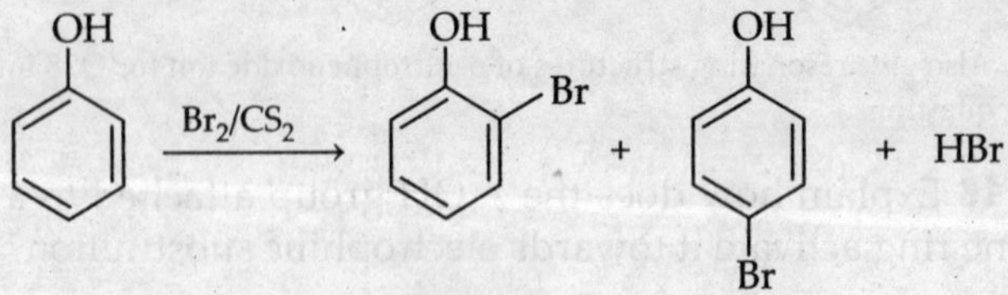

Phenol   *o*-Bromophenol   *p*-Bromophenol

(iii) 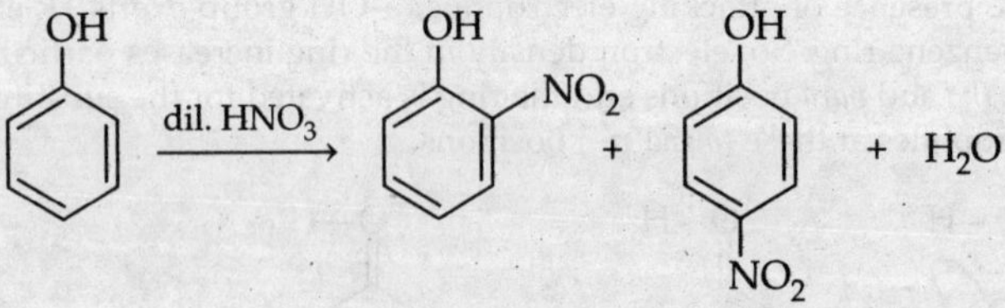

Phenol   *o*-Nitrophenol   *p*-Nitrophenol

(iv) 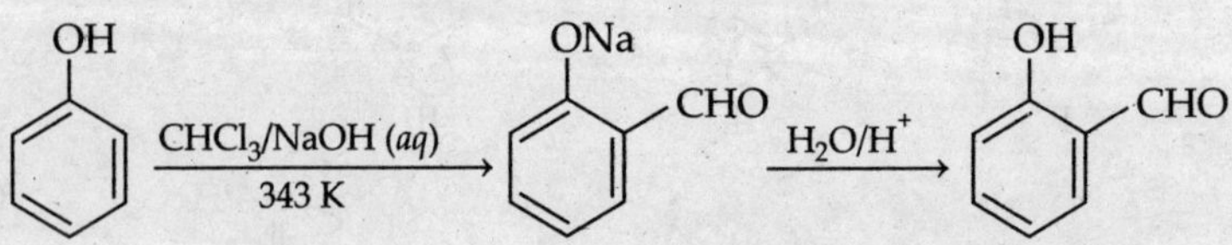

Phenol   Salicylaldehyde

Question 18 Explain the following with an example.

(i) Kolbe's reaction. (ii) Reimer-Tiemann reaction.
(iii) Williamson ether synthesis. (iv) Unsymmetrical ether.

Thinking Process

(i) (Reaction of phenol with NaOH and CO_2), Salicylic acid is formed.
(ii) Reaction of phenol with $CHCl_3$ + *aq.* NaOH $\longrightarrow$ salicylaldehyde.
(iii) Alkyl halide + sodium. alkoxide $\longrightarrow$ Ether + Sodium halide.
(iv) Ethers containing two different alkyl/aryl groups.

Sol. (i) **Kolbe's reaction** When phenol reacts with sodium hydroxide, reactive phenoxide ion is formed. So, electrophilic aromatic substitution takes place with CO_2 under a pressure of 4-7 atm and at 400 K temperature followed by acidification and *ortho* hydroxybenzoic acid (Salicylic acid) is formed. This is called Kolbe's reaction.

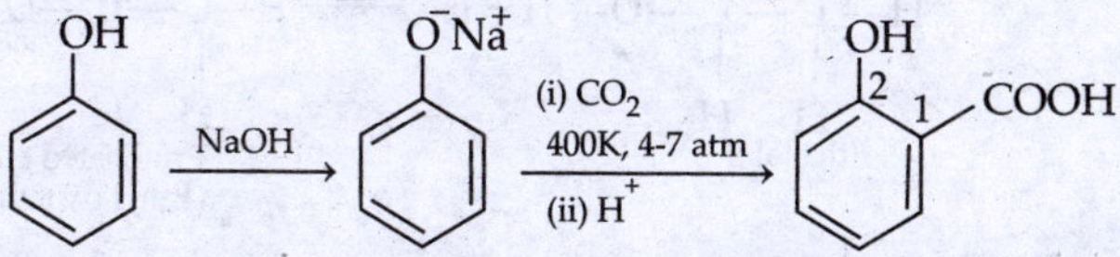

Phenol Sodium phenoxide 2-Hydroxybenzoic acid (Salicylic acid)

(ii) **Reimer-Tiemann reaction** When phenol is treated with chloroform in the presence of sodium hydroxide, −CHO group is introduced at *ortho* position of phenol ring. This is called Reimer-Tiemann reaction.

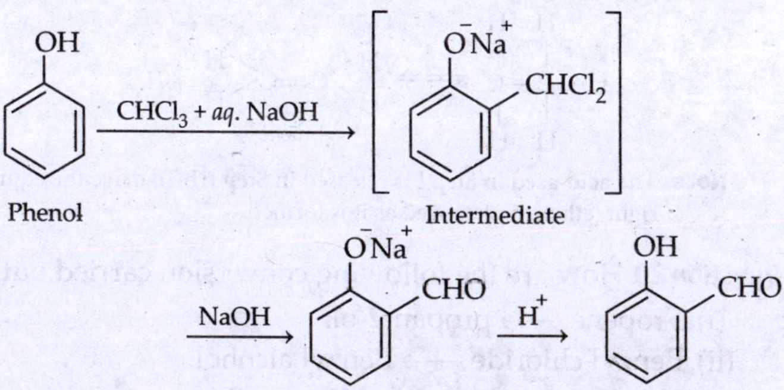

Salicylaldehyde

(iii) **Williamson ether synthesis** Ethers (symmetrical and unsymmetrical) are prepared by this method. It involves the reaction of an alkyl halide with sodium alkoxide or sodium phenoxide to form ether.

$$R—X + R'—ONa \longrightarrow R—O—R' + NaX$$

e.g., 1. $(CH_3)_3—C—ONa + CH_3Br \longrightarrow CH_3O—C—(CH_3)_3 + NaBr$

2. $C_6H_5OH + NaOH \longrightarrow C_6H_5ONa \xrightarrow{RX} C_6H_5—O—R$

(iv) **Unsymmetrical ether** An ether in which alkyl or aryl groups attached to the oxygen atom are different, is known as unsymmetrical ether. For example, ethyl methyl ether ($C_2H_5OCH_3$), methyl phenyl ether ($CH_3—O—C_6H_5$), etc.

Question 19 Write the mechanism of acid catalysed dehydration of ethanol to yield ethene.

◎ *Thinking Process* Step involved in acid catalysed dehydration are

(i) Protonation of alcohol. (ii) Formation of carbocation.

(iii) Elimination of a proton.

Sol. Mechanism of acid catalysed dehydration of ethanol

Step I : Protonation of ethanol

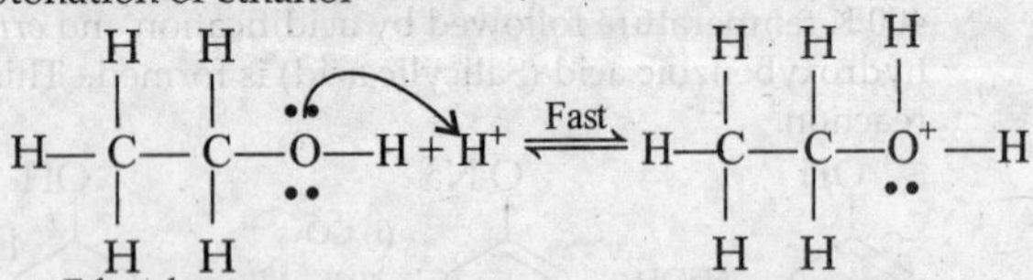

Ethanol

Protonated ethanol (Ethyl oxonium ion)

Step II : Formation of carbocation

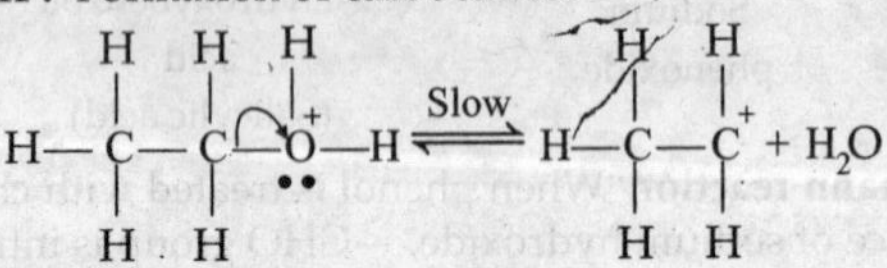

Step III : Elimination of a proton

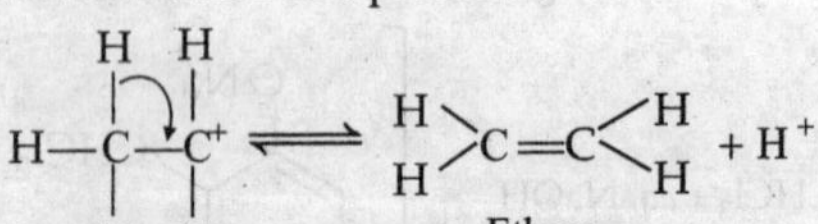

Ethene

Note The acid used in Step I is released in Step III. To drive the equilibrium to the right, ethene is removed as it is formed.

Question 20 How are the following conversion carried out?

(i) Propene ⟶ propan-2-ol.

(ii) Benzyl chloride ⟶ Benzyl alcohol.

(iii) Ethyl magnesium chloride ⟶ Propan-1-ol.

(iv) Methyl magnesium bromide ⟶ 2-Methylpropan-2-ol.

◎ *Thinking Process*

(i) Acidic hydration of propene.

(ii) Alkaline hydrolysis of benzyl chloride.

(iii) Reaction with methanal in dry ether followed by acid hydrolysis.

(iv) Reaction with propanone in dry ether followed by acid hydrolysis.

Sol. (i) $CH_3—CH=CH_2 + \text{conc.} H_2SO_4 \longrightarrow$
Propene

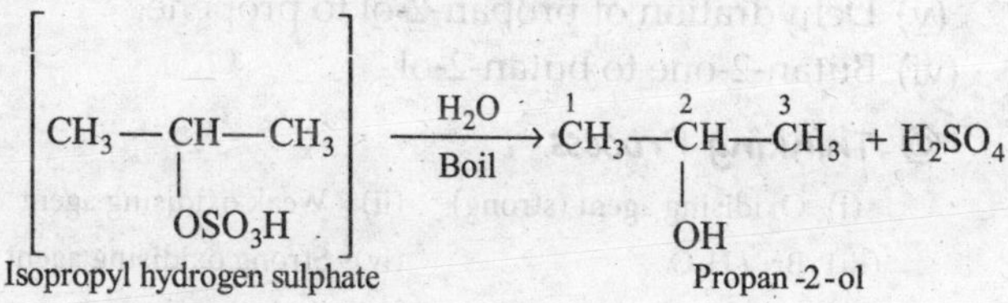

(ii)

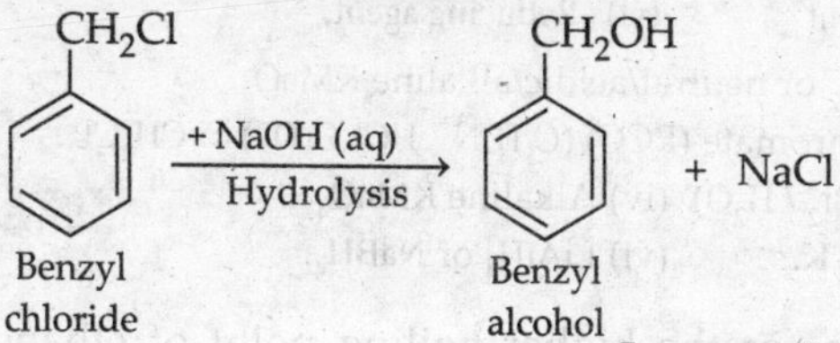

(iii)

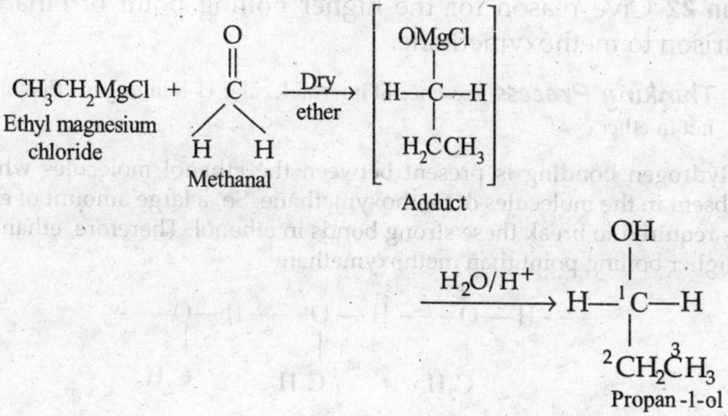

(iv)

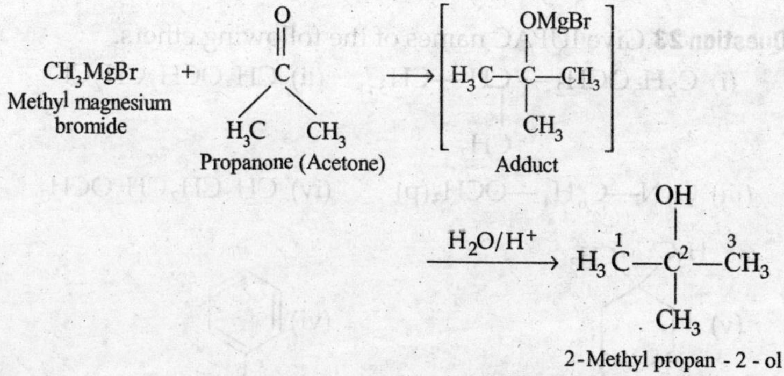

Question 21. Name the reagents used in the following reactions.

(i) Oxidation of a primary alcohol to carboxylic acid.

(ii) Oxidation of a primary alcohol to aldehyde.

(iii) Bromination of phenol to 2,4,6-tribromophenol.

(iv) Benzyl alcohol to benzoic acid.
(v) Dehydration of propan-2-ol to propene.
(vi) Butan-2-one to butan-2-ol.

Thinking Process

(i) Oxidising agent (strong) (ii) Weak oxidising agent
(iii) Br_2 / H_2O (iv) Strong oxidising agent
(v) Dehydrating agent (vi) Reducing agent.

Sol. (i) Acidified $K_2Cr_2O_7$ or neutral/acidic/alkaline $KMnO_4$.
(ii) Pyridine chlorochromate (PCC) ($C_5H_5N^+$ HCl CrO_3^-) in CH_2Cl_2.
(iii) Bromine water (Br_2 / H_2O). (iv) Alkaline $KMnO_4$
(v) 85% H_3PO_4 at 440 K. (vi) $LiAlH_4$ or $NaBH_4$.

Question 22 Give reason for the higher boiling point of ethanol in comparison to methoxymethane.

Thinking Process Presence of intermolecular H-bonding in ethanol, but not in ether.

Sol. Hydrogen bonding is present between the ethanol molecules which is absent in the molecules of methoxymethane. So, a large amount of energy is required to break these strong bonds in ethanol. Therefore, ethanol has higher boiling point than methoxymethane.

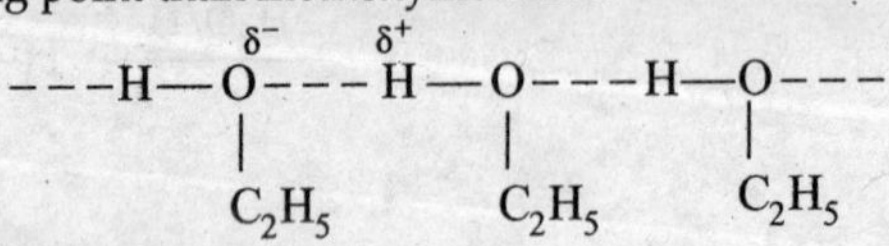

Question 23 Give IUPAC names of the following ethers.

(i) $C_2H_5OCH_2—CH(CH_3)—CH_3$ (ii) $CH_3OCH_2CH_2Cl$

(iii) $O_2N—C_6H_4—OCH_3$(p) (iv) $CH_3CH_2CH_2OCH_3$

(v) 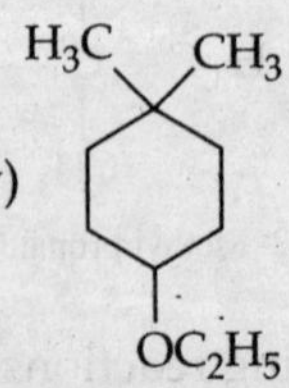

(vi) 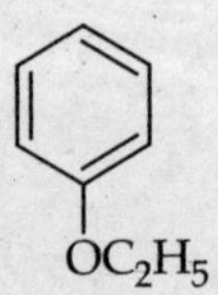

Thinking Process Recall the rules of IUPAC nomenclature see solution 1 of excercise.

Sol. (i) $C_2H_5—O—\overset{1}{C}H_2—\overset{2}{C}H(CH_3)—\overset{3}{C}H_3$

1-Ethoxy-2-methylpropane

(ii) $CH_3—O—\overset{1}{C}H_2—\overset{2}{C}H_2—Cl$

2-Chloro-1-methoxyethane

(iii) $O_2N—C_6H_4—OCH_3$ (p) or 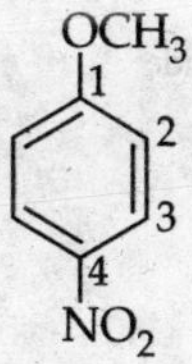

4-Nitroanisole

4-Nitroanisole

(iv) $\overset{3}{C}H_3\overset{2}{C}H_2\overset{1}{C}H_2OCH_3$

1-Methoxypropane

(v) 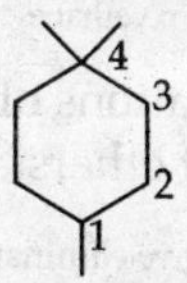

1-Ethoxy-4,4-dimethyl cyclohexane

(vi) 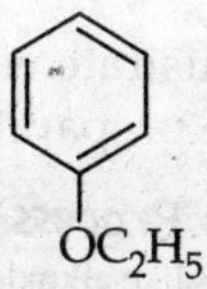

Ethoxybenzene

Question 24 Write the names of reagents and equations for the preparation of the following ethers by Williamson's synthesis.

(i) 1-propoxypropane (ii) Ethoxybenzene

(iii) 2-methoxy-2-methylpropane (iv) 1-methoxyethane

◎ *Thinking Process*

(i) $R—X + R'—O—Na \xrightarrow[\text{synthesis}]{\text{Williamson's}} R—O—R' + NaX$

(ii) Alkyl halide should be primary.

Sol. (i) $CH_3CH_2CH_2O^-Na^+ + CH_3CH_2CH_2—Br \xrightarrow{\text{Heat}}$
Sodium propoxide 1-Bromopropane

$CH_3CH_2CH_2—O—CH_2CH_2CH_3 + NaBr$
1-Propoxypropane

(ii) 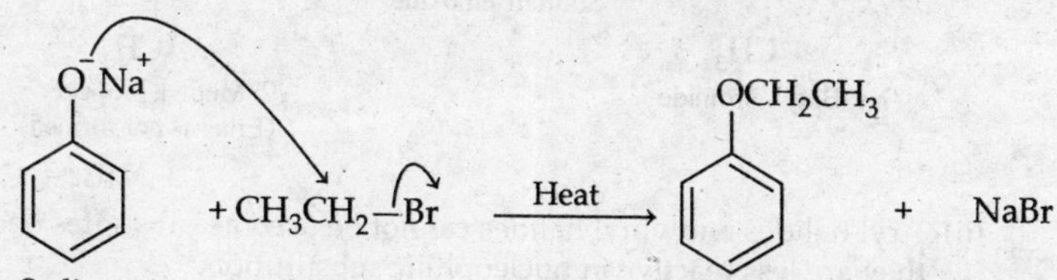

Sodium phenoxide Bromo-ethane Ethoxy-benzene

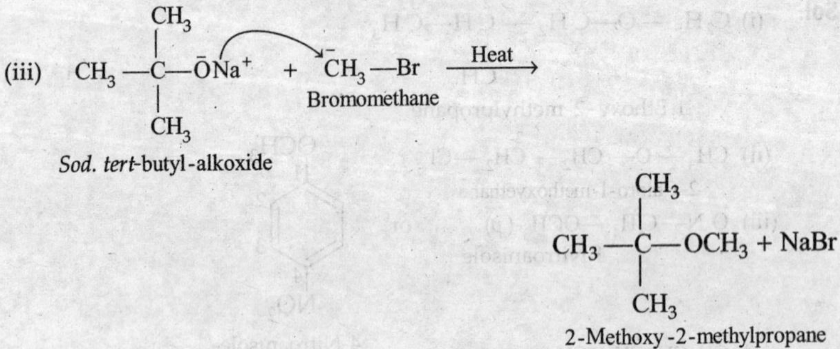

(iv) $CH_3CH_2\bar{O}Na^+ + CH_3—Br \xrightarrow{\text{Heat}} CH_3CH_2—O—CH_3 + NaBr$

Sodium ethoxide   Bromomethane   1-methoxyethane

Question 25. Illustrate with examples the limitations of Williamson's synthesis for the preparation of certain types of ethers.

◎ ***Thinking Process*** Tertiary alkyl halides readily give elimination product with strong bases like alkoxide ions. The C—*X* bond of alkyl halide does not possess double bond character *i. e.,* should not be in conjugation with multiple bond.

Sol. (i) In Williamson's synthesis reaction for the preparation of ether, the alkyl halide used must be primary as tertiary halides readily undergo elimination with strong bases like C_2H_5ONa. This is to be best understood by taking the example of preparation of ethyl tertiary butyl ether. For which the reactants used are ethyl bromide and sodium tertiary butoxide, but not the tertiary butyl chloride and sodium ethoxide.

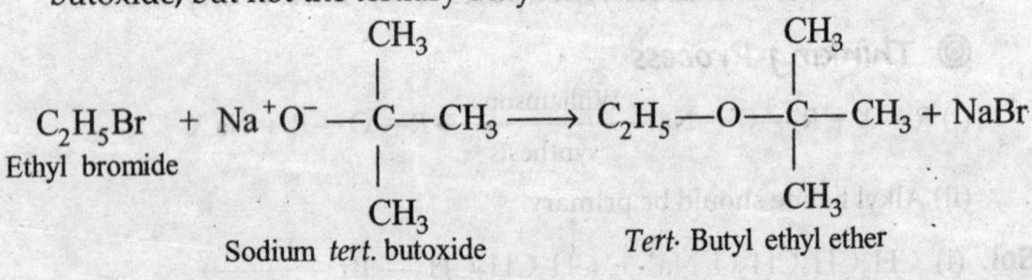

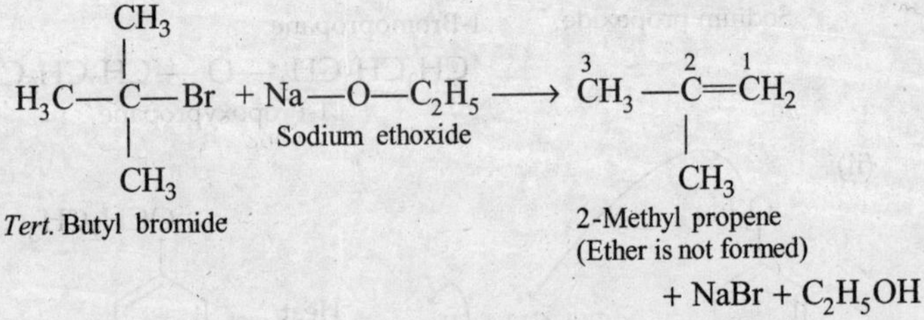

(ii) Aryl halides and vinyl halides cannot be used as substrates because they are less reactive in nucleophilic substitution.

Question 26 How is 1-propoxypropane synthesised from propan-1-ol? Write mechanism of this reaction.

◎ *Thinking Process*

(i) Williamson's synthesis or
(ii) Dehydration of propan-1-ol.

Sol. Any one of the following two methods can be employed

(i) **Williamson's synthesis**

(a) $\underset{\text{Propan-1-ol}}{3CH_3CH_2CH_2OH} + PBr_3 \longrightarrow \underset{\text{1-Bromopropane}}{3\,CH_3CH_2CH_2Br} + H_3PO_3$

(b) $\underset{\text{Propan-1-ol}}{2\,CH_3CH_2CH_2OH} + 2Na \longrightarrow \underset{\text{Sodium propoxide}}{2\,CH_3CH_2CH_2O^-Na^+} + H_2$

Reaction mechanism

$$\underset{\text{Sod. propoxide}}{CH_3CH_2CH_2\overset{-}{O}Na^+} + \underset{\text{1-Bromopropane}}{CH_3CH_2CH_2—Br} \xrightarrow[\text{Heat }(S_N2)]{\text{Dry ether}}$$

$$\underset{\text{1-Propoxypropane}}{CH_3CH_2CH_2—O—CH_2CH_2CH_3} + NaBr$$

(ii) **By dehydration of 1-propanol with conc. H_2SO_4 at 413 K.**

$$\underset{\text{Propan-1-ol}}{CH_3CH_2CH_2OH} + H^+ \xrightarrow{H_2SO_4} \underset{\text{Protonated 1-propanol}}{CH_3CH_2CH_2—\overset{+}{O}H_2}$$

$$\underset{\text{Propan-1-ol}}{CH_3CH_2CH_2—\ddot{\underset{\cdot\cdot}{O}}H} + CH_3CH_2CH_2—\overset{+}{O}H_2 \xrightarrow[-H_2O,]{413\text{ K}}$$

$$CH_3CH_2CH_2—\overset{+}{\underset{H}{O}}—CH_2CH_2CH_3$$

$$\xrightarrow[\text{(Fast)}]{-H^+} \underset{\text{1-Propoxypropane}}{CH_3CH_2CH_2—O—CH_2CH_2CH_3}$$

Question 27 Preparation of ethers by acid dehydration of secondary or tertiary alcohols is not a suitable method. Give reason.

◎ *Thinking Process* Due to steric hindrance, alkenes are formed by S_N1 mechanism.

Sol. Ethers are formed as a result of acid dehydration by S_N2 mechanism (from primary alcohols). If secondary or tertiary alcohols are used, due to steric hindrance, alkenes are formed and not ethers.

$$\underset{\substack{\text{Propan-2-ol} \\ (2^\circ \text{ alcohol})}}{CH_3-\underset{\underset{CH_3}{|}}{CH}-OH} \xrightarrow[413\text{ K}]{\text{Conc. } H_2SO_4} \underset{\substack{\text{Propene} \\ \text{(Major)}}}{CH_3-CH=CH_2}$$

$$+ \underset{\substack{\text{Di-isopropyl ether} \\ \text{(Minor)}}}{CH_3-\overset{\overset{CH_3}{|}}{CH}-O-\overset{\overset{CH_3}{|}}{CH}-CH_3}$$

$$\underset{\substack{\textit{tert.}\text{ Butyl alcohol} \\ (3^\circ)}}{CH_3-\overset{\overset{CH_3}{|}}{\underset{\underset{CH_3}{|}}{C}}-OH} \xrightarrow[413\text{ K}]{\text{Conc. } H_2SO_4} CH_3-\overset{\overset{CH_3}{|}}{C}=CH_2 + H_2O$$

Question 28 Write the equation of the reaction of hydrogen iodide with : (i) 1-propoxypropane (ii) methoxybenzene and (iii) benzyl ethyl ether.

◎ *Thinking Process* Alcohols and alkyl or aryl iodides are formed. Generally primary halide (or lower halide) is formed in this reaction.

Sol. (i) $\underset{\text{1-Propoxypropane}}{CH_3CH_2CH_2-O-CH_2CH_2CH_3} \xrightarrow[373\text{ K}]{HI}$

$$\underset{\text{Propan-1-ol}}{CH_3CH_2CH_2-OH} + \underset{\text{Iodopropane}}{CH_3CH_2CH_2-I}$$

(ii)

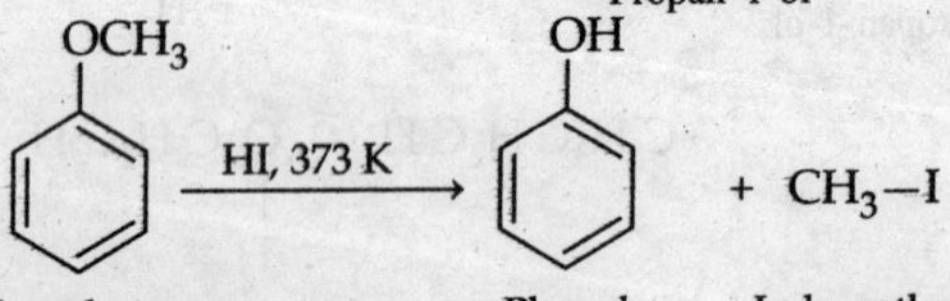

Methoxybenzene Phenol Iodomethane

(iii)

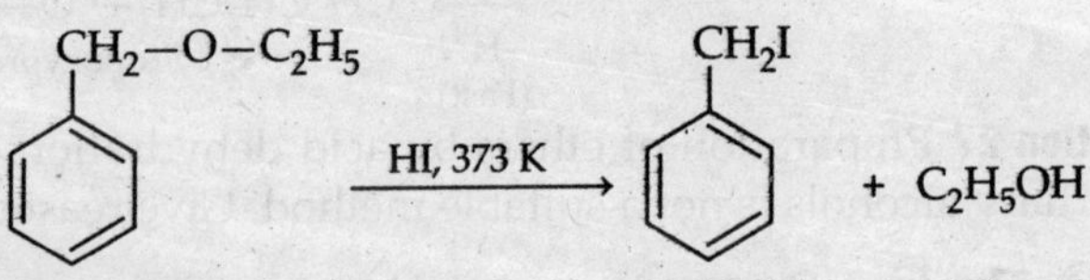

Benzyl ethyl ether Benzyl iodide Ethanol

Question 29 Explain the fact that in aryl alkyl ethers

(i) the alkoxy group activates the benzene ring towards electrophilic substitution.

(ii) it directs the incoming substituents to *ortho* and *para* positions in benzene ring.

◎ ***Thinking Process*** Consider $+R$ effect of the alkoxy group and more electron density at *o*- and *p*-positions.

Sol. In aryl alkyl ethers, $+R$ effect of the alkoxy group ($-OR$) increases the electron density in the benzene ring thereby activating the benzene ring towards electrophilic substitution reactions.

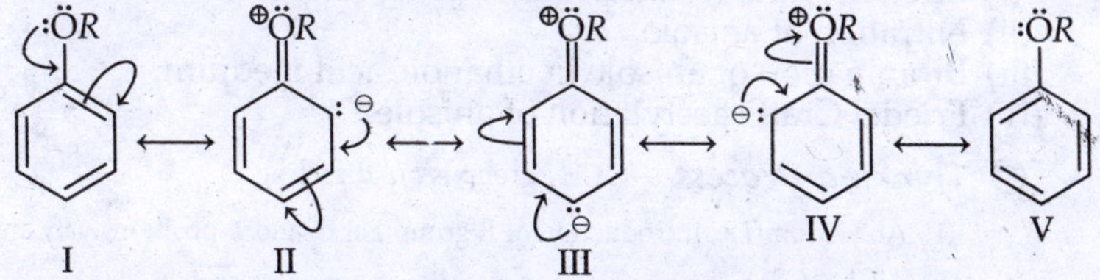

Electron density is more at *o*- and *p*-positions so *o*- and *p*-products are mainly formed during electrophilic substitution reactions. *e.g.*,

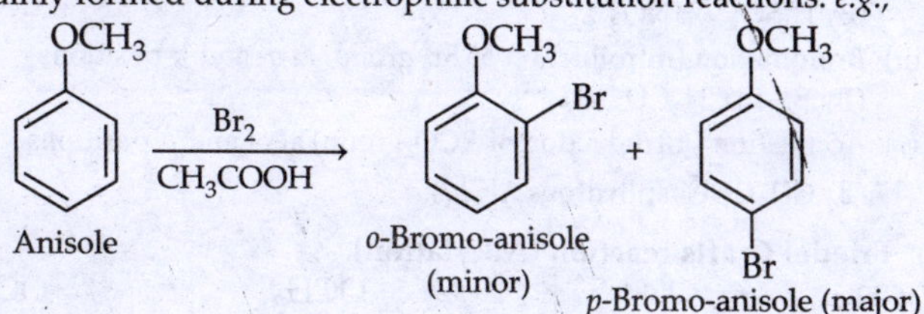

Question 30 Write the mechanism of the reaction of HI with methoxymethane.

◎ ***Thinking Process*** Steps involved in this process are

(i) protonation (ii) formation of methanol and iodomethane,

Sol. When equimolar amounts of HI and methoxymethane are taken, a mixture of methyl alcohol and iodomethane are formed.

Mechanism

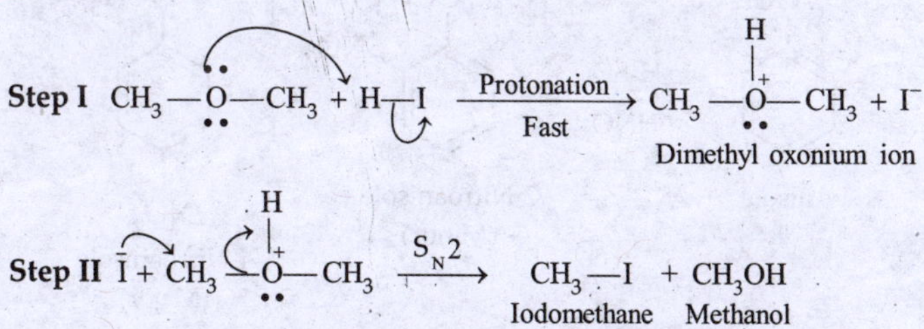

If HI is present in excess, CH_3OH formed in step II is further converted into CH_3I.

$$\textbf{Step III} \quad CH_3—\ddot{\underset{\cdot\cdot}{O}}—H + H—I \xrightarrow[\text{fast}]{\text{Protonation}} CH_3—\overset{\overset{H}{|}}{\underset{\cdot\cdot}{O^+}}—H + I^-$$

Protonated methanol

$$\textbf{Step IV} \quad I^- + CH_3—\overset{\overset{H}{|}}{\underset{\cdot\cdot}{O^+}}—H \xrightarrow[\text{Slow}]{S_N2} CH_3—I + H_2O$$

Iodomethane

Question 31 Write equations of the following reactions.

(i) Friedel Crafts reaction–alkylation of anisole.
(ii) Nitration of anisole.
(iii) Bromination of anisole in ethanoic acid medium.
(iv) Friedel Crafts acetylation of anisole.

◎ ***Thinking Process*** —OCH_3 group is *o*/*p* directing.

(i) Alkylation (*i.e.*, introduction of *R* group) at *o*- and *p*-positions. (By anhyd. $AlCl_3$ / CS_2).
(ii) Nitration (*i.e.*, introduction of NO_2 group) at *o*- and *p*-positions (By H_2SO_4 / HNO_3).
(iii) Bromination (introduction of Br_2 group) at *o*- and *p*-positions (By Br_2 in CH_3COOH).
(iv) Acetylation (introduction of *R*CO-group) at *o*- and *p*-positions (By CH_3COCl/anhydrous $AlCl_3$).

Sol. (i) **Friedel Crafts reaction (Alkylation)**

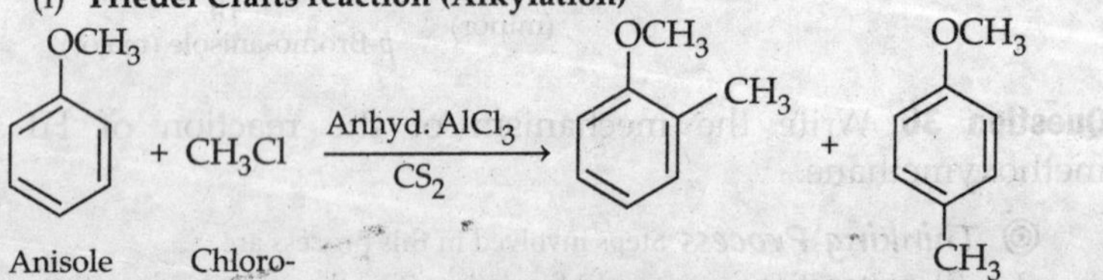

Anisole + Chloro-methane → 2-Methoxy toluene (Minor) + 4-Methoxy toluene (Major)

(ii) **Nitration of anisole**

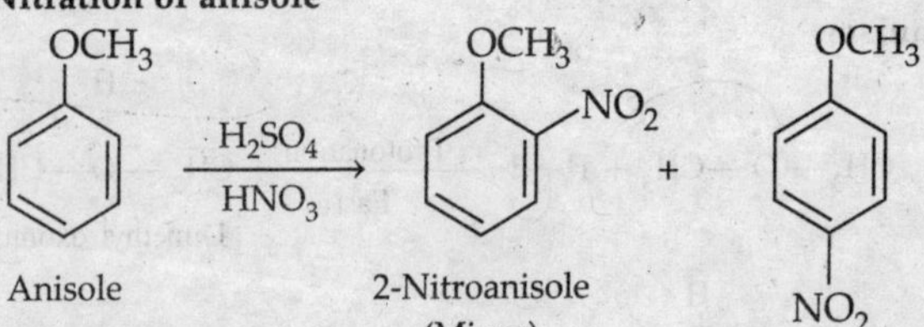

Anisole → 2-Nitroanisole (Minor) + 4-Nitroanisole (Major)

(iii) **Bromination of anisole**

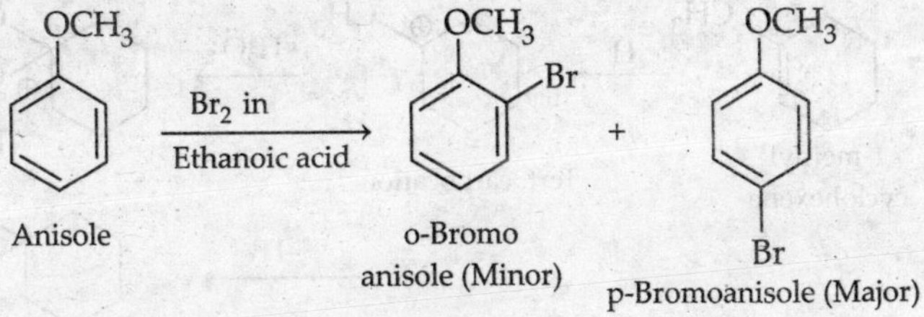

(iv) **Friedel Crafts acetylation of anisole**

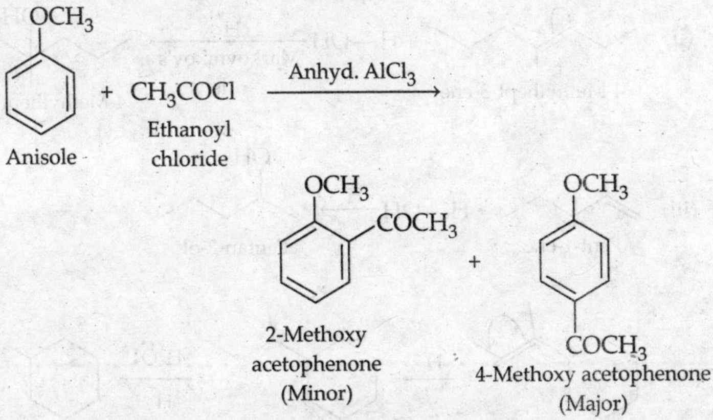

Question 32 Show how would you synthesise the following alcohols from appropriate alkenes?

(i) 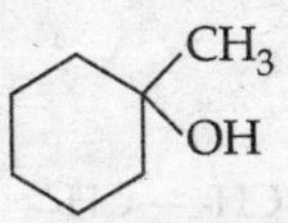

(ii) 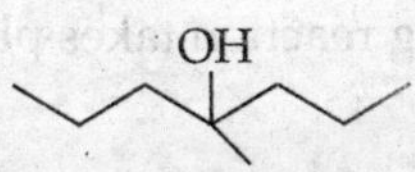

(iii) 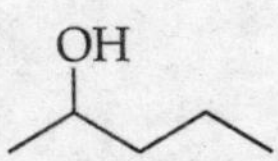

(iv) 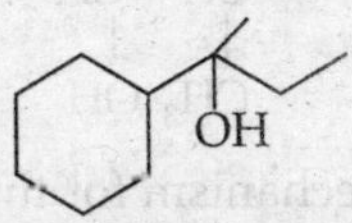

◎ ***Thinking Process*** By hydration (addition of H_2O) of appropriate alkenes in accordance with Markovnikov's rule.

Sol.

(i) 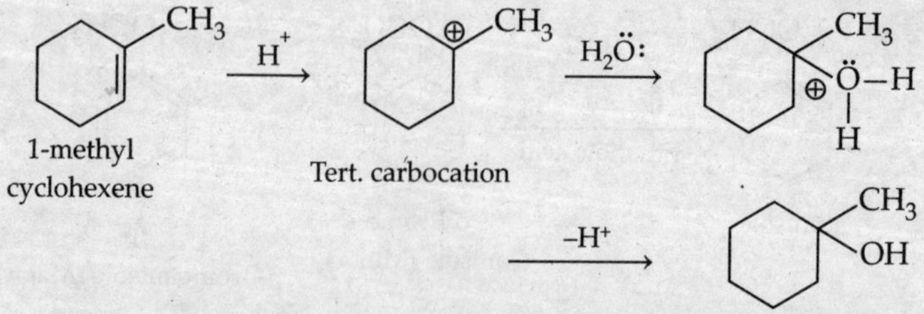

1-methyl cyclohexene → Tert. carbocation → 1-methylcyclo-hexan-1-ol

(ii) 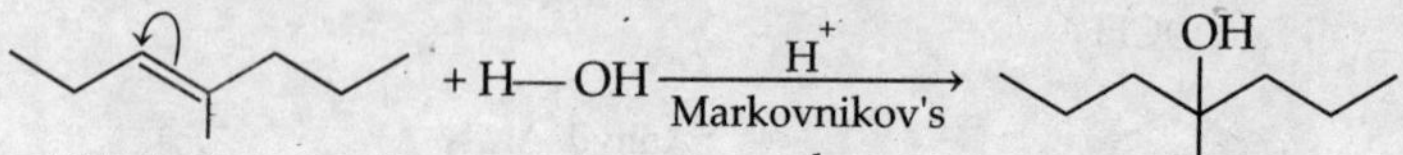

4-Methylhept-3-ene → 4-Methylheptan-4-ol

(iii) 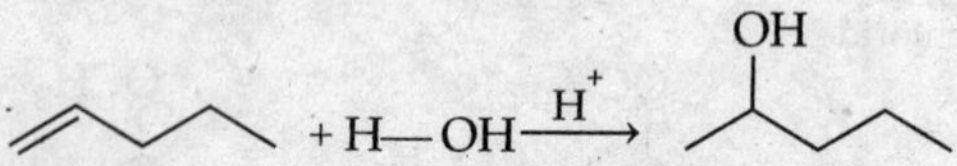

Pent-1-ene → Pentan-2-ol

(iv) 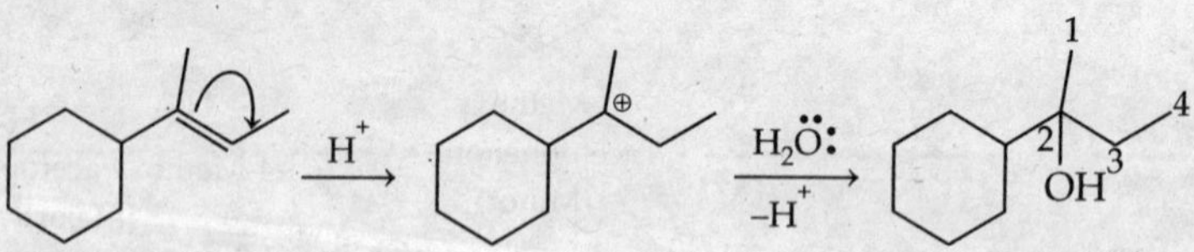

2-Cyclohexylbut -2-ene → 2-Cyclohexyl butan-2-ol

Question 33 When 3-methylbutan-2-ol is treated with HBr, the following reaction takes place

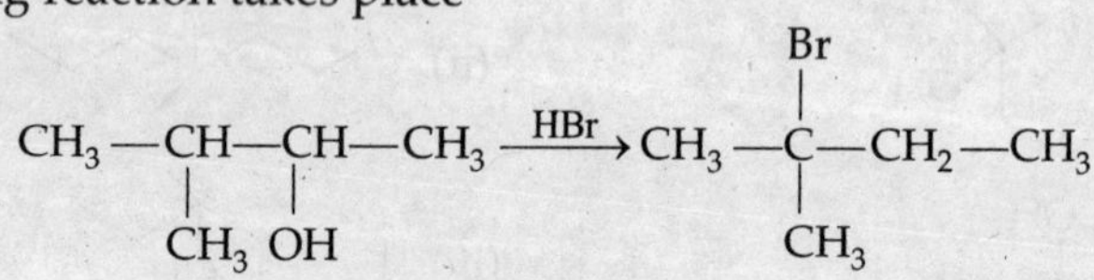

Give a mechanism for this reaction.

◎ ***Thinking Process*** The secondary carbocation formed in the process rearranges to a more stable tertiary carbocation by a hydride ion shift from 3rd carbon atom.

Sol. Mechanism

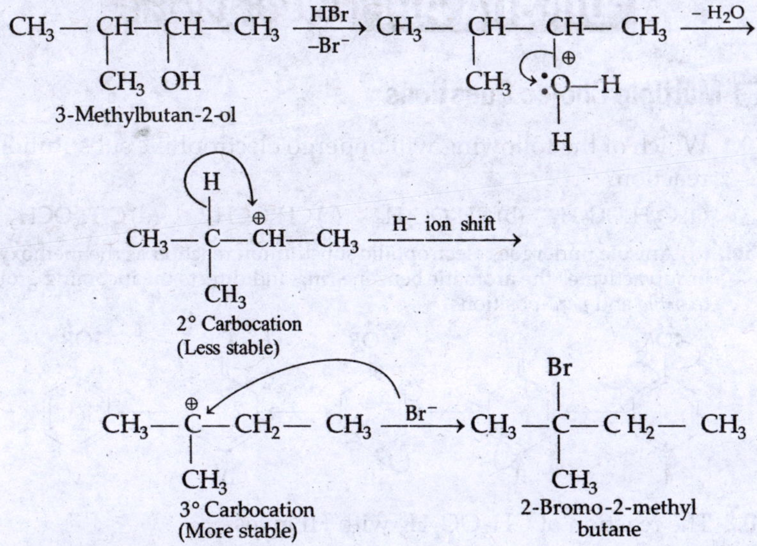

3-Methylbutan-2-ol

2° Carbocation (Less stable)

3° Carbocation (More stable)

2-Bromo-2-methyl butane

Mistake Alert **One can make a mistake of not writing the hydride ion (H^-) shift step for carbocation rearrangement.**

DIKSHA APP Questions

☐ Multiple Choice Questions

Q.1 Which of the following will undergo electrophilic substitution reaction?

(a) $C_2H_5OC_2H_5$ (b) $CH_3OC_2H_5$ (c) CH_3OCH_3 (d) $C_6H_5OCH_3$

Sol. (d) Anisole undergoes electrophilic substitution reaction as the methoxy group activates the aromatic benzene ring and directs the incoming group to *ortho* and *para*-positions.

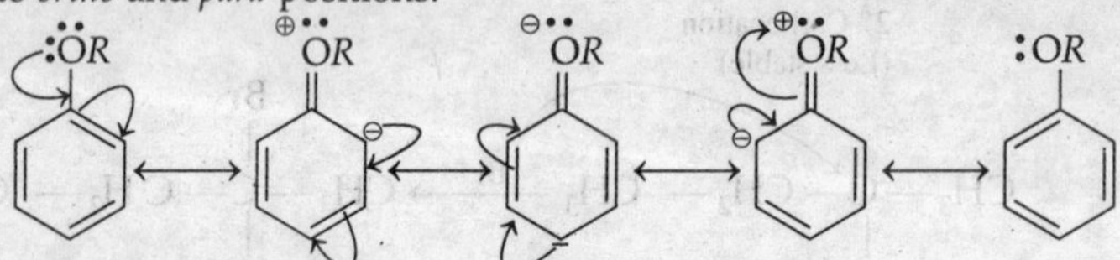

I II III IV V

Q.2 The reaction of $CH_3OC_2H_5$ with HI gives

(a) CH_3I only (b) C_2H_5OH only

(c) $CH_3I + C_2H_5OH$ (d) $C_2H_5I + CH_3OH$

Sol. (c) The reaction of an ether with concentrated HI starts with protonation of ether molecule.

Step 1

$$CH_3-\ddot{\underset{\cdot\cdot}{O}}-CH_2CH_3 + H-I \rightleftharpoons CH_3-\overset{H}{\underset{\cdot\cdot}{\overset{+}{O}}}-CH_2CH_3 + I^-$$

Step 2 Iodide a good nucleophile. It attacks the least substituted carbon of oxonium ion formed in step 1 and displaces an alcohol molecule by S_{N^2} mechanism.

$$I^- + CH_3-\overset{H}{\underset{\cdot\cdot}{\overset{+}{O}}}-CH_2CH_3 \longrightarrow \left[I + CH_3-\overset{H}{\underset{\cdot\cdot}{\overset{+}{O}}}-CH_2CH_3\right]^- \downarrow CH_3I + CH_3CH_2OH$$

Q.3 Th alcohol known as wood spirit is

(a) CH_3OH (b) $CH_3CH_2CH_2OH$

(c) C_2H_5OH (d) None of these

Sol. (a) Methanol CH_3OH is also known as 'wood spirit'. It was produced by destructive distillation of wood. Therefore, option (a) is correct.

Q.4 Denaturation of ethanol is carried out by adding

(a) CH_3OH and C_6H_6 (b) CH_3OH and pyridine
(c) KCN (d) CH_3OH and HCOOH

Sol. (b) Ethyl alcohol (ethanol) is denatured by adding substances that make it undrinkable and unsuitable for consumption while retaining its industrial utility. Common denaturing agents include: methanol and pyridine.

Therefore, option (b) is correct.

Q.5 Aspirin is obtained by the acetylation of

(a) *p*-Dihydroxybenzene (b) *o*-Hydroxybenzoic acid
(c) *o*-Dihydroxybenzene (d) *m*-Hydroxybenzoic acid

Sol. (b) Acetylation of *o*-hydroxybenzoic acid or salicylic acid produces aspirin.

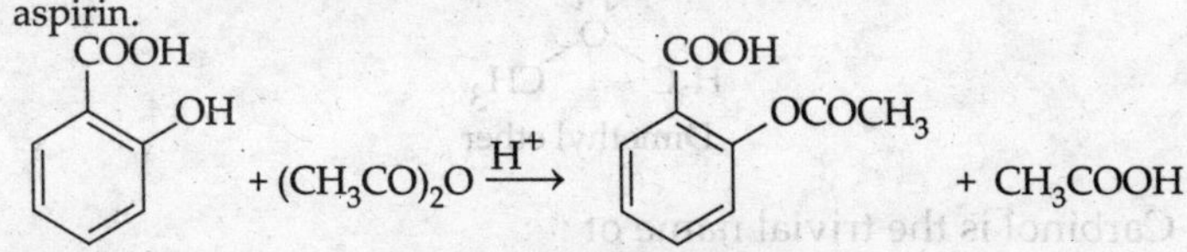

Salicylic acid Acetylsalicylic acid (Aspirin)

Therefore, option (b) is correct.

Q.6 A tertiary alcohol is obtained by the reaction of Grignard reagent with

(a) Butanone (b) Propanone
(d) Acetone (d) All of the above

Sol. (d) Ketones reacts with Grignard reagent to give tertiary alcohols.

$$R\!-\!\overset{\overset{\displaystyle O}{\|}}{C}\!-\!R + R'MgX \longrightarrow R\!-\!\underset{\underset{\displaystyle R}{|}}{\overset{\overset{\displaystyle R'}{|}}{C}}\!-\!OMgX$$

$$\xrightarrow{H_2O} R\!-\!\underset{\underset{\displaystyle R}{|}}{\overset{\overset{\displaystyle R'}{|}}{C}}\!-\!OH + Mg(OH)X$$

Therefore, option (d) is correct.

Q.7 Which of the following is a dihydric alcohol?

(a) Glycerol (b) Catechol
(c) Resorcinol (d) Ethylene glycol

Sol. (d) Alcohols containing two hydroxyl groups are called dihydric alcohols. Ethylene glycol is a dihydric alcohol.

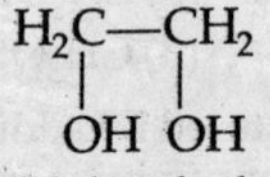

Ethylene glycol

Q.8 The hybridisation of the central oxygen atom in ether is

(a) sp^2 (b) sp^3d^2

(c) sp^3 (d) sp

Sol. (c) The central oxygen atom in ether has two bond pairs and two lone pair of electrons, and it is sp^3 hybridized.

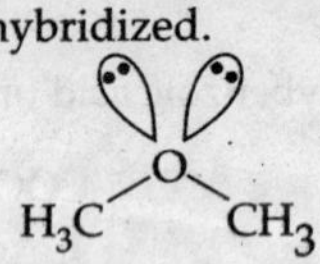

Dimethyl ether

Q.9 Carbinol is the trivial name of :

(a) $(CH_3)_3COH$ (b) C_2H_5OH

(c) CH_3OH (d) $CH_3CH_2CHOHCH_3$

Sol. (c) Methanol, CH_3OH is commonly known as carbinol.

Therefore, option (c) is correct.

Q.10 The IUPAC name of $CH_3OCH(CH_3)_2$ is

(a) 1-Methoxy propane

(b) 3-Methoxy propane

(c) Methyl isopropyl ether

(d) 2-Methoxy propane

Sol. (d) 2-Methoxy propane is the IUPAC name of $CH_3OCH(CH_3)_2$.

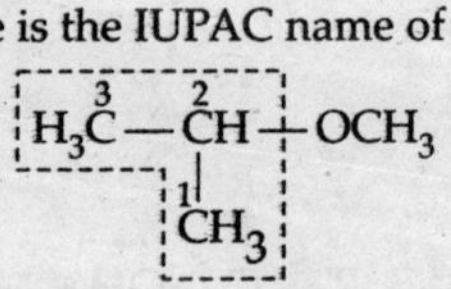

Q.11 Which of the following is not an alcohol?

(a) $CH_2=CHCH_2OH$ (b) C_6H_5OH

(c) CH_2OHCH_2OH (d) $C_6H_5CH_2OH$

Sol. (b) C_6H_5OH is phenol and not an alcohol.

Q.12 Cyclohexanol is a

(a) tertiary alcohol (b) phenol

(c) secondary alcohol (d) primary alcohol

Sol. (c) Cyclohexanol is a secondary alcohol.

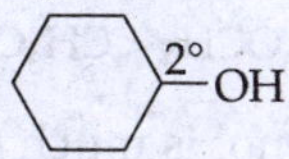

Cyclohexanol
Secondary alcohol

☐ Short Answer Type

Q.1 (a) Why is cumene the most widely used method for the preparation of phenol?

(b) Arrange the following in increasing order of their boiling point:

$$CH_3CH_2OH, CH_3CHO, CH_3—O—CH_3$$

Sol. (a) Phenol is manufactured from the hydrocarbon, cumene. Cumene (Isopropylbenzene) is oxidised in the presence of air to cumene hydroperoxide. It is converted to phenol and acetone by treating it with dilute acid. Acetone, a by-product of this reaction, is also obtained in large quantites by this method.

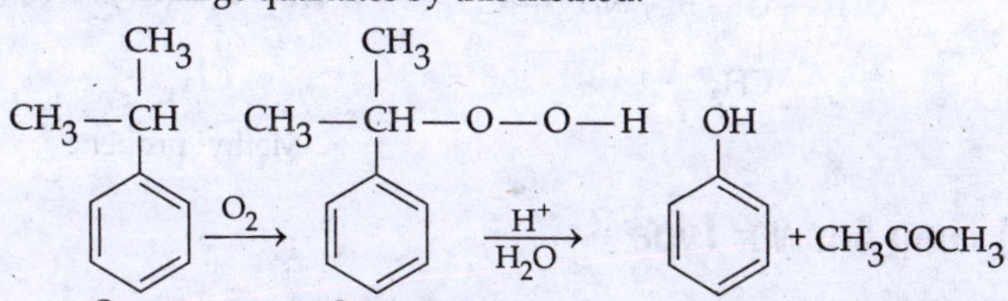

Cumene Cumene hydroperoxide Phenol Acetone

This acetone produced is also commercially important, therefore, cumene is the most widely used method for preparation of phenol.

(b) Alcohols have the highest boiling point because there is inter-molecular hydrogen bonding present between the alcohol molecules. Aldehydes have a higher boiling point than ether because aldehydes have carbonyl carbon, i.e., >C=O, which is highly polar due to the significant difference in electronegativity between carbon and oxygen.

This polarity leads to strong dipole-dipole interactions between aldehyde molecules. Ethers have an oxygen atom bonded to two carbon atoms, but the ether linkage (C–O–C) is less polar compared to the carbonyl group in aldehydes. The stronger dipole-dipole interactions in aldehydes lead to higher boiling points as compared to ethers.

$$CH_3OCH_3 < CH_3CHO < CH_3CH_2OH$$

Q.2 (a) C—O bond in phenol is much shorter than ethanol. Why?

(b) Why $(CH_3)_3CBr$ on reaction with $CH_3O^-Na^+$ gives alkene as major product and not an ether?

Sol. (a) The C—O bond in phenol has partial double bond character due to resonance. Also the carbon attached to oxygen is sp^2 hybridised in phenol and is more electronegativel as compared to that in ethanol which is sp^3 hybridised.

The partial double-bond character in the C—O bond of phenol, makes it shorter and stronger compared to the C—O bond in ethanol.

(b) In the reaction of $(CH_3)CBr$ and $CH_3O^-Na^+$, elimination is favoured over substitution as CH_3O^- is not only a nucleophile but also a strong base. It reacts with alkyl halides leading to β-elimination.

This reaction gives alkene as a major product instead of ether.

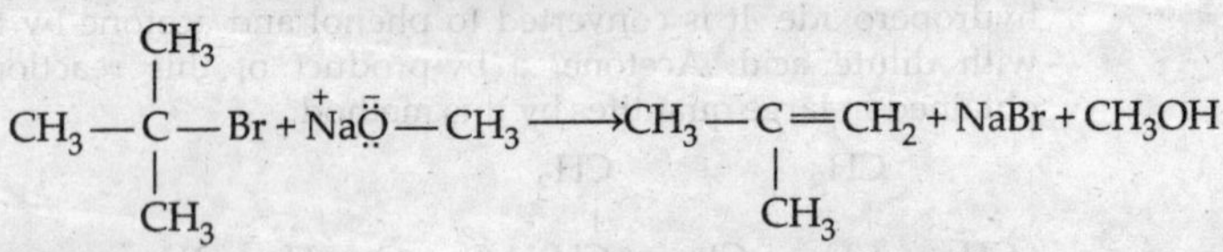

2-Methyl propene

☐ Long Answer Type

Q.1 (a) Give one chemical test to distinguish between:

(i) Phenol and benzoic acid

(ii) Propan-1-ol and Propan-2-ol

(iii) Methanol and ethanol

(b) Why is bimolecular dehydration not appropriate for preparation of ethyl methyl ether? Write a suitable method for its preparation.

Sol. (a) (i) Add $NaHCO_3$ to each test tube containing phenol and benzoic acid. Phenol does not react with $NaHCO_3$ but benzoic acid gives effervescence.

(In (i))

$$\underset{\text{(Phenol)}}{C_6H_5OH} + NaHCO_3 \longrightarrow \text{No reaction}$$

$$\underset{\text{Benzoic acid}}{C_6H_5COOH} + NaHCO_3) \rightarrow C_6H_5COONa + CO_2 + H_2O\text{(effervescence)}$$

(ii) Propan-2-ol gives iodoform test whereas Propan-1-ol does not.

In (ii))

$$\underset{\text{Propan-1-ol}}{CH_3—CH_2—CH_2OH} \xrightarrow[NaOH]{I_2} \text{No reaction}$$

$$\underset{\text{Propan-2-ol}}{CH_3—CH—CH_3} \xrightarrow[NaOH]{I_2} CH_3—\overset{O}{\overset{\|}{C}}—O^{\ominus}Na^{\oplus} + \underset{\substack{\text{(Yellow ppt.)}\\ \text{(Iodoform)}}}{CHI_3 \downarrow}$$

(iii) Ethanol gives yellow ppt. with I_2 & NaOH (Iodoform test) whereas methanol does not. In (iii)

$$\underset{\text{Methanol}}{CH_3OH} \xrightarrow[NaOH]{I_2} \text{No reaction}$$

$$\underset{\text{Ethanol}}{C_2H_5OH} \xrightarrow[NaOH]{I_2} \underset{\text{(Iodoform yellow ppt)}}{CHI_3 \downarrow + HCOO^{\ominus}Na^{\oplus}}$$

(b) Bimolecular dehydration is best for making symmetrical dialkyl ethers (like dimethyl ether or diethyl ether) from primary alcohols. This is because the reaction involves two molecules of the same alcohol and forms a symmetrical ether, which is easy to control. When using two different primary alcohols like ethanol and methanol, the reaction becomes less predictable.

Both alcohols are similarly basic, so it is hard to control which alcohol gets protonated (*i.e.*, which —OH group becomes a good leaving group). Both alcohols could potentially act as nucleophiles, leading to a mix of products. This results in a combination of symmetrical ethers (diethyl ether and dimethyl ether) and the desired unsymmetrical ether (ethyl methyl ether).Ethyl methyl ether can be prepared by Williamson synthesis.

$$\underset{\text{Methylchloride}}{CH_3Cl} + \underset{\text{Sod. ethoxide}}{C_2H_5ONa} \longrightarrow \underset{\text{Ethylmethyl ether}}{CH_3OC_2H_5} + NaCl$$

Aldehydes, Ketones and Carboxylic Acids

CHAPTER 08

Important Points

01 Carbonyl group ($>C{=}O$) has been classified into two categories-aldehydes (RCHO) and ketones (RCOR). Aldehydes and ketones are functional isomers.

02 Aldehydes are prepared by

(a) dehydrogenation and controlled oxidation of primary alcohols.

(b) controlled reduction of acyl halides. **(Rosenmund reduction)**

$$\underset{\text{Benzoyl chloride}}{C_6H_5-\overset{\overset{O}{\|}}{C}-Cl} \xrightarrow[\text{Pd–BaSO}_4]{H_2} \underset{\text{Benzaldehyde}}{C_6H_5-CHO}$$

(c) Aromatic aldehydes are prepared by oxidation of methyl benzene by CrO_3 or CrO_2Cl_2 in the presence of acetic anhydride.

$$\underset{\text{Toluene}}{C_6H_5-CH_3} + CrO_2Cl_2 \xrightarrow{CS_2} \underset{\text{Chromium complex}}{C_6H_5-CH(OCrOHCl_2)_2} \text{ (Etard reaction)}$$

$$\xrightarrow{H_3O^+} C_6H_5-CHO$$

$$C_6H_5-CH_3 + CrO_3 + (CH_3CO)_2O \xrightarrow{273\text{–}283K}$$

$$C_6H_5-CH(OCOCH_3)_2 \xrightarrow[\Delta]{H_3O^+} \underset{\text{Benzaldehyde}}{C_6H_5-CHO}$$

(d) Benzaldehyde is prepared by side chain chlorination of toluene, followed by hydrolysis.

$$\underset{\text{Toluene}}{C_6H_5-CH_3} \xrightarrow{Cl_2/hv} \underset{\text{Benzal chloride}}{C_6H_5-CHCl_2} \xrightarrow[373\text{ K}]{H_2O} \underset{\text{Benzaldehyde}}{C_6H_5-CHO}$$

(e) Benzaldehyde is prepared by treating benzene or its derivative with carbon monoxide and HCl in the presence of anhyd. $AlCl_3$ or CuCl. **(Gatterman-Koch reaction)**

$$\underset{\text{Benzene}}{C_6H_5} \xrightarrow[\text{Anhyd. } AlCl_3/CuCl]{CO,\ HCl} \underset{\text{Benzaldehyde}}{C_6H_5—CHO}$$

(f) Aldehydes can also be prepared from nitriles and esters.

$$RCN + SnCl_2 + HCl \longrightarrow RCH{=}NH \xrightarrow{H_3O} RCHO$$

(Stephen reaction)

- $RCN \xrightarrow[2.\ H_2O]{1.\ AlH(i\text{-}Bu)_2} R—CHO$

- $CH_3(CH_2)_9—\overset{O}{\overset{\|}{C}}—OC_2H_5 \xrightarrow[2.\ H_2O]{1.\ DIBAL\text{-}H} CH_3(CH_2)_9—\overset{O}{\overset{\|}{C}}—H$

03 Ketones are prepared by

(a) oxidation of secondary alcohols.

(b) hydration of alkynes.

(c) reaction of acyl chloride with dialkylcadmium.

$$2\,R—Mg—X + CdCl_2 \longrightarrow R_2Cd + 2Mg(X)Cl$$

$$2\,R'—\underset{O}{\underset{\|}{C}}—Cl + R_2Cd \longrightarrow 2\,R'—\underset{O}{\underset{\|}{C}}—R + CdCl_2$$

(d) Ketone is prepared by reacting a nitrile with Grignard reagent, followed by hydrolysis.

$$R—C{\equiv}N \xrightarrow[\text{ether}]{C_6H_5MgBr} R—C(=NMgBr)—C_6H_5 \xrightarrow{H_3O^+} R—C(=O)—C_6H_5$$

Propiophenone
(1-Phenylpropanone)

(e) Aromatic ketones can also be prepared by **Friedel-Crafts acylation reaction.**

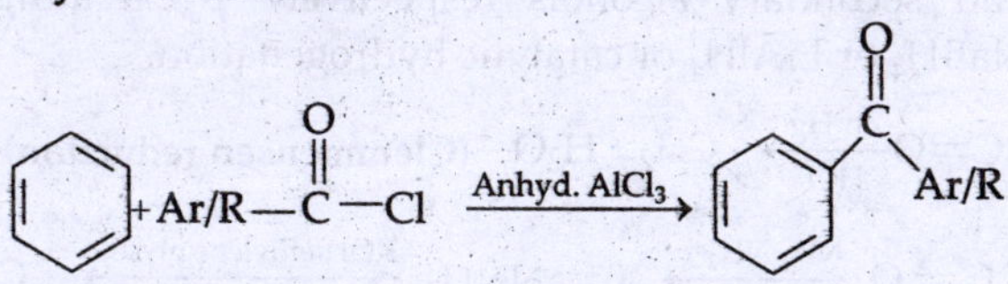

04 Nucleophilic addition and nucleophilic addition-elimination reactions of aldehydes and ketones are :

(a) Cyanohydrin formation

$$HCN + OH^- \rightleftharpoons :\bar{C}N + H_2O$$

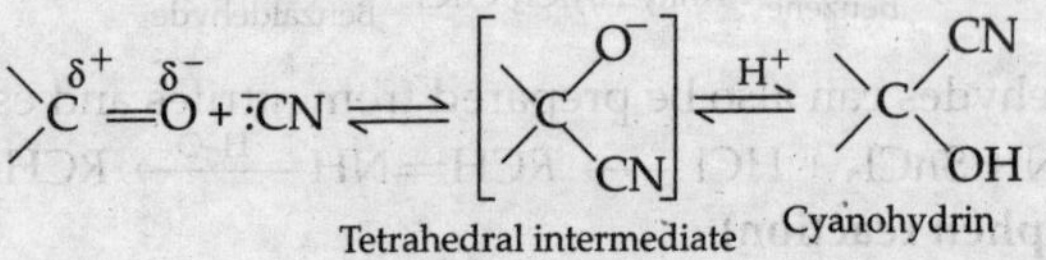

(b) Addition of sodium hydrogensulphite to form addition products.

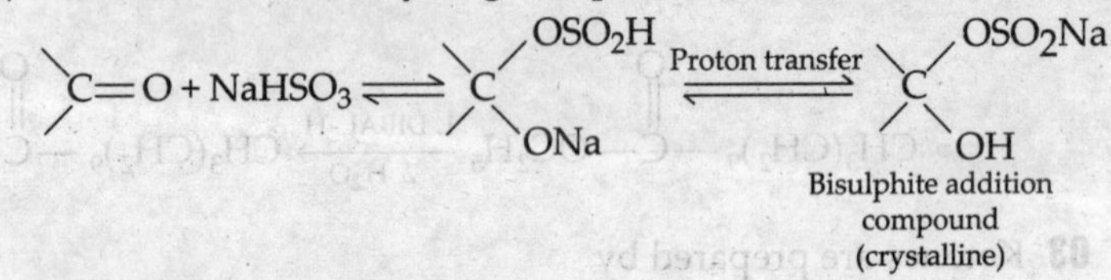

(c) Addition of Grignard reagents.

(d) Hemiacetal and acetal formation.

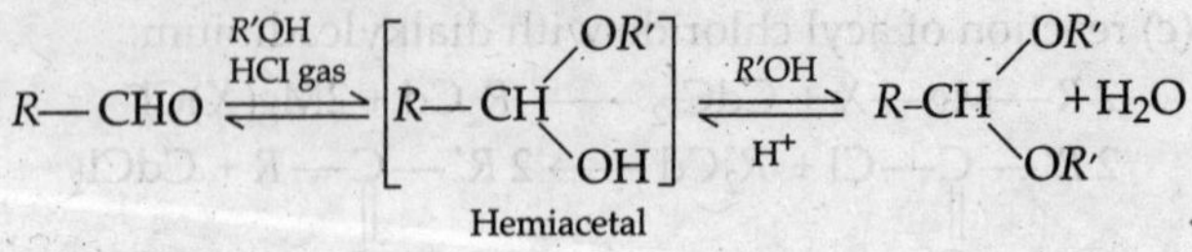

(e) Nucleophiles such as ammonia and its derivatives $H_2N—Z$ can be added to aldehydes and ketones.

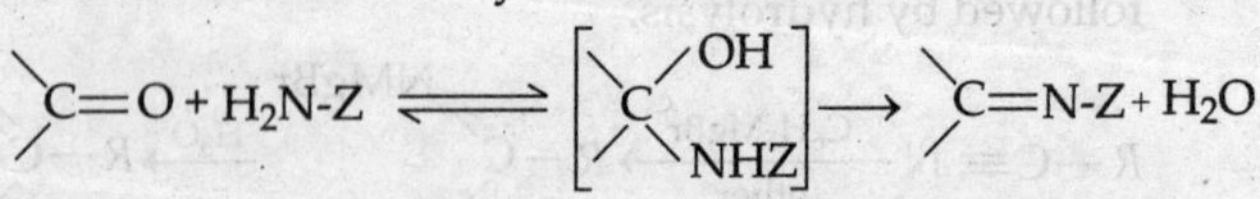

Z = Alkyl, aryl, OH, NH_2, C_6H_5NH, $NHCONH_2$

05 Aldehydes and ketones undergo reduction to form alcohols and hydrocarbons.

(a) Aldehydes and ketones undergo reduction to form primary and secondary alcohols respectively, by treating it with $NaBH_4$ or $LiAlH_4$ or catalytic hydrogenation.

(b) 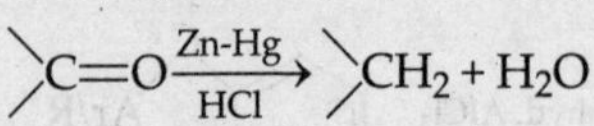 **(Clemmensen reduction)**

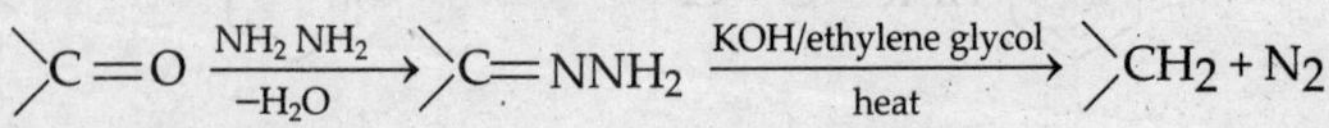

(Wolff-kishner reduction)

06 (a) Aldehydes on oxidation with nitric acid, potassium permanganate, potassium dichromate, etc., produces carboxylic acids.

$$R\text{—}CHO \xrightarrow{[O]} R\text{—}COOH$$

(b) Aldehydes are even oxidised by mild oxidising agents like Tollen's reagent and Fehling's reagent.

$$RCHO + 2[Ag(NH_3)_2]^+ + 3\bar{O}H \longrightarrow RCOO^- + 2Ag + 2H_2O + 4NH_3$$

(Tollen's reagent)

$$R\text{—}CHO + 2Cu^{2+} + 5OH^- \longrightarrow RCOO^- + \underset{\text{Red-brown ppt}}{Cu_2O} + 3H_2O$$

(Fehling's reagent)

(c) Ketones are oxidised by strong oxidising agents and at high temperatures, to yield mixture of carboxylic acids having lesser number of carbon atoms than the parent ketone.

$$R\text{—}\overset{1}{C}H_2\text{—}\overset{2}{C}(=O)\text{—}\overset{3}{C}H_2\text{—}R' \xrightarrow{[O]} R\text{—}COOH + R'\text{—}CH_2COOH$$

(By cleavage of $C_1 — C_2$ bond)

+

$$R\text{—}CH_2COOH + R'\text{—}COOH$$

(By cleavage of $C_2 — C_3$ bond)

(d) Methyl ketones are oxidised by haloform reaction.

$$R\text{—}\overset{O}{\overset{\|}{C}}\text{—}CH_3 \xrightarrow{NaOX} R\text{—}\overset{O}{\overset{\|}{C}}\text{—}ONa + CHX_3 \; (X = Cl, Br, I)$$

07 Boiling points of aldehydes and ketones are less than that of alcohols of comparable molecular masses.

08 Aldehydes can be distinguished from ketones by Tollen's reagent and Fehling's solution.

09 (a) Aldol condensation (Aldehydes/ketones with (α – H).

$$\underset{\text{Ethanal}}{2CH_3 - CHO} \underset{}{\overset{\text{dil. NaOH}}{\rightleftharpoons}} \underset{\substack{\text{3–Hydroxybutanal} \\ \text{(Aldol)}}}{CH_3 - \underset{OH}{\underset{|}{C}H} - CH_2 - CHO}$$

$$\xrightarrow[-H_2O]{\Delta} \underset{\substack{\text{But-2-enal} \\ \text{(Aldol condensation} \\ \text{product)}}}{CH_3 - CH{=}CH - CHO}$$

(b) **Cannizzaro reaction** (Aldehydes/ketones with no (α – H))

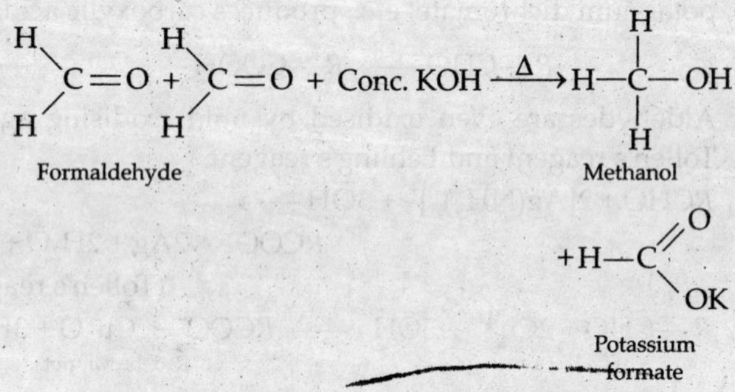

10 Carboxylate ions have more acidic strength than phenoxide ion due to delocalisation of lone pair of electrons over more electronegative two oxygen atoms.

11 Carboxylic acids are prepared by

(a) Oxidation of primary alcohols, aldehydes and alkenes.

$$RCH_2OH \xrightarrow[\text{2. } H_3O^+]{\text{1. alkaline } KMnO_4} RCOOH$$

(b) Aromatic carboxylic acids are prepared by side chain oxidation of alkyl benzenes.

$$\underset{\text{Toluene}}{C_6H_5—CH_3} \xrightarrow[\text{Heat}]{KMnO_4\text{–}KOH} C_6H_5—COOK \xrightarrow{H_3O^+} \underset{\text{Benzoic acid}}{C_6H_5—COOH}$$

(c) Hydrolysis of nitriles and amides.

$$R—CN \xrightarrow[H_2O]{\overset{+}{H} \text{ or } \overset{-}{OH}} R—\overset{\overset{O}{\|}}{C}—NH_2 \xrightarrow[\Delta]{\overset{+}{H} \text{ or } \overset{-}{OH}} RCOOH$$

(d) Treatment of Grignard reagents with carbon dioxide.

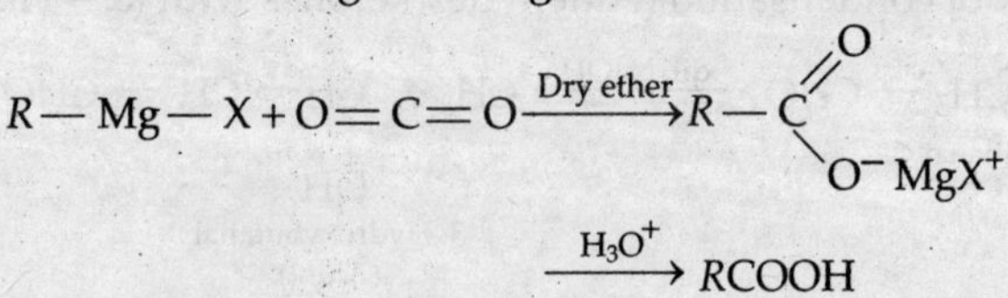

(e) Hydrolysis of acyl halides and anhydrides.

$$RCOCl \xrightarrow{H_2O} RCOOH + Cl^-$$

$$RCOCl \xrightarrow{\bar{O}H/H_2O} RCOO + Cl^- \xrightarrow{H_3O} RCOOH$$

$$\underset{\text{Benzoic anhydride}}{(C_6H_5CO)_2O} \xrightarrow{H_2O} \underset{\text{Benzoic acid}}{2\,C_6H_5COOH}$$

(f) Hydrolysis of esters.

$$\underset{\text{Ethyl benzoate}}{C_6H_5—COOC_2H_5} \underset{}{\overset{H_3O^+}{\rightleftharpoons}} \underset{\text{Benzoic acid}}{C_6H_5—COOH} + C_2H_5OH$$

12 Electron withdrawing groups increases the acidity of carboxylic acids and electron donating groups decreases the acidity of carboxylic acids.

13 Chemical reactions of carboxylic acids are

$$RCOOH \xrightarrow{NaHCO_3} RCO\overset{\ominus}{O}\overset{\oplus}{Na} + H_2O + CO_2 \text{ (Brisks effervescene)}$$

$$RCOOH \xrightarrow[\overset{+}{H},\Delta \text{ or } P_2O_5\ \Delta]{RCOOH} \underset{\text{(Anhydride)}}{R—\overset{O}{\overset{\|}{C}}—O—\overset{O}{\overset{\|}{C}}—R}$$

$$RCOOH \xrightarrow[\overset{+}{H},]{R^1OH} RCOOR^1 + H_2O$$

$$RCOOH \xrightarrow{PCl_5} RCOCl + POCl_3 + HCl$$

$$RCOOH \xrightarrow{PCl_3} 3ROCl + H_3PO_3$$

$$RCOOH \xrightarrow{SOCl_2} ROCl + SO_2 + HCl$$

$$RCOOH \xrightarrow{NH_3} RCOO^-N^+H_4 \xrightarrow[-H_2O]{\Delta} \underset{\text{(Amide)}}{RCONH_2}$$

$$RCOOH \xrightarrow[\text{(ii) } H_3O^+]{\text{(i) } LiAlH_4\text{/ether or } B_2H_6} RCH_2OH$$

- Decarboxylation

$$R\text{—COONa} \xrightarrow[\text{Heat}]{\text{NaOH and CaO}} R\text{—H} + Na_2CO_3$$

- Halogenation of alpha-hydrogen [Hell-Volhard-Zelinsky reaction (HVZ reaction)]

$$R\text{—}CH_2\text{—COOH} \xrightarrow[\text{(ii) } H_2O]{\text{(i) } X_2\text{/Red phosphorus}} R\text{—}\underset{\substack{| \\ X}}{\text{CH}}\text{—COOH}$$

X = Cl, Br

α-Halocarboxylic acid

14 Aromatic aldehydes, ketones and — COOH group in benzoic acid is *meta*-directing as well as deactivating in nature. So, it undergoes electrophilic substitution reaction at *meta* position.

15 Formalin is (40%) aqueous solution of formaldehyde which is used to preserve the biological specimens.

16 Benzoic acid is used as a food preservative. Esters of benzoic acid are used in perfumery. Methanoic acid is used in rubber, textile, dyeing, leather and electroplating industries. Ethanoic acid is used as a solvent and as vinegar in food industry. Hexanedioic acid is used in the manufacture of nylon–6, 6.

Intext Questions

Question 1 Write the structures of the following compounds.

(i) α-Methoxypropionaldehyde (ii) 3-Hydroxybutanal
(iii) 2-Hydroxycyclopentane carbaldehyde
(iv) 4-Oxopentanal (v) Di- *sec*. butyl ketone
(vi) 4-Fluoroacetophenone

◎ ***Thinking Process*** Recall the rules of IUPAC nomenclature. The suffix 'al' represents the presence of —CHO group and 'one' represents $-\overset{\overset{\displaystyle O}{\|}}{C}-$ group.

Sol.

(i) 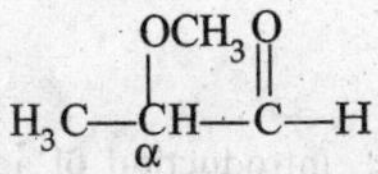

α-Methoxypropionaldehyde

(ii) 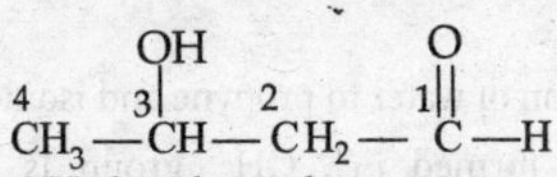

3-Hydroxybutanal

(iii) 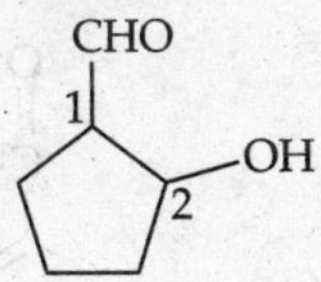

2-Hydroxycyclopentane carbaldehyde

(iv) 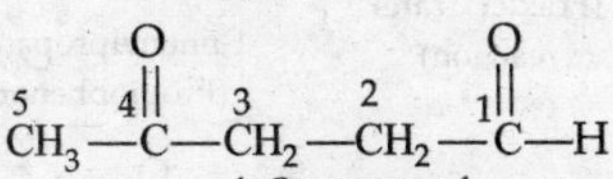

4-Oxopentanal

(v) 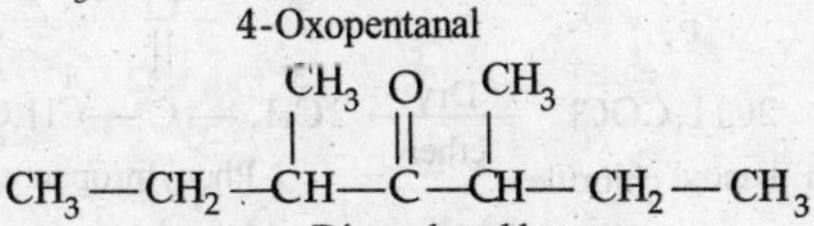

Di-*sec.* butyl ketone

(vi) 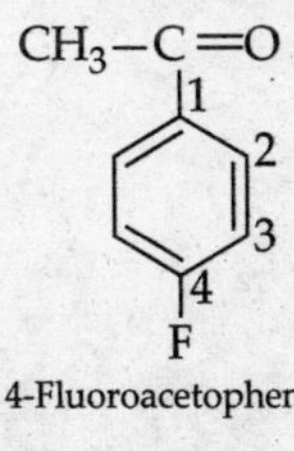

4-Fluoroacetophenone

Question 2 Write the structures of products of the following reactions :

(i) 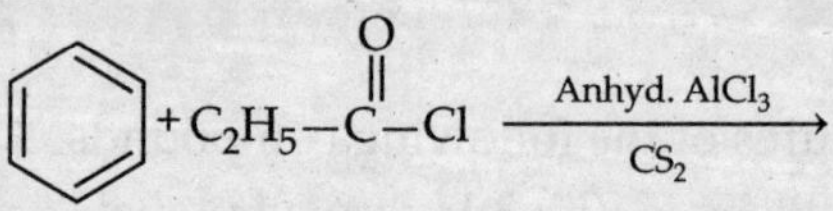

(ii) $(C_6H_5CH_2)_2Cd + 2CH_3COCl \longrightarrow$

(iii) $H_3C-C\equiv C-H \xrightarrow{Hg^{2+},\, H_2SO_4}$

(iv) 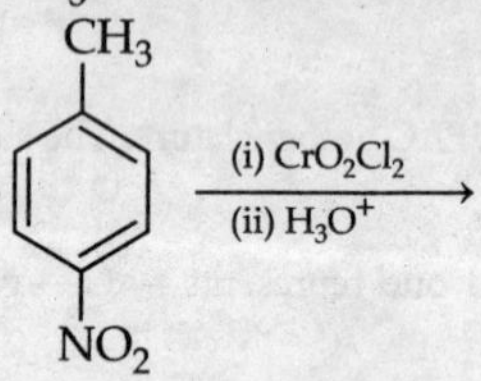

◎ *Thinking Process*

(i) Friedel Crafts reaction (Acylation). *i.e.*, introduction of acyl group in benzene ring.

(ii) Formation of ketone.

(iii) Hydration of propyne *i. e.*, addition of water to propyne and isomerization.

(iv) Etard's reaction (Aldehyde is formed *i.e.*, CH_3 group is converted into-CHO group.).

Sol.

(i) 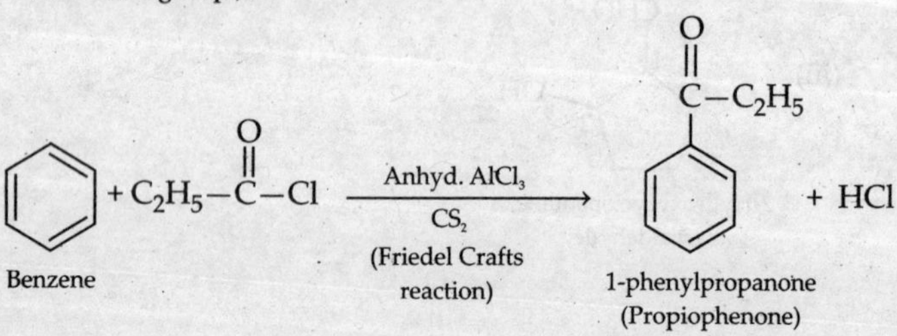

(ii) $\underset{\text{Dibenzylcadmium}}{(C_6H_5CH_2)_2Cd} + \underset{\text{Ethanoyl chloride}}{2CH_3COCl} \xrightarrow[\text{ether}]{\text{Dry}} \underset{\text{1-Phenylpropanone}}{2\overset{3}{C}H_3-\overset{\overset{O}{\|}}{\overset{2}{C}}-\overset{1}{C}H_2C_6H_5}$

$+ \underset{\text{Cadmium chloride}}{CdCl_2}$

(iii) 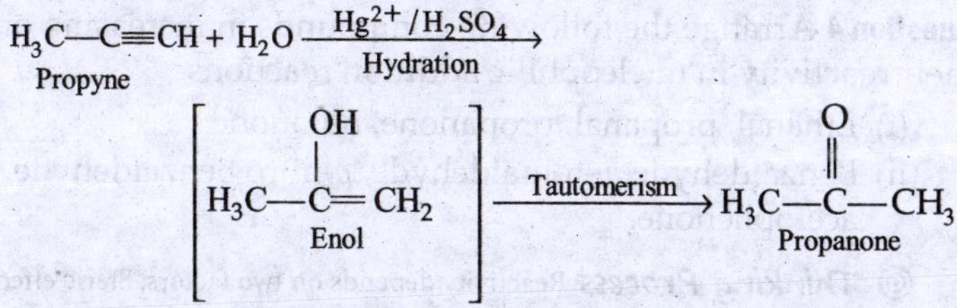

(iv) 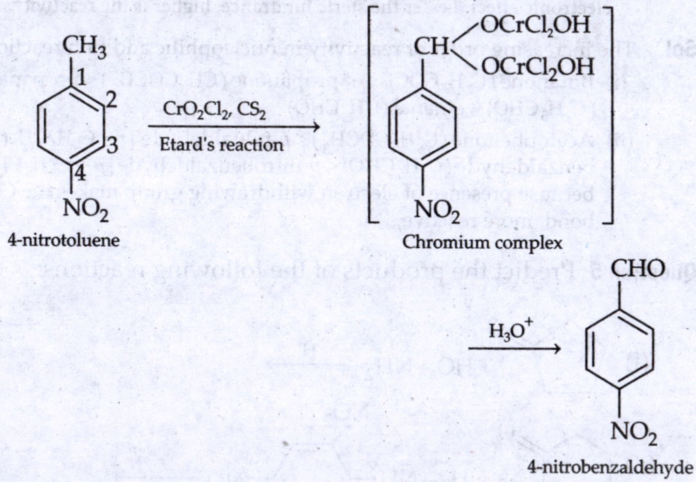

Question 3 Arrange the following compounds in increasing order of their boiling points. CH_3CHO, CH_3CH_2OH, CH_3OCH_3, $CH_3CH_2CH_3$

◎ ***Thinking Process*** **Boiling point is related to attractive forces. Stronger the attractive force, higher is the boiling point.**

Sol. $CH_3CH_2CH_3 < CH_3OCH_3 < CH_3CHO < CH_3CH_2OH$

Hydrocarbons are non-polar having weakest attractive forces; Ethers are polar (dipolar forces); Aldehydes have strong dipolar interactions; Alcohols have maximum inter molecular forces due to hydrogen bonding.

Question 4 Arrange the following compounds in increasing order of their reactivity in nucleophilic addition reactions.

(i) Ethanal, propanal, propanone, butanone.

(ii) Benzaldehyde, *p*-tolualdehyde, *p*-nitro benzaldehyde, acetophenone.

◎ ***Thinking Process*** Reactivity depends on two factors: Steric effect and electronic effect. Lesser the steric hindrance, higher is the reactivity.

Sol. The increasing order of reactivity in nucleophilic addition reactions is:

(i) Butanone ($C_2H_5COCH_3$) < propanone (CH_3COCH_3) < propanal (C_2H_5CHO) < ethanal (CH_3CHO)

(ii) Acetophenone ($C_6H_5COCH_3$) < *p*-tolualdehyde [$p-C_6H_5CH_3(CHO)$] < benzaldehyde (C_6H_5CHO) < *p*-nitrobenzaldehyde [$p-C_6H_5CHO(NO_2)$] because presence of electron withdrawing group makes the $C=O$ bond, more reactive.

Question 5 Predict the products of the following reactions:

(i) 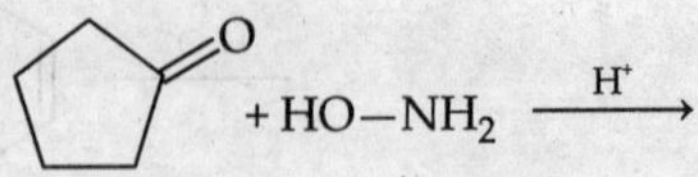

(ii) 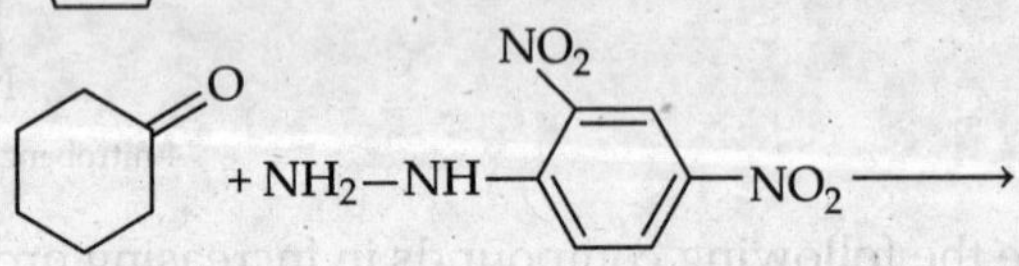

(iii) $R-CH=CH-CHO + NH_2-\overset{\overset{\displaystyle O}{\|}}{C}-NH-NH_2 \xrightarrow{H^+}$

(iv) 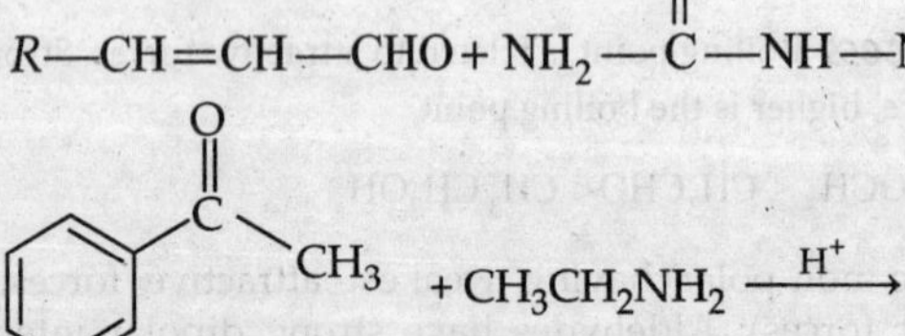

◎ ***Thinking Process*** Elimination of H_2O from carbonyl and amine group and formation of $C=N$ bond.

Sol.

(i) 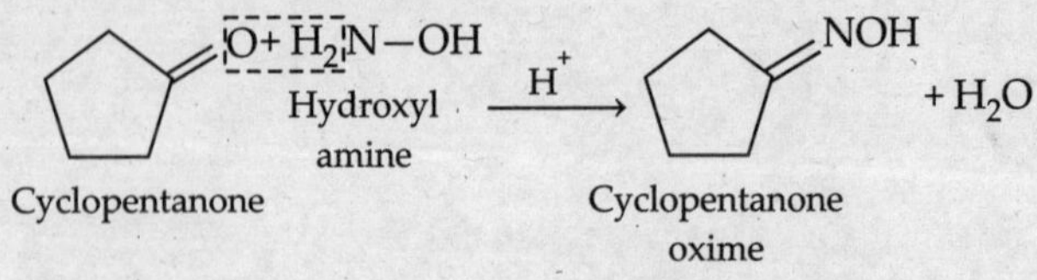

(ii) 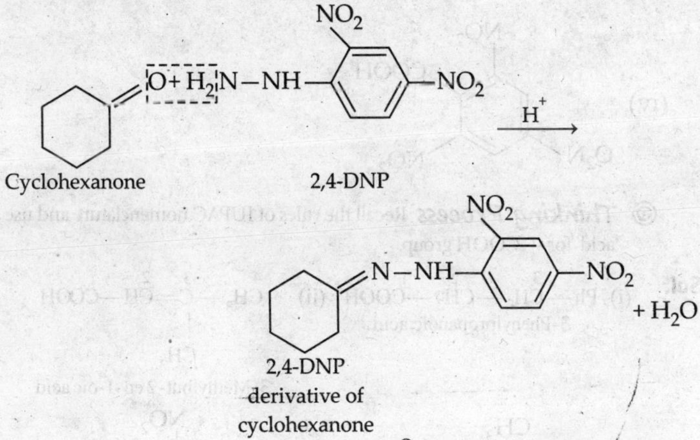

(iii) $R—CH{=}CH—CH{=}O + H_2N—NH—\overset{O}{\overset{\|}{C}}—NH_2$

Unsaturated aldehyde   Semicarbazide

$$\xrightarrow{H^+} R—CH{=}CH—CH{=}N—NH—\overset{O}{\overset{\|}{C}}—NH_2 + H_2O$$

(iv) 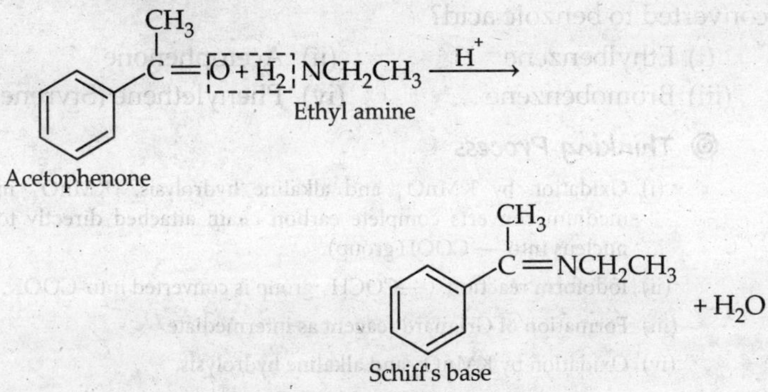

Note Reaction (ii) is used as a test for carbonyl group.

Question 6 Give the IUPAC names of the following compounds :

(i) $PhCH_2CH_2COOH$

(ii) $(CH_3)_2C{=}CHCOOH$

(iii) 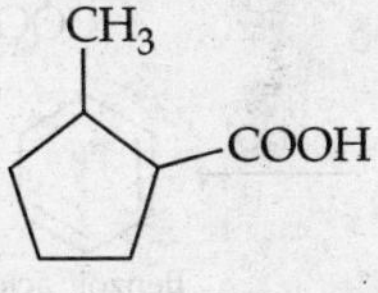

(iv) 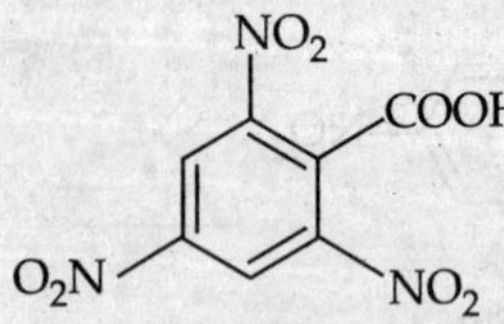

◎ *Thinking Process* Recall the rules of IUPAC nomenclature and use suffix 'oic acid' for —COOH group.

Sol. (i) $\overset{3}{Ph—CH_2}—\overset{2}{CH_2}—\overset{1}{COOH}$

3-Phenylpropanoic acid

(ii) $\overset{4}{CH_3}—\overset{3}{C}(CH_3)=\overset{2}{CH}—\overset{1}{COOH}$

3-Methylbut-2 en-1-oic acid

(iii) 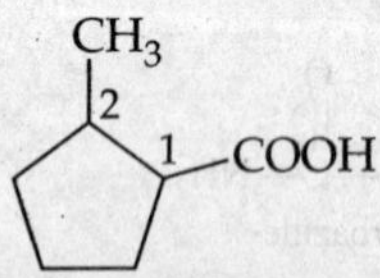

2-Methylcyclopentane carboxylic acid

(iv) 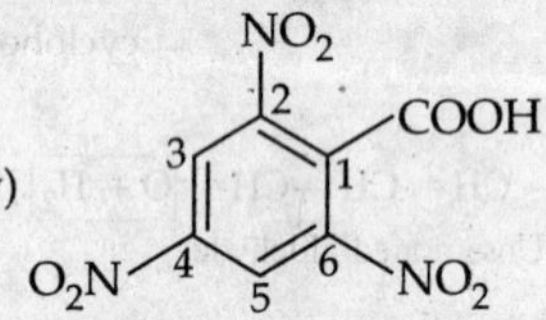

2,4,6-Trinitrobenzoic acid

Question 7 Show how each of the following compounds can be converted to benzoic acid?

(i) Ethylbenzene (ii) Acetophenone

(iii) Bromobenzene (iv) Phenylethene (Styrene)

◎ *Thinking Process*

(i) Oxidation by $KMnO_4$ and alkaline hydrolysis. ($KMnO_4$ in alkaline medium converts complete carbon chain attached directly to benzene nucleus into — COOH group).

(ii) Iodoform reaction. (—$COCH_3$ group is converted into-COOK.)

(iii) Formation of Grignard reagent as intermediate.

(iv) Oxidation by $KMnO_4$ and alkaline hydrolysis.

Sol.

(i) 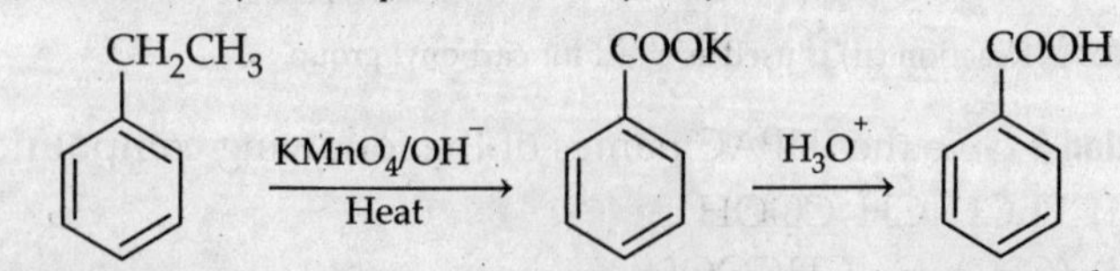

Ethyl benzene Potassium benzoate Benzoic acid

(ii) 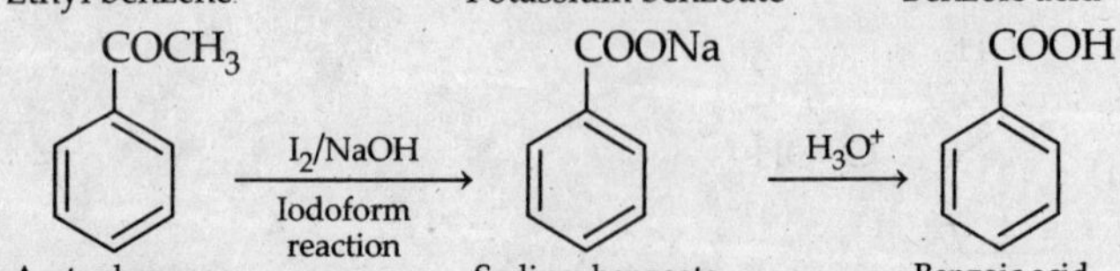

Acetophenone Sodium benzoate Benzoic acid

(iii) 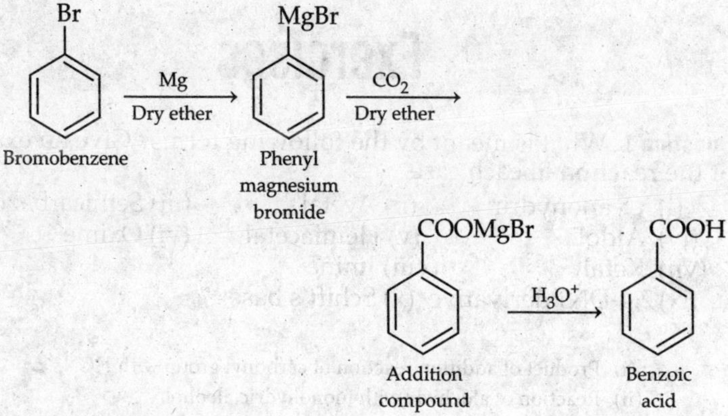

(iv) 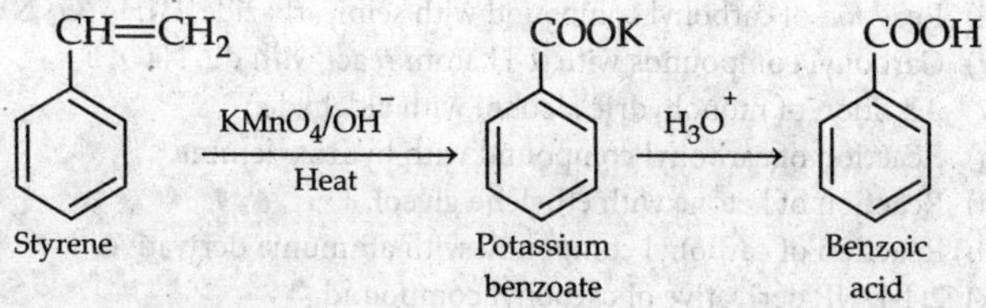

Question 8 Which acid of each pair shown here would you expect to be stronger?

(i) CH_3COOH or CH_2FCOOH

(ii) CH_2FCOOH or $CH_2ClCOOH$

(iii) $CH_2FCH_2CH_2COOH$ or CH_3CHFCH_2COOH

(iv) 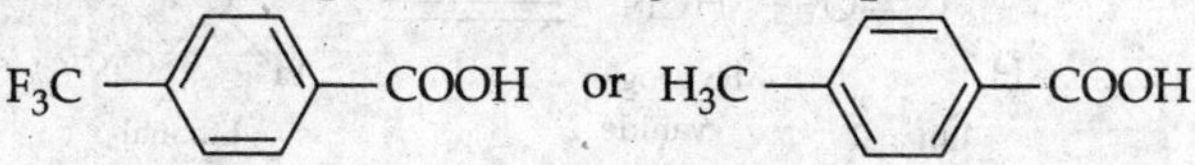

◎ *Thinking Process*

(i) Presence of an electron withdrawing group like F($-I$ showing group) makes a carboxylic acid stronger.

(ii) Higher the $-I$ effect, stronger is the acid. The order of $-I$ effect is I < Br < Cl < F.

(iii) As the distance between $-I$ showing group and —COOH group increases, acidity decreases.

Sol. (i) CH_2FCOOH is stronger acid.

(ii) CH_2FCOOH is a stronger acid.

(iii) CH_3CHFCH_2COOH is a stronger acid.

(iv) 

is a stronger acid.

Exercises

Question 1 What is meant by the following terms? Give an example of the reaction in each case.

(i) Cyanohydrin (ii) Acetal (iii) Semicarbazone
(iv) Aldol (v) Hemiacetal (vi) Oxime
(vii) Ketal (viii) Imine
(ix) 2,4-DNPderivative (x) Schiff's base

(i) Product of addition reaction of carbonyl group with HCN.
(ii) Reaction of aldehyde with monohydric alcohol.
(iii) Reaction of carbonyl compound with semicarbazide, ($NH_2CO \cdot NHNH_2$)
(iv) Carbonyl compounds with α-H atom react with dil. NaOH.
(v) Addition of monohydric alcohol with aldehyde.
(vi) Reaction of carbonyl compound with hydroxylamine.
(vii) Reaction of ketone with ethylene glycol.
(viii) Reaction of carbonyl compound with ammonia derivatives.
(ix) 2,4-DNP derivative of carbonyl compound.
(x) Reaction of carbonyl compound with primary amines.

Sol. (i) **Cyanohydrin** Addition products formed by the reaction of aldehydes and ketones with hydrogen cyanide (HCN) are known as cyanohydrins.

For example

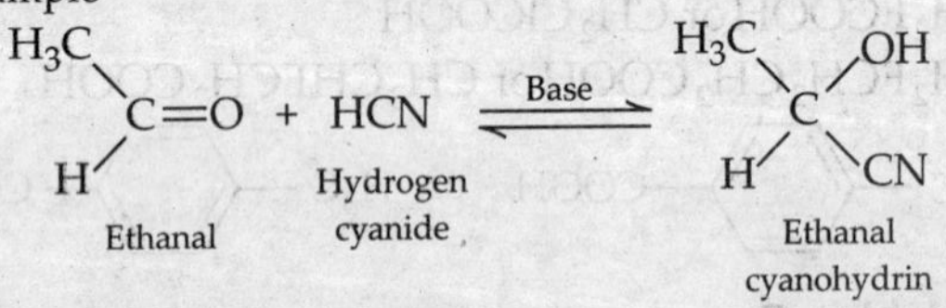

(ii) **Acetal** When an aldehyde reacts with two equivalents of a monohydric alcohol in the presence of dry HCl gas, *gem*-dialkoxy compounds are formed; which are known as acetals. In acetal, two alkoxy groups are present on the terminal C-atom. For example :

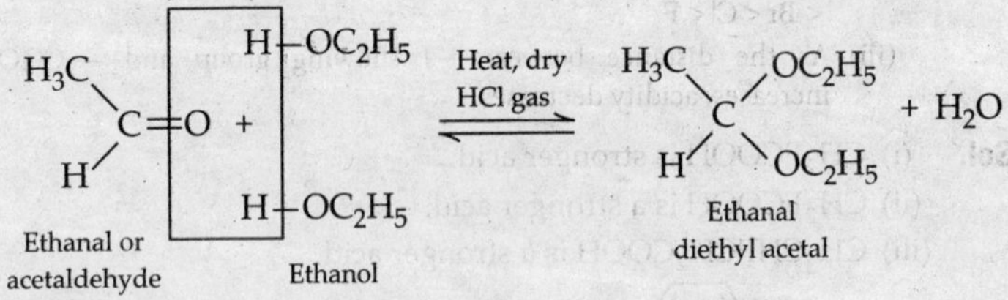

(iii) **Semicarbazone** The compounds formed on the reaction of aldehydes /ketones with semicarbazide are called semicarbazones. For example :

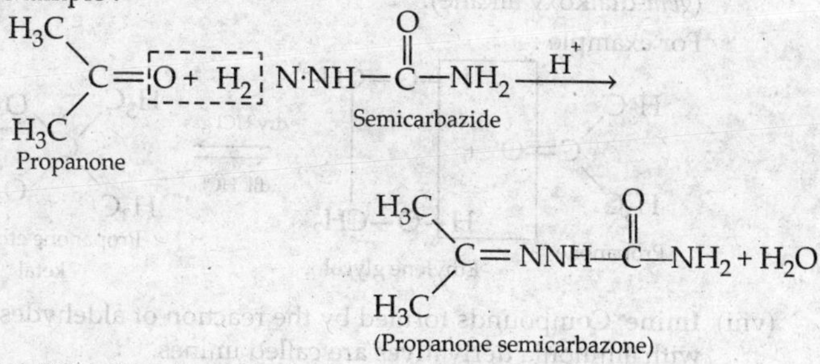

(iv) **Aldol** When an aldehyde (or ketone) having at least one α-hydrogen atom undergo a reaction in the presence of dilute alkali as catalyst to form aldol or β-hydroxyaldehydes (or ketal in case of ketones), the reaction is called aldol condensation.

For example :

$$\underset{\text{Ethanal}}{2CH_3-CHO} \xrightarrow{\text{Dil. NaOH}} \overset{4}{C}H_3-\overset{3}{C}H(OH)-\overset{2}{C}H_2-\overset{1}{C}HO$$

3-Hydroxybutanal (Aldol)

(v) **Hemiacetal** When an aldehyde reacts with one molecule of a monohydric alcohol in presence of dry HCl gas, *gem*-alkoxy alcohols are formed. These are known as hemiacetals.

For example :

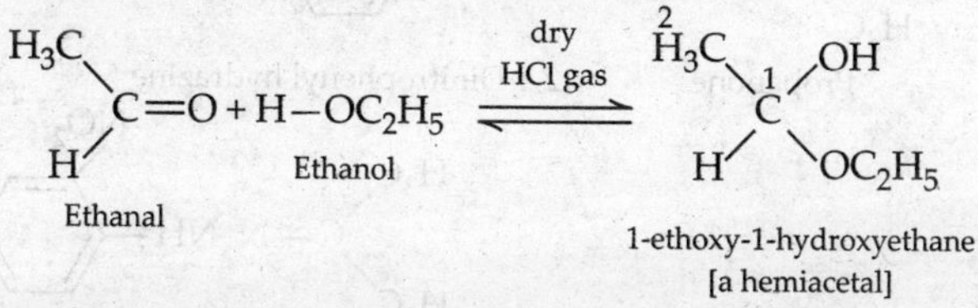

(vi) **Oxime** When an aldehyde or ketone reacts with hydroxylamine in weak acidic medium, the product obtained is known as oxime.

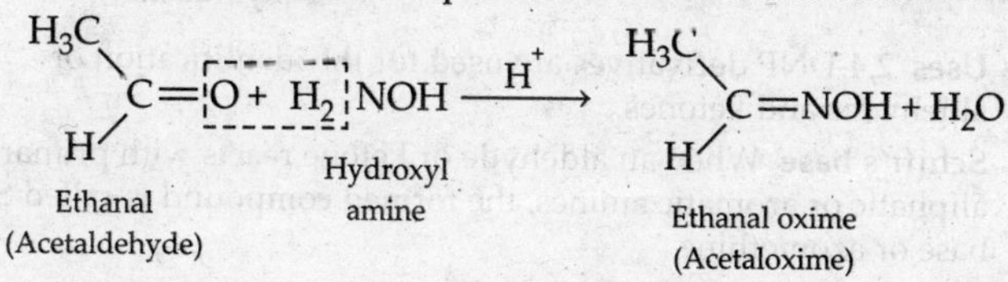

(vii) **Ketal** The compound formed by heating a ketone with ethylene glycol in the presence of dry HCl gas is known as ketal (*gem*-dialkoxy alkane).

For example :

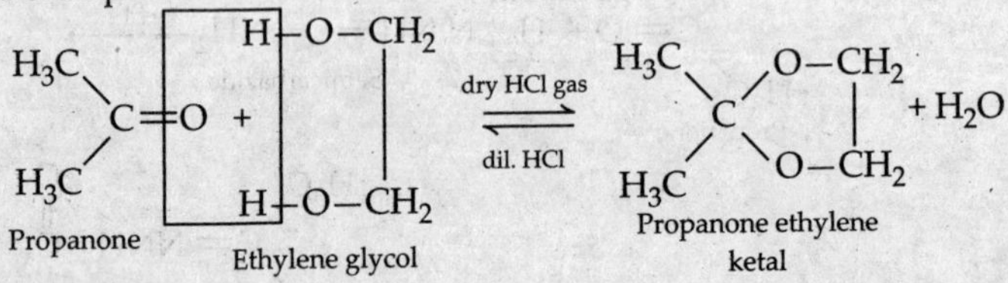

(viii) **Imine** Compounds formed by the reaction of aldehydes and ketones with ammonia derivatives are called imines.

These compounds contain $>C=NZ$ group. General reaction is :

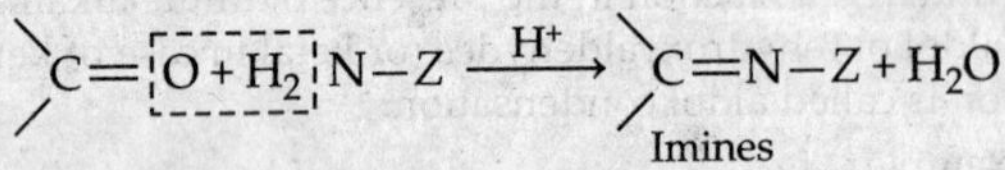

Z = Alkyl, aryl, OH, NH_2, C_6H_5NH, $NHCONH_2$, etc.

(ix) **2,4-DNP derivative** 2, 4-dinitrophenyl hydrazine reacts with aldehyde or ketone to produce 2,4-dinitrophenyl hydrazones (*i.e.*, 2,4-DNP derivative). The reaction takes place in weak acidic medium.

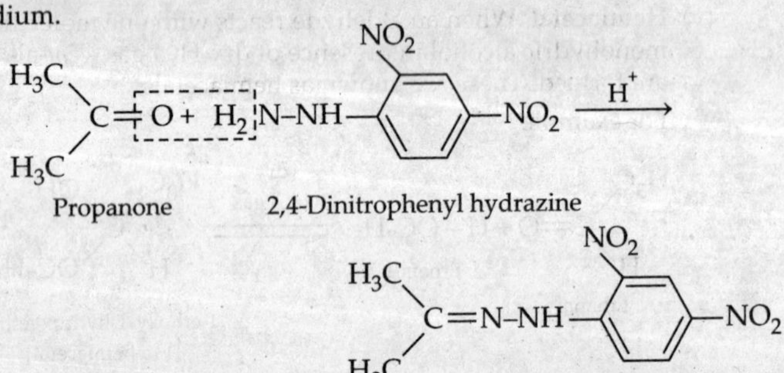

Uses 2,4-DNP derivatives are used for the identification of aldehydes and ketones.

(x) **Schiff's base** When an aldehyde or ketone reacts with primary aliphatic or aromatic amines, the formed compound is called Schiff' base or azomethine.

$$\underset{\text{Aldehyde}}{R-CH=O} + \underset{\text{Primary amine}}{H_2N-R'} \xrightarrow{H^+} \underset{\text{Schiff's base}}{R-CH=N-R'} + H_2O$$

Question 2 Name the following compounds according to IUPAC system of nomenclature :

(i) $CH_3CH(CH_3)CH_2CH_2CHO$
(ii) $CH_3CH_2COCH(C_2H_5)CH_2CH_2Cl$
(iii) $CH_3CH{=}CHCHO$
(iv) $CH_3COCH_2COCH_3$
(v) $CH_3CH(CH_3)CH_2C(CH_3)_2COCH_3$
(vi) $(CH_3)_3CCH_2COOH$
(vii) $OHCC_6H_4CHO$-*p*

◎ ***Thinking Process*** Write complete structure, choose the longest chain and do the numbering.
Recall the rules of IUPAC nomenclature to give name. Use 'al' for —CHO and 'one' for >C=O group.

Sol. (i) 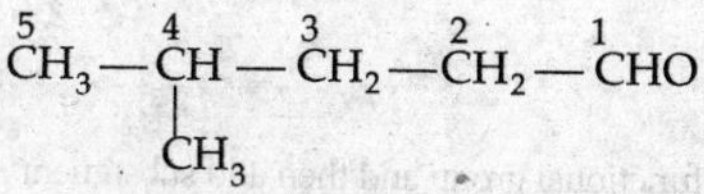

4-Methylpentanal

(ii) 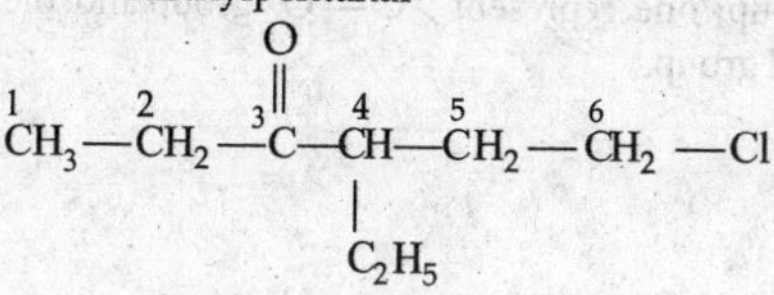

6-Chloro-4-ethylhexan-3-one

(iii) 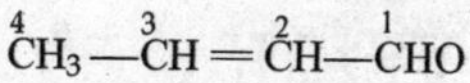

But-2-en-1-al

(iv) 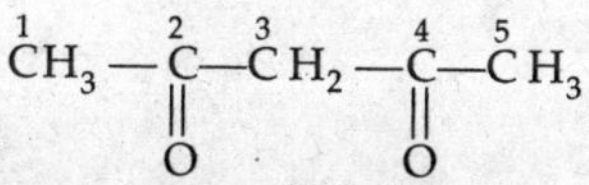

pentane-2, 4-dione

(v) 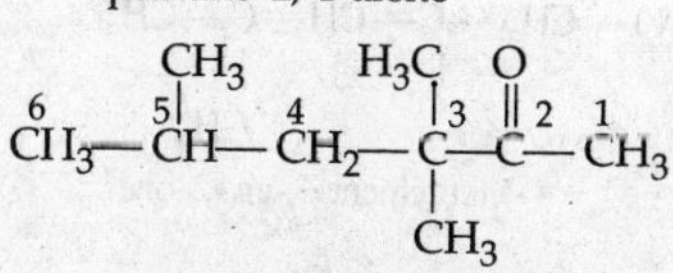

3, 3, 5-Trimethylhexan-2-one

(vi) 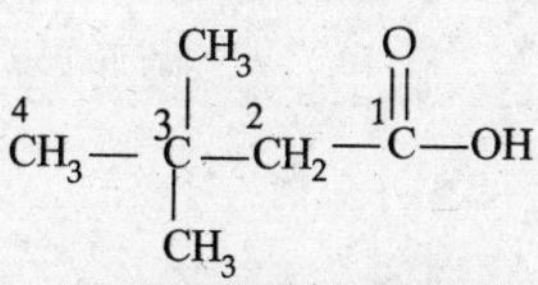

3,3-Dimethylbutanoic acid

(vii) 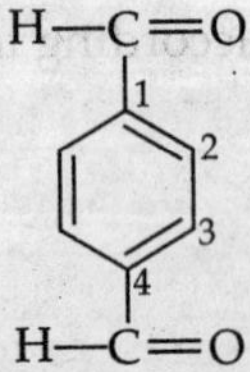

Benzene-1,4-dicarbaldehyde

Question 3 Draw the structures of the following compounds.

(i) 3-Methylbutanal (ii) *p*-Nitropropiophenone
(iii) *p*-Methylbenzaldehyde (iv) 4-Methylpent-3-en-2-one
(v) 4-Chloropentan-2-one
(vi) 3-Bromo-4-phenylpentanoic acid
(vii) *p*, *p*′-Dihydroxybenzophenone
(viii) Hex-2-en-4-ynoic acid

◎ ***Thinking Process***

(i) First draw the main chain with functional group and then add substituent groups.
(ii) 'al' represents —CHO group; 'one' represent >C=O group and 'oic acid' represents —COOH group.

Sol. (i) 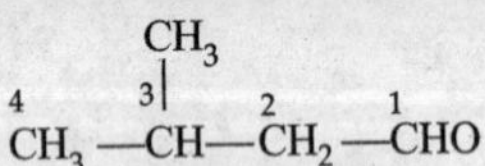

3-Methylbutanal

(ii) 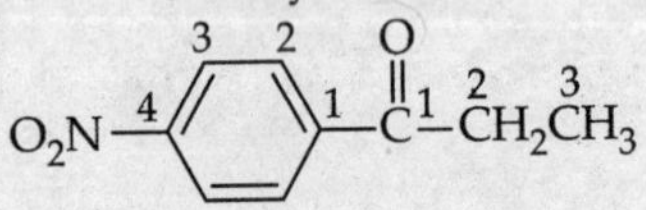

p -Nitropropiophenone

(iii) 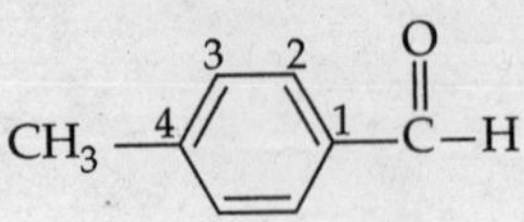

p- Methylbenzaldehyde

(iv) 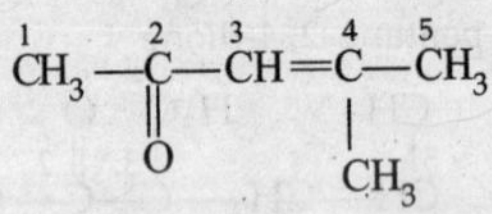

4-Methylpent-3-en-2-one

(v) 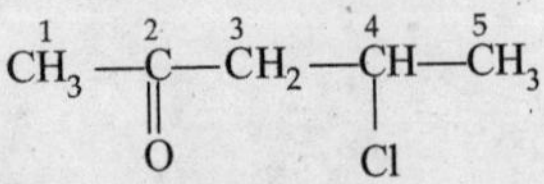

4-Chloropentan-2-one

(vi) 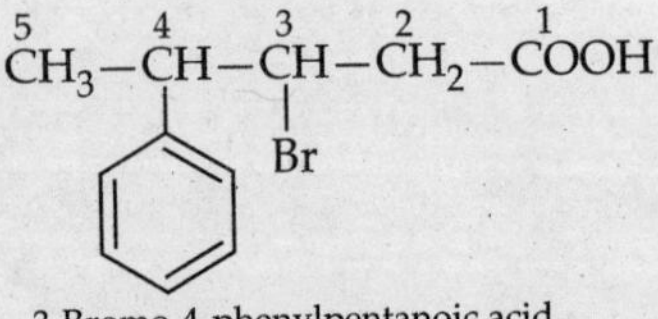

3-Bromo-4-phenylpentanoic acid

(vii) 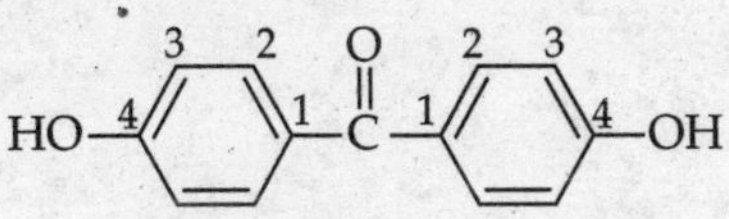

p,p'- Dihydroxybenzophenone

(viii) $\overset{6}{C}H_3-\overset{5}{C}\equiv\overset{4}{C}-\overset{3}{C}H=\overset{2}{C}H-\overset{1}{C}OOH$

Hex-2-en-4-yn -oic acid

Question 4 Write the IUPAC names of the following ketones and aldehydes, wherever possible, give also common names.

(i) $CH_3CO(CH_2)_4CH_3$

(ii) $CH_3CH_2CHBr\,CH_2CH(CH_3)CHO$

(iii) $CH_3(CH_2)_5CHO$

(iv) $Ph—CH = CH—CHO$

(v) 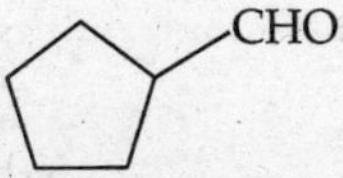

(v) PhCOPh

◎ ***Thinking Process*** As in Q. 2 of exercise.

Sol.

(i) $\overset{1}{C}H_3-\underset{\underset{O}{\|}}{\overset{2}{C}}-\overset{3}{C}H_2-\overset{4}{C}H_2-\overset{5}{C}H_2-\overset{6}{C}H_2-\overset{7}{C}H_3$

IUPAC name : Heptan-2-one

Common name : Methyl *n*-pentyl ketone

(ii) $\overset{6}{C}H_3-\overset{5}{C}H_2-\underset{\underset{Br}{|}}{\overset{4}{C}H}-\overset{3}{C}H_2-\underset{\underset{CH_3}{|}}{\overset{2}{C}H}-\overset{1}{C}HO$

IUPAC name : 4-Bromo-2-methylhexanal

Common name : γ-bromo-α-methyl caproaldehyde

(iii) $\overset{7}{C}H_3-\overset{6}{C}H_2-\overset{5}{C}H_2-\overset{4}{C}H_2-\overset{3}{C}H_2-\overset{2}{C}H_2-\overset{1}{C}HO$

IUPAC name : Heptanal

Common name : *n*-Heptyl aldehyde

(iv) 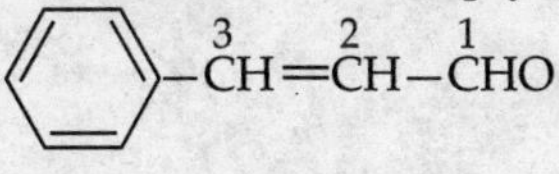

IUPAC name : 3-Phenylprop-2-en-1-al

Common name : β-Phenyl acrolein

(v) 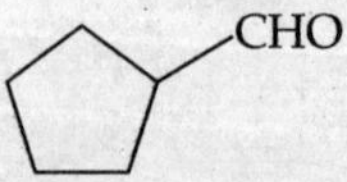

IUPAC name : Cyclopentane carbaldehyde

(vi) $C_6H_5—\overset{O}{\overset{\|}{C}}—C_6H_5$

IUPAC name : Diphenylmethanone

Common name : Benzophenone

Question 5 Draw structures of the following derivatives.

(i) The 2,4-dinitrophenylhydrazone of benzaldehyde

(ii) Cyclopropanone oxime (iii) Acetaldehydedimethylacetal

(iv) The semicarbazone of cyclobutanone

(v) The ethylene ketal of hexan-3-one

(vi) The methyl hemiacetal of formaldehyde

◎ ***Thinking Process***

(i) Product of the reaction of benzaldehyde and 2,4-dinitrophenyl hydrazine (by removing one water molecule).

(ii) Product of the reaction of hydroxyl amine (NH_2OH) with cyclopropanone (by removing one water molecule).

(iii) Product of the reaction of acetaldehyde (CH_3CHO) with two molecules of methanol (CH_3OH).

(iv) Product of the reaction of cyclobutanone (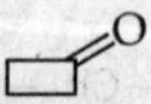) with semicarbazide ($NH_2 \cdot NHCONH_2$) by removing water molecule.

(v) Product of the reaction of hexan-3-one with epoxide 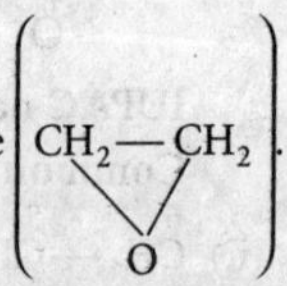.

(vi) Product of the reaction of formaldehyde (HCHO) with one molecule of methanol (CH_3OH).

Sol.

(i) 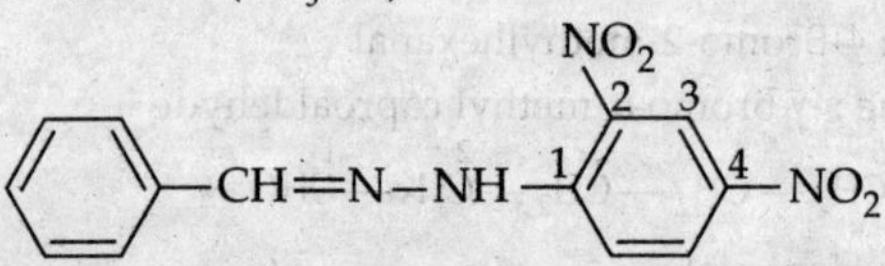

(ii) 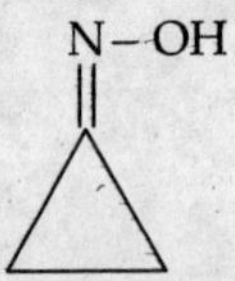

(iii) 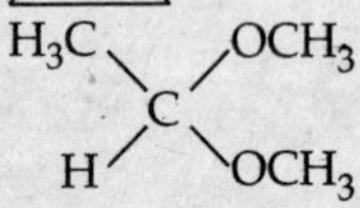

(iv) 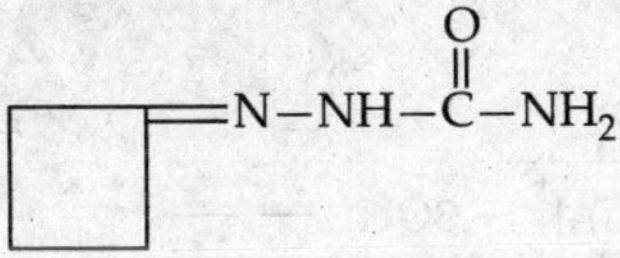

(v) 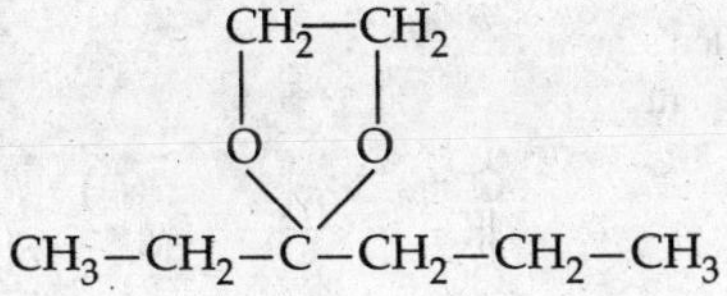

(vi) 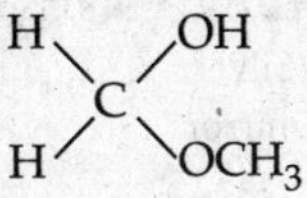

Question 6 Predict the products formed when cyclohexane carbaldehyde reacts with following reagents.

(i) PhMgBr and then H_3O^+ (ii) Tollen's reagent

(iii) Semicarbazide and weak acid

(iv) Excess ethanol and acid

(v) Zinc amalgam and dilute hydrochloric acid

◎ ***Thinking Process***

(i) Nucleophilic addition of RMgBr (Grignard reagent) to —CHO group, followed by hydration; Carbinol is formed.

(ii) Oxidation of —CHO group to —COOH and reduction of Ag^+ to Ag (silver), *i.e.*, silver mirror is formed.

(iii) Removal of H_2O from $C{=}O$ and NH_2 group so semicarbazone is formed.

(iv) Nucleophilic additiop followed by substitution; Acetal is formed.

(v) Conversion of —CHO group to $—CH_3$, *i.e.*, Cycloalkane is formed (Clemmensen's reduction).

Sol. (i) 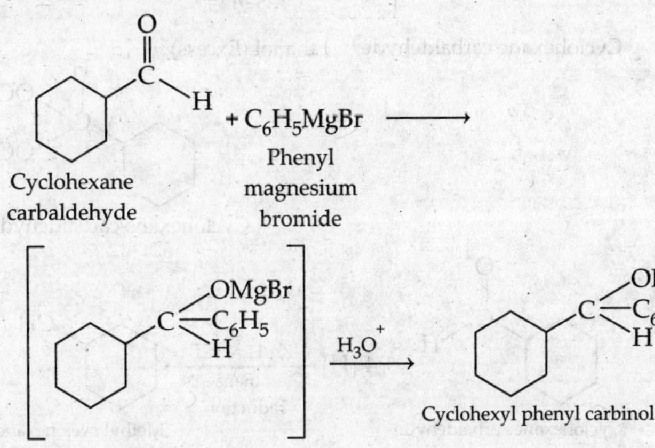

(ii) 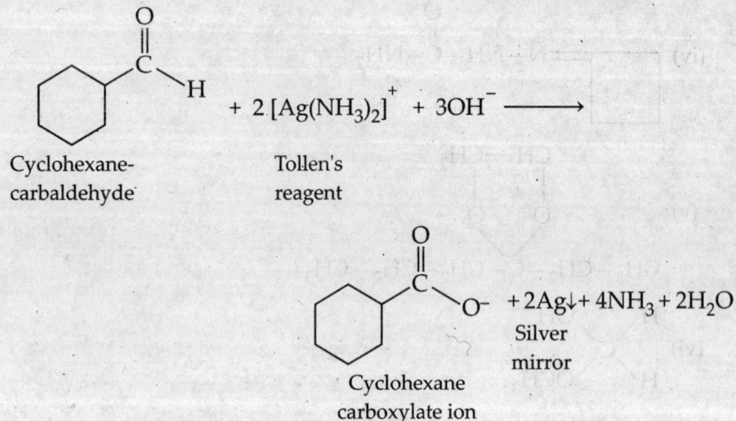

Cyclohexane-
carbaldehyde
+ 2 [Ag(NH3)2]+ + 3OH−
Tollen's
reagent
+ 2Ag↓ + 4NH3 + 2H2O
Silver
mirror
Cyclohexane
carboxylate ion

(iii) 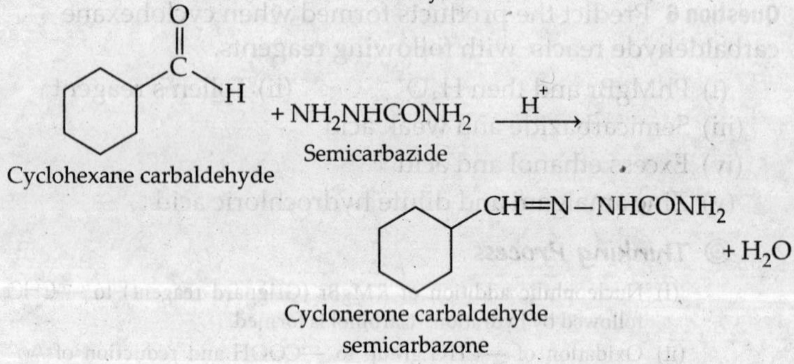

Cyclohexane carbaldehyde
+ NH2NHCONH2
Semicarbazide
H+
CH=N−NHCONH2
+ H2O
Cyclonerone carbaldehyde
semicarbazone

(iv) 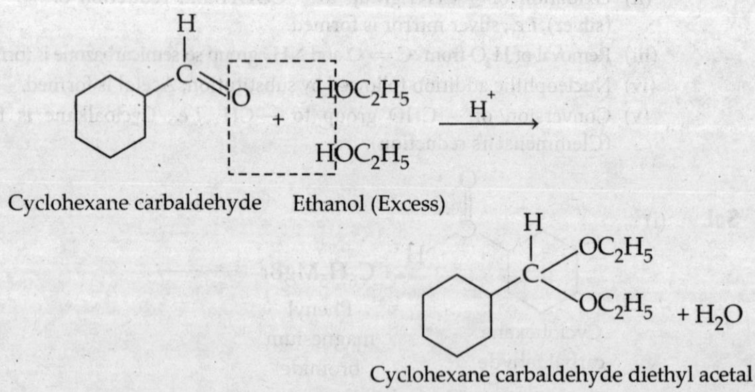

Cyclohexane carbaldehyde
HOC2H5
HOC2H5
Ethanol (Excess)
H+
OC2H5
OC2H5
+ H2O
Cyclohexane carbaldehyde diethyl acetal

(v) 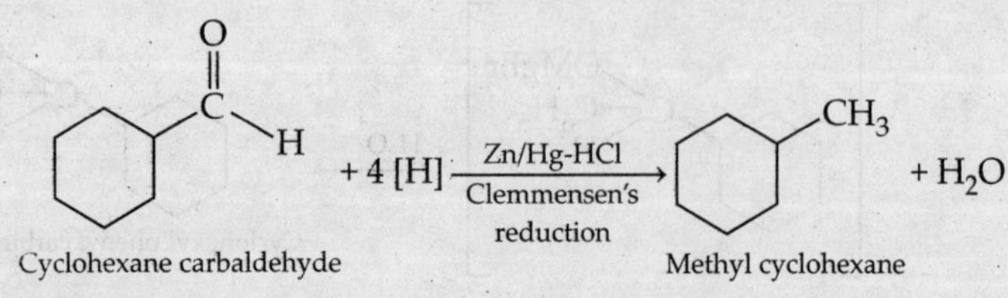

Cyclohexane carbaldehyde
+ 4 [H]
Zn/Hg-HCl
Clemmensen's
reduction
CH3
+ H2O
Methyl cyclohexane

Question 7 Which of the following compounds would undergo aldol condensation, which the Cannizzaro reaction and which neither? Write the structures of the expected products of aldol condensation and Cannizzaro reaction.

(i) Methanal
(ii) 2-Methylpentanal
(iii) Benzaldehyde
(iv) Benzophenone
(v) Cyclohexanone
(vi) 1-Phenylpropanone
(vii) Phenylacetaldehyde
(viii) Butan-1-ol
(ix) 2,2-Dimethylbutanal

◎ ***Thinking Process***

(a) Compounds (aldehydes or ketones) having one or more α-H-atoms undergo aldol condensation.
(b) Compounds (aldehydes) without α-H-atoms undergo Cannizzaro reaction.
(c) Compounds (ketones) without α-H-atoms will neither undergo aldol condensation nor Cannizzaro reaction.
So write the structure of each compound to find the answer.

Sol. (a) Compounds which undergo aldol condensation (having α-hydrogen atom) are following :

(i) **2-Methylpentanal**

$$2\,CH_3CH_2CH_2—\overset{\alpha-H}{CH}(CH_3)—CHO \xrightarrow[\text{Aldol condensation}]{\text{Dil. NaOH}}$$

2-Methylpentanal

$$\overset{7}{C}H_3\overset{6}{C}H_2\overset{5}{C}H_2\,\overset{4}{C}H(CH_3)—\overset{3}{C}H(OH)—\overset{2}{C}(CH_3)(\overset{1}{C}HO)—CH_2CH_2CH_3$$

3-Hydroxy-2,4-dimethyl 2-propyl heptanal

(v) **Cyclohexanone**

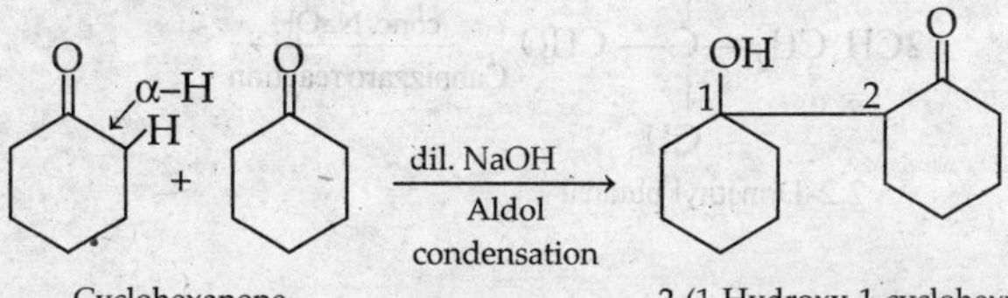

Cyclohexanone   2-(1-Hydroxy-1-cyclohexyl) cyclohexan-1-one

(vi) **1-Phenylpropanone**

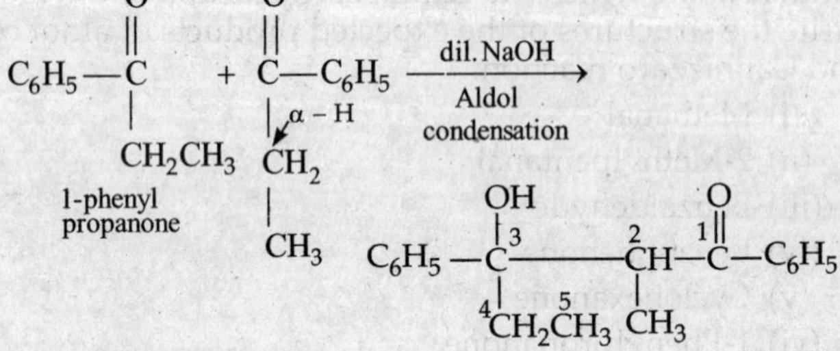

(vii) **Phenyl acetaldehyde**

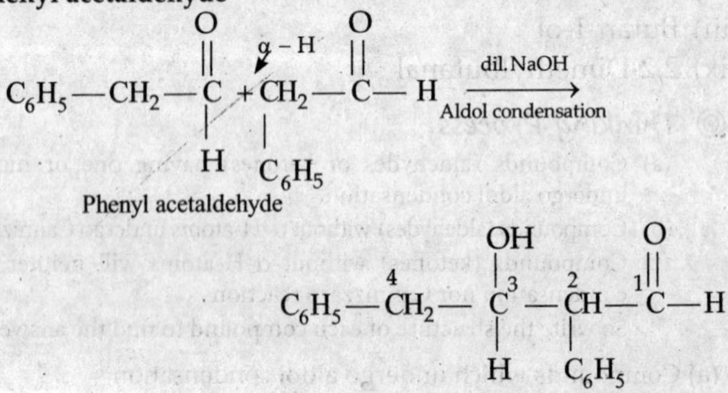

3-Hydroxy-2,4-diphenylbutanal

(b) **Compounds which undergo Cannizzaro reaction :**

(Without α-hydrogen atoms; only aldehydes)

(i) **Methanal**

$$\underset{\text{Methanal}}{2HCHO} \xrightarrow[\text{Cannizzaro reaction}]{\text{Conc.NaOH}} \underset{\text{Methanol}}{CH_3OH} + \underset{\text{Sodium methanoate}}{HCOONa}$$

(iii) **Benzaldehyde**

$$\underset{\text{Benzaldehyde}}{2C_6H_5CHO} \xrightarrow[\text{Cannizzaro reaction}]{\text{Conc}\cdot\text{NaOH}} \underset{\text{Benzyl alcohol}}{C_6H_5CH_2OH} + \underset{\text{Sodiumbenzoate}}{C_6H_5COONa}$$

(ix) **2,2-Dimethylbutanal**

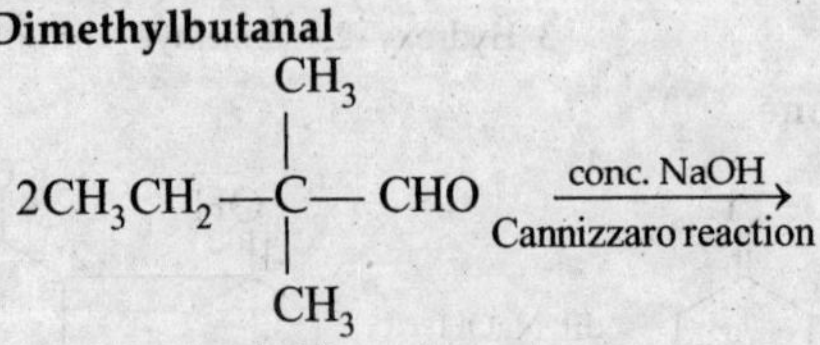

2,2-Dimethyl butanal

Structure contd...

$$\overset{4}{C}H_3\overset{3}{C}H_2-\overset{2}{C}(CH_3)_2-\overset{1}{C}H_2OH$$

2, 2-Dimethylbutan -1-ol

$$\overset{4}{C}H_3\overset{3}{C}H_2-\overset{2}{C}(CH_3)_2-\overset{1}{C}OONa$$

Sodium -2,2-dimethylbutanoate

(c) Compounds which undergo neither of the two reactions- Cannizzaro/ Aldol :

(iv) **Benzophenone** It is a ketone, so it does not undergo Cannizzaro's reaction. Without α-hydrogen, it cannot participate in aldol condensation.

(viii) **Butan-1-ol** It is an alcohol. So, it cannot participate in any of the above 2 reactions.

Question 8 How will you convert ethanal into the following compounds?

(i) Butane-1,3-diol (ii) But-2-enal (iii) But-2-enoic acid

◎ *Thinking Process* Given conversions involve the following steps

(i) (a) Aldol condensation (b) Reduction

(ii) (a) Aldol condensation (b) Dehydration

(iii) (a) Aldol condensation (b) Dehydration
(c) Reaction with Tollen's reagent.

Sol. (i) **Ethanal to butane-1, 3-diol**

$$\underset{\text{Ethanal}}{2CH_3CHO} \xrightarrow[\text{Aldol condensation}]{\text{dil.NaOH}} \underset{\text{3-Hydroxybutanal}}{\overset{4}{C}H_3\overset{3}{C}H(OH)\overset{2}{C}H_2\overset{1}{C}HO}$$

$$\xrightarrow[+2[H]]{LiAlH_4} \underset{\text{Butan-1,3-diol}}{CH_3CH(OH)CH_2CH_2OH}$$

(ii) **Ethanal to but-2-en-al**

$$\underset{\text{Ethanal}}{2CH_3CHO} \xrightarrow[\text{Aldol condensation}]{\text{dil.NaOH}} \underset{\text{3-Hydroxybutanal}}{\overset{4}{C}H_3\overset{3}{C}H(OH)\overset{2}{C}H_2\overset{1}{C}HO}$$

$$\xrightarrow[-H_2]{\text{Heat}} \underset{\text{But-2-enal}}{\overset{4}{C}H_3\overset{3}{C}H=\overset{2}{C}H\overset{1}{C}HO}$$

(iii) **Ethanal into but-2-enoic acid**

$$\underset{\text{Ethanal}}{2CH_3CHO} \xrightarrow[\text{(ii) Heat, } -H_2O]{\text{(i) Aldol condensation}} \underset{\text{But-2-en-al}}{\overset{4}{C}H_3\overset{3}{C}H{=}\overset{2}{C}H\overset{1}{C}HO}$$

$$\xrightarrow[{[Ag(NH_3)_2]OH}]{\text{Tollen's reagent}} \underset{\text{But-2-enoic acid}}{\overset{4}{C}H_3{-}\overset{3}{C}H{=}\overset{2}{C}H{-}\overset{1}{C}OOH}$$

Question 9 Write structural formulas and names of four possible aldol condensation products from propanal and butanal. In each case, indicate which aldehyde acts as nucleophile and which as electrophile?

◎ *Thinking Process* Because of the presence of α-H atoms, propanal and butanal both undergo self and cross aldol condensation.

Sol. α-hydrogen atoms are present in propanal as well as butanal. So, they can undergo aldol condensation in four ways :

(i) **Condensation involving propanal only**

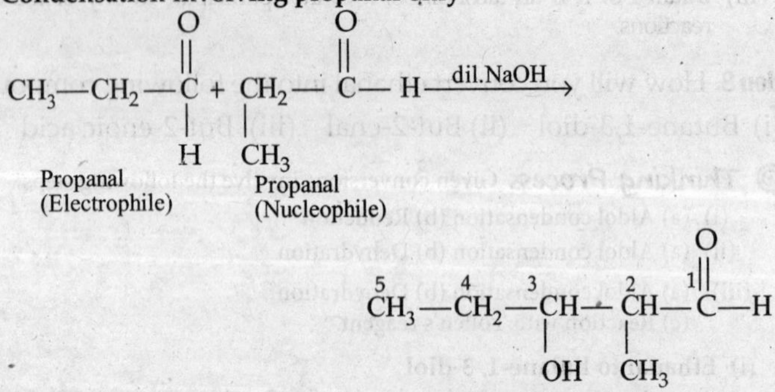

3-Hydroxy-2-methylpentanal

(ii) **Condensation involving butanal only**

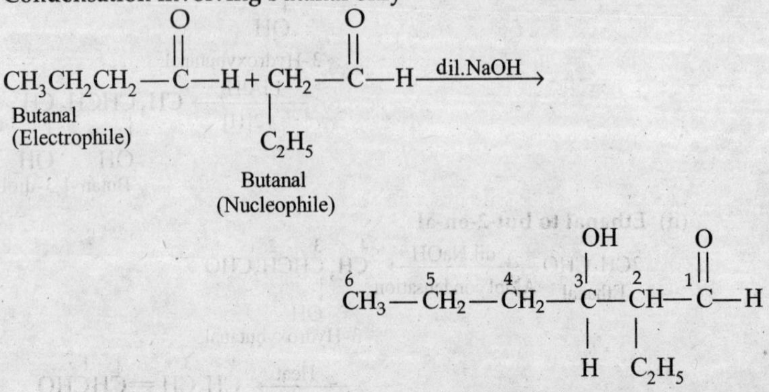

2-Ethyl-3-hydroxyhexanal

(iii) **Condensation involving butanal (electrophile) and propanal (nucleophile)**

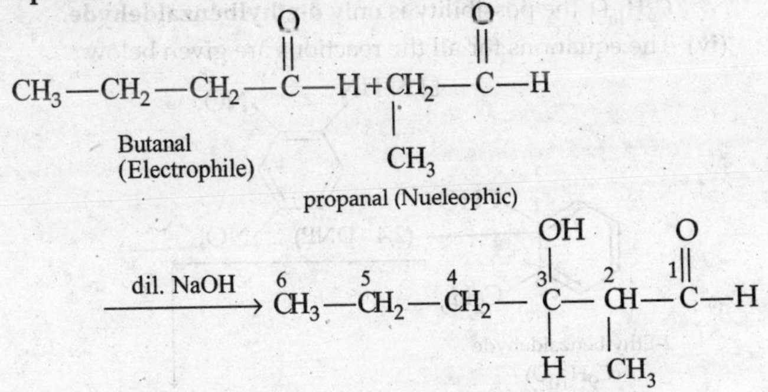

3-Hydroxy-2-methylhexanal

(iv) **Condensation involving propanal (electrophile) and butanal (nucleophile)**

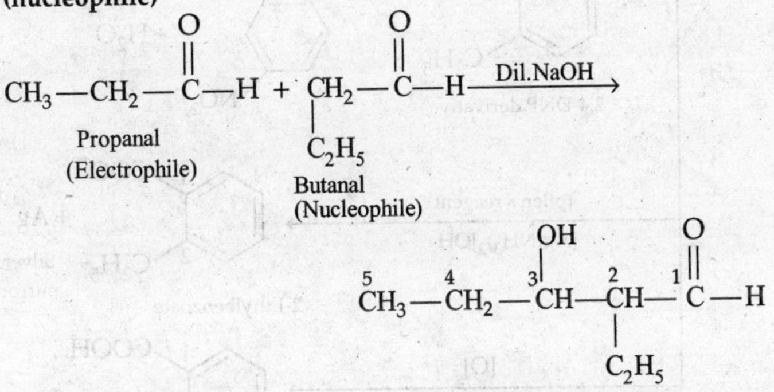

2-Ethyl-3-hydroxypentanal

Question 10 An organic compound with the molecular formula $C_9H_{10}O$ forms 2,4-DNP derivative, reduces Tollen's reagent and undergoes Cannizzaro reaction. On vigorous oxidation, it gives 1,2-benzene dicarboxylic acid. Identify the compound.

◎ *Thinking Process*

(i) Identify the functional group from the reactions given by it.

(ii) Find position of the functional group, from 1, 2-benzene dicarboxylic acid.

(iii) Write the structure of actual compound.

(iv) Give all reactions.

Sol. (i) The compound with molecular formula $C_9H_{10}O$ forms a 2,4-DNP derivative and reduces Tollen's reagent, so it is an aldehyde.

(ii) It undergoes Cannizzaro reaction, so the aldehyde group should be directly attached to the benzene ring.

(iii) On vigorous oxidation, it gives 1,2-benzene dicarboxylic acid, so it should be an *ortho* substituted benzaldehyde. For molecular formula $C_9H_{10}O$, the possibility is only **o-ethylbenzaldehyde.**

(iv) The equations for all the reactions are given below :

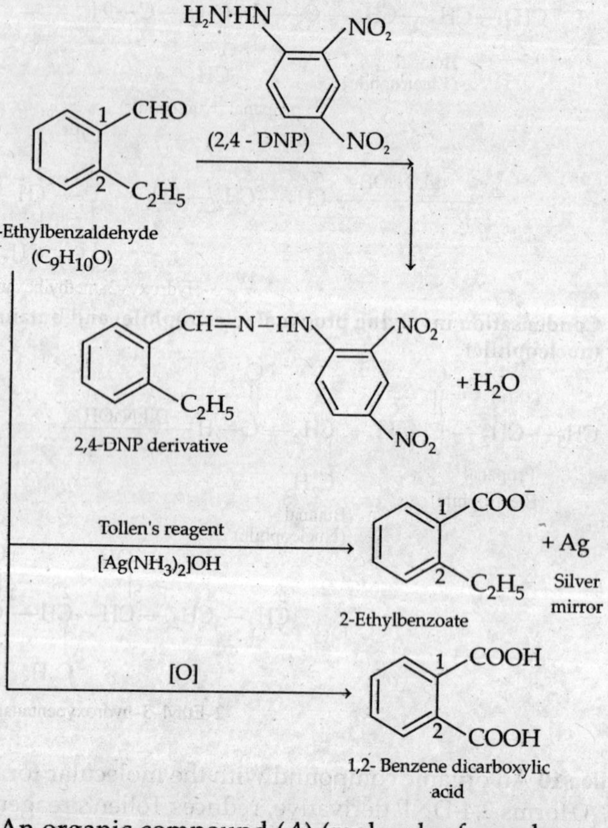

Question 11 An organic compound (A) (molecular formula ($C_8H_{16}O_2$)) was hydrolysed with dilute sulphuric acid to give a carboxylic acid (B) and alcohol (C). Oxidation of (C) with chromic acid produced (B). (C) on dehydration gives but-1-ene. Write equations for the reactions involved.

Thinking Process

(i) Ester produces a carboxylic acid and an alcohol on hydrolysis.

(ii) Ester (A) has 8 C-atoms, calculate the number of carbon atoms in acid and alcohol.

(iii) Guess the alcohol and the acid according to the given reactions.

(iv) Now guess the ester.

(v) Write all the related equations.

Sol. (i) Since, [*A*] produces carboxylic acid [*B*] and an alcohol [*C*] on hydrolylsis, compound [*A*] is an ester.

(ii) Alcohol [C] on oxidation produces acid [*B*]. It means both [*B*] and [C] have same number of carbon atoms, *i.e.*, four each.

(iii) [C] on dehydration produces but-1-ene. Also, [*B*] is produced on oxidation of [C]. These two facts shows that [C] is a primary alcohol [1°].

(v) The equations for all the above reactions are :

$$\underset{\text{Butylbutanoate}[A]}{CH_3CH_2CH_2—\overset{\overset{O}{\|}}{C}—OCH_2CH_2CH_2CH_3} \xrightarrow[\text{Hydrolysis}]{\text{Dil.}H_2SO_4}$$

$$\underset{\text{Butanoic acid }[B]}{CH_3CH_2CH_2—\overset{\overset{O}{\|}}{C}—OH} + \underset{\text{Butan-1-ol }[C]}{CH_3CH_2CH_2CH_2OH}$$

$$\underset{\substack{\text{Butan-1-ol}\\ [C]}}{CH_3CH_2CH_2CH_2OH} \xrightarrow[\substack{H_2CrO_4\\ \text{(oxidation)}}]{[O]} \underset{\substack{\text{Butanoic acid}\\ [B]}}{CH_3CH_2CH_2COOH}$$

$$\underset{[C]}{CH_3CH_2CH_2CH_2OH} \xrightarrow[\text{Dehydration }(-H_2O)]{\text{Conc. }H_2SO_4} \underset{\text{But-1-ene}}{CH_3CH_2CH = CH_2}$$

Question 12 Arrange the following compounds in increasing order of their property as indicated:

(i) Acetaldehyde, acetone, di-*tert*. butyl ketone, methyl *tert*. butyl ketone (reactivity towards HCN).

(ii) $CH_3CH_2CH(Br)COOH$, $CH_3CH(Br)CH_2COOH$, $(CH_3)_2CHCOOH$, $CH_3CH_2CH_2COOH$ {acid strength}.

(iii) Benzoic acid, 4-nitrobenzoic acid, 3,4-dinitro benzoic acid, 4-methoxybenzoic acid (acid strength).

Thinking Process

(i) Greater the steric hindrance, lesser the reactivity of carbonyl compound towards nucleophilic addition, *i. e.*, towards HCN.

(ii) Presence of electron withdrawing group (EWG) makes an acid more acidic. As the distance between EWG and —COOH increases, acidity decreases.

(iii) Same as (ii).

Sol. (i) The reactivity of a compound depends on the steric hindrance due to the groups present around the carbonyl group. Greater the steric hindrance, less will be the reactivity of the compound. **Reactivity towards HCN** is in following order. Di-tertiary butyl ketone < Methyl tertiary butyl ketone < Acetone < Acetaldehyde.

(ii) Alkyl group with $+I$ effect decreases the acidic strength whereas with $-I$ effect increases the acidic strength $-I$ effect decreases with distance.

Increasing order of acidic strength is :

$$(CH_3)_2CHCOOH < CH_3CH_2CH_2COOH$$
$$< CH_3CH(Br)CH_2COOH < CH_3CH_2CH(Br)COOH$$

In $(CH_3)_2CHCOOH$, there are —CH_3 groups on α-carbon, which increases the electron density by $+I$ effect on α-carbon. This provides hinderance for the release of H^+ from —COOH group.

(iii) Electron donating group (—OCH_3) decreases the acidic strength where as electron withdrawing group (—NO_2) increases the same.

Increasing order of acidic strength is

4-Methoxybenzoic acid < benzoic acid < 4-nitrobenzoic acid < 3,4-dinitrobenzoic acid.

Question 13 Give simple chemical tests to distinguish between the following pairs of compounds.

(i) Propanal and propanone (ii) Acetophenone and benzophenone
(iii) Phenol and benzoic acid (iv) Benzoic acid and ethyl benzoate
(v) Pentan-2-one and pentan-3-one
(vi) Benzaldehyde and acetophenone (vii) Ethanal and propanal

◎ *Thinking Process*

(i) Iodoform test (Given by CH_3CO—or $CH_3CH(OH)$ group containing compounds.)

(ii) Sodium bicarbonate test. (Given by —COOH group containing compounds.)

Sol. (i) **Propanal and propanone** Propanone responds to iodoform test whereas propanal (CH_3CH_2CHO) due to absence of CH_3CO— group does not.

$$\underset{\text{Propanone}}{\boxed{CH_3CO}CH_3} + \underset{\text{Sodium hypoiodite}}{3NaOI} \xrightarrow[\text{Heat}]{NaOH,\ I_2} \underset{\text{(yellow ppt.) Iodoform}}{CHI_3\downarrow} + \underset{\text{Sodium acetate}}{CH_3COONa} + 2NaOH$$

(ii) **Acetophenone and benzophenone** Acetophenone gives positive iodoform test whereas benzophenone ($C_6H_5COC_6H_5$) does not.

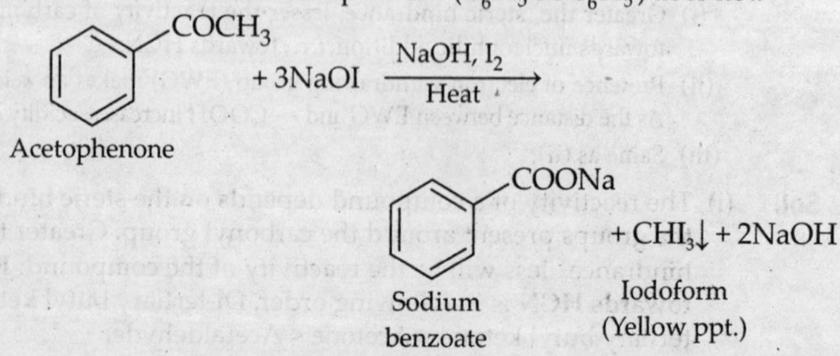

(iii) **Phenol and benzoic acid** Benzoic acid reacts with sodium bicarbonate to produce effervescence of carbon dioxide whereas phenol (C_6H_5OH) does not.

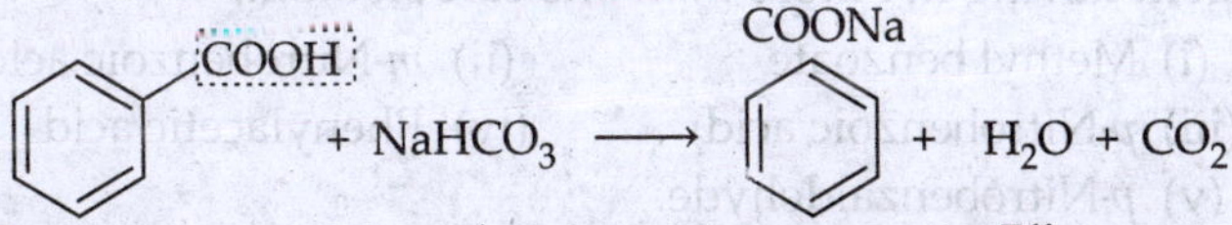

Benzoic acid   Sodium benzoate   Effervesence

(iv) **Benzoic acid and ethyl benzoate** Benzoic acid reacts with sodium bicarbonate to produce effervescence of carbon dioxide whereas ethyl benzoate (Ph-COO$-C_2H_5$) does not.

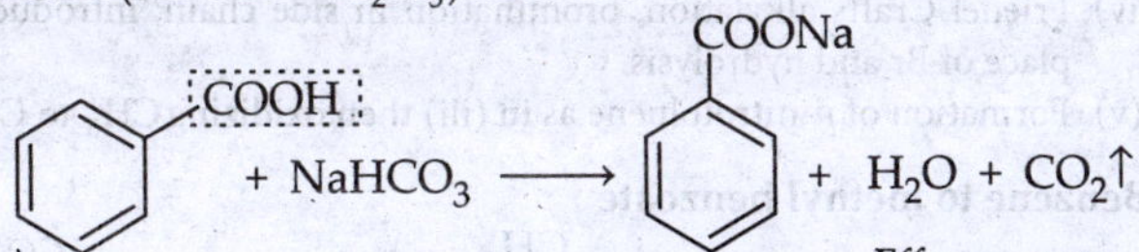

Benzoic acid   Sodium benzoate   Effervescence

(v) **Pentan-2-one and pentan-3-one** Pentan-2-one responds positively towards iodoform test whereas pentan-3-one ($C_2H_5COC_2H_5$) does not.

$$\underset{\text{Pentan-2-one}}{\overset{1}{CH_3}-\overset{2}{CO}-\overset{3}{CH_2}-\overset{4}{CH_2}-\overset{5}{CH_3}} + 3NaOI \xrightarrow[\text{Heat}]{NaOH,\ I_2} \underset{\text{Yellow ppt.}}{CHI_3\downarrow} + CH_3CH_2CH_2COONa + 2NaOH$$

(vi) **Benzaldehyde and acetophenone** Acetophenone responds towards iodoform test positively whereas benzaldehyde (C_6H_5CHO) does not.

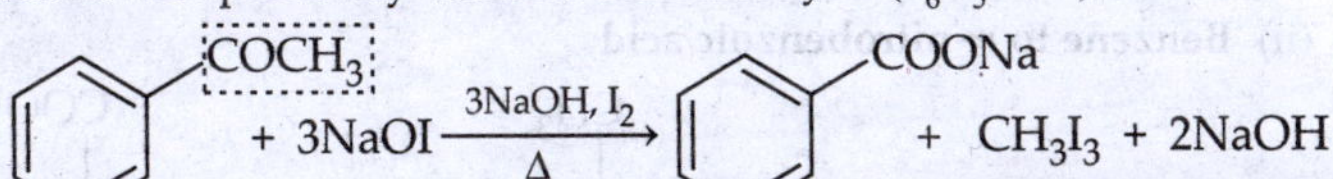

Benzoic acid   Sodium benzoate   Iodoform (yellow ppt.)

(vii) **Ethanal and propanal** Ethanal responds positively towards iodoform test whereas propanal (CH_3CH_2CHO) does not.

$$\underset{\text{Ethanal}}{CH_3CHO} + 3NaOI \xrightarrow[\text{Heat}]{I_2/NaOH} \underset{\substack{\text{Yellow ppt.}\\ \text{(Iodoform)}}}{CHI_3\downarrow} + HCOONa + 2NaOH$$

Mistake Alert Only those aldehydes and ketones respond towards iodoform test positively which have at least one methyl group attached to the carbonyl carbon atom.

Question 14 How will you prepare the following compounds from benzene? You may use any inorganic reagent and any organic reagent having not more than one carbon atom.

(i) Methyl benzoate (ii) *m*-Nitrobenzoic acid
(iii) *p*-Nitrobenzoic acid (iv) Phenylacetic acid
(v) *p*-Nitrobenzaldehyde.

◎ ***Thinking Process*** The given conversions involve the following processes

(i) Friedel Crafts alkylation, oxidation, esterification.

(ii) Introducing —COOH as in (i) then nitration.

(iii) Friedel Crafts alkylation ; then nitration; $CH_3 \xrightarrow{\text{Oxidation}} COOH$

(iv) Friedel Crafts alkylation, bromination in side chain, introducing CN in place of Br and hydrolysis.

(v) Formation of *p*-nitrotoluene as in (iii) then oxidizing CH_3 to CHO.

Sol. (i) **Benzene to methyl benzoate**

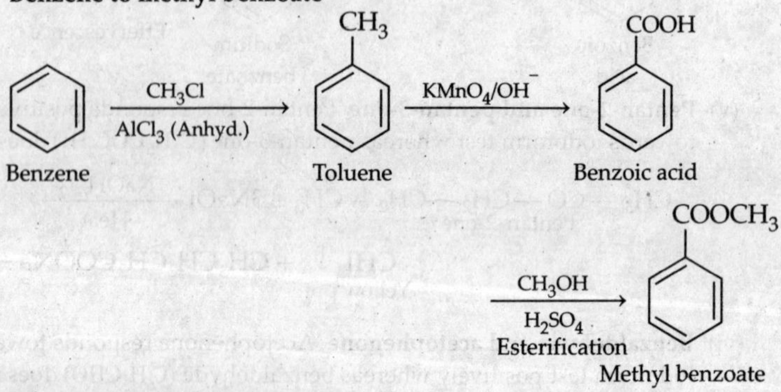

(ii) **Benzene to *m*-nitrobenzoic acid**

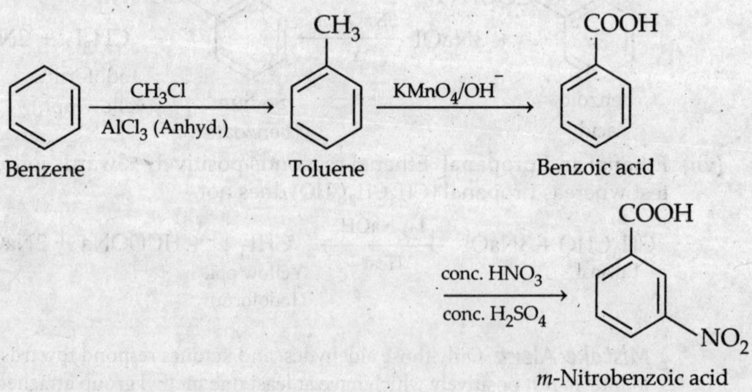

(iii) **Benzene to *p*-Nitrobenzoic acid**

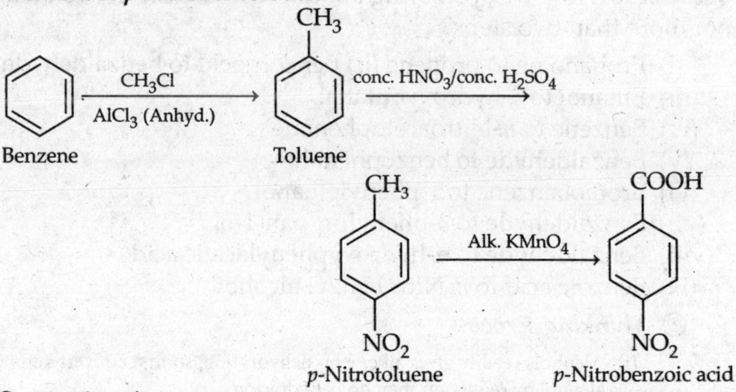

Mistake Alert Before oxidising —CH_3 to —COOH, first do nitration as —COOH is meta directing, but we need —NO_2 at para position in the question (—CH_3 is o-/p-directions).

(iv) **Benzene to phenylacetic acid**

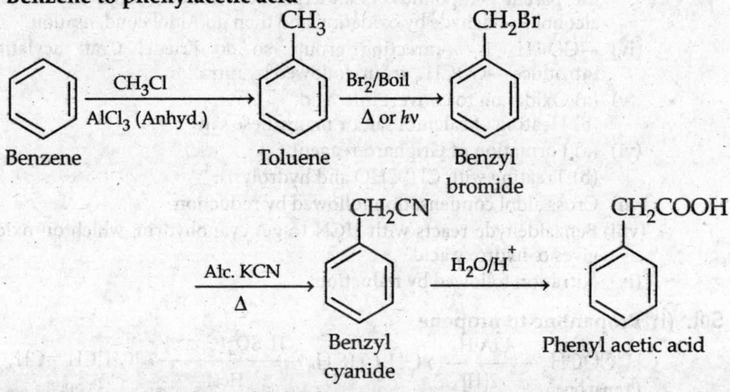

(v) **Benzene to *p*-nitrobenzaldehyde**

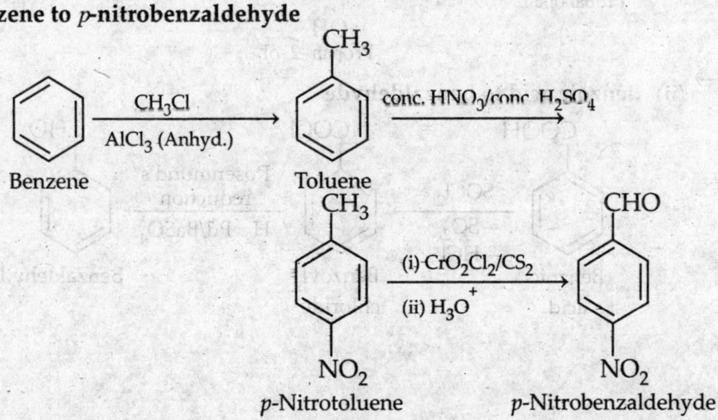

Question 15 How will you bring about the following conversion in not more than two steps?

(i) Propano ne to propene (ii) Benzoic acid to benzaldehyde
(iii) Ethanol to 3-hydroxybutanal
(iv) Benzene to *m*-Nitroacetophenone
(v) Benzaldehyde to benzophenone
(vi) Bromobenzene to 1-phenylethanol
(vii) Benzaldehyde to 3-phenylpropan-1-ol
(viii) Benzaldehyde to α-hydroxyphenylacetic acid
(ix) Benzoic acid to *m*-Nitrobenzyl alcohol

Thinking Process

(i) Alcohols readily gives alkene on dehydration, so first convert ketone into alcohol by reduction then do dehydration.
(ii) Benzaldehyde is easily obtained from benzoyl chloride so convert benzoic acid into benzoyl chloride and then do Rosenmund's reduction.
(iii) Carbonyl compounds gives a compound having double carbon atoms than the parent compounds, if undergo aldol condensation, so first convert alcohol to aldehyde by oxidation and then do Aldol condensation.
(iv) $-COCH_3$ is *m*-directing group, so do Friedel Craft acylation to introduce $-COCH_3$ group followed by nitration.
(v) (a) Oxidation to convert into acid.
(b) Heating of calcium salt or manganese salt.
(vi) (a) Formation of Grignard reagent.
(b) Treating with CH_3CHO and hydrolysis.
(vii) Cross aldol condensation followed by reduction.
(viii) Benzaldehyde reacts with HCN to get cyanohydrin, which on oxidation gives α-hydroxy acid.
(ix) Nitration followed by reduction.

Sol. (i) **Propanone to propene**

$$\underset{\text{Propanone}}{CH_3COCH_3} \xrightarrow[2[H]]{LiAlH_4} \underset{\text{Propan-2-ol}}{CH_3\underset{|}{C}HCH_3 \atop \quad OH} \xrightarrow[\text{Heat}]{H_2SO_4(\text{Conc.})} \underset{\text{Propene}}{CH_3CH{=}CH_3}$$

(ii) **Benzoic acid to benzaldehyde**

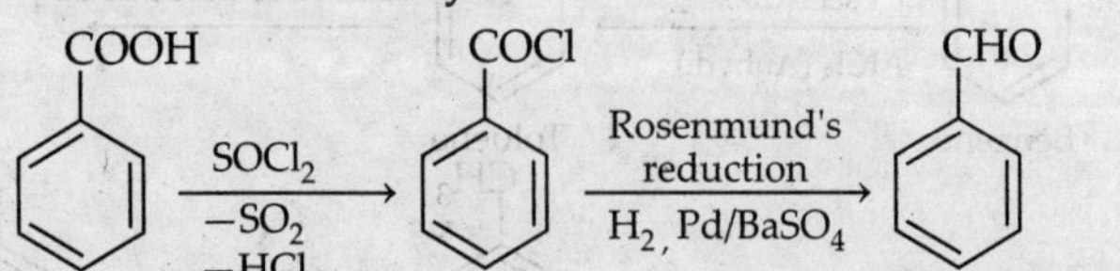

Benzoic acid — Benzoyl chloride — Benzaldehyde

(iii) **Ethanol to 3-hydroxybutanal**

$$CH_3CH_2OH \xrightarrow[\text{CrO}_3 \text{ in anhy. medium or KMnO}_4/\text{dil } H_2SO_4]{\text{Oxidation}} \underset{\text{Ethanal}}{CH_3CHO}$$

$$\xrightarrow[\text{condensation dil. NaOH warm}]{\text{Aldol}} \underset{\text{3-Hydroxybutanal}}{CH_3\underset{\mid \atop OH}{CH}CH_2CHO}$$

(iv) **Benzene to *m*-Nitroacetophenone**

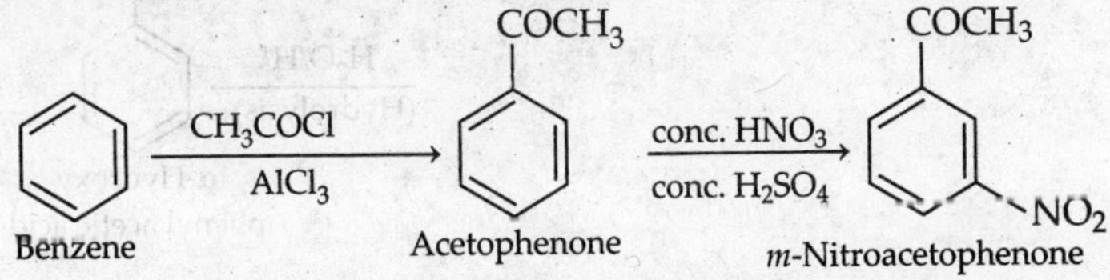

(v) **Benzaldehyde to benzophenone**

$$\underset{\text{Benzaldehyde}}{C_6H_5CHO} \xrightarrow[\text{KMnO}_4]{\text{Oxidation}} \underset{\text{Benzoic acid}}{C_6H_5COOH} \xrightarrow[\text{Heat}]{\text{Ca(OH)}_2 \text{or Mno}} \underset{\text{Benzophenone}}{C_6H_5COC_6H_5}$$

(vi) **Bromobenzene to 1-phenylethanol**

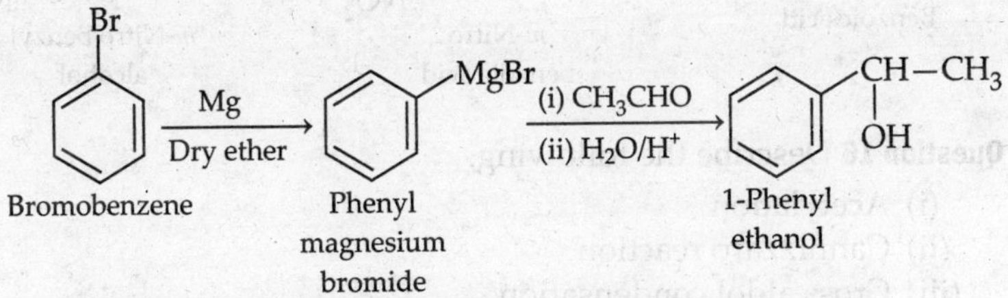

(vii) **Benzaldehyde to 3-phenylpropan-1-ol**

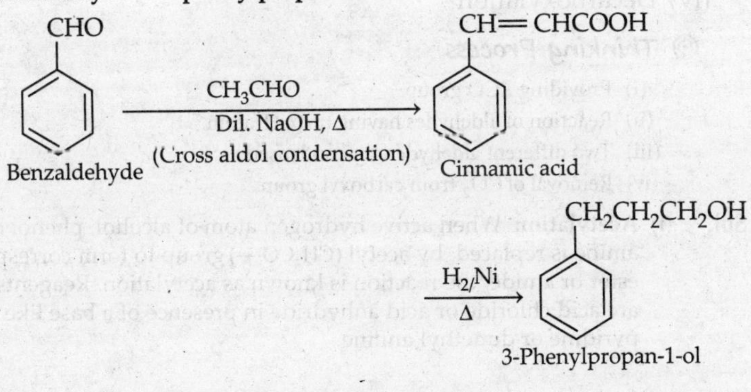

(viii) **Benzaldehyde to α-hydroxyphenyl acetic acid**

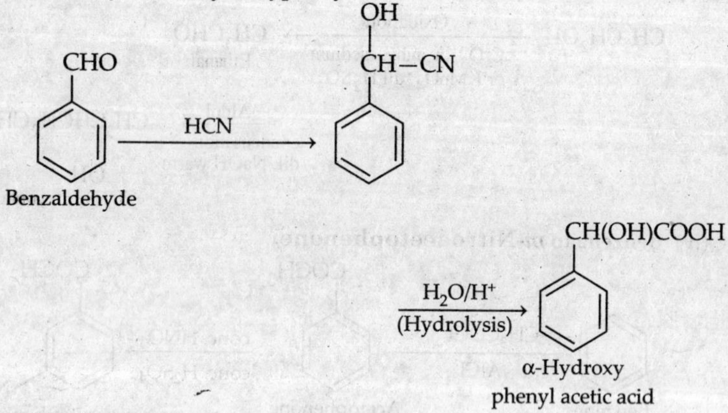

(ix) **Benzoic acid to *m*-nitrobenzyl alcohol**

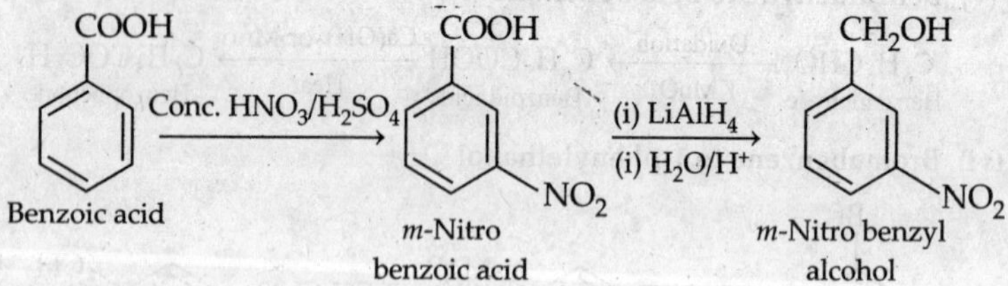

Question 16 Describe the following.

(i) Acetylation
(ii) Cannizzaro reaction
(iii) Cross aldol condensation
(iv) Decarboxylation

◎ *Thinking Process*

(i) Providing *R*CO group.
(ii) Reaction of aldehydes having no α-H-atom.
(iii) Two different aldehydes are condensed.
(iv) Removal of CO_2 from carboxyl group.

Sol. (i) **Acetylation** When active hydrogen atom of alcohol, phenol or an amine is replaced by acetyl (CH_3CO—) group to form corresponding ester or amide, the reaction is known as acetylation. Reagents used are acid chloride or acid anhydride in presence of a base like pyridine or dimethyl aniline.

For example :

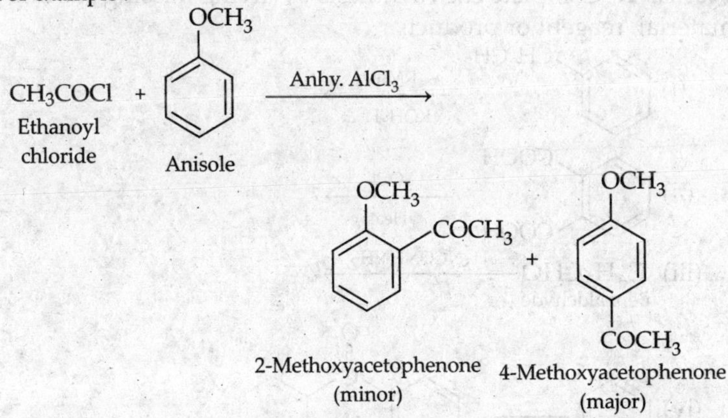

(ii) **Cannizzaro reaction** Aldehydes which do not have any α-hydrogen atom, undergo self oxidation and reduction (disproportionation) reaction on treating with concentrated alkali. This reaction is called Cannizzaro reaction. As a result, one molecule of aldehyde is reduced to alcohol while another is oxidized to carboxylic acid salt. For example :

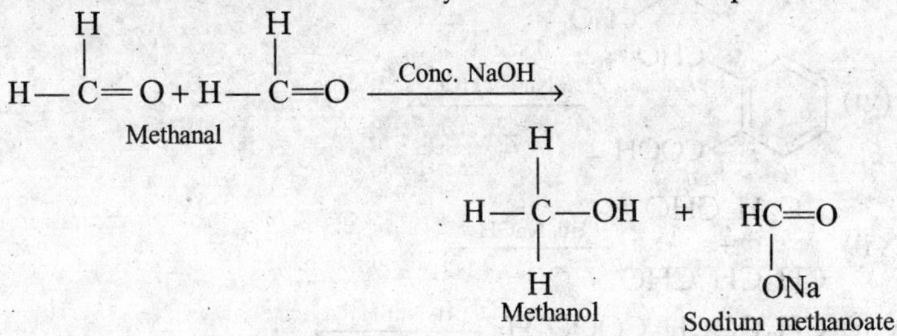

(iii) **Cross aldol condensation** When aldol condensation is carried out between two different aldehydes and or ketones, it is called cross aldol condensation. If both the reactants contain α-hydrogen atoms, it gives a mixture of four products.

For example :

Please consult solution of Q. 9.

(iv) **Decarboxylation** Carboxylic acids lose carbon dioxide molecule to produce hydrocarbons on heating their sodium salts with sodalime (a mixture of NaOH and CaO in ratio 3 : 1). This reaction is called decarboxylation.

For example :

$$\underset{\text{Sodium ethanoate}}{CH_3COONa} + \underset{\text{Sodium hydroxide}}{NaOH} \xrightarrow[\text{Heat}]{CaO} \underset{\text{Methane}}{CH_4} + \underset{\text{Sodium carbonate}}{Na_2CO_3}$$

Question 17 Complete each synthesis by giving missing starting material, reagent or products.

(i) 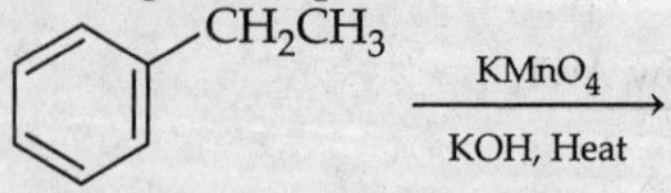

(ii) 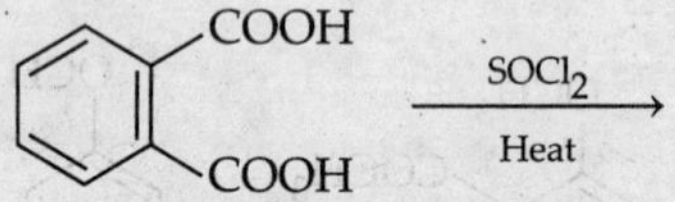

(iii) $C_6H_5CHO \xrightarrow{H_2NCONHNH_2}$
Benzaldehyde

(iv) 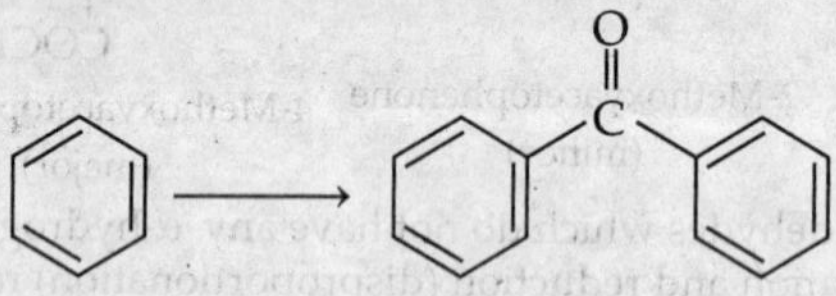

(v) 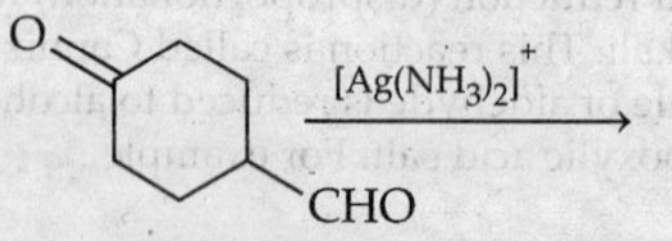

(vi) 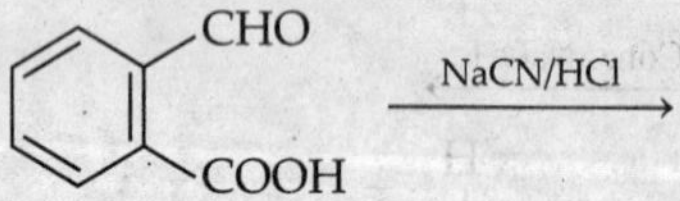

(vii) $C_6H_5CHO + CH_3CH_2CHO \xrightarrow{\text{dil. NaOH}}$

(viii) $CH_3COCH_2COOC_2H_5 \xrightarrow[\text{(ii) } H^+]{\text{(i) } NaBH_4}$

(ix) 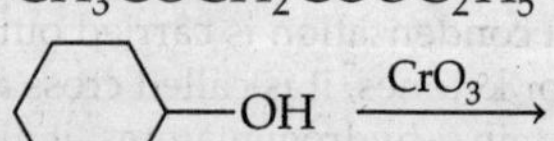

(x) 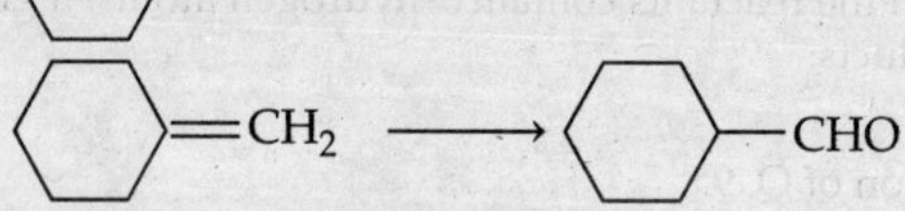

(xi) 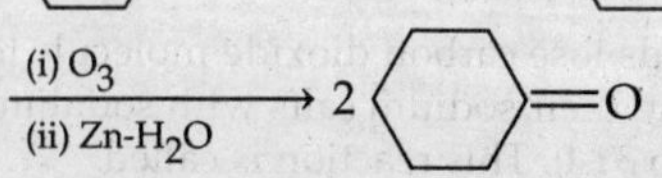

◎ Thinking Process

(i) Oxidation, *i.e.,* conversion of alkyl chain directly attached to benzene nucleus into —COOK group.

(ii) Chlorination, *i.e.,* conversion of —OH into —Cl.

(iii) Addition elimination reaction, *i.e.,* removal of H_2O from carbonyl and amine group.

(iv) Friedel Crafts reaction, *i.e.,* reaction with *R*COCl in the presence of anhy. $AlCl_3$.

(v) Oxidation of —CHO into —COOH.
(vi) Formation of cyanohydrin, *i.e.*, nucleophilic addition of HCN to —CHO group.
(vii) Claisen-Schmidt condensation.
(viii) Selective reduction of ketone group into alcohol.
(ix) Oxidation of alcohol into ketone.
(x) Formation of alcohol by hydroboration followed by its conversion to aldehyde.
(xi) Oxidation, (ozonolysis)

Sol.

(i) 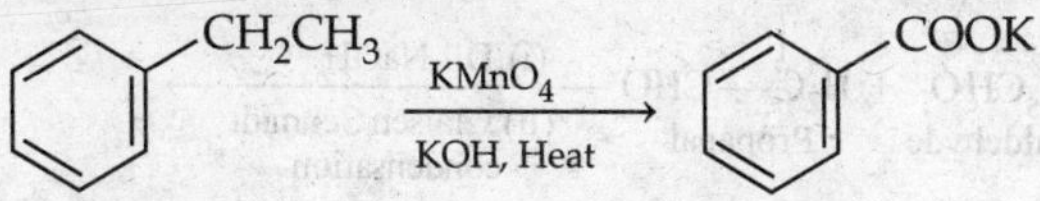

Ethyl benzene → Potassium benzoate

(ii) 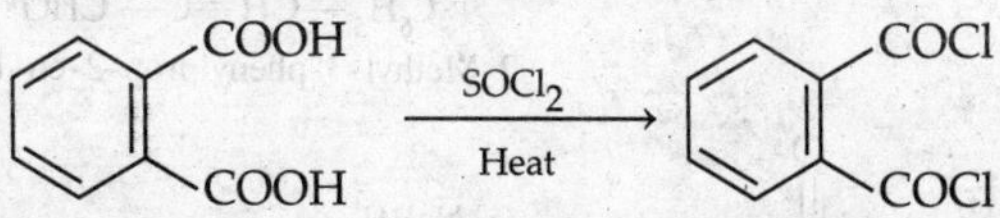

Phthalic acid → Phthaloyl chloride

(iii) $C_6H_5CH\,O + H_2\,NNHCONH_2 \longrightarrow$
Benzaldehyde Semicarbazide

$$C_6H_5CH{=}N{-}NH{-}\overset{\displaystyle O}{\overset{\|}{C}}{-}NH_2 + H_2O$$
Benzaldehyde semicarbazone

(iv) 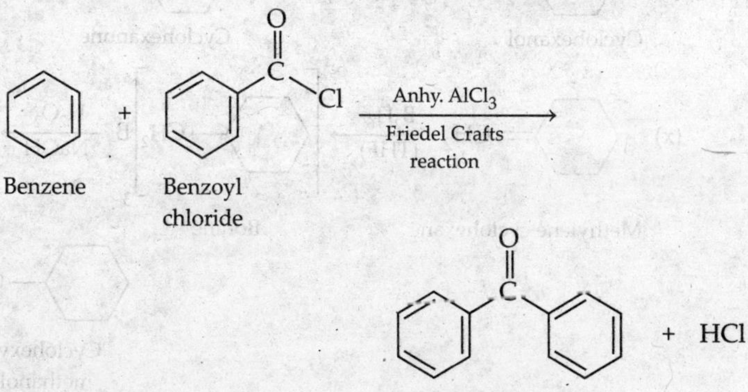

Benzophenone

(v) 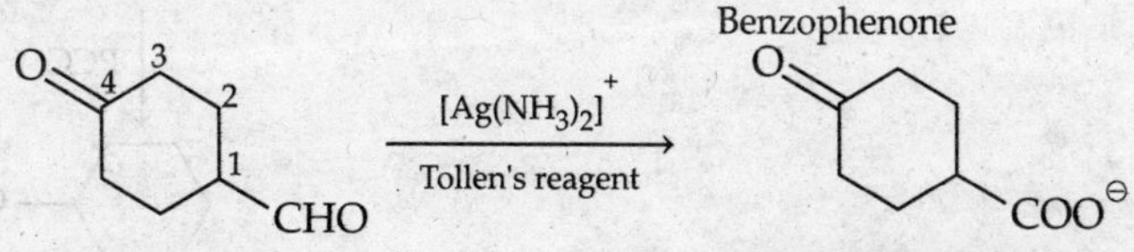

4-Oxo-cyclohexane carbaldehyde → 4-Oxo-cyclohexane carboxylate anion

(vi) 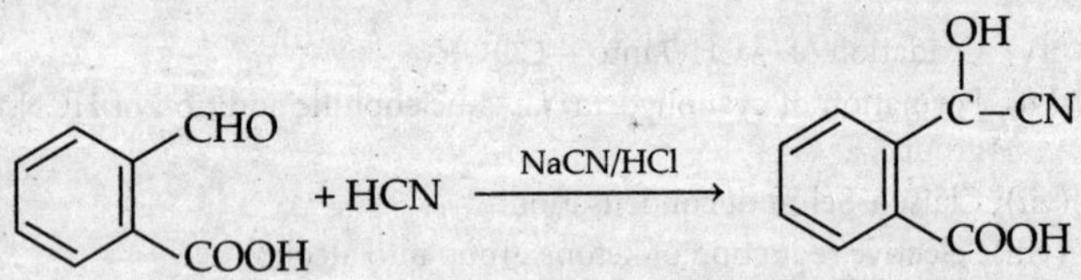

2-formyl benzoic acid → 2-[1-hydroxycyano methyl] benzoic acid

(vii)

$$\underset{\text{Benzaldehyde}}{C_6H_5CHO} + \underset{\text{Propanal}}{H_2\overset{\overset{CH_3}{|}}{C}-CHO} \xrightarrow[\text{(ii) Claisen Schmidt condensation}]{\text{(i) Dil·NaOH}} \overset{3}{C_6H_5-CH}=\overset{\overset{CH_3}{|}}{\overset{2}{C}}-\overset{1}{CHO}$$

2-Methyl-3-phenylprop-2-en-1-al

(viii)

$$\overset{4}{CH_3}-\overset{\overset{O}{\|}}{\overset{3}{C}}-\overset{2}{CH_2}-\overset{\overset{O}{\|}}{\overset{1}{C}}-O-C_2H_5 \xrightarrow[\text{(ii) } H^+]{\text{(i) } NaBH_4} \overset{4}{CH_3}-\overset{\overset{OH}{|}}{\overset{3}{CH}}-\overset{2}{CH_2}-\overset{\overset{O}{\|}}{\overset{1}{C}}-O-C_2H_5$$

Ethyl-3-oxo-butanoate → Ethyl-3-hydroxylbutanoate

(ix) 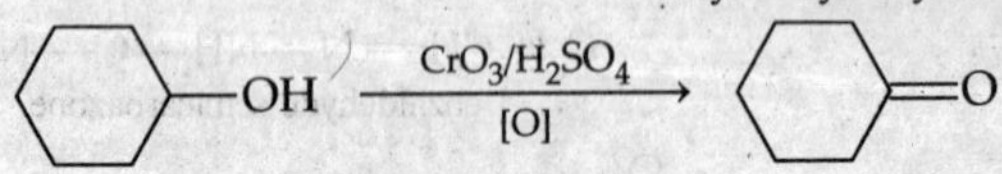

Cyclohexanol → Cyclohexanone

(x) 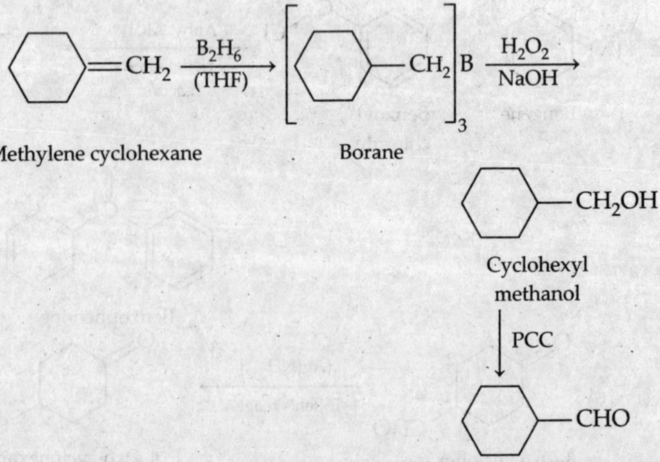

Methylene cyclohexane → Borane → Cyclohexyl methanol → Cyclohexane carbaldehyde

(xi) 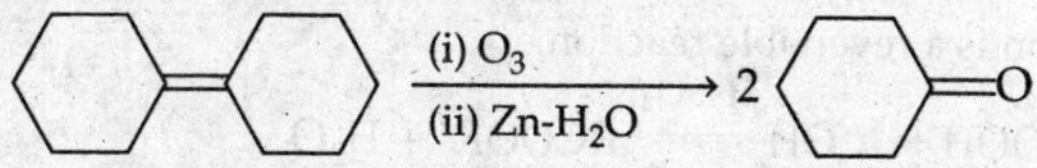

Cyclohexylidene cyclohexane → Cyclohexanone

Mistake Alert Only keto ($>C=O$) group is reduced to alcohol (—OH), not ester (—COO—), when treated with $NaBH_4$ reducing agent.

Question 18 Give plausible explanation for each of the following :

(i) Cyclohexanone forms cyanohydrin in good yield but 2,2,6-trimethylcyclohexanone does not.

(ii) There are two $—NH_2$ groups in semicarbazide. However, only one is involved in the formation of semicarbazones.

(iii) During the preparation of esters from a carboxylic acid and an alcohol in the presence of an acid catalyst, the water or the ester should be removed as soon as it is formed.

Thinking Process

(i) $+I$ effect due to methyl groups: steric hindrance, makes a carbonyl compound less reactive.

(ii) Lone pair of electrons involved in conjugation with CO.

(iii) Consider the reversible nature of the reaction.

Sol. (i)

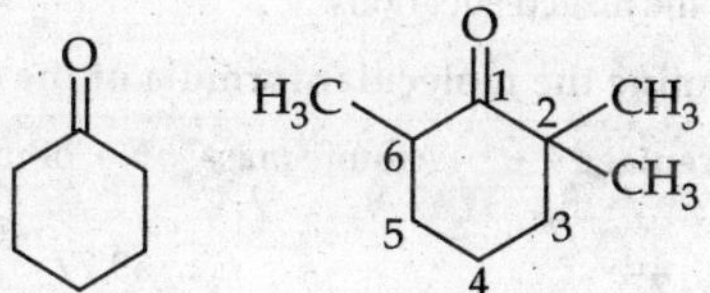

Cyclohexanone 2,2,6-Trimethyl cyclohexanone

In 2,2,6 trimethylcyclohexanone, three methyl groups are presents at α-position with respect to the ketonic ($>C=O$) group. Therefore, these groups cause steric hindrance during the nucleophilic attack of CN^- ion so cyanohydrin is not formed. Due to the absence of methyl groups in cyclohexanone, there is no steric hindrance and cyanohydrin is formed.

(ii) **Resonance in semicarbazide**

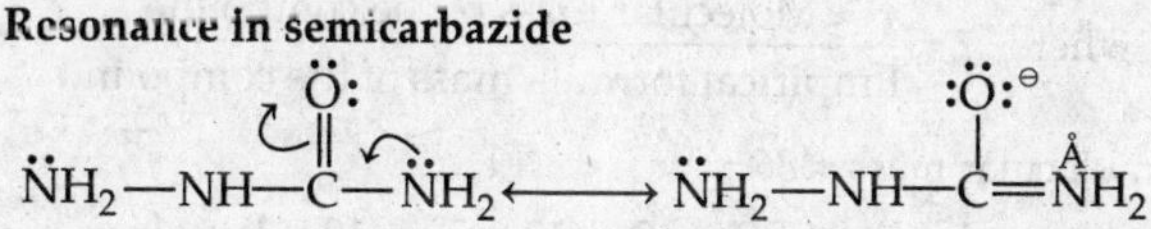

Semicarbazide has two amino (NH_2) groups, out of which one is involved in resonance as shown above. Electron-density on this NH_2 decreases and it does not act as a nucleophile. But the other NH_2 group (attached to NH) has lone pair of electrons which are not involved in resonance. So, this pair is available for the nucleophilic attack on carbonyl group ($>C=O$) of aldehydes and/or ketones.

(iii) Esterification is a reversible reaction.

$$RCOOH + R'OH \underset{}{\overset{H_2SO_4}{\rightleftharpoons}} \underset{\text{Ester}}{RCOOR'} + H_2O$$

When the sufficient amount of products is formed, the rate of forward reaction decreases and the reverse reaction begins. To avoid this condition *i.e.*, in order to shift the equilibrium in forward direction, the concentration of products (ester and/or water) should be decreased. (Le-Chatelier's principle). So, water or ester should be removed from time to time.

Question 19 An organic compound contains 69.77% carbon, 11.63% hydrogen and rest oxygen. The molecular mass of the compound is 86. It does not reduce Tollen's reagent but forms an addition compound with sodium hydrogen sulphite and give positive iodoform test. On vigorous oxidation it gives ethanoic and propanoic acid. Write the possible structure of the compound.

Thinking Process

(i) Derive empirical and molecular formula by first finding moles. $\left(\text{as moles} = \dfrac{\text{Percentage mass}}{\text{Atomic mass}}\right)$

(ii) According to the given chemical reactions, derive the structural formula.

(ii) Write all the related equations.

Sol. Step I To determine the molecular formula of the compound.

Element	Percentage	Atomic mass	No. of moles	Simplest molar ratio
C	69.77	12	$\frac{69.77}{12} = 5.81$	$\frac{5.81}{1.16} = 5$
H	11.63	1	$\frac{11.63}{1} = 11.63$	$\frac{11.63}{1.16} = 10$
O	(100 − 69.77 − 11.63) = 18.60	16	$\frac{18.60}{16} = 1.16$	$\frac{1.16}{1.16} = 1$

Empirical formula of the given organic compound = $C_5H_{10}O$.

Molecular formula = $n \times$ (empirical formula)

$$\text{where, } n = \frac{\text{Molecular mass of the compound}}{\text{Empirical formula mass of the compound}}$$

Given, molecular mass = 86

Empirical formula mass of $C_5H_{10}O = (12 \times 5) + (10 \times 1) + (16)$

$$= 60 + 10 + 16 = 86$$

$$\therefore \quad n = \frac{86}{86} = 1$$

$$\text{Molecular formula} = 1 \times C_5H_{10}O = C_5H_{10}O$$

Step II Predicting the structure of the compound.

Criteria 1. Formation of addition compound with $NaHSO_3$ depicts the presence of aldehyde or ketone.

2. The given compound does not reduce Tollen's reagent but gives positive iodoform test, so it is a methyl ketone.

3. On oxidation, the compound forms a mixture of ethanoic and propanoic acid, so it is

$$\overset{1}{C}H_3-\overset{2}{\underset{\|}{\overset{O}{C}}}-\overset{3}{C}H_2-\overset{4}{C}H_2-\overset{5}{C}H_3.$$

Pentan-2-one

Step III Chemical equations :

1. $$\overset{1}{C}H_3-\overset{2}{\underset{\|}{\overset{O}{C}}}-\overset{3}{C}H_2-\overset{4}{C}H_2-\overset{5}{C}H_3 + NaHSO_3 \longrightarrow CH_3-\underset{SO_3^-Na^+}{\overset{OH}{C}}-CH_2-CH_2-CH_3$$

Sodium bisulphite addition product

2. $$\overset{1}{C}H_3-\overset{2}{\underset{\|}{\overset{O}{C}}}-\overset{3}{C}H_2-\overset{4}{C}H_2-\overset{5}{C}H_3 + 3I_2 + 4NaOH \xrightarrow[\text{reaction}]{\text{Iodoform}} \underset{\text{Iodoform (yellow ppt.)}}{CHI_3}\downarrow + CH_3-CH_2-CH_2-COONa + 3NaI + 3H_2O$$

3. $$\underset{\text{Pentan-2-one}}{\overset{1}{C}H_3-\overset{2}{\underset{\|}{\overset{O}{C}}}-\overset{3}{C}H_2-\overset{4}{C}H_2-\overset{5}{C}H_3} \xrightarrow[H_2SO_4]{K_2Cr_2O_7} \underset{\text{Ethanoic acid}}{CH_3COOH} + \underset{\text{Propanoic acid}}{CH_3-CH_2-COOH}$$

Question 20 Although phenoxide ion has more number of resonating structures than carboxylate ion, carboxylic acid is a stronger acid than phenol. Why?

Thinking Process Comparative effectiveness of delocalisation of negative charge is responsible for the acidic strength. A resonating structure having negative charge on more electronegative atom, is more stable.

Sol. 1. Phenoxide ion has non-equivalent resonance structures in which the negative charge is at the less electronegative carbon atom.

2. The negative charge is delocalised over two electronegative oxygen atoms in carboxylate ion whereas in phenoxide ion the negative charge less effectively delocalised over one oxygen atom and less electronegative carbon atoms.

- Phenoxide ion has the following resonating structures:

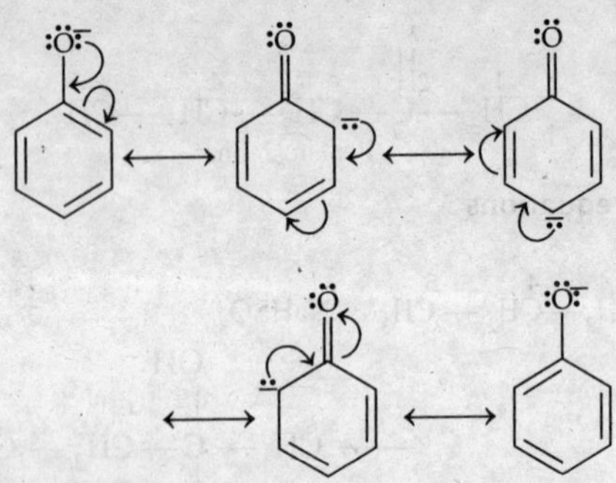

- Carboxylate ion has the following resonating structure

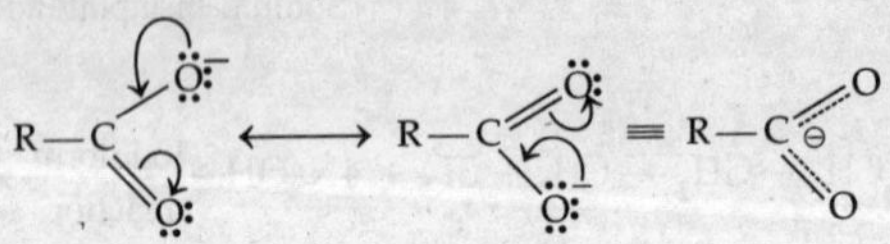

DIKSHA APP Questions

☐ Multiple Choice Questions

Q.1 Industrial uses of methanoic acid, are:

(a) as food preservative.

(b) as solvent.

(c) in rubber, textile, leather and electroplating industries.

(d) manufacturing of soaps and detergents.

Sol. (c) Formic acid (methanoic acid) is used in rubber, textile, leather and electroplating industries.

Q.2 Carboxylic acids do not undergo Friedel crafts reaction because

(a) COOH group is *meta* directing.

(b) COOH group is resonance stabilised.

(c) carboxyl group is deactivating and gets bonded to Friedal craft catalyst.

(d) All of the above

Sol. (c) Carboxylic acids do not undergo Friedel-Crafts reactions because they contain a strong electron-withdrawing group (the carboxyl group, —COOH), which deactivates the aromatic ring.

This deactivation prevents the ring from reacting with electrophiles, which are necessary for Friedel-Crafts alkylation or acylation reactions. Additionally, carboxylic acids can react with the Lewis acids typically used in Friedel-Crafts reactions.

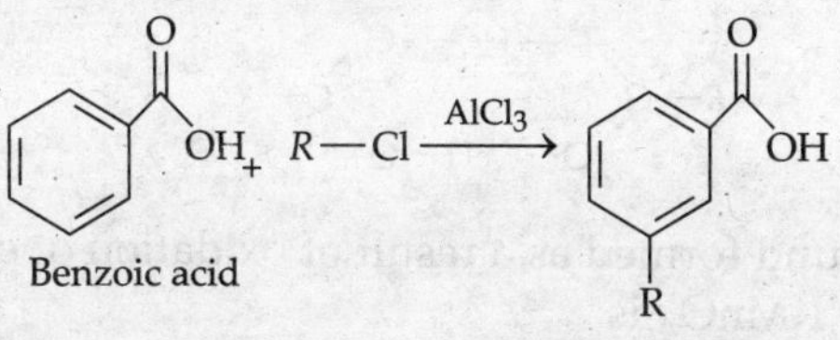

Q.3 Which of the following acid is the strongest?

(a) CH_3COOH (b) $CH_2ClCOOH$

(c) $CHCl_2COOH$ (d) CCl_3COOH

Sol. (d) CCl_3COOH is the strongest acid because the three chlorine atoms withdraw electron density through their high electronegativity. This stabilizes the negative charge on the conjugate base (CCl_3COO^-), making it easier for the acid to donate a proton (H^+).

Q.4 Which of the following has highest boiling point?

(a) CH_3COCl (b) $(CH_3CO)_2O$

(c) CH_3COOH (d) CH_3CHO

Sol. (c) Carboxylic acids have the highest boiling points among organic compounds due to their ability to form strong hydrogen bonds and dimers. In the liquid phase, carboxylic acids often form dimers through hydrogen bonding between two carboxyl groups, significantly increasing the boiling point as compared to compounds that only exhibit weaker intermolecular interactions.

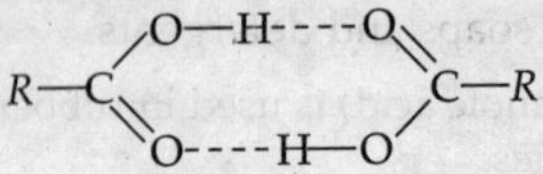

Q.5 Carboxylic acids have higher boiling point than aldehydes, ketones and even alcohols of comparable molecular mass. It is due to their

(a) formation of intramolecular hydrogen bonding.

(b) formation of carboxylate ion.

(c) more extensive association of carboxylic acid *via* vander Waal's force of attraction.

(d) Formation of intermolecular hydrogen bonding.

Sol. (a) Carboxylic acids have the highest boiling points among organic compounds due to their ability to form strong hydrogen bonds and dimers. In the liquid phase, carboxylic acids often form dimers through intermolecular hydrogen bonding between two carboxyl groups, thus significantly increasing the boiling point.

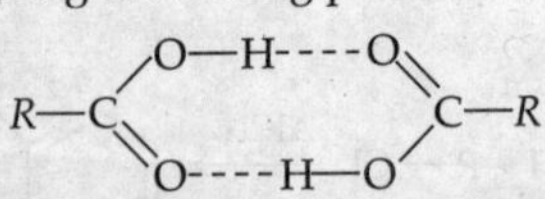

Q.6 The compound formed as a result of oxidation of ethyl benzene by $KMnO_4$ is

(a) benzyl Alcohol (b) acetophenone

(c) benzophenone (d) benzoic Acid

Sol. (d) Oxidation of ethyl benzene by $KMnO_4$ gives benzoic acid.

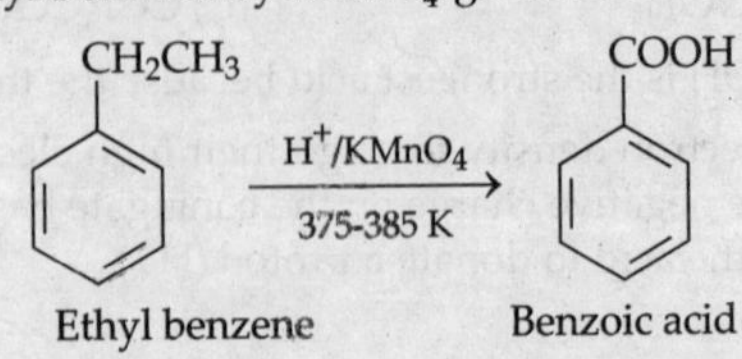

Q.7 What is the IUPAC name of

$$CH_3-\underset{\displaystyle OH}{\underset{|}{CH}}-CH_2-\underset{\displaystyle COOH}{\underset{|}{CH}}-CH_3$$

(a) 4-hydroxy-1-methylpentanoic acid
(b) 4-hydroxy-2-methylpentanoic acid
(c) 2-hydroxy-4-methylpentanoic acid
(d) 2-hydroxy-2-methylpentanoic acid

Sol. (b) The IUPAC name of the given compound is 4-hydroxy-2-methylpentanoic acid.

Q.8 The carboxylic acid group does not give the usual addition and elimination reactions of aldehydes and ketones because

(a) O—H bond is more polar than C=O group.
(b) COOH group gets ionised.
(c) carboxylate ion gets stabilised by resonance.
(d) COOH group does not contain carbonyl group.

Sol. (c) Carboxylic acids do not undergo the typical addition and elimination reactions of aldehydes and ketones because the carboxylate ion is resonance stabilised. Due to this resonance, the negative charge is delocalized over both the carbonyl oxygen and the hydroxyl group. This reduces the reactivity of the carbonyl carbon in the carboxylic acid making it less prone to undergo typical addition and elimination reactions.

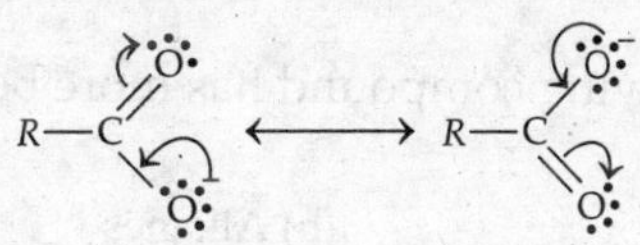

Q.9 Formaldehyde is used

(a) as antiseptic and germicide.
(b) for making synthetic plastic and resins.
(c) for the preservation or biological specimens.
(d) All of the above.

Sol. (d) Formaldehyde is used as an antiseptic and germicide. It is used for making synthetic plastic and resins. It is also used for the preservation of biological specimens.

Q.10 Which of the following is most reactive towards nucleophilic addition reactions?

(a) CH_3COCH_3 (b) CH_3CHO
(c) $CH_3COC_2H_5$ (d) HCHO

Sol. (d) Aldehydes are more reactive than ketones toward nucleophiles because they have only one alkyl group, which results in less steric hindrance compared to ketones, which have two alkyl groups. Additionally, the two alkyl groups in ketones reduces the electrophilicity of carbonyl carbon due to their $+I$ effect.
Consequently, formaldehyde is least sterically hindered and has more electrophilic carbonyl carbon, so it is most reactive towards nucleophilic addition reactions.

Q.11 Aldehydes and Ketones form hydrocarbon by?

(a) Clemmensen reduction
(b) Cannizzaro reaction
(c) Rosenmund's reduction
(d) Aldol Condensation

Sol. (a) When carbonyl group of aldehydes or ketones is reduced to a CH_2 group on treatment with zinc amalgam and concentrated hydrochloric acid then the reaction is called as Clemmensen reduction.

$$>C=O \xrightarrow[\text{HCl}]{\text{Zn-Hg}} >CH_2 + H_2O$$

Q.12 Which of the following compound has more boiling point than ketones?

(a) Alcohol (b) Alkanes
(c) Aldehydes (d) Ether

Sol. (a) Alcohols have a higher boiling point than ketones because there is inter-molecular hydrogen bonding present between the alcohol molecules. Whereas, ketones have weaker dipole-dipole interactions between molecules.

Q.13 Which of the following aldehyde is present as gas?

(a) Acetaldehyde
(b) Formaldehyde
(c) Butyraldehyde
(d) Benzaldehyde

Sol. (b) Formaldehyde (HCHO) is the aldehyde that is commonly found as a gas at room temperature.

Q.14 Which of the following reagents can be used to prepare a ketone from acid chloride?

(a) $LiAlH_4$
(b) Grignard Reagent
(c) Dimethyl cadmium
(d) Cadmium chloride

Sol. (c) Treatment of acyl chloride with dialkylcadmium, prepared by the reaction of cadmium chloride with Grignard reagent, gives ketones.

$$2R—Mg—X + CdCl_2 \longrightarrow R_2Cd + 2Mg(X)Cl$$

$$2R'—\underset{\underset{O}{\|}}{C}—Cl + R_2Cd \longrightarrow 2R'—\underset{\underset{O}{\|}}{C}—R + CdCl_2$$

Q.15 In the equation $CH_3COCl \xrightarrow[BaSO_4]{H_2/Pd} X$; X is

(a) Acetaldehyde
(b) Propionaldehyde
(c) Acetone
(d) Acetic Acid

Sol. (a) This reaction is Rosenmund reduction and it gives acetaldehyde as the product (X).

Q.16 In the carbonyl group, the carbon atom undergoes

(a) sp hybridisation
(b) sp^2 hybridisation
(c) sp^3 hybridisation
(d) sp^3d hybridisation

Sol. (b) In carbonyl group, carbon atom in sp^2 hybridised. This hybridization involves three sp^2 orbitals forming sigma bonds with the oxygen and any other substituents, while the remaining p orbital on the carbon overlaps with a p orbital on the oxygen to form the pi-bond, resulting in the carbonyl double bond.

Q.17 The IUPAC name of

$$CH_3—\underset{\underset{Cl}{|}}{CH}—\underset{\underset{CH_3}{|}}{CH}—CHO$$

(a) 3-chloro-2-methylbutanal
(b) 2-chloro-3-methylbutanal
(c) 2-methyl-3-chlorobutanal
(d) 3-methyl-2-chlorobutanal

Sol. (a) The IUPAC name of the given compound is 3-chloro-2-methylbutanal.

□ Short Answer Type

Q.1 Illustrate the following reactions giving suitable example in each case.

1. Clemmensen Reduction
2. Cross Aldol condensation

Sol. (i) When carbonyl group of aldehydes or ketones is reduced to a CH_2 group on treatment with zinc amalgam and concentrated hydrochloric acid, then the reaction is called as Clemmensen reduction, then the reaction

$$>C=O \xrightarrow[HCl]{Zn\text{-}Hg} >CH_2 + H_2O$$

(ii) Cross aldol condensation: When aldol condensation is carried out between two different aldehydes and/or ketones, it is called cross aldol condensation. If both of them contain α-hydrogen atoms. It gives a mixture of four products. This is illustrated below by aldol reaction of a mixture of ethanal and propanal.

$$\begin{matrix} CH_3CHO \\ + \\ CH_3CH_2CHO \end{matrix} \xrightarrow[2.\ \Delta]{1.\ NaOH} \underset{\substack{\text{But-2-enal} \\ \text{from two molecules} \\ \text{of ethanal}}}{CH_3-CH=CH-CHO} + \underset{\substack{\text{2-Methylpent-2-enal} \\ \text{from two molecules} \\ \text{of propanal}}}{CH_3CH_2-CH=\underset{\substack{| \\ CH_3}}{C}-CHO}$$

simple or self aldol products

$$\underset{\text{2-Methylbut-2-enal}}{CH_3-CH=\underset{\substack{| \\ CH_3}}{C}-CHO} + \underset{\text{Pent-2-enal}}{CH_3-CH_2-CH=CHCHO}$$

from one molecule of ethanal and one molecule of propanal

cross aldol products

☐ Long Answer Type

Q.1 A. Give chemical tests to distinguish between the following:

1. Benzoic Acid and ethyl benzoate
2. Benzaldehyde and acetophenone

B. Complete each synthesis by giving missing reagents or products in the following:

1. 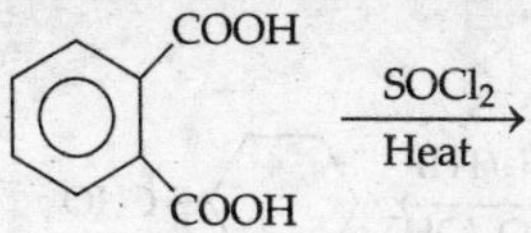

2. $C_6H_5CHO \longrightarrow H_2NCONHNH_2$

3. 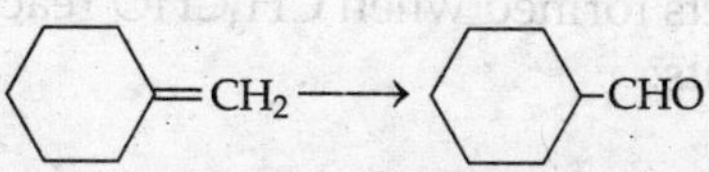

Sol. A. 1. **Benzoic acid and ethyl benzoate** Benzoic acid reacts with sodium bicarbonate to produce effervescence of carbon dioxide whereas ethyl benzoate (Ph—COO—C_2H_5) does not.

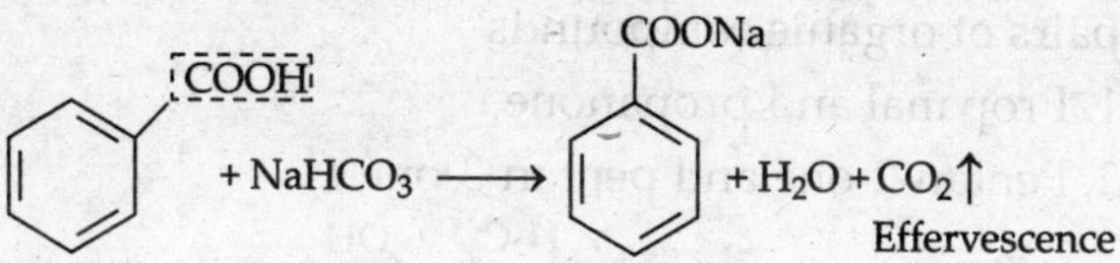

Benzoic acid — Sodium benzoate — Effervescence

2. **Benzaldehyde and acetophenone** Acetophenone responds towards iodoform test positively whereas benzaldehyde (C_6H_5CHO) does not.

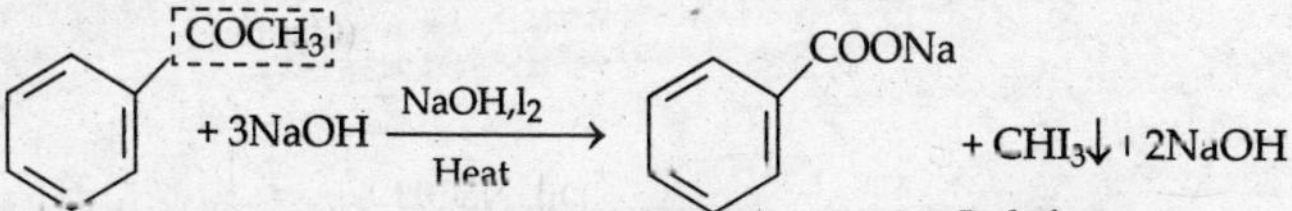

Acetophenone — Sodium benzoate — Iodoform (Yellow ppt.)

B.

1. 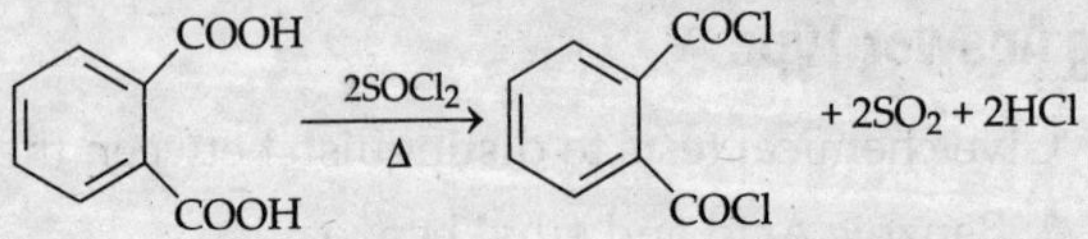

2. $C_6H_5CHO \xrightarrow{H_2NCONHNH_2} C_6H_5CH{=}N{-}NH{-}CONH_2 + H_2O$

3. 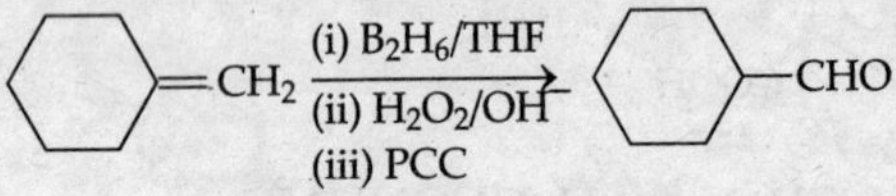

Q.2 A. Write the products formed when CH_3CHO reacts with the following reagents:

1. HCN
2. $H_2N{-}OH$
3. CH_3CHO in the presence of dilute NaOH

B. Give simple chemical test to distinguish between following pairs of organic compounds

1. Propanal and propanone
2. Pentan-2-one and pentan-3-one

Sol. A.

1. 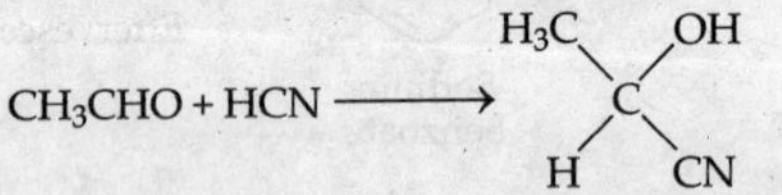

(Cyanohydrin)

2. $CH_3CHO + NH_2OH \longrightarrow CH_3CH{=}N{-}OH$

(Oxime)

3. $CH_3CHO + CH_3CHO \xrightarrow[\text{Aldol reaction}]{\text{Dil. NaOH}} CH_3{-}\underset{\substack{|\\OH}}{CH}{-}CH_2{-}\overset{O}{\overset{\|}{C}}{-}H$

3-Hydroxybutan-1-al

B. 1. **Propanal and propanone** Propanone responds to iodoform test whereas propanal (CH_3CH_2CHO) due to absence of CH_3CO— group does not.

$$\underset{\text{Propanone}}{\boxed{CH_3CO}\,CH_3} + \underset{\substack{\text{Sodium}\\\text{hypoidoite,}}}{3NaOI} \xrightarrow[\text{Heat}]{NaOH, I_2} \underset{\substack{\text{(yellow ppt.}\\\text{iodoform)}}}{CHI_3\downarrow} + \underset{\text{Sodium acetate}}{CH_3COONa} + 2NaOH$$

2. **Pentan-2-one and pentan-3-one** pentan-2-one responds positively iodoform test whereas pentan-3-one ($C_2H_5COC_2H_5$) does not.

$$\underset{\text{Pentan-2-one}}{CH_3—CO—CH_2—CH_2—CH_3} + \underset{\substack{\text{sodium}\\\text{hypoiodite}}}{3NaOI} \xrightarrow[\text{Heat}]{NaOH, I_2}$$

$$\underset{\substack{\text{(yellow ppt.)}\\\text{(Iodoform)}}}{CHI_3\downarrow} + CH_3CH_2CH_2COONa + 2NaOH$$

Amines

CHAPTER 09

Important Points

01 Amines are the derivatives of ammonia. These are classified as primary ($-NH_2$), secondary ($>NH$) and tertiary ($\geqslant N$). The attached groups may be alkyl (aliphatic) or aryl (aromatic).

02 Amines behave as Lewis bases due to the presence of an electron pair on nitrogen atom.

03 Amines can be prepared by:

(a) 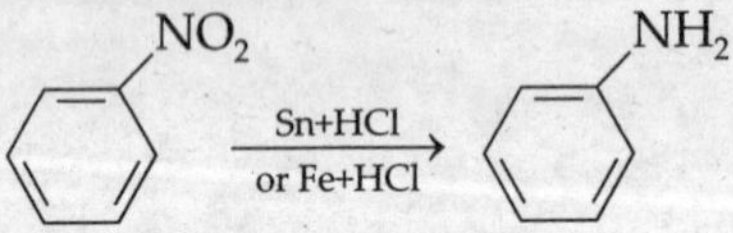
(Reduction of nitro compounds)

(b) Ammonolysis of alkyl halides.

$$\ddot{N}H_3 + R-X \longrightarrow R-\overset{+}{N}H_3X^- \xrightarrow{NaOH} R-NH_2 + H_2O + \overset{+}{Na}X^-$$

Nucleophile   Substituted ammonium salt

(c) $R-C\equiv N \xrightarrow[Na(Hg)/C_2H_5OH]{H_2/Ni} R-CH_2-NH_2$ (Reduction of nitriles)

(d) $R-\overset{O}{\overset{\|}{C}}-NH_2 \xrightarrow[(ii)\ H_2O]{(i)\ LiAlH_4} R-CH_2-NH_2$ (Reduction of amides)

(e) Gabriel phthalimide synthesis.

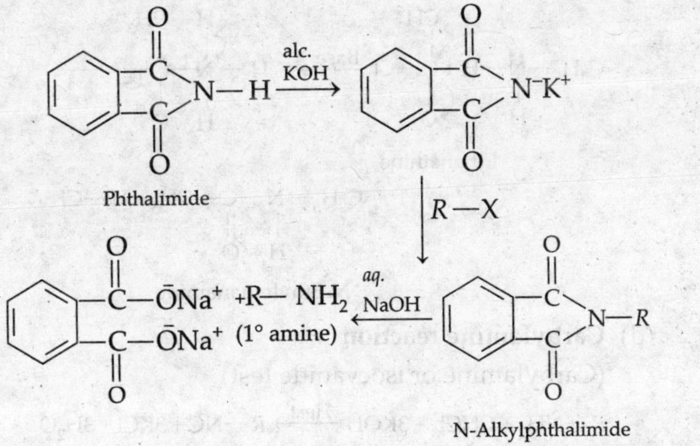

Phthalimide

N-Alkylphthalimide

(f) Hoffmann bromamide degradation reaction.

$$R-\overset{O}{\overset{\|}{C}}-NH_2 + Br_2 + 4NaOH \longrightarrow R-NH_2 + Na_2CO_3 + 2NaBr + 2H_2O$$

04 The order of boiling point of isomeric amines is :
Primary > Secondary > Tertiary

05 The order of basic strength of methyl substituted and ethyl substituted amines in aqueous medium is :

$$(C_2H_5)_2NH > (C_2N_5)_3N > C_2H_5NH_2 > NH_3$$
$$(CH_3)_2NH > CH_3NH_2 > (CH_3)_3N > NH_3$$

06 Aniline is a weaker base than ammonia.

07 Some chemical reactions of amines are:

(a) Amines are basic in nature so, they react with acids to form salts

$$R-\ddot{N}H_2 + \overset{+}{H}X \rightleftharpoons R-\overset{+}{N}H_3\,X^-\ \text{(Salt)}$$

(b) $$C_2H_5NH_2 + C_2H_5Br \xrightarrow[\text{(Alkylation)}]{-HBr} (C_2H_5)_2NH \xrightarrow[-HBr]{C_2H_5Br} (C_2H_5)_3\ddot{N} \xrightarrow{C_2H_5Br} (C_2H_5)_4\overset{+}{N}Br$$

(c) Acylation

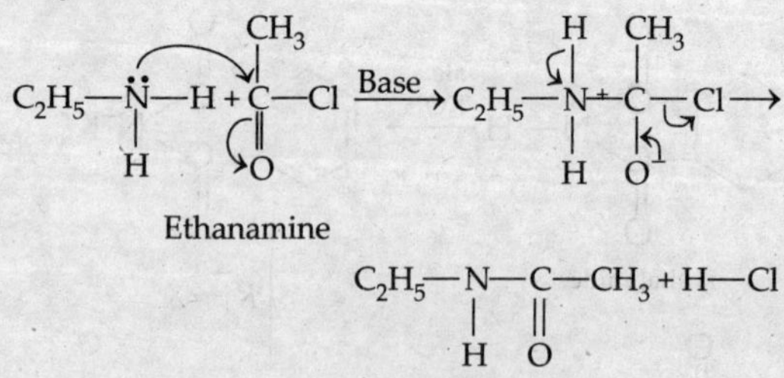

Ethanamine

N-Ethylethanamide

(d) **Carbylamine reaction**

(Carbylamine or isocyanide test)

$$R\text{—}NH_2 + CHCl_3 + 3KOH \xrightarrow{\text{Heat}} R\text{—}NC + 3KCl + 3H_2O$$

1° Amine

(e) **Reaction with nitrous acid**

(i) $R\text{—}NH_2 + HNO_2 \xrightarrow{NaNO_2 + HCl} [R\text{—}\overset{+}{N_2}\overset{-}{Cl}] \xrightarrow{H_2O} ROH + N_2 + HCl$

(1° Aliphatic Amine) (Diazonium salt) (Alcohol)

(ii) $C_6H_5\text{—}NH_2 \xrightarrow[273\text{–}278\ K]{NaNO_2 + 2HCl} C_6H_5\text{—}\overset{+}{N_2}Cl^- + NaCl + 2H_2O$

Aniline (Diazotisation reaction) (Benzenediazonium chloride)

(iii) Secondary and tertiary amines react with nitrous acids in a different manner and do not form diazonium salt.

(f) Reaction with benzenesulphonyl chloride (Hinsberg's reagent)

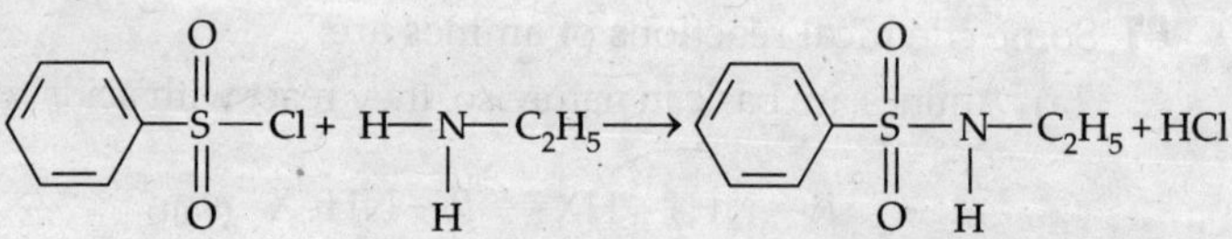

(Hinsberg's reagent) (Primary amine) *N*-Ethylbenzenesulphonamide (soluble in alkali)

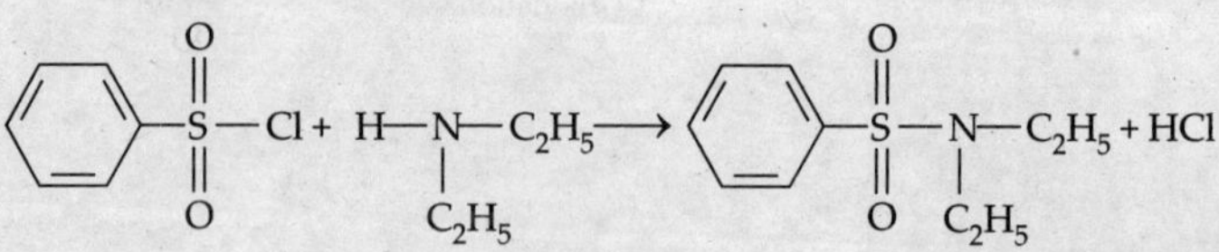

(secondary amine) *N, N* Diethylbenzene sulphonamide (Insoluble in alkali)

Tertiary amines do not react with Hinsbergs reagent.

(g) **Electrophilic substitution reactions**

Amino group in aniline is mainly ortho and para directing in nature.

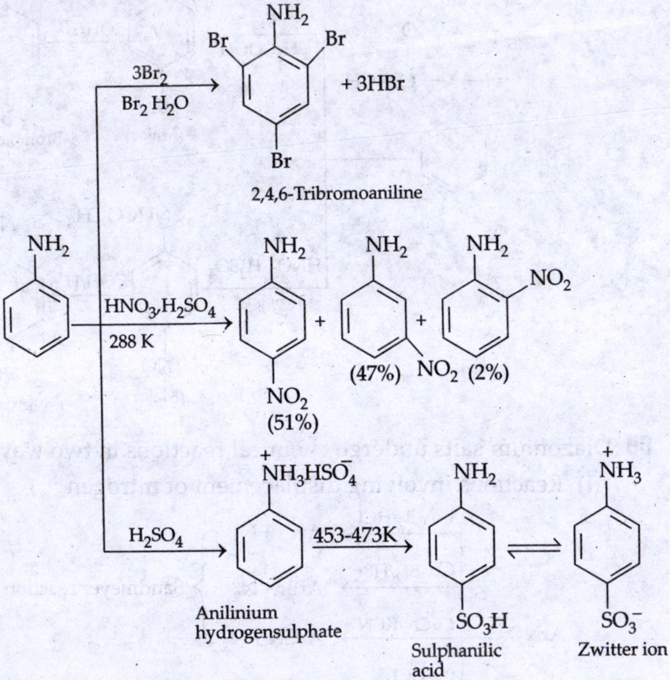

08 Aromatic amines are highly reactive. So, to get monosubstituted product (controlled reaction), we can protect $-NH_2$ group by acetylation with acetic anhydride.

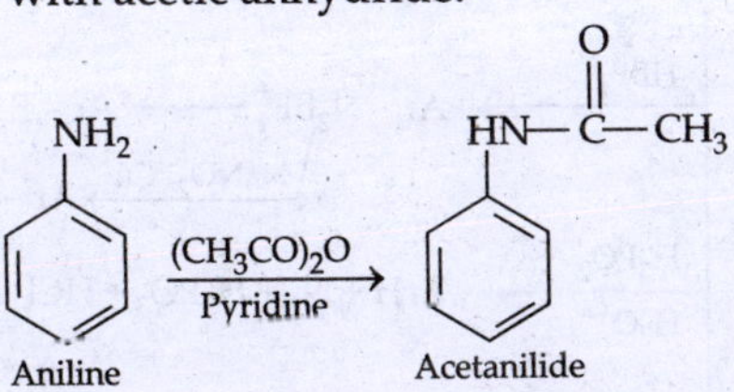

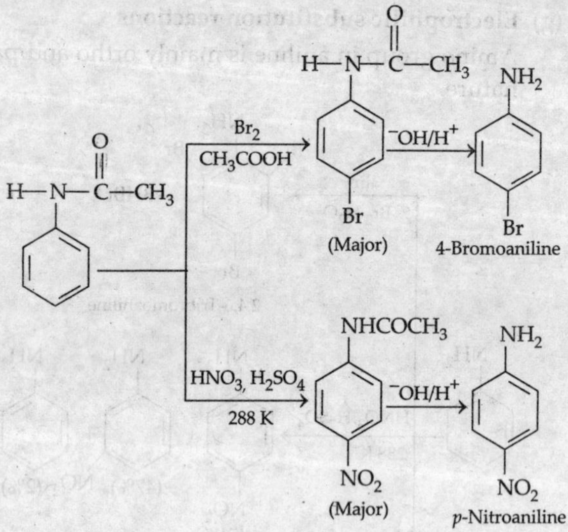

09 Diazonium salts undergo chemical reactions in two ways :

(i) Reactions involving displacement of nitrogen

$$Ar\overset{+}{N}_2\overset{-}{X} \xrightarrow{Cu_2Cl_2/HCl} ArCl + N_2$$
$$Ar\overset{+}{N}_2\overset{-}{X} \xrightarrow{Cu_2Br_2/HBr} ArBr + N_2$$
$$Ar\overset{+}{N}_2\overset{-}{X} \xrightarrow{CuCN/KCN} ArCN + N_2$$
} Sandmeyer reaction

$$Ar\overset{+}{N}_2\overset{-}{X} \xrightarrow{Cu/HCl} ArCl + N_2 + CuX$$
$$Ar\overset{+}{N}_2\overset{-}{X} \xrightarrow{Cu/HBr} ArBr + N_2 + CuX$$
} Gattermann reaction

$$Ar\overset{+}{N}_2Cl^- \xrightarrow{KI} ArI + KCl + N_2$$
$$Ar\overset{+}{N}_2Cl^- \xrightarrow{HBF_4} Ar-\overset{+}{N}_2BF_4^- \longrightarrow Ar-F + BF_3 + N_2$$
$$Ar-\overset{+}{N}_2BF_4^- \xrightarrow{NaNO_2,\ Cu} Ar-NO_2 + N_2 + NaBF_4$$
$$Ar\overset{+}{N}_2Cl^- \xrightarrow[H_2O]{H_3PO_2} ArH + N_2 + H_3PO_3 + HCl$$
$$Ar\overset{+}{N}_2Cl^- \xrightarrow{CH_3CH_2OH} ArH + N_2 + CH_3CHO + HCl$$
$$Ar\overset{+}{N}_2Cl^- \xrightarrow{H_2O} ArOH + N_2 + HCl$$

(ii) Reactions involving retention of diazo group (Coupling reactions)

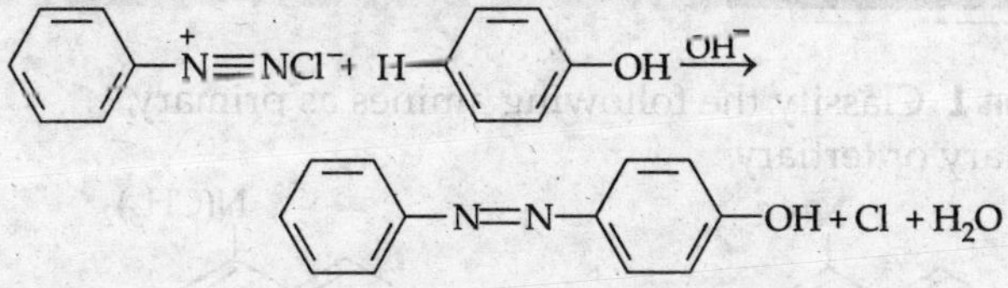

p-Hydroxyazobenzene (orange dye)

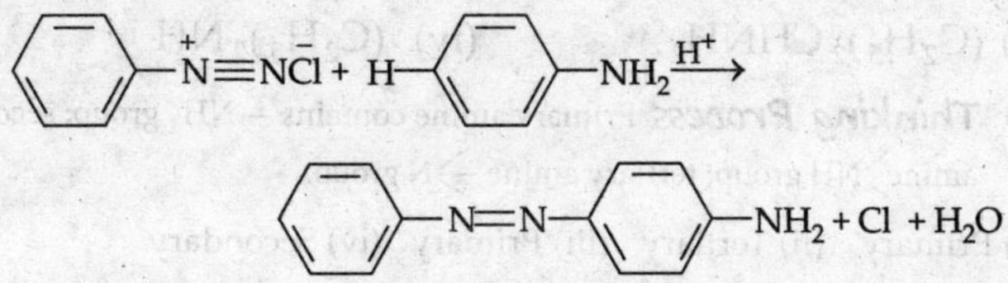

p-Aminoazobenzene
(yellow dye)

Intext Questions

Question 1 Classify the following amines as primary, secondary or tertiary.

(i) 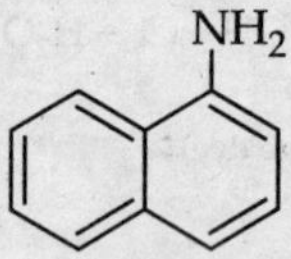

(ii) 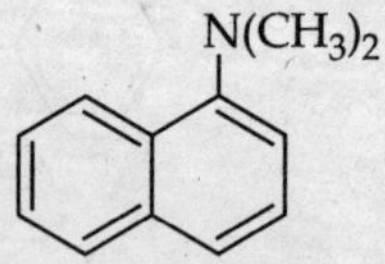

(iii) $(C_2H_5)_2CHNH_2$ (iv) $(C_2H_5)_2NH$

Thinking Process Primary amine contains $—NH_2$ group; secondary amine $>NH$ group; tertiary amine $\geq N$ group.

Sol. (i) Primary (ii) Tertiary (iii) Primary (iv) Secondary

Question 2 (i) Write structures of different isomeric amines corresponding to the molecular formula, $C_4H_{11}N$.

(ii) Write IUPAC names of all the isomers.

(iii) What type of isomerism is exhibited by different pairs of amines?

Thinking Process

(i) Recall the definition of isomerism; rules of IUPAC nomenclature; types of isomerism.

(ii) Draw all the structures possible for molecular formula $C_4H_{11}N$ and give their IUPAC name according to rules.

(iii) Also compare all the structures to find the property like chain length, position of functional group, nature of functional group, etc. In which the structures differ.

Sol. (i) and (ii) Eight isomers of $C_4H_{11}N$ are :

(a) $\overset{4}{C}H_3—\overset{3}{C}H_2—\overset{2}{C}H_2—\overset{1}{C}H_2—NH_2$
Butan-1-amine (Primary)

(b) $\overset{3}{C}H_3—\overset{2}{C}H(CH_3)—\overset{1}{C}H_2—NH_2$
2-Methylpropan-1-amine
(Primary)

(c) $\overset{4}{C}H_3—\overset{3}{C}H_2—\overset{2}{C}H(\overset{1}{C}H_3)—NH_2$
Butan-2-amine
(Primary)

(d) $CH_3—\overset{2}{C}(\overset{1}{C}H_3)(\overset{3}{C}H_3)—NH_2$
2-Methylpropan-2-amine
(Primary)

(e) $C_2H_5—N(C_2H_5)—H$
N-Ethylethanamine
(Secondary)

(f) $C_3H_7—N(CH_3)—H$
N-Methylpropan-1-amine
(Secondary)

(g) $CH_3—CH(CH_3)—NH—CH_3$
N-Methylpropan-2-amine
(Secondary)

(h) $CH_3—N(C_2H_5)—CH_3$
N, N-Dimethylethanamine
(Tertiary)

(iii) Isomerism exhibited by different amines are;

(a) **Chain isomers** *i.e.*, have different carbon chains. (a) and (b); (c) and (d); (f) and (g).

(b) **Position isomers** *i.e.*, functional group occupy different positions. (b) and (c); (b) and (d); (a) and (d)

(c) **Metamers** *i.e.*, different alkyl groups are attached to the same functional group. (e) and (f) ; (g) and (e)

(d) **Functional isomers** All primary amines are the functional isomers of secondary and tertiary amines and vice-versa.

Question 3 How will you convert

(i) Benzene into aniline?

(ii) Benzene into N, N-dimethylaniline ?

(iii) $Cl—(CH_2)_4—Cl$ into hexan-1,6-diamine?

◎ *Thinking Process*

(i) Nitration followed by reduction, as NH_2 cannot be introduced directly into benzene ring.

(ii) After forming aniline, methylation of amino group.

(iii) Reaction with alc. KCN followed by reduction.

Sol. (i) **Benzene into aniline**

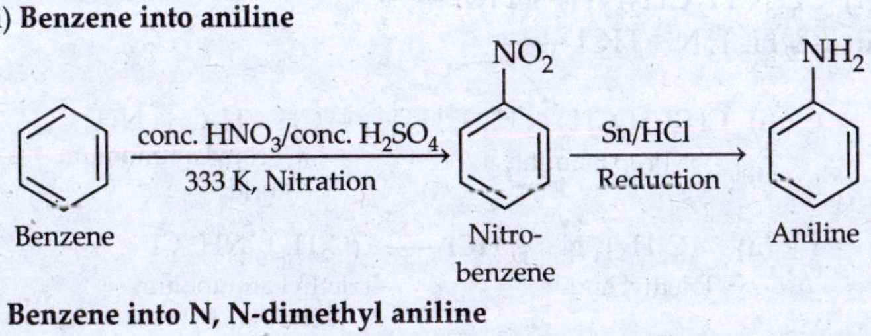

(ii) **Benzene into N, N-dimethyl aniline**

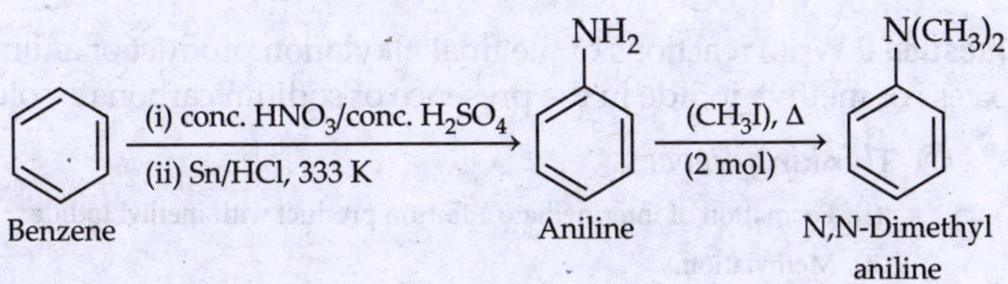

(iii) **$Cl—(CH_2)_4—Cl$ into hexan-1,6- diamine**

$$Cl—(CH_2)_4—Cl + 2KCN \xrightarrow[-KCl]{Alcohol} CN(CH_2)_4—CN$$

$$\xrightarrow[\text{or } LiAlH_4]{H_2/Pt} \underset{\text{Hexan-1,6-diamine}}{NH_2CH_2(CH_2)_4CH_2NH_2}$$

Mistake Alert NH_2 group cannot be introduced directly on benzene ring. So, first do nitration followed by reduction to get aniline.

Question 4 Arrange the following in increasing order of their basic strength :

(i) $C_2H_5NH_2, C_6H_5NH_2, NH_3, C_6H_5CH_2NH_2$ and $(C_2H_5)_2NH$

(ii) $C_2H_5NH_2, (C_2H_5)_2NH, (C_2H_5)_3N, C_6H_5NH_2$

(iii) $CH_3NH_2, (CH_3)_2NH, (CH_3)_3N, C_6H_5NH_2, C_6H_5CH_2NH_2$

Thinking Process

(i) Presence of electron donating *R* group increases the basicity of amines. However, 3° amines in aqueous solution are less basic due to steric hindrance.

(ii) Aliphatic amines are more basic than aromatic amines because in later lone pair takes part in delocalization, so less available for donation.

Sol. (i) $C_6H_5NH_2 < NH_3 < C_6H_5CH_2NH_2 < C_2H_5NH_2 < (C_2H_5)_2NH$

(ii) $C_6H_5NH_2 < C_2H_5NH_2 < (C_2H_5)_3N < (C_2H_5)_2NH$

(iii) $C_6H_5NH_2 < C_6H_5CH_2NH_2 < (CH_3)_3N < CH_3NH_2 < (CH_3)_2NH$

Question 5 Complete the following acid-base reactions and name the products:

(i) $CH_3CH_2CH_2NH_2 + HCl \longrightarrow$

(ii) $(C_2H_5)_3N + HCl \longrightarrow$

Sol. (i) $$\underset{n\text{-Propanamine}}{CH_3CH_2CH_2\ddot{N}H_2} + HCl \longrightarrow \underset{n\text{-Propyl ammonium chloride}}{CH_3CH_2CH_2\overset{+}{N}H_3\overset{-}{Cl}}$$

(ii) $$\underset{\text{Triethyl amine}}{(C_2H_5)_3\ddot{N}} + HCl \longrightarrow \underset{\text{Triethyl ammonium chloride}}{(C_2H_5)_3\overset{+}{N}H\overset{-}{Cl}}$$

Question 6 Write reactions of the final alkylation product of aniline with excess of methyl iodide in the presence of sodium carbonate solution.

Thinking Process

(i) Formation of intermediate addition product with methyl iodide.

(ii) Methylation.

Sol. **Hoffmann's ammonolysis reaction** In the presence of excess methyl iodide, aniline (primary amine) forms quarternary ammonium salt.

$$\underset{\text{Aniline}}{C_6H_5\ddot{N}H_2} + CH_3{-}I \longrightarrow \underset{\text{N-methyl anilinium iodide}}{[C_6H_5\overset{+}{N}H_2CH_3]I^-}$$

$$2[C_6H_5\overset{+}{N}H_2CH_3]I^- + Na_2CO_3 \longrightarrow \underset{\text{N-methylaniline}}{2C_6H_5NHCH_3} + 2NaI + CO_2 + H_2O$$

$$C_6H_5\ddot{N}HCH_3 \xrightarrow[Na_2CO_3]{CH_3I} \underset{\text{N,N-dimethyl aniline}}{C_6H_5N(CH_3)_2}$$

$$C_6H_5\ddot{N}(CH_3)_2 + CH_3{-}I \longrightarrow \underset{\text{N,N,N-trimethyl anilinium iodide}}{[C_6H_5\overset{+}{N}(CH_3)_3\overset{-}{I}]}$$

$$[C_6H_5N(CH_3)_3]I^- + Na_2CO_3 \longrightarrow \underset{\text{N,N,N-trimethyl anilinium carbonate}}{[C_6H_5\overset{+}{N}(CH_3)_3]_2CO_3^{2-}} + 2NaI$$

Question 7 Write chemical reaction of aniline with benzoyl chloride and write the name of the product obtained.

◎ *Thinking Process* Elimination of HCl and formation of amide (—CO—NH—) linkage.

Sol.

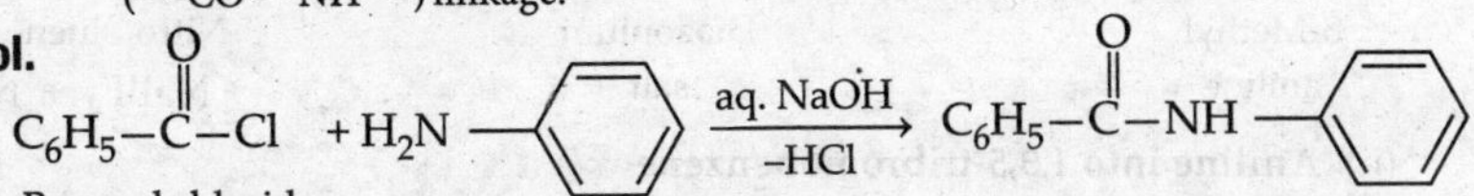

Benzoyl chloride Aniline N-phenyl benzamide (Benzanilide)

Question 8 Write structures of different isomers corresponding to the molecular formula C_3H_9N. Write IUPAC names of the isomers which will liberate nitrogen gas on treatment with nitrous acid.

◎ *Thinking Process*

(i) Write all the structures possible for molecular formula C_3H_9N. Give their IUPAC name and classify them into 1° (—NH_2 group), 2° (>NH group) and 3° (—N< group)

(ii) Primary amines (1°) will liberate N_2 on reaction with HNO_2.

Sol. C_3H_9N has four isomers :

(a) $CH_3CH_2CH_2NH_2$
Propan-1-amine (1°)

(b) $CH_3CH(NH_2)CH_3$
Propan-2-amine (1°)

(c) $CH_3NHC_2H_5$
N-Methylethanamine (2°)

(d) $CH_3N(CH_3)CH_3$
N,N-dimethyl methanamine (3°)

Primary amines react with HNO_2 to produce N_2 gas.

(a) $\underset{\text{Propan-1-amine}}{CH_3CH_2CH_2NH_2} + HONO \longrightarrow \underset{\text{Propan-1-ol}}{CH_3CH_2CH_2OH} + N_2 + H_2O$

(b) $\underset{\text{Propan-2-amine}}{CH_3—\underset{\displaystyle NH_2}{\underset{|}{C}}HCH_3} + HONO \longrightarrow \underset{\text{Propan-2-ol}}{CH_3\underset{\displaystyle OH}{\underset{|}{C}}HCH_3} + N_2 + H_2O$

Question 9 Convert : (i) 3-Methyl aniline into 3-nitrotoluene.

(ii) Aniline into 1,3,5-tribromobenzene.

◎ ***Thinking Process*** The given conversions involve the following steps.

(i) Diazotisation followed by reaction with HBF_4 and nitration.

(ii) Bromination, diazotisation and reduction (by H_3PO_2).

Sol. (i) **3-methyl aniline into 3-nitrotoluene**

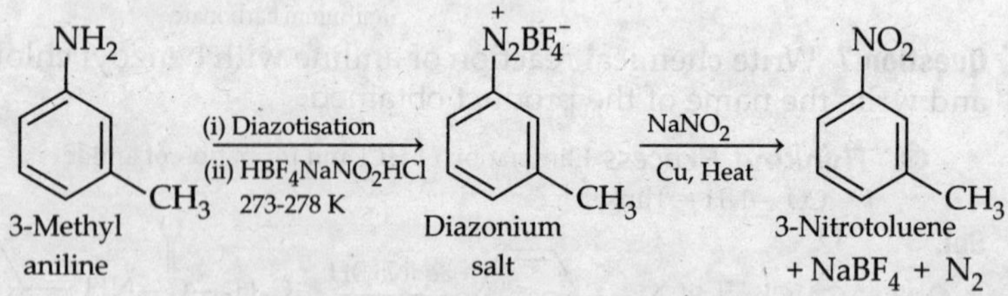

(ii) **Aniline into 1,3,5-tribromobenzene**

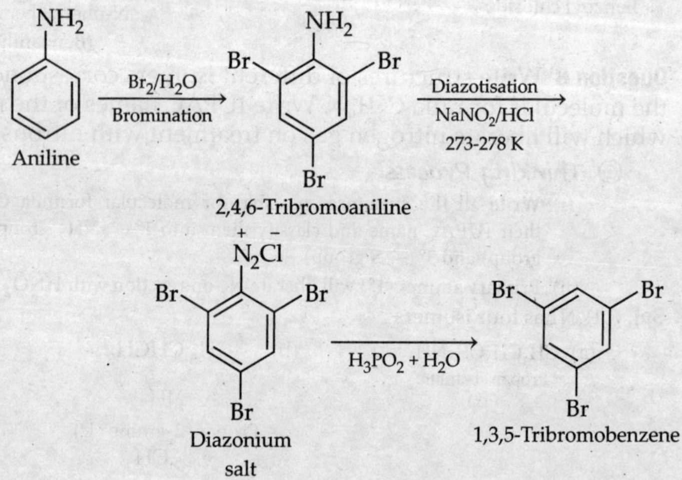

Exercises

Question 1 Write IUPAC names of the following compounds and classify them into primary, secondary and tertiary amines.

(i) $(CH_3)_2CHNH_2$ (ii) $CH_3(CH_2)_2NH_2$

(iii) $CH_3NHCH(CH_3)_2$ (iv) $(CH_3)_3CNH_2$

(v) $C_6H_5NHCH_3$ (vi) $(CH_3CH_2)_2NCH_3$

(viii) m-$BrC_6H_4NH_2$

◎ *Thinking Process*

(i) Recall the rules of IUPAC nomenclature and write their name.

(ii) Classify them as 1°, 2°, 3° (primary —NH_2, secondary >NH, tertiary >N)

Sol. (i) $\overset{1}{C}H_3—\overset{2}{C}H(\overset{3}{C}H_3)—NH_2$

Propan-2-amine (Primary)

(ii) $\overset{3}{C}H_3—\overset{2}{C}H_2—\overset{1}{C}H_2—NH_2$

Propan-1-amine (Primary)

(iii) $CH_3—NH—\overset{2}{C}H(\overset{1}{C}H_3)—\overset{3}{C}H_3$

N-Methylpropan-2-amine (Secondary)

(iv) $\overset{1}{C}H_3—\overset{2}{C}(CH_3)(\overset{3}{C}H_3)—NH_2$

2-Methylpropan-2-amine (Primary)

(v) $C_6H_5—NH—CH_3$

N-Methylbenzenamine (Secondary)

(vi) $CH_3—CH_2—N(CH_3)—CH_3—CH_2$

N-Ethyl-N-methylethan-amine (Tertiary)

(vii)

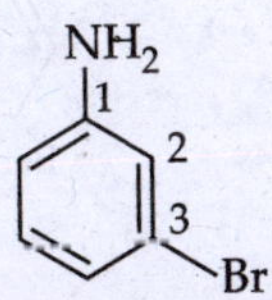

3-Bromobenzenamine or 3-Bromoaniline (Primary)

Question 2 Give one chemical test to distinguish between the following pairs of compounds.

(i) Methylamine and dimethylamine

(ii) Secondary and tertiary amines

(iii) Ethylamine and aniline (iv) Aniline and benzylamine

(v) Aniline and N-methylaniline.

Thinking Process

(i) Write the structures of amines and classify them into 1°, 2°, 3° benzyl amine or aromatic amine.

(ii) Only 1° amines (all types) give carbylamine reaction. 1° and 2° aliphatic amines give Libermann's nitroso reaction.

(iii) Aromatic amines give dye test, *i.e.*, diazotization followed by coupling.

Sol.

(i) **Methylamine and dimethyl amine** can be distinguished by carbylamine test. Methyl amine (primary) responds to **carbylamine reaction**. When heated with chloroform and KOH, it produces foul smell. Dimethyl amine (secondary) does not respond to this test.

$$\underset{\text{Methyl amine}}{CH_3NH_2} + CHCl_3 + 3KOH \xrightarrow{\text{Heat}} \underset{\substack{\text{Methyl isocyanide} \\ \text{(Foul smell)}}}{CH_3—NC} + 3KCl + 3H_2O$$

(ii) **Secondary and tertiary amines** can be distinguished by Hinsberg's test. Secondary amines react with Hinsberg's reagent (benzenesulphonyl chloride, $C_6H_5SO_2Cl$) to form a product which is insoluble in alkali. Tertiary amines do not react with this reagent.

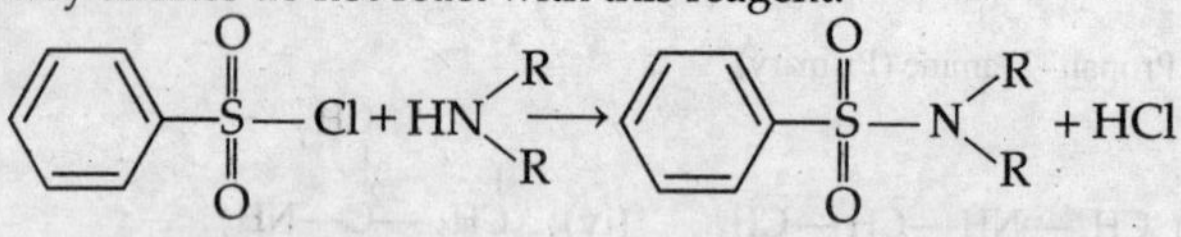

(Insoluble in alkali)

(iii) Ethyl amine (primary aliphatic amine) and aniline (primary aromatic amine) can be distinguished by **azo dye test**.

Aniline responds to this test whereas ethyl amine does not.

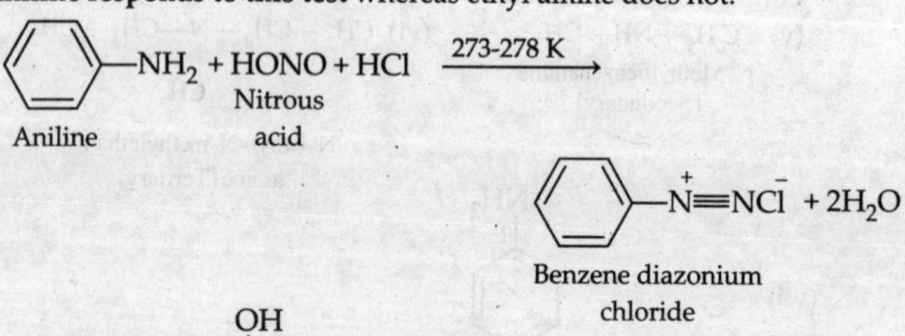

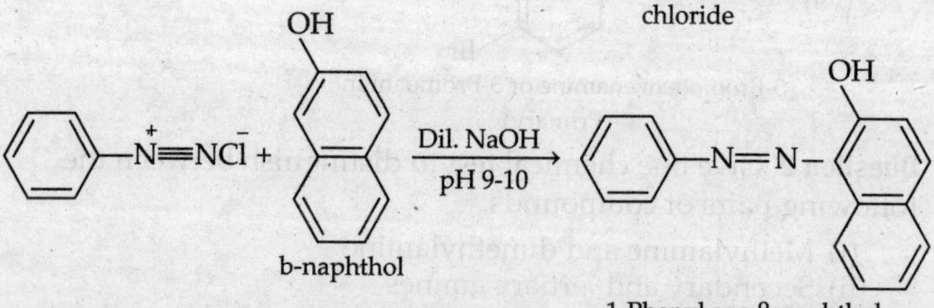

(iv) **Aniline and benzyl amine (nitrous acid test)** Benzyl amine reacts with nitrous acid to form a diazonium salt which is unstable. It evolves N_2 gas by decomposing at even low temperature.

$$\underset{\text{Benzyl amine}}{C_6H_5CH_2NH_2} \xrightarrow[HCl]{HNO_2} [C_6H_5CH_2-\overset{+}{N}\equiv N\overset{-}{Cl}]$$

$$\xrightarrow[\text{Decomposes}]{H_2O} \underset{\text{Benzyl alcohol}}{C_6H_5CH_2OH} + N_2\uparrow + HCl$$

Aniline reacts with nitrous acid to from benzene diazonium chloride which does not decompose to give N_2, and gives an orange-red dye when reacted with β-naphthol.

$$\underset{\text{Aniline}}{C_6H_5NH_2} \xrightarrow[273\text{-}278\,K]{HNO_2, HCl} \underset{\text{Benzene diazonium chloride}}{C_6H_5\overset{+}{N}\equiv N\overset{-}{Cl}}$$

(v) **Aniline and N-methylaniline (carbylamine test)** Aniline gives carbylamine test because it is a primary amine whereas *n*-methyl aniline (secondary amine) does not give this test.

$$\underset{\text{Aniline}}{C_6H_5NH_2} + CHCl_3 + \underset{(\text{Alc.})}{3\,KOH} \xrightarrow{\Delta} \underset{\substack{\text{Phenyl isocyanide}\\(\text{Foul smell})}}{C_6H_5NC} + 3KCl + 3H_2O$$

Question 3 Account for the following:

(i) pK_b of aniline is more than that of methylamine.
(ii) Ethylamine is soluble in water whereas aniline is not.
(iii) Methylamine in water reacts with ferric chloride to precipitate hydrated ferric oxide.
(iv) Although amino group is *o*- and *p*- directing in aromatic electrophilic substitution reactions, aniline on nitration gives a substantial amount of *m*-nitroaniline.
(v) Aniline does not undergo Friedel Crafts reaction.
(vi) Diazonium salts of aromatic amines are more stable than those of aliphatic amines.
(vii) Gabriel phthalimide synthesis is preferred for synthesising primary amines.

Thinking Process

(i) Higher the pK_b value, lesser is the basicity, *i.e.*, tendency to donate electrons.
(ii) Hydrogen bonding, which is shown by compounds containing N—H, F—H or O—H bond. Bulkiness of the group attached to such bond decreases the extent of H-bonding.
(iii) Consider reaction mechanism.
(iv) Formation of anilinium ion which is *m*-directing.
(v) Aniline is a Lewis base so form salt with Lewis acid.
(vi) Stability due to resonance
(vii) No production of secondary and tertiary amines.

Sol. (i) In aniline, the electron pair on nitrogen atom is involved in conjugation with ring and is less available for protonation than in methyl amine. Therefore, pK_b value of aniline is more than that of methylamine and aniline is less basic. (As higher the pK_b value, less is the basicity).

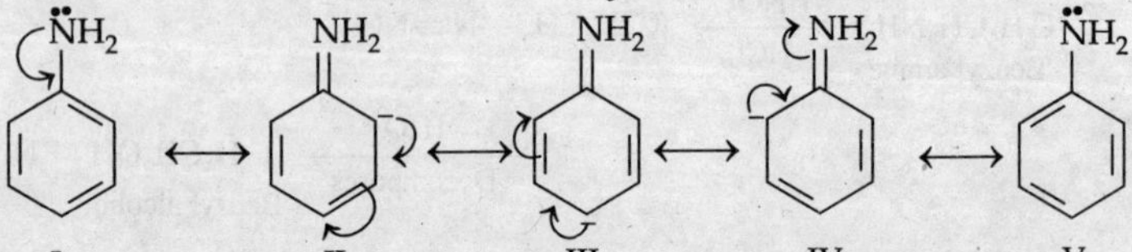

I II III IV V

(ii) Ethylamine is soluble in water due to hydrogen bonding.

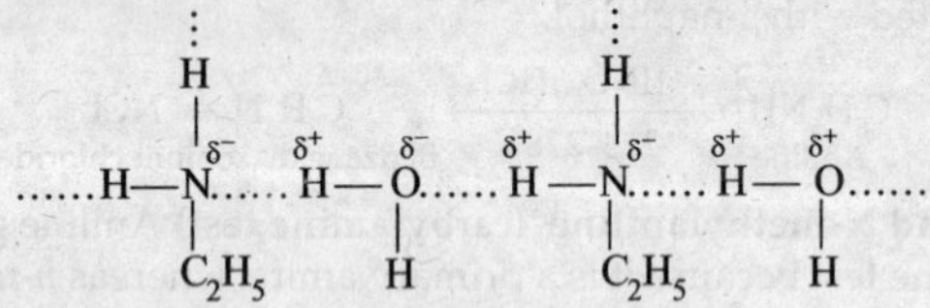

In aniline due to bulky hydrocarbon part, the extent of hydrogen bonding is less and it is not soluble in water.

(iii) Methylamine being more basic than water due to the $-CH_3$ group's +I effect, accepts a proton from water and OH^- ions are produced.

$$\underset{\text{Methylamine}}{CH_3\ddot{N}H_2} + H{-}OH \longrightarrow CH_3\overset{+}{N}H_3 + \overset{-}{O}H$$

OH^- ion reacts with Fe^{3+} to form a precipitate of hydrated ferric oxide.

$$FeCl_3 \longrightarrow Fe^{3+} + 3\overline{Cl}$$

$$2Fe^{3+} + 6OH^- \longrightarrow 2Fe(OH)_3 \text{ or } Fe_2O_3\cdot 3H_2O$$

Hydrated ferric oxide (Brown ppt.)

(iv) In presence of conc. HNO_3 and conc. H_2SO_4, most of aniline gets protonated to form anilinium ion. Now, aniline and anilinium ions both are present in the reaction mixture. In aniline—NH_2 group is *o*- and *p*-directing but anilinium ion is *m*-directing. Because of more amount of anilinium ion, a lot of *m*-nitroaniline is formed.

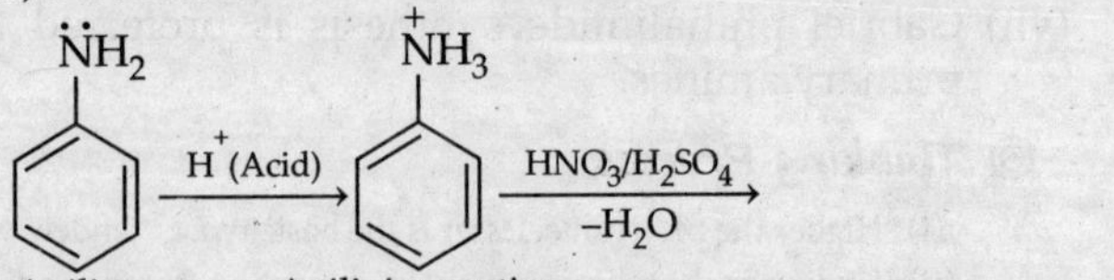

Aniline Anilinium cation

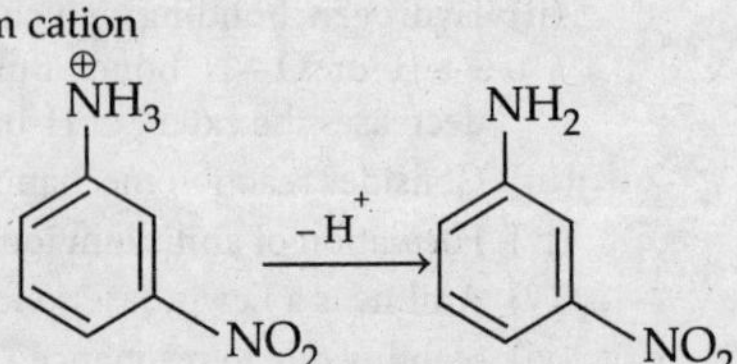

m-Nitroanilinium cation *m*-Nitroaniline

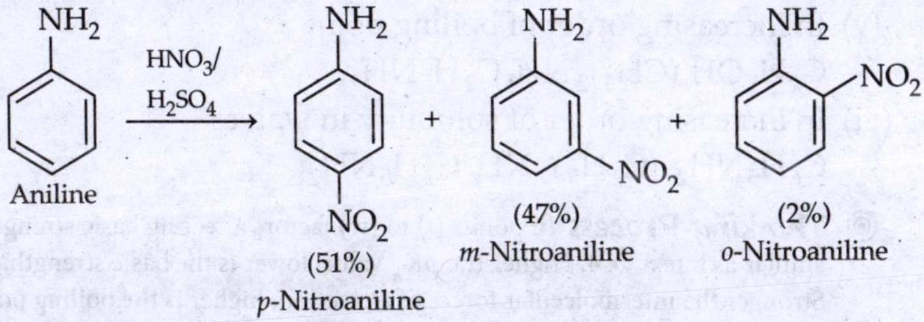

(v) Aniline being a lewis base forms a complex with $AlCl_3$, a Lewis acid. As a result, nitrogen of aniline becomes positively charged and acts as a strong deactivating group for electrophilic substitution reaction. Consequently, aniline does not undergo Friedel Crafts reaction.

$$\underset{\substack{\text{Aniline}\\\text{(Lewis base)}}}{C_6H_5\ddot{N}H_2} + \underset{\text{(Lewis acid)}}{AlCl_3} \longrightarrow \underset{\text{Complex}}{[C_6H_5NH_2]^+[AlCl_3]^-}$$

(vi) Diazonium salts of aromatic amines are more stable than those of aliphatic amines because these are resonance stabilised while no such resonance stabilisation is possible in the corresponding diazonium salts of aliphatic amines.

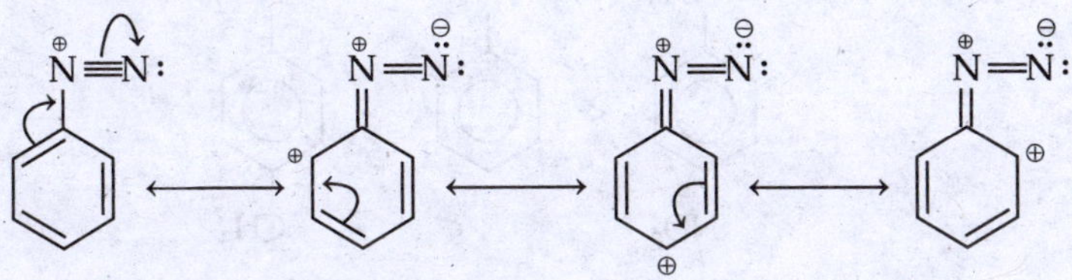

(vii) Gabriel phthalimide synthesis produces primary amines only without the traces of secondary or tertiary amines. So, this method is preferred for the synthesis of primary amines.

Question 4 Arrange the following

(i) In decreasing order of the pK_b values

$C_2H_5NH_2, C_6H_5NHCH_3, (C_2H_5)_2NH$ and $C_6H_5NH_2$.

(ii) In increasing order of basic strength :

$C_6H_5NH_2, C_6H_5N(CH_3)_2, (C_6H_5)_2NH$ and CH_3NH_2.

(iii) In increasing order of basic strength :

(a) Aniline, *p*-nitroaniline and *p*-toluidine

(b) $C_6H_5NH_2, C_6H_5NHCH_3, C_6H_5CH_2NH_2$.

(iv) In decreasing order of basic strength in gas phase :

$C_2H_5NH_2, (C_2H_5)_2NH, (C_2H_5)_3N$ and NH_3.

(v) In increasing order of boiling point
$C_2H_5OH, (CH_3)_2NH, C_2H_5NH_2$.

(vi) In increasing order of solubility in water
$C_6H_5NH_2, (C_2H_5)_2NH, C_2H_5NH_2$.

◎ **Thinking Process** In points (i) to (iv) factors affecting basic strength similar as intext Q. 4. Higher the pK_b value, lower is the basic strength. (v) Stronger the intermolecular forces of attraction, higher is the boiling point. Moreover, molecules capable of forming H-bond also have high boiling point. (vi) Higher the tendency to form H-bond, more is the solubility. Extent of H-bonding is more in 1° amine than in 3° and 2° amines as more H-atoms are present in order 1° > 2° > 3°, to form extensive H-bonding. Among aniline and ethylamine, aniline solubility is less due to the presence of bulky benzenering.

Sol. (i) $C_6H_5NH_2 > C_6H_5NHCH_3 > C_2H_5NH_2 > (C_2H_5)_2NH$.

(ii) $C_6H_5NH_2 < C_6H_5N(CH_3)_2 < CH_3NH_2 < (C_2H_5)_2NH$.

(iii) (a) *p*-nitroaniline < aniline< *p*-toluidine. Electron donating groups increases the basicity of aniline and electron withdrawing groups decreases the basicity of aniline.

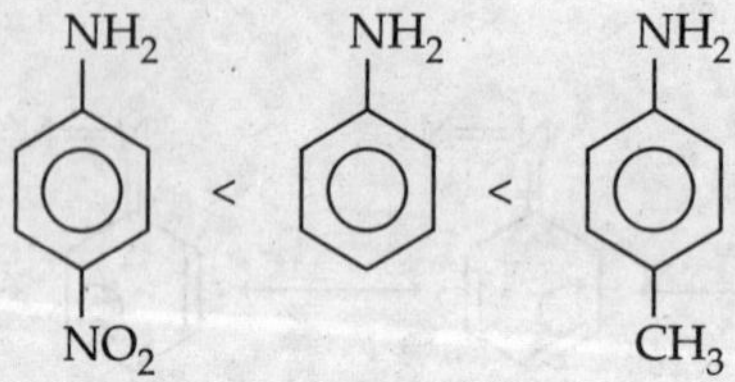

(b) $C_6H_5NH_2 < C_6H_5NHCH_3 < C_6H_5CH_2NH_2$.

(iv) In gas phase, there is no solvation effect, the basic strength depends mainly on $+I$ effect. So, higher the $+I$ effect, more is the basic strength. $(C_2H_5)_3N > (C_2H_5)_2NH > C_2H_5NH_2 > NH_3$.

(v) Oxygen is more electronegative, so it forms strongest H-bond and C_2H_5OH has the highest boiling point. $C_2H_5NH_2$ has 2N—H bonds. So, it can undergo H-bonding more extensively than $(CH_3)_2NH$, therefore $C_2H_5NH_2$ has greater boiling point than $(CH_3)_2NH$.
$(CH_3)_2NH < C_2H_5NH_2 < C_2H_5OH$.

(vi) $C_6H_5NH_2 < (C_2H_5)_2NH < C_2H_5NH_2$.

Question 5 How will you convert:

(i) Ethanoic acid into methanamine?
(ii) Hexanenitrile into 1-aminopentane?
(iii) Methanol to ethanoic acid?
(iv) Ethanamine into methanamine?
(v) Ethanoic acid into propanoic acid?
(vi) Methanamine into ethanamine?

(vii) Nitromethane into dimethylamine?

(viii) Propanoic acid into ethanoic acid?

◎ ***Thinking Process*** The given conversion involve the following steps :

(i) Chlorination of carboxyl group by $SOCl_2$, formation of amide by reacting with NH_3, Hofmann bromamide reaction, *i.e.*, reaction with Br_2 / KOH.

(ii) Hydrolysis followed by reaction with and ammonia to form amide and then, Hofmann bromamide reaction.

(iii) Chlorination (reaction with PCl_5 or $SOCl_2$), substituting Cl by CN (using alc. KCN), hydrolysis.

(iv) Reaction with HNO_2, oxidation, amide formation (by reaction with NH_3), then Hofmann bromamide reaction.

(v) Reduction (by $LiAlH_4$), iodination, cyanide formation, hydrolysis.

(vi) Alcohol formation *i.e.*, reaction with HNO_2, iodination, cyanide formation, reduction.

(vii) Reduction into NH_2 by Sn/HCl, carbylamine reaction, reduction.

(viii) Amide formation (reaction with NH_3), Hofmann's bromamide reaction, reaction with nitrous acid, oxidation.

Sol. (i) **Ethanoic acid into methanamine**

$$\underset{\text{Ethanoic acid}}{CH_3COOH} \xrightarrow{SOCl_2} \underset{\text{Ethanoyl chloride}}{CH_3COCl} \xrightarrow{NH_3\text{(excess)}} \underset{\text{Ethanamide}}{CH_3CONH_2}$$

$$\xrightarrow[\text{Hofmann bromamide reaction}]{Br_2/KOH} \underset{\text{Methanamine}}{CH_3NH_2}$$

(ii) **Hexanenitrile to 1-aminopentane**

$$\underset{\text{Hexanenitrile}}{CH_3(CH_2)_4CN} \xrightarrow[\text{Hydrolysis}]{H_3O^+} \underset{\text{Hexanoic acid}}{CH_3(CH_2)_4COOH} \xrightarrow{SOCl_2} \underset{\text{Hexanoyl chloride}}{CH_3(CH_2)_4COCl}$$

$$\xrightarrow{NH_3} \underset{\text{Hexanamide}}{CH_3(CH_2)_4CONH_2} \xrightarrow{Br_2/KOH} \underset{\text{1-Aminopentane}}{CH_3(CH_2)_4NH_2}$$

(iii) **Methanol to ethanoic acid**

$$\underset{\text{Methanol}}{CH_3OH} \xrightarrow{PCl_5} \underset{\text{Chloro methane}}{CH_3Cl} \xrightarrow{\text{KCN(alc.)}} \underset{\text{Ethane nitrile}}{CH_3CN} \xrightarrow{H_3O^+} \underset{\text{Ethanoic acid}}{CH_3COOH}$$

(iv) **Ethanamine to methanamine**

$$\underset{\text{Ethanamine}}{CH_3CH_2NH_2} \xrightarrow[\text{(ii) } H_2O]{\text{(i) HONO}} \underset{\text{Ethanol}}{CH_3CH_2OH} \xrightarrow[K_2Cr_2O_7/H_2SO_4]{[O]} CH_3CHO \xrightarrow[K_2Cr_2O_7/H_2SO_4]{[O]}$$

$$CH_3COOH \xrightarrow[\text{Heat}]{NH_3} \underset{\text{Ethanamide}}{CH_3CONH_2} \xrightarrow{Br_2/KOH} \underset{\text{Methanamine}}{CH_3NH_2}$$

(v) **Ethanoic acid into propanoic acid**

$$\underset{\text{Ethanoic acid}}{CH_3COOH} \xrightarrow[\text{[H]}]{LiAlH_4} \underset{\text{Ethanol}}{CH_3CH_2OH} \xrightarrow{P/I_2} \underset{\text{Iodoethane}}{CH_3CH_2I}$$

$$\xrightarrow{KCN(alc.)} \underset{\text{Propane nitrile}}{CH_3CH_2CN} \xrightarrow{H_2O/H^+} \underset{\text{Propanoic acid}}{CH_3CH_2COOH}$$

(vi) **Methanamine to ethanamine**

$$\underset{\text{Methanamine}}{CH_3NH_2} \xrightarrow[\text{(ii) } H_2O]{\text{(i) HONO}} \underset{\text{Methanol}}{CH_3OH} \xrightarrow{P/I_2} \underset{\text{Methyl iodide}}{CH_3I}$$

$$\xrightarrow{KCN(alc.)} \underset{\text{Methyl nitrile}}{CH_3CN} \xrightarrow[4[H]]{Na(Hg)/C_2H_5OH/\text{Reduction}} \underset{\text{Ethanamine}}{CH_3CH_2NH_2}$$

(vii) **Nitromethane into dimethylamine**

$$\underset{\text{Nitro methane}}{CH_3NO_2} \xrightarrow[\text{[H]}]{Sn/HCl} \underset{\text{Amino methane}}{CH_3NH_2} \xrightarrow{CHCl_3/KOH} \underset{\text{Methyl isocyanide}}{CH_3NC}$$

$$\xrightarrow[\text{[H]}]{Na(Hg)/C_2H_5OH} \underset{\text{Dimethylamine}}{CH_3NHCH_3}$$

(viii) **Propanoic acid into ethanoic acid**

$$\underset{\text{Propanoic acid}}{CH_3CH_2COOH} \xrightarrow{NH_3/\text{Heat}} \underset{\text{Propanamide}}{CH_3CH_2CONH_2} \xrightarrow{Br_2/KOH} \underset{\text{Ethylamine}}{CH_3CH_2NH_2}$$

$$\xrightarrow[\text{(ii) } H_2O]{\text{(i) HONO}} \underset{\text{Ethanol}}{CH_3CH_2OH} \xrightarrow[\text{[O]}]{K_2Cr_2O_7/H_2SO_4} \underset{\text{Ethanal}}{CH_3CHO}$$

$$\xrightarrow[\text{[O]}]{K_2Cr_2O_7/H_2SO_4} \underset{\text{Ethanoic acid}}{CH_3COOH}$$

Question 6 Describe a method for the identification of primary, secondary and tertiary amines. Also write chemical equations of the reactions involved.

◎ *Thinking Process* Give reaction with Hinsberg's reagent (*i.e.*, $C_6H_5SO_2Cl$) as it reacts differently with 1°, 2° and 3° amines.

Sol. Hinsberg's reagent (benzene sulphonyl chloride- $C_6H_5SO_2Cl$) reacts with primary, secondary and tertiary amines in a different manner. This is used for the distinction of three types of amines.

(i) **Primary amine** The reaction of benzene sulphonyl chloride with primary amine proudces *N*-alkyl benzene sulphonamide. Hydrogen attached to nitrogen in the product is acidic so it is soluble in alkali.

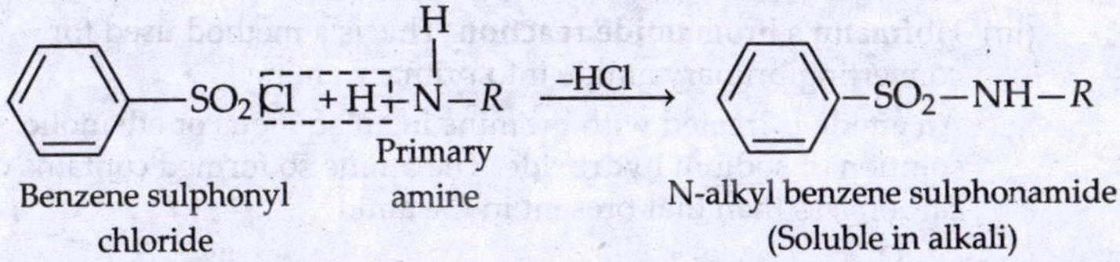

(ii) **A secondary amine** reacts with Hinsberg's reagent to from N,N-dialkyl benzene sulphonamide which remains insoluble in alkali (as no acidic H on nitrogen is present).

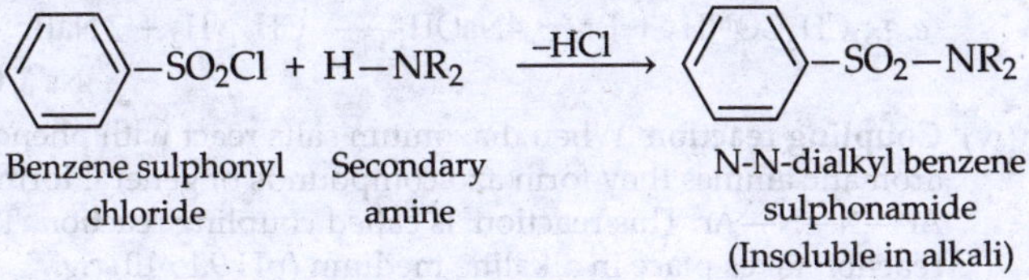

(iii) **A tertiary amine** does not react with benzene sulphonyl chloride.

Question. 7 Write short notes on the following :

(i) Carbylamine reaction (ii) Diazotisation

(iii) Hofmann's bromamide reaction

(iv) Coupling reaction

(v) Ammonolysis

(vi) Acetylation

(vii) Gabriel phthalimide synthesis.

Sol. (i) **Carbylamine reaction** When aliphatic and aromatic primary amines are heated with chloroform and ethanolic potassium hydroxide, carbylamines or isocyanides are formed. These substances produced have foul smell. Secondary and tertiary amines do not give this reaction. This reaction is used to detect primary amines.

$$R\text{—}NH_2 + CHCl_3 + 3KOH \xrightarrow{\text{Heat}} R\text{—}NC + 3KCl + 3H_2O$$

(ii) **Diazotisation** Aromatic amines react with nitrous acid at low temperatures (273-278K) to form diazonium salts. This reaction is called diazotisation reaction.

$$NaNO_2 + HCl \longrightarrow HONO + NaCl$$

$$C_6H_5NH_2 + HONO + HCl \xrightarrow{273\text{-}278K} C_6H_5N_2Cl + NaCl + 2H_2O$$

Aniline (Primary aromatic amine) → Benzene diazonium chloride

Note When primary aliphatic amines react with nitrous acid, aliphatic diazonium salts are formed (Unstable), which liberate nitrogen gas and alcohols.

$$R\text{—}NH_2 + HNO_2 \xrightarrow{NaNO_2 + HCl} [R\text{—}\overset{+}{N_2}\overset{-}{Cl}] \xrightarrow{H_2O} ROH + N_2 + HCl$$

(iii) **Hofmann's bromamide reaction** This is a method used for converting primary amide into primary amine.
An amide is treated with bromine in an aqueous or ethanolic solution of sodium hydroxide. The amine so formed contains one carbon less than that present in the amide.

$$\underset{\text{Amide}}{R-\overset{\overset{\displaystyle O}{\|}}{C}-NH_2} + Br_2 + 4NaOH \longrightarrow \underset{\text{Amine}}{R-NH_2} + Na_2CO_3 + 2NaBr + 2H_2O$$

e.g., $CH_3CONH_2 + Br_2 + 4NaOH \longrightarrow CH_3NH_2 + 2NaBr + Na_2CO_3 + 2H_2O$

(iv) **Coupling reaction** When diazonium salts react with phenols or aromatic amines they form azo compounds of general formula, Ar—N=N—Ar. This reaction is called coupling reaction. The reaction takes place in alkaline medium (pH 9 to 10) *e.g.*

(a) 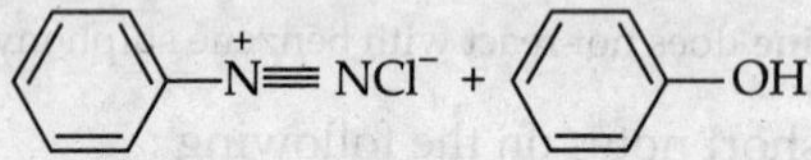

Benzene diazonium chloride　　Phenol

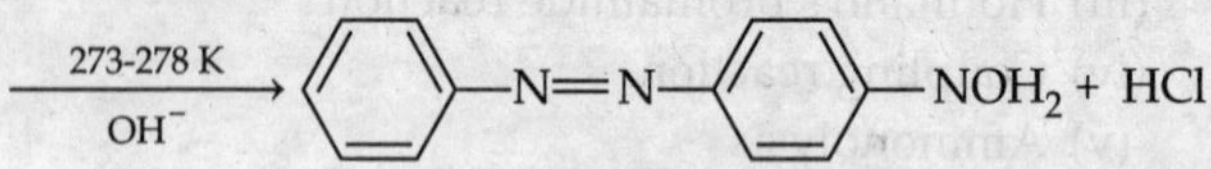

p-Hydroxyazobenzene
(Orange dye)

(b) 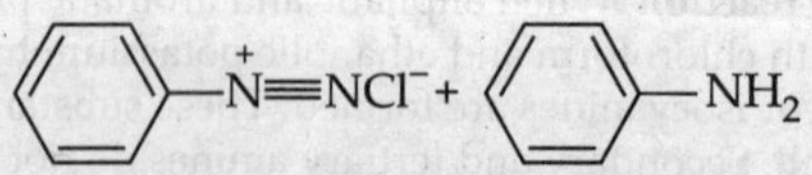

Benzene diazonium chloride　　Aniline

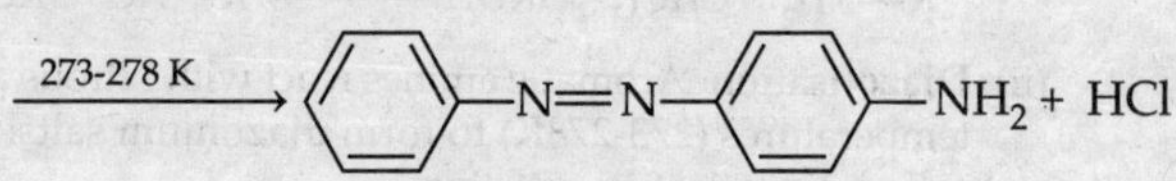

p-Aminoazobenzene
(Yellow dye)

(v) **Ammonolysis** The process of cleavage of C—*X* bond by ammonia molecule is known as ammonolysis.

$$\underset{\text{Nucleophile}}{\ddot{N}H_3} + R-X \longrightarrow \underset{\text{Substituted ammonium salts}}{R-\overset{+}{N}H_3X^-}$$

$$\underset{(1°)}{R-NH_2} \xrightarrow{+R-X} \underset{(2°)}{R_2NH} \xrightarrow{+R-X} \underset{(3°)}{R_3N} \longrightarrow \underset{\text{Quaternary ammonium salt}}{R_4N^+X^-}$$

(vi) **Acetylation** The process in which acetyl ($CH_3CO—$) group is introduced in a molecule, is called acetylation. Reagents used for this purpose are acetyl chloride or acetic anhydride.

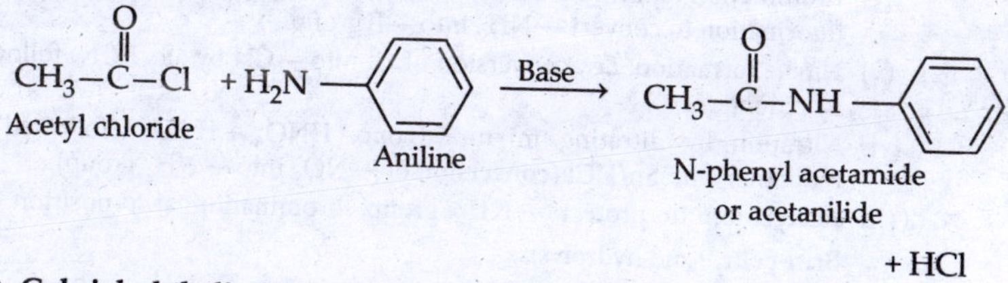

(vii) **Gabriel phthalimide synthesis** This method is used for the preparation of aliphatic primary amines. Phthalimide on reaction with ethanolic potassium hydroxide forms potassium salt of phthalimide. This potassium salt on heating with alkyl halide followed by alkaline hydrolysis produces primary amine.

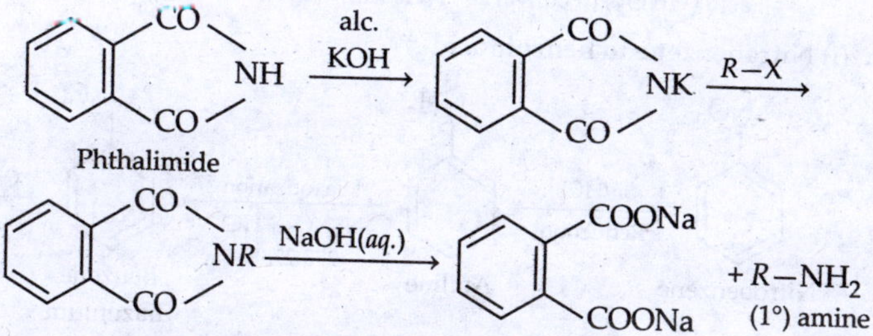

Question 8 Accomplish the following conversions :

(i) Nitrobenzene to benzoic acid
(ii) Benzene to *m*- bromophenol
(iii) Benzoic acid to aniline
(iv) Aniline to 2,4,6-tribromofluorobenzene
(v) Benzyl chloride to 2-phenylethanamine
(vi) Chlorobenzene to *p*-chloroaniline
(vii) Aniline to *p*- bromoaniline
(viii) Benzamide to toluene
(ix) Aniline to benzyl alcohol.

Thinking Process The given conversions involve the following steps :

(i) Reduction, (by Sn/HCl to convert $—NO_2$ to $—NH_2$), diazotisation, cyanide formation, hydrolysis (to convert —CN into —COOH).

(ii) Nitration, *i.e.*, introduction of $—NO_2$ group in benzene nucleus by nitrating agent, bromination (by Br_2 / $FeBr_3$) at *m*-position, reduction by Sn/HCl to convert $—NO_2$ into $-NH_2$, diazotisation (conversion of $—NH_2$ into $—N_2Cl$ group) followed by hydrolysis (conversion of $—N_2Cl$ into —OH group).

(iii) Amide formation, *i.e.,* reaction with NH_3 followed by Hofmann bromamide reaction, *i.e.,* conversion of —$CONH_2$ group into —NH_2.

(iv) Bromination to introduce Br atom at 2,4 and 6 position, diazotisation and fluorination to convert —NH_2 into —F group.

(v) Nitrile formation, *i.e.,* conversion of Cl into —CN by alc. KCN, followed by reduction.

(vi) Nitration by nitrating mixture (conc. $HNO_3 + H_2SO_4$) followed by reduction with Sn/HCl (conversion of —NO_2 into —NH_2 group).

(vii) Acetylation to protect —NH_2 group, bromination at *p*-position (by Br_2 / $FeBr_3$) and hydrolysis.

(viii) Hofmann bromamide reaction to convert —$CONH_2$ into —NH_2; diazotisation and reaction with H_3PO_2 to convert —N_2Cl into —H; Friedel Crafts alkylation to introduce —CH_3 group.

(ix) Diazotisation and cyanide formation by reacting with HNO_2 and CuCN; reduction to convert —CN into —CH_2NH_2 and reaction with nitrous acid (HNO_2) to convert —NH_2 into —OH.

Sol. (i) **Nitrobenzene to benzoic acid**

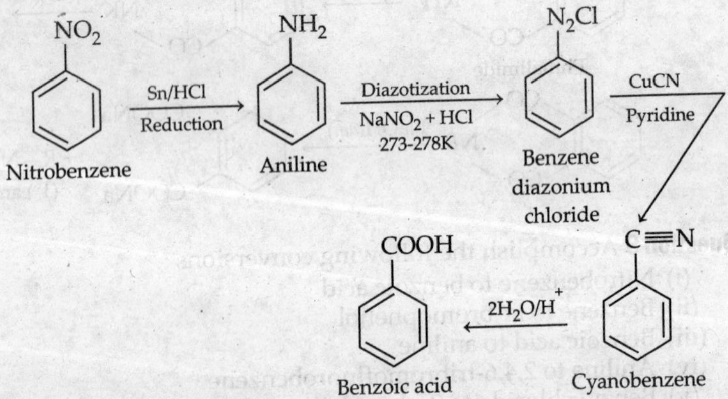

(ii) **Benzene to *m*-bromophenol**

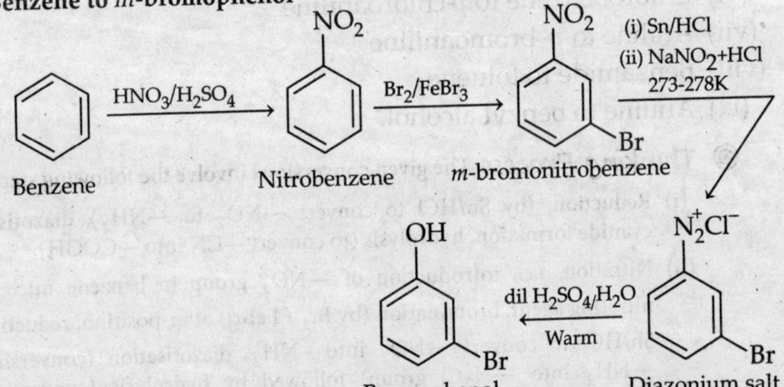

(iii) **Benzoic acid to aniline**

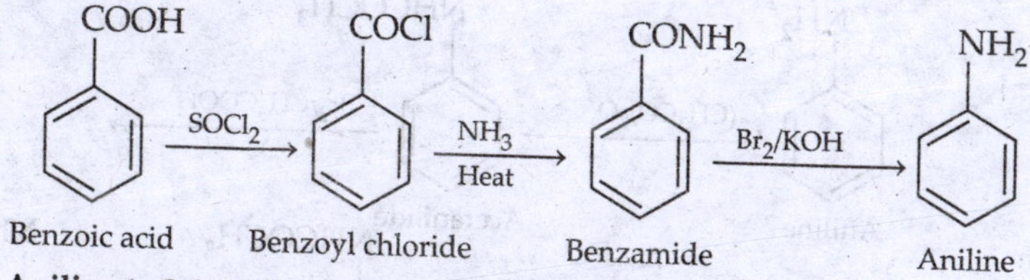

(iv) **Aniline to 2,4,6-tribromofluorobenzene**

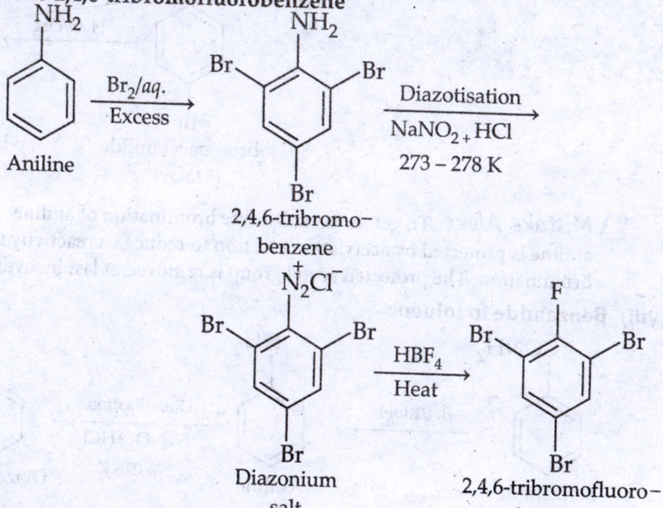

(v) **Benzyl chloride to 2-phenylethanamine**

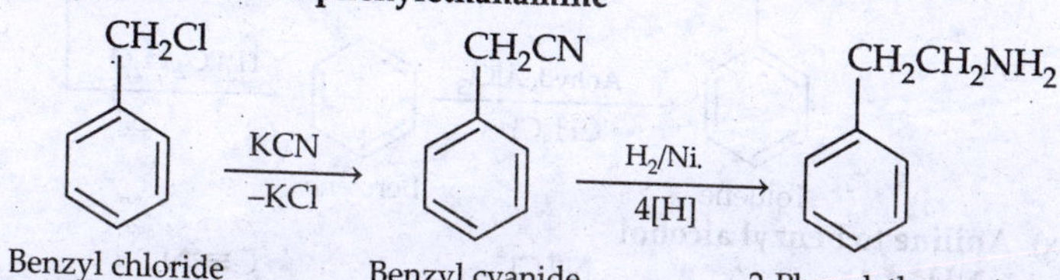

(vi) **Chlorobenzene to *p*-Chloroaniline**

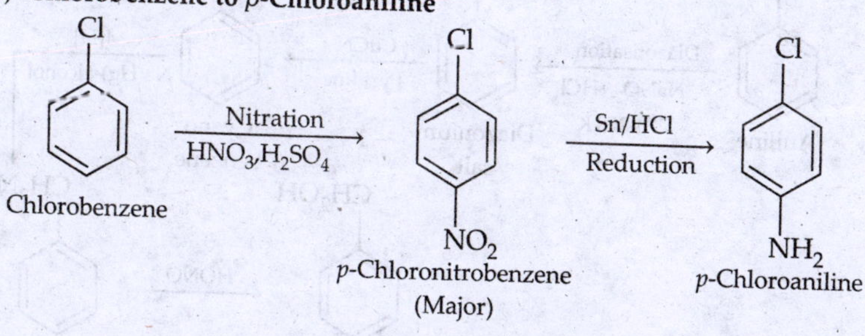

(vii) **Aniline to *p*-bromoaniline**

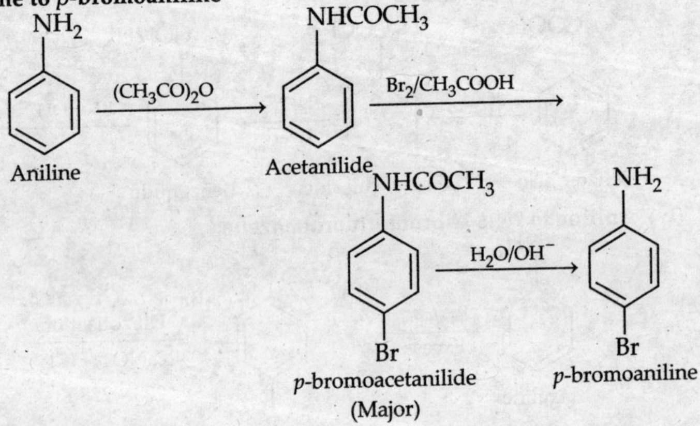

Mistake Alert To get mono-substitute bromination of aniline —NH_2 of aniline is protected by acetylation reaction to reduce its reactivity towards bromination. The protected acetyl group is removed at last by hydrolysis.

(viii) **Benzamide to toluene**

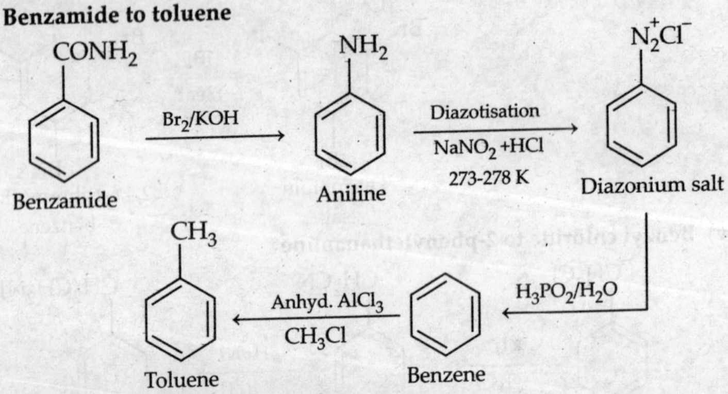

(ix) **Aniline to benzyl alcohol**

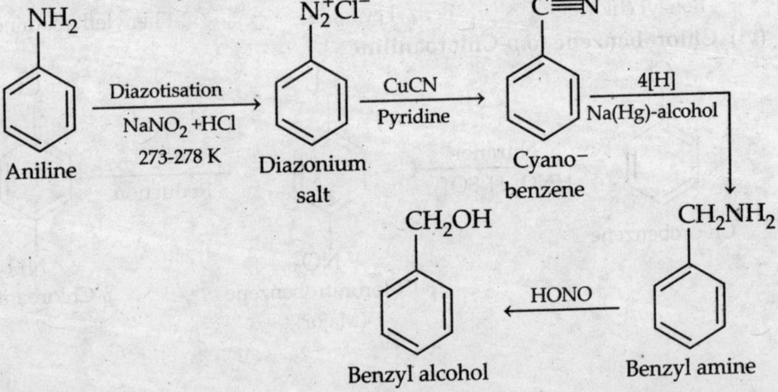

Alternative Solution of (ix)

(a) Convert the toluene prepared in (viii) into benzylchloride and then do hydrolysis to get benzyl alcohol.

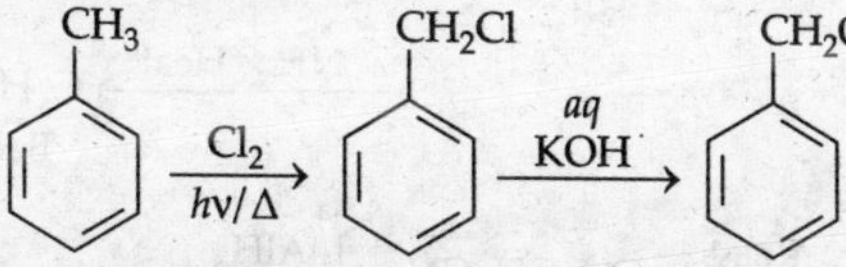

(b) Convert the cyanobenzene prepared in (ix) to benzoic acid by hydrolysis and then reduce —COOH to —CH_2OH group by $LiAlH_4$.

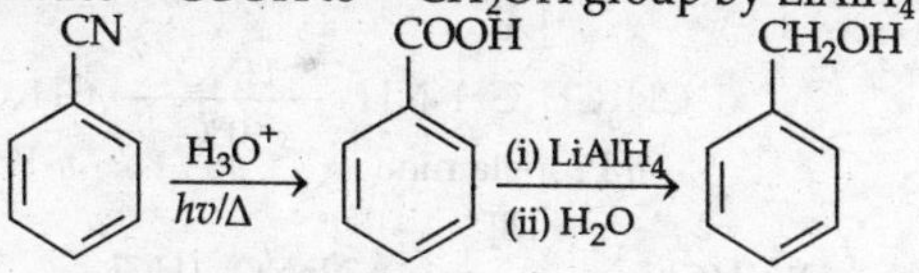

Question 9 Give the structures of *A*, *B* and *C* in the following reactions

(i) $CH_3CH_2I \xrightarrow{NaCN} A \xrightarrow[\text{Partial hydrolysis}]{OH^-} B \xrightarrow{NaOH + Br_2} C$

(ii) $C_6H_5N_2Cl \xrightarrow{CuCN} A \xrightarrow[H^+]{H_2O} B \xrightarrow[\Delta]{NH_3} C$

(iii) $CH_3CH_2Br \xrightarrow{KCN} A \xrightarrow{LiAlH_4} B \xrightarrow[0°C]{HNO_2} C$

(iv) $C_6H_5NO_2 \xrightarrow{Fe/HCl} A \xrightarrow[273\text{ K}]{NaNO_2 + HCl} B \xrightarrow[\Delta]{H_2O/H^+} C$

(v) $CH_3COOH \xrightarrow[\Delta C]{NH_3} A \xrightarrow{NaOBr} B \xrightarrow{NaNO_2/HCl} C$

(vi) $C_6H_5NO_2 \xrightarrow{Fe/HCl} A \xrightarrow[273\text{ K}]{HNO_2} B \xrightarrow{C_6H_5OH} C$

◎ **Thinking Process** Different processes involved are as follows :

(i) Nitrile formation, amide formation, amine formation.
(ii) Nitrile formation, hydrolysis, ammonolysis (amide formation).
(iii) Nitrile formation, reduction, formation of alcohol.
(iv) Reduction, diazotisation, hydrolysis.
(v) Amide formation, amine formation, alcohol formation.
(vi) Reduction, diazotisation, coupling.

Sol. (i) $\underset{\text{Ethyl iodide}}{CH_3CH_2I} \xrightarrow{NaCN} \underset{\substack{\text{Ethyl cyanide}\\ [A]}}{CH_3CH_2CN} \xrightarrow[\substack{\text{Partial}\\ \text{hydrolysis}}]{OH^-}$

$$\underset{\substack{\text{Propionamide}\\ [B]}}{CH_3CH_2CONH_2} \xrightarrow{NaOH + Br_2} \underset{\substack{\text{Ethanamine}\\ [C]}}{CH_3CH_2NH_2}$$

(ii) $\underset{\substack{\text{Benzene}\\ \text{diazonium}\\ \text{chloride}}}{C_6H_5N_2Cl} \xrightarrow{CuCN} \underset{\substack{\text{Cyano}\\ \text{benzene}\\ [A]}}{C_6H_5CN} \xrightarrow{H_2O/H^+} \underset{\substack{\text{Benzoic acid}\\ [B]}}{C_6H_5COOH}$

$\xrightarrow{NH_3,\ \text{Heat}} \underset{\substack{\text{Benzamide}\\ [C]}}{C_6H_5CONH_2}$

(iii) $\underset{\text{Ethyl bromide}}{CH_3CH_2Br} \xrightarrow{KCN} \underset{\substack{\text{Ethyl cyanide}\\ [A]}}{CH_3CH_2CN} \xrightarrow{LiAlH_4}$

$\underset{\substack{n\text{-Propylamine}\\ [B]}}{CH_3CH_2CH_2NH_2} \xrightarrow[0°C]{HNO_2} \underset{n\text{-Propylalcohol}}{CH_3CH_2CH_2OH}$

(iv) $\underset{\text{Nitrobenzene}}{C_6H_5NO_2} \xrightarrow{Fe/HCl} \underset{\substack{\text{Aniline}\\ [A]}}{C_6H_5NH_2} \xrightarrow[273\,K\text{-}378]{NaNO_2/HCl}$

$\underset{\substack{\text{Diazonium salt}\\ [B]}}{C_6H_5N_2^+Cl^-} \xrightarrow[\text{Heat}]{H_2O/H^+} \underset{\substack{\text{Phenol}\\ [C]}}{C_6H_5OH}$

(v) $\underset{\text{Acetic acid}}{CH_3COOH} \xrightarrow[\text{Heat}]{NH_3} \underset{\substack{\text{Acetamide}\\ [A]}}{CH_3CONH_2} \xrightarrow{NaOBr}$

$\underset{\substack{\text{Methylamine}\\ \text{align}\\ [B]}}{CH_3NH_2} \xrightarrow{NaNO_2/HCl} \underset{\substack{\text{Methanol}\\ [C]}}{CH_3OH}$

(vi) $\underset{\text{Nitro benzene}}{C_6H_5NO_2} \xrightarrow{Fe/HCl} \underset{\substack{\text{Aniline}\\ [A]}}{C_6H_5NH_2} \xrightarrow[273K]{HNO_2}$

$\underset{\substack{\text{Diazonium salt}\\ [B]}}{C_6H_5N_2^+Cl^-} \xrightarrow{C_6H_5OH} \underset{\substack{p\text{-Hydroxyazobenzene}\\ [C]}}{C_6H_5N=NC_6H_4(OH)(p)}$

Question 10 An aromatic compound '*A*' on treatment with aqueous ammonia and heating forms compound '*B*' which on heating with Br_2 and KOH forms a compound '*C*' of molecular formula C_6H_7N. Write the structures and IUPAC names of compounds *A*, *B* and *C*.

Sol. (i) **To determine the structures of *B* and C** Compound '*B*' on heating with Br_2 and KOH forms compound '*C*'. So, '*B*' is amide and '*C*' is amine. Molecular formula C_6H_7N of '*C*' tells us that it is aniline (**$C_6H_5NH_2$**).

$$\underset{\substack{\text{Benzamide}\\[B]}}{C_6H_5CONH_2} \xrightarrow{Br_2/KOH} \underset{\substack{\text{Aniline}\\[C]\\(C_6H_7N)}}{C_6H_5NH_2}$$

(ii) **To determine the structure of A** Compound '*A*' on treatment with aqueous ammonia forms '*B*', so '*A*' is benzoic acid.

$$\underset{\substack{\text{Benzoic acid}\\[A]}}{C_6H_5COOH} \xrightarrow[\text{Heat}]{\text{Aqueous } NH_3} \underset{\substack{\text{Benzamide}\\[B]}}{C_6H_5CONH_2}$$

Question 11 Complete the following reactions :

(i) $C_6H_5NH_2 + CHCl_3 + \text{alc. KOH} \longrightarrow$

(ii) $C_6H_5N_2Cl + H_3PO_2 + H_2O \longrightarrow$

(iii) $C_6H_5NH_2 + H_2SO_4(\text{conc.}) \longrightarrow$

(iv) $C_6H_5N_2Cl + C_2H_5OH \longrightarrow$

(v) $C_6H_5NH_2 + Br_2(aq) \longrightarrow$

(vi) $C_6H_5NH_2 + (CH_3CO)_2O \longrightarrow$

(vii) $C_6H_5N_2Cl \xrightarrow[\text{(ii)} NaNO_2/Cu, \Delta]{\text{(i) } HBF_4}$

Thinking Process

(i) Carbylamine reaction, *i.e.*, conversion of —NH_2 into —NC group.

(ii) H_3PO_2 / H_2O converts —N_2Cl into —H and oxidation of H_3PO_2.

(iii) Formation of $C_6H_5N^+H_3HSO_4^-$ product.

(iv) Conversion of —N_2Cl into —H and oxidation of alcohol

(v) Bromination, *i.e.*, Br atoms occupy 2,4 and 6 positions.

(vi) Acetylation reaction.

(vii) Fluorination, *i.e.*, introduction of F atom and its conversion to —NO_2 group.

Sol. (i) $$\underset{\text{Aniline}}{C_6H_5NH_2} + CHCl_3 + KOH \xrightarrow[\substack{\text{Carbylamine}\\\text{reaction}}]{\text{Heat}} \underset{\substack{\text{Phenyl isocyanide}\\\text{(Foul smell)}}}{C_6H_5N \equiv C} + 3KCl + 3H_2O$$

(ii) $$\underset{\substack{\text{Benzene diazonium}\\\text{chloride}}}{C_6H_5N_2Cl} + H_3PO_2 + H_2O \xrightarrow[\text{Reduction}]{} \underset{\text{Benzene}}{C_6H_6} + N_2 + H_3PO_3 + HCl$$

(iii) $C_6H_5NH_2 + H_2SO_4 \longrightarrow$ 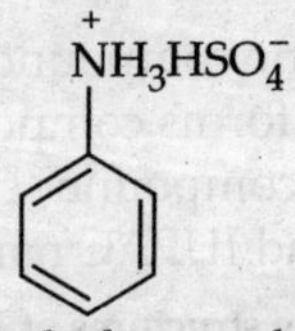

Aniline Conc. Anilinium hydrogen sulphate

(iv) $C_6H_5N_2Cl + C_2H_5OH \xrightarrow{\text{Reduction}} C_6H_6 + CH_3CHO + N_2 + HCl$

Benzene diazonium chloride Benzene Ethanal

(v) $C_6H_5NH_2 + Br_2\,(aq.) \longrightarrow$ 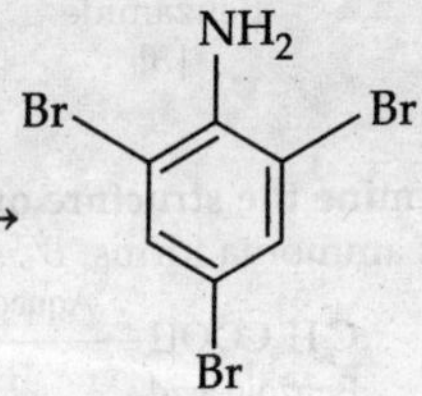 $+ 3HBr$

Aniline

2,4,6-Tribromoaniline

(vi) $C_6H_5NH_2 + (CH_3CO)_2O \longrightarrow H_5C_6NHCOCH_3$

Aniline Ethanoic anhydride N-phenyl ethanamide or acetanilide

(vii) $C_6H_5N_2Cl \xrightarrow[\text{(ii)}NaNO_2/Cu,\ \text{Heat}]{\text{(i)}HBF_4} C_6H_5NO_2 + NaBF_4 + N_2$

Benzene diazonium chloride Nitro benzene

Question 12 Why cannot aromatic primary amines be prepared by Gabriel phthalimide synthesis?

◎ ***Thinking Process*** Gabriel phthalimide synthesis involves breaking of C—*X* bond where, *X* is halogen) and in aromatic halides C—*X* bond acquires double bond character.

Sol. In Gabriel phthalimide reaction, potassium salt of phthalimide is formed. It reacts readily with alkyl halide to form the corresponding alkyl derivative.

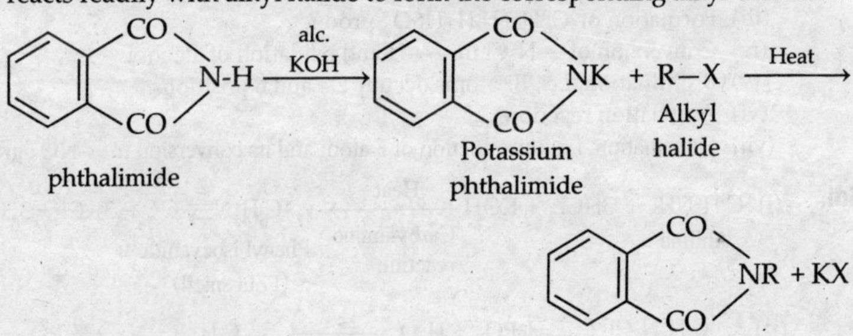

phthalimide Potassium phthalimide

N-alkyl phthalimide

But aryl halide does not react with potassium phthalimide because C—X bond in haloarene (alkyl halide) is difficult to be cleaved due to partial double bond character. So, aromatic primary amines cannot be prepared by Gabriel phthalimide synthesis.

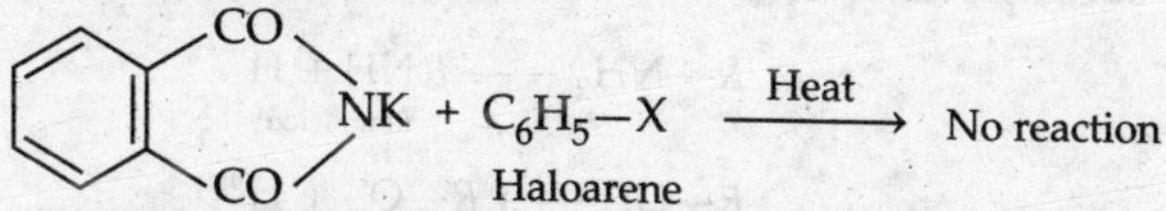

Potassium phthalimide

Question 13 Write the reactions of (i) aromatic and (ii) aliphatic primary amines with nitrous acid.

◎ **Thinking Process** Diazonium salts are formed, but alkyl amines form unstable diazonium salts which decompose to produce alcohol.

Sol. (i) **Aromatic primary amines** react with nitrous acid at low temperatures (273-278 K) to form diazonium salts.

$$\underset{\text{Aniline}}{C_6H_5—NH_2} \xrightarrow[273\text{-}278\,K]{NaNO_2 + HCl} \underset{\text{Benzene diazonium chloride}}{C_6H_5—\overset{+}{N}_2\overset{-}{Cl}} + NaCl + 2H_2O$$

Note Nitrous acid is produced by the reaction of $NaNO_2$ and HCl insitu.

(ii) **Aliphatic primary amines** react with nitrous acid to form aliphatic diazonium salts (unstable), which produce nitrogen gas and alcohols after decomposition.

$$\underset{\text{Alkyl amine}}{R—NH_2} + HNO_2 \xrightarrow{NaNO_2 + HCl}$$

$$[R—\overset{+}{N}_2\overset{-}{Cl}] \xrightarrow{H_2O} \underset{\text{Alcohol}}{ROH} + N_2 + HCl$$

Question 14 Give plausible explanation for each of the following :

(i) Why are amines less acidic than alcohols of comparable molecular masses?

(ii) Why do primary amines have higher boiling point than tertiary amines?

(iii) Why are aliphatic amines stronger bases than aromatic amines?

◎ **Thinking Process**

(i) Consider polarity of N—H and O—H bonds.

(ii) More is the ease of H—bond formation, higher is the boiling point.

(iii) Resonance and protonation in case of aromatic amines.

Sol. (i) Amines are less acidic than alcohols of comparable molecular masses because N—H bond is less polar than O—H bond, since O is more electronegative than N. Hence, amines release H^+ ion with more difficultly as compared to alcohol. Also, alcohols and amines loses a proton to form :

$$R\text{—}NH_2 \longrightarrow R\overset{\ominus}{N}H + H^{\oplus}$$
(amide ion)

$$R\text{—}OH \longrightarrow R\text{—}O^{\ominus} + H^{\oplus}$$
(alkoxide ion)

Since, O is more electronegative, it can accomodate the negative charge more easily than N, therefore it is more stable. Thus, alcohols are more acidic than amines of comparable masses.

(ii) Intermolecular hydrogen bonding is present in primary amines but not in tertiary amines (H-atom absent in amino group). So, primary amines have higher boiling point than tertiary amines as extra energy is required to break the H bonding and separate the primary amine molecules.

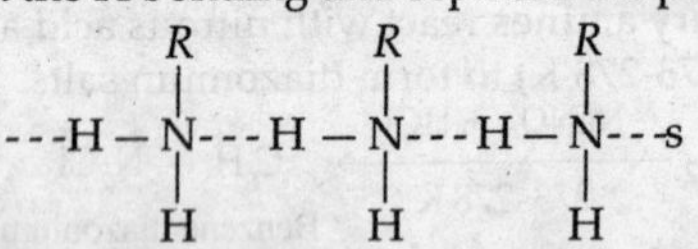

(iii) Aliphatic amines are stronger bases than aromatic amines due to following reason: Electron pair on the nitrogen atom of aromatic amines is involved in conjugation with the π-electron pairs of the ring as follows

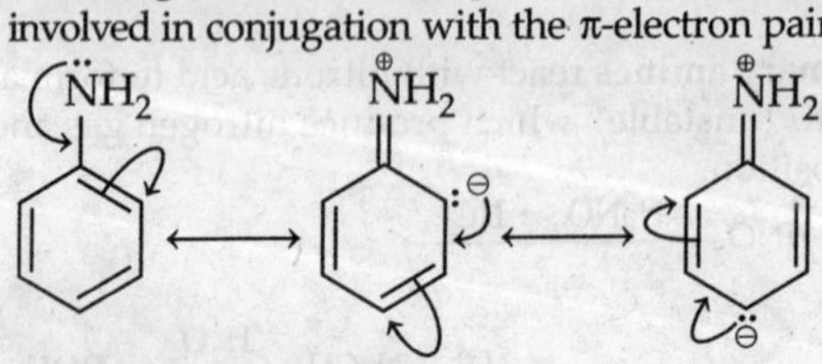

I II III

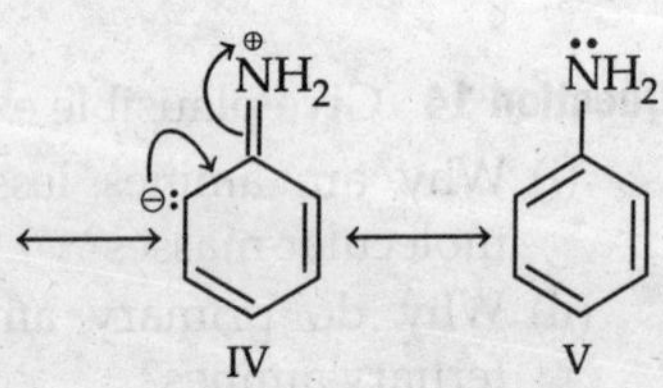

IV V

So, this lone pair on nitrogen is less available for protonation.

Thus, aniline is a weaker base than alkyl amines, in which $+I$ effect of alkyl group increases the electron density on the nitrogen atom.

DIKSHA APP Questions

☐ Multiple Choice Questions

Q.1 The nitrogen containing organic compound which plays an important role as good intermediate for the introduction of —F, —CN, —OH, —NO_2 groups in the aromatic ring is

(a) aniline (b) diazonium salt
(c) nitrobenzene (d) None

Sol. (b) Diazonium salt is nitrogen containing organic compound, which acts as a very good intermediate for the introduction of —F, —CN, —OH, —NO_2 groups in the aromatic ring because diazonium group is a very good leaving group and it can be easily substituted by displacing nitrogen from the aromatic ring. The nitrogen formed escapes from the reaction mixture as a gas.

Q.2 The reaction of benzenediazonium chloride with aniline yields yellow dye. The name of the yellow dye is:

(a) *p*-hydroxyazobenzene (b) *p*-aminoazobenzene
(c) *p*-nitroazobenzene (d) *o*-nitroazobenzene

Sol. (b) The coupling reaction between benzenediazonium chloride and aniline yield a yellow dye (*p*-aminoazobenzene).

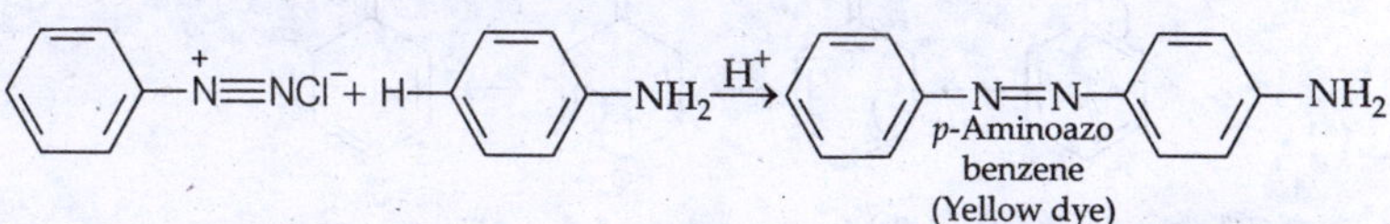

$+ Cl^- + H_2O$

Q.3. The products obtained when benzenediazoniumfluoroborate is heated with aqueous sodium nitrite solution in the presence of copper are:

(a) fluorobenzene and nitrogen gas
(b) fluorobenzene, N_2 gas and $NaBF_4$
(c) nitrobenzene, N_2 gas and $NaBF_4$
(d) nitrobenzene and $NaBF_4$

Sol. (c) The products obtained when benzenediazonium fluoroborate is heated with aqueous sodium nitrite solution in the presence of copper are: nitrobenzene, N_2 gas and $NaBF_4$.

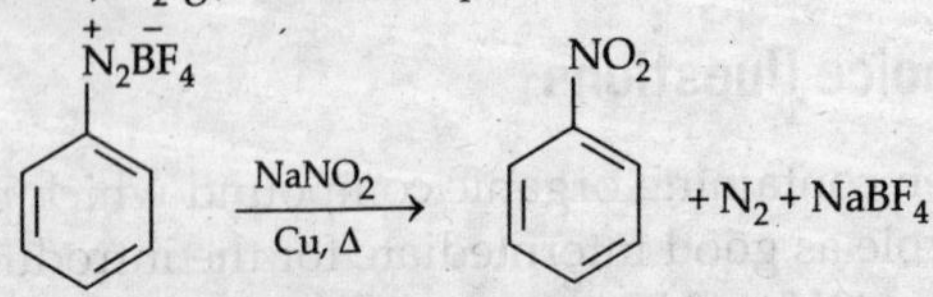

Q.4 For the transformation of *m*-bromobenzenediazonium chloride into bromobenzene the reagent used is

(a) $LiAlH_4$ (b) H_3PO_2 (c) H_3O^+ (d) H_2 / Pt

Sol. (b) Hypophosphorus acid (phosphinic acid) is a mild reducing agent which reduces *m*-bromobenzenediazonium chloride to bromobenzene and itself gets oxidised to phosphorous acid.

$m\text{-Br-}C_6H_4N_2Cl + H_3PO_2 \longrightarrow C_6H_5Br + HCl + H_3PO_3$

Therefore, option (b) is correct.

Q.5 Which of the following will be the most stable diazonium salt?

(a) CH_3N_2X (b) $C_6H_5N_2X$ (c) $CH_3CH_2N_2X$ (d) $C_6H_5CH_2N_2X$

Sol. (b) $C_6H_5N_2X$ is the most stable diazonium salt due to presence of resonance.

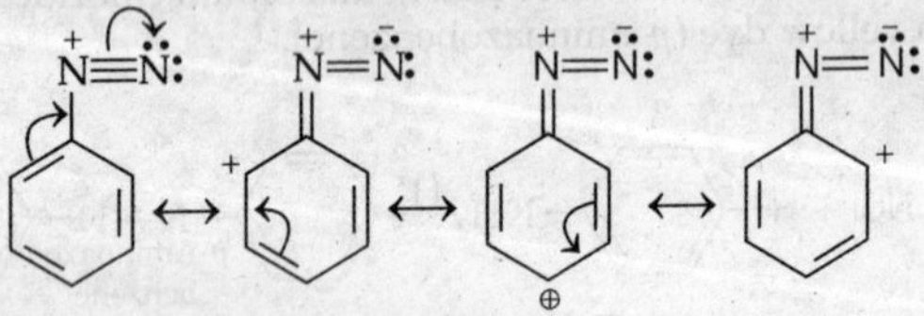

Therefore, option (b) is correct.

Q.6 Which is **not** true for benzenediazonium chloride?

(a) It is readily soluble in water. (b) It is colourless crystalline solid.

(c) It decomposes easily in dry state. (d) None of these

Sol. (d) Benzene diazonium chloride is a colourless crystalline solid. It is readily soluble in water and it decomposes easily in the dry state.

Q.7 The diazonium salt is not generally stored and is used immediately after its preparation because

(a) It is highly stable and further can't react.

(b) It is unstable

(c) Resonance makes it unfit for reaction.

(d) None of the above

Sol. (b) The diazonium salt is unstable. So, due to its instability, it is not stored and is used immediately after its preparation.

Q.8 The conversion of primary aromatic amines into diazonium salt is known as

(a) diazomerisation (b) diazotisation

(c) diazonium process (d) All of these

Sol. (b) The conversion of primary aromatic amines into diazonium salt by reacting it with nitrous acid at 273-278K is known as diazotisation.

$$C_6H_5NH_2 + NaNO_2 + 2HCl \xrightarrow{273\text{-}278\,K} C_6H_5N_2^+Cl^- + NaCl + 2H_2O$$

Q.9 An organic compound (C_3H_9N) (*A*), when treated with nitrous acid, gave an alcohol and N_2 gas was evolved. (*A*) on warming with $CHCl_3$ and caustic soda gave (*C*), which on reduction gave isopropylmethylamine. Predict the compound (*A*).

(a) $(CH_3)_2CH—NH_2$ (b) $CH_3—CH_2—NH—CH_3$

(c) $(CH_3)_2N—CH_3$ (d) $CH_3—CH_2—CH_2—NH_2$

Sol. (a) Since *A* reacts with nitrous acid to produce an alcohol and nitrogen gas, then *A* must be a primary amine as the general reaction for primary amines with nitrous acid involves the formation of an alcohol and nitrogen gas. Compound *A* when reacted with chloroform $(CHCl_3)$ and caustic potash (KOH), undergoes carbylamine reaction, forming an isocyanide (carbylamine). The isocyanide product is reduced to isopropylmethylamine. This suggests that the original amine *A* must be isopropylamine. The structure of compound *A* is isopropylamine, which has the formula $(CH_3)_2CHNH_2$.

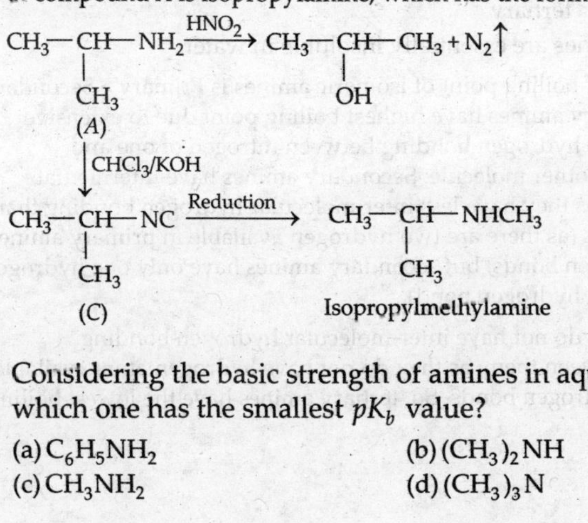

Q.10 Considering the basic strength of amines in aqueous solution, which one has the smallest pK_b value?

(a) $C_6H_5NH_2$ (b) $(CH_3)_2NH$

(c) CH_3NH_2 (d) $(CH_3)_3N$

Sol. (b) The pK_b value is the measure of basicity of a compound. Lower pK_b values indicates stronger bases. In the case of methyl substituted amines, the order of basic strength in aqueous solution is: secondary > primary > tertiary. (This order is decided after considering three factors: $+I$ effect of alkyl groups, solvation effect and steric hinderance.)

Q.11 The solubility in water of $C_6H_5NH_2$ (I), $(C_2H_5)_2NH$(II) and $C_2H_5NH_2$ (III) increase in the order of:

(a) II < III < I (b) I < II < III

(c) III < II < I (d) II < I < III

Sol. (b) Aniline has a phenyl group attached to the amine group. The large, nonpolar phenyl ring decreases its solubility in water as compared to smaller, more polar aliphatic amines. Diethylamine has two ethyl groups attached to the amine group. While it can form hydrogen bonds with water, the presence of two bulky ethyl groups reduces its solubility as compared to smaller amines. Ethylamine has a smaller structure, than diethylamine and aniline. It is a primary amine with just one ethyl group, which allows it to interact more effectively with water through hydrogen bonding, making it the most soluble among these compounds.

Q.12 Which statement is wrong about amine?

(a) aniline and other arylamines are usually colourless but get coloured on storage due to atmospheric oxidation.

(b) amines are less polar than alcohol.

(c) the order of boiling point of isomeric amines is : Primary < secondary < tertiary.

(d) higher amines are essentially insoluble in water.

Sol. (c) The order of boiling point of isomeric amines is Primary > Secondary > Tertiary. Primary amines have highest boiling point due to extensive inter-molecular hydrogen bonding between nitrogen of one and hydrogen of another molecule. Secondary amines have intermediate boiling points as they have less inter-molecular hydrogen bonding than primary amines (as there are two hydrogen available in primary amines to form hydrogen bonds, but secondary amines have only one hydrogen which can form hydrogen bond).

Tertiary amines do not have inter-molecular hydrogen bonding interaction between them, as they do not have hydrogen atom available for forming hydrogen bonds. So, tertiary amines have the lowest boiling point.

Q.13 Ammonolysis of benzyl chloride and the amine gives an organic compound, which react with two moles of CH_3Cl to give

(a) benzyl amine
(b) N-methyl-N-phenylmethanamine
(c) N, N-dimethylphenylmethanamine
(d) None of the above

Sol. (c) Benzyl chloride reacts with ammonia to form benzylamine. Benzylamine reacts with two moles of methyl chloride to form N, N-dimethylbenzylamine.

$$\underset{\text{Benzyl chloride}}{C_6H_5—CH_2—Cl} \xrightarrow{NH_3} \underset{\text{Benzylamine}}{C_6H_5—CH_2NH_2}$$

$$\xrightarrow{2CH_3Cl} \underset{\text{N, N-Dimethyl benzylamine}}{C_6H_5—CH_2—\underset{\underset{CH_3}{|}}{N}—CH_3}$$

Q.14 Gabriel phthalimide reaction is used for preparation of

(a) primary aromatic amine.
(b) secondary amine.
(c) primary aliphatic amine.
(d) tertiary amine.

Sol. (c) Gabriel Phthalimide Synthesis is a method used to prepare primary aliphatic amines. Phthalimide reacts with potassium hydroxide (KOH), to form the potassium salt of phthalimide, which is then treated with an alkyl halide ($R—X$) to form N-alkylphthalimide. N-alkylphthalimide is hydrolyzed using NaOH to yield the primary aliphatic amine and phthalic acid.

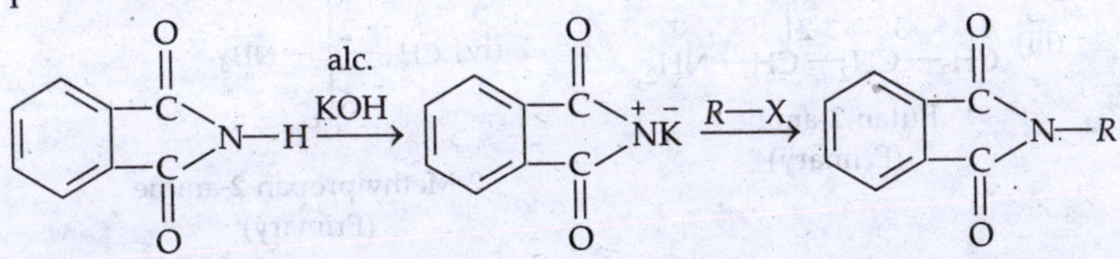

Phthalimide N-Alkylphthalimide

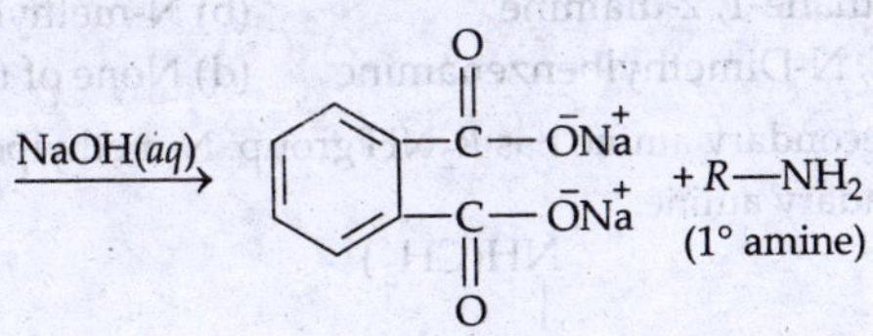

Q.15 The IUPAC name of the following compound is
$(CH_3)_2N-CH=CH_2$
(a) N,N-dimethylethenamine
(b) N-ethyl-N-methylmethanamine
(c) N-vinyl-N-methylmethanamine
(d) None of the above

Sol. (a) The IUPAC name of the given compound is N,N-dimethylethenamine.

Q.16 The correct IUPAC name for $CH_2=CH-CH_2-NH-CH_3$ is
(a) Allylmethylamine (b) N-methylprop-2-en-1-amine
(c) 3-aminobutene (d) N-methylbutene

Sol. (b)The IUPAC name of the given compound is N-methylprop-2-en-1-amine.

Q.17 How many primary amines (structural isomers) are possible for the formula $C_4H_{11}N$?
(a) 1 (b) 2 (c) 3 (d) 4

Sol. (d) There are four primary amines (structural isomers) possible for the formula $C_4H_{11}N$.

(i) $\overset{4}{CH_3}-\overset{3}{CH_2}-\overset{2}{CH_2}-\overset{1}{CH_2}-NH_2$
Butan-1-amine
(Primary)

(ii) $\overset{3}{CH_3}-\overset{2}{CH}(CH_3)-\overset{1}{CH_2}-NH_2$
2-Methylpropan-1-amine
(Primary)

(iii) $\overset{4}{CH_3}-\overset{3}{CH_2}-\overset{2}{CH}(\overset{1}{CH_3})-NH_2$
Butan-2-amine
(Primary)

(iv) $CH_3-\overset{2}{C}(\overset{1}{CH_3})(\overset{3}{CH_3})-NH_3$
2-Methylpropan-2-amine
(Primary)

Q.18 Which of the following is a secondary amine?
(a) Ethane-1, 2-diamine (b) N-methylpentan-2-amine
(c) N, N-Dimethylbenzenamine (d) None of the above

Sol. (b) Secondary amine has R_2NH group. N-methylpentan-2-amine is a secondary amine.

$CH_3-CH_2-CH(NH(CH_3))-CH_2-CH_3$

Q.19 Like ammonia, nitrogen atom of amines is

(a) trivalent.

(b) carries an unshared paired electron.

(c) sp^3 hybridized and pyramidal geometry.

(d) All of the above

Sol. (d) Like ammonia, nitrogen atom in amines is trivalent. It carries an unshared pair of electron, which makes amines basic in nature. It has sp^3 hybridisation and pyramidal shape.

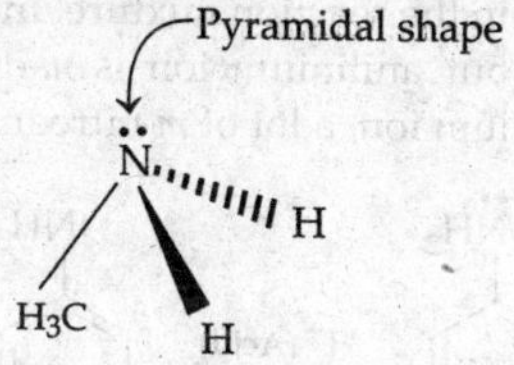

Therefore, option (d) is correct.

Q.20 Bond angle in 3° amine (trimethylamine) increases from 107° to 108°. Why?

(a) Steric hindrance between the three bulky alkyl groups.

(b) Availability of a free pair of electron on nitrogen.

(c) It is due to its pyramidal shape.

(d) None of the above

Sol. (a) The bond angle in tertiary amines increases slightly from 107° to 108° due to steric hinderance among the three bulky alkyl groups attached to the nitrogen. The increased steric repulsion between these groups causes the bond angles to expand slightly to minimize overcrowding and reduce steric strain.

□ Short Answer Type

Q.1 Give reason:

a. Aniline does not undergo Friedel-Craft Reaction.

b. Although amino group is *ortho* and *para* directing in aromatic electrophilic substitution reactions, aniline on nitration gives a substantial amount of *m*-nitroanillne.

c. Aniline is weaker base than cyclohexylamine.

Sol. (a) Aniline being a Lewis base forms a complex with $AlCl_3$, a Lewis acid. As a result, nitrogen of aniline becomes positively charged and acts as a strong deactivating group for electrophilic substitution reaction. Consequently, aniline does not undergo Friedel Crafts reaction.

$$\underset{\text{(Lewis base)}}{\underset{\text{Aniline}}{C_6H_5\ddot{N}H_2}} + \underset{\text{(Lewis acid)}}{AlCl_3} \longrightarrow \underset{\text{Complex}}{[C_6H_5NH_2]^+[AlCl_3]^-}$$

(b) In presence of conc. HNO_3 and conc. H_2SO_4, most of aniline gets protonated to form anilinium ion. Now, aniline and anilinium ions both are present in the reaction mixture. In aniline —NH_2 group, is *o*- and *p*-directing but anilinium ion is *m*-directing. Because of more amount of anilinium ion, a lot of *m*-nitroaniline is formed.

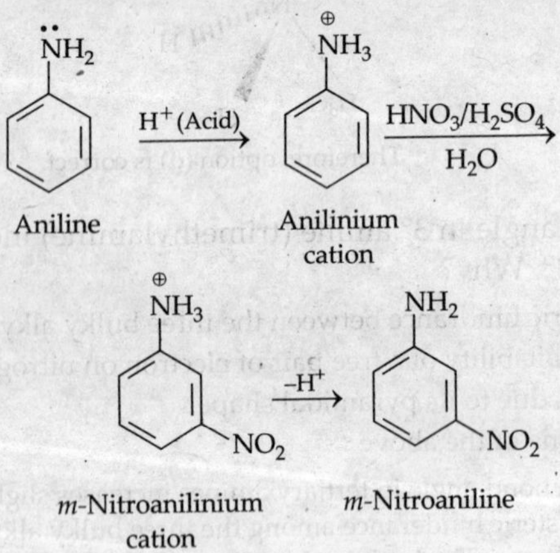

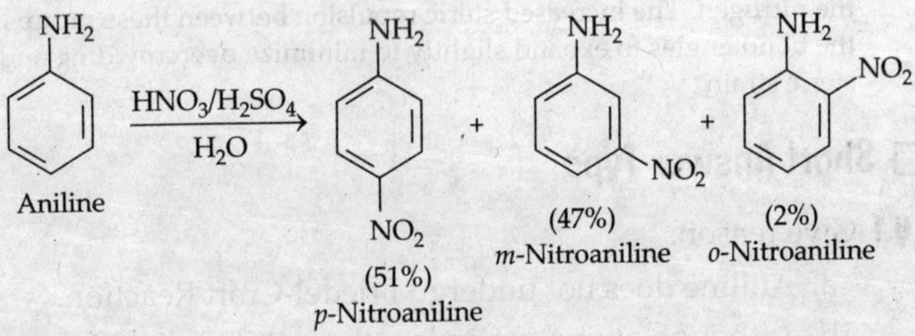

(c) In aniline lone pair on nitrogen undergoes resonance with the ring, so it is not available to transfer whereas in cyclohexylamine, cyclohexyl group is electron donating group so it increase the electron density at nitrogen, hence it become electron rich and electrons are easily available for transfer.

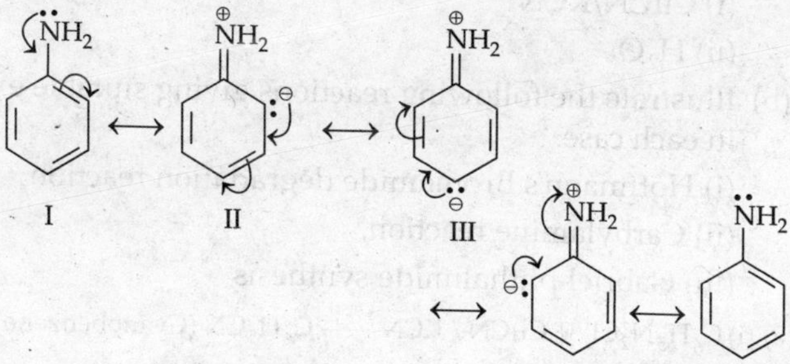

I, II, III, IV, V

Q.2 a. How do you convert the following?

(i) Aniline to phenol

(ii) Ethanamide to methanamaine

b. How will you distinguish the CH_3NH_2 and $(CH_3)_2NH$

Sol. a.

(i)

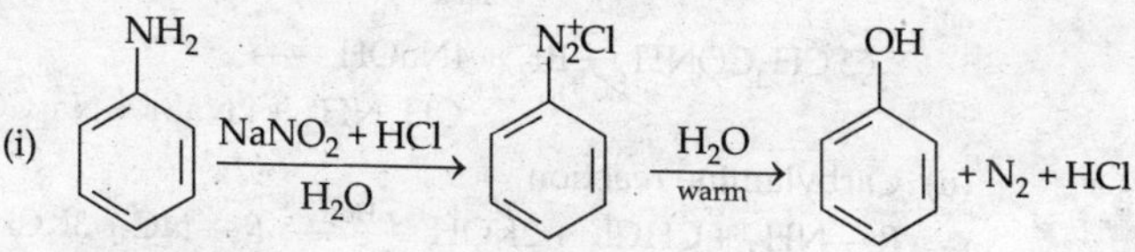

Aniline — Benzene diazonium chloride — Phenol

(ii) $CH_3-\overset{O}{\overset{\|}{C}}-NH_2 + Br_2 + 4KOH \xrightarrow{\text{Hoffmann bromamide reaction}} \underset{\text{Methanamine}}{CH_3NH_2} + 2KBr + K_2CO_3 + 2H_2O$

b. Methylamine and dimethyl amine can be distinguished by carbylamine test. Methyl amine (primary amine) responds to carbylamine reaction. When heated with chloroform and KOH, it produces foul smell. Dimethyl amine (secondary) does not respond to this test.

$$\underset{\text{Methyl amine}}{CH_3NH_2} + CHCl_3 + 3KOH \xrightarrow{\text{Heat}} \underset{\substack{\text{Methyl isocyanide} \\ \text{(Foul smell)}}}{CH_3-NC} + 3KCl + 3H_2O$$

☐ Long Answer Type

Q.1 (a) Write the structures of main products when benzene diazonium chloride reacts with the following reagents:

(i) CuCN/KCN

(ii) H_2O

(b) Illustrate the following reactions giving suitable example in each case:

(i) Hoffmann's Bromamide degradation reaction

(ii) Carbylamine reaction.

(iii) Gabriel phthalimide synthesis

Sol. (a) (i) $C_6H_5N_2^+Cl^- + CuCN / KCN \longrightarrow C_6H_5CN$ (Cyanobenzene)

(ii) $C_6H_5N_2^+Cl^- + H_2O \longrightarrow C_6H_5OH$ (Phenol)

(b) (i) Hoffmann's bromamide degradation reaction

$$\underset{\text{Amide}}{R{-}\overset{\overset{\displaystyle O}{\|}}{C}{-}NH_2} + Br_2 + 4NaOH \longrightarrow \underset{\text{Amine}}{R{-}NH_2} + Na_2CO_3 + 2NaBr + 2H_2O$$

e.g., $CH_3CONH_2 + Br_2 + 4NaOH \longrightarrow CH_3NH_2 + 2NaBr + Na_2CO_3 + 2H_2O$

(ii) Carbylamine reaction

$$R{-}NH_2 + CHCl_3 + 2KOH \xrightarrow{\text{Heat}} R{-}NC + 3KCl + 3H_2O$$

(iii) Gabriel phthalimide synthesis

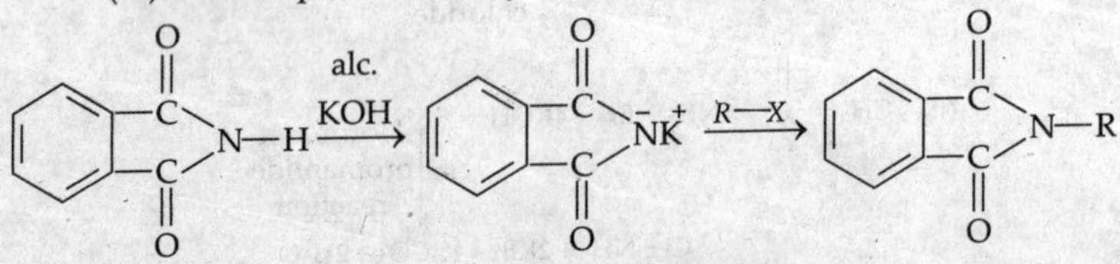

Phthalimide N-Alkylphthalimide

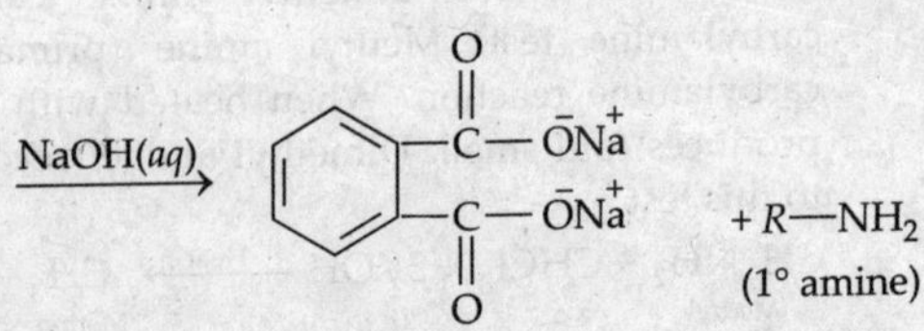

Q.2 (a) Write chemical equations involved when aniline is treated with the following reagents

(i) Br_2 (*aq*)

(ii) HCl

(iii) $NaNO_2$ + HCl at 0°C-5°C

(b) Write chemical reaction of aniline with benzoyl chloride and write the name of the product obtained.

(c) Arrange the following in increasing order of boiling point:
C_2H_5OH, $(CH_3)_2NH$, $C_2H_5NH_2$

Sol. (a)

(i) 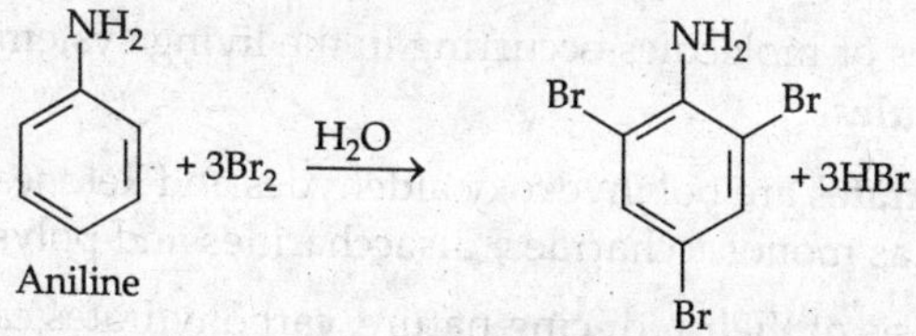

Aniline

2,4,6-Tribromoaniline

(ii) 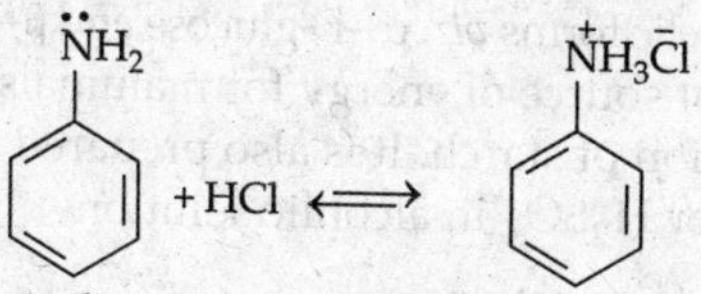

Aniline

Anilinium chloride

(iii) $$\underset{\text{Aniline}}{C_6H_5—NH_2} \xrightarrow[273\text{-}278\ K]{NaNO_2 + 2HCl} \underset{\text{Benzenediazonium Chloride}}{C_6H_5—\overset{+}{N}_2\overset{-}{Cl}} + NaCl + 2H_2O$$

(b) $C_6H_5NH_2 + C_6H_5COCl \longrightarrow C_6H_5NHCOC_6H_5 + HCl$

The name of product obtained compound is N-phenylbenzamide

(c) $(CH_3)_2NH < C_2H_5NH_2 < C_2H_5OH$,

Ethanol has strong hydrogen bonding due to its hydroxyl group (—OH), leading to the highest boiling point. Ethylamine has weaker hydrogen bonding as compared to ethanol because $-NH_2$ group is less effective in hydrogen bonding than the —OH group in ethanol (since oxygen is more electronegative than nitrogen). Dimethylamine has even weaker hydrogen bonding as compared to ethylamine as it has only one H-atom attached to Nitrogen to form less effective H-bonding as compared to 2H-atoms present in ethylamine which forms stronger H-bonding. Therefore, ethylamine has higher boiling point than dimethylamine.

Biomolecules

CHAPTER 10

Important Points

01 Substances or molecules occurring in the living systems are called **biomolecules.**

02 **Carbohydrates** are polyhydroxy aldehydes and ketones. These are classified as monosaccharides, disaccharides and polysaccharides.

03 On the basis of their reducing nature, carbohydrates can be grouped as reducing sugars and non-reducing sugars.

04 Glucose exists in two cyclic forms *viz,* α–D-glucose and β–D-glucose. It is the most important source of energy for mammals and is obtained by the digestion of starch. It is also prepared by boiling sucrose with dil. HCl or H_2SO_4 in alcohlic solution.

05 Glucose undergoes many reactions

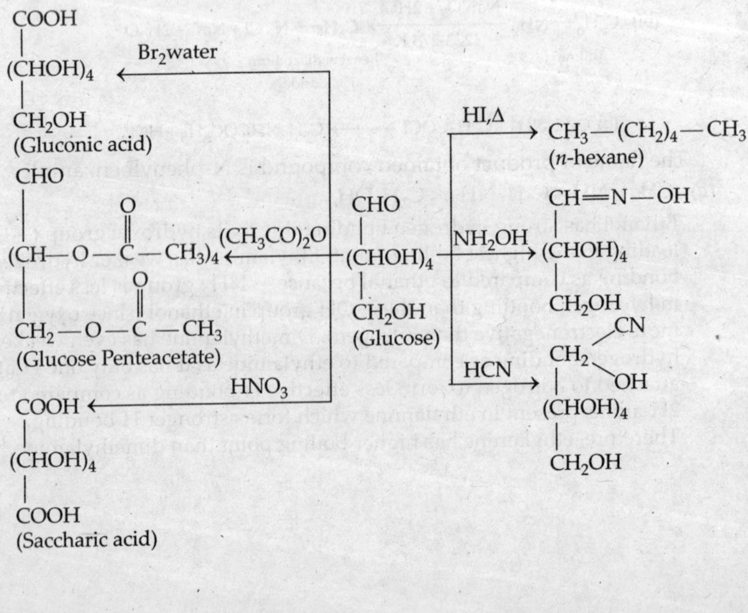

06 Monosaccharides are held together by **glycosidic linkages** to form disaccharides or polysaccharides.

07 If a monosaccharide contains an aldehyde group, it is known as an **aldose** and if it contains a keto group, it is known as a **ketose.**

08 (a) Sucrose = α-D-Glucose + β-D-Glucose (C_1-C_2 linkage)

(b) Maltose = α-D-Glucose + α-D-Glucose (C_1-C_4 linkage)

(c) Lactose = β-D-Glucose + β-D-Glucose (C_1-C_4 linkage)

09 **Starch** is the main storage polysaccharide of plants.

It is a polymer of α-glucose and it consists of two components : Amylase (water soluble) and amylopectin (water insoluble).

10 **Amylase** has two α-D-glucose units joined together by C_1-C_4 glycosidic linkage. **Amylopectin** has two α-D-glucose units held together C_1-C_4 glycosidic linkage and the branching occurs by C_1-C_6 glycosidic linkage. Both these components have α-glycosidic linkage.

11 Cellulose is the constituent of cell wall of plant cells. It is a polysaccharide of β-D-glucose units joined by β-glycosidic linkage between C_1 and C_4.

12 The carbohydrates are stored in animal body as **glycogen** (animal starch). Its structure is similar to amylopectin and it has more branching. When body needs glucose, enzymes break down glycogen to form glucose. It is present in liver, muscles and brain.

13 **Amino acids** are the smallest units of proteins. These consist of an amino and a carboxyl group.

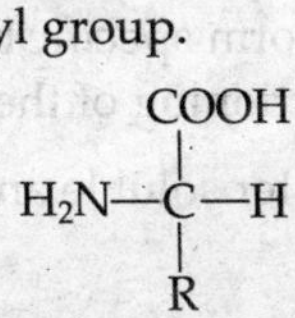

(Structure of commonly occuring amino acid)

14 Structure of proteins can be studied at four levels-primary, secondary, teriary and quarternary.

15 Some amino acids can be synthesised in the body and are known as **non-essential amino acids**. Whereas, some amino acids are not synthesised in the body and must be obtained through diet, they are known as **essential amino acids.**

16 In proteins, amino acids are connected to each other by peptide bond or **peptide linkage**. It is the amide bond formed between —COOH and —NH_2 group. By forming peptide linkage between amino acids, we can get dipeptides, tripeptides or polypeptides.

17 Proteins are classified into two types

(a) **Fibrous proteins**

- Insoluble in water.
- Polypeptide chains run parallel and are held together by hydrogen and disulfide bonds, to give fibre-like structure.
- For example, keratin, myosin, etc.

(b) **Globular proteins**

- Water soluble.
- Chains of polypeptides coil around to give a spherical shape.
- For example, albumins, insulin, etc.

18 Due to temperature change or pH change, secondary and tertiary structure are destroyed but primary structure remains intact. The process is called **denaturation of proteins.**

19 **Enzymes** are the biocatalysts and they are specific in function.

20 **Vitamins** are organic compounds which are required in the diet in small amounts to perform specific biological functions for healthy growth and functioning of the body.

21 Vitamins B and C are water soluble and vitamins A, D, E and K are fat soluble.

22 **Nucleic acids** are the polymers of nucleotides. DNA and RNA are two nucleic acids.

23 **DNA** (Deoxyribose Nucleic Acid) transmits the hereditary characters from one generation to another.

RNA (Ribonucleic Acid) synthesises protein in the cell.

24 Nucleic acid consists of pentose sugar, nitrogenous base and phosphoric acid. A combination of base and sugar is called nucleoside. A combination of nucleoside and phosphoric acid is called **nucleotide.**

25 DNA has **double stranded α-helix** structure.

26 DNA contains four bases : adenine (A), guanine (G), cytosine (C) and thymine (T). RNA contains four bases : Adenine (A), Guanine (G), Cytosine (C) and Uracil (U).

27 RNA has single stranded helix structure. It is of three types and they all perform different functions : messenger RNA (*m*-RNA), ribosomal RNA (*r*-RNA) and transfer RNA (*t*-RNA).

28 **Hormones** are the chemical substances produced by ductless glands called **endocrine glands**, such as thyroid, adrenals, etc., in the body and they are poured directly into the blood stream, which transports them to the site of action. They act as intercellular messenger. They help to maintain the balance of biological activities in the body.

Intext Questions

Question 1 Glucose or sucrose are soluble in water but cyclohexane or benzene (simple six membered ring compounds) are insoluble in water. Explain.

◎ ***Thinking Process*** Molecules which have polar nature or are capable to form hydrogen bond are generally soluble in water.

Sol. In glucose ($C_6H_{12}O_6$), 5 — OH groups are present and in sucrose ($C_{12}H_{22}O_{11}$), 8 — OH groups are present, which are polar in nature. They are involved in intermolecular hydrogen bonding with water molecules, so these compounds are readily soluble in water.

Benzene (C_6H_6) and cyclohexane (C_6H_{12}) are hydrocarbons. They do not have any polar group so they cannot make hydrogen bonds with water. Therefore, they are insoluble in water.

Question 2 What are the expected products of hydrolysis of lactose?

◎ ***Thinking Process*** Lactose is a disaccharide of glucose and galactose. On hydrolysis, it will produce monosaccharides.

Sol. Lactose forms two molecules of monosaccharides on hydrolysis— One molecule of β-D-(+)-glucose and one molecule of β-D-(−)-galactose.

$$\underset{\substack{\text{Lactose} \\ \text{(A disaccharide)}}}{C_{12}H_{22}O_{11}} + H_2O \xrightarrow[\text{Lactase}]{H_3O^+ \text{ or}} \underset{\beta\text{-D-(+)-Glucose}}{C_6H_{12}O_6} + \underset{\beta\text{-D-(−)-Galactose}}{C_6H_{12}O_6}$$

Question 3 How do you explain the absence of aldehyde group in the pentaacetate of D-glucose?

◎ ***Thinking Process*** Free aldehyde group (—CHO) gives reaction with Tollen's reagent, Fehling reagent, etc.

Sol. D-glucose, an aldohexose gives the characteristic reactions of aldehydic group (*e.g.*, with HCN, Tollen's reagent, Fehling reagent, etc.), but pentaacetate of D-glucose does not give these reactions.

It means that either —CHO group is absent or it is not available for the chemical reactions in pentaacetyl glucose. Infact, the aldehydic group is a part of hemiacetal structure which pentaacetyl glucose has. So, it is not available for reaction.

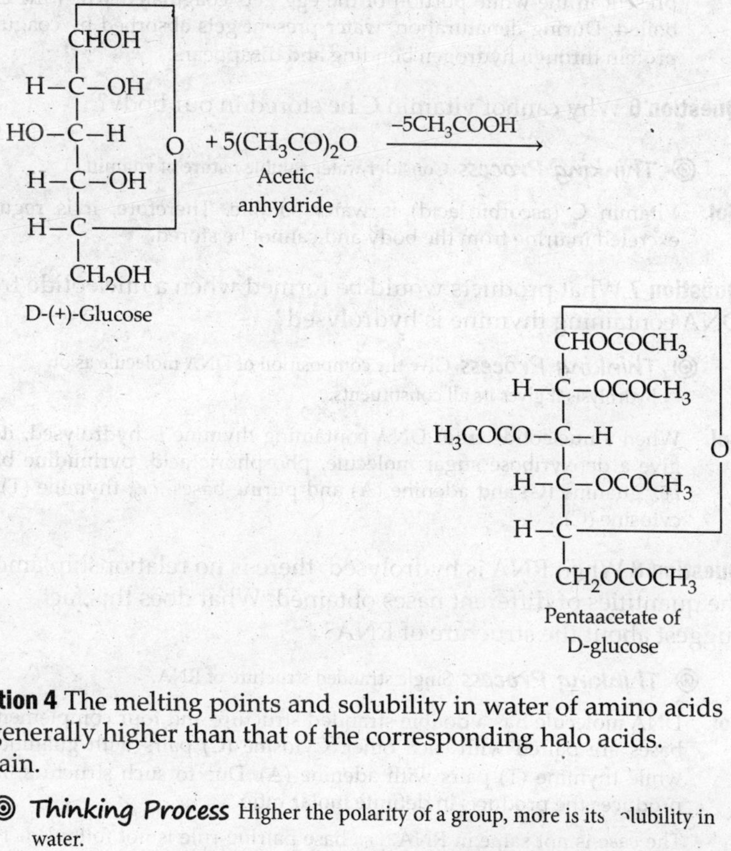

Question 4 The melting points and solubility in water of amino acids are generally higher than that of the corresponding halo acids. Explain.

◎ ***Thinking Process*** Higher the polarity of a group, more is its solubility in water.

Sol. Amino acids are dipolar in nature as they exist in zwitter ionic form ($\overset{+}{N}H_3$ — CHR — COO^-) and have strong dipolar interactions. Therefore, these have high melting points. When dissolved in water, these form hydrogen bonds with water molecules, therefore, these are soluble in water. (except at isoelectric point, where they have least solubility) In case of halo acids, these are not dipolar. Only their carboxyl group is involved in hydrogen bonding, not the halogen atom. Therefore, halo acids, have lower melting points and lesser solubility than amino acids.

Question 5 Where does the water present in the egg go after boiling the egg?

Sol. When an egg is boiled, its globular protein gets denatured. The albumin present in the white portion of the egg gets coagulated when the egg is boiled. During denaturation, water present gets absorbed by coagulated protein through hydrogen bonding and disappears.

Question 6 Why cannot vitamin C be stored in our body?

◎ ***Thinking Process*** Consider water soluble nature of vitamin C.

Sol. Vitamin C (ascorbic acid) is water soluble. Therefore, it is regularly excreted in urine from the body and cannot be stored.

Question 7 What products would be formed when a nucleotide from DNA containing thymine is hydrolysed?

◎ ***Thinking Process*** Give the composition of DNA molecule as on hydrolysis it gives its all constituents.

Sol. When a nucleotide from DNA containing thymine is hydrolysed, it will give a deoxyribose sugar molecule, phosphoric acid, pyrimidine bases, *i.e.*, guanine (G) and adenine (A) and purine bases, *i.e.*, thymine (T) and cytosine (C).

Question 8 When RNA is hydrolysed, there is no relationship among the quantities of different bases obtained. What does this fact suggest about the structure of RNA?

◎ ***Thinking Process*** Single stranded structure of RNA.

Sol. DNA molecule has a double stranded structure and four complementary bases are paired with each other. Cytosine (C) pairs with guanine (G) while thymine (T) pairs with adenine (A). Due to such structure, DNA produces the products in definite molar ratio.

The case is not same in RNA. *i.e.*, base pairing rule is not followed. Thus, when RNA is hydrolysed, the quantities of different bases are different. This suggests that RNA has single stranded structure.

Exercises

Question 1 What are monosaccharides?

Sol. The carbohydrates which cannot be further hydrolysed into simpler unit of polyhydroxy aldehyde or ketone are called monosaccharides. Their general formula is $(CH_2O)_n$ where, $n = 3$ to 7. These are of two types: aldoses (—CHO group present) and ketoses (ketone group present).

Question 2 What are reducing sugars?

Sol. Those sugars which act as reducing agents are called reducing sugars. They contain an aldehyde (—CHO) group or a ketone (>C═O), group. All monosaccharides and disaccharides (except sucrose) are reducing sugars. *e.g.*, glucose, fructose, lactose, etc. They reduce Fehling's solution and Tollen's reagent.

Question 3 Write two main functions of carbohydrates in plants.

◎ ***Thinking Process*** Recall different carbohydrates present in plants with their functions.

Sol. **Functions of carbohydrates in plants.**

(i) Cell walls of plants are made up of cellulose, a polysaccharide.

(ii) Carbohydrates are stored in the form of starch (a polysaccharide) as the reserve food material.

Question 4 Classify the following into monosaccharides and disaccharides. Ribose, 2-deoxyribose, maltose, galactose, fructose and lactose.

◎ ***Thinking Process*** Monosaccharides do not undergo hydrolysis whereas disaccharides give two molecules of monosaccharides when subjected to hydrolysis.

Sol. **Monosaccharides :** Ribose, 2-deoxyribose, galactose and fructose.

Disaccharides : Maltose and lactose.

Question 5 What do you understand by the term glycosidic linkage?

Sol. **Glycosidic linkage** The linkage between two monosaccharide units through oxygen atom is called glycosidic linkage. It is formed by a loss of water molecules.

Disaccharides and polysaccharides are formed by this linkage. *e.g.,* In sucrose molecule, glycosidic linkage can be shown as below:

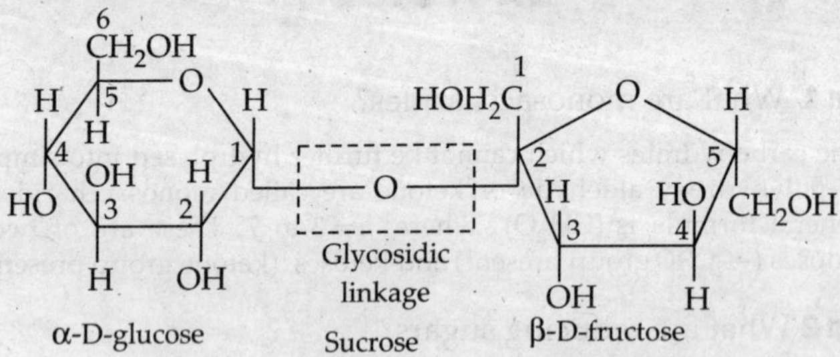

Question 6 What is glycogen? How is it different form starch?

Sol. **Glycogen** is a polysaccharide (carbohydrate). The carbonhydrates are stored in animal body as glycogen. It is present in liver, muscles and brain. When the body needs glucose, enzymes break down the glycogen into glucose.

Starch is a polysaccharide. It is the main storage polysaccharide of plants. It consists of two components **amylose** and **amylopectin**. Amylose is water soluble and makes 15-20% of starch.

Amylopectin is insoluble in water and makes 80-85% of starch. Glycogen mainly resembles amylopectin in structure. Both glycogen and amylopectin are branched polymers of glucose but glycogen is more highly branched than amylopectin. Glycogen chain consists of 10-14 glucose units whereas amylopectin chains consist of 20-25 glucose units.

Question 7 What are the hydrolysis products of

(i) sucrose and (ii) lactose?

◎ *Thinking Process*

(i) Sucrose is a disaccharide of glucose and fructose and lactose is a disaccharide of glucose and galactose.

(ii) Disaccharides on hydrolysis give monosaccharides.

Sol. (i) **Sucrose** is dextrorotatory but after hydrolysis, it produces dextrorotatory glucose and laevorotatory fructose.

$$\underset{\substack{\text{Sucrose} \\ \text{(Invert sugar)}}}{C_{12}H_{22}O_{11}} + H_2O \xrightarrow{\text{Invertase}} \underset{\text{D-(+)-glucose}}{C_6H_{12}O_6} + \underset{\text{D-(−)-fructose}}{C_6H_{12}O_6}$$

Since, the laevorotation of fructose $(-92.4°)$ is more than dextroratation of glucose $(+52.5°)$, the mixture is laevorotatory. Thus, on hydrolysis of sucrose, changes in the sign of solution, from *dextro* (+) to *laevo* (–) happens. Hence, the product it is known as invert sugar.

(ii) **Lactose** on hydrolysis produces β-D-galactose and β-D-glucose.

$$\underset{\text{Lactose}}{C_{12}H_{22}O_{11}} + H_2O \xrightarrow{\text{Lactase}} \underset{\beta\text{-D-Galactose}}{C_6H_{12}O_6} + \underset{\beta\text{-D-Glucose}}{C_6H_{12}O_6}$$

Question 8 What is the basic structural difference between starch and cellulose?

Sol. The basic difference between starch and cellulose is due to the difference in linkage between the glucose units.

Starch consists of amylose and amylopectin, both made up of α-D(+)-glucose units. Amylose consists of linear chains of glucose linked in C_1-C_4 manner. Amylopectin consists of these linear chains further linked in C_1-C_6 manner. In both the componento α-D-glycosidic link age is present.

In cellulose, only β -D(+)-glucose molecules are linked to each other in C_1-C_4 manner through β-D-glycosidic linkage

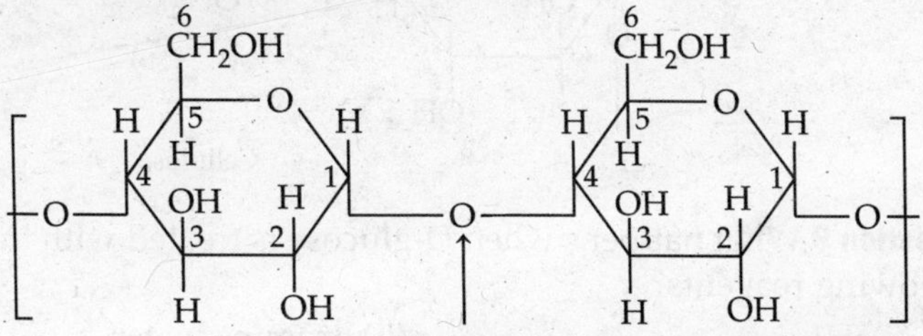

α-linkage Amylose

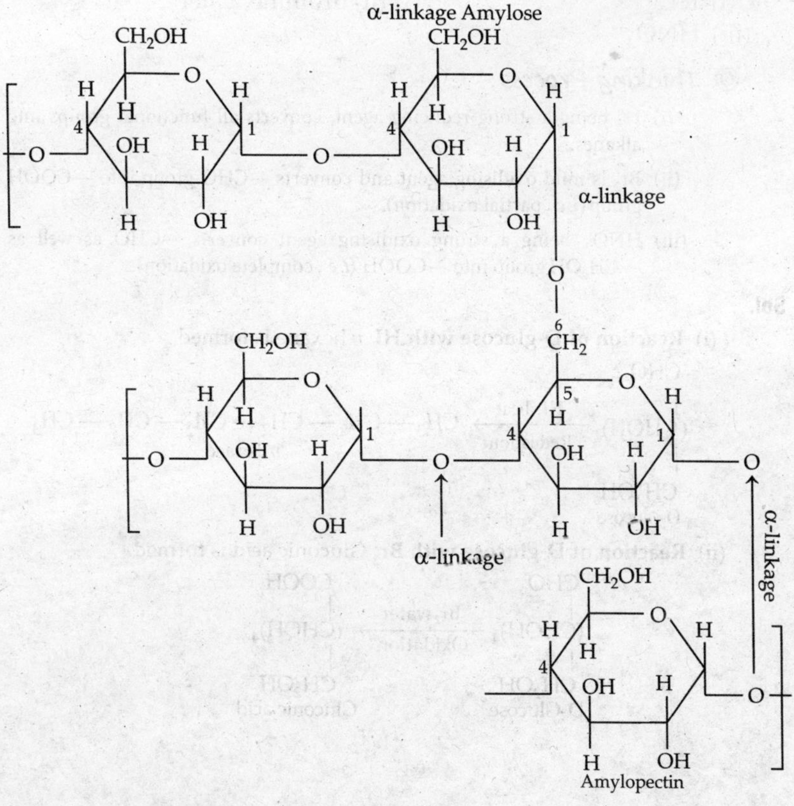

Amylopectin

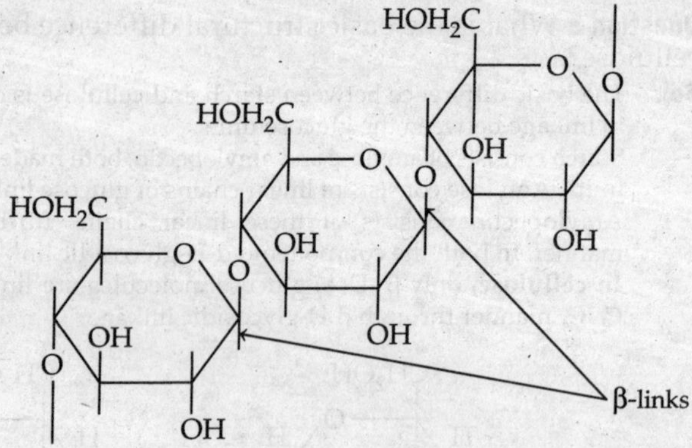

Cellulose

Question 9 What happens when D-glucose is treated with the following reagents?

(i) HI (ii) Bromine water

(iii) HNO_3

◎ *Thinking Process*

(i) HI being a strong reducing agent, converts all functional groups into alkanes.

(ii) Br_2 is mild oxidising agent and converts —CHO group into —COOH group (*i.e.*, partial oxidation).

(iii) HNO_3 being a strong oxidising agent converts —CHO as well as —CH_2OH group into —COOH (*i.e.*, complete oxidation).

Sol.

(i) **Reaction of D-glucose with HI** *n*-hexane is formed.

$$\underset{\text{D-Glucose}}{\begin{array}{c} CHO \\ | \\ (CHOH)_4 \\ | \\ CH_2OH \end{array}} \xrightarrow[\text{Reduction}]{\text{HI, heat}} \underset{n\text{-hexane}}{CH_3—CH_2—CH_2—CH_2—CH_2—CH_3}$$

(ii) **Reaction of D-glucose with Br_2** Gluconic acid is formed.

$$\underset{\text{D-Glucose}}{\begin{array}{c} CHO \\ | \\ (CHOH)_4 \\ | \\ CH_2OH \end{array}} \xrightarrow[\text{Oxidation}]{Br_2\text{ water}} \underset{\text{Gluconic acid}}{\begin{array}{c} COOH \\ | \\ (CHOH)_4 \\ | \\ CH_2OH \end{array}}$$

(iii) **Reaction of D-glucose with** Saccharic acid is formed.

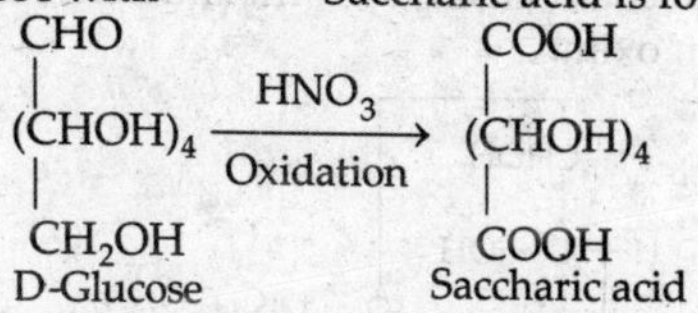

Mistake Alert Br_2 water causes partial oxidation of glucose, while HNO_3 causes complete oxidation of glucose, as HNO_3 is a strong oxidising agent than Br_2 water.

Question 10 Enumerate the reactions of D-glucose which cannot be explained by its open chain structure.

Thinking Process Give reactions which are characteristic of aldehydic group but not shown by glucose as in it free —CHO group is not present.

Sol. Following reactions cannot be explained by the open chain structure of D-glucose.

(i) Although aldehyde group is present in glucose, it does not give 2,4-DNP test, Schiff's test and it does not react with $NaHSO_3$.

(ii) Formation of α- and β- methyl glucosides cannot be explained by its open chain structure. These are only formed when we assume its ring structure.

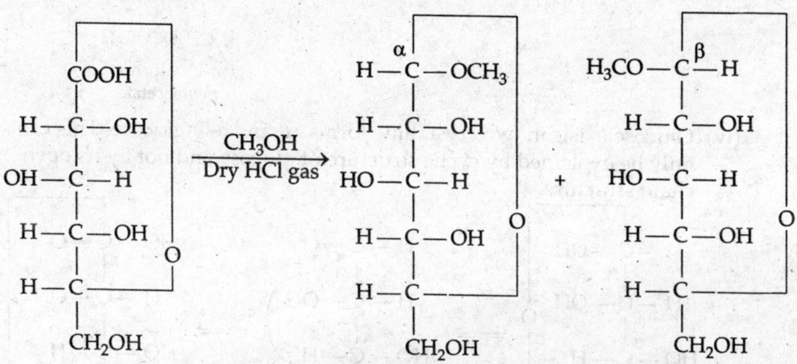

Methyl α-D-glucoside Methyl α-D-glucoside

(iii) Like methyl glycosides, glucose pentaacetate also exists in two anomeric forms : α D-glucose pentaacetate and β-D-glucose pentaacetate. These pentaacetates do not have a free —OH group at C_1 and hence are not hydrolysed in aqueous solution to produce the open chain aldehyde form and hence do not react with NH_2OH to form oxime.

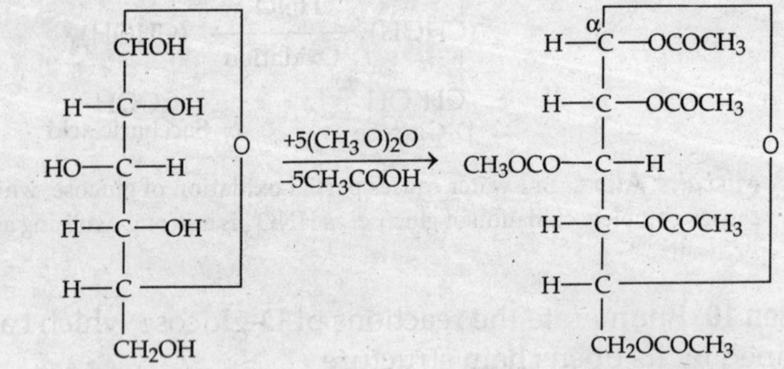

A mixture of α-and β- D-glucose

α-D-Glucose pentaacetate

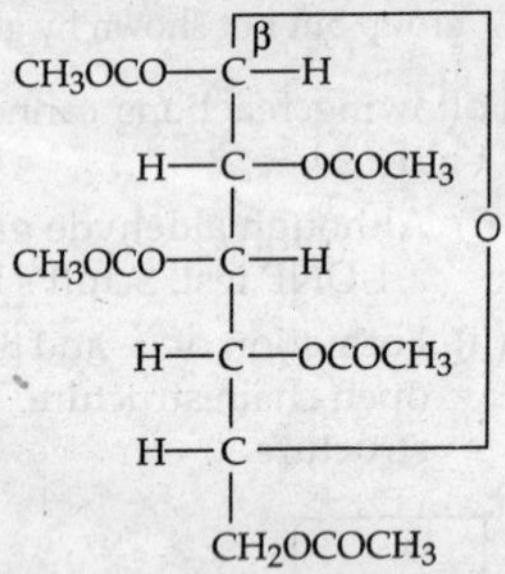

α-D- Glucose pentaacetate

(iv) Glucose exists in two crystalline forms, α- and β-D-glucose. This can only be explained by cyclic structure of glucose and not by its open chain structure.

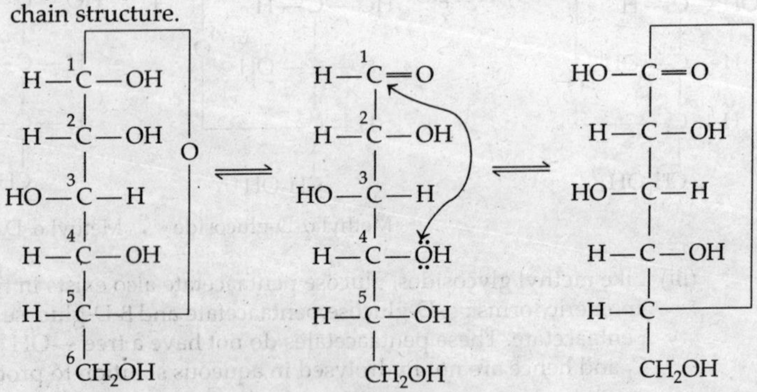

β-D (+)-Glucose

α - D -(+) -Glocuse

Mistake Alert The two cyclic forms of glucose (α-and β) exists in equilibrium with open chain structure, therefore, we use '$\rightleftharpoons$' arrow in the equation and not '$\longrightarrow$'

Question 11 What are the essential and non-essential amino acids? Give two examples of each type.

Sol. **Essential amino acids** Amino acids which cannot be synthesised in the body and must be taken in diet are called essential amino acids *e.g.*, valine, leucine, phenylalanine etc.

Non-essential amino acids Amino acids which can be synthesised in the body are known as non-essential amino acids. *e.g.*, glycine, alanine, glutamic acid. etc. Out of 20 amino acids which make up the bioproteins, 10 are non-essential amino acids and rest are essential amino acids.

Mistake Alert One can make a mistake in confusing the essential amino–acids with non-essential amino acids.

Question 12 Define the following as related to proteins.

(i) Peptide linkage (ii) Primary structure (iii) Denaturation.

Sol.

(i) **Peptide linkage** Peptide linkage is an amide linkage formed between —COOH group and —NH_2 group.

When carboxyl group of one amino acid reacts with the amino group of the other, a water molecule is eliminated and peptide linkage is formed. (This gives a dipeptide.)

$$\underset{\text{Glycine}}{H_2N-CH_2-COOH} + \underset{\text{Alanine}}{H_2N-\underset{\underset{CH_3}{|}}{CH}-COOH} \xrightarrow{-H_2O}$$

$$\underset{\text{Glycylalanine (Gly-Ala)}}{H_2N-CH_2-\underset{\text{Peptide linkage}}{CO-NH}-\underset{\underset{CH_3}{|}}{CH}-COOH}$$

(ii) **Primary structure** Each polypeptide in a protein has amino acids linked with each other in a specific sequence and this sequence of amino acids is called primary structure of that particular protein. Any change in the primary structure creates different protein.

(iii) **Denaturation** When a protein in its native form, is subjected to physical change as change in temperature, or chemical change like change in pH, the hydrogen bonds are disturbed. The protein globules unfold, helix get uncoiled and protein loses its biological activity. This is called denaturation of protein. Secondary and tertriary structures are destroyed but the primary structure remains as such. Coagulation of egg while on boiling, curdling of milk, etc., are the examples of denaturation.

Question 13 What are the common types of secondary structure of proteins?

◎ *Thinking Process* Describe the two types : α-helix and β-pleated structure.

Sol. The secondary structure of protein refers to the shape in which a long polypeptide chain can exist. Secondary structure is of two types:

(i) **α-helix** In α-helix, a polypeptide chain forms all possible hydrogen bonds by twisting into a right handed screw (helix) with the $>$NH group of each amino acid residue hydrogen bonded to the $>C{=}O$ of an adjacent turn of the helix.

(ii) **β-pleated structure** In β-pleated structure, all peptide chains are stretched out to nearly maximum extension and then laid side by side which are held together by intermolecular hydrogen bonds. The structure resembles the pleated folds of drapery and also called β-pleated sheet.

Question 14 What type of bonding helps in stabilising the α-helix structure of proteins?

Sol. The α-helix structure of proteins is stabilized by hydrogen bonding In α-helix, a polypeptide chain forms all possible hydrogen bonds by twisting into a right handed screw (helix) with $>$NH group of each amino acid residue hydrogen bonded to the $>C{=}O$ of an adjacent turn of the helix.

Question 15 Differentiate between globular and fibrous proteins.

Sol.

S.No.	Globular proteins	Filbrous proteins
1.	Polypeptide chains are arranged as coils.	Polypeptide chains are parallel to each other.
2.	They have spherical shape.	They have thread like structure.
3.	They are water soluble.	They are insoluble in water.
4.	Examples : insulin, albumins etc.	Examples:keratin, myosin etc.

Question 16 How do you explain the amphoteric behaviour of amino acids?

◎ *Thinking Process* Amphoteric behaviour is due to the presence of basic group (—NH_2) and acidic group (—COOH).

Sol. Amino acids have amino (—NH_2) group, basic in nature and carboxyl (—COOH) group which is acidic in nature. In aqueous medium, NH_2 group accepts a proton and COOH group loses a proton forming a dipolar ion, called the zwitter ion.

In this form, amino acids behave both as acids and bases, so they are amphoteric in nature.

$$H_2\ddot{N}-\underset{\substack{|\\R}}{CH}-COOH \rightleftharpoons H_3\overset{+}{N}-\underset{\substack{|\\R}}{CH}-COO^- \text{ (Dipolar ion)}$$

Question 17 What are enzymes?

Sol. Enzymes are defined as the biological or biocatalysts which catalyse or speed up the reactions occurring in the living beings. Majority of the enzymes are globular proteins. Enzymes are specific and selective in action.

For example, the enzyme that catalyses hydrolysis of maltose into glucose is named as maltase.

$$\underset{\text{(Maltose)}}{C_{12}H_{22}O_{11}} \xrightarrow{\text{Maltase}} \underset{\text{(Glucose)}}{2C_6H_{12}O_6}$$

Enzymes are needed only in small quantities for the progress of a reaction. They are said to reduce the magnitude of activation energy, thus speed up a chemical reaction.

Question 18 What is the effect of denaturation on the structure of proteins?

Sol. During the denaturation of a protein , its secondary and tertiary structures are destroyed but primary structure remains intact. During this process globular protein convert into fibrous proteins and the biological activity of the protein is lost.

For example Coagulation of egg white on boiling, curdling of milk due to bacterial action, etc.

Question 19 How are vitamins classified? Name the vitamin responsible for the coagulation of blood.

Sol. (a) Vitamins are classified into two groups on the basis of their solubility in water or fat :

(i) **Fat soluble vitamins** Vitamins which are soluble in fat and oils are but insoluble in water are called fat soluble vitamins. For example, vitamins A, D, E and K. They are stored in liver and adipose (fat storing) tissues.

(ii) **Water soluble vitamins** These vitamins are soluble in water and insoluble in fat. For example, vitamin B-complex and vitamin C. These vitamins are readily excreted in urine and cannot be stored in our body. So, these must be supplied regularly in diet.

(b) Vitamin K is responsible for the coagulation of blood.

Question 20 Why are vitamin A and vitamin C essential to us? Give their important sources.

◎ *Thinking Process* Discuss about deficiency diseases related to these vitamins and their sources.

Sol. Vitamins are essential for us because they protect us from different diseases. Every vitamin is specific in its function.

Vitamin	Deficiency disease	Sources
Vitamin A	Xerophthalmia (Hardening of cornea of eye) or night blindness	Fish liver oil, carrots, butter and milk.
Vitamin C	Scurvy (bleeding gums)	Citrus fruits, amla and green leafy vegetables.

Question 21 What are nucleic acids? Mention their two important functions.

Sol. **Nucleic acids** The biomolecules which are found in the nuclei of living organisms in the form of nucleoproteins or chromosomes are called nucleic acids. They are the genetic material of the cell.

Nucleic acids are of two types; DNA (deoxyribonucleic acid) and RNA (ribonucleic acid).

Functions of Nucleic Acids

(1) DNA is the reserve of genetic information. DNA, due to its replication property, transmits hereditary characteristics from one generation to another.

(2) RNA and DNA help in the protein synthesis in the cell. RNA synthesizes the protein and DNA has the message for this synthesis.

Question 22 What is the difference between a nucleoside and a nucleotide?

Sol.

Nucleoside	Nucleotide
1. It is a combination of base and sugar.	1. It is a combination of nucleoside and phosphoric acid.
2. Examples (a) Adenosine = Adenine + Ribose	2. Examples (a) Adenylic acid = Adenosine +Phosphoric acid.
(b) Guanosine = Guanine + Ribose	(b) Guanylic acid = Guanosine + Phosphoric acid.
(c) Cytidine = Cytosine + Ribose	(c) Cytidylic acid = Cytidine +Phosphoric acid.
(d) Deoxythymidine = Thymine + Deoxyribose	(d) Uridylic acid = Uridine + Phosphoric acid.
3. Structure 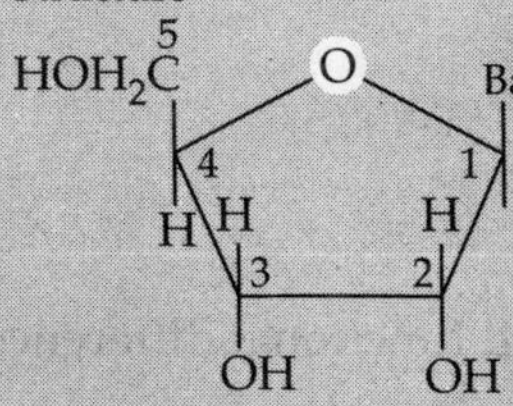 Nucleoside	3. Structure 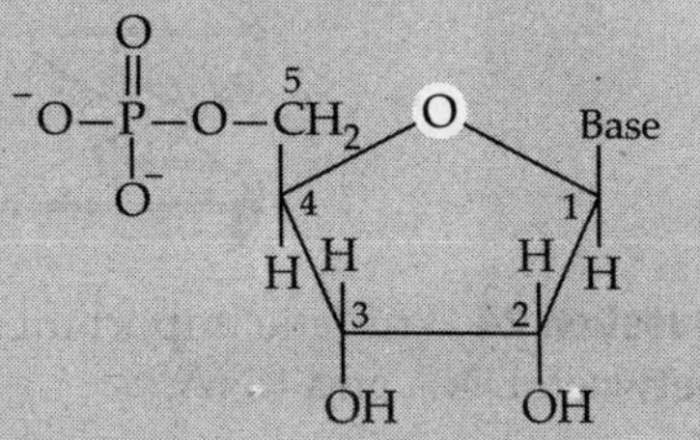 Nucleotide

Question 23 The two strands in DNA are not identical but are complementary. Explain.

◎ *Thinking Process*

(i)Discuss the bonding and pairing of bases.

(ii)Draw the double helical structure of DNA molecule.

Sol. The two strands in DNA molecule are held together by hydrogen bonding, which is according to a specific rule. Adenine forms hydrogen bond with thymine and guanine forms hydrogen bond with cytosine. Due to this base pairing principle, the sequence of bases in one strand automatically fixes the sequence of bases in the other strand. So, the strands are complementary to each other.

Thus, the two strands are not identical but are complimentary.

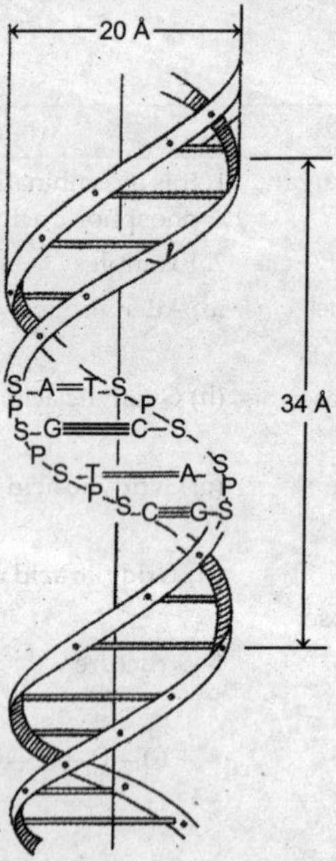

The double strand helix structure of DNA

Question 24 Write the important structural and functional differences between DNA and RNA.

Sol.

S. No.	DNA	RNA
	Structural Differences	
1.	The pentose sugar present in DNA is D-2-deoxyribose.	The pentose sugar present in RNA is D-ribose.
2.	DNA contains cytosine and thymine as pyrimidine bases.	RNA contains cytosine and uracil as pyrimidine bases.
3.	It has a double-stranded α-helix structure.	It has a single stranded α-helix structure.
4.	Its molecule is relatively long with high molecular mass.	Its molecule is relatively short with low molecular mass.
	Functional Differences	
5.	It has unique property of replication.	It usually does not replicate.
6.	It controls the transmission of hereditary characters.	It controls protein synthesis.

Question 25 What are the different types of RNA found in the cell?

Sol. Three different types of RNA present in the cell are :

1. Ribosomal RNA (*r*-RNA)
2. Messenger RNA (*m*-RNA) 3. Transfer RNA (*t*-RNA)

DIKSHA APP Questions

☐ Multiple Choice Question

Q.1 How many amino acids are present in insulin?

(a) 25 (b) 51
(c) 22 (d) 32

Sol. (b) Insulin is composed of 51 amino acids. It consists of two peptide chains: Chain *A* contains 21 amino acids and Chain *B* contains 30 amino acids. These two chains are linked by disulphide bonds, forming the functional insulin molecule.

Q.2 Which of the following hormones contain iodine?

(a) Adrenaline (b) Insulin
(c) Thyroxine (d) Testosterone

Sol. (c) The hormones that contain iodine are thyroid hormones, specifically thyroxine. These hormones are produced by the thyroid gland and are crucial for regulating metabolism, growth and development.

Q.3 The presence or absence of hydroxyl group on which carbon atom of sugar differentiates RNA and DNA?

(a) Carbon 2 (b) Carbon 3
(c) Carbon 4 (d) Carbon 1

Sol. (a) The presence or absence of a hydroxyl group on the carbon-2 atom of the sugar differentiates RNA from DNA. RNA (Ribonucleic Acid) contains a hydroxyl group (—OH) on the 2' carbon of the ribose sugar. DNA (Deoxyribonucleic Acid) lacks a hydroxyl group on the 2' carbon of the deoxyribose sugar, having only a hydrogen atom (-H) instead.

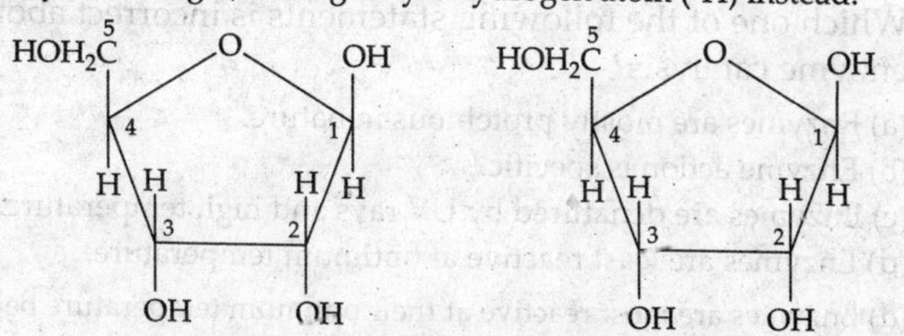

β-D-ribose β-D-2-deoxyribose

Q.4 RNA is different from DNA because RNA contains

(a) ribose sugar and Thymine (b) ribose sugar and Uracil

(c) de oxyribose sugar and Thymine (d) deoxyribose sugar and Uracil

Sol. (b) RNA differs from DNA because: RNA has ribose sugar and DNA has deoxyribose sugar . DNA has Adenine (A), Guanine (G), Cytosine (C) and Thymine (T) bases. Whereas, RNA has Adenine (A), Guanine (G), Cytosine (C) and Uracil (U) bases.

Q.5 Two vitamins absorbed from intestine along with fats are

(a) vitamin A and D (b) vitamin A and B

(c) vitamin A and C (d) vitamin D and C

Sol. (a) Two vitamins which are absorbed from intestine along with fats are Vitamin A and D as, these two vitamins are fat soluble vitamins.

Q.6 Which of the following vitamins causes Xerophthalmia and Night blindness?

(a) Vitamin D (b) Vitamin A (c) Vitamin C (d) Vitamin E

Sol. (b) Deficiency of Vitamin A causes Xerophthalmia (hardening of cornea of eye) and night blindness. Therefore, option (b) is correct.

Q.7 The enzyme which converts glucose and fructose to ethyl alcohol is:

(a) Diastase (b) Invertase (c) Maltase (d) Zymase

Sol. (d) Zymase is a complex of enzymes found in yeast that is responsible for the fermentation of sugars, like glucose and fructose, into ethanol.

$$\underset{\text{Glucose or fructose}}{C_6H_{12}O_6} \xrightarrow[\text{in yeast}]{\text{Zymase}} \underset{\text{Ethanol}}{2C_2H_5OH} + \underset{\text{Carbon dioxide}}{2CO_2}$$

Q.8. Which one of the following statements is incorrect about enzyme catalysis?

(a) Enzymes are mostly proteinous in nature.

(b) Enzyme action is specific.

(c) Enzymes are denatured by UV rays and high temperature.

(d) Enzymes are least reactive at optimum temperature.

Sol. (d) Enzymes are most reactive at their optimum temperature because, at this temperature, they work most efficiently.
Therefore, statement in option (d) is incorrect.

Q.9 Where does the water present in the egg go after boiling the egg?

(a) Water gets converted into steam which escapes into the atmosphere.
(b) Water brings about hydrolysis of protein present in the egg to form the constituent alpha amino acid.
(c) Water helps in the denaturation of the egg protein.
(d) Water gets absorbed/adsorbed in the coagulated egg protein through H-bonding.

Sol. (d) When an egg is boiled, the globular proteins present inside the egg gets denatured and coagulate. After boiling the egg, the water present in it is absorbed by the coagulated protein through H-bonding.

Q.10 Which one of the following is an essential amino acid?

(a) Cysteine (b) Serine (c) Tyrosine (d) Isoleucine

Sol. (d) Essential amino acids are not synthesized in the human body and it must be obtained through diet. Isoleucine is an essential amino acid

Q.11 Which of the following statements is not true about glucose?

(a) It is an aldohexose. (b) On heating with HI it forms *n*-hexane.
(c) It is present in furanose form.
(d) It does not give 2, 4-DNP test.

Sol. (c) Glucose forms six membered cyclic structure, which is called pyranose structure. It does not form a five membered ring, so it cannot be present in furanose form.

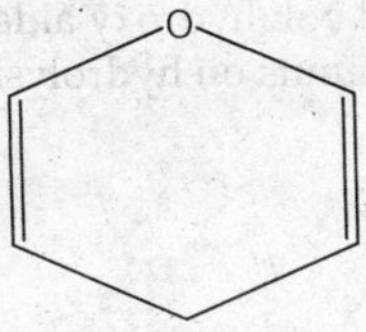

Pyran

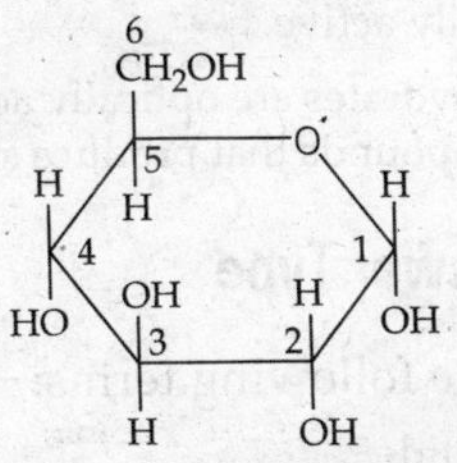

α-D-(+)-Glucopyranose

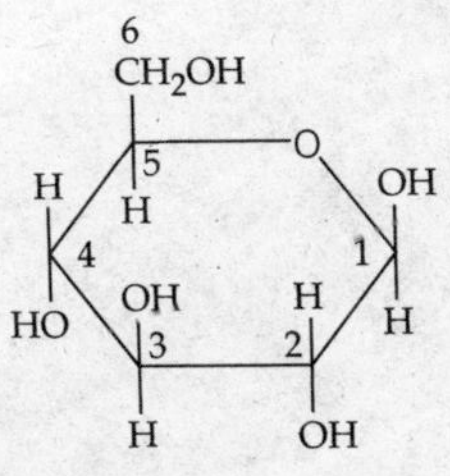

β-D-(+)-Glucopyranose

Q.12 Which one of the following is a non-reducing sugar?

(a) Glucose (b) Sucrose
(c) Maltose (d) Lactose

Sol. (b) Sucrose is a non-reducing sugar. In sucrose, the reducing groups of glucose and fructose are bonded by glycosidic linkage. So, it does not have a free aldehyde or ketone group capable of acting as a reducing agent.

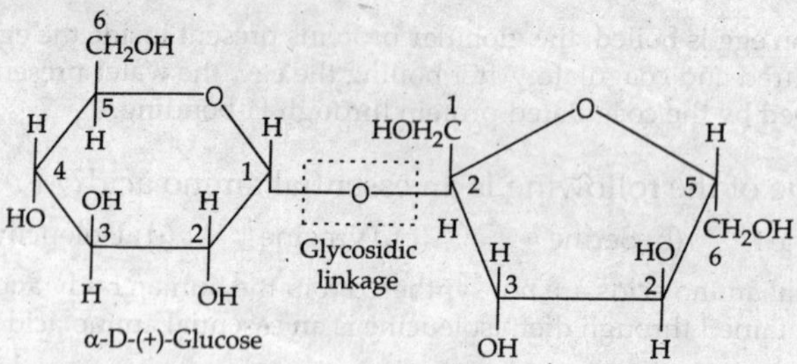

Sucrose

Q.13 Carbohydrate may be defined as

(a) optically inactive polyhydroxy aldehyde.
(b) optically inactive polyhydroxy ketones.
(c) optically active polyhydroxy aldehydes or ketones or substance which give these on hydrolysis.
(d) polyhydroxy aldehyde or ketones which mayor may not be optically active.

Sol. (c) Carbohydrates are optically active polyhydroxy aldehydes or ketones or the compounds that produce such units on hydrolysis.

□ Short Answer Type

Q.1 Define the following terms:

(a) Nucleotide
(b) Zwitter ion
(c) Glycosidic linkage

Sol. (a) Nucleotides are the monomers of nucleic acids consisting of heterocyclic base, pentose sugar and phosphate group.

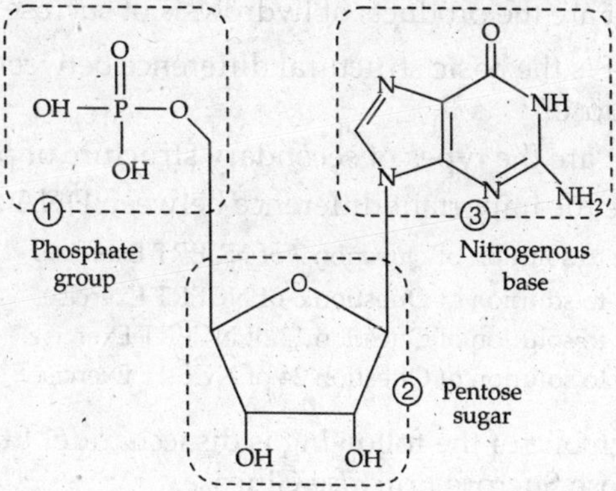

(b) The dipolar ion whose one end is positively charged and the other end is negatively charged is called zwitter ion. *e.g.*, $H_3N^+CH_2COO^-$ (Zwitter ion of glycine).

(c) Refer to solution of Question 5 of NCERT Exercises.

Q.2 (a) Write the name of the disease caused by deficiency of vitamin B_{12}?

(b) Name the base that is found In nucleotide of RNA but not in DNA?

(c) Glucose on reaction with HI gives *n*-hexane. What does it suggest about the structure of glucose?

Sol. (a) The disease cause by deficiency of vitamin B_{12} is pernicious anaemia (RBC deficient in haemoglobin).

(b) Uracil is the base that is found in nucleotide of RNA but not in DNA.

(c) Glucose on reaction with HI gives *n*-hexane. This suggests that all the six carbon atoms of glucose are linked in a straight chain.

$$\begin{matrix} CHO \\ | \\ (CHOH)_4 \\ | \\ CH_2OH \end{matrix} \xrightarrow{HI, \Delta} \underset{(n\text{-Hexane})}{CH_3—CH_2—CH_2—CH_2—CH_2—CH_3}$$

☐ Long Answer Type

Q.1 (a) What are the products of hydrolysis of sucrose and lactose?

(b) What is the basic structural difference between starch and cellulose?

(c) What are the types of secondary structure of proteins?

(d) Write the important difference between DNA and RNA?

Sol. (a) Refer to solution of Question 7 of NCERT Exercise.

(b) Refer to solution of Question 8 of NCERT Exercise.

(c) Refer to solution of Question 13 of NCERT Exercise.

(d) Refer to solution of Question 24 of NCERT Exercise.

Q.2 (a) Which one of the following is disaccharide? Starch, Maltose,Sucrose,Fructose,Glucose

(b) What is the difference between fibrous protein and globular protein?

(c) What are essential amino acid, why should these be part of our diet?

(d) Name the sugars present in Nucleic acids?

Sol. (a) Sucrose and Maltose are disaccharides.

(b) Refer to solution of Question 15 of NCERT Exercises.

(c) Those amino acids which are not synthesized by our body are called essential amino acids. These must be a part of our diet as these are needed for synthesis of proteins.

(d) The sugars present in nucleic acids are: ribose and 2-deoxyribose sugars.

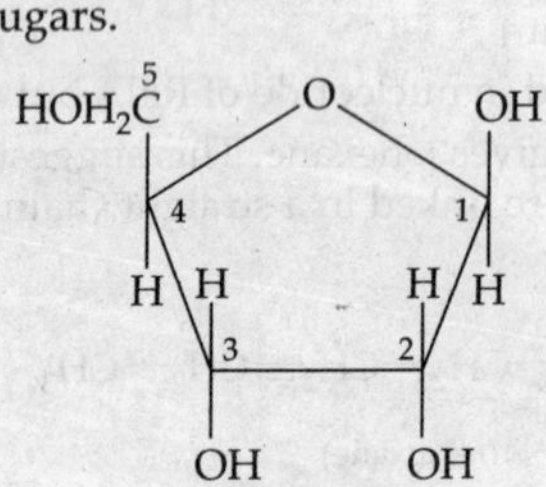

β-D-ribose

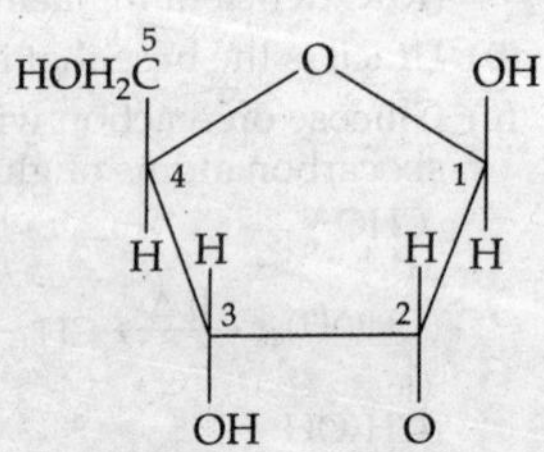

β-D-2-deoxyribose